China Business Guide

2004 Edition

ChinaKnowledge Press

Map of China

KAZAKHSTAN

KYRGYZSTAN

Xinjiang

Qinghai

Tibet

INDIA

NEPAL

BHUTAN

Yur

MYANMAR

LAO

- Capital of China
- Municipalities
- Special Administrative Regions
- Autonomous Regions
- Provinces

RUSSIA
MONGOLIA
Heilongjiang
Jilin
Liaoning
BEIJING
Inner Mongolia
NORTH KOREA
SOUTH KOREA
Tianjin
Hebei
Ningxia
Shanxi
Shandong
JAPAN
Gansu
Shaanxi
Henan
Jiangsu
Anhui
Shanghai
Chongqing
Hubei
Sichuan
Zhejiang
Jiangxi
Hunan
Guizhou
Fujian
Guangdong
Taiwan
Guangxi
Hong Kong
Macau

We would appreciate it if readers could alert us as to errors and omissions by writing in to:

China Knowledge Press Private Limited

China Business Guide Editor
8 Temasek Boulevard
#37-01A Suntec Tower Three
Singapore 038988

ISBN 9814163007

Printed in Singapore

FOREWORD

China's emergence as the world's largest factory and top consumer market has fueled interest among business people all over the world. Today, China is quickly integrating itself into the world trading ecosystem and changing equations of production. In the process, it inadvertently induces global operating efficiency and puts pressure on foreign enterprises to stay competitive.

In the first quarter of 2004, China attracted USD 13.1 billion worth of Foreign Direct Investment (FDI) and has, since 2001, overtaken the US and UK as the largest recipient of FDI. Its spectacular GDP growth of 9.7% in the first half of 2003, in spite of the outbreak of SARS, can only strengthen one's conviction in China's economic resilience. The pessimism of detractors has proven to be somewhat myopic in perspective.

Newspapers and trade publications in the UK, Germany, France, US, Malaysia, Singapore, Hong Kong and China had unanimously reviewed our first edition, and concurred on the usefulness and information value of the Guide for business travelers and even seasoned entrepreneurs in China.

Unlike other business guides on China, this Guide covers the entire country: the four municipalities, twenty-two provinces, five autonomous regions and two Special Administrative regions (excluding Taiwan). For all of these thirty-three administrative regions, we offer a general account of the region, the most up-to-date figures, vital statistics, maps, and current business news.

For business people looking to set up manufacturing facilities, we have added information gathered from over two years' worth of research, surveys and site visits to more than two hundred state-level industrial parks and development zones. This saves the potential investor time and effort in gathering the requisite information.

Apart from the well-developed coastal cities and the booming Pearl River Delta and Yangtze River Delta regions, this Guide also offers updates on the development of the western regions, and suggests ways to tap the huge market potential of the lesser developed northeastern region comprising Jilin, Heilongjiang and Liaoning.

The Guide crystallizes the practical knowledge and experience of our experts in the China market, and research undertaken by analysts and consultants who have provided valuable advice to entrepreneurs, foreign diplomats and government bodies.

Synthesizing our wide range of business guides and industry reports into a single volume for easy reference, we are happy to present you yet another comprehensive and practical guide.

We hope China Business Guide is your most informative companion and business tool to tap into The Land of Opportunities, China.

Charles Chaw C. Loong
Managing Director
China Knowledge Press

May 2004
Singapore

CONTENTS

ABOUT CHINA

Introduction

China, one of the earliest cradles of civilization, is the third largest country in the world with 5000-year-old history of dynasties and revolutions. It also has the largest population in the world, comprising about one fifth of the human population. Spanning over 31 provinces and autonomous regions, China has a vast land area of approximately 9,600,000 km^2.

It is one of the fastest growing economies in the world offering great opportunities to foreign investors and traders.

CHINA General Fact Sheet 2003	
Area (km^2)	approx 9.6 million
Geographic coordinates	35°North, 105°East
Population	1.3 billion
Population growth	0.60%
Birth rate	12.96 births/ 1,000
Death rate	6.74 deaths/ 1,000
Sex ratio	1.09 male/ female
Life expectancy	72 years
Literacy rate	86%
Capital	Beijing
National holiday	1 October (1949)
National Symbols	
~Flag	(see above)
~Anthem	The March of the Volunteers
~Animal	Giant Panda
~Landmark	The Great Wall of China
~Flower (Unofficial)	Peony

Great Wall of China

One of the seven wonders in the world, the Great Wall of China, also known as "Wan Li Chang Cheng", spans 6700km and was built by China's first Emperor, Qin Shihuang. It was constructed to fend off invasion attempts by the tribal people from the Northern part of China.

The Great Wall has since become a national monument and a tourist attraction. The Great Wall has also inspired many stories and legends. One of the most famous is about Meng Jiang Nü, whose sorrow over her husband's death caused part of the great wall to collapse. This story exemplifies the hardship and grief experienced by the commoners during the construction of the Great Wall.

Many operas and songs have been written about the Great Wall and it has become an important part of the Chinese culture.

Ancient Chinese History

Period	Dynasties		Events
1.7 million years ago - 2100 BC	Primitive Society (Stone Age)	原始社会	The Yuanmou Man, dating back to 1.7 million years, was the earliest mankind found living in China. Evidence of the use and control of fire, an essential part of human life, was also discovered. As society progressed, there was a gradual transience from a matriarchal to patriarchal society; from a society where intermarriages among the same family were the norm, to an exogamous society.
2100 - 1600 BC	Xia	夏	The first dynasty founded by Yu the Great. A slavery society.
1600 - 1100 BC	Shang	商	Oracle script, the oldest form of communication, was invented. A civilization based on agriculture and handicraft. Currency in the form of seashells was first used.
1100 - 770 BC	Western Zhou	西周	Start of the feudal serf society. Bartering was also used in trade.
770 - 403 BC	Eastern Zhou 东周	Spring-Autumn Period 春秋时代	Divisive rule by feudal states. Emergence of the feudal landlord class.
403 - 221 BC		Warring States Period 战国时代	Seven feudal states were at its strongest. During this period different schools of thought developed into the "Hundred Schools of Thought", and China's oldest existing literature The Five Classics, consisting of five different books, were written. Advances were made in astronomy, calendric system and medical studies.
221 - 206 BC	Qin	秦	The first unified, central state in China. First Emperor of China Qin Shihuang constructed the Great Wall of China, standardised the writing, currency and metric system. The dynasty was overthrown by China's first countrywide revolution lead by the peasants.
206 BC - 24 AD	Han 汉	Western Han 西汉	One of the golden eras in China history.

			China officially became a Confucian state and literature and arts flourished. Paper was invented. The dynasty reached its prosperous peak during the reign of Emperor Han Wendi and Emperor Han Jingdi.
25 - 189		Eastern Han 东汉	The empire expanded westward, opening the "Silk Road" that facilitated trading. The later part of the Han dynasty witnessed a power struggle between the consort clans (外戚) and the court eunuchs (宦官).
190 - 280	Three Kingdoms Period	三国	The three kingdoms Wei, Shu and Wu fought for control of China. Wei (ruled by Cao Cao) was the most powerful. Nearing the end of the Cao clan's rule, in 280 AD, the Sima clan succeeded in conquering the other two states to take over China.
280 - 316	Jin 晋	Western Jin 西晋	The Sima clan led this unstable empire. Due to the rampant corruption and the lack of strong leadership, the Jin dynasty was overthrown.
317 - 420		Eastern Jin 东晋	
317 439	Sixteen Kingdoms	十六国	This was a time of great division.
439 581	Northern Dynasty	北朝	Gunpowder and the wheel barrow were invented. Historians also noted great advancement in medicine, mathematics, geography, astronomy and cartography.
420 589	Southern Dynasty 南朝	Song 宋 (420-479) Qi 齐 (479-502) Liang 梁 (502-557) Chen 陈 (557-589)	
581 - 618	Sui	隋	After a long period of division, China is reunified, political and economic reforms were made. The Grand Canal was completed and the Great Wall of China was reconstructed. Major progress was made in the ship building industry.
618 - 907	Tang	唐	The "Golden Age" of China. Emperor Tang Taizong, went into the annals of history as one of the greatest rulers of China, by implementing a series of policies known as the Zhenguan reign period reforms, and thus brought China to a new height of prosperity.

			Under Tang rule, Chinese territory covered an even larger area than that of the Han Dynasty. Literature, arts, sciences and technology flourished. China's most renowned poets, Li Bai, Du Fu and Bai Juyi lived during that time. Block printing and gunpowder was invented. Many schools of Buddhism were opened. The dynasty was interrupted by the second Zhou Dynasty (690 - 705 AD) which was ruled by Empress Wu Zetian, the first female emperor in Chinese history.
907 - 960	Five Dynasties and Ten Kingdoms	五代十国	A period of political unrest when short dynasties and kingdoms existed. Paper money was first used in China to replace the existing copper money.
960 - 1127	Song 宋	Northern Song 北宋	The Northern Song dynasty basically unified the southern part of China, however powerful kingdoms such as Liao and Xixia existed. Commerce and foreign trade prospered. Movable-type printing and compass were invented.
1127 - 1279		Southern Song 南宋	Southern Song was established after Jin Kingdom overthrew Northern Song and Liao. The famous Song warrior Yue Fei belongs to this era.
1271 - 1368	Yuan	元	Kublai Khan (1215-94), the grandson of Genghis Khan, overthrew the Song dynasty to mark the beginning of Mongolian rule in China. Novels and drama flourished during this period as Vernacular Chinese became popular.
1368 - 1644	Ming	明	Founded by Emperor Ming Taizu (Zhu Yuanzhang) in 1368, Ming Dynasty was believed to be one of the most powerful nations at that time. Zheng He, the great Chinese marine navigator, led huge fleets and voyaged to many countries.
1644 - 1911	Qing	清	The Qing Dynasty was founded by the Manchus. During its early reigns, China enjoyed peace, prosperity and strong economic growth. International trade was allowed to grow.

Under the Qing's rule, Han Chinese was a subjugated class. There were many regulations restricting their daily lifestyles and activities. Intermarriages between Manchus and Han Chinese were forbidden in order to preserve the purity of their race.

After mid-Qing, the glorious days of the empire were tainted by unsolved problems of corruption within the ruling body and mass poverty. Over time, a series of uprisings broke out. In addition to these internal struggles, conflicts with the West also surfaced. In 1840, the first Opium War broke out.

In 1911, the Xinhai Revolution led by Dr. Sun Yat-sen, led to the collapse of Qing Dynasty, thus ending centuries of monarchial rule in China.

Contemporary Chinese History (1949-present)

Year	Event	Brief Description
1949	Establishment of the People's Republic of China	1 October 1949 marked the official founding of the PRC. Mao Zedong, Chairman of the Central People's government council, became the leader of the PRC.
1956-1957	The Hundred Flowers Campaign	During a Supreme State Conference on 2 May 1958, Mao Zedong declared his intention to "let a hundred flowers bloom, let a hundred schools of thought contends." This marks the short-lived liberalization of academic, artistic and literary pursuits.
1957-1962	The Great Leap Forward	The CCP, governing body of PRC, launched this campaign to speed up the economic and technological development of the country.
1966-1976	The Cultural Revolution	The Cultural Revolution which spanned ten tumultuous years had a devastating impact on China. This was the period in which the radical leftists in the party implemented misguided policies that crippled the Chinese economy. Instead of advancing, China moved backward. As a result, its economic development was staggered about 20 years.

1971	Official United Nations recognition of the People's Republic of China	In 1971, during the 26th session of the UN General Assembly, the historic Resolution 2758 (XXVI) was adopted, by an overwhelming majority, which recognizes in unequivocal terms that "the representatives of the Government of the People's Republic of China are the only lawful representatives of China to the United Nations."
1972	US President Richard Nixon's First Visit to China	Nixon's 1972 trip to China opened a new chapter in Sino-American dealings. This move made in the spirit of "détente", normalized relations between the two countries for the first time since the establishment of the People's Republic of China. The late Chairman Mao had given special attention to the visit and the two leaders had an open discussion on major issues of mutual concern. Prior to the visit, hostility, mistrust and the clash of ideologies made it impossible for the two countries to develop a meaningful relationship. Since then, their strained relationship thawed. It also paved way for cultural, scientific and trade exchanges between these two powers and eventually led to US diplomatic recognition of the PRC (1979). On 28 February 1972, the Shanghai Communiqué was signed by the People's Republic of China and the United States of America. It did not conform to the usual style of communiqués as both sides expressed their differing views as well as points of agreement on bilateral and international issues. It was a historic moment, a breakthrough in Sino-US relations in which diplomatic contact was established and would become more frequent in the years to come.
1976	Demise of Chairman Mao	Mao Zedong died on September 9, 1976, in Beijing. His death affected millions of Chinese people. Mourners from all over the nation went to Beijing to pay their respects to their leader. This also marks the end of the Cultural Revolution, a tragic chapter in the history of Contemporary China.
1978	The Third Plenary Session	Turning point in the history of contemporary China. The year 1978

		marked the start of economic reform and liberalization in China. In July 1977, Deng Xiaoping who had made valuable contributions during the earlier years and won the respect of both the people and the Party was reinstated to his former posts. He assumed leadership of China in 1978. The Third Plenary Session of the Party's Eleventh Central Committee was convened in December 1978. In a dramatic speech, Deng Xiaoping advocated critical thinking and the search for truth from facts, stressing the importance of economic development and essentially repudiated extreme leftist policies of the past that crippled the Chinese economy.
1979	US Diplomatic Recognition of the People's Republic of China	This event marked the exchange of ambassadors and the establishment of a US embassy in China.
1989	The Tian'anmen Event	Student uprisings at Tian'anmen Square in Beijing on 4 June 1989.
1992	Deng Xiaoping's Spring Speech	During his tour of South China, Deng delivered a series of speeches calling for greater commitment to market reforms. China embarked on the road to reform and market economy in 1978. The pace of reform, however, slowed dramatically in 1989. It was only in 1992, during Deng Xiaoping's visit to South China that the tide turned definitively. After stepping down as party chief and premier, Deng attempted to revitalize the economic reform program that he had undertaken, and during his trip south, became the most outspoken proponent of the market economy. Dubbed "南巡 nanxun" or "southern inspection tour", this is a term coined to describe the trips made by the emperors around China to get a better picture of the lives their people led. Deng Xiaoping's 1992 visit was a revolutionary event. In an attempt to cut China loose from the bonds holding the country back from attaining its full economic potential, Deng gave a series of astonishing speeches declaring that China should stop acting "like a woman with bound feet", and should "stride boldly forward" into the marketplace. Shenzhen was selected as the spot for this "Spring Speech" because

		Deng felt that the remarkable rise of Shenzhen into a booming entrepreneurial town is symbolic of the power of market economy. The speech of 1992 had a tremendous impact on China. It reaffirmed the economic course China had been pursuing under Deng's leadership and was a message to the international community that market reform in China would continue. Following the speech, foreign direct investment into China soared.
1993	Jiang Zemin was elected as the President of the PRC	This marked the succession of the third generation of Chinese leaders.
1997	Return of Hong Kong to China	This was a historic event which marked the end of British sovereignty over Hong Kong.
1997	Demise of Deng Xiaoping	The country mourned the death of a great leader.
1999	Return of Macau	Two years after Hong Kong, Macau was returned in 1999.
2001	Successful bid for Olympics 2008	Beijing won the bid to host the Olympics in 2008
2001	China enters the WTO	November 2001 marked the official entry of China into the WTO, reaffirming its commitment to lowering tariff and other barriers to trade.
2003	Hu Jintao was elected President of the PRC	Hu is now general secretary of the CPC Central Committee, president of the PRC, and vice chairman of the Central Military Commission.

Beijing History

Period	Dynasties	Description
1045 B.C.		The legendary story of how the Huang Di battled against tribal leader Chiyou in Zhoulu, a town east of present day Beijing. His successor, Emperor Yao was said to build Youdu where Ji city was actually established.
226 B.C.	Qin	Emperor Qin Shihuang occupied Ji and was named the administrative centre of Guangyang Commandery. For a thousand years, Ji remained one of the strategic trading and military centre as well as an object of frequent power struggles. He also built the Great Wall of China.

581 - 618	Sui	Was named Zhuojun by Emperor Yang of the Sui Dynasty. He also used it as a military base for amassing troops and supplies for war against Korea.
618 - 907	Tang	Called Youshou by Emperor Taizong where he used the place to build a Temple for Compassion for loyalists (Minzhongsi).
916 - 1125	Liao	Khitans occupied Ji and named it Nanjing, second capital of Liao
1153	Jin	Called Zhongdu, capital of Jin where the Nüzhen (Jurchen) conquered Liao.
1215	Yuan	Occupied by Genghis Khan and called Yanjing only a province rather than a capital
1272	Yuan	Kublai Khan rebuilt Yanjing and called it Dadu, the capital of Yuan. It became an important political centre when the Mongolians unified China. The reconstruction of Dadu consisted of 3 major projects - imperial palaces, city walls, moats and canals.
1368	Ming	The founding emperor, Zhu Yuanzhang seized Dadu and made Nanjing its capital.
1406	Ming	Started the construction of Forbidden City. Major walls as high as 12 metres were built around the city of Beiping by Emperor Yongle. In addition, the palace and gardens were also built during this time and completed in 1420.
1421	Ming	Emperor Yongle formally transferred the capital to Beiping and named it Beijing for the first time.
1564	Ming	Expanded further south to form the present day city size by Emperor Jiajing.
1644	Qing	Became the Qing Capital.
1860	Qing	British-French Allied Forces invaded the city and burnt down Yuanmingyuan.
1900	Qing	Eight-Power Allied Forces invaded the city to suppress Boxer Movement.
1911		Sun Yat-Sen's revolution put an end to the rule of Qing. And founded the Republic of China (then renamed Beiping).
1937		Japan invaded Beiping.
1945		Surrender of Japan.
1949		On 1 October, Chairman Mao established the People's Republic of China, resumed name of Beijing as capital.

Topography

Climate & Seasons

China experiences a diverse range of climatic conditions in different parts of the country, from scorching heat in the Southern Wuhan, Chongqing & Nanjing, to subzero coldness in the Northern Beijing, Inner Mongolia and Heilongjiang. The diversity is further enhanced by the changing of seasons, each lasting about three months. Though blessed with the four seasons, some parts of China are susceptible to more extreme weather conditions, including floods, typhoons, droughts and earthquakes.

Changjiang & Yellow River

Changjiang, also known as Yangtze River, originates from the Tanggula Mountains, passing through Chongqing, Wuhan, Nanjing and Shanghai before it flows into the East China Sea. It is the third longest river in the world after Nile and the Amazon, stretching a distance of 6, 400km. Affectionately termed China's Lifeline, Changjiang supports many activities of the Chinese population.

Yellow River, also known as Huanghe, lies further north to Changjiang. It stretches from Lanzhou to Beijing, carrying yellow muddy substance known as loess. Although the loess deposits on the banks of the river are useful resources, the yellow river is prone to flooding and is a threat the population residing nearby.

Terrain, Flora & Fauna

On the vast land of China lie many different forms of topography like deserts (on the Western side), high plateaus, plains, deltas and most prominently, mountains. The variety of landscapes has cultivated a huge array of flora and fauna.

Majority of the people reside in the rural areas.

Among the many species found in the Chinese forests, the bamboo is perhaps the most famous. This plant is the main food source of the giant panda and also a useful raw material. Other well-known plants found in China include lotus, magnolia, maple, ginkgo and spruce.

The giant panda is one of the most widely recognized symbols of China. The natural habitat for this national treasure is the temperate zone in central China, where bamboo grows in abundance. The giant panda is an endangered species. Currently only about 1,000 are left in the wilderness while over a hundred are living in Chinese zoos. Other endangered animals are the south china tiger, snow leopard, Changjiang dolphin and the red-crowned crane.

People

Demographics

China has a population of about 1. 3 billion (estimated at July 2003) with an annual growth rate of 0.6% and male to female ratio of 1.09. The majority of the people reside in the rural area, with about 30% of them living in the urban regions. The population structure is as follows:

The labour force is 744 million (estimated 2001) and the breakdown is on the next page:

The unemployment rate is at 4% in the urban regions and more substantial in the rural areas.

The literacy rate has been on the rise for the past years because the Chinese Government has progressively made education

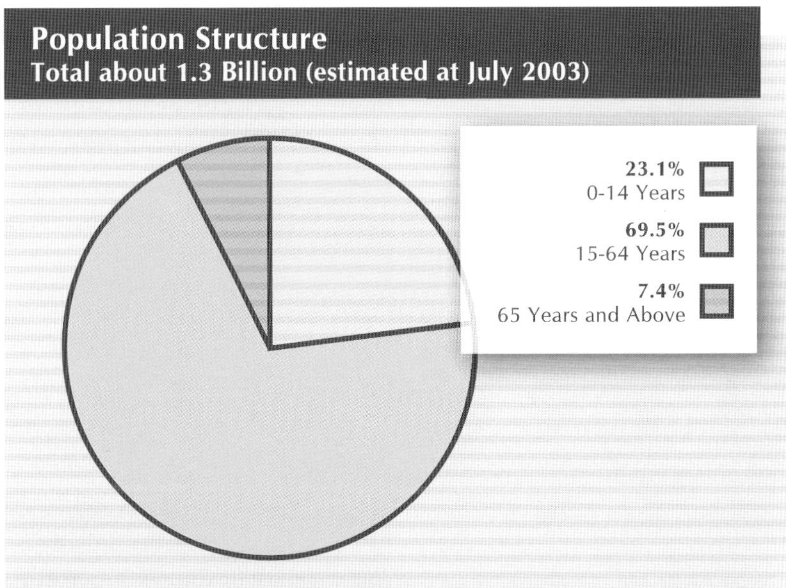

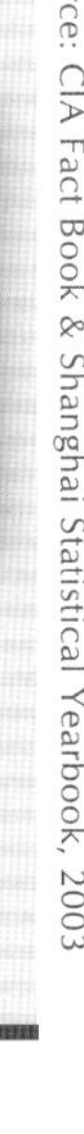

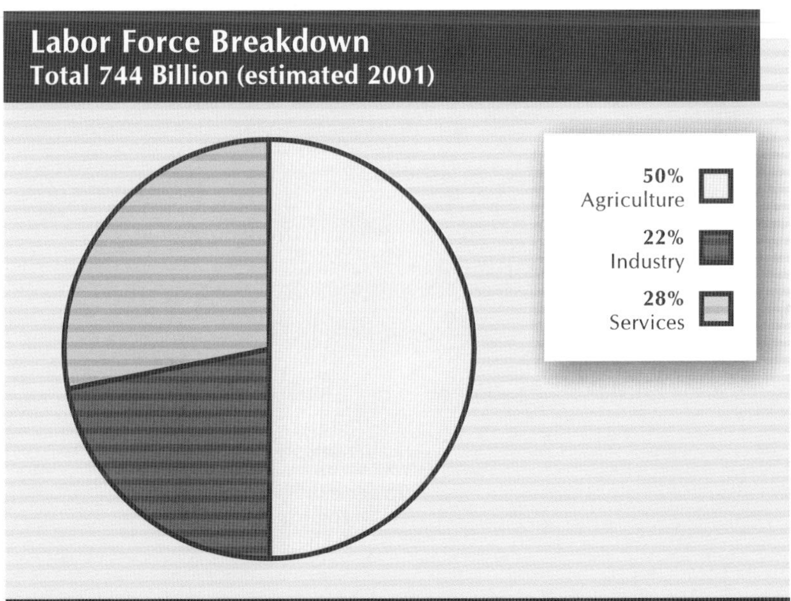

Source: CIA Fact Book & Shanghai Statistical Yearbook, 2003

compulsory in many provinces. As a result, the current literacy rate in China stands at 86%.

Ethnic Groups

China has many ethnic groups, with the Han Chinese constituting about 92% of the total population. The Han people speak and write the Chinese language, which is also the working language in China. The remaining 8% of the population makes up 55 different minor groups. Yunnan alone hosts 24. Autonomous states like Guangxi, Ningxia, Inner Mongolia, Tibet and Xinjiang are also the home to the larger minority groups.

In each region, different dialects are spoken. Eight of the main dialects are Chinese, Shanghainese (Wu), Cantonese (Yue), Minbei (Fuzhou), Minnan (Taiwanese), Hakka, Xiang and Gan. The use of English is becoming more prevalent as China is fast developing into an economic powerhouse and a tourist capital.

Religion & Philosophy China is a country with many religions. The people have the legal right to choose their own religion. All religions hold equal status and exist in harmony.

Buddhism was the first religion to enter China during the later Han and has greatly influenced China's history and culture. The translation of scriptures led to the

Chinese people have freedom to choose their own religion

development of the Chinese language. Stories in Buddhism also played an important role in shaping early Chinese thinking. The Buddhists in China attend occasional services, practice rituals, and support a temple on a regular basis. It has been estimated that 68 million Chinese consider themselves Buddhists.

Islam started in China's Xinjiang regions during the Tang dynasty, and slowly extended to other parts of China. It is an important religion and has converted many ethnic groups like the Kazak, Baoan and Dongxiang. One autonomous region, Ningxia, has been designated for Muslims. Today, there are believed to be more than four million Chinese Muslims.

Christianity entered China as early as the 7th century, but only became actively practiced after the 17th century. Following the entry into China of the Western powers in the 19th century, a large number of Catholic and Protestant missionaries came into the country. However, these missionaries had difficulty converting the Chinese because Christianity was associated in the people's mind with Western Imperialism. Christians are estimated to comprise about one percent of China's population today.

Taoism was founded in China during the Han dynasty, and originated from Laozi's school of philosophy. Laozi believed that human and nature should co-exist in harmony, and this philosophy has been central to the evolution of acupuncture, herbal medicine, tai chi and meditation into what they are today.

Confucianism is a school of philosophy rather than a religion. It was founded during the Spring-Autumn period by Confucius but only became influential during the Han dynasty when the Han rulers adopted Confucianism teachings. This philosophy pervaded Chinese thought and has a huge impact on Chinese culture and society even till now.

Traditionally Taoism and Confucianism are moral guides to the ethical behaviour. Both schools of thought started during the Golden Age of Chinese thought. Taoism taught individuals to maintain inner peace while living in harmony with the nature and surroundings while Confucianism sought to inculcate a set of behaviourism that will create a cordial and fair society. They have been the central influence on the Chinese way of thinking up till today.

A nation rich in culture.

Culture

Chinese Calligraphy 书法

Chinese calligraphy is an ancient art. Chinese characters evolved from pictures and signs, and this unique form of art came into being during the development of writing. Literally translated, calligraphy means beautiful writing. Four basic tools of Chinese calligraphers are brush, ink, ink slab and paper, commonly referred to as the "Four Treasures of the Scholar (文房四宝)". Using fine paper, brushes and ink, calligraphers have developed a wide variety of writing styles, handed down from generation to generation. The distinctiveness of Chinese calligraphy lies in the aesthetic appeal of these varied writing styles.

Chinese calligraphy is an avenue of self-expression among the educated society in China. Practicing and appreciating Chinese calligraphy was a common past-time of the royal family, court officials and scholars during the imperial era. Great calligraphers surfaced in each dynasty, and their works became representative of their time. Once a critical standard for the literati, calligraphy has since evolved into a unique branch of art in China. Mastery of this art requires great patience, discipline, and grace.

Chinese Painting

Chinese painting is a traditional art form whose roots can be traced back to the ancient times. Like calligraphy, it is a hobby the literati engaged in. Painting is usually done using a brush on paper or silk, often with black ink. Classical Chinese painting can be broadly classified into three categories: landscapes, figures and birds-and-flowers. More than decorative art, Chinese paintings also serve as important records of the past. Images of emperors and their concubines, philosophers, and generals were immortalized by such paintings while landscapes and bird-and-flower paintings demonstrated the importance of nature in the Chinese way of thinking.

Martial Arts (Wushu – 武术)

More commonly known as Kung Fu in the Western countries, it features high flying kicks, strong vicious punches and suave kung fu choreography. Beyond the physical fights and exercises, it also incorporates Chinese philosophy, meditation and aesthetics. In the past, Wushu is used to train soldiers in survival combat skills. However in these days, many people are practicing Wushu for health, defence, mental discipline, entertainment and competitive reasons. It is a recognized sport of the Olympics Games. The most famous Wushu schools are Shaolin Temple and Mt. Wudang and among them only Shaolin teaches hundreds of styles of Wushu. Just to name a few, they are Chang Quan (long fist), Nan Quan (southern fist), Taiji Quan, Xingyi Quan and Bagua Quan.

Chinese Opera

A traditional form of stage entertainment fusing elements of mime, dance, song, dialogue, swordplay and acrobatics into one.

All these combined with expressions, delicate movements and dramatic gestures present a spectacular performance. Unlike the Western opera, the Chinese do not use complicated and expensive stage props and backdrops. Chinese opera conveys the message to the audience through the acting skills of performers. Specific and extravagant costumes, facial make-ups, musical motifs and recitations complement such perfect acting to portray each character more distinctively. The more elaborate the costume and the head-dress or head-gear, the more important the character is. Another prominent feature of Chinese opera is the painted faces of the performers. Colours shown on the faces usually reflect a physical attribute of the character and they also indicate his personality.

Opera is a form of popular Chinese stage entertainment

Most Westerners find the singing from the opera to be "noisy" and shrill. Songs are usually accompanied by loud gongs, crashing cymbals, and droning stringed instruments. There are almost 300 forms of opera (depending on the places of their origins). Beijing opera is considered the most refined and popular. Others include Pingju, Kunqu, Shaoxing, Henan, Sichuan, Shanxi, Huangmei, Huagu and Yangko.

Tea Culture

Tea is made from the supple leaves of the Camellia Sinensis plant, native to both China and India. Tea was "supposedly" discovered by Shen Nong (the Divine Farmer) in 2700 BC. Since then tea has been part of the daily lives of the Chinese and is used

Tea drinking is an art in Chinese culture

in several products such as ice-cream, shampoo, medicine and even special dishes such as smoked tea duck. Because of their passion for tea-drinking, the Chinese are extremely critical about tea and had high requirements about the tea quality (colour and fragrance), water and tea wares. The finest tea is grown on high altitudes of 3,000 to 7,000 feet. Water used also plays an important role and it is often gathered from springs, rain or snow. Among them, spring and rainwater in autumn are considered the prefect ingredients for brewing tea. Water is considered perfect when its tastes are sweet, pure, cool, clean and flowing. The famous tea wares used are purple clay wares (紫茶壶) made from Yixing, Jiangsu province and Jingdezhen, Jiangxi Province.

Many conventions govern tea drinking in Chinese cultures. The host will only pour tea about seven tenth full, because the other three tenth is said to be filled with friendship and affection. The guest should finish the tea in three gulps. Tea plays an important role in Chinese social life. Serving a cup of tea is more than mere politeness; it is also a symbol of togetherness, a gesture of sharing and enjoyment as well as friendship and respect.

Geomancy (Fengshui – 风水)

Fengshui means wind and water in Chinese. It is frequently practiced in architecture, which links the whole process from site selection, designing, construction and interior and exterior decorating. It combines the trinity forces of Heaven, Earth and Human as well as the emphasis on cohabitation with the surrounding environment of the structure. The art of fengshui advocates the presence of magnetic field termed as the Qi field. Fengshui is often used to avoid evil qi and gain auspicious ones. An example of the best orientation is to build the structure facing a river or lake in the south and back against a hill in the north.

Chinese Zodiac

The ancient Chinese invented 10 Heavenly Stems and 12 Earthly Branches for chronological purposes. Since most of the commoners then were illiterate, the 12 Earthly Branches were replaced by 12 animals in order to be easily remembered. These 12 animals are rat, ox, tiger, rabbit, dragon, snake, horse, sheep, monkey, rooster, dog and pig which form the Chinese zodiac signs. They are based on year rather than month as in the Western horoscopes and most of an individual personality and profile is revealed from his/her birth time.

RAT

1912, 1924, 1936, 1948, 1960, 1972, 1984, 1996.
The first animal in the zodiac cycle. People born in the year of rat are usually imaginative, charming and generous to loved ones. However, they are often hot-tempered and critical. Rats get along well with Dragons and Monkeys but should avoid Horses.

OX

1913, 1925, 1937, 1949, 1961, 1973, 1985, 1997.
People born in the year of Ox are natural leaders and will also make excellent parents. They are also upright, inspiring, easy-going and conservative. Ox gets along well with Snakes and Roosters but not with Sheep.

TIGER

1914, 1926, 1938, 1950, 1962, 1974, 1986, 1998.
Those born under this sign are usually aggressive, sensitive, charming and emotional. They bland well with Horses and Dogs but not Monkey.

RABBIT

1915, 1927, 1939, 1951, 1963, 1975, 1987, 1999.
Usually affectionate, talented, tranquillity and obliging. They are sometimes over emotional and superficial to avoid conflicts. Their best partners are Sheep or Pigs instead of Roosters.

DRAGON

1916, 1928, 1940, 1952, 1964, 1976, 1988, 2000.
The most popular zodiac sign among all. Those born under this sign are considered as intelligent, gifted, popular, full of vitality and successful. Dragons are compatible with Snakes or Rooster but not with Sheep

SNAKE

1917, 1929, 1941, 1953, 1965, 1977, 1989, 2001.
These people are usually clever, passionate and romantic. Some believe that those women born under this zodiac sign are often beautiful. Good partnership with Rooster or Ox but not Pig.

HORSE

1918, 1930, 1942, 1954, 1966, 1978, 1990, 2002.
They are deemed to be hardworking, friendly and cheerful but sometimes impatient. They get along well with Tigers and Dogs instead of Rats.

SHEEP

1919, 1931, 1943, 1955, 1967, 1979, 1991, 2003.
People under this sign are usually creative, artistic, passionate, honest and charming. But they can be pessimistic, too dependent on material comforts and timid at times. They are most compatible with Rabbits and Pigs but not with Ox.

MONKEY

1920, 1932, 1944, 1956, 1968, 1980, 1992, 2004.
Monkeys are intelligent and entertaining but can be discouraged easily. Best match with Dragons and Rats but not Tigers.

ROOSTER

1921, 1933, 1945, 1957, 1969, 1981, 1993, 2005.
They are perceived as courageous, hardworking, arrogant and reckless. Roosters work well with Snakes and Ox but not with Rabbits.

DOG

1922, 1934, 1946, 1958, 1970, 1982, 1994, 2006.
Those born under this sign are usually honest, quiet, stubborn and faithful. However, they can be introvert and cynical sometimes. Best match are Tigers and Horses but not with Dragons.

PIG

1923, 1935, 1947, 1959, 1971, 1983, 1995, 2007.
They are honest, reliable, sincere and shy. Pigs should be aware of other Pigs and are compatible with Sheep and Rabbits.

Cuisine

"To the People, Food is Heaven" ~ ancient Chinese Proverb 民以食为天 and therefore the Chinese place strong emphasis on their cuisine. Most of the dishes are required to "express" certain qualities, such as colour, fragrance and taste. Chinese cuisine can be broadly categorized by region: namely Shandong, Sichuan, Guangdong (Cantonese), Fujian, Jiangsu, Zhejiang, Hunan and Anhui.

Shandong Cuisine – emphasizes the freshness and aroma of the food. Most of the dishes are non- greasy. Garlic and shallots are used in abundance as seasonings, enriching the flavour and enhancing its taste. A typical menu will include Bird's Nest燕窝, Yellow River Carp in Sweet and Sour 酸甜鲤鱼.

Sichuan Cuisine – frequent use of chillies and peppers are to emphasize the spiciness of the food, even for vegetables. Like the Shandong cuisine, garlic is also widely used in food preparation. In addition, ginger and fermented beans are included in cooking process. A typical menu will include Hot Pot 麻辣火锅 , Kung Bao Chicken宫保鸡丁, Mapo Doufu 麻婆豆腐.

Guangdong (Cantonese) Cuisine – most of the dishes taste light, crisp and fresh. Uniqueness of the cuisine depends a lot on the meat and the different fowls used. Most of the food is prepared by the steaming or stir-frying method in order to retain its original flavour. The presentation of the dishes is also very important. A typical menu will include Shark Fin Soup 鱼翅汤, Steamed Sea Bass 清蒸鲈鱼 and Roasted Piglet烤乳猪.

Fujian Cuisine – unlike the Cantonese cuisine, Fujian uses seafood as the main ingredient. Most chefs highlight the sweet and sour taste in their cooking. A typical menu will include Snow Chicken 雪花鸡.

Jiangsu Cuisine – also known as Huaiyang Cuisine. Similar to the

Fujian cuisine, the seafood is largely used as the main ingredient. The Jiangsu cuisine stresses the freshness and sweetness of food. A typical menu will include Stewed Crab with Clear Soup 清汤炖蟹, Long-boiled and Dry-shredded Meat 熬干肉丝 and Duck Triplet 三煮鸭.

Zhejiang Cuisine – gains reputation for the freshness, tenderness, softness and smoothness of its dishes with their mellow fragrance. A typical menu includes Sour West Lake Fish 酸西湖鱼, Longjing Shelled Shrimp龙井壳虾 and Beggar's Chicken 叫化鸡 .

Hunan Cuisine – compared to Sichuan cuisine, chilli, pepper and shallots are also necessities in Hunan Cuisine. Thus, most of the food prepared Hunan style is flavourful. A typical menu includes Dong'an Chicken 东安鸡 and Peppery & Hot Chicken 胡椒鸡.

Anhui Cuisine – renowned for their stewing and braising techniques. Ham and candied sugar is often added to enhance the taste. A typical menu includes Stewed Snapper 炖鱼and Huangshan Braised Pigeon 烤乳猪.

Dining Etiquette

Chopsticks – a familiar tool in Chinese dining. This utensil is usually a headache to most foreigners. There are a number of taboos restricting the way chopsticks can be used. Dropping them is considered bad luck. Do not cross the chopsticks unless in a dim sum restaurant, because the gesture indicates that one is ready to foot the bill. Never ever stick chopsticks upright in the rice bowl, because this is an omen of death and thus considered extremely impolite to the seniors and host present. Finally, do not tap the bowl with chopsticks. It is deemed as an insult to the host.

Table manners – most people eat together, and usually the host will serve dishes with his/her own chopsticks to guests to show hospitality. For westerners, it is

National Holidays & Festivals

There are ten national holidays in China.

Holiday	Date
*New Year's Day 元旦	1 January
*Chinese New Year 农历新年	January or February (Golden Week)
International Women's Day	3 March
Tree Planting Festival	12 March
*International Labour Day	1 May (Golden Week)
Youth Day	4 May
International Children's Day	1 June
Anniversary of the founding of the People's Liberation Army	1 August
Teacher's Day	10 September
*National Day	1 October (Golden Week)

* denotes Public holidays

acceptable to leave the food alone if one feels uncomfortable about consuming it. Never try to turn over the fish; this is usually done by the host or the waiter. It is deemed as bad luck as it signifies a capsizing fishing boat.

Major Festivals

CHINESE NEW YEAR / SPRING FESTIVAL 春节

Chinese New Year or Spring Festival begins on the first day of the first month of the lunar calendar and officially lasts for three days. It is a major event and as the first traditional festival of the year, the celebrations are grand and colourful.

The Chinese decorate their homes with couplets, paintings and other festive ornaments. Red is the colour of choice because it represents good luck and fortune. On the eve of Chinese New Year, it is customary for the entire family to gather and have a sumptuous reunion dinner 年夜饭. The next morning will be spent visiting with relatives and friends, exchanging greetings and good wishes for the year ahead. On the streets, celebratory events like the lion dance and the dragon dance are held to herald a new year.

The 15th day of the first lunar month is known as Yuan Xiao元宵 or Lantern Festival. On this day, each city will be filled with lights as people take to the streets with colourful lanterns. In the villages, celebrations include fireworks displays.

TOMB SWEEPING DAY 清明节

This is a day to worship one's ancestors. On the 5th day of April, people will visit the graves of their ancestors to clean the site and offer prayers. Hence the name: Tomb Sweeping Day.

DRAGON BOAT FESTIVAL 端午节

The Dragon Boat Festival takes place on the 5th day of the 5th month of the lunar calendar. It is a day to commemorate the poet, Qu Yuan, of the Warring Period.

Qu Yuan was a patriotic man who loved his country. He tried repeatedly to convince his emperor of the merits of his suggestions to the problems the country was facing at that time. However, he was ultimately betrayed by a traitor and exiled. In 278 BC, the Qin army invaded the city of Chu. Qu Yuan drowned himself in the Mi Lo River that year on the 5th day of the 5th month. Legend has it that the people living beside the river rowed out immediately to retrieve his body upon hearing of his death but were unable to find it. Hence, they made rice dumplings to feed the fish in the river in hopes that they would leave his body alone. This soon became an annual event known as the dragon boat race and dumplings became the customary festive food.

MID-AUTUMN FESTIVAL 中秋节

The 15th day of the eighth month of the lunar calendar coincides with mid-autumn and hence is dubbed the Mid-Autumn Festival. On that day, during the imperial era, the Chinese will offer intricate small and round hand-made cakes to the Moon Goddess. After the ceremony, these cakes will be distributed to members of the family, symbolizing unity, togetherness, reunion and harmony. Such a practice endured to this day and each Mid-Autumn night, the family will gather to enjoy these cakes under the moonlight. This soon became known as the Moon Cake Festival.

Social & Business Etiquette

Etiquette in China is as much related to superstition as to courtesy. It is a complex issue most foreign investors fail to understand because of the wide gulf between cultures. Chinese social and business etiquette differs substantially from that of the Western countries. It is however, something that the Chinese place great importance upon. In order to build up business relations with Chinese companies, it is essential to first have a clear understanding of the Chinese cultural context. The success of a business venture will usually depend as much on the foreigner's attention to such issues as anything else.

Chinese culture is strongly influenced by Confucian principles and values pervade both the workplace and society at large. Modesty is a highly valued trait. Men are more empowered than women, the head of the household is a position which commands great respect, and education rather than wealth is seen as a social filter. Professors are among the most respected people in society.

Greetings

Much emphasis should be placed on protocol in business dealings with the Chinese. It is always advisable to address a Chinese person by the surname together with a courtesy title. For business leaders or government officials, the surname together with the professional title will be the most appropriate (for instance: Mayor Li or Director Huang). A handshake is an acceptable greeting although a slight bow or nod will suffice. It is considered polite to bring a gift to one's first meeting with his business partner. Gifts indicate that one is

Interpersonal relationships are important when doing business in China.

sincere in building a relationship. It is the thought that counts, not the material value, hence, gifts are not opened in one's presence.

Relationships (关系 Guanxi)

A particularity of doing business in China is the importance of interpersonal relationships or Guanxi. It is essential for the foreign businessman to establish a personal relationship with his Chinese counterpart in order to build trust. One begins this by doing small favours, like buying a meal or bringing a gift. Interpersonal relationships, more than legal terms, are critical in securing a binding contract.

Negotiating

The first person to enter the room is usually assumed to be the leader of the group. Business cards should always be presented and received with both hands, and exchanged individually. It is extremely rude to deal out business cards across the table. Always scan the business card and then lay in down on the table. Putting it away without first looking at it is deemed as an insult to the person.

Meetings will usually begin with small talk. Foreign businessmen should resist the urge to get down to business directly as this will be taken to imply that they are uninterested in building a relationship. The negotiating process is slow because of this need to first establish a relationship.

The Chinese live in a high context environment where information is not as explicitly codified and other contextual information and implicit signs matter more in the transmission of messages. Non-verbal communication plays a key role. When negotiating or during business meetings, it is to one's advantage to play close attention to body language and other signs. The Chinese will usually not explicitly refuse an offer as this is seen as offensive but will communicate their wishes less directly.

It is a sign of disrespect to have one's business partner deal with one's subordinate (for example making lunch appointment with one via one's secretary). Similarly, sending a young executive to a business meeting with a senior Chinese businessman also indicates that the foreign investor is not taking his partner seriously.

Entertainment

When invited to a business meal, the bill is never divided among the guests. The person who invited others is expected to pay and should insist on doing so even if the guests protest. The Chinese also entertain lavishly and expect the same in return. Toasting is an integral part of business etiquette. The host of a banquet offers the first toast and the guest is expected to return it midway through the

Entertainment is an important aspect of business activity.

banquet. It is considered bad form to drink by oneself in company. Coaxing each other to drink is the norm. Toasts will be proposed throughout the meal, a popular toast is干杯ganbei (bottoms up!). Declining a drink outright is considered rude but medical reasons are great excuses to avoid heavy drinking.

Food is another important aspect of Chinese culture. When inviting a Chinese to one's home, always prepare a proper meal rather than serve finger food and snacks. As a guest, it is also considered polite to sample each dish and leave a little food on one's plate at the end of every meal. Belching can also indicate one's satisfaction with the food.

Symbols and Gestures

Symbols have different meanings in different cultures. There are many gestures and symbols in Chinese culture which have alternative interpretations. For instance, using a finger to scrape one's face while looking at someone else means "Shame on you" to a Chinese. Other inappropriate gestures include sticking one's chopsticks upright in a bowl, or sending chrysanthemums as both are seen as symbols of death. Pens, on the other hand, are very good gifts because penmanship is highly valued in the Chinese culture. It is very easy for an ignorant foreigner to offend the Chinese with an inappropriate gift or gesture.

The conventions surrounding etiquette in China are mostly practiced by the older businessmen. The younger generation, however, are increasingly westernized and are not governed by as many customs. Moreover, the Chinese also do not expect a foreigner to understand all their particularities and will make allowances. The basic rule to keep in mind is just to be polite. Learning a few Chinese words and phrases will be very useful in showing one's interest and sincerity in building a relationship.

Political System & State Structure

China is a country of many political parties. Apart from the Communist Party of China (CPC) which holds real power, there are eight non-Communist parties.

Following the First Plenary Session of Chinese People's Political Consultative Conference (CPPCC) in September 1949, participated by CPC and other democratic parties, the People's Republic of China was elected and founded. Since then, all the non-Communist parties participated in important decisions concerning the state's political issues; and many members of the non-Communist parties have been represented in CPPCC committees in various levels.

Many members of the non-Communist parties hold leading posts on the standing committees of the people's congresses, the committees of CPPCC, government organisations, and economic, cultural, scientific and technological departments at various levels. The non-Communist parties of China are not the opposition parties, but parties that coexist and engage in mutual supervision with CPC.

Political Parties

Communist Party of China (CPC)

Founded in July 1921, the CPC has more than 60 million members today. From 1921 to 1949, the CPC had led the Chinese people in overthrowing the rule of imperialism, feudalism and bureaucrat-capitalism with the establishment of the People's Republic of China (PRC). After the founding of New China, the CPC had led the people in defending the country's independence and safety, and had successfully completed the country's transition from new democracy to socialism.

Unprecedented large-scale socialist constructions have since been carried out systematically, achieving economic and cultural progress unparalleled in the history of China.

Political System & State Structure

COMMITTEE

Hu Jintao
President, also General Secretary of Communist Party

Zeng Qinghong
Vice-President, also on Standing Committee of Political Bureau

Wen Jiabao
Premier of the State Council, also on Standing Committee of Political Bureau

Standing Committee of State Council
Premier, 4 Vice Premiers, 5 State Councilors. Secretary General Members at ministerial level

State Council
Ministries and commissions, offices, bureaus and institutions

LEGISLATURE

Wu Bangguo
Chairman of Standing Committee of National People's Congress(NPC), also on Standing Committee of Political Bureau

Vice Chairmen Standing Committee of NPC (about 150 members) Meets between NPC annual sessions

JUDICIARY

Xiao Yang
President Supreme People's Court

Jia Chungwang
Procurator - General Supreme People's Procuratorate

MILITARY

Central Military Commission(State)

Jiang Zemin
Chairman, also chairman of Communist Party Central Military Commission

NATIONAL PEOPLE'S CONGRESS (NPC)

Approximately 3,000 delegates meet in plenary session once a year for 2-3 weeks

CHINESE PEOPLE'S POLITICAL CONSULTATIVE CONGRESS (CPPCC)

Jia Qinglin

Chairman, CPPCC also on Standing Committee of Political Bureau

Standing Committee of CPPCC
Chairman, Vice Chairman, Secretary General

The CPPCC meets once a year in plenary session, in conjunction with NPC Delegates include intellectuals, academics, business people, technical experts, overseas Chinese, professionals, democratic parties

Source: China Knowledge Press

The CPC holds real power in China

In September 1997, the CPC convened its historically significant 15th National Congress, where Deng Xiaoping Theory was declared as the guiding ideology of the whole Party.

The Congress has identified the period up to year 2010 as the key period for China's modernization drive. China is expected to actively promote fundamental changes in the economic structure, to establish a socialist market economy that is able to sustain steady and rapid development of the economy. These will lay a solid foundation to realize the country's modernization in the middle of the next century.

The highest leading bodies of the Communist Party of China are the national Party congress (which is held once every five years) and the Central Committee elected at the national Party congress. The Central Committee holds meetings at least once a year. The Central Political Bureau (Politburo), the Politburo's Standing Committee and the general secretary of the Central Committee are elected at a plenary session of the Central Committee, which also decides on members of the Central Secretariat. The Central Political Bureau and its Standing Committee exercise the functions and powers of the Central Committee when it is not in session. The Central Secretariat attends to the day-to-day work of the Politburo and its Standing Committee. The Central Committee's general secretary is responsible for convening meetings of the Central Political Bureau and its Standing Committee, and directs the work of the Central Secretariat. Hu Jintao is the current general secretary.

China Revolutionary Committee of the Kuomintang

Founded in January 1948, the party has more than 60,000 members. The current Central Committee chairman is He Luli. It is for the most part composed of former Kuomintang members and those who have historical connections with Kuomintang.

China Democratic League

Founded in October 1941, it now has more than 144,000 members, mostly intellectuals at fairly senior levels. The current Central Committee chairman is Ding Shisun.

China Democratic National Construction Association

Founded in December 1945, this party has more than 78,000 members, most are from the economic field or academic specialists. The current Central Committee chairman is Cheng Siwei.

China Association for the Promotion of Democracy

Founded in December 1945, this party currently has more than 74, 000 members. Its membership is mainly drawn from intellectuals working in educational, cultural, scientific and publishing fields. The current Central Committee chairman is Xu Jialu.

Chinese Peasants and Workers' Democratic Party

Founded in August 1930, it currently has more than 74,000 members, most of whom work in the fields of public health, culture and education or science and technology. The current Central Committee chairman is Jiang Zhenghua.

China Zhi Gong Dang

Founded in October 1925, this party currently has more than 18,000 members. Most of them are returned overseas Chinese, relatives of overseas Chinese, and representative individuals and specialists and scholars with overseas connections. The current Central Committee chairman is Luo Haocai.

Jiusan Society

Founded in December 1944, this party currently has more than 78, 000 members. They are mostly high-and-medium-level intellectuals working in science and technology, culture and education, or public health. The current Central Committee chairman is Han Qide.

Taiwan Democratic Self-Government League

Founded in November 1947, this party has more than 1,800 members who are mainly people born or with family roots in Taiwan, but are currently residing in mainland China. The current Central Presidium chairman is Zhang Kehui.

Social Organizations

There are a large number of social organizations in China, of which the major ones are the All-China Federation of Trade Unions, the All-China Youth Federation, the All-China Women's Federation, and the All-China Federation of Industry and Commerce.

Porcelain is a popular traditional art.

All-China Federation of Trade Unions

This major organization is the supreme leading body of all the local trade union organizations in China. Founded in May 1925, it currently has 89.13 million members. The current Executive Committee chairman is Wang Zhaoguo.

All-China Youth Federation

Founded in May 1949, this is a

federation comprising of all the youth organizations in China. The current chairman is Sun Jinling. Of the organizational members of the All-China youth Federation, the Communist Youth League of China is the core, being a mass organization made up of China's advanced youth. Founded in May 1922, it currently has 68.71 million members. The current Central Committee first secretary is Zhou Qiang.

All-China Women's Federation

Founded in Aprial 1949, this mass organization was founded to get women from all ethnic groups and all walks of life united to fight for women's further emancipation. The current Executive Committee chairwoman is Gu Xiulian.

All-China Federation of Industry and Commerce

Founded in October 1953, this people's association organised by people in industry and commerce functions as a non-govenmental chamber of commerce for promoting business people's domestic and overseas ties. Its current Executive Committee chairman is Huang Mengfu.

Fiscal Policy & Taxation System

Between 1949 and 1978, China's fiscal policy and taxation system fell in line with that of a planned economy, thus covering all aspects of social life. Since opening up to the rest of the world, reforms have been gradually introduced, allowing China's financial sector to break away from the system of unified distribution of revenues and expenditures that complied with that of a planned economy. Reforms are aimed at diversifying the range of fiscal tools, with the system of distribution intended to control economic operations indirectly and to guide resource distribution.

Since 1984, the Central Government has shifted the national budgetary system from one of single entry to that of double entry. In 1992, reforms were greatly stepped up in order to meet the needs of microeconomic control. By 1994, the skeletal structure of a financial system meeting the needs of a socialist market economy, with tax distribution at its heart, was in place. The main components are:

(i) A multi-tier financial system based upon the rational division of central taxes, local taxes and taxes shared by the central and local governments

(ii) A new system of turnover tax with value added tax as the mainstay, consumption and business taxes as supplements, and the income tax system being established and continually refined

(iii) A double entry budgetary system consisting of regular and constructive budgets

(iv) Promoting balance in the total economic output and the country's economic structure by means of utilising the budget, taxation, state debt and allowances.

Fiscal Solvency

With economic development and reforms in fiscal policy and taxation, the goal of fiscal solvency is within sight. In 1978, the state financial revenue was RMB 113.2 billion yuan. By 2002, the figure had climbed to RMB 1890.4 billion yuan, in no small part due to a proactive fiscal policy stimulating the economy; the government's investment and spending programme was largely paid for by issuing debt.

Taxation is becoming an important source of the state financial revenue. In 1978, tax revenue came up to a total of RMB 51.93 billion yuan. By 2002, the figure was RMB 1763.6 billion yuan. The accumulated taxation income was RMB 11954.6 billion yuan from 1978 to 2002.

Since the introduction of reforms, the distribution relationship between the central and local government finances has been gradually smoothened. A system of

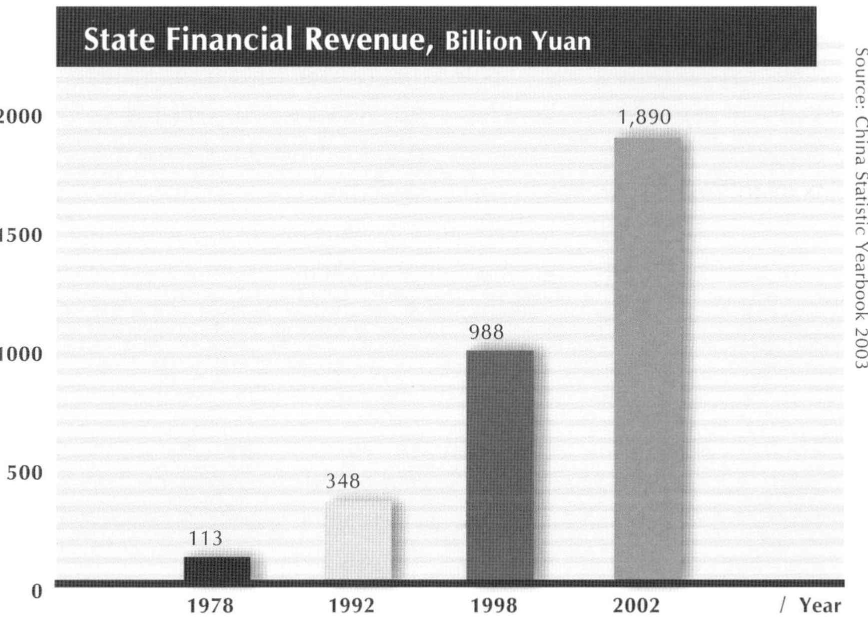
State Financial Revenue, Billion Yuan
2000
1500
1000
500
0
113
348
988
1,890
1978
1992
1998
2002
/ Year
Source: China Statistic Yearbook 2003

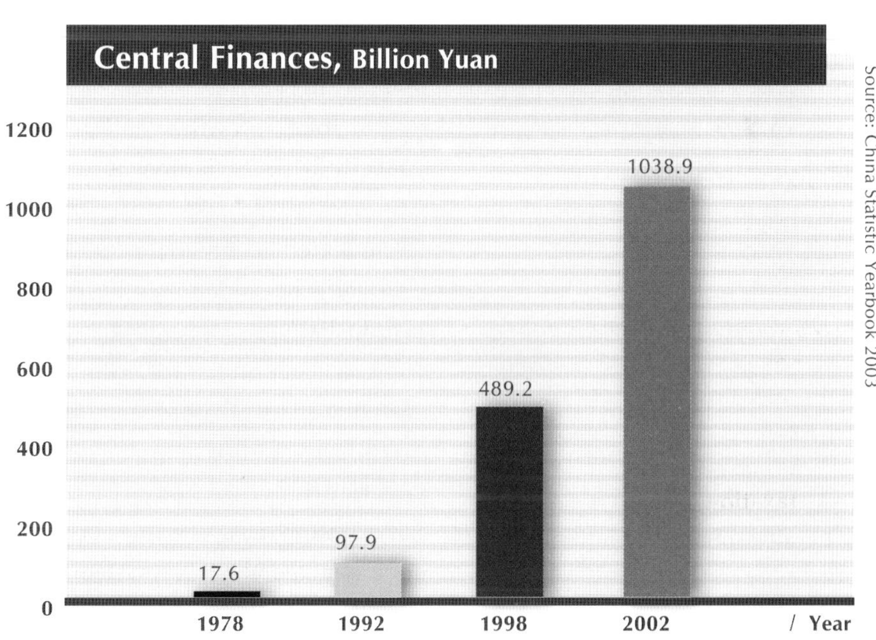
Central Finances, Billion Yuan
1200
1000
800
600
400
200
0
17.6
97.9
489.2
1038.9
1978
1992
1998
2002
/ Year
Source: China Statistic Yearbook 2003

tax distribution under which central finances are growing in a stable and controlled fashion has been built, and the basis for standard transfer payments established. Looking at state financial revenue, central finances accounted for RMB 17.6 billion yuan, 15.5% of the total. By 2002, the figure was RMB 1038.9 billion yuan, 55% of the total.

Taxation

Before reform, China practiced a single taxation system. As taxation lacked any real relation to the economic activity of enterprises, the system suffered from a lack of vitality. In 1981, the Chinese government took the first step in overhauling the taxation system, collecting income tax from Sino-foreign joint ventures as well as solely foreign-funded enterprises. From a single tax category, a compound taxation system in which turnover and income taxes were the mainstay and other tax categories in coordination with it was being shaped, allowing for better control of the state's finances. By 1994, the structural adjustment of the taxation system taking the market economy as the norm was comprehensively realised and, by and large, completed. In 1996, the rate of customs duties was lowered, and a greater degree of import supervision was exercised.

Tax incentives serve as one of the most important factors for foreign investors. Currently, there are 13 types of taxes applicable to foreign-funded enterprises, foreign enterprises and foreigners. These include enterprise income tax, value-added tax, consumption tax, business tax, personal income tax, resource tax, land value-added tax, stamp tax, tax on urban real estate, tax for use of car and ship license plates, slaughter tax, contract tax and construction tax for cultural undertakings. Various tax concessions or breaks are available to foreign-invested enterprises (FIEs) under certain circumstances.

BUSINESS IN CHINA

CHINA'S ECONOMY

China's economy zoomed at an enviable rate of 9.9% year-on-year growth in the fourth quarter of 2003, with per capita income reaching an all-time high of USD 1,090. The impressive performance of the Chinese economy is attributed to the government's pro-active fiscal and monetary policies, growing fixed asset investments etc.

China's foreign exchange reserves rose sharply to a record USD 403.3 billion by the end of 2003, which is 116.8 billion dollars more than a year ago. In 2003, the country attracted USD 115.07 billion worth of investment, up 39% over the previous year.

In 2003, China's total foreign trade volume reached a record of USD 851.2 billion, up 37.1%, much higher than the forecast of 780-800 billion. However, imports outstripped the growth in exports and rose 39.9% to USD 412.84 billion. Exports surged by 34.6% to USD 438.37 billion.

CHINA ECONOMIC Fact Sheet 2003

GDP	USD 1,411 billion
GDP growth rate	9.1%
GDP composition- by sector	
agriculture	14.8%
industry & construction	53.0%
services	32.2%
Labour force	744 million
Labour force - by occupation	
agriculture	50%
industry	22%
services	28%
Exports	USD 438.4 billion
Imports	USD 412.8 billion
Currency	Yuan
Internet users	79.5 million

Data Source: National Bureau of Statistics of China website (Feb 26, 2004)

TRADE

In 2002, China's imports and exports totalled USD 621 billion, of which imports were USD 295 billion, and exports USD 326 billion, producing an annual trade surplus of USD 31 billion., ranking seventh in total imports and exports among chief trading countries. The trade volume between China and its top ten trading partners totalled USD 424.5 billion.

Foreign Trade Laws & Management

Foreign Trade Law

China has instituted a legal system of foreign trade centred around the Foreign Trade Law, which prescribes the management of foreign trade dealers, import and export, commodities and techn-ology, foreign exchange, customs control, import and export commodity inspection, animal and plant quarantine, protection of intellectual property rights, and economic and trade arbitration related to foreign interests and proceedings.

The Foreign Trade Law took effect from July 1, 1994, standardizing foreign trade activities in China in the following ways:

- Ensuring uniformity in its foreign trade system;
- Safeguarding a fair and free foreign trade order;
- Ensuring the independent operational authority of foreign trade dealers;
- Encouraging development of foreign trade; and
- Promoting trade relations with other countries and regions on the basis of equality and mutual benefits.

Foreign Trade Management

1. Imports

Trading of all goods and technology are permitted except for those stipulated otherwise. China enforces quotas and license management on certain imports, thus shielding domestic enterprises from direct foreign competition.

Import Commodity Management

Commodities subjected to quota and import license management (26)		Commodities which are not subjected to quota management but are subjected to import license management (7)
A. General commodities (14)	B. Machinery and electronic products (12)	
Refined oil, wool, polyester fibers, acrylic fibers, polyester chips, natural rubber, automobile tires, sodium cyanide, refined sugar, chemical fertilizers, tobacco and related products, cellulose diacetate fiber tows cotton and trichloroethane (methylchloro form).	Automobiles and related key parts, motorcycles and related engines and frames, color TV sets and tubes, radios and tape recorders and related modules, refrigerators and related compressors, video recording equipment and related key parts, cameras and related bodies, watches, air-conditioners and related compressors, audio and video tape copying equipment, automobile cranes and related chassis, and air-flow looms.	Cereals, plant oil, liquor, color sensitive materials, chemicals under supervision and control (including 12 kinds of chemicals that can be used as chemical weapons, 14 kinds of key carriers for chemical weapons and 17 kinds of raw materials for making chemical weapons), chemicals that can be easily used to produce drugs, and CD and VCD production equipment.
Apply to the Ministry of Foreign Trade and Economic Cooperation for the import license on the strength of the "Certificate for the Import Quota of General Commodities" signed and issued by the state development planning department.	Apply to the Ministry of Foreign Trade and Economic Cooperation for the import license on the strength of the "Import Quota Certificate" signed and issued by the state managerial department in charge of the import and export of machinery and electronic products.	See notes below.

Note:

1) To import cereals, plant oil, liquor and colour sensitive materials, a dealer has to apply to the Ministry of Foreign Trade and Economic Cooperation for the import license on the strength of the "Registration Certificate for the Import of Special Commodities" and other documents signed and issued by the import registration department authorized by the State Development Planning Commission.

2) To import chemicals under supervision and control, a dealer has to apply to the Ministry of Foreign Trade and Economic Cooperation for the import license on the strength of the approval document and other documents issued by the State Economy and Trade Commission.

3) To import chemicals that can easily be used to make drugs, a dealer has to apply to the Ministry of Foreign Trade and Economic Cooperation for the import license on the strength of the approval document issued by the department.

4) To import CD and VCD production equipment, a dealer has to apply to the Ministry of Foreign Trade and Economic Cooperation for the import license on the strength of the approval document issued by the State Press and Publication Administration and the "Registration Form for the Import of Machinery and Electronic Products" signed and issued by the managerial department in charge of the import and export of machinery and electronic products.

Under the Foreign Trade Law, all commodities subjected to quota and license management can only be imported after approval from the Ministry of Foreign Trade and Economic Cooperation.

a. *Non-Quota Management of the Import of Machinery & Electronic Products*

Besides quota management, China also exercises non-quota management of the import of machinery and electronic products (machinery and equipment, electronic products, related parts & accessories, devices & components). Among them, imports with technology desired by China, which are procured primarily through international bidding, are classified as Special Products.

Those not subjected to quota management will be under the automatic registration system, in which all importers must submit registration forms. Imported machinery and electronic products must comply with bilateral or multilateral trade agreements, as well as state laws and regulations concerning environmental protection measures. To import special tobacco machinery, radio transmission equipment, satellite TV reception facilities, and special devices and companions for satellite ground reception facilities, a dealer must first obtain approval from the relevant state industrial department.

The State Machinery and Electronic Products Import and Export Office is in charge of managing these imports.

b. *Automatic Registration for Import of Special Products*

To better monitor the import of staple raw materials and sensitive commodities, China requires automatic registration of them. These commodities include cereals, plant oil, liquor, crude oil, asbestos, colour sensitive materials, pesticides, plastics raw materials, synthetic rubber, plywood, chemical fibre cloth, rolled steel, billets, and 14 types of non-ferrous metals (copper, aluminium, etc).

The State Development Planning Commission is in charge of guiding, coordinating and management of this work.

c. *Imports by Verified Companies*

The Ministry of Foreign Trade and Economic Cooperation verifies and approves a list of companies which trade in staple raw materials which are:

- Vital to the economy and people's livelihood;
- Monopolistic in nature;
- Sensitive in price, operation and management

There are 19 types of imported commodities that are in this category: Wheat, crude oil, refined oil (referring to gasoline, diesel oil and kerosene), chemical fertilizers (nitrogenous, phosphate, potash and compound fertilizer), rubber (natural rubber), rolled steel (slabs, wire, shaped steel, tubes and tin-plated iron), timber (logs), plywood (veneer, decorative skin plates and pasted skin plates), wool (raw, washed and top wool), acrylic fibres, cotton (raw cotton), tobacco and related products, refined sugar, plant oil, waste steel, waste cooper, waste aluminium, waste paper and waste plastics.

d. *Wastes, Chemicals & Poisonous Chemicals*

China prohibits the import of wastes for dumping, stacking and disposal within its territories. The import of wastes for the use as raw materials is also restricted. Even for permitted wastes, examination and approval must be obtained from the prefectural environmental protection department or the State Environmental Protection Administration.

As of May 1, 1994, any chemical import not registered in China (except pesticides) must apply to the State Environmental Protection Administration for environmental management of chemicals, and provide samples for tests.

No enterprise may engage in entrepot trade of wastes.

e. *Used Machinery & Electronics Products*

As of November 1, 1998, the following products cannot be imported without permission from the Ministry of Foreign Trade and Economic Cooperation: Used machinery and electronics products in relation to production safety, human safety and environmental production (including pressure container, radiation, engineering machinery, electrical appliances, medical apparatus, food machinery, agricultural machinery, printing machine, textile machinery, colour expansion equipment, and amusement) as well as used machinery and electronics products, quota products, special products, registered used machinery and electronics products (used imported machinery and electronic products provided free by foreign businesses from foreign-funded and processing trade enterprises) manufactured before and in 1980.

2. Exports

a. Quota and Licence Management

Commodities subjected to China's export quota and licence management may be divided into four categories:

i) Planned quota management

Staple commodities essential to the national economy and people's livelihood, and important China traditional exports are subjected to planned quota management. There are 36 types of such commodities, 11 of which are subjected to unified joint operation (only for designated companies): Soybeans (including broken soybeans), corn (including broken corn), coal (including coal pulp), tungsten (tungsten ore, paratungstate ammonium, tungsten peroxide and tungstic acid), antimony (antimony ingots and antimony oxide), crude oil, refined oil, cotton, silk and silk in gray.

ii) Voluntary quota management

Export commodities which hold a leading position on the global or certain market, or those which are specially requested by foreign countries, are all subjected to voluntary quota management.

iii) Passive quota management

There are 24 types of export commodities subjected to quota restrictions in other countries. The annual export amount of such commodities is decided by both countries each year, with major managerial procedures implemented in accordance with bilateral agreements.

iv) Others

This category includes important brands, high quality and special exports which have high export value, as well as commodities that require management. In such cases, only general licence management is required. These products are subjected to free market mechanism.

Export licence management is practised in the first three categories. In 2001, 66 types of commodities were subjected to this. The Ministry of Foreign Trade and Economic Cooperation and provincial trade departments are the authorities in charge.

To promote fair competition and maintain a normal order in foreign trade, the Chinese government implemented a bidding system for some of the export commodities which are under quota.

b. Commodities Banned From Export

i. Commodities that jeopardise national security;

ii. Selected cultural relics, animals or plants on the verge of extinction, and products manufactured by reform-through-labour units;

iii.Commodities that infringe international obligations of the People's Republic of China;

iv. Musk, natural bezoar, black

moss and platinum, which are in dire domestic shortage.

3. Customs Control

Customs offices at all levels supervise and control the entry and exit of goods, luggage, articles, mails and commodities. They are also responsible for collecting tariffs, curb smuggling, as well as working out customs statistics and handling of other customs business.

a. Tariff Management

i. Import and export duties

As of January 1, 1992, China adopted the internationally accepted System for Standardizing Commodity Names and Classification (namely, the HD catalog) and joined the Convention on Standardizing International Commodity Names and Classification. The Customs Procedure on Imports and Exports promulgated on January 1, 1996, adopted the 1996 edition of Standardization System Catalogue revised by the World Customs Organization.

The import duty includes general and preferential tax rates. The latter applies to imported goods from countries where an agreement on mutually beneficial tariffs has been signed. For other imported goods, a general tax rate applies.

In 2001, China collected export duty on 22 types of commodities, including tungsten ore and silicon iron.

ii. Value-added tax and consumption tax

From January 1, 1994, certain goods imported into China are subjected to a value-added tax, in addition to the import duty and consumption tax. The consignee of the goods, or the unit or the individual handling the customs declaration procedures pays these taxes.

iii. Tax refund for exports

China's Procedures on Managing Tax Refunding (Exemption) for Export Goods stipulate that enterprises exporting goods may obtain refunds on the value-added tax and consumption taxes.

b. Free Trade Zones

Free trade zones are economic zones established with the approval of the State Council, and over which customs office exercises special supervision and control. They are the most highly liberalized of all economic zones. Their main function is to handle re-export trade and processing for export and bonded warehouses.

China's policies on free trade zones are:

- Enterprises within a free trade zone may freely conduct trade activities with overseas enterprises;
- All kinds of trade and commercial activities conducted by enterprises within a free trade zone with domestic enterprises outside the zone (within China) shall be regarded as foreign trade business. These enterprises may sign trade contracts only with Chinese enterprises authorized to handle imports and exports;
- Enterprises within a free trade zone do not have domestic import and export operational authority. Since June of 1990, 14 trade zones have been set up with State Council approval.

4. Intellectual Property Protection

To promote trade and economic cooperation, and technological and cultural exchanges between China and other countries, and to safeguard social and public interests, the customs office may detain import and export goods suspected of infringing intellectual property rights and that will enter or leave China soon.

5. Legally-Prescribed Commodity Quarantine and Animal & Plant Quarantine

Legally Prescribed Commodity Quarantine refers to commodities quarantined for quality, safety and hygiene reasons, after compulsory inspections by the China State Entry-Exit Inspection and Quarantine Bureau. The list of legally prescribed commodities will then be announced.

Other unlisted commodities will be subjected to inspection by the consignee and the user. Should quality problems be found, the consignee or the user should immediately apply to the local Entry-Exit Inspection and Quarantine Bureau for commodity inspection. The inspection results may be used as the basis for claim negotiations between the two trade partners.

6. Food Hygiene and Pharmaceutical Inspection

Under the Food Border Hygienic Quarantine Law, all imported foodstuffs, food additives, containers, packaging materials, related tools and equipment, as well as foodstuffs for export, are subjected to hygiene supervision and inspection by the Entry-Exit Inspection and Quarantine Bureau.

China practices a registration approval system on the import of medicine (for medical use, finished products, semi-finished products and auxiliary medicine). Medicines imported into China must get the Registration Certificate of Imported Medicine from the China State Medicine Supervision Bureau, and pass the inspection of the Port Medicine Inspection Institute authorized by the State Medicine Supervision Bureau. The application for registration must be made by the representative office of foreign pharmaceutical companies stationed in China, or by their registration agents in China. In addition, these imports must undergo clinical tests in accordance with the Chinese regulations on the Methods of Examination and Approval of New Medicines and The Scope of Management of the Clinical Tests of Medicine.

In the Registration Certificate of Imported Medicine, the importer of these medicines must include the final packaging of the medicine, state the name of the medicine, its chief components and registration number in Chinese and also provide a Chinese manual. The medicine can only enter China through a port with a Port Medicine Inspection Institute.

The export of traditional Chinese medicine is managed under Methods on the Quarantine of Animals and Plants and Regulations on Endangered Species.

Management of special pharmaceuticals is as follows:

- *Blood Products*

The state bans any unit or individual from importing blood products. In case of urgent clinical treatment, the importer shall apply for approval in advance to the Health Bureau of a province, an autonomous region or a municipality.

- *Psychoactive drugs and radioactive medicine*

The import and export of psychoactive drugs and radioactive medicine are subjected to examination and approval by the Ministry of Health, which issues the relevant permits and has designated the China Pharmaceutical Tonics Import and Export Corporation to oversee such imports and exports. The Ministry of Health publishes the varieties and classification of psychoactive drugs each year.

- *Narcotic drugs*

The import and export of narcotic drugs is similarly subjected to examination and approval by the Ministry of Health, which issues the relevant permits. The Ministry of Health will also notify the government of the exporting country and the International Narcotic Drug Control Secretariat.

Processing Trade & Border Trade

Processing Trade

Processing refers to economic activities in which all or a part of raw materials, parts and packing materials are imported from overseas through bonded procedures and processed or assembled by onshore enterprise. These finished products will be exported overseas.

The processing of all products requires the examination and approval of the foreign trade bureau at provincial level or lower, except for commodities such as sugar, vegetable oil, wool, natural rubber and crude oil, whose trade balance is closely monitored by the state and hence approval can be obtained only from the provincial foreign trade bureau.

Food stuff are subject to hygienic supervision

The Chinese Customs classifies the commodities into three categories:

- The prohibited category refers to commodities banned from import under the Foreign Trade Law as well as those unable to be monitored by the Customs.
- The restricted category refers to commodities with huge price disparities between China and foreign countries.
- The permitted category covers all other commodities.

Border Trade

China supports and encourages the development of border trade:

- **Mutual trade between border population**

This refers to trade between the

border and neighbouring government-approved areas or appointed fairs within 20 km of the border, within a stipulated quantity and quality. Border trade is exempted from import tax and import related value-added tax for trading volumes of up to RMB 3,000 yuan per day.

- Small amount border trade

A type of border trade. All commodities, excluding tobacco, wine and cosmetics, which are imported through small amount border trade at the appointed ports, will be taxed half of the import tax and import related value-added tax. These include imported materials exchanged through foreign economic and technological cooperation with border areas. Certain preferential treatment is given to commodities exchanged through small amount border trade.

Anti-Dumping Policy

Dumping is defined as the introduction of imported products into the China market at an export price below its value in ordinary trade. In the past, dumping of imported products has threatened and even caused substantial damages to some established industries in China. It has also discouraged the growth of other related industries.

Anti-dumping or anti-subsidy measures have been adopted in accordance with the Anti-Dumping and Anti-Subsidy regulations of China.

1. Applications for Anti-Dumping Investigation

A domestic producer can apply in writing for anti-dumping investigations to the Ministry of Foreign Trade and Economic Cooperation.

2. Anti Dumping Procedures

The Ministry of Foreign Trade and Economic Cooperation accepts anti-dumping applications and decides whether to place a case on record after discussions with the State Economic and Trade Commission, and notify related parties of their interest:

a. The Ministry of Foreign Trade and Economic Cooperation makes anti-dumping investigations together with the General Administration of Customs and issues the initial ruling; the State Economic and Trade Commission is in charge of investigating the damages and issues the initial ruling, together with relevant industrial departments;

b. In accordance with the investigations and the ruling, the Ministry of Foreign Trade and Economic Cooperation proposes whether to levy the anti-dumping tax;

c. In accordance with the proposal, the State Council Tariff and Tax Regulations Commission decides on whether to levy the anti-dumping tax, and sets the tax rate and the collection duration; and

d. The General Administration of Customs implements the anti-dumping measures.

3. Duration of Investigation

The duration of anti-dumping investigations is usually about 12 months from the date when the case is recorded. It may be extended to 18 months under special circumstances.

4. Administration for Anti-Dumping Investigations

In their investigations, departments may issue questionnaires to all concerned parties and conduct a sample survey. At the request of any party, all concerned parties will be given the opportunity to air their views.

5. Anti-Dumping Measures

If the initial ruling states that there is evidence of dumping and its damages to a domestic industry, the following temporary anti-dumping measures may be taken:

- ***Temporary anti-dumping tax***

Levying the temporary anti-dumping tax, in accordance with

Local industries flourish as the economy expands.

prescribed procedures, for four months from the date of announcement of the measures. The period may be extended to nine months under special circumstances.

- ***Cash and other form of guarantees***

Exporters who dump products or the government of the exporting country may apply for price commitment to the Chinese Ministry of Foreign Trade and Economic Cooperation. After discussions with the State Economic and Trade Commission, the Ministry of Foreign Trade and Economic Cooperation can accept the price commitment through negotia-tion, thus halting anti-dumping investigations. But if the price commitment is not executed, anti-dumping investigations may resume.

Should the final ruling state that there is evidence of dumping and its damages to a domestic industry, the anti-dumping tax may be levied. The duration of the tax and price commitment is five years.

PROFESSIONAL SERVICES

Accounting

Current Situation of Accounting Services

China's accounting services have developed quickly in recent years. By 1995, 11 foreign CPA firms had established 17 representative offices in China, and had recruited 26 member firms in 14 cities. Nine Chinese-foreign joint venture CPA firms have been approved to provide services for foreign or Chinese companies within a defined scope. By October 1998, there were over 20 international CPA firms in the market and more than 30 representative offices in Beijing, Shanghai, and other major cities. Ten cooperative firms and four member CPA firms were established.

With the development of the market economy and new social labour reforms, accounting services expanded quickly and the number of professionals increased. By end-2001, China had a total of 4287 CPA firms, of which 72 were licensed to audit securities firms. There were 55,897 practicing CPAs and 75,000 non-practicing CPAs. The total revenue in 2002 was about RMB 8.8 billion yuan.

Recent Structural Reforms in CPA

When the CPA system was established in the early 1980s, most accounting firms were funded and managed by various government institutions. These arrangements supported the rapid development of the CPA profession but no longer met the needs of the market economy as reforms deepened. The general objectives of the CPA structural reforms were to establish a management system for accounting firms commensurate with a mixed economy, and to directly expose accounting firms to legal obligations. Specific objectives were to develop accounting firms characterized by independent operation, self-assumption of risks, self-discipline and self-development, while strengthening the risk awareness of CPAs, improving their professional ethics and ensuring quality.

The building industry continues to boom

Architecture

In the year 2002, China experienced robust economic growth of 8.2%. Investment in fixed capital alone rose by 18%. Beijing Olympics looms ahead in 2008 and the Shanghai World Expo follows two years later. These factors combined gave rise to a booming Chinese architecture industry.

With the emergence of China's upper middle class, the country is moving towards a Western-style economy, a far cry from the uniformity and utilitarianism of its Communist past. The Chinese of today like architecture, buildings and space to reflect some aspects of traditional Western architecture. Projects that reflect this trend include a suburban development north of Beijing called Orange County with its faux Los Angeles architecture concept, and the New World City, a 100-acre community within Beijing.

The Chinese authorities aim to channel USD 55 billion, i.e. 15% of their annual expenditure on buildings to foreign firms. The planning of the aquatics centre for the Beijing Olympics 2008 is risk.

commissioned to Edaw, a US-based firm, a clear indication that China is committed to importing foreign architecture.

China presently owns over 120 Sino-Foreign architectural design offices and more than 140 world-class engineering and architectural consulting enterprises have established offices in China. The Landscape Architecture China 2003 held in Guangzhou alone attracted many first-class architectural design enterprises such as KPF, SASAKI, B+H and Kisho Kurokawa.

Laws on Architectural Services

Following China's accession to the World Trade Organisation, laws concerning the provision of architectural services have been revised in the spirit of liberalizing the sector. Foreign firms are to be given greater access to the domestic market.

The decrees, known as 113 and 114, permit foreign firms to work in China either as wholly foreign-owned entities or as joint ventures. According to the British Embassy, however, the terms underscoring such ventures are so strict that they are in fact more prohibitive than before. The Chinese are applying the same rules to foreign firms as to domestic companies.

Under Chinese regulations, for example, in order to establish a wholly foreign-owned design firm in China, a quarter of the staff must be qualified expatriate architects or engineers. In the case of joint-ventures with a Chinese company, the proportion is restricted to one-eighth. To design family housing, a firm must have a turnover of at least USD 25.7 million and at least 300 staff who are degree-holders.

Networking or *guanxi* with key political contacts is still a major factor in securing a deal, ensuring the smooth execution of a project, and in facilitating clients profiling.

Banking & Finance

Prior to 1978, lending was not based on commercial estimates of

State-owned enterprises (SOEs) were given preferential treatment, resulting in a large amount of bad debts and non-performing loans. Constituting up to 60% of bank lending, the four state-owned commercial banks (SOCBs) became technically insolvent by 2000. According to official figures, 25.4% of all loans by Chinese banks are unlikely to be repaid in full. Independent experts placed the true figure at 50%.

In 1984, The People's Bank of China (PBOC) was designated the nation's central bank. In 1994, Beijing established the State Development Bank, the China Export-Import Bank, and the Agricultural Development Bank to perform policy-lending functions of the four main SOCBs, focusing on government-directed policy lending for infrastructure development and SOE operating costs. The intention was to let SOCBs concentrate on providing a greater array of banking services on commercial terms

In 1 Dec 2002, Chinese authorities introduced new rules that allowed selected foreign investors to buy and sell domestic shares and bonds for the first time. With 1200 publicly traded companies and nearly USD 500 billion in total capitalization, the two domestic stock markets were transformed in slightly over a decade into Asia's third-largest. Foreign fund management companies, insurers, commercial banks, securities companies and other asset management firms can apply to become foreign investors. Approved foreign institutions will be permitted to conduct limited investment in local-currency-denominated Class A shares and in government, corporate and convertible bonds.

By end of October 2002, financial institutions' aggregate book value profit increased by RMB 54.7 billion yuan to RMB 28.7 billion yuan. Outstanding broad money (M2) increased 17% to RMB 17.73 trillion yuan; narrow money (M1) up 17.9% to RMB 6.7 trillion yuan and money in circulation (M0) was up by 10.6% to RMB 1.6 trillion yuan. New deposits in January-October increased by RMB 673.5 billion yuan to a total of RMB 2,331.8 billion yuan, of which new corporate deposits accounted for RMB 620 billion yuan and new personal savings deposits at RMB 1,104.8 billion yuan. Non-performing loans by state-owned commercial banks dropped by 90.7 yuan, down 3.8%.

In 2003, China is planning the building of a deposit-insurance system that will incorporate protection of depositors' funds, banking industry supervision and the resolution of bankrupt institutions.

Major Players

Three state policy banks: China Development Bank, Export and Import Bank of China, and Agricultural Development Bank of China.

Four state-owned specialized banks: China Construction Bank, Agricultural Bank of China, Industrial and Commercial Bank of China and Bank of China.

Three state-controlled banks: China Merchants Bank, Huaxia Bank and China Minsheng Banking Corporation.

Regional commercial banks: Shenzhen Development Bank, Hainan Development Bank, Fujian Industrial Bank, Guangdong Development Bank and Pudong Development Bank.

Legal Services

The number of lawyers in China has jumped to the present 110,000 from a mere 200 two decades ago. There are now nearly 10,000 law offices in China including lawyers specializing in securities, finance and real estate sectors. There is a great demand for lawyers in the knowledge-based economy. Legal services form an important component to a sound investment environment that is essential for overseas investors.

Since July 1992, when China first opened its legal offices to overseas markets, the Ministry of Justice has approved 92 law offices from 11 countries and 28 Hong Kong law firms to establish representative offices in China. The law firms from foreign countries have branch offices in 10 Chinese cities including Beijing and Shanghai. Since January 2003, the geographic and quantitative limitations of foreign law offices in China have been removed and the one-firm-one-office restriction lifted. In 2004, the removal of these restrictions will be further enforced.

Currently, China has approved 115 law firms of 16 foreign countries to set up representative offices in Mainland China, and 12 of them have opened their second representative offices along with four Hong Kong law firms. The representative offices of foreign law firms have offered legal services in China in sectors such as investment, banking, technology transfer, insurance, intellectual property, estate agency, investment and lawsuit arbitration.

Foreign law firms set up branches in major cities

INDUSTRY HIGHLIGHTS

AUTOMOBILE

Recently China's car industry has grown at an unprecedented rate, driven to a large extent by remarkable economic progress since 1980.

Once a country's per capita GDP exceeds USD 1,000, its private car purchases start to rise quickly. By 1998, a total population of 300 million had per capita income exceeding USD 1,000. Shanghai's per capita GDP in 1998 was RMB 25,192 yuan (USD 3,043). By 2002, Shanghai's per capita GDP had reached RMB 33,780 (USD 4,081). As for Beijing, its GDP per capita in 1998 was RMB 16,142 yuan (USD 1,950). By 2002, its GDP per capita had increased to RMB 23,411 yuan (USD 2,828). In Tianjin's case, its GDP per capita was RMB 13964 yuan (USD 1,687) in 1998. However by 2002, its GDP per capita had risen to about to RMB 20,592 yuan (USD 2,488).

Automobile demand by 2005 is forecast to reach 5.8 million, with luxury cars accounting for 2 million. The forecast for 2010 is 10 million and 4 million, respectively. These figures underscore the China market's immense promise. Rapid increase in demand has stimulated production levels. As indicated by the following chart, total passenger car production has risen from 607,000 in 2000 to 703,600 in 2001 (an increase of 16%). From 2001 to 2002, the passenger car industry rose to 1,092,000, posting a robust increase of 55%.

The figures in the chart below right indicate that the value of China's motor vehicles exports (includes chassis) rose from USD 193.74 million in 2000 to USD 208.11 million in 2001, posting a healthy 7% growth. From 2001 to 2002, the value of motor vehicles exports increased to USD 261.15 million, delivering a robust growth rate of 25%. These figures reflect the growing international competitiveness of China's fledgling automobile industry.

Given China's rising affluence, it is no surprise that the luxury car

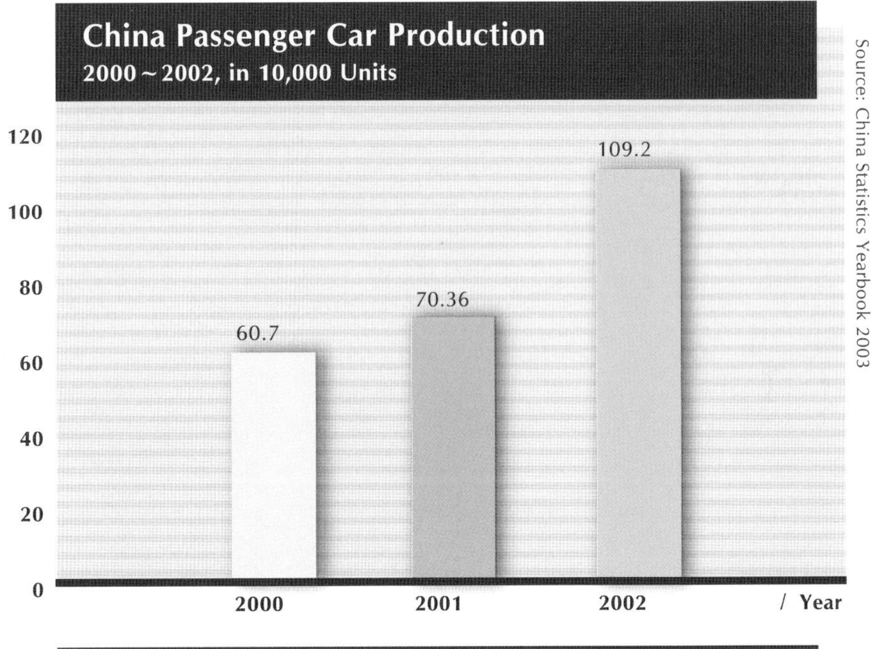
China Passenger Car Production
2000 ~ 2002, in 10,000 Units
120
100
80
60
40
20
0
60.7
70.36
109.2
2000
2001
2002
/ Year
Source: China Statistics Yearbook 2003

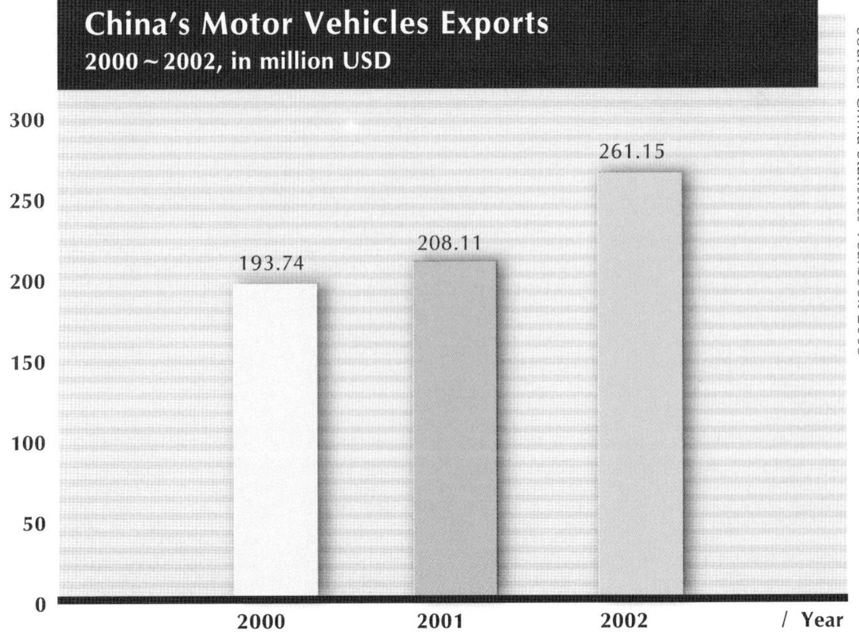
China's Motor Vehicles Exports
2000 ~ 2002, in million USD
300
250
200
150
100
50
0
193.74
208.11
261.15
2000
2001
2002
/ Year
Source: China Statistics Yearbook 2003

market has performed well, growing at a rate of 41.3% in April and 73.8% for July, respectively in 2002. (Total July production was 94,900 units.) Most Chinese are not affluent by Western standards, but foreign carmakers have identified a key market — one-third of new cars sold in China are in the luxury range. Shanghai's Bentley dealership with an annual sales target of 20, sold 15 cars in 2003, double the number sold last year.

Demand for automobiles in China has surpassed the expectations of many industry players and observers. The effects of joining WTO in 2001 would be likely to further accelerate this key sector.

Significant WTO Rules

1. The Removal of Tariffs and Quotas

The coming end of tariffs and quotas would have a significant positive impact. Although all quotas must be officially removed by 2005, the country has begun steps to facilitate their removal in order to raise international competitiveness. Weak domestic firms may be wiped out, while more competitive ones will be compelled to raise their level of innovation, production standards and overall efficiency in the face of this foreign 'onslaught'. Many of these domestic companies have formed joint ventures (JV) with their overseas competitors in order to acquire knowledge of advanced production techniques, research and development methods, and marketing and distribution expertise.

Common examples of 50/50 JVs are Shanghai Volkswagen Automotive Corp (Volkswagen AG & Shanghai Automotive Industry Corp), Dongfeng Motor Co Ltd (Nissan Motor Co Ltd and Dongfeng Motor Corporation), and Yanfeng Visteon Automotive Trim System Co (Visteon Corporation of the US and Shanghai Automotive Co).

2. Abolition of Subsidies

In the WTO, subsidies are defined as monetary support provided by a member to its individual industries. Under WTO rules, subsidies per se are not prohibited, as long as the subsidy does not harm another member's interests. WTO classifies subsidies into three main categories:

a. **Non-Actionable ("Green Light Subsidies")** refer to both non-specific and specific subsidies meant for research assistance, spending on education, and promoting development of poor regions. Such subsidies are permitted.

b. **Actionable ("Yellow Light Subsidies")** are specific, either injuring another member's domestic industry, or nullifying or impairing benefits under GATT. They may cause serious prejudice to another member's interests (including damage to a WTO member in the market of the subsidizing country or in a third country market). This clause does not apply to developing countries – which form the majority of WTO membership.

c. **Prohibited ("Red Light Subsidies")** are contingent in law or in fact on exporting or on using domestic (local content) rather than imported inputs. Least developed countries are exempted, as are developing countries with per capita income less than USD 1,000. (Again this is a substantial group of countries but their trade volume is low, especially in exports.) Other developing countries must get rid of prohibited subsidies by 2003.

When China started its domestic car industry, the main objective was to reduce China's dependence on imported automobiles. Under today's WTO rules, most of its subsidies would be prohibited.

3. Trade-related investment measures

This refers to measures that the host country imposes on foreign investment. In China's auto industry, such measures are prohibited under WTO guidelines, if they obstruct foreign investment.

4. Transparency

Under WTO rules, the Chinese government is required to improve the level of transparency by disclosing all policies and measures on trade. WTO guidelines indicate that many old practices of the Chinese central planning system have to be abolished. A WTO audit committee will review China's economy and compliance record every three years. The same committee reviews the US, European, Japanese and Canadian economies every two years. Other countries are reviewed every four to eight years.

Changes in Auto Sector Policies

As the auto sector grows and progresses, China is changing the policy environment as well. A principal aim is to acquire advanced foreign auto manufacturing technology including auto parts. Some new broad policies are given below.

Foreign investors entering JV arrangements with domestic auto firms must consider China's need to rationalize its foreign exchange outflow in order to maintain equilibrium in its balance of payments. This is to prevent the inflow of "hot money", which could hurt the financial stability of the country.

Under the new automotive policies, Chinese auto companies will not be permitted to use SKD or CKD methods to produce cars. The government discourages car production by assembling imported parts and components, and cars thus produced in China will be taxed as imported products. This new policy aims to:

- raise the standards for new automobile factories
- lift the levels of R&D and service in existing factories

- explore the feasibility of original new products
- encourage technological progress in the industry

Under the new policies, several activities in the sector remain prohibited. For example, foreign investors may not establish in China:

- sales and marketing offices, and may not do so through joint ventures.
- motorcycles manufacturers and their respective parts suppliers without a local partner. They may not conduct import/export in these industries independently.
- services for the maintenance and servicing of cars and motorcycles, and may not use JVs with domestic partners to promote such services.
- independent freight forwarding or logistical services. They can do so only in the form of a JV with a domestic firm.
- credit financing, rental, or insurance facilities for automobiles and motorcycles, and may not use JVs to promote such services.

Liberalization of Trading Rights

China is relaxing import/export regulations to liberalize its trading environment. For example, registration fees for mid-sized companies were reduced to RMB 5 million yuan in 2002, RMB 3 million yuan in 2003, and will be cut further to RMB 1 million yuan in 2004.

Many foreign investors with a minority stake in a JV were given full trading rights in 2002; the same was due by end-2003 for foreign investors with larger JV stakes. By end-2004, all foreign investors in Chinese JVs will enjoy full trading rights.

China pledged to dismantle its approval system for trading rights by end-2004. This would benefit local investors, as well as foreign and independent investors from WTO's 148 member countries.

Importers will still face restrictions on product distribution, as distribution rights will be arranged under the General Agreement on Trade in Services (GATS) rules. WTO regulations forbid discrimination against imports by foreign investors and by independent investors from WTO member countries.

Distribution

By end-2002, all foreign auto companies in JVs with local auto firms were permitted to participate in all distribution activities. By end-2003, the foreign party was allowed to hold a controlling interest in the distribution network, and quotas on these companies were ended. By end-2004, all regulations limiting the foreign auto companies' capacity to establish their own distribution network would be removed.

Retailing

As soon as China joined WTO in December 2001, foreign investors were permitted to operate retail auto outlets with JV partners in five Special Economic Zones (Shenzhen, Zhuhai, Shantou, Xiamen, and Hainan) and in eight major cities (Beijing, Shanghai, Tianjin, Guangzhou, Dalian, Qingdao, Zhengzhou, and Wuhan).

The number of JV retail networks in Beijing and Shanghai currently does not exceed four, and in other areas does not exceed two. The two foreign auto companies are permitted to establish distribution operations in Beijing with branches. Both companies hold a 40% stake in their respective joint ventures.

By end-2002, restrictions were removed on retailing operations of foreign auto companies. By end-2003, foreign investors can have a controlling interest in their JV retailing operations in all major cities including Chongqing and Ningbo.

By end-2004, foreign investors in JV arrangements with more than 30 retail outlets still may not hold a controlling interest. This rule is to be phased out by end-2006.

Franchising

By end-2004, there will be no restrictions on franchise establishment. China agreed to consult with WTO members in developing regulations on sales away from a fixed location. The foreign investor (the franchisor) must have assets of at least USD 5 million, and can acquire a controlling interest. By end-2004, the foreign party may set up its own independent company.

Financial Services

All geographical and client restrictions on the foreign currency business were removed by end-2002. Foreign financial companies may directly service Chinese firms by end-2006. Foreign banks licensed for RMB business in a particular region may service clients in other regions that have opened for such business.

As for RMB business, it was restricted to Shanghai, Shenzhen, Tianjin and Dalian upon accession to the WTO; expanding to Guangzhou, Zhuhai, Qingdao, Nanjing and Wuhan within 1 year; to Jinan, Fuzhou, Chengdu and Chongqing within 2 years; to Kunming, Beijing and Xiamen within 3 years; to Shantou, Ningbo, Shenyang and Xi'an within 4 years. There will be no geographic restrictions after five years of China's accession to the WTO, that is, by end 2006.

Licensing of Foreign Firms to Conduct RMB Business

Effective Date	Areas Covered in China
Upon WTO Accession	Shanghai, Shenzhen, Tianjin, and Dalian
End - 2002	Expanding to Guangzhou, Zhuhai, Qingdao, Nanjing, and Wuhan
End - 2003	Expanding to Jinan, Fuzhou, Chengdu, and Chongqing
End - 2004	Expanding to Kunming, Beijing, and Xiamen
End - 2005	Expanding to Shantou, Ningbo, Shenyang, and Xian
End - 2006	No Restrictions

Data Source: Fudan University, School of Economics, China Center for Economic Studies.

Currently, auto financing is relatively limited in China, as only 15% of car purchases are financed as opposed to around 75% in the West.

Auto financing is a new phenomenon, with the four large state banks and other local commercial banks authorized to undertake auto financing only since the late 1990s. According to the 2003 KPMG report, Chinese banks to date have not aggressively targeted this market; they lack the specific auto financing and marketing expertise of overseas auto finance providers. The same report asserts that the traditional reluctance in China to take on debt and the high national savings rate may also impact the take-up rates for auto finance. Although the government said that it would liberalize auto financing in line with WTO rules, it is still formulating concrete measures.

Meanwhile, two foreign auto manufacturers have entered interim deals with commercial banks to offer auto financing to

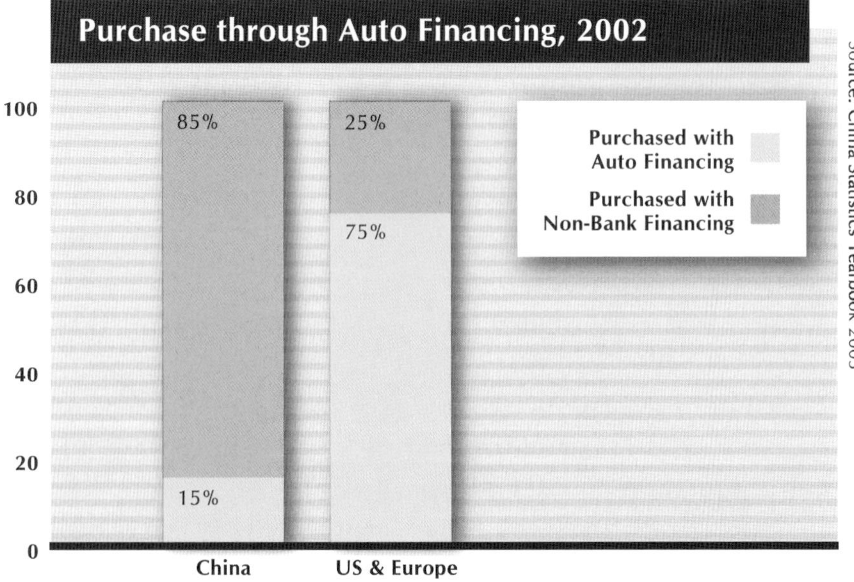

their customers; Volkswagen signed a deal with the Bank of China in January 2003 and Ford signed a deal with China Construction Bank in June 2003. With the gradual liberalization of China's financial markets, auto financing is expected to be a key driver of growth for China's automobile industry, which in turn would spur growth of its nascent auto parts industry.

Insurance Services

China is gradually opening up its insurance industry, particularly for life, non-life, and reinsurance policies. However foreign companies may not underwrite vehicle insurance.

Transportation Services

In December 2001, foreign companies were allowed to establish delivery firms using heavy trucks and vans through JVs with domestic companies. By end-2004, they may set up independent firms.

Warehousing Services

In December 2001, foreign companies were allowed to establish warehousing services through JVs in which they may not hold more than a 49% stake. In December 2002, foreign parties were allowed to acquire a controlling interest; by end-2004, they may set up independent firms.

Maintenance Services

In December 2001, geographic and regional restrictions were removed on automobile servicing firms wishing to establish maintenance services. But they had to do so through JVs. By end-2002 however, foreign entities were allowed to hold a controlling interest in the JV; by end-2004, they may set up independent firms.

Freight Forwarding Services

In December 2001, foreign freight forwarding firms established for more than three years were allowed to set up JVs in which they hold less than a 50% stake.

The minimum JV amount was USD 1 million.

By end-2002, foreign parties were allowed to acquire a controlling interest in the JV. By end-2003, the foreign investor was allowed to set up subsidiaries by investing a minimum of USD 120,000 in each subsidiary.

By end-2004, foreign freight forwarding firms may set up independent firms. They will receive the same treatment as their local competitors, but may operate for only 20 years. By end-2006, foreign investors involved in JVs for more than two years may establish a second JV with domestic firms.

Advertising Services

In December 2001, foreign companies were allowed to establish JVs with a stake up to 49%. By end-2003, they could acquire a controlling interest, and by end-2005 they may set up an independent firm.

Testing and Maintenance Services

Foreign automakers with more than three years equipment testing and maintenance experience in China may establish JVs with domestic companies to launch testing, analysis, and maintenance facilities with an initial investment of at least USD 350,000. By end-2005, foreign investors may establish an independent firm.

Future Development

The astounding growth of China's automobile industry has inevitably bred fears of overcapacity. Max Warburton at Goldman Sachs stated that global automotive manufacturers are taking "a colossal, lemming-like leap over the cliff" as they plan to invest an estimated USD 10 billion into car factories over the next three years.

However Phil Murtaugh, the Chairman of General Motors China, warned against taking future capacity estimates at face value, pointing out that naysayers tend to count the full potential output of China's 90-odd small carmakers (most of which are near bankruptcy). He pointed out that there are still 80-90 plants in China that have never built 10,000 cars in their entire history.

David Thursfield, head of international business at Ford Motors, said that the company's recently launched operations are already profitable due to strong demand and high prices. Frederick Henderson, the Asia-Pacific president for GM said that in five years China will become Asia's largest automotive market, pushing ahead of Japan.

The explosive growth of China's automobile industry has evidently become critical to the global strategy of the world's largest automakers. Akio Toyoda, the great grandson of the founder of Toyota Motor Corp and the man responsible for Toyota's China operations, stated that "There's no future for us globally if we messed up in China". The company is aggressively playing catch-up to rivals such as Volkswagen AG and GM, which control about 35% and 10% of China's passenger-car market respectively vis-à-vis Toyota's 2%.

Another leading Japanese auto maker, Nissan, together with its Chinese JV Dongfeng, has plans to increase automobile sales in China to 620,000 by 2007 from the expected 300,000 units this year. These bullish examples allay any fears of overcapacity for the time being.

Nonetheless, if China's economy maintains its current momentum, most automotive manufacturers expect demand for cars to grow at 15-20% for the rest of the decade, creating a market that, as asserted by Bernd Pischetsrieder, chief executive of Volkswagen, is on track to become the second largest in the world after the United States.

EDUCATION

Since the founding of the People's Republic of China in 1949, the Chinese government has always place education on its higher agenda, which has promulgated multiple codes to protect the education rights of its population from different angles, especially the different ethnic groups, children, women and the disabled.

Through uninterrupted efforts in the past five decades, China has made significant progress in its education sector. Ever since the reforms and opening up policies of 1978, the most significant reforms were the restoration of the higher-education examination system, the nationwide implementation of nine years compulsory education in planned stages. At the same time, primary schooling is common in areas with a concentrated 91% of Chinese population; higher education, occupational and polytechnic education, diversified adult education and ethical education have also developed rapidly. All these contributed to a multilayered, diversified and discipline-inclusive education system in China and facilitated the cross-border communication and cooperation in education sector.

The guiding principle, to paraphrase a message written for Jingshan School by Deng Xiaoping in 1983, has been to gear education towards the demands of modernization, of the world and of the future. It is a principle that has played an important role in the success of China's educational undertakings.

By the end of 2002, there were about 2000 tertiary institutions, including universities and colleges. In China, the number of students' enrolment by level and type of school was 9.04 million of which 1.84 million were the year's new intake of students. 93% of the country had instituted compulsory primary education, and about 99% of school-age children were enrolled in schools. The dropout rate decreased, and the official

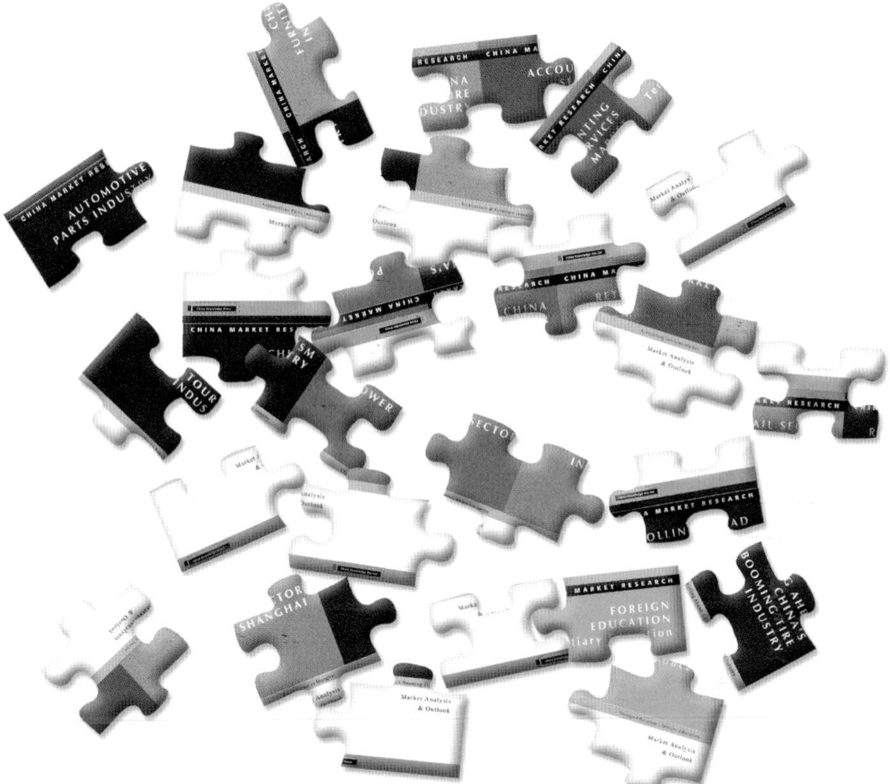

Full Research Reports

List of our major research report users:

- Small to Medium Corporations and Multinationals
- Financial and Asset Management Institutions
- Universities and Academia
- Statutory Boards and Business Libraries
- Private investors
- Investment Research Firms
- Governments
- Information Solutions Providers
- Public Libraries
- Commercial Banks

Market Analysis & Outlook

ISBN: 981-4163-06-6
US: $395.00

Market Analysis & Outlook

ISBN: 981-04-8991-9
US: $395.00

Market Analysis & Outlook

ISBN: 981-4163-09-0
US: $395.00

Market Analysis & Outlook

ISBN: 981-04-8762-2
US: $395.00

Market Analysis & Outlook

ISBN: 981-04-9003-8
US: $395.00

Market Analysis & Outlook

ISBN: 981-04-9252-9
US: $395.00

Market Analysis & Outlook

ISBN: 981-4163-08-2
US: $395.00

Market Analysis & Outlook

ISBN: 981-4163-10-4
US: $395.00

Market Analysis & Outlook

ISBN: 981-04-8760-6
US: $395.00

Market Analysis & Outlook

ISBN: 981-4163-07-4
US: $1,250.00

CHINA MARKET RESEARCH
CHINA OUTDOOR ADVERTISING INDUSTRY

Market Analysis & Outlook

ISBN: 981-4163-36-8
US: $395.00

literacy rate of young and middle-aged people was reduced to less than 5 percent, which is above average of a Third World country, although still short of a developed country's standards.

Formerly, all education right up to university level was fully state-funded. Upon graduating, university graduates would then accept any jobs the state deemed fit to assign to them. However, students now may pay their own way through school and are at liberty to take up any employment of their choice.

China has also acknowledged the economic value of having a literate population fluent in foreign languages, with English being the most popular foreign language so far.

Education Management & Administration System

China has set up an education system with the government as the major investor and social partners as co-investors. In the current stage, the local government is playing a key role in compulsory education, while the central and provincial government is dominant in higher education. In occupational and adult education, social partners including industrial organizations, businesses and public institutions are playing a more and more important role. The Ministry of Education of PRC is the supreme education administration body in China, which is responsible for carrying out related laws, regulations, guidelines and policies of the central government; planning development of the education sector; integrating and coordinating educational initiatives and programs nationwide; maneuvering and guiding education reforms countrywide. Since 1978, the Ministry of Education, within its jurisdiction, has issued more than 200 sets of administrative rules and regulations, significantly facilitating development of education of different natures.

With regards to the education budget, financial allocation is still the major source, while multiple fund channels have been opened up. China's educational fund has increased on a yearly basis since 1978.

Education System & Development

China's education system is made up of 4 components: basic education, occupational/polytechnic education, common higher education and adult education.

Basic education comprises of pre-school education, primary (6 years), junior (3 years) and senior (3 years) middle schooling. The Chinese government has always listed basic education as one of its top priorities. Since 1986 when the Law of Compulsory Education of the People's Republic of China was promulgated, primary schooling has been common in most parts of China, while junior middle schooling is being popularized in large cities and economically developed areas. There were 20 million pupils enrolled in 456,900 primary schools in 2002, where 97.02% of primary school children completed their studies and continued their education.

Medium-level occupational and polytechnic education is mainly provided by medium-level professional schools, polytechnic schools, occupational middle schools as well as short-term occupational and technical training programs of various forms. Since the 1980s, occupational and polytechnic education in China experienced rapid development. The proportion of enrolment of high-school-equivalent occupational and polytechnic schools in total enrolment of high schools had increased from 18.9% in 1980 to 61.5% in 2002.

Common higher education comprises of junior college, bachelor, master and doctoral degree programs. Junior college program usually last 2~3 years; bachelor program 4 years; master program 2~3 years; doctoral program 3 years. In five decades since 1949, China has made significant achievements in higher education. There were 2003 regular and adult Higher Education Institutions (HEIs) in China, including 1396 regular HEIs and 607 adult HEIs, in 2002. Total enrolment was 5.6 million undergraduates in 2002.

Adult education comprises of schooling education, anti-illiteracy education and other programs oriented and catered to adult groups. China's adult education has evolved rapidly since the Liberation. There are currently 652048 adult schools of various levels and types. By the end of 2002, there were about 1396 tertiary institutions, including universities and colleges, in China, with 9.03 million students of which 1.84 million were the year's new intake of students.

International Communication & Cooperation

Since China inaugurated the opening and reform initiative in 1978, international communication and cooperation in the education sector has migrated onto a new stage, cheering the healthy development of studying overseas, the increasing number of foreigners studying in China, and the expanding cross-border academic communication. International communication and cooperation has brought us with beneficial reference, impelled education reform and development in China and enhanced the mutual understanding and friendship between China and other countries.

In more than two decades since 1979, China had sent some 320,000 students to more than 100 countries and regions, hosted 340,000 students from more than 160 countries and regions; dispatched out 1,800 teachers and experts, and appointed 40,000 foreign experts and teachers. The number of Chinese experts and academics involved in overseas international conferences and that of foreign experts and academics once presenting at international academic symposiums held in China both amounted to 11,000.

For the past two decades or more, China has also made sound achievements in bilateral and multilateral education cooperation, which has gotten educational aid from UNESCO, UNIECF, UNFPA, UNDP, World Bank and many other international organizations, including a loan of USD 14.7 billion from World Bank for the education development program, and the aid of more than USD 100 million from other organizations. In recent years, the educational aid given by Hong Kong, Macau and Taiwan to mainland China has increased, thus witnessing a steady educational communication and cooperation between both sides.

Market Size & Potential

The education market size and potential in China is expanding rapidly. As of 2002, the number of students studying in regular institutions of higher learning stood at 9 million, an increase of 25.6% from 2001. The number enrolled for professional and postgraduate degrees rose 17% to 5.4 million. The total annual market size was thus 14.4 million students for higher learning education. Based on an average annual growth rate of 15%, this number could double by 2008. Demand for further education and knowledge is evidenced by the increasing number of people in different age groups continuing their education and by rising annual consumer expenditure. According to some experts, China requires 100,000 new MBA degree holders annually. But only 46% (54 million) of all high school graduates enroll in regular higher education institutes.

There also exists some scope for market investment opportunity in China education. At present, financing for primary and secondary education is

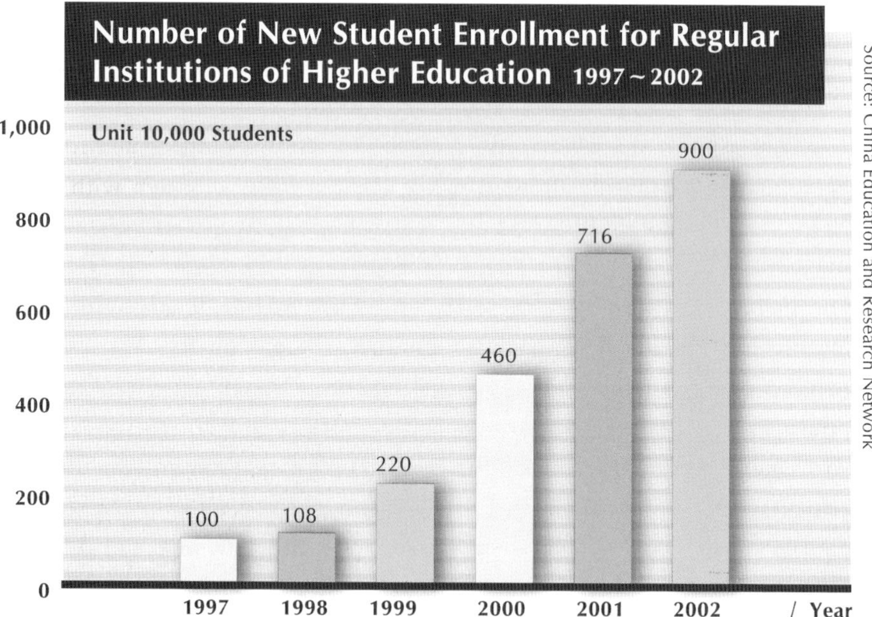

insufficient. In the compulsory education stages, financing is primarily the responsibility of the government. Many residents in cities and developed areas want schools with a high quality. The establishment of non-state-run schools can and has met the needs for more options, while increasing educational resources. According to official statistics, China had more than 60,000 non-state-run schools with over 10 million students on campus by the year 2000. Many state-run schools have reformed and introduced a system under which schools are run by the state with financing from various social sectors, thus raising non-state investment. Propelled by the increasing needs of society for high-quality education, this trend is likely to continue. Most teaching facilities in many areas of compulsory education have not met the basic standards as prescribed by the state and local governments. For instance, the actual availability rate of science instruments in primary schools is only about one third of the basic standard, and that of experimental instruments in junior middle schools is about 50%. This translates into a huge market for teaching equipment.

Despite rapid development over the last 20 years, China's higher education cannot meet growing social needs; the result is a sharp supply-demand gap. Various kinds of non-state-run educational establishments have been growing up and overseas educational establishments have rushed into the market, which has enormous expansion potential. Over the next ten years, the internet and network are expected to be one of the largest investment areas in the educational market, up to RMB 100 billion yuan. Facilities need to be maintained and renewed in the course of operation, and teaching software needs to be updated.

Regulatory Environment

Since the early 1980s, there has been a fundamental structural change in financing education from a centralized system with a diversified revenue base. In 1985, the State Council promulgated the official policy for financial reform in basic education, consisting of two major components: decentralization in administration and financing, and diversification in mobilizing resources.

By the early 1990s, a decentralized financing system for primary and secondary education was in place, with budget sources (government allocation) and out-of-budget sources (surcharges and levies, social contributions, school-generated resources, and school fees). Between 1986 and 1992, in 1992 constant prices, the government budget allocation increased by 3.5% per year, and out–of-budget funds by 19.7% per year. Per-student budget spending was increased by 9.6% per year at the primary level and by 5.1% per year at the significant changes in the distribution of revenue for primary and secondary education.

In the "Report on the Implementation of the Central and Local Budgets for 2001 and on the Draft Central and Local Budgets for 2002", Finance Minister Xiang Huaicheng noted that China had increased its investment in science and education gradually. Despite this progress, China's investment in education is only one-third the average level of developed countries and half the average level of developing countries.

Outbound Education Market

According to the agencies surveyed, the most favoured destinations are the United States, Australia, New Zealand, United Kingdom, Canada, and Singapore. In this group, Australia and New Zealand are the most popular due to relatively lower living expenses and a relaxed and conducive study environment. England is next, with its relatively easy application of student visas, good reputable schools, and high quality of education. Canada and the United States are still popular destinations as they provide good English language exposure. The degrees conferred in these countries are internationally recognized. Singapore ranks last in this group as it is not a "pure English-speaking" country and its schools are not as well known to Chinese students. Students who prefer an Asian environment over a Western country and those with less confidence in speaking English may prefer Singapore.

Other nations such as Russia, Ukraine, France, and Germany appeal to Chinese students as well. Russia and Ukraine are popular among students for historical, career, and trade reasons. Both countries grant visas easily. France is the choice destination for arts as a profession. Most students going to Germany and France get scholarship assistance; self-funding for higher education there is rare.

ENERGY

China is the world's second largest energy consumption country (next to the U.S.). Energy consumption has been fueled by the ever fastest economic growth in the past two decades. In 2002, China's total energy consumption reached 1.48 billion tons of standard coal, about 2.6 times the value in 1978. The composition of primary energy is shown below.

COAL

Coal is vital to China's energy sector, accounting for about 66.1% of total primary energy consumption in 2002. Among them, power generation accounts for the majority of coal consumption. Now, electricity generated by coal-fired units accounts for about 70% of total generation in China. And it is expected that nearly 60% of total generation will still be generated by coal-fired units in 2020. China's total coal resource in the

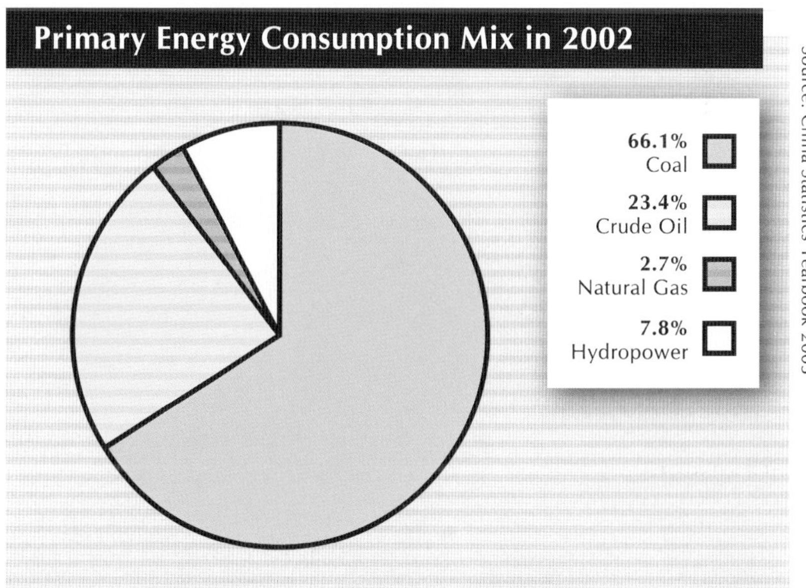

Source: China Statistics Yearbook 2003

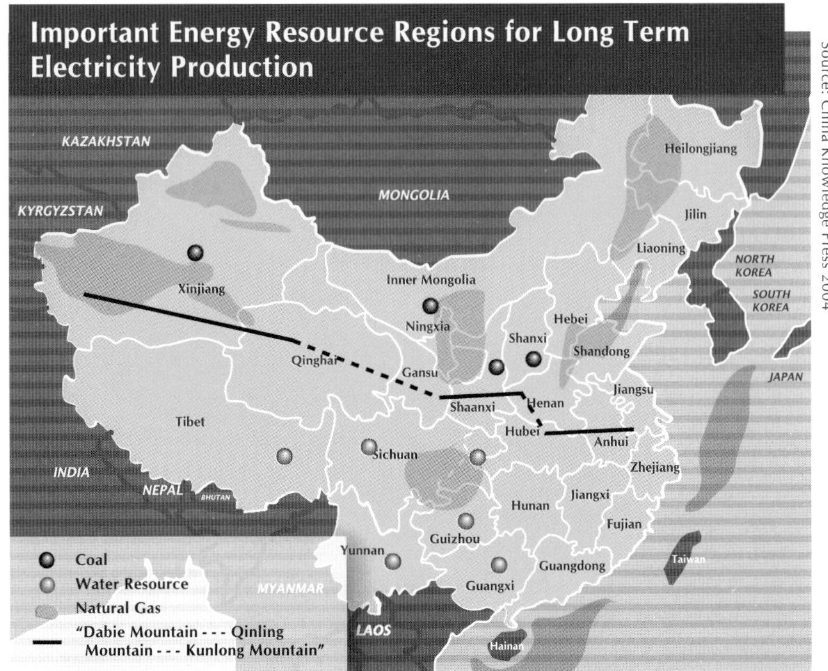

shallow layers of the Earth (less than 1,000m) is about 2.6 trillion tonnes. About 94% of the resources are in the region north of the Dabie Mountain - Qinling Mountain - Kunlong Mountain" range. Among them the Three Western Region (Shanxi, Shaanxi and the western part of Inner Mongolia) and Xinjiang accounts for 81.3%, Northeast 1.6% and East China 2.8%.

Now the biggest coal production province is Shanxi. Other big production provinces are Henan, Shandong, Heilongjiang, Inner Mongolia, Hebei, Guizhou, Sichuan, Liaoning. Shaanxi and Anhui are the second tier of coal production provinces.

China's coal industry met a serious oversupply problem in the late 1990s. In part to improve the quality of production and eliminate unsafe and inefficient producers, and in part to lower the level of overcapacity, many small town and village enterprise mines were closed. In 2000, the shares of the then largest producers were estimated to have increased to 22% from 16% in 1990.

China's coal demand is projected to rise significantly in the future. According to IEA (2003), coal production is expected to increase from 1.23 trillion tons in 2000 to 2.30 trillion tons in 2030, and USD 123 billion investment will be needed to reach that capacity.

At the same time, due to environmental concern and the thirst for oil, China has expressed a strong interest in coal liquefaction technology. Liquid fuels produced from coal liquefaction will be used as substitute products for oil, which has become increasingly dependent on imports.

OIL

Since 1993, China has become a oil net import country. China has surpassed Japan as the No.2 petroleum user after the U.S. in 2003. And it is increasing its oil purchases even faster than its strong economic growth. Imports for the first 10 months of 2003 were up 30% compared to the same period in 2002. According to IEA, imports are expected to increase to 4 million barrels a day by 2010, and 10 million barrels by 2030, roughly the same import level of the U.S. in 2003. At the same time, domestic oil output remains flat (for the first 10 months of 2003, the output of crude oil was only up 1.3% from the same period last year). In 2003 and 2004, China is expected to account for about a third of the increase in global oil demand.

China's oil industry has undergone major changes in recent years. In 1998, the Chinese government reorganized most state owned oil and gas assets into two vertically integrated firms — the China National Petroleum Corporation

(CNPC) and the China Petrochemical Corporation (Sinopec). Before the restructuring, CNPC had been engaged mainly in oil and gas exploration and production, while Sinopec had been engaged in refining and distribution. In 1998, the Chinese government ordered an asset swap which transferred some exploration and production assets to Sinopec and some refining and distribution assets to CNPC. This created two regionally focused firms, CNPC in the north and west, and Sinopec in the south, though CNPC is still tilted towards crude oil production and Sinopec towards refining. Another major company is the China National Offshore Oil Corporation (CNOOC), which handles offshore exploration and production and accounts for more than 10% of China's domestic crude production. Since the reform, the regulated prices are closer to the international prices.

The Big Three - Sinopec, CNPC, and CNOOC - all have successfully carried out initial public offerings (IPOs) of stock within the last three years. CNPC separated out most of its high quality assets into a subsidiary called PetroChina in early 2000, and carried out its IPO of a minority interest on both the Hong Kong and New York stock exchanges in April 2000. The IPO raised over USD 3 billion, with BP the largest purchaser at 20% of the shares offered. Sinopec carried out its IPO in New York and Hong Kong in October 2000, raising about USD 3.5 billion. Like the PetroChina IPO, only a minority stake of 15% was offered. About USD 2 billion of this amount was purchased by the three global super-majors - ExxonMobil, BP, and Shell. CNOOC held its IPO of a 27.5% stake in February 2001, after an earlier attempt in September 1999 was cancelled. Shell bought a large block of shares valued at around USD 200 million.

NATURAL GAS

Historically, natural gas has not been a major fuel in China. In 2002, it only accounts for 2.7% of total primary energy consumption. Until the 1990s, natural gas was used mainly as a feedstock for fertilizer plants, with little use for electricity generation.

Natural gas is deemed as a kind of clean energy. Compared to coal, it creates much less pollution problems. After a breakthrough in prospecting during the 8th Five Year Period (1991-1995), cumulative verified reserves of natural gas in this five year period reached 630 billlion cubic meters (bcm), which was almost equal to the total verified reserves in the last 40 years. This breakthrough, combined with the constraints of oil output, makes China to make up its mind to increase natural gas's shares in energy mix significantly and to invest heavily on natural gas. IEA estimates that the gas demand would increase from 32 bcm in 2000 to 61 bcm in 2010, and to 162 bcm in 2030. And it is estimated that a cumulative investment of just under USD 100 billion in supply infrastructure will be needed over the period 2001-2030 to meet projected increases in demand. Distribution networks will attract the largest amounts of capital — more than a third of total investment.

According to the results of prospecting, most of the natural gas reserves are distributed in the central, northwest and coastal waters while the main natural gas consumption regions are in the East, where the economy is more advanced.

In order to exploit the rich natural gas resource in the Western region, a gigantic project — "West-to-East Gas Pipeline" is under construction. The west end of the pipeline is Lunnan in Tarim Basin, which had verified gas reserves about 540 bcm (390 bcm exploitable) at the end of 2002 (the verified gas reserves will be above 1,000 bcm in 2010). The east end of the pipeline is Shanghai, the center of Yangtze River Delta, the most dynamic economic zone in China.

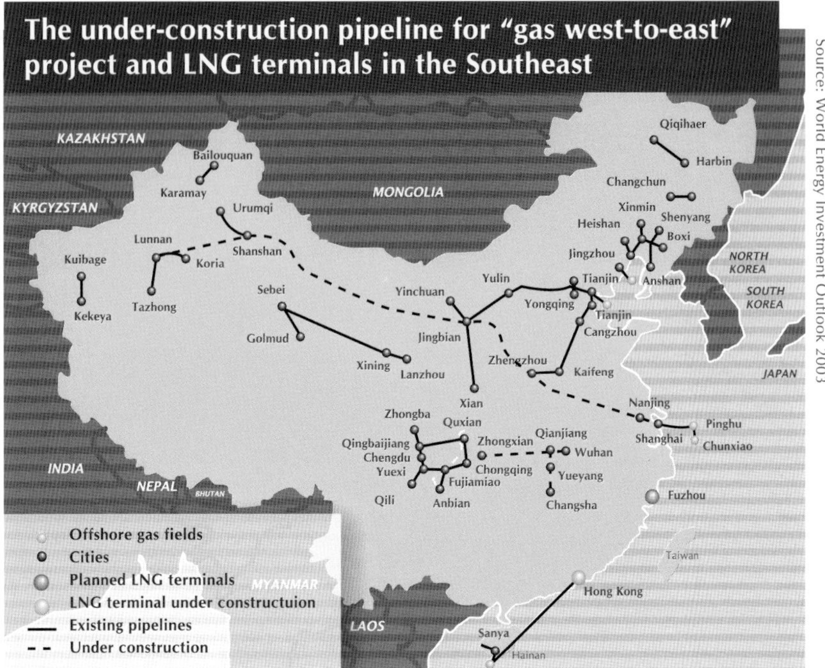

The under constructed pipeline for "gas west-to-east" project and LNG terminals in the Southeast

The 4,200km long pipeline will pass through nine provinces. The project's fixed investment will hit RMB 38.4 billion yuan. Considering the related construction projects such as the city pipeline nets, industrial utilization etc., the complete investment will total RMB 140 billion yuan. It is scheduled that the whole pipeline will be in operation in 2005, with 12 bcm of natural gas as its annual volume of transmission. And about 40% of gas for the west-to-east project will be used for power generation.

At the same time, imported LNG has become another alternative energy resource for the Southeast region. In order to boost its economy with clean energy,

Guangdong launched China's first LNG project in 2002, which involves the construction of an LNG import terminal (in Guangzhou) and high-pressure gas pipelines. The first phase of the project will be completed in 2005, mainly supplying to Guangdong. Australia won the Guangdong LNG contract, which is worth around A$20-$25 billion in export income for Australia over the 25-year supply period. Besides Guangzhou, another LNG is going to be built soon in Fuzhou, the capital of Fujian province. And other few terminals around the coast areas are under feasibility study. Besides Australia, Indonesia will be another important LNG importer in the future. China is also engaging or discussing with Russia and other few Central Asian countries about potential pipeline projects.

ELECTRICITY

The Chinese electricity industry was born in 1882. By 1949, when the People's Republic of China was founded, China's power sector is with 1.85GW installed capacity and 6,500km transmission lines. After 30 years' of relatively fast expansion, China's installed capacity increased to 63GW in 1979. The growth accelerated after the mid 1980s due to surging demand for electricity boosted by increased investment and residential consumption associated with market reforms. By the end of 2002, the installed capacity increased further to 353GW with 1640TWh electricity generated.

China is now the world's second largest electricity producer, both in capacity and generated electricity. According to the estimation from the Tenth Five-Year Plan of China, the installed capacity will increase to 390GW by 2005. China's power sector will witness an unprecedented growth in the next 20 to 30 years. IEA estimates that about 800GW of new capacity would be needed in the next 30 years, while ChinaKnowledge predicts that the same capacity would be added in less than 20 years. According to IEA, nearly

USD 2 trillion investment on electricity infrastructure over the next three decades would be needed, of which more than USD 1trillion will be for transmission and distribution. And China Knowledge predicts that about USD 1.2 trillion would be needed from 2004 to 2020, with USD 630 billion on new capacity alone.

Coal-fired plants are the predominant force in China's power sector. At the end of 2002, coal-fired plants account for 70% of the total 353GW of installed generation capacity; hydro installation is about 23% and oil-fired plants for 6%. Gas is merely 0.2%. Nuclear is about 1.3%, and other renewable technology is almost negligible.

In order to enhance utilization efficiency and reduce pollution, the Chinese government is restructuring the thermal power sector by encouraging the building of large power plants with capacity of over

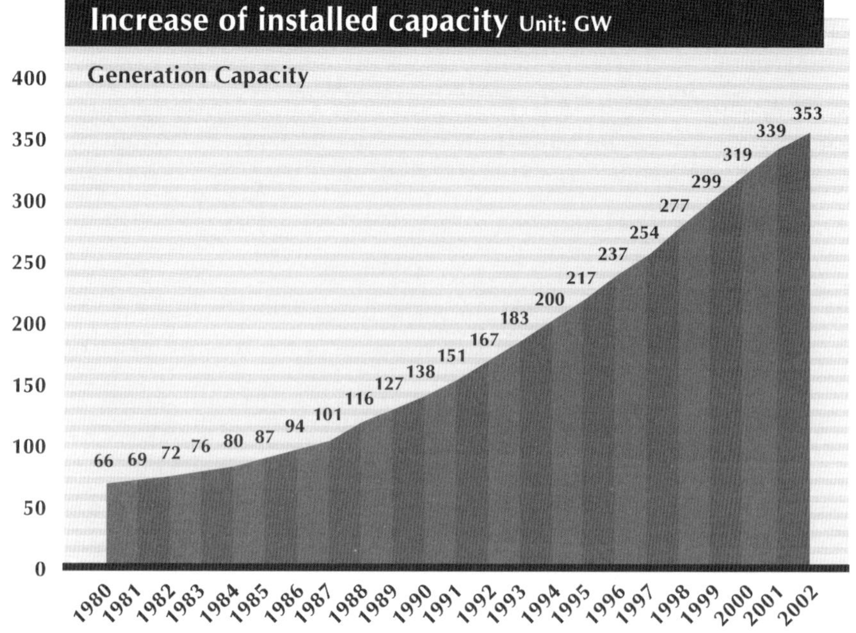

300,000Kilowatts(KW), as well as increase the weightage of hydro, nuclear and gas-fired power generators.

Similar to the other sectors in the energy industry, China's power sector is undergoing a deregulation process. The door of China's power sector was opened for the first time in the mid 1980s. The generation sub-sector was made accessible to provincial/local governments, domestic and foreign companies.

By the late 1990s, although China's power industry has made remarkable progress, the regulatory system by and large was left intact. Central planning still played a decisive role. Between 1997 and 2000, due to the fastly expanding power sector, plus the effects of Asia financial crisis and closure of many inefficient State Owned Enterprises (SOEs), many provinces in China witnessed a temporary power supply surplus. This provided a chance for China's power sector to have a thorough structural reform.

The first step is to separate government administration from power enterprises. This was marked by the closure of the Ministry of Electric Power Industry (MOEPI) and establishment of State Power Co. (SPC) in 1997-1998. Some assets of SPC and some Independent Power Producers (IPPs) were further listed in stock

Tremendous increase in hydropower

Investment requirement 2001~2030

Sector	Investment (USD)	Percentage of Global Investment
COAL	**Total $122.7 billion** Mining $120.6 billion Ports $2.1 billion	**34.0 %**
OIL	**Total $119 billion** Exploration & development $69 billion Refining $50 billion	**4.2 %**
GAS	**Total $100 billion** Exploration & development $31 billion Transmission & Storage $29 billion LNG $5 billion Distribution $35 billion	**3.2 %**
ELECTRICITY	**Total $1913 billion** New power plants and refurbishment $845 billion Transmission network extension $345 billion Distribution $723 billion	**19.0 %**

Source: IEA (2003)

exchanges. The second step is to separate generation with transmission and distribution, and to create an electricity market. It was started by the break-up of SPC. On December 29th 2002, SPC's virtual monopoly came to an end. 11 independent companies were established by splitting up the former SPC's assets.

Among these 11 new entities, five of them are generation companies. They are China Huaneng, China Datang, China Huadian, GuoDian Power and China Power Investment, each one with about 20GW generation capacity (on equity basis). On the transmission side, two grid companies were formed. They are the State Grid Corp and the Southern Power Grid Corp. Four consulting and construction companies were also established to play an ancillary role in the future electricity market. They are China Power Engineering Consulting Group, China Water Resources and Hydropower Engineering Consulting Corp, China Water Resources and Hydropower Engineering Construction Corp and China Gezhoupa Group.

STOCK MARKET

Introduction

Stock trading activities started in China in 1987 initiated by the Shenzhen Development Bank. Trading became more active and by the end of 1989, thousands of shareholding companies were set up all over the country. On 26th November 1990, the Shanghai Stock Exchange was founded, followed shortly after by the Shenzhen Stock Exchange in July 1991. These marked the beginning of stock markets in Chinese history.

Two main types of shares, A shares and B shares, are offered on the exchanges. A shares are offered exclusively to Chinese nationals. The purchase of B shares was initially restricted to foreigners but in 2001, the China Securities Regulatory Commission (CSRC) decided to open B shares to domestic investors because of the continuous slim trading and small capitalisation of the B shares market. The stock exchanges experienced several periods of boom and bust after establishment.

Shanghai Stock Exchange (SSE)

The Shanghai Stock Exchange (SSE) is a non-profit membership institution governed by the CSRC which based its development on the principle of 'legislation, supervision, self-regulation and standardization'. At the start of 2003, 715 companies were listed on the exchange with more than 35.6 million investors, 181,000 of them being institutional investors. The total market capitalization reached RMB 2,536.4 billion yuan.

The SSE has a modern trading system that supports electronic trading at a speed as high as 8000 transactions per second. The closest asking and bidding prices are automatically matched. With a trading floor size of 3,600 metre square, the SSE is the largest in the Asia-Pacific region. It can also provide real-time transaction information to domestic and foreign investors alike via its connection to the largest domestic satellite and optical communication network.

Shenzhen Stock Exchange (SZSE)

The Shenzhen Stock Exchange (SZSE) was established shortly after the SSE. It plays a significant part in terms of the total market capitalization, trading turnover and number of listed companies, and is one of the supporting pillars of the national economy. It is linked to many overseas markets and is actively extending its network to other countries.

In the year 2002, in conjunction with the launch of 'Qualified Foreign Institutional Investors' (QFII) system which allowed foreign investors to invest directly in A shares, the SZSE set up other guidelines to be followed. To date, SZSE has 615 listed stocks from 508 companies, with 33.17 million investors. Among the 215 members, 53 are overseas market participants broking or underwriting the B shares. The

market capitalization of the SZSE accounted for 13.52% of the GDP in 2002.

Like the SSE, SSZE offers real-time information of trading activities with the help of satellite technology and leased lines. The capacity of the system far exceeds the amount of trading actually carried out at the present moment: a figure of 20 million versus 4.5 million.

Types of Stocks

Besides the universal classification of common stock and preferred stock, a security is also defined by the shareholder's status and nationality. This classification works to control the transferability of shares: State shares are theoretically non-transferable. Foreign shares may be traded only in a special, closed market while individual shares may be transferred only between Chinese citizens.

• ***A Shares***

Also known as individual shares, A shares are previously owned only by Chinese citizens. A shares have the full functions of classic stock, and may be freely traded and transferred within the domestic market. With the implementation of the QFII, qualified foreign investors could participate directly in the investing of A shares.

• ***Foreign Capital Shares***

These include B shares and overseas-listed shares. B shares were originally restricted to foreign investors. However, since February 2001, they have been opened to domestic investors. B shares, like any other shares, are denominated in RMB, but are traded in US dollars and Hong Kong dollars in the SSE and SZSE respectively.

H shares are fundamentally Chinese state-owned shares listed on the Hong Kong Stock Exchange. They are subscribed for and listed in Hong Kong dollars, but denominated in RMB.

In the year 2002 the total market capitalization of the two exchanges reached nearly RMB 4 trillion yuan, establishing China as one of the largest stock markets in Asia. Against the backdrop of a strong long-term outlook and accelerated liberalization, China's stock market has a promising future.

WTO & the China Stock Market

With China's entry into the WTO, basic improvements in the efficiency, transparency and liquidity of China's stocks have been achieved. Specifically, changes mandated by WTO's General Agreement of Trade in Services (GATS) is liberalising China's financial and accounting services markets, and increasing financial intermediaries. These help to foster development in China's stock market and also to reduce the costs of information, monitoring and corporate control.

It is expected that a highly internationalised stock market will emerge which fully complies with all the GATS requirements. China's stock market will become an important component of the global commercial platform.

Privatization of State-Owned Stocks

The majority of stocks in China are state-owned, with the government controlling about two-thirds of the listed companies. In addition, the price differences between floating and non-floating (state-owned) shares are huge, sometimes to the extent that floating stocks are double the price of non-floating stocks. In the short run, as some state-owned stocks are being privatised, excessive speculation may occur which will destabilize the investment environment. Yet as the government steps up regulation, increases transparency and seeks better methods to sell state-owned stocks such that stability is maintained, China's stock market landscape will change for the better.

Sponsor System for Domestic Listing

From February 2004, a sponsor listing system will be implemented. Initial Public Offering (IPO) applicants will be required to seek sponsorship of a qualified underwriter who shall bear liabilities to ensure the quality and accuracy of the information disclosed. Investment bankers are motivated by this sponsor system to screen and select the better listing projects because of the enormous implications, like suspension of business, if any major fault arises. This system will aid the development the stock market in China and also sets a higher standard for the listing of companies.

Prime Sectors

- **Real Estate** - As demand for housing sky rockets in China, listed real estate companies will be hot in demand. This sector has huge growth potential; it is advisable to place higher emphasis on the larger companies with strong financial standing and established share prices.

- **Medical** - Medical and pharmaceutical industries are characterized by high risks and high returns. This is especially true for companies which have unique characteristics and strengths at a time when health concerns are growing.

- **Information and Electronics** - These industries are at the forefront of technology. China, like the rest of the world, has an ever-increasing need for information and electronics. These high-tech industries are able to create added value. The current conditions are also extremely favourable with the prevalence of relatively low-cost skilled workers in the market.

STOCK EXCHANGE SHARES LISTING

Shanghai Stock Exchange B Shares Listing

Code	Name
900901	SVA Electron Co., Ltd.
900902	Shanghai Erfangji Co., Ltd.
900903	Dazhong Transportation (Group) Co., Ltd.
900904	Shanghai Wing Sung Data Technology Co., Ltd.
900905	China First Pencil Co., Ltd.
900906	China Textile Machinery Stock Ltd.
900907	Shanghai Rubber Belt Co., Ltd.
900908	Shanghai Chlor Alkali Chemical Co., Ltd.
900909	Shanghai Tyre & Rubber Co., Ltd.
900910	Shanghai Highly (Group) Co., Ltd.
900911	Shanghai Jinqiao Export Processing Zone Development Co., Ltd.
900912	Shanghai Outer Gaoqiao Free Trade Zone Development Co., Ltd.
900913	Shanghai Lian Hua Fibre Co., Ltd.
900914	Shanghai Jinjang Tower Co., Ltd.
900915	Shanghai Forever Co., Ltd.
900916	Phoenix Co., Ltd.
900917	Shanghai Haixin Group Co., Ltd.
900918	Shanghai Yaohua Pilkinton Glass Co., Ltd.
900919	Shanghai Dajiang (Group) Co., Ltd
900920	Shanghai Diesel Engine Co., Ltd.
900921	Hero(Group) Co., Ltd.
900922	Shanghai Sanmao Textile Co., Ltd.
900923	Shanghai Friendship Group Co., Ltd.
900924	Shanggong Co., Ltd.
900925	Shanghai Shangling Electric Appliance Co., Ltd.
900926	Shanghai Baosight Software Co., Ltd.
900927	Shanghai Material Trade Center Co., Ltd.
900928	Shanghai Automation Instrumentation Co., Ltd.
900929	Shanghai China International Travel Service Co., Ltd.
900930	Shanghai Posts & Telecommunications Co., Ltd.
900932	Shanghai Lujiazui Finance & Trade Zone Development Co., Ltd.
900933	Hua Xin Cement Co., Ltd.

900934 Shanghai New Asia (Group) Co., Ltd.
900935 Shanghai Jintai Co., Ltd.
900936 Inner Mongolia Eerduosi Cashmere Products Co., Ltd.
900937 Heilongjiang Electric Power Co., Ltd.
900938 Tientsin Marine Shipping Co., Ltd.
900939 Shanghai Huili Building Material Co., Ltd.
900940 Shanghai Worldbest Co., Ltd.
900941 Eastern Communications Co., Ltd.
900942 Huangshan Tourism Development Co., Ltd.
900943 Shanghai Kai Kai Industrial Co., Ltd.
900945 Hainan Airlines Co., Ltd.
900946 Jinan Qingqi Motorcycle Co., Ltd.
900947 Shanghai Zhenhua Port Machinery Co., Ltd.
900948 Inner Mongolia Yitai Coal Co., Ltd.
900949 Zhejiang Southeast Electric Power Co., Ltd.
900950 Jiangsu Xincheng Real Estate Co., Ltd.
900951 Dahua Group Dalian Chemical Industry Co., Ltd.
900952 Jinzhou Port Co., Ltd.
900953 Worldbest Kama Machinery Co., Ltd.
900955 Shanghai Matsuoka Co., Ltd.
900956 Huangshi Dongbei Electrical Appliance Co., Ltd.
900957 Shanghai Lingyun Curtain Wall Science & Technology Co., Ltd.

Shenzhen Stock Exchange A Shares Listing

Agriculture

<u>Code</u> <u>Name</u>
000509 Sichuan Tiange Technology Group Co.,Ltd.
000663 Fujian Yongan Forestry Group Joint-Stock
000713 Hefei Fengle Seed Co., Ltd.
000735 Haikou Agriculture & Industry & Trade
000769 Dailian Feifei Aojia Modern Agriculture
000798 CNFC Overseas Fishery Co., Ltd.
000829 Jiangxi Gannan Fruit Co., Ltd.
000860 Beijing Shunxin Agriculture Co., Ltd.

000918 Hunan Yahua Seeds Co., Ltd.
000972 Xinjiang Chalkis Co., Ltd.
000998 Yuan Longping High-Tech Agriculture Co.

Conglomerates

Code	Name
000686	The Liulu Industrial Co.,Ltd of Jinzhou
000690	Guangdong Baolihua Industry Co., Ltd.
000691	Hainan Huandao Industry Co., Ltd.
000701	Xiamen Xinde Co., Ltd.
000716	Guangxi Strong Co., Ltd.
000722	Hengyang Gold Fruit Agriculture Industry
000793	Hainan Minsheng Gas Corp.
000835	Beijing Longyuan-Shuangdeng Industrial
000881	China Dalian International Cooperation

Construction

Code	Name
000023	Shenzhen Universe (Group) Co., Ltd.
000065	Norinco International Cooperation Ltd.
000090	Shenzhen Tonge (Group) Co., Ltd.
000415	Xinjiang Huitong Co., Ltd.
000730	SSEPEC
000758	China NFC Co., Ltd.
000797	China Wuyi Co., Ltd.

Finance

Code	Name
000001	Shenzhen Development Bank Co., Ltd.
000562	Hongyuan Securities Co., Ltd.
000563	Shanxi International Trust & Investment

IT

Code	Name
000863	Shenzhen Dawncom Business Technology
000892	Chongqing Changfeng Communication Co.
000909	Soyea Technology Co., Ltd.
000938	Tsinghua Unisplendour Corp., Ltd.
000948	Yunnan Nantian Electronics Information
000977	Langchao Electronic Information Industry
000981	Gansu Languang S & T Co., Ltd.
000997	Fujian Newland Computer Co., Ltd.

Manufacturing

Code	Name
000012	CSG Technology Holding Co., Ltd.
000016	Konka Group Co., Ltd.
000017	Shenzhen China Bicycle Co., Ltd.
000018	Victor Onward Textile Industrial Co., Ltd.
000019	Shenzhen Shenbao Industrial Co., Ltd.
000020	Shenzhen Huafa Electronics Co., Ltd.
000026	Shenzhen Fiyta Holdings Ltd.
000028	Shenzhen Accord Pharmaceutical Co., Ltd.
000030	Shenzhen Lionda Holdings Co., Ltd.
000036	Shenzhen Union Holdings China Co., Ltd.
000039	China International Marine Containers
000045	Shenzhen Textile (Holdings) Co., Ltd.
000048	Shenzhen Kondarl (Group) Co., Ltd.
000050	Shenzhen Tianma Microelectronics Co., Ltd.
000055	Shenzhen Fangda Group Co., Ltd.
000058	Shenzhen SEG Co., Ltd.
000059	Shenzhen Liaohe Tongda Chemicals Co., Ltd.
000060	Shenzhen Zhongjin Lingnan Nonfemet Co.
000068	Shenzhen SEG Samsung Glass Co., Ltd.
000070	Shenzhen SDG Information Co., Ltd.

000078 Shenzhen Neptunus Bioengineering Co., Ltd.
000150 Macat Optics & Electronics Co., Ltd.
000153 Anhui Xinli Pharmaceutical Co., Ltd.
000155 Sichuan Chemical Co., Ltd.
000156 Hunan Anplas Co., Ltd.
000157 Changsha Zoomlion Heavy Industry S & T
000158 Shijiazhuang Changshan Textile Co., Ltd.
000301 Wujiang Silk Co., Ltd.
000400 A-XJ Electric Co., Ltd.
000401 Tangshan Jidong Cement Co., Ltd.
000403 Sanjiu Yigong Biopharmaceutical & Chemical
000404 Huayi Compressor Co., Ltd.
000407 Shandong Shengli Co., Ltd.
000408 Hebei Huayu Co., Ltd.
000409 Stone Group Hi-Tech Co., Ltd.
000410 Shenyang Machine Tool Co., Ltd.
000413 Shijiazhuang Baoshi Electronic Glass Co.
000416 Qingdao Jiante Biological Investment Co.
000418 Wuxi Little Swan Co., Ltd.
000420 Jilin Chemical Fibre Co., Ltd.
000422 Hubei Yihua Chemical Industry Co., Ltd.
000423 Shandong Dong-E E-Jiao Co., Ltd.
000425 Xuzhou Science & Technology Co., Ltd.
000488 Shandong Chenming Paper Holdings Ltd.
000498 Dandong Chemical Fibre Co., Ltd.
000506 Sichuan Dongtai Industry Co., Ltd.
000510 Sichuan Jinlu Group Co., Ltd.
000513 Livzon Pharmaceutical Group Inc.
000515 Chongqing Yu-Gang Tioxide Co., Ltd.
000518 Jiangsu Sihuan Bioengineering Co., Ltd.
000519 Chengdu Yinhe Innovation Technology CO.
000520 Sinopec Wuhan Phoenix Co., Ltd.
000521 Hefei Meiling Co., Ltd.
000522 Guangzhou Bai Yun Shan Pharmaceutical
000523 Lonkey Industrial Co., Ltd.

000525 Nanjing Redsun Co., Ltd.
000527 GD Midea Holding Co., Ltd.
000528 Guangxi Liugong Machinery Co., Ltd.
000529 Guangdong Meiya Group Co., Ltd.
000530 Dalian Refreigeration Co., Ltd.
000533 Guangdong Macro Co., Ltd.
000535 KMK Co., Ltd.
000536 Fujian Mindong Electric Power Co., Ltd.
000538 Yunnan Baiyao Group Co., Ltd.
000541 Foshan Electrical & Lighting Co., Ltd.
000544 White Dove (Group) Co., Ltd.
000545 Jilin Henghe Pharmaceutical Co., Ltd.
000549 Torch Investment Co., Ltd.
000550 Jiang Ling Motors Corp., Ltd.
000551 Create Technology & Science Co., Ltd.
000552 Gansu Changfeng Baoan Industry Co., Ltd.
000553 Hubei Sanonda Co., Ltd.
000557 Guangxia (Yinchuan) Industry Co., Ltd.
000559 Wanxiang Qianchao Co., Ltd.
000561 Chang Ling (Group) Co., Ltd.
000565 Chongqing Sanxia Paints Co., Ltd.
000566 Hainan Qingqihaiyao Co., Ltd.
000568 Luzhou Laojiao Co., Ltd.
000569 Chuantou Changcheng Special Steel Co.
000570 Changchai Co., Ltd.
000571 Hainan Sundiro Holding Co., Ltd.
000576 The Jianmen Sugar Cane Chemical Factory
000581 Weifu High-Technology Co., Ltd.
000585 NE Electrical T&T Machinery Manufacturing
000587 Guangming Group Furniture Co., Ltd.
000589 Guizhou Tyre Co., Ltd.
000590 Tsinghua Unisplendour Guhan
000591 Chongqing Tongjunge Co., Ltd.
000595 Xibei Bearing Co., Ltd.
000596 Anhui Gujing Distillery Co., Ltd.

000597 Northeast Pharmaceutical Group Co., Ltd.
000598 Blue Star Cleaner Co., Ltd.
000599 Qingdao Doublestart Shoe Manufacturing Co.
000603 Weida Medical Applied Technology Co., Ltd.
000605 Sihuan Pharmaceutical Co., Ltd.
000606 Qinghai Gelatin Co., Ltd.
000607 Chongqing Holley Share Co., Ltd.
000609 Beijing Yanhua Up-Dated Hi-Tech Co., Ltd.
000612 Jiaozuo Wangfang Aluminum Manufacturing
000615 Hubei Golden Ring Co., Ltd.
000617 Jinan Diesel Engine Co., Ltd.
000618 Jilin Chemical Industrial Co., Ltd.
000619 Wuhu Conch Profiles and Science Co., Ltd.
000620 Heilongjiang Sunfield S & T Co., Ltd.
000622 Yueyang Hengli Air-Cooling Equipment,Inc
000623 Jilin Aodong Medicine Industry Groups
000625 Chongqing Changan Automobile Co., Ltd.
000627 Hubei Biocause Pharmaceutical Co., Ltd.
000629 Panzhihua New Steel & Vanadium Co., Ltd.
000630 Anhui Tongdu Copper Stock Co., Ltd.
000631 Lan Bao Technology Information Co., Ltd.
000635 Ningxia Ninghe National Chemicals Co.
000636 Fenghua Advance Technology Co., Ltd.
000637 Maoming Petro-Chemical Shihua Co., Ltd.
000639 Zhuzhou Qingyun Development Co., Ltd.
000650 Jiujiang Chemical Fibre Co., Ltd.
000651 Gree Electric Appliances Inc. of Zhuhai
000655 Shandong Zibo Huaguang Ceramics Co., Ltd.
000656 Chongqing Dongyuan Steel Co., Ltd.
000657 China Tungsten and Hightech Materials Co.
000659 Zhuhai Zhongfu Stock Entreprise Co., Ltd.
000661 Changchun High & New Technology Inc.
000665 Wuhan Plastics Industrial Group Co., Ltd.
000666 Jingwei Textile Machinery Co., Ltd.
000673 Datong Cement Co., Ltd.

000676 Henan Star Hi-Tech Co., Ltd.
000677 Weifang Sea Dragon Co., Ltd., Shandong
000678 Xiangyang Automobile Bearing Co., Ltd.
000680 Shantui Construction Machinery Co., Ltd.
000681 Far East Industrial Stock Co., Ltd.
000683 Inner Mongolian Yuanxing Natural Alkali
000687 Baoding Swan Co., Ltd.
000695 Tianjin Beacon Paint & Coatings Co., Ltd.
000697 Xianyang Pianzhuan Co., Ltd.
000698 Shenyang Chemical Industry Co., Ltd.
000699 Jiamusi Paper Co., Ltd.
000700 Jiangnan Mould & Plastic Technology Co.
000707 Hubei Shuanghuan S & T Stock Co., Ltd.
000708 Daye Special Steel Co., Ltd.
000709 Tangshan Iron and Steel Co., Ltd.
000710 Chengdu Tianxing Instrument and Meter
000712 Guangdong Golden Dragon Development Inc.
000717 SGIS Songshan Co., Ltd.
000718 Jilin Paper Manufacturing Co., Ltd.
000719 Jiaozuo Xin'an S & T Co., Ltd.
000723 Fuzhou Tianyu Electric Co., Ltd.
000725 BOE Technology Group Co., Ltd.
000726 Luthai Textile Co., Ltd.
000727 Nanjing Huadong Electronics I & T Co.
000728 Beijing Huaer Co., Ltd.
000729 Beijing Yanjing Brewery Co., Ltd.
000731 Siichuan Meifeng Chemical Industry Co.
000732 Fujian Sannong Group Co., Ltd.
000733 China Zhenhua (Group) S & T Co., Ltd.
000736 Chongqing International Enterprise Investment Co., Ltd.
000737 Nafine Chemical Industry Group Co., Ltd.
000738 Nan Fang Motor Co., Ltd.
000739 Qingdao Dongfang Group Co., Ltd.
000750 Guilin Jiqi Pharmaceutical Co., Ltd.
000751 Huludao Zinc Industry Co., Ltd.

000752 Tibet Galaxy S & T Development Co., Ltd.
000755 Shanxi Sanwei Group Co., Ltd.
000756 Shandong Xinhua Pharmaceutical Co., Ltd.
000757 Sichuan Direction Photoelectricity Co.
000760 Hubei Axle Co., Ltd.
000761 Bengang Steel Plates Co., Ltd.
000763 Jinzhou Petrochemical Co., Ltd.
000766 Tonghua Golden-Horse Pharmaceutical Co.
000768 Xi'an Aircraft International Corp.
000777 Sufa Technology Industry Co., Ltd., CNNC.
000778 Xinxing Ductile Iron Pipes Co., Ltd.
000779 Lanzhou Shanmao Industrial Co., Ltd.
000780 Inner Mongolia Prairie Xingfa Co., Ltd.
000782 Guangdong Xinhui Meida Nylon Co., Ltd.
000783 Shijiazhuang Refining-Chemical Co., Ltd.
000786 Beijing New Building Material Co., Ltd.
000788 Southwest Synthetic Pharmaceutical Co.
000789 Jiangxi Wannianqing Cement Co., Ltd.
000790 Chengdu Hoist Inc., Ltd.
000791 Northwest Yongxin Chemical Industry Co.
000792 Qinghai Salt Lake Potash Co., Ltd.
000795 Taiyuan Twin Tower Aluminum Oxide Co.
000799 Hunan Jiuguijiu Co., Ltd.
000800 FAW Car Co., Ltd.
000801 Sichuan Hushan Electronic Co., Ltd.
000803 Sichuan Meiya Silk (Group) Co., Ltd.
000806 Beihai Yinhe Hi-Tech Industrial Co., Ltd.
000807 Yunnan Aluminium Co., Ltd.
000809 Sichuan No.1 Textile Stock Co., Ltd.
000810 China Resources Jinhua Co., Ltd.
000811 Yantai Moon Co., Ltd.
000812 Shaanxi Jinye Science T & E Co., Ltd.
000813 Xinjiang Tianshan Woollen Textiles Co.
000815 Ningxia Meili Paper Industry Co., Ltd.
000816 Jiangsu Jianghuai Engine Co., Ltd.

000818 Jinhua Group Chlor-Alkali Co., Ltd.
000819 Yueyang Xingchang Petro-Chemical Co., Ltd.
000820 Jincheng Paper Co., Ltd.
000821 Hubei Jingshan Light Industry Machinery
000822 Shandong Haihua Co., Ltd.
000823 Guangdong Goworld Co., Ltd.
000825 Shanxi Taigang Stainless Steel Co., Ltd.
000826 SDIC Yuanyi Industry Co., Ltd.
000827 Dalian Changxing Industry Co., Ltd.
000828 Guangdong Fortune S & T Co., Ltd.
000830 Shandong, Luxi Chemical Co., Ltd.
000831 Shanxi Guanlu Co., Ltd.
000832 Heilongjiang Longdi Co., Ltd.
000833 Guangxi Guitang (Group) Co., Ltd.
000837 Qinchuan Machinery Development Co., Ltd.
000838 Southwest Chemical Machinery Co., Ltd.
000848 Hebei Chengde Lolo Co., Ltd.
000850 Anhui Huamao Textile Co., Ltd.
000851 Cuizhou China No.7 Grinding Wheel Co.
000852 Kingdream Public Co., Ltd.
000856 Tangshan Ceramic Corp., Ltd.
000858 Wuliangye Yibin Co., Ltd.
000859 Anhui Guofeng Plastic Industry Co., Ltd.
000861 Maoming Yongye (Group) Co., Ltd.
000862 Wuzhong Instrument Co., Ltd.
000866 Sinopec Yangzi Petrochemical Co., Ltd.
000868 Anhui Ankai Automobile Co., Ltd.
000869 Yantai Changyu Pioneer Wine Co., Ltd.
000876 Sichuan New Hope Agribusiness Co., Ltd.
000877 Xinjiang Tianshan Cement Co., Ltd.
000878 Yunnan Copper Industry Co., Ltd.
000880 Shandong Juli Co., Ltd.
000883 Hubei Triring Co., Ltd.
000887 Anhui Feicai Vehicle Co., Ltd.
000890 Jiangsu Fasten Co., Ltd.

000893 Guangzhou Refrigeration Co., Ltd.
000895 Henan Shuanghui Investment & Development
000898 Angang New Steel Co., Ltd.
000901 Harbin Fenghua-Aerospace Hi-Tech Co., Ltd.
000902 China Garments Co., Ltd.
000903 Kunming Yunnei Power Co., Ltd.
000908 Hunan Tianyi S & T Co., Ltd.
000910 Jiangsu Dare Advanced Packing Material
000911 Nanning Sugar Manufacturing Co., Ltd.
000912 Sichuan Lutianhua Co., Ltd.
000913 Zhejiang Qianjiang Motorcycle Co., Ltd.
000915 Shandong Shanda WIT S & T Co., Ltd.
000919 Jinling Pharmaceutical Co., Ltd.
000920 South Huiton Co., Ltd.
000921 Guangdong Kelon Electronic Holding Co.
000922 Acheng Relay Co., Ltd.
000923 Xuanhua Construction Machinery
000925 Zhejiang Haina S & T Co., Ltd.
000926 Hubei Fuxing S & T Co., Ltd.
000927 Tianjin Automotive Xiali Co., Ltd.
000928 Jilin Carbon Co., Ltd.
000929 Lanzhou Huanghe Enterprise Co., Ltd.
000930 Anhui BBCA Biochemical Co., Ltd.
000932 Hunan Valin Steel Tube & Wire Co., Ltd.
000935 Sichuan Shuangma Cement Co., Ltd.
000936 Jiangsu Huaxicun Co., Ltd.
000949 Xinxiang Chemical Fiber Co., Ltd.
000950 Chongqing Min-Feng Agrochem Co., Ltd.
000951 SHANDONG Xiaoya Electrical Appliance
000952 Hubei Guangji Pharmaceutical Co., Ltd.
000953 Guangxi Hechi Chemical Co., Ltd.
000955 Hainan Xinlong Nonwovens Co., Ltd.
000957 Zhongtong Bus & Holding Co., Ltd.
000959 Beijing Shougang Co., Ltd.
000960 Yunnan Tin Co., Ltd.

000961 Dalian Jinniu Co., Ltd.
000962 Ningxia Orient Tantalum Industry Co., Ltd.
000963 Huadong Medicine Co., Ltd.
000965 Tianjin Cement Co., Ltd.
000967 Zhejiang Shangfeng Industrial Holdings
000969 Advanced Technology & Materials Co., Ltd.
000970 Beijing Zhong Ke San Huan High-Tech Co.
000971 Hubei Maiya Co., Ltd.
000973 Foshan Plastics Group Co., Ltd.
000976 Guangdong Kaiping Chunhui Co., Ltd.
000979 Anhui Koyo (Group) Co., Ltd.
000980 Huangshan Jinma Co., Ltd.
000982 Ningxia St.Edenweiss Co., Ltd.
000985 Daqing Huake Co., Ltd.
000988 Huagong Tech Co., Ltd.
000989 Hunan Jiuzhitang Co., Ltd.
000990 Chengzhi Co., Ltd.
000995 Gansu Huangtai Wine-Marketing Industry
000999 Sanjiu Medical & Pharmaceutical Co., Ltd.
001696 Chengdu Zongshen Lianyi Industry Co., Ltd.

Media

Code	Name
000504	Beijing CCID Media Investments Co., Ltd.
000693	Chengdu Unionfriend-Taikang Network Co.
000917	Hunan TV & Broadcast Intermediary Co.

Mining

Code	Name
000406	Sinopec Shengli Oil Field Dynamic Group
000594	Neimenggu Hongfeng Industry Co., Ltd.
000762	Tibet Mineral Development Co., Ltd
000817	Liaohe Jinma Oilfield Co., Ltd.

000933 Shenhuo Coal Industry & Electricty Co.
000937 Hebei Jinniu Energy Resources Co., Ltd.
000956 Sinopec Zhongyuan Petroleum Co., Ltd.
000968 Shanxi Shenzhou Coal Electricity Coking Co., Ltd.
000983 Shanxi Xishan Coal & Electricity Power Co., Ltd.

Real Estate

Code	Name
000402	Finance Street Holding Co., Ltd.
000502	Hainan New Energy Co., Ltd.
000505	Hainan Pearl River Holdings Co., Ltd.
000511	Shenyang Ingenious Development Co., Ltd.
000514	Chongqing Yukaifa Co., Ltd.
000558	Lander Real Estate Co., Ltd.
000592	Fujian CFC Industries Co., Ltd.
000608	Super Shine Co., Ltd.
000628	Chengdu Brilliant Development Group,Inc.
000667	Yunnan Huayi Investment Group Co., Ltd.
000889	Qinhuangdao Hualian Business Building Co.

Social Services

Code	Name
000711	Heilongjiang Long-Far Co., Ltd.
000721	Xi'an Catering & Service (Group) Co., Ltd.
000802	Beijing Jingxi Tourism Development Co.
000888	Emei Shan Tourism Co., Ltd.
000897	Tianjin Jinbin Development Co., Ltd.
000931	Beijing Centergate Technologies Co., Ltd.
000975	Chongqing Wujiang Electric Power Co.
000978	Guilin Tourism Corp., Ltd.

Transportation

Code	Name
000582	Beihai Xinli Industrial Co., Ltd.
000652	Tianjin TEDA Co., Ltd.
000753	Fujian Minnan Economy Development Co.
000776	Yan Bian Highway Construction Co., Ltd.
000886	Hainan Expressway Co., Ltd.
000900	Xiandai Investment Co., Ltd.
000905	Xiamen Road & Bridge Co., Ltd.
000916	Huabei Expressway Co., Ltd.
000996	Jielee Industry Co., Ltd.

Utilities

Code	Name
000534	Shantou Electric Power Development Co.
000539	Guangdong Electric Power Development Co.
000543	Anhui Wenergy Co., Ltd.
000601	Guangdong Shaoneng Group Co., Ltd.
000692	Shenyang Huitian Thermal Power Co., Ltd.
000720	Shandong Luneng Taishan Cable Co., Ltd.
000767	Shanxi Zhangze Electric Power Co., Ltd.
000875	Jilin Power Share Co., Ltd.
000899	Jiangxi Ganneng Co., Ltd.
000939	Wuhan Kaidi Electric Power Co., Ltd.
000958	Shijiazhuang Dongfang Thermoelectric Co.
000966	Hubei Changyuan Electric Power Co., Ltd.
000993	Fujian Mindong Electric Power Co., Ltd.
001896	Henan Yuneng Holdings Co., Ltd.

Wholesale & Retail

Code	Name
000672	Baiyin Copper Commercial Building Co., Ltd.
000679	Dalian Friendship (Group) Co., Ltd.
000705	Zhejiang Zhenyuan Co., Ltd.
000715	CITIC Development-Shenyang Commercial
000759	Wuhan Zhongbai Group Co., Ltd.
000765	Wuhan Huaxin Hi-Tech Co., Ltd.
000785	Wuhan Zhongnan Commercial Group Co., Ltd.
000796	Baoji Department Store (Group) Co., Ltd.
000882	China Commerce Co., Ltd.
000906	Southern Building Materials Co., Ltd.
000987	Guangzhou Friendship Co., Ltd.

Shenzhen Stock Exchange B Shares Listing

Agriculture

Code	Name
200992	Shandong Zhonglu Oceanic Fisheries Co.

Conglomerates

Code	Name
200011	Shenzhen P & R Development (Group) Ltd.
200025	Shenzhen Tellus Holding Co., Ltd.

IT

Code	Name
200468	Nanjing Postal Telecommunications Co.

Manufacturing

Code	Name
200012	CSG Technology Holding Co., Ltd.
200016	Konka Group Co., Ltd
200017	Shenzhen China Bicycle Co., Ltd.
200018	Victor Onward Textile Industrial Co., Ltd
200019	Shenzhen Shenbao Industrial Co., Ltd
200020	Shenzhen Huafa Electronics Co., Ltd.
200026	Shenzhen Fiyta Holdings Ltd.
200028	Shenzhen Accord Pharmaceutical Co., Ltd.
200030	Shenzhen Lionda Holdings Co., Ltd.
200039	China International Marine Containers
200041	Shenzhen Benelux Enterprise Co., Ltd.
200045	Shenzhen Textile (Holdings) Co., Ltd.
200054	Shenzhen North Jianshe Motorcycle Co.
200055	Shenzhen Fangda Group Co., Ltd.
200058	Shenzhen SEG Co., Ltd.
200160	Chengde Dixian Textile Co., Ltd.
200168	Guangdong Rieys Co., Ltd.
200413	Shijiazhuang Baoshi Electronic Glass Co.
200418	Wuxi Little Swan Co., Ltd.
200488	Shandong Chenming Paper Holdings Ltd.
200512	Tsann Kuen (China) Enterprise Co., Ltd.
200513	Livzon Pharmaceutical Group Inc.
200521	Hefei Meiling Co., Ltd.
200530	Dalian Refrigeration Co., Ltd.
200541	Foshan Electrical & Lighting Co., Ltd.
200550	Jiang Ling Motors Corp., Ltd.
200553	Hubei Sanonda Co., Ltd.
200570	Changchai Co., Ltd.
200581	Weifu High-Technology Co., Ltd.
200596	Anhui Gujing Distillery Co., Ltd.
200625	Chongqing Changan Automobile Co., Ltd.
200706	Wafangdian Bearing Co., Ltd.

200725	BOE Technology Group Co., Ltd.
200726	Luthai Textile Co., Ltd.
200761	Bengang Steel Plates Co., Ltd.
200770	Wuhan Boiler Co., Ltd.
200771	Hangzhou Steam Turbine Co., Ltd.
200869	Yantai Changyu Pioneer Wine Co., Ltd.
200986	Foshan Huaxin Packaging Co., Ltd.

Mining

Code	Name
200053	Shenzhen Chiwan Petroleum Supply Base

Real Estate

Code	Name
200002	China Vanke Co., Ltd.
200029	Shenzhen Real Estate & Properties Co.
200505	Hainan Pearl River Holdings Co., Ltd.

Social Services

Code	Name
200613	Hainan Dadonghai Tourism Centre Co., Ltd.

Transportation

Code	Name
200022	Shenzhen Chiwan Wharf Holdings Ltd.
200057	Shenzhen Great Ocean Shipping Co., Ltd.
200152	Shandong Airlines Co., Ltd.
200429	Guangdong Expressway Development Co.

Utilities

Code	Name
200024	China Merchants Shekou Holdings Co., Ltd.
200037	Shenzhen Nanshan Power Station Co., Ltd.
200539	Guangdong Electric Power Development Co.

Wholesale & Retail

Code	Name
200013	Shenzhen Petrochemical Industry Co., Ltd.
200056	Shenzhen International Enterprise Co.

KEY STATISTICS

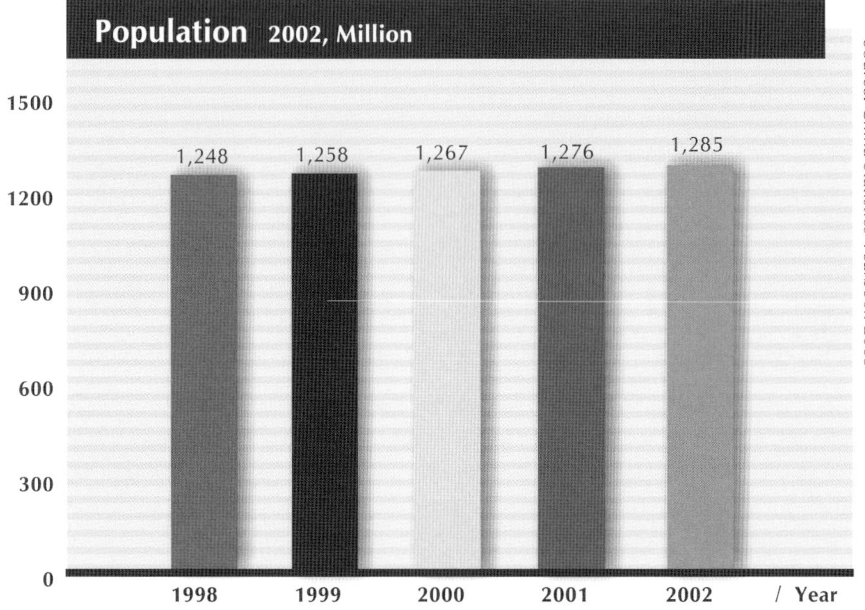

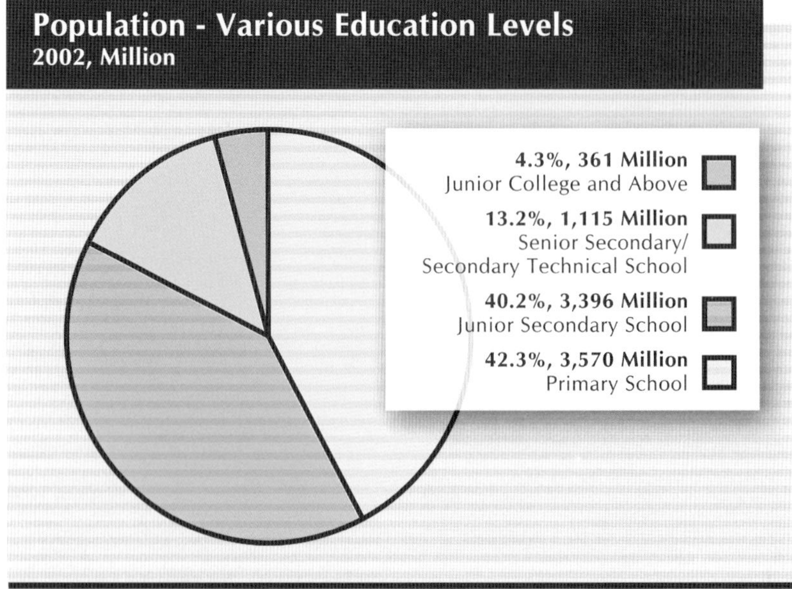

Inside the World's Largest Factory

TV Documentary

The episode titles are as follows:

I Manufacturing in Transition
II Free Trade Zones and Beyond
III Suzhou - Singapore : 10 years and after
IV Shanghai Bonds
V "Silicon Valley" of China

ChinaKnowledge Media *Production*

Order Form

Please Indicate the Title and Quantity that You Want to Order:

China Knowledge Press Titles (All Prices In US$)	Retail Price	Quantity
Inside the World's Largest Factory VCD (5 titles) I Manufacturing in Transition II Free Trade Zones and Beyond III The Singapore Model - 10 years and after IV Shanghai Bonds V "Silicon Valley" of China	USD 90	☐ 1 set ~~USD 90~~ **USD 54** ☐ 2 sets ~~USD 180~~ **USD 108** ☐ 3 sets ~~USD 270~~ **USD 162** ☐ 4 sets ~~USD 360~~ **USD 216** ☐ 5 sets ~~USD 450~~ **USD 270**

Total: USD

Payment Method (Please tick one)

☐ Telegraphic Transfer to ("China Knowledge Press Pte Ltd.")
A/c No. 0048-001013-01-3-022
Swift code: DBSSSGSG

☐ Charge to my American Express Card
Card No. :
Expiry Date: Signature: ______

Shipping & Delivery charges to:	
Asia	US$ 15
Australia/New Zealand	US$ 15
US, UK & Europe	US$ 25
Other Countries	US$ 30
Shopping & Delivery charges are waived for orders above US$1,000.	

Below is my: ☐ Home Address ☐ Office Address

Family Name: ☐Dr. ☐Mr. ☐Ms. ☐Mdm. ______

Given Name: ______

Job Title: ______ Company Name: ______

Address: ______ Country: ______

Telephone: ______ Email: ______

Business Activity: ______

All cheques made payable to "China Knowledge Media Pte Ltd"

Please send your completed order form with payment to our distributor:

China Knowledge Media Pte Ltd
8 Temasek Boulevard
#37-01A Suntec Tower Three
Singapore 038988
Tel: (65) 6235 1483 Fax: (65) 6235 2374

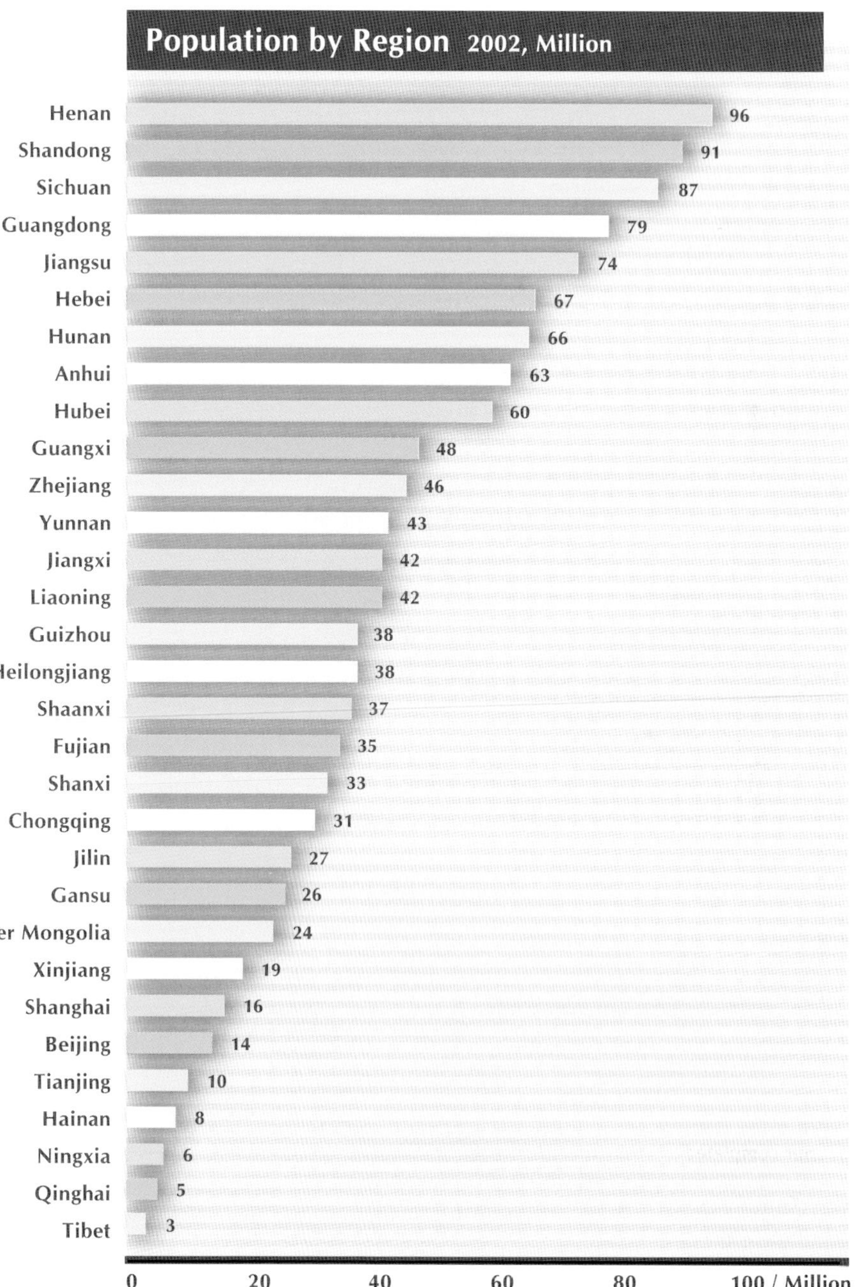
Population by Region 2002, Million
Henan 96
Shandong 91
Sichuan 87
Guangdong 79
Jiangsu 74
Hebei 67
Hunan 66
Anhui 63
Hubei 60
Guangxi 48
Zhejiang 46
Yunnan 43
Jiangxi 42
Liaoning 42
Guizhou 38
Heilongjiang 38
Shaanxi 37
Fujian 35
Shanxi 33
Chongqing 31
Jilin 27
Gansu 26
nner Mongolia 24
Xinjiang 19
Shanghai 16
Beijing 14
Tianjing 10
Hainan 8
Ningxia 6
Qinghai 5
Tibet 3
0
20
40
60
80
100 / Million
Source: China Statistics Yearbook 2003

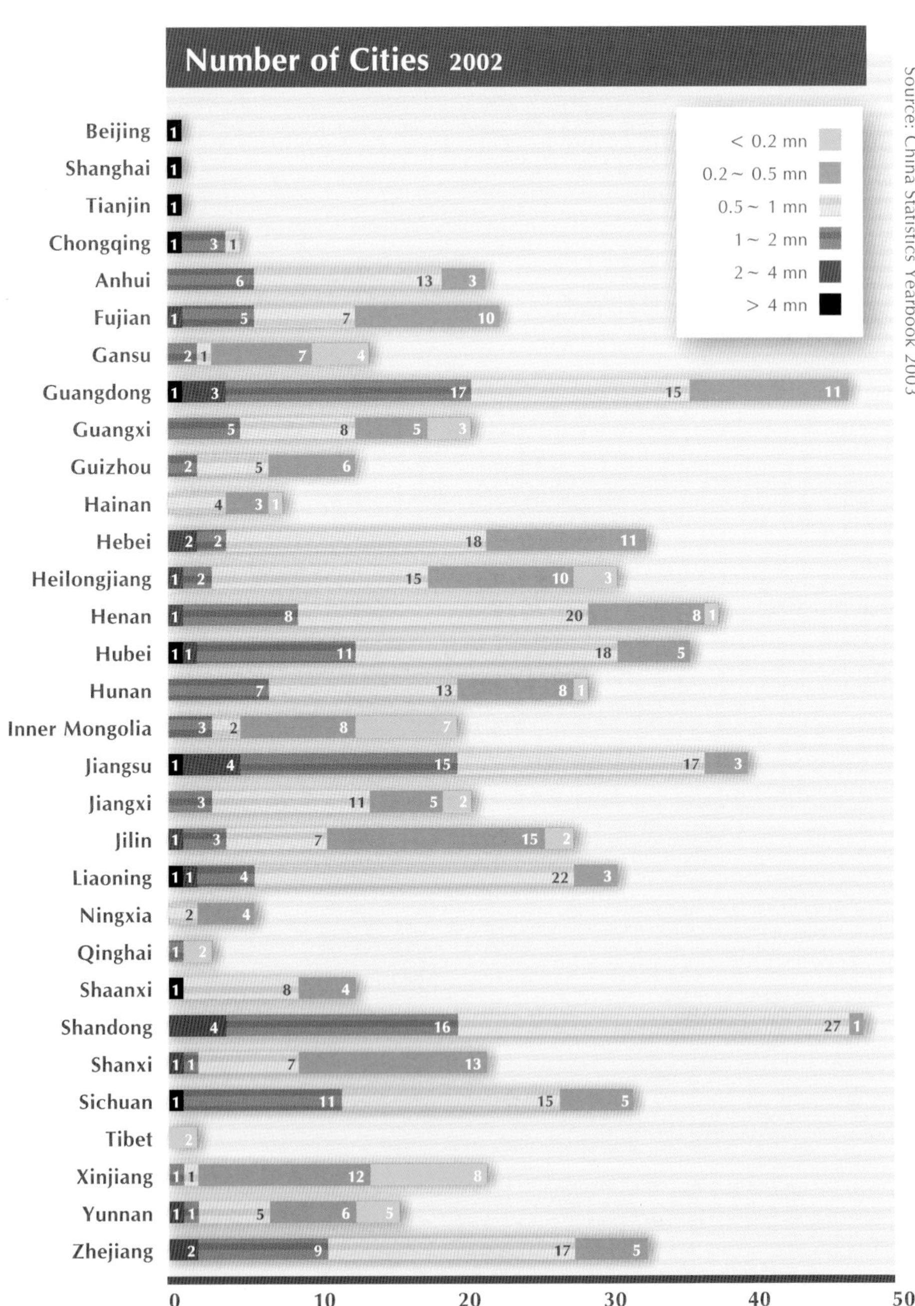

Number of Cities 2002
Source: China Statistics Yearbook 2003
< 0.2 mn
0.2 ~ 0.5 mn
0.5 ~ 1 mn
1 ~ 2 mn
2 ~ 4 mn
> 4 mn
Beijing 1
Shanghai 1
Tianjin 1
Chongqing 1 3 1
Anhui 6 13 3
Fujian 1 5 7 10
Gansu 2 1 7 4
Guangdong 1 3 17 15 11
Guangxi 5 8 5 3
Guizhou 2 5 6
Hainan 4 3 1
Hebei 2 2 18 11
Heilongjiang 1 2 15 10 3
Henan 1 8 20 8 1
Hubei 1 1 11 18 5
Hunan 7 13 8 1
Inner Mongolia 3 2 8 7
Jiangsu 1 4 15 17 3
Jiangxi 3 11 5 2
Jilin 1 3 7 15 2
Liaoning 1 1 4 22 3
Ningxia 2 4
Qinghai 1 2
Shaanxi 1 8 4
Shandong 4 16 27 1
Shanxi 1 1 7 13
Sichuan 1 11 15 5
Tibet 2
Xinjiang 1 1 12 8
Yunnan 1 1 5 6 5
Zhejiang 2 9 17 5
0 10 20 30 40 50

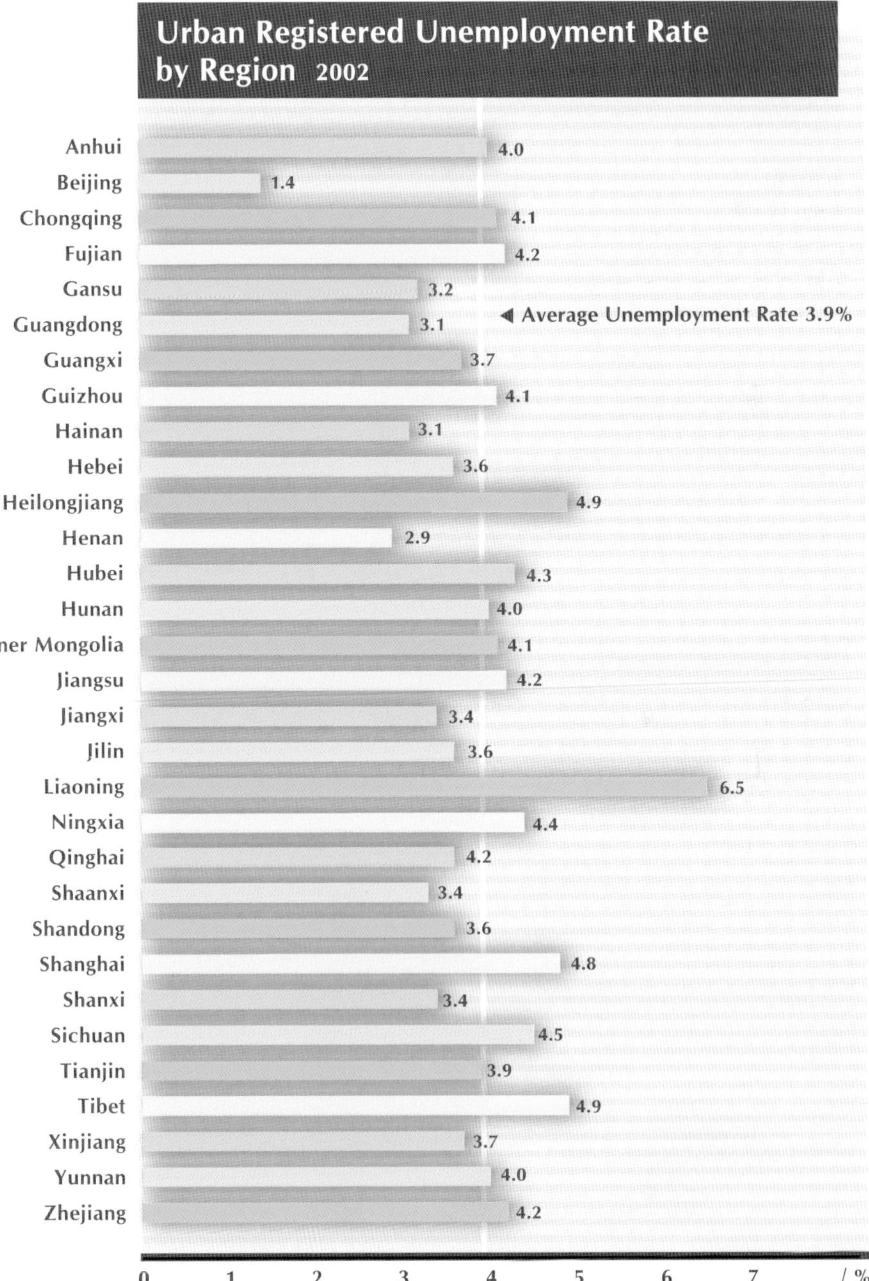
Urban Registered Unemployment Rate by Region 2002
Source: China Statistics Yearbook 2003
Anhui 4.0
Beijing 1.4
Chongqing 4.1
Fujian 4.2
Gansu 3.2
Guangdong 3.1
Average Unemployment Rate 3.9%
Guangxi 3.7
Guizhou 4.1
Hainan 3.1
Hebei 3.6
Heilongjiang 4.9
Henan 2.9
Hubei 4.3
Hunan 4.0
Inner Mongolia 4.1
Jiangsu 4.2
Jiangxi 3.4
Jilin 3.6
Liaoning 6.5
Ningxia 4.4
Qinghai 4.2
Shaanxi 3.4
Shandong 3.6
Shanghai 4.8
Shanxi 3.4
Sichuan 4.5
Tianjin 3.9
Tibet 4.9
Xinjiang 3.7
Yunnan 4.0
Zhejiang 4.2
0 1 2 3 4 5 6 7 / %

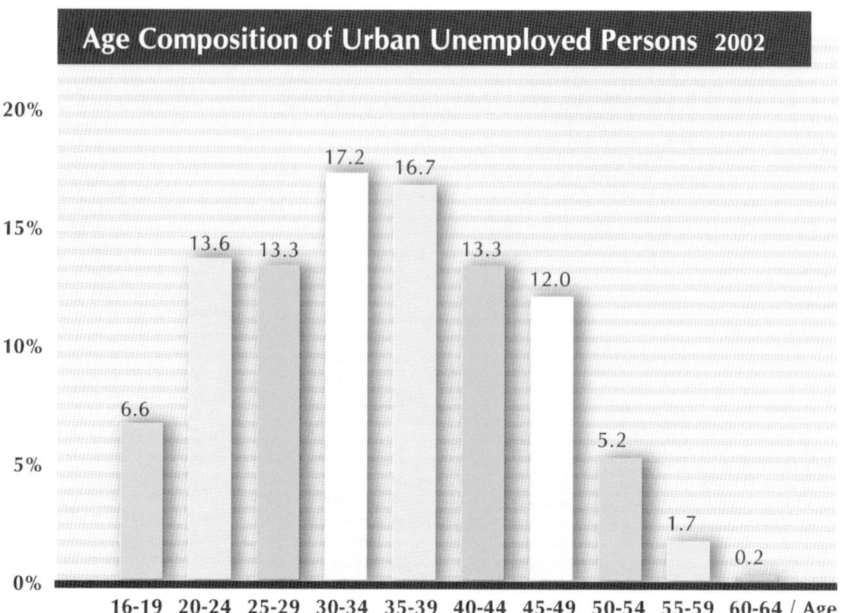
Age Composition of Urban Unemployed Persons 2002
20%
15%
10%
5%
0%
6.6
13.6
13.3
17.2
16.7
13.3
12.0
5.2
1.7
0.2
16-19 20-24 25-29 30-34 35-39 40-44 45-49 50-54 55-59 60-64 / Age
Source: China Statistics Yearbook 2003

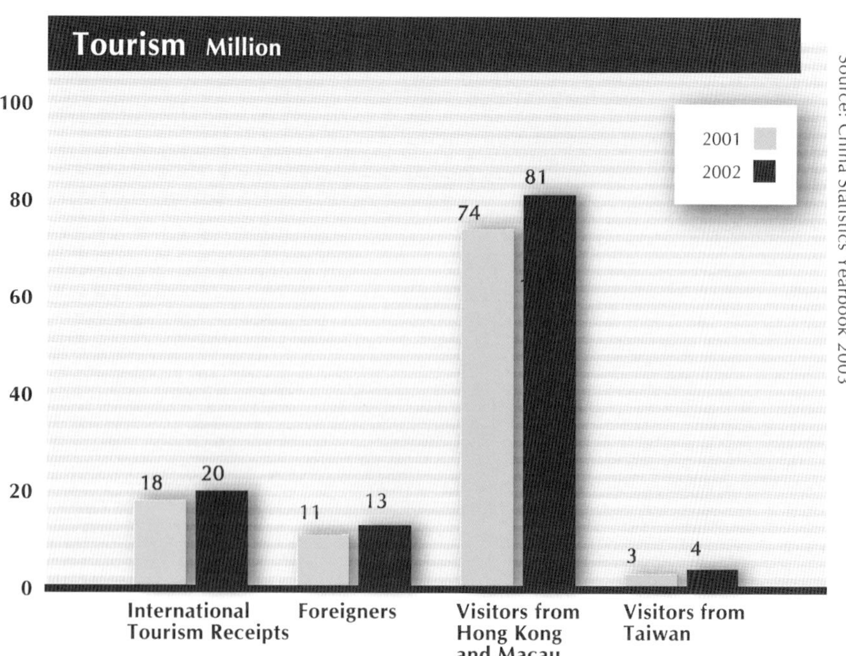
Tourism Million
100
80
60
40
20
0
2001
2002
18
20
11
13
74
81
3
4
International Tourism Receipts
Foreigners
Visitors from Hong Kong and Macau
Visitors from Taiwan
Source: China Statistics Yearbook 2003

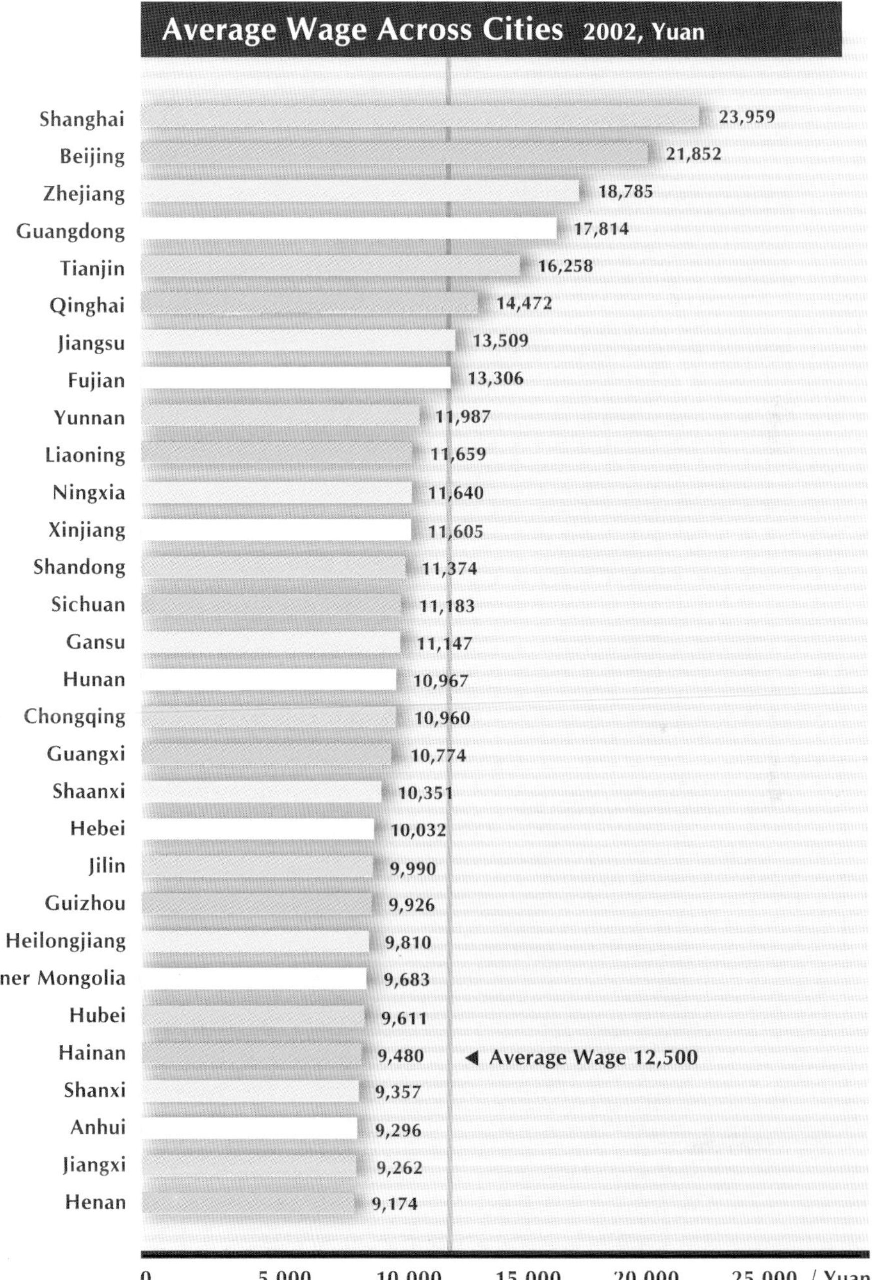

Source: China Statistics Yearbook 2003

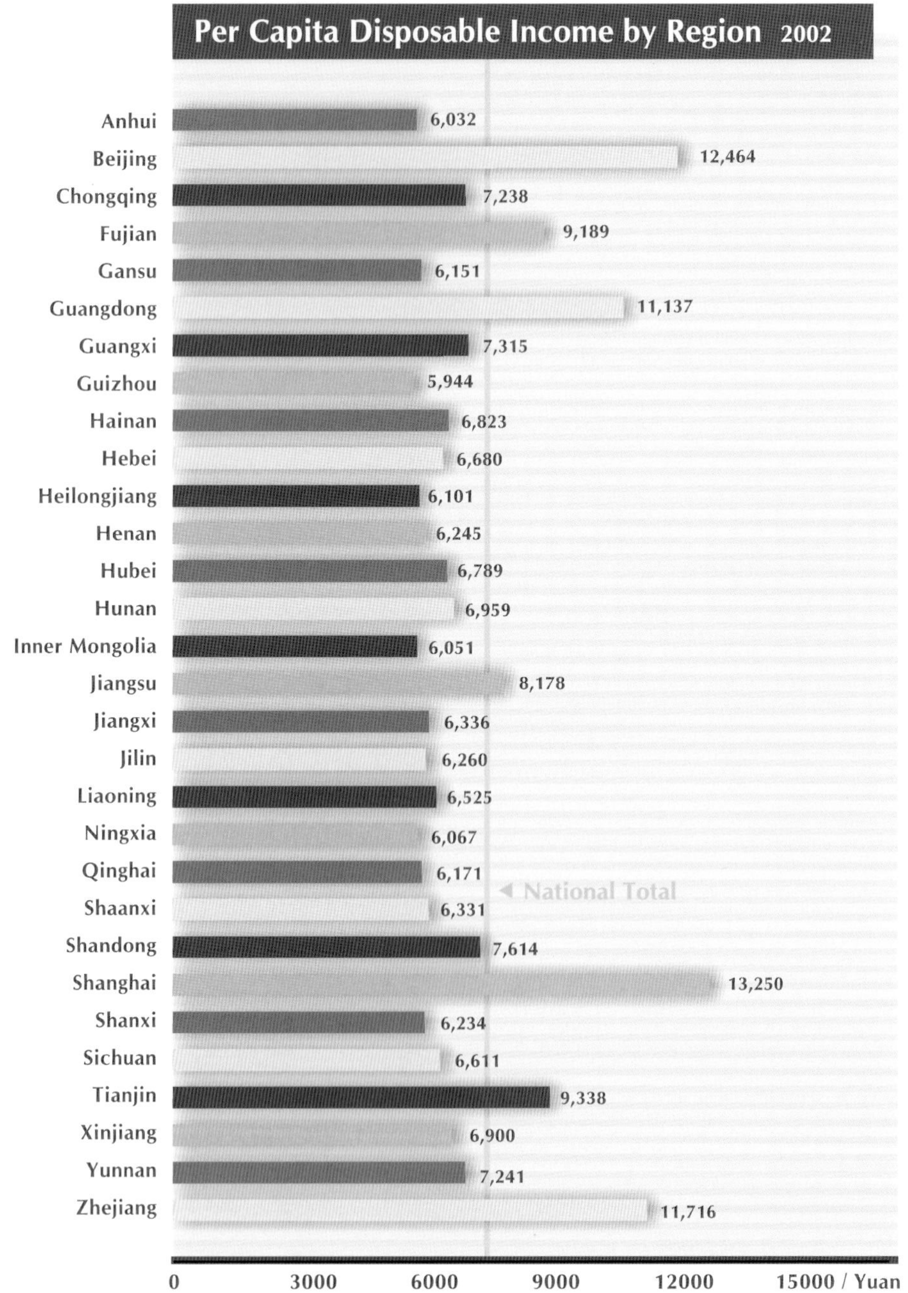
Per Capita Disposable Income by Region 2002
Source: China Statistics Yearbook 2003
Anhui 6,032
Beijing 12,464
Chongqing 7,238
Fujian 9,189
Gansu 6,151
Guangdong 11,137
Guangxi 7,315
Guizhou 5,944
Hainan 6,823
Hebei 6,680
Heilongjiang 6,101
Henan 6,245
Hubei 6,789
Hunan 6,959
Inner Mongolia 6,051
Jiangsu 8,178
Jiangxi 6,336
Jilin 6,260
Liaoning 6,525
Ningxia 6,067
Qinghai 6,171
Shaanxi 6,331
Shandong 7,614
Shanghai 13,250
Shanxi 6,234
Sichuan 6,611
Tianjin 9,338
Xinjiang 6,900
Yunnan 7,241
Zhejiang 11,716
◄ National Total
0
3000
6000
9000
12000
15000 / Yuan

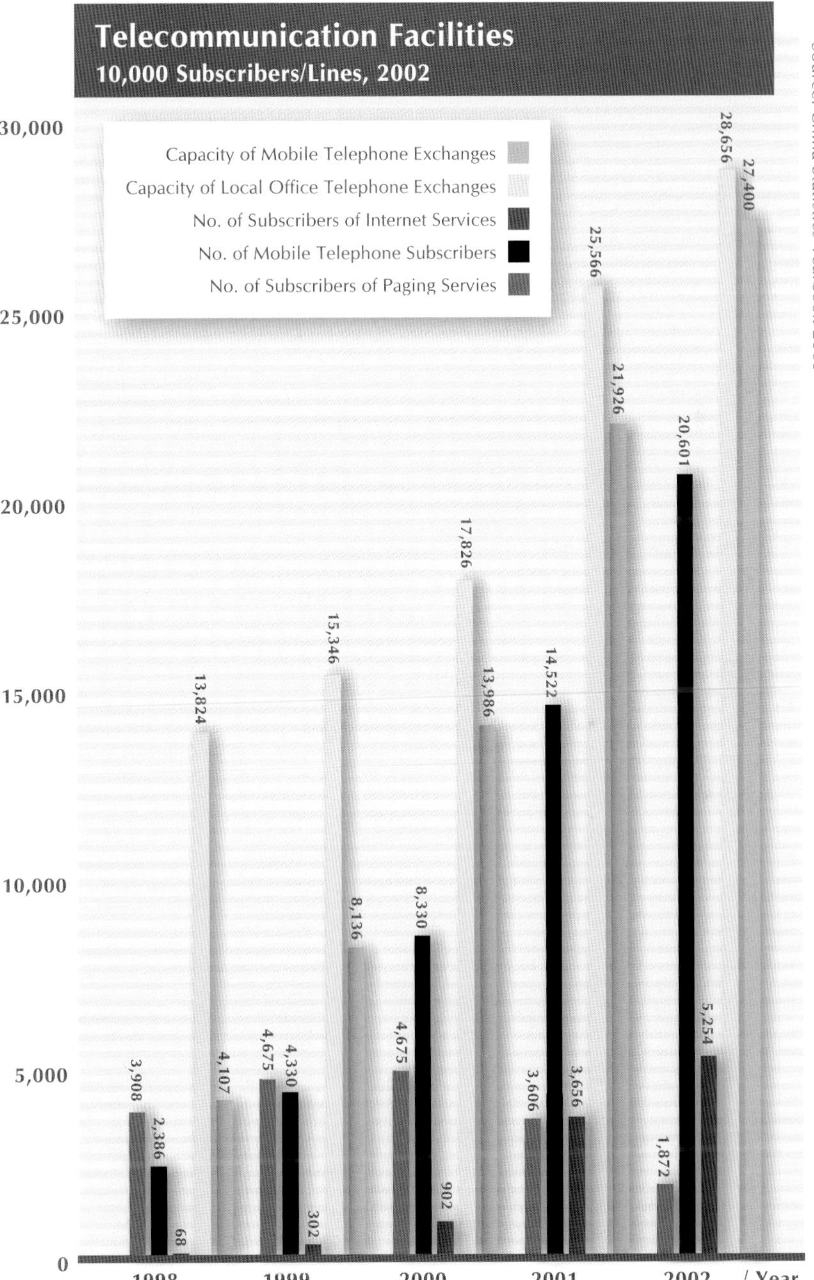
Telecommunication Facilities
10,000 Subscribers/Lines, 2002
Capacity of Mobile Telephone Exchanges
Capacity of Local Office Telephone Exchanges
No. of Subscribers of Internet Services
No. of Mobile Telephone Subscribers
No. of Subscribers of Paging Servies
30,000
25,000
20,000
15,000
10,000
5,000
0
3,908
2,386
68
13,824
4,107
4,675
4,330
302
15,346
8,136
4,675
8,330
902
17,826
13,986
3,606
14,522
3,656
25,566
21,926
1,872
20,601
5,254
28,656
27,400
1998
1999
2000
2001
2002
/ Year
Source: China Statistics Yearbook 2003

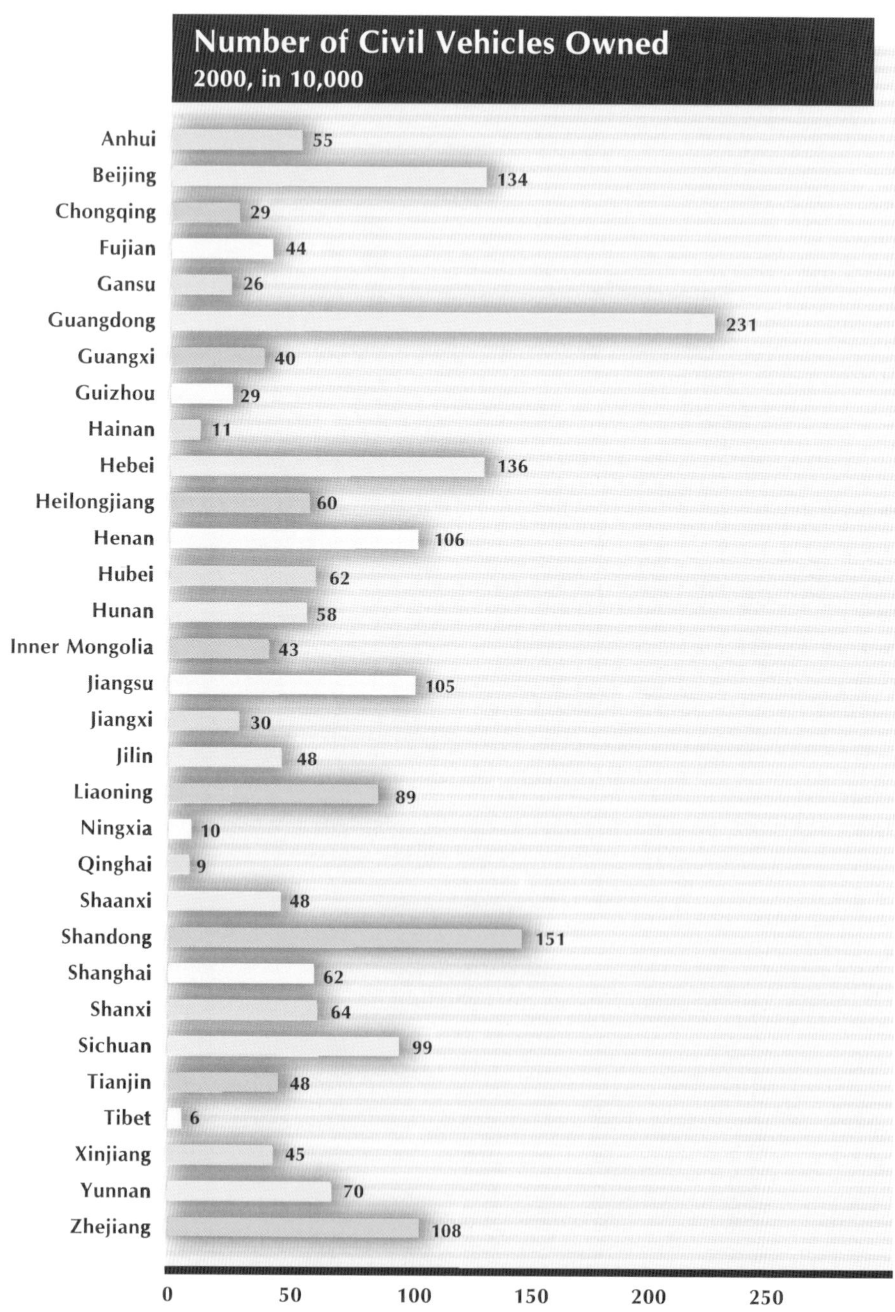
Number of Civil Vehicles Owned
2000, in 10,000
Anhui 55
Beijing 134
Chongqing 29
Fujian 44
Gansu 26
Guangdong 231
Guangxi 40
Guizhou 29
Hainan 11
Hebei 136
Heilongjiang 60
Henan 106
Hubei 62
Hunan 58
Inner Mongolia 43
Jiangsu 105
Jiangxi 30
Jilin 48
Liaoning 89
Ningxia 10
Qinghai 9
Shaanxi 48
Shandong 151
Shanghai 62
Shanxi 64
Sichuan 99
Tianjin 48
Tibet 6
Xinjiang 45
Yunnan 70
Zhejiang 108
0
50
100
150
200
250
Source: China Statistics Yearbook 2003

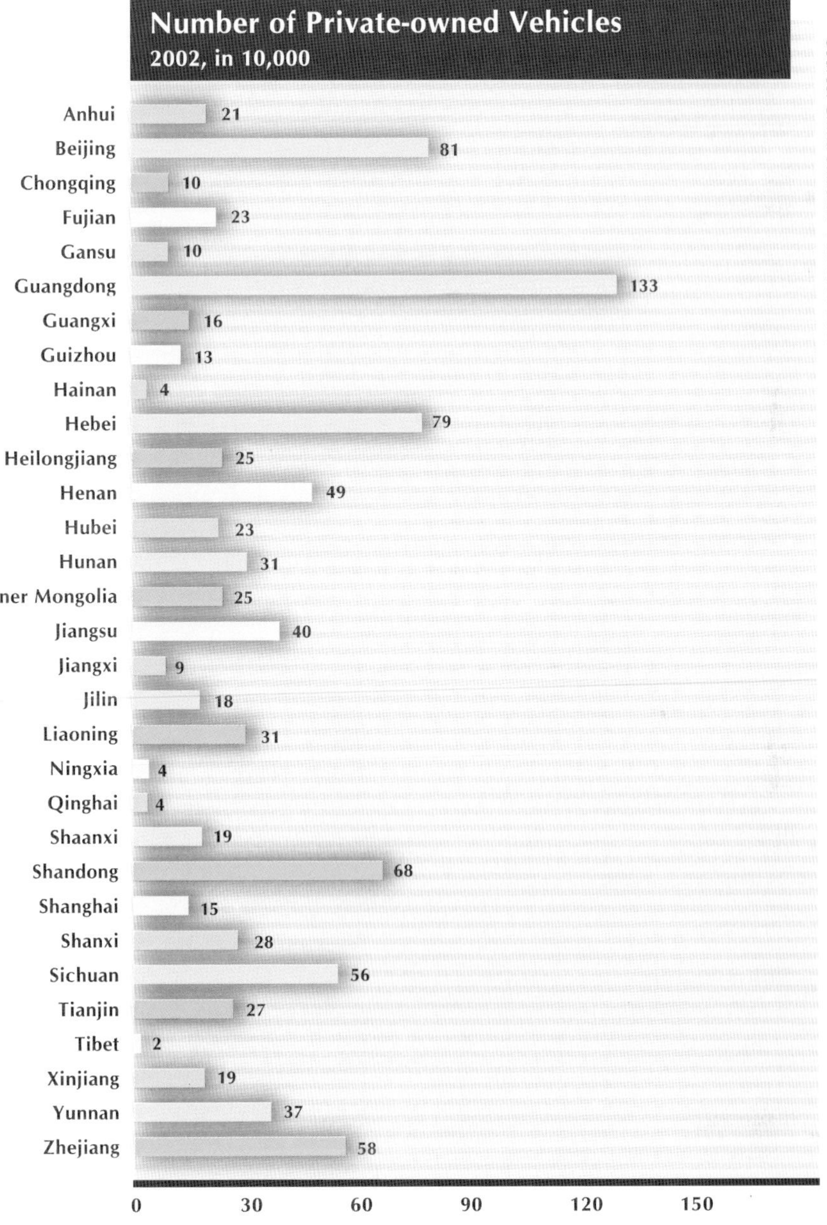
Number of Private-owned Vehicles
2002, in 10,000
Anhui
21
Beijing
81
Chongqing
10
Fujian
23
Gansu
10
Guangdong
133
Guangxi
16
Guizhou
13
Hainan
4
Hebei
79
Heilongjiang
25
Henan
49
Hubei
23
Hunan
31
nner Mongolia
25
Jiangsu
40
Jiangxi
9
Jilin
18
Liaoning
31
Ningxia
4
Qinghai
4
Shaanxi
19
Shandong
68
Shanghai
15
Shanxi
28
Sichuan
56
Tianjin
27
Tibet
2
Xinjiang
19
Yunnan
37
Zhejiang
58
0
30
60
90
120
150
Source: China Statistics Yearbook 2003

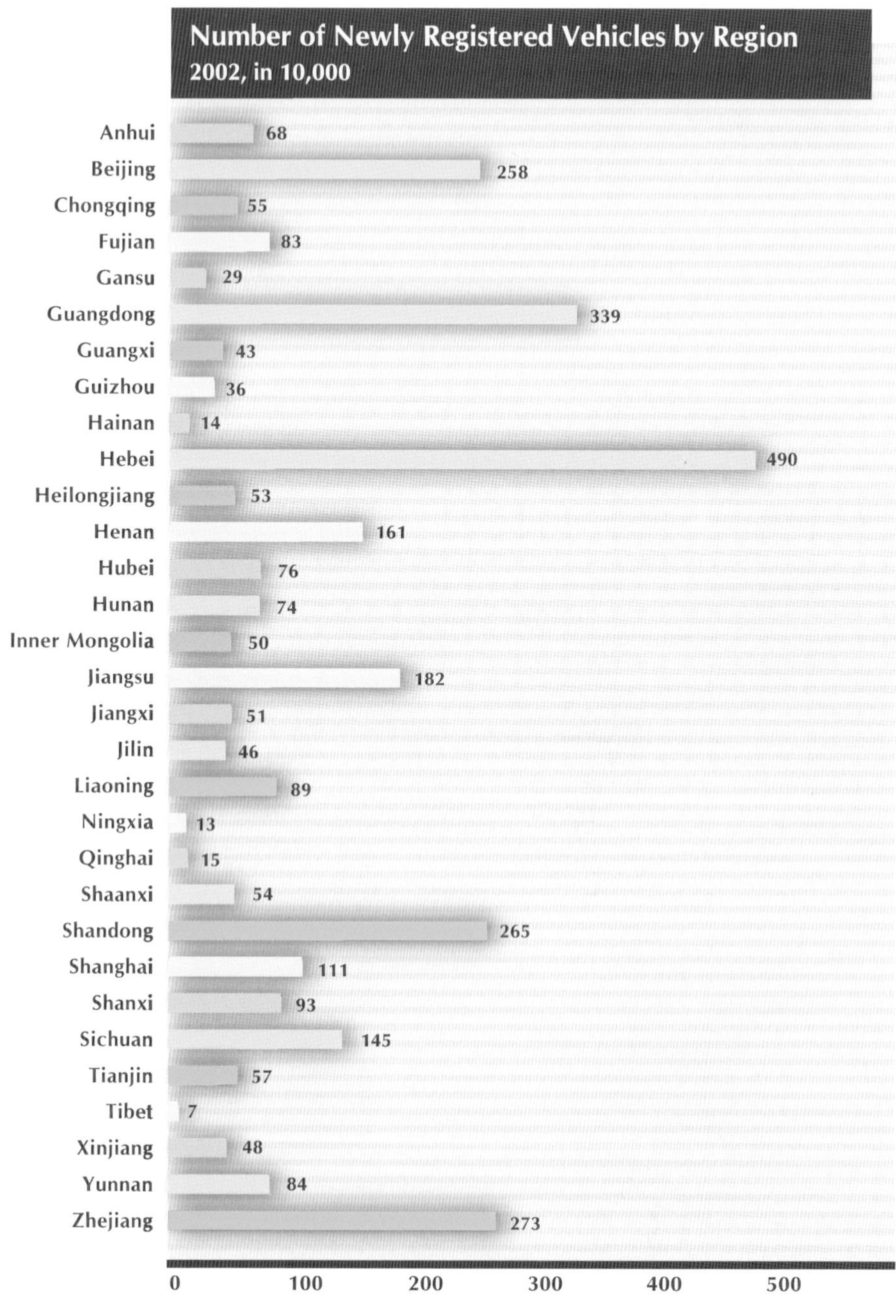
Number of Newly Registered Vehicles by Region
2002, in 10,000
Source: China Statistics Yearbook 2003
Anhui 68
Beijing 258
Chongqing 55
Fujian 83
Gansu 29
Guangdong 339
Guangxi 43
Guizhou 36
Hainan 14
Hebei 490
Heilongjiang 53
Henan 161
Hubei 76
Hunan 74
Inner Mongolia 50
Jiangsu 182
Jiangxi 51
Jilin 46
Liaoning 89
Ningxia 13
Qinghai 15
Shaanxi 54
Shandong 265
Shanghai 111
Shanxi 93
Sichuan 145
Tianjin 57
Tibet 7
Xinjiang 48
Yunnan 84
Zhejiang 273
0
100
200
300
400
500

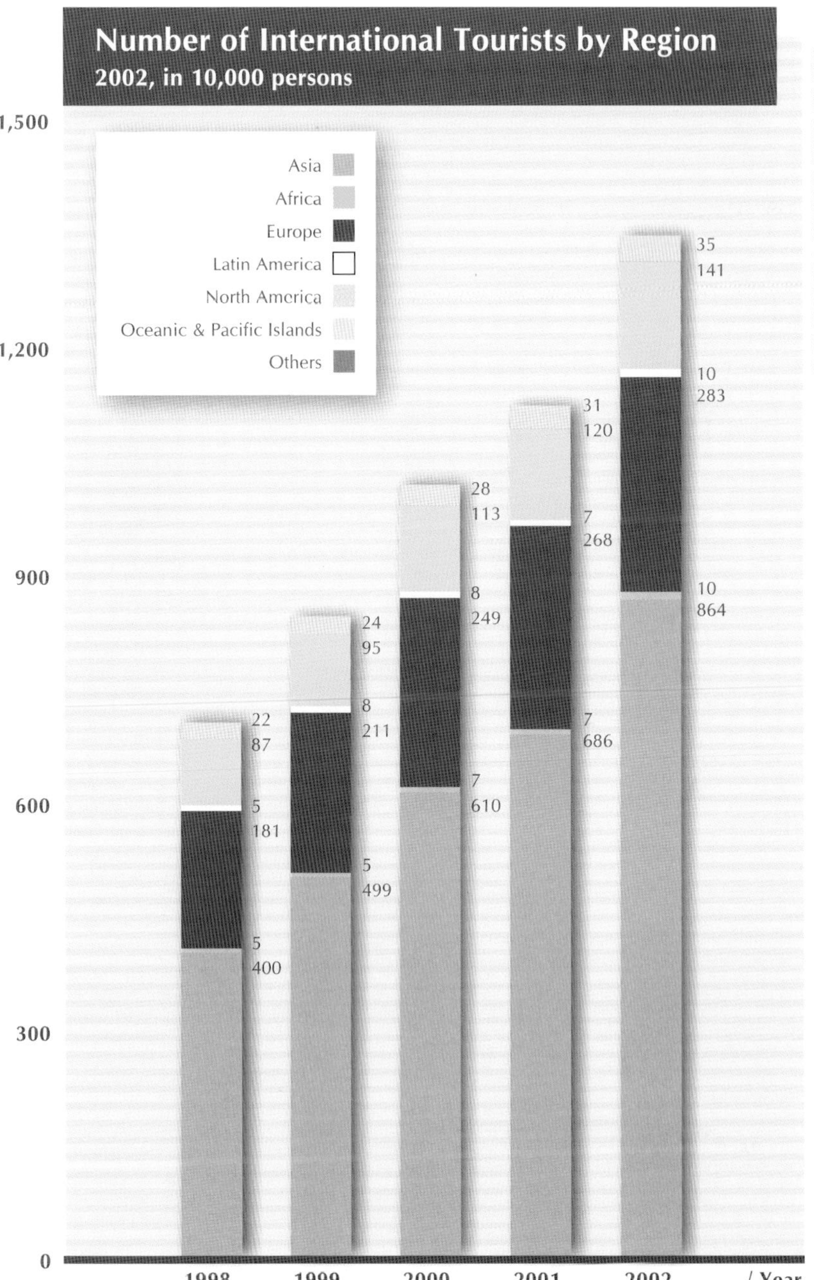
Number of International Tourists by Region
2002, in 10,000 persons
1,500
1,200
900
600
300
0
Asia
Africa
Europe
Latin America
North America
Oceanic & Pacific Islands
Others
22
87
5
181
5
400
24
95
8
211
5
499
28
113
8
249
7
610
31
120
7
268
7
686
35
141
10
283
10
864
1998
1999
2000
2001
2002
/ Year
Source: China Statistics Yearbook 2003

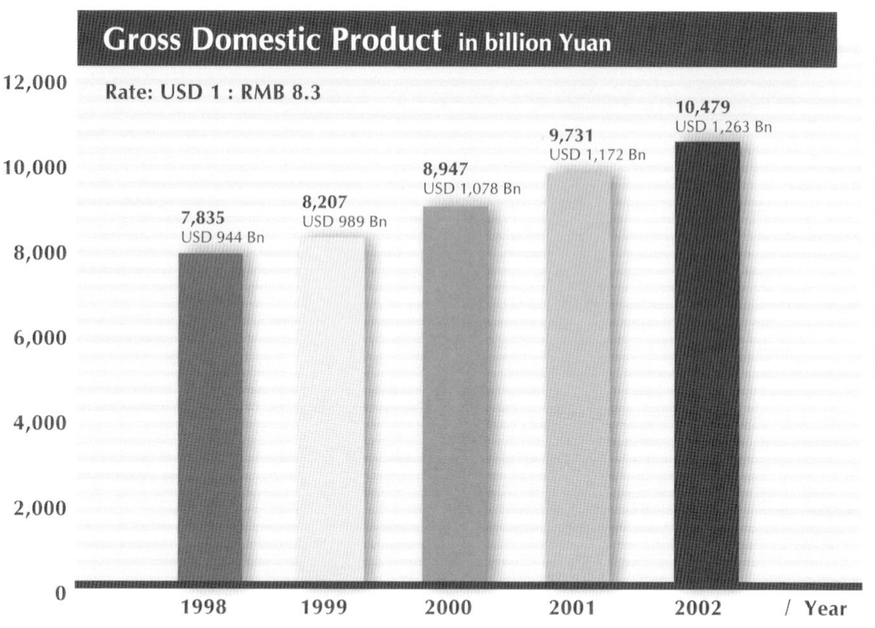
Gross Domestic Product in billion Yuan
Rate: USD 1 : RMB 8.3
12,000
10,000
8,000
6,000
4,000
2,000
0
7,835
USD 944 Bn
8,207
USD 989 Bn
8,947
USD 1,078 Bn
9,731
USD 1,172 Bn
10,479
USD 1,263 Bn
1998
1999
2000
2001
2002
/ Year
Source: China Statistics Yearbook 2003

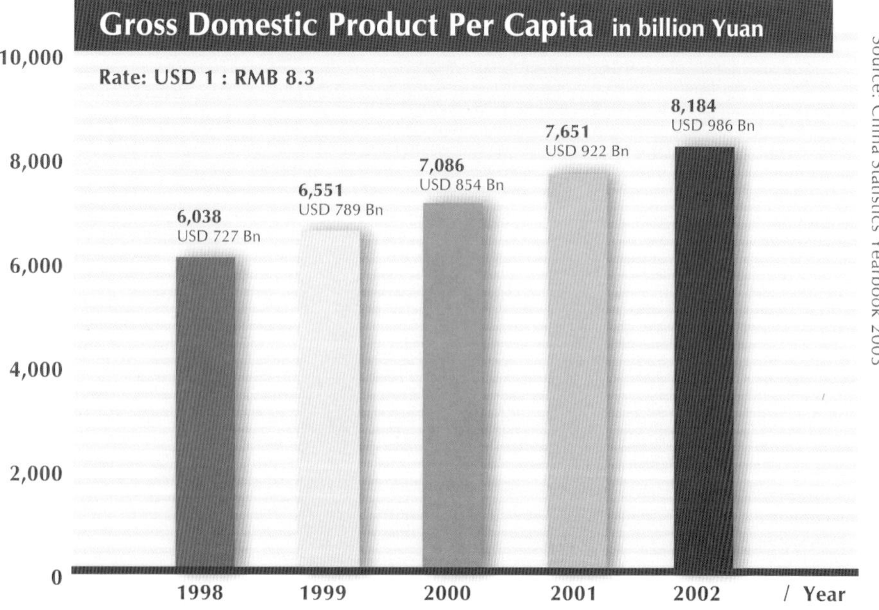
Gross Domestic Product Per Capita in billion Yuan
Rate: USD 1 : RMB 8.3
10,000
8,000
6,000
4,000
2,000
0
6,038
USD 727 Bn
6,551
USD 789 Bn
7,086
USD 854 Bn
7,651
USD 922 Bn
8,184
USD 986 Bn
1998
1999
2000
2001
2002
/ Year
Source: China Statistics Yearbook 2003

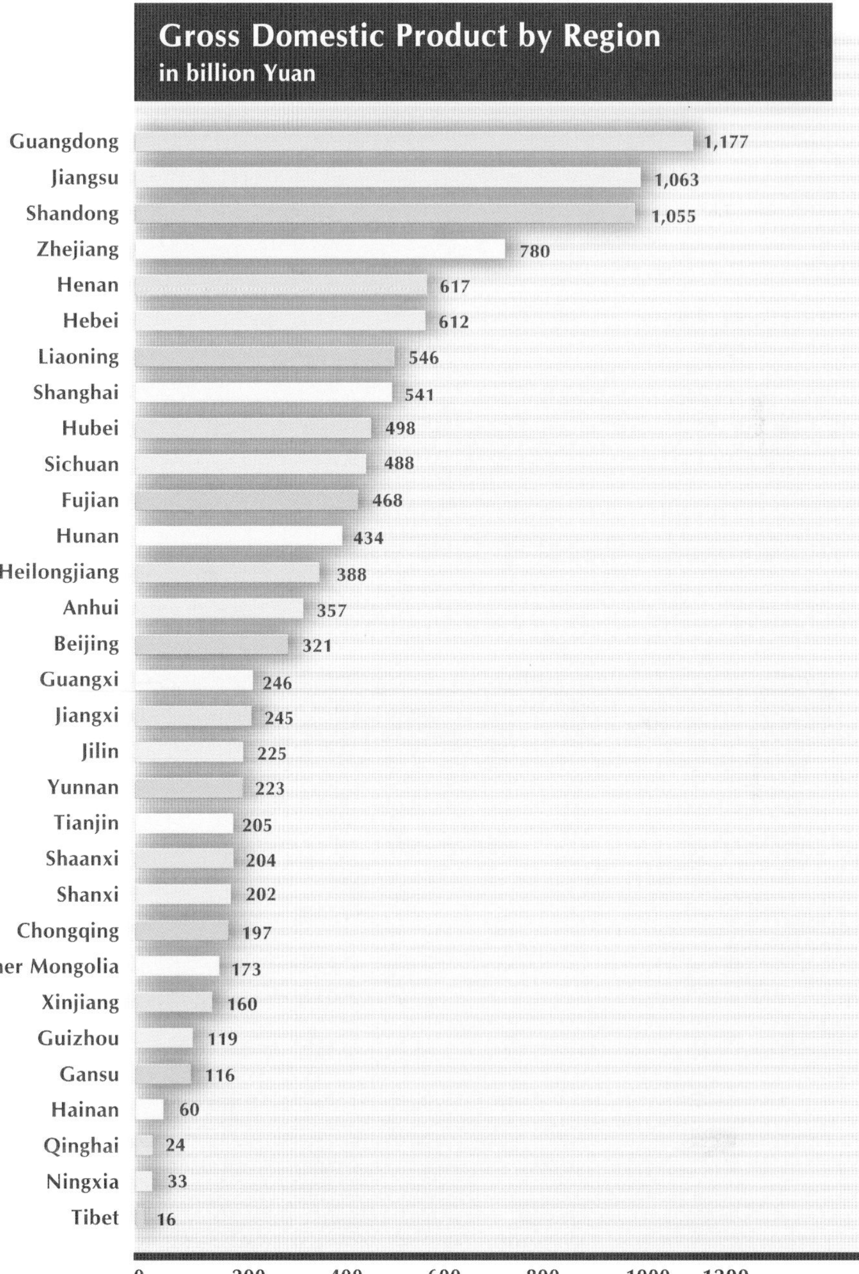
Gross Domestic Product by Region
in billion Yuan
Guangdong 1,177
Jiangsu 1,063
Shandong 1,055
Zhejiang 780
Henan 617
Hebei 612
Liaoning 546
Shanghai 541
Hubei 498
Sichuan 488
Fujian 468
Hunan 434
Heilongjiang 388
Anhui 357
Beijing 321
Guangxi 246
Jiangxi 245
Jilin 225
Yunnan 223
Tianjin 205
Shaanxi 204
Shanxi 202
Chongqing 197
nner Mongolia 173
Xinjiang 160
Guizhou 119
Gansu 116
Hainan 60
Qinghai 24
Ningxia 33
Tibet 16
0
200
400
600
800
1000
1200
Source: China Statistics Yearbook 2003

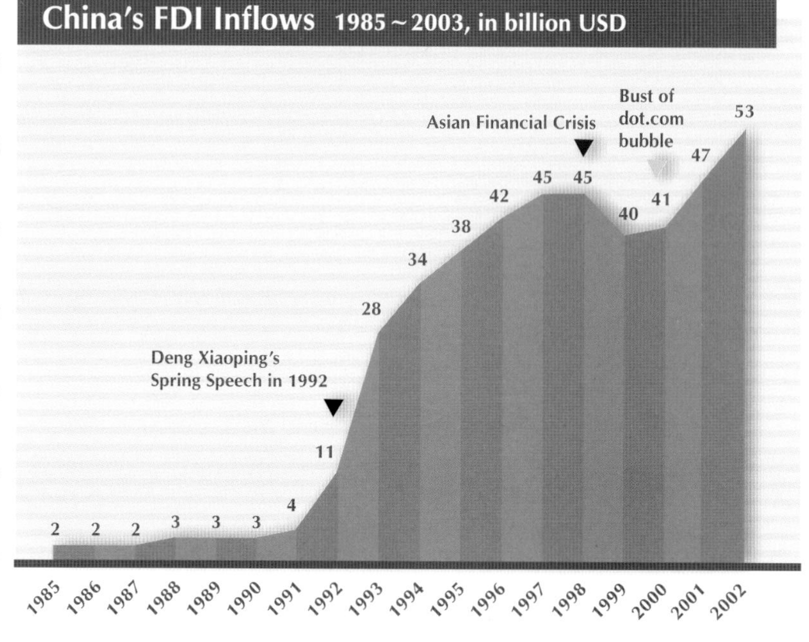
China's FDI Inflows 1985 ~ 2003, in billion USD
60
50
40
30
20
10
0
Deng Xiaoping's
Spring Speech in 1992
Asian Financial Crisis
Bust of
dot.com
bubble
2
2
2
3
3
3
4
11
28
34
38
42
45
45
40
41
47
53
1985
1986
1987
1988
1989
1990
1991
1992
1993
1994
1995
1996
1997
1998
1999
2000
2001
2002
Source: China Statistics Yearbook 2003

Foreign Direct Investment - Contractual Value
in billion USD
100
80
60
40
20
0
52
41
62
69
83
1998
1999
2000
2001
2002
/ Year
Source: China Statistics Yearbook 2003

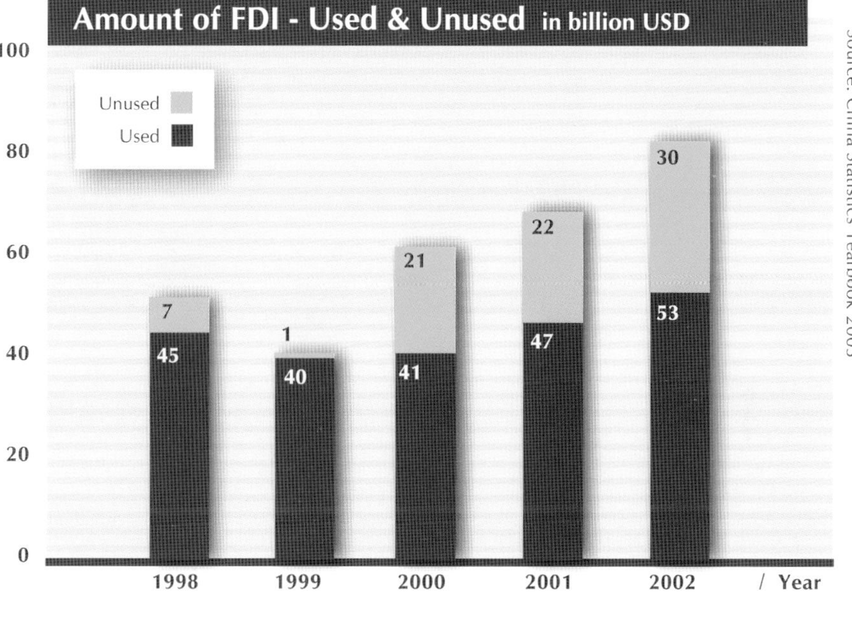
Amount of FDI - Used & Unused in billion USD
100
80
60
40
20
0
Unused
Used
7
45
1
40
21
41
22
47
30
53
1998
1999
2000
2001
2002
/ Year
Source: China Statistics Yearbook 2003

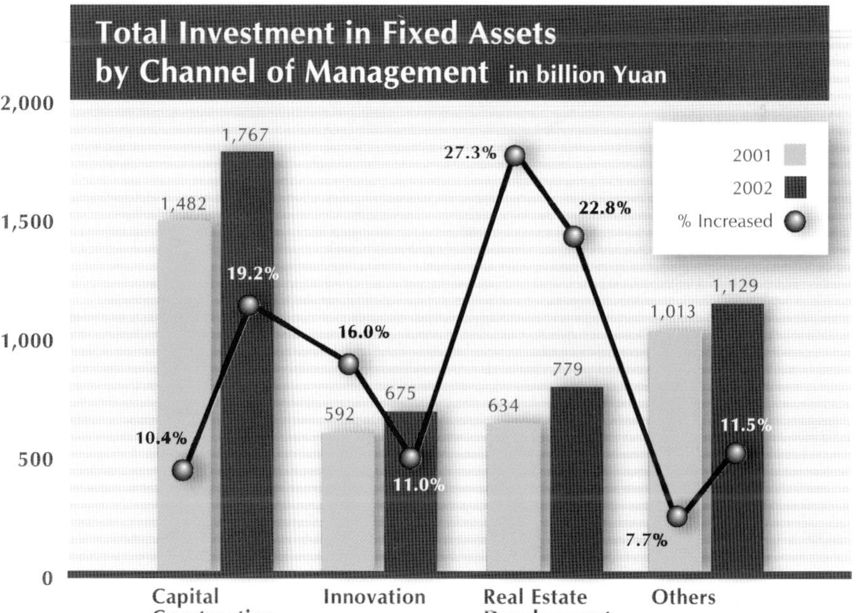
Total Investment in Fixed Assets by Channel of Management in billion Yuan
2,000
1,500
1,000
500
0
2001
2002
% Increased
1,482
1,767
10.4%
19.2%
592
675
16.0%
11.0%
634
779
27.3%
22.8%
1,013
1,129
7.7%
11.5%
Capital Construction
Innovation
Real Estate Development
Others
Source: China Statistics Yearbook 2003

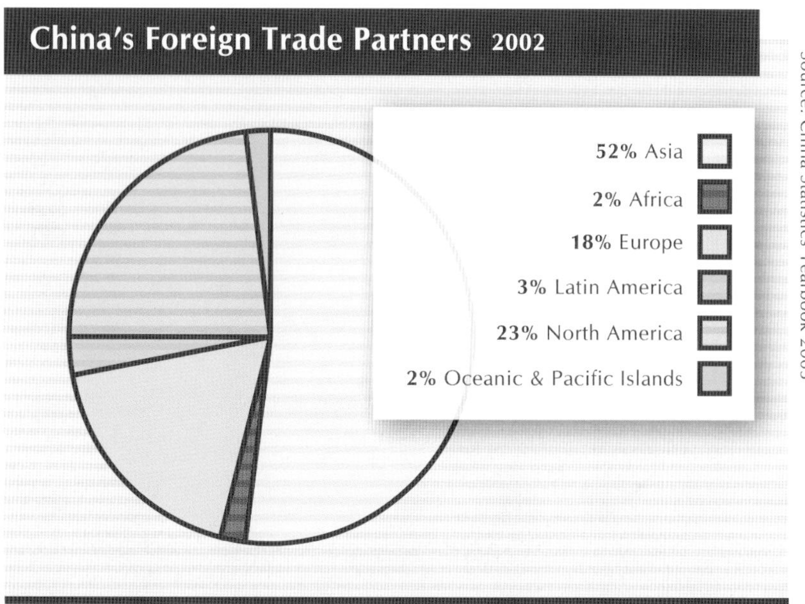
China's Foreign Trade Partners 2002
52% Asia
2% Africa
18% Europe
3% Latin America
23% North America
2% Oceanic & Pacific Islands
Source: China Statistics Yearbook 2003

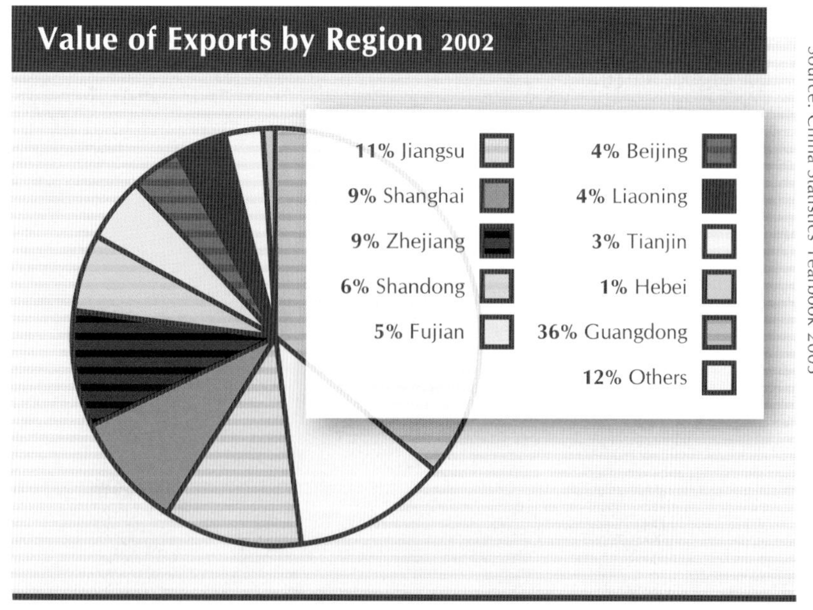
Value of Exports by Region 2002
11% Jiangsu
9% Shanghai
9% Zhejiang
6% Shandong
5% Fujian
4% Beijing
4% Liaoning
3% Tianjin
1% Hebei
36% Guangdong
12% Others
Source: China Statistics Yearbook 2003

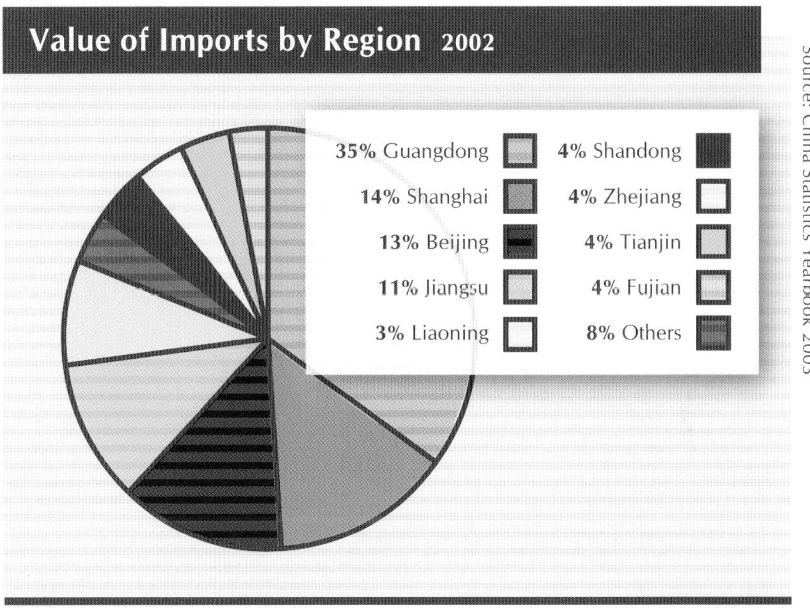

Source: China Statistics Yearbook 2003

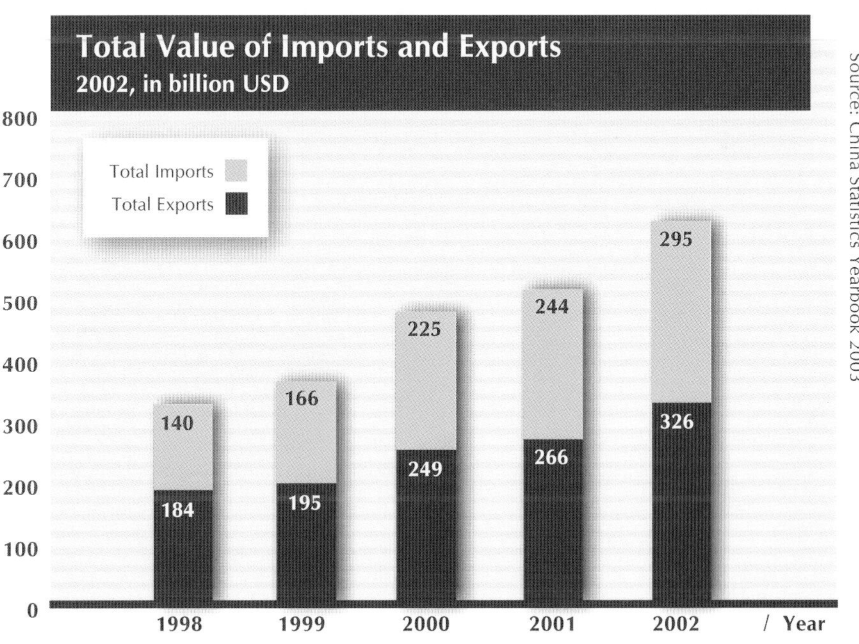

Source: China Statistics Yearbook 2003

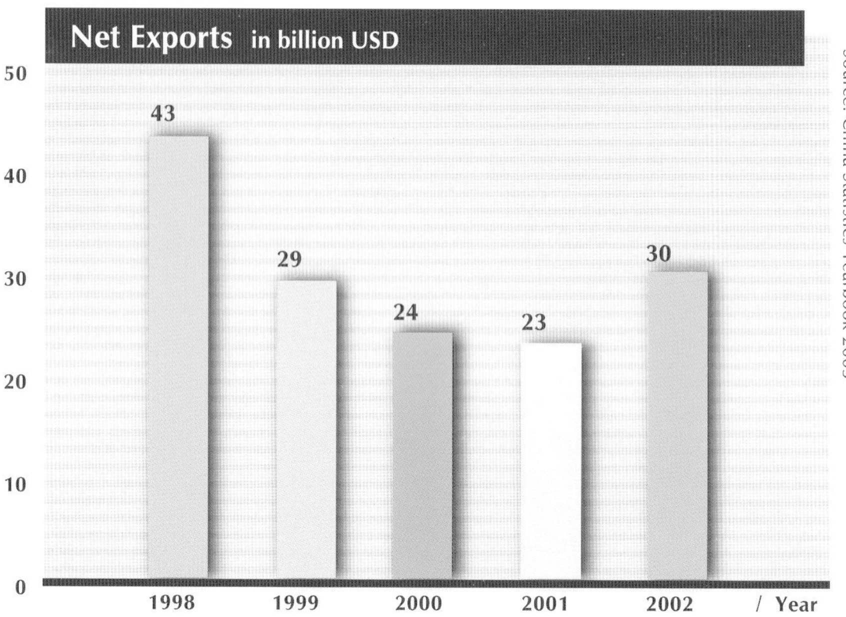
Net Exports in billion USD
50
40
30
20
10
0
43
29
24
23
30
1998
1999
2000
2001
2002
/ Year
Source: China Statistics Yearbook 2003

Total Value of Import & Export Goods of Foreign-Funded Enterprises in billion USD
350
300
250
200
150
100
50
0
117
119
126
133
160
170
Imports
Exports
2000
2001
2002
/ Year
Source: China Statistics Yearbook 2003

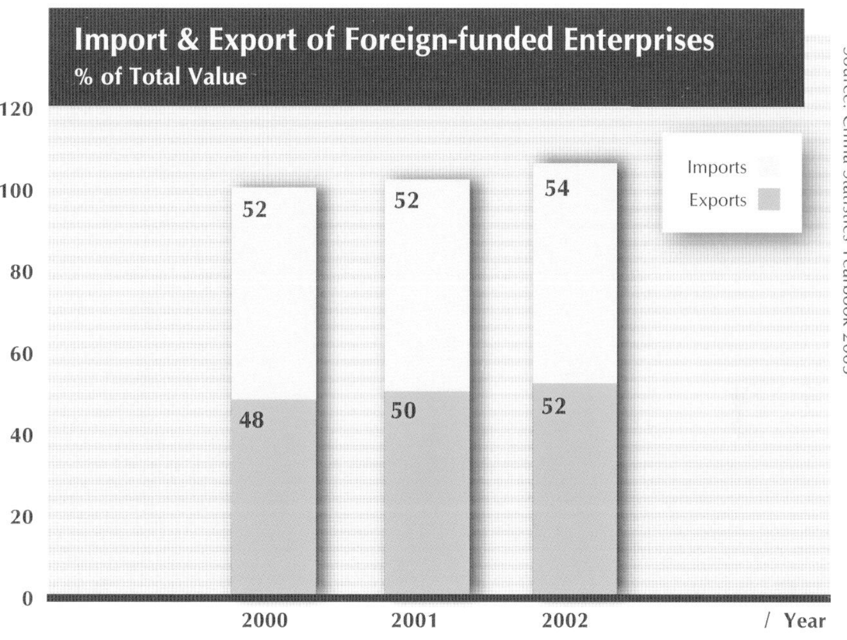

Source: China Statistics Yearbook 2003

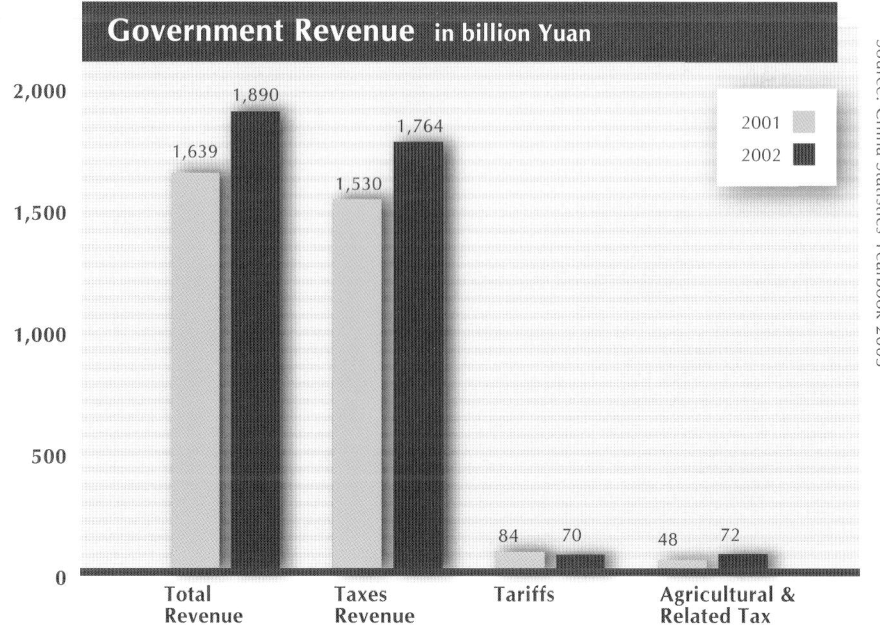

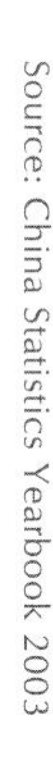

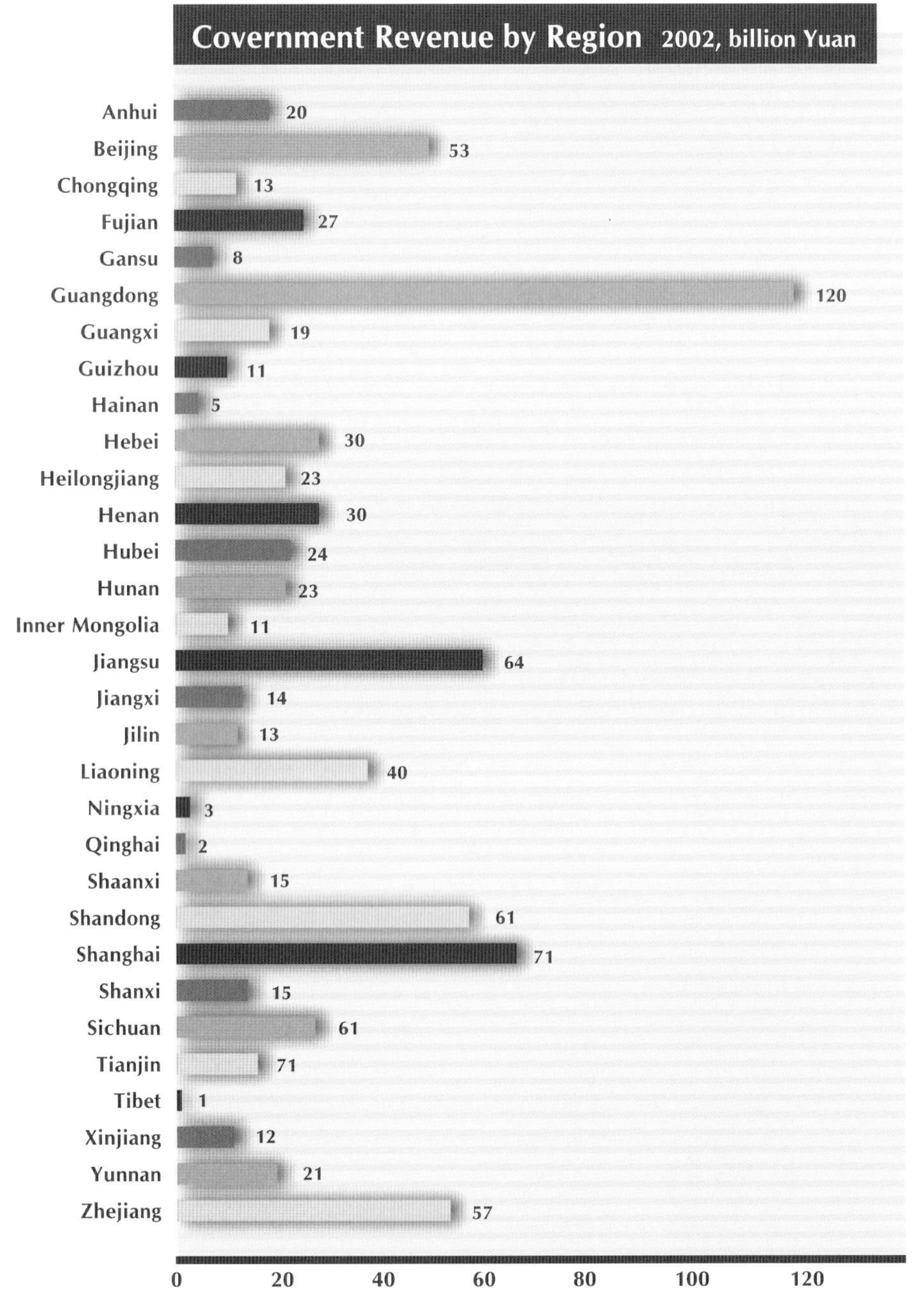
Covernment Revenue by Region 2002, billion Yuan
Source: China Statistics Yearbook 2003
Anhui 20
Beijing 53
Chongqing 13
Fujian 27
Gansu 8
Guangdong 120
Guangxi 19
Guizhou 11
Hainan 5
Hebei 30
Heilongjiang 23
Henan 30
Hubei 24
Hunan 23
Inner Mongolia 11
Jiangsu 64
Jiangxi 14
Jilin 13
Liaoning 40
Ningxia 3
Qinghai 2
Shaanxi 15
Shandong 61
Shanghai 71
Shanxi 15
Sichuan 61
Tianjin 71
Tibet 1
Xinjiang 12
Yunnan 21
Zhejiang 57
0
20
40
60
80
100
120

Government Debts Issuance in billion Yuan
600
500
400
300
200
100
0
331
372
418
460
568
1998
1999
2000
2001
2002
/ Year
Base Year 1978 = 100

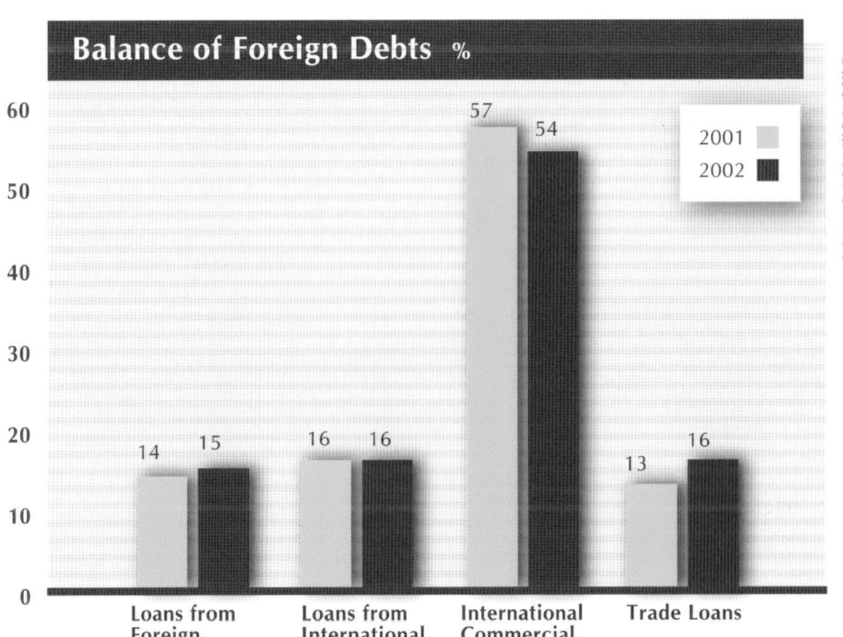
Balance of Foreign Debts %
60
50
40
30
20
10
0
2001
2002
14
15
16
16
57
54
13
16
Loans from Foreign Governments
Loans from International Financial Institutions
International Commercial Loans
Trade Loans
Base Year 1978 = 100

Consumer Price Index
Base Year 1985 = 100
350
300
250
200
0
208
259
303
328
337
334
330
331
333
331
1993
1994
1995
1996
1997
1998
1999
2000
2001
2002
Source: China Statistics Yearbook 2003

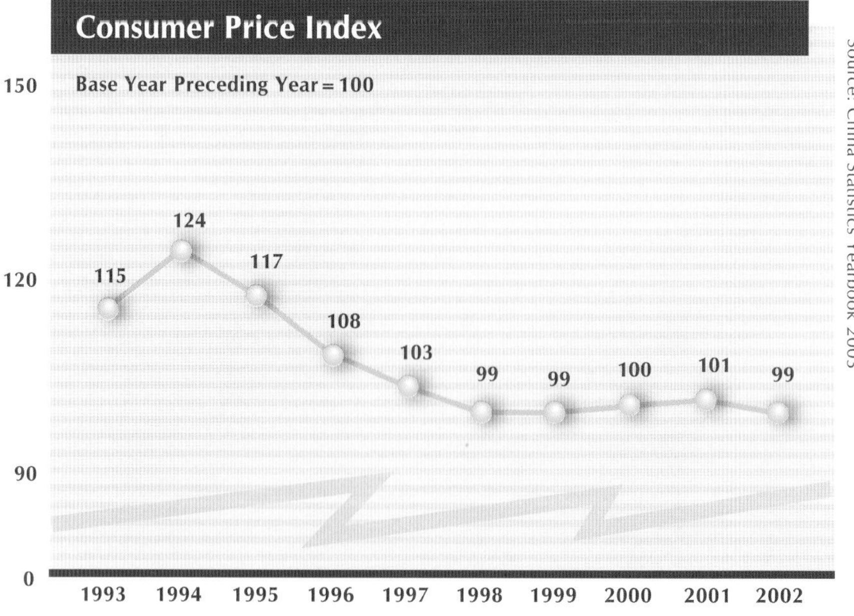
Consumer Price Index
Base Year Preceding Year = 100
150
120
90
0
115
124
117
108
103
99
99
100
101
99
1993
1994
1995
1996
1997
1998
1999
2000
2001
2002
Source: China Statistics Yearbook 2003

Retail Price Index
Base Year 1978 = 100
400
350
300
250
200
0
255
310
356
378
381
371
360
354
352
347
1993
1994
1995
1996
1997
1998
1999
2000
2001
2002
Source: China Statistics Yearbook 2003

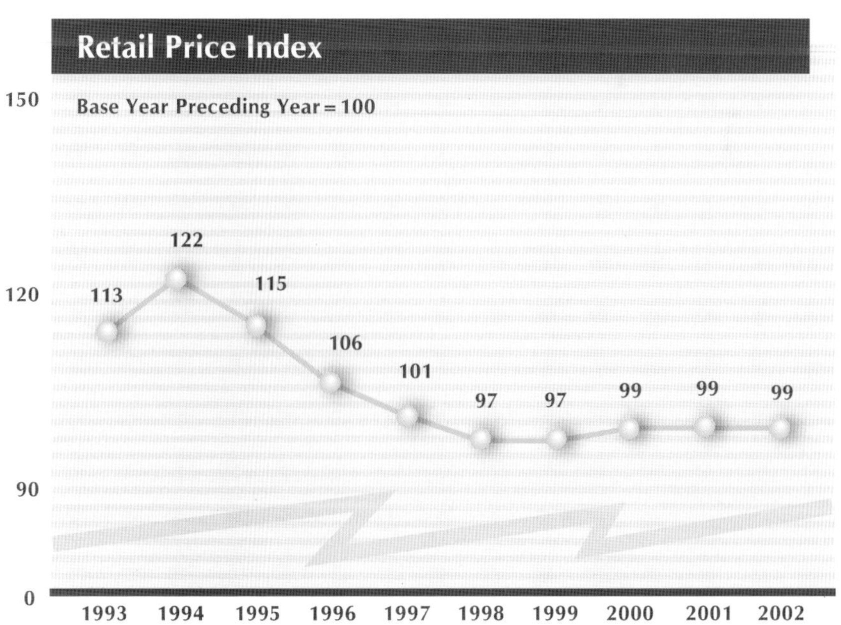
Retail Price Index
Base Year Preceding Year = 100
150
120
90
0
113
122
115
106
101
97
97
99
99
99
1993
1994
1995
1996
1997
1998
1999
2000
2001
2002
Source: China Statistics Yearbook 2003

Price Indices of Real Estate in China

Base Year 1978 = 100

	2000	2001	2002
Selling Price Indices of House	101	102	104
Transactions Price Indices of Land	100	102	107
Renting Price Indices of Houses	102	103	101

Source: China Statistics Yearbook 2003

Money Supply at Year-End in billion Yuan

	2000	2001	2002
Currency in Circulation (MO)	1,465	1,569	1,728
Money (M1)	5,315	5,987	7,088
Money & Quasi-Money (M2)	13,461	15,830	18,501

Source: China Statistics Yearbook 2003

SPECIAL TOPICS

WORLD TRADE ORGANIZATION (WTO) & CHINA

China's entry into the WTO was a long anticipated event, realized after 15 years of negotiations. On 10th November 2001, China became the 143rd member of the WTO. With its accession, China has reaffirmed its commitment to the mission and objectives of the WTO, primary among them being to encourage and facilitate free trade.

Impact On China and The Global Community

This historic event has far-reaching implications on the country. China's investment environment will undergo two fundamental changes. Firstly, consistent with the spirit and letter of the WTO, both tariffs and other non-tariff barriers to trade will be progressively reduced. Most of the protected industries will be opened up in phases while other sectors will see a gradual loosening of constraints governing foreign investment. By 2004, three years from the date of accession, foreign companies will be able to import to and do business in virtually all parts of China.

Secondly, WTO membership entails a transition to a transparent, rule-based economy. Investing in China and Chinese companies will become easier than before, with less restrictions and clearer regulations. Together, these changes will spur deeper reforms, and produce more open and efficient markets.

Implications on the Domestic Companies

China's commitment to free trade will expose domestic companies in previously protected industries to stiff competition. Imported products are allowed to compete on an equal footing with domestic products while state-owned enterprises are no longer permitted to benefit from export subsidies. The phasing out approach is taken in an attempt to reduce the adverse immediate impact of such measures on Chinese companies.

In the long run, Chinese enterprises will benefit tremendously from various aspects of knowledge transfer from the multinationals, including management expertise, financial engineering, and business innovation. These knowledge transfers will help promote the upgrading of industrial structure as a whole and drive them towards becoming more international. Foreign competition will also increase the efficiency as well as competitiveness of such companies and the surviving ones will be much better positioned domestically and even internationally.

In keeping with the principles of the WTO, non-performing firms should be allowed to fail. China's accession had hence sparked a whole series of consolidation and restructuring in various state-owned enterprises. This will result in a more streamlined market with fewer but better players.

Within some sectors, great opportunities abound even in the immediate term. China's entry meant greater access into more markets for its exports. Sectors like manufacturing are expected to realize substantial growth.

Opportunities for Foreign Enterprises

China's integration into the multilateral trading system will open up the world's largest market to foreign enterprises, creating many exciting business opportunities.

Agriculture

China agreed to limit farm subsidies to 8.5% of the value of domestic farm production. Promises were also made to cut duties on agricultural products and US priority products. In 2003, China's average tariff rate on farm products was reduced to 16.8% from 18.1% in 2002, while all non-tariff measures on farm products have been eliminated.

Telecommunications

Foreign operators have many opportunities to expand their presence in this formerly highly protected sector. By the end of 2004, they will be allowed to hold up to a 49% stake in mobile telecommuni-cations firms. Tariffs on high-tech products like telecoms equipment will be eliminated by 2005. Domestic and International Fixed Services will be opened up the most slowly. Only by 2007 will all geographic restrictions be lifted and a 49% foreign ownership will be permitted in all cities.

Textiles

Chinese enterprises will benefit from the Agreement on Textiles and Garments signed during the Uruguay round of trade talks. Textile and garment exports are likely to register significant growth, with expected growth rate of 63.8% for textiles and a doubling for garments by 2005. The prospects for the chemical fibre industry are less bright due to its late development, weak industry foundation and dependence on tariff protection.

Insurance

China will relax the many restrictions constraining the development of this sector. Non-life insurers from abroad will be allowed to set up branches or joint ventures in China, holding up to a 51 percent stake in the joint ventures. By the end of 2003, these firms will be allowed to establish solely foreign-funded subsidiaries in China. They are permitted to engage in "general insurance policies" and large-scale commercial insurance and offer non-life services to overseas enterprises, property insurance to foreign-funded in China, and related liability insurance and credit insurance services. By 2003, they will be able to provide all kinds of non-life insurance services to Chinese and foreign customers. Foreign life insurers will only be permitted to establish solely foreign-funded subsidiaries five years after WTO entry, offering a host of services to an unrestricted clientele. All geographical restrictions on foreign life and non-life insurance firms will be phased out by 2004.

As of 2002, there are 40 domestic and foreign capital insurance companies in China, including five solely state-owned enterprises, nine share-holding companies, 13 Sino-foreign joint ventures and 13 branches of foreign insurance companies. Foreign insurance companies have about 1 percent share in the Chinese insurance market, with tremendous room for growth in market share.

Distribution and Retail

China has agreed to phase out restrictions on distribution services for most products within three years of its entry. Foreign firms will be allowed to control up to a 65% stake in retail stores. By the end of 2004, wholly foreign-owned retail companies may be established and all geographical restrictions and quotas on the number of foreign-invested retail enterprises will be eliminated. While prior to China's entry, foreign firms are forced to distribute products made in China via domestic intermediaries, this has now changed. They are no longer compelled to do so and now have the choice to set up their own networks. This creates great opportunities for the development of the wholesale industry in China.

The Banking Sector

The banking sector is one of the most highly regulated industries in China. Foreign banks had very limited access to the Chinese market.

Prior to China's entry into the WTO, the clientele of foreign banks were restricted to Foreign-Invested Enterprises (FIEs). They were also kept out of the Renminbi (RMB) business. The RMB license which gives banks the right to conduct RMB business was only granted to selected qualified foreign banks first in Shanghai (1996) then in Shenzhen (1998). Even then, many clientele, geographic and institutional restrictions were imposed. Foreign banks were confined to serving FIEs only at the location where they are registered.

With China's accession into the WTO, the process of liberalization was accelerated. Most of the restrictions on foreign currency business were lifted. Foreign banks may immediately offer comprehensive foreign exchange services to Chinese enterprises and Chinese citizens without exam-ination and approval of individual cases. They are also permitted to develop the business of foreign exchange, inter-bank loan, the issue of foreign exchange credit cards and foreign credit cards agency.

A more cautious approach will be taken with RMB business. An initial schedule was drawn up to phase out geographic and clientele restrictions in stages over a period of five years. At the time of accession, foreign banks can only operate a RMB business in four cities. By 2004, the number would have increased to thirteen. The China Banking Regulatory Commission (CBRC) recently confirmed this, a clear indication of the commitment of the Chinese government to fulfilling their obligations.

Restrictions on operating across locations will also be relaxed. Foreign banks licensed to conduct RMB business at one city will be permitted to service customers of other cities opened for RMB business. Such a foreign bank in Shanghai, for example, will be able to provide RMB services to clients at Fuzhou by 2004 (according to the schedule). Furthermore, within five years of accession, foreign banks will be granted full access to the Chinese market. They will be permitted to set up local outlets in all cities, and the criteria for approval will be the same as that for Chinese banks. By 2006, all clientele constraints will be lifted. Foreign banks will be permitted to conduct RMB business with both Chinese enterprises and Chinese citizens.

Schedule for Liberalizing RMB Business

a. Lifting of Geographic Constraints on foreign banks:

Time Period	Coverage
Time of Entry : 2001	Shanghai, Shenzhen, Tianjin & Dalian were opened to applications by foreign banks for a RMB license
2002	Guangzhou, Zhuhai, Qingdao, Nanjing, Wuhan
2003	Jinan, Fuzhou, Chengdu & Chongqing opened
2004	Kunming, Beijing, Xiamen
2005	Shantou, Ningbo, Shenyang, Xi'an
2006	All geographic restrictions will be phased out

b. Lifting of Clientele Restrictions on foreign banks:

Time Period	Coverage
2003	Foreign banks granted access to Chinese Enterprises
2006	Foreign Banks will be given National Treatment

Over the next three years, foreign banks will continue to see the relaxation of more restrictions, in keeping with China's obligations to the WTO as well as a desire on the part of Chinese government to restructure and reinvigorate the domestic banking sector. Opportunities abound for foreign banks.

The Progress Thus Far

China has taken many steps to fulfill its obligations. Transparency on foreign trade policies has been improved. A new Regulation on Import and Export Duties, for example, has recently been released, a revised version in which clearer and more specific provisions were added defining relevant tariff rates and resulted in an improved legal system on revenue collection. It will take effect on January 1 2004. More than 3,000 customs documents which went against the rules and practices of the WTO have in fact been amended or are in the process of revision since 2000.

China has also honoured promises to lower tariffs and non-tariff trade barriers, while many restrictions limiting foreign investments were lifted. The average tariff level of over 5,000 imported goods has been reduced from 12% to 11% at the beginning of 2003. By 2005, in accordance with the WTO agreement, the figure will be reduced to 10%.

In 2003, the Chinese government has amended laws regulating commercial banks, foreign trade, and import and export tariffs. Regulations concerning administrative approbation, Sino-foreign education cooperation and qualification certification have also been revised. Meetings are underway to update China's Foreign Trade Law and address intellectual property rights issues in order to facilitate the development of foreign trade.

The Ministry of Finance (MOF) reaffirmed China's commitment to reform the state-owned enterprises (SOEs), declaring that efforts to regulate and withdraw undue subsidies will be stepped up. "Policy subsidies", for instance, which are compensation subsidies granted to offset losses incurred by some SOEs as a result of low prices set by the government, will be revised. The year 2004 will see more adjustments made to existing policies which do not comply with the WTO.

The Road Ahead

China's accession has many implications. To the world, it means access to a huge market of 1.4 billion. As the country opens up, industries like automotive, banking, insurance and telecommunications will be hit with stiff competitive pressures. In the long term, however, this can only be good for China since it will spur the process of reform and force domestic companies to increase their efficiency.

China's entry will also benefit the country in more obvious ways. Protectionist policies of its trading partners within the WTO against Chinese exports will have to be eliminated. This implies a host of opportunities for the relevant sectors. Textiles is one such industry expected to register high growth. Quotas on Chinese textile exports will formally end in 2005 under a WTO-wide accord.

As more policies to align the country with the international market are implemented, the domestic economic structure will undergo a fundamental change. Together with Beijing Olympics 2008, Shanghai World Expo 2010 and the increasing internationalization of major Chinese cities, China will become increasingly integrated with the global community. The Chinese market shows enormous promise.

BEIJING 2008 OLYMPICS

July 13, 2001, was a historic day which China and its people had long anticipated. It was the day when Beijing was selected by the International Olympic Committee to host the 2008 Olympic Games. Beijing's successful bid is both a triumph for the Chinese leadership and a boost to national pride. It satisfied China's longing for international recognition.

To China, the years in the run-up to 2008 are expected to be a period of significant developments both in terms of sports and culture. It will challenge the wits and courage of the people in China to prepare themselves for this potentially life-changing event. The tremendous business opportunities brought forth by 2008 Olympics will push the nation's development into the new economy.

As the host of the 2008 Olympics, the city of Beijing will benefit considerably from the massive investment spending in the pipeline and numerous job opportunities it will create. In the run-up to 2008, Beijing plans to spend a total of USD 34 billion on the Olympic Games, including USD 22 billion earmarked for modernising the nation's capital. In one of the most ambitious infrastructure projects so far, Beijing will build extensive Olympic-related sports venues and associated facilities, enhance its transportation and telecommunications networks, and install environmental protection systems

While a small part of the planned infrastructure projects will be financed by the Beijing Organising Committee of Olympic Games (BOCOG), the rest will be financed by the Chinese National Government, Beijing Municipal Government and private investors within and outside China. Moreover, to meet international standards, it is believed that the design, construction and manage-ment of most of the Olympic-related infrastructure facilities, including the Olympic park will be put up for international bidding. Action plans have been drawn up for the overall organization of the Olympic Games and nine specific planning areas.

Meanwhile, the marketing hype that goes with the Olympic will also have a significant impact on the awareness of Beijing, and help accelerate the growth of the city's tourism industry. Judging from the experience in other host cities of the Olympics, tourist arrivals in Beijing could increase by 20% during the year of the Games, which would provide a strong boost to retail sales in the city. According to some rough estimates, increased infrastructure spending and the gain in tourism income would add an average of about 2-3% per year to Beijing's GDP growth in the next four years. In 2002, Beijing's economy grew by 13%.

While many are quick to point to monetary benefits of hosting the Olympic Games, which seem to be quite limited outside of Beijing, the real significance of the sporting event lies beyond economics. In the run-up to the Beijing Olympics, China will become more integrated into the global community, not just in terms of sports but also culturally. The hosting of the sporting event will also expose China to greater international scrutiny and foster better understanding of the county. Through engaging China more closely with the wider world, the Olympic Games will help strengthen the forces of liberalism in the country and hasten the pace of social, if not political, change.

Over the next four years, Beijing will continue to commit all its resources and talents to prepare itself for the hosting of a successful Olympic Games. Opportunities abound for a wide range of businesses in the run-up to 2008.

Key Strategic Preparation Phases

There are a few key strategic phases for the preparation of the Olympic 2008.

The pre-preparation phase was from December 2001 to June 2003. During this phase, action plans were formulated and the organizational structure of BOCOG was established. Preparation for construction of Olympic construction facilities, infrastructure and marketing programs had been put into operation.

The development phase is from July 2003 to June 2006. During this period, the task set forth in the "10th year Plan" will be completed, and the construction of the Olympic venues and other related facilities and the preparation in other areas will be in full swing. By June 2006, the major construction projects of Olympic venues and facilities will be completed and basic preparations ready.

The improvement and operation phase will be from July 2006 to the opening of the 2008 Olympic Games. During this phase, all the venues and facilities, which fully meet the requirements of the Games, will be in place. Examination and improvements will be made to the venues; test events will be conducted to ensure smooth operation; and all services will be available.

Key Infrastructure Projects

The Beijing Municipal Government has made plans to build up the entire infrastructure required for the 2008 Olympics. The infrastructure projects in the pipeline will translate into a host of investment opportunities for the business community, as follows:

Natural Environment & Infrastructure Development

Consider-able improvement in the ecological environment of the city is needed to achieve the goal of a green Olympics. Much focus will be placed on the prevention of air pollution and the protection of drinking water sources through the means of economic restructuring, the increased use of cleaner high quality energies, thus establishing a more restrictive emission standard and strengthened ecological protection and construction. By 2008, the indexes of SO_2, NOx and CO in the urban city will meet the WTO standards and the density of the particles will reach the level of major cities in developed countries, fully meeting the standard for hosting the Olympic Games.

The first task towards a green Olympic will be to prevent coal burning pollution. Introducing and developing the use of cleaner high-quality energy such as natural gas and electricity will optimize urban energy structure. The second long-distance gas pipeline and its supporting facilities will be built from North Shaanxi to Beijing. The structure of electrical power supply will be improved, with the newly added power consumption load to be taken mainly by power sources outside Beijing. The power networks in downtown areas will be expanded and those in rural areas upgraded so as to improve the quality and reliability of power supply. The Beijing No. 3 Thermal Power Station and Gaojing Power Station will be transformed into gas burning power stations and eight gas burning thermal power stations, including the one in Caoqiao, will be built or expanded, all able to supply cooling, heating and electrical powers.

New energy resources such as geothermal energy, solar energy, wind energy and biological energy will be exploited, and energy saving will be encouraged. By 2008, the annual supply of natural gas in the city will reach 5 billion cubic metres; the consumption of coal and coke will account for less than 20% of the terminal energy structure; and urban area to be heated by thermal power will cover around 100 million square kilometres.

Besides preventing pollution by coal burning, pollution by automobile emission need to be reduced as well. Starting from 2003, a standard parallel to the European Standard II will be enforced regarding the pollutant emission of new vehicles, and before 2008, a standard parallel to the European Standard III will be put into effect. The regulations regarding vehicle scrapping and testing will be tightened. EP Marks will be issued to qualified motor vehicles and joint law enforcement by EP agencies and traffic control departments will be strengthened. The application of cleaner gaseous fuel in buses and taxis will be promoted. By 2007, 90% of the buses and 70% of taxis will use clean fuel. The development of new technologies, such as electrical automobiles will be pushed forward.

Stricter control on particle pollution will also be required on all construction sites to meet the requirement for environmental protection in this respect. Starting from January 2003, in the areas within the Fourth Ring Road in Beijing, any loose cargo must be transported in closed containers.

The system of "house responsibility for cleaning" and the regulations regarding urban afforestation will be further implemented. By 2005, all open grounds in urban areas will be covered with trees or grass, and the cleaning of all the main motorways in the urban area will be mechanized.

Emission of all industrial pollutants will be reduced by exercising control on the total emission volume. All key enterprises will be required to practice clean production and introduce the ISO14001 environment manage-ment system. Special attention will be given to pollution control in metallurgical, chemical, electricity and cement industries. In an effort to remove the enterprises located in the urban districts, by 2008, the chemical industrial zone in the Southeast suburbs and some 200 polluting enterprises within the Fourth Ring Road will be relocated. The Capital Iron & Steel Plant will reduce its steel production by 2 million tons and its production structure will be readjusted.

Drinking water sources will be protected in coordination with the upstream areas; China will endeavour to achieve this goal as defined in the "Plan for the Sustainable Utilization of Water Resources in the Capital in the Early 21st Century (2001-2005)". More effective measures will be adopted to guarantee the quality of the water in Miyun and Guanting Reservoirs and their upstream and restore the function of Guanting Reservoir as a drinking water source. Under-ground drinking water sources will be protected through economic restructuring, water saving, agricultural pollution prevention and urban wastewater treatment system improvements etc.

Urban Transport Development & Management

Modernization process of the road network construction and traffic management in Beijing will be promoted, aimed at providing convenient, quick, safe, orderly and efficient services. The construction of rail transport systems, urban road transport systems, inter-city transport systems, and city transport hubs will be accelerated. All of these will provide favourable conditions for the further socioeconomic and urban development of Beijing and the first class urban transportation services for the Olympic Games as well.

Construction of the urban rail transport network composed of such projects as Beijing Urban Light Rail, Ba-Tong Subway Line, Subway Line No. 5, Subway Line No. 4, Olympic Subway Line, and the fast rail from Dongzhimen to Beijing Capital International Airport. By 2008, 148.5 kilometres of new rail transport will be added, reaching a total of 202 kilometres, and the subway will be carrying about 10% of the passengers in the city.

New expressways including the Fifth Ring Road, the Sixth Ring Road, Beijing-Miyun Road, and a number of first and second grade motorways will be completed. By 2008, the length of expressways in the whole city will reach 718 kilometres; motorways will reach 14,700 kilometres, and the road density will reach 87.3 km per square kilometres. The density of urban streets will be increased in the course of the old city renovation. By 2007, the construction and expansion of 318 kilometres of urban streets will be completed.

In order to satisfy the special demands before, during and after the Olympic Games as well as the needs of the city's future development, the Beijing Capital International Airport will be expanded, making it a large hub for international as well as domestic air traffic.

Development of Information & Telecommunications Systems

While applying IT extensively to urban development to build a "digital Beijing", the focus will be on the "digital Olympics" program, the building of tele-communications infrastructure and network system, to create a favourable IT environment and provide excellent information services.

By 2008, information services will be inexpensive, rich in content, free of language barriers, and personalized and available for anyone, at anytime and anywhere. This will not only contribute greatly to the success of an excellent Olympic Games, but also showcase to the world the level and achievements of China's IT.

Some landmark IT buildings will be built, which can serve as multi-function centres for the Olympic Games. To provide sufficient frequencies for the Olympic Games, the overall planning and management of radio frequencies will be strengthened. A technical support system for radio management will be established in Beijing to facilitate the overall improvement of frequency management, radio signal monitoring, radio interference analysis and radio equipment testing ability. Comprehensive measures will be taken to provide a clean electromagnetic environment so as to ensure the smooth operation of all radio communication devices. The advanced communications facilities will be built to provide a broadband digital communications system that is reliable, flexible, expandable, reusable, and adaptable to new technologies.

Focus will also be placed on the development of the software for management systems and information service systems related to the Olympic Games. Weather forecast and monitoring will be reinforced to provide timely and accurate meteorological services for large-scale gatherings and sports events. E-commerce services covering ticketing, tourism, merchandizing, shopping, projects tendering and procurement will also be provided.

Artificial intelligence technologies will be used in an effort to overcome the "language barrier" during the Olympic Games. Smartcard technology will also be used to provide the participants with safe and convenient services in accreditation, security check and payment etc; meanwhile, a card-based payment network and a favourable card-based payment environment will be established.

Sports Venue

37 stadiums are planned to be used for the 28 sports events during 2008 Olympic Games. The Olympic venues will be situated in the six cities: Beijing, Shenyang, Qinhuangdao, Tianjin, Qingdao and Shanghai. 27 sports events will take place in the 32 stadiums located in Beijing. Sailing and football preliminary matches will take place in five venues outside Beijing.

The 32 stadiums in Beijing are concentrated in the following areas: Olympic Green District,

Western Community District, University District and Northern Tourist. The whole layout is described as "One Centre with Three Districts".

The Olympic Green will be the "main and central district" where the Games will take place. With 13 sports venues for the Olympic Games, it is the area where major sports events are to take place and 70% of the gold medals will be awarded. Nine stadiums are located in the "Western Community District". The new project, Wukesong Sports Centre, will be a place for residents in Southwest Beijing to conduct their cultural and sports activities.

Four stadiums are located in the "University District" including the Capital Stadium which will be used by universities and the local community for their cultural and sports activities. Two stadiums, situated in "Northern Tourist District" including Beijing Countryside Horse Racetrack, will try to facilitate tourism in the suburban area after the Olympic Games. In other areas, 4 stadiums will be expanded and renovated,

Olympic Green

The Olympic Green, located on the north end of the central axis of Beijing, occupies an area of 1,135 hectares, which contains a forest park of 680 hectares and a central area of 405 hectares for the Games. The Olympic Green, supplemented by the venues and facilities for the Asian Games, will boast convenient traffic, concentrated population, good urban infrastructure, and well developed service facilities for commercial and cultural activities etc. In the planning of the Olympic Green, we will bear in mind the long-term development of the city and the needs of the citizens for material and cultural life, making it a multi-functional public centre for sports, meetings, exhibitions, entertainment and shopping, with broad spaces and landscaped surroundings.

The major sports facilities to be built in the Olympic Green include:

National Stadium: with a seating capacity of 80,000 people; it will be the venue for the opening and closing ceremonies, athletics and football finals.

National Indoor Stadium: with a seating capacity of 18,000 people; it will be the venue for gymnastics, handball and volleyball finals. It will be a multi-functional structure.

National Swimming Centre: with a seating capacity of 18,000 people; it will be the main venue for swimming competitions. It will serve as a public sports centre after the Olympic Games.

Other related facilities to be built in the Olympic Green include:

Olympic Village: with complete supporting facilities, the Olympic Village will consist of 360,000 square metres of apartments available to the athletes, coaches and team officials during the Games. These apartments will be sold as commercial housing after the Games.

Other facilities: a number of other buildings will also be planned and built in the Green, which will serve as the competition venues for table tennis, badminton, fencing and wrestling and as the Main Press Centre (MPC) and the International Broadcasting Centre (IBC). After the Games, these buildings will be turned into convention and exhibition centres, and cultural facilities such as Capital Youth Palace and Urban Planning Exhibition Hall etc. In addition, other supporting service facilities will also be available for accommodation, commerce and offices etc.

e.g. Workers' Stadium, to create a favourable environment for cultural and sporting needs of the community's residents.

Investment Policies

Due to higher investment demand, longer constructing cycle and lower rating standard, the government will finance many infrastructure constructions projects. This creates significant barriers for investors from home and abroad, resulting in a large gap between infrastructure construction and local economic development needs. In order to change the status and accelerate deregulation in infrastructure construction, Beijing Municipal Government has recently established a mechanism, granting appropriate compensation to domestic and foreign investors who invest in infrastructure construction in the city. Beijing Municipal Government has launched favourable policies and measures oriented to infrastructure projects to attract investors to construction and operation of infrastructure projects in city. Meanwhile, the price of infrastructure products, which was unreasonable, will be put in order gradually.

1. Diversified investment sources. Any business that has the financial resources to enter into the industry, no matter whether it is a state-owned or private, domestic or international enterprise, may seek to become an investor of the operation-destined infrastructure projects in Beijing. For some operation-destined infrastructure projects, competitive bidding will be adopted in choosing the investment partners

2. In case the current rate is unable to reach the designated level, favourable policies will be offered to the infrastructure projects financed by enterprises selected via competitive bidding. Meanwhile, the franchise rights there may be granted to the enterprises by the government. The preferential policy: infrastructure

projects will be exempted from some taxes and charges. For example, sewage and garbage treatment projects will be exempted from the land royalty charge for construction of "four sources", construction of public utilities and blood control etc.

3. In order to substantively carry out the preferential policies customised for infrastructure construction, ensuring reasonably attractive-return to investors who invest in infrastructure projects in Beijing, the Beijing Municipal Government will take the following measures:

a) The government will establish a compensation fund to fill in the gap between the contract price and the government-set price. Compensating approach: the government will define the quality of services/products, technical specifications, as well as the capacity /throughout it undertakes to purchase, and determine the compensation as per the contract price. The government will take into account tolerance of end users, and set the price of services/products accordingly. If the price determined is lower than the contract price, the government will compensate the investors by paying the difference. The valid term of the contract price will vary with projects, but no less than three years in general. After three years, in the event that the government adjusts the prices of upstream products, or the variation of exchange rate exceeds a certain threshold, the contract price can be adjusted appropriately upon approval. If the price set by the government is still lower than the contract price, the government will continue to compensate the investors by further filling in the price gap.

b) In order to balance the construction funds or budget, depending on specific operation-destined infrastructure project, Beijing Development and Planning Commission will, after substantive study in collaborating with related authorities, such as urban planning and land administration, propose the granting of rights to investors to use land specially allocated for development and construction of high profits return project, and seek approval form the Municipal government before implementation.

c) Upon examination by competent authorities and approval by the Municipal Government, fixed-term franchise rights will be granted to the investors on operating such business as advertisement in the infrastructure projects financed and operated by them. The investors will also be encouraged to develop such culture and sports businesses as tourism and entertainment in conjunction with the infrastructure projects under construction.

d) Under the condition that is statutorily permitted, the government will assist the investors to apply for loans from foreign governments and international financial organizations etc and support them in capital securitisation.

e) For projects that need a large amount of investment that is difficult to be recovered in the short term, the government may be involved in the investments and operation by contributing a certain proportion of the capital stocks

e) The government will coordinate the public unity conditions for investors during the project construction and operation.

4. In order to provide an immediate access to the infrastructure projects and other investment-bidding projects, the Beijing Municipal Government, by assigning Beijing Development and Planning Commission as the undertaker and the Municipal Economic Information Centre as the developer, has formally opened the "Beijing Investment Platform" in August 2000. Its main functions are: Firstly, to

enhance investment bidding and propaganda thereof for infrastructure projects that will be implemented in the cit, facilitating on-line inquiry about Beijing's investment bidding project and related policies and regulations. Secondly, to publicise the bid invitation information to attract interested investors and enhance transparency of govern-ment contract awarding. Thirdly, to realise online follow up management and services for initial preparation of crucial investment projects in Beijing. Fourthly, to realise online communication, negotiation and consultation among investors, project owners and administrative bodies. Lastly, to extensively capture investment intention from investors and comments made by all social lines on Beijing's infrastructure construction. At present the English edition has been put into use.

Olympics Marketing Plan

The Beijing Organising Committee for the Olympic Games (BOCOG) launched the marketing plan of the Beijing 2008 Olympic Games on 1 September 2003. The marketing plan of the Beijing Olympics forms the basis for both domestic and overseas companies to take part in the broadcasting, ticketing, sponsorship and licensing programmes of the Beijing 2008 Olympic Games.

The marketing plan of the Olympics is actually a partnership between the Olympic Movement and the business community. While the International Olympic Committee (IOC) manages a series of Olympic marketing programmes to solicit support for the Olympic Movement and the Olympic Games in terms of technology and capital, the global business community also finds the marketing programmes an effective marketing platform for their companies. For example, Samsung enjoyed breakthrough in its sales and corporate image after becoming a sponsor of the Olympic Games.

The Olympic marketing programmes are composed of four main programme areas, which are television broadcasting, Olympic Games ticketing, corporate sponsorship and Olympic licensing. Among these four programme areas, sponsorship and licensing are the two which most likely would derive more business opportunities for Hong Kong companies, including small- and medium-sized ones.

Television broadcast partnership

Olympic Games is the most-watched sporting event in the world. Since the Seoul Olympics in 1988, the number of countries televising the Games increased from 160 to 220 in the 2000 Sydney Olympics. The long term broadcasting rights strategy developed by the IOC is now the most important source of the Olympic marketing revenue.

Olympic Games ticketing

The ticketing programme is for the public to purchase tickets for the different events of the Olympic Games. In 2000, more than 6.7 million tickets were sold in the Sydney Olympics and generated USD 551 million in revenue.

Corporate sponsorship

Sponsorship is a relationship between the Olympic Movement and corporations. There are different levels of sponsorship entitling companies to different marketing rights in various regions, category exclusivity and the use of designated Olympic images and marks. Companies can also become suppliers to the Olympic Movement, providing the Olympics with the necessary support and products. In return, suppliers at different levels are granted the corresponding marketing rights. In the Sydney Olympics 2000, there were 11 Olympic Partner Programme (TOP) sponsors who had worldwide Olympic marketing rights and 13 domestic Olympic Games sponsors which had Olympic marketing rights within Australia only. Besides, there were altogether 80 Sydney Olympics 2000 supporters, suppliers and sporting goods suppliers who had relatively less marketing rights.

Olympic licensing

Licensing programmes are agreements that grant rights of use of Olympic marks, imagery, themes, including emblems and mascots, to companies to produce products to commemorate the Olympic Games or specific Olympic teams. The company, or licensee, pays for the right with royalty fee which is usually between 10% and 15% of the product sales revenue. In the Sydney Olympics 2000, there were 100 licensees who produced a full range of apparel, collectibles and other merchandise (3,000 product lines in total). The Sydney Olympic

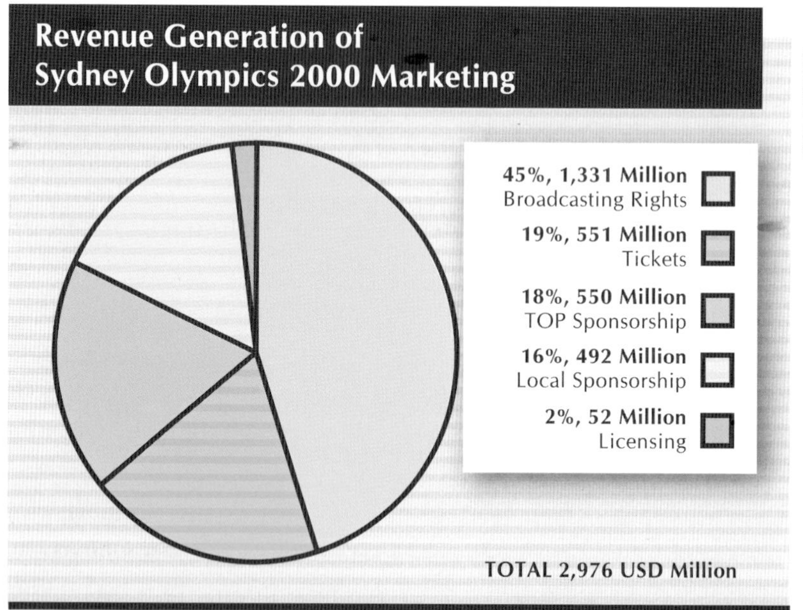

Note : The revenue generated by IOC and the Sydney Organising Committee for the Olympic Games (SOCOG) was USD 1,881 million and USD 1,095 million respectively.

merchandise was available in 2,000 retail outlets throughout Australia since 1997.

Three-Tier Administrative Structure of Olympic Marketing IOC, OCOGs and NOCs

Administration of the Olympics marketing is a three-tier structure, each having its own corresponding marketing programmes within specific boundaries.

The highest level is the International Olympic Committee (IOC). The IOC, as the holder of the rights to the Olympic Games and the Olympic marks, is responsible for the overall direction and management of Olympic marketing programmes. Marketing programmes directly under the IOC are those worldwide programmes such as worldwide sponsorship and broadcasting.

The second tier is the Organising Committee for the Olympic Games (OCOGs) and the third tier is the National Olympic Committees (NOCs). Under the direction of the IOC, the OCOG manages Olympic Games marketing programmes that are targeted to the Olympic host country. The NOCs manage national Olympic marketing programmes that are targeted within their home countries.

Sponsorship

The three tiers of Olympic marketing structure govern three different levels of sponsorship programmes:

Worldwide Sponsorship, also known as the Olympic Partner Programme (TOP), was created and is directly managed by the IOC. TOP partners are multinational organisations which will provide direct support, services or expertise for the staging of the Games. Agreements with these multinational organisations are on a four-year term, including one Olympic Winter Games and one Summer Games. The TOP partners, in return, are granted exclusive marketing rights, including the use of all Olympic imagery, and opportunities within their designated product category. They may exercise these rights on a worldwide basis.

<u>**Olympic Games Sponsorship,**</u> also known as OCOG sponsorship, is managed by the OCOG under the direction of the IOC. These programmes are not supposed to be worldwide, but are targeted within the host country of the Olympic Games. Olympic Games sponsors, or OCOG sponsors, are granted marketing rights within the host country or territory only.

<u>**National Sponsorship,**</u> or NOC sponsorship, is managed by local Olympic Committees that support their sports development and their Olympic teams. These programmes grant marketing rights within the NOC country or territory only.

So far, nine international corporations have signed contracts to become IOC's TOP partners. They are Coca-Cola, General Electric, John Hancock, Kodak, Panasonic, Samsung Electronics, Schlumberger, Swatch and Visa International. Reportedly, IOC hopes to invite more companies (including Chinese enterprises) to participate in the partner programme in addition to the existing nine TOP partners.

As for sponsors, the Beijing Olympics marketing plan has not placed any special restrictions on their industry category. Sponsors can come from any industry provided that the category does not contradict the Olympic spirit and is in line with the actual needs of the Games and the marketing rules. However, according to common practice, there is usually only one sponsor in each category, creating exclusive marketing opportunities for the sponsoring company. Sponsors to BOCOG can enjoy various rights and benefits, including:

- Use of BOCOG and/or COC marks and designations for the purposes of advertising and marketing promotions;
- Product/service exclusivity in specific categories;
- Hospitality opportunities at the Olympic Games;
- Preferred option to purchase TV ad space and billboards during the Games period;
- Preferred option to purchase sponsoring opportunities of cultural programmes and signature events such as the Torch Relay;
- BOCOG sponsor recognition programmes and acknowledgements.

The following criteria will be applied in the process of selecting sponsors:

Corporate Strength and Accountability

Companies must be prestigious enterprises, enjoying market leadership, boasting good growth prospects, financial strength, and the ability to generate adequate cash flow in order to meet the sponsorship investment requirements.

Quality and Reliability of Product/Service

Companies should be able to supply sufficient top-notch and reliable products/technology/service as required to ensure the sound operation of the Games.

Financial Pledge/Investment

Companies should make competitive financial offers, which is one of the key criteria for selecting sponsors.

Brand Alignment

Companies must possess a good reputation and social image, identify with and boost the ideals of the Olympic Movement and the concepts of the Beijing

Olympic Games. In addition, their products should be environment-friendly.

Marketing Activation

Companies should invest an adequate amount of financial and other resources in their promotions, advertising and general activation efforts in order to fully leverage on the Olympic marketing platform and thereby assist in promoting and propagating the Olympic ideals and Beijing Games.

BOCOG will recruit sponsors in different ways, including open recruitment, selective recruitment (i.e. sending out invitations to companies satisfying the necessary technical requirements) and individual recruitment (i.e. direct negotiations with individual companies).

Licensing

Similar to the sponsorship programme, the licensing programme also has a three-tier structure. The first tier is the IOC licensing programme. The IOC operates a limited worldwide licensing programme in certain categories such as film, video games and other multimedia opportunities. The second tier is for the OCOG to grant licensees the rights to use OCOG or Olympic Games marks to create souvenirs or merchandise relating to the Olympic Games for sale to the public. The merchandise is usually of a festive or commemorative nature, such as pins, T-shirts and caps. The third tier is for an NOC to grant licensees the rights to use NOC or national Olympic team marks to create souvenirs relating to the national Olympic team.

The licensing programme of the Beijing Olympics will serve to promote the Olympic image with an appealing blend of Chinese culture and Beijing element. According to Ms Yuan Bin, deputy director of BOCOG Marketing Department, major licensed product categories include sporting goods, cultural products, leisure goods, arts and crafts, and souvenirs. The programme will adopt a segmented market strategy, ensuring that Beijing Olympics licensed products will be available in a broad range of styles and prices targeting different consumer groups. Where fees are concerned, licensees have to pay a minimum guarantee and a royalty advance to BOCOG.

BOCOG will take into account the following factors in selecting licensees:

- Licensees will be selected on the bases of market research, qualification assessment, and first-hand investigation;
- The overall investigation will cover financial status, production capacity, quality control, design ability, environmental protection, anti-counterfeit measures, marketing strategy, distribution channels, after-sale services, logistics, etc;
- Licensees should have the financial ability to pay guarantees and royalties on time.

Licensees should maintain good performance as the contract term may vary and contract renewal is subject to prior performance. This will help achieve the "Made-in-China = High Quality" objective.

EXPO 2010 SHANGHAI CHINA

China is the largest developing nation in the world, with the highest growth potential. Over the past 20 years, China has come a long way. The city of Shanghai, in particular, has seen tremendous development. One of the four most rapidly developing cities in the world, Shanghai is fast evolving into a business capital and cosmopolitan city. The quality of life in the city has also risen. Against this backdrop of social and economic success, Shanghai won the bid to host World Expo 2010, becoming the first developing nation in its 150 years of history to do so.

Shanghai: tremendous development

The World Expo is to Shanghai what the Olympics is to Beijing. Dubbed the "Economic Olympics", World Expos are highly profitable and can be a big catalyst to the development of a city.

This exhibition is to be held at a site in Pudong. The design of the site is yet to be confirmed at the time of writing. Spain, Italy and Canada are among those who have submitted proposals for the consideration of the Organizing Committee. The proposed duration for the Expo spans from 1st May to 31st October 2010.

During this period, the entire city of Shanghai will be put on display for all the visitors as well as participants of the Expo to see and experience for themselves the extent of Shanghai and China's progress. It is also an opportunity to foster greater cross-cultural understanding, expand international communications and China's presence in the global community.

Within the 4 sq km exhibition site strategically situated along the Huangpu River, a technological wonderland will be created in which each nation presents their interpretation of the central theme, "Better City, Better Life". Companies from every invited country will showcase the latest in their scientific and technological innovations.

Sending a powerful message to the world

The form and format of display will vary from company to company. Each is responsible for the layout and design of its own exhibition space as well as the mode of presentation. This can range from demonstrations of technology products by company representatives, to stimulation rides to hands-on trial by visitors. Visual aids in the form of charts, or brochures will also be provided. Most organizations will include multimedia shows and other atypical forms of exhibition to give the visitor a unique and interesting experience. In addition to its main objectives of educating via entertaining, the World Expo is also a valuable channel for large-scale marketing. Multinationals like Nokia and Siemens have launched a couple of their latest models during such fairs, generating much hype and free publicity due to the media attention surrounding the event.

Historical Overview

The first World Fair was held in London, England, in 1851. Then the

A land of colour and promise

most powerful country in the world, the British showcased their products and manufacturing processes and invited other countries to participate in the exhibition. Later on, this evolved into a large-scale international non-profit event to promote economic, scientific and technological progress.

Vision

The series of World Expositions is a celebration of the human spirit, articulating people's ideals, dreams and desires, and showcasing their achievements, innovations and scientific breakthroughs. Each event has a specific theme reflecting the hopes and realities of their times and all who participate are offered a taste of life outside their own community.

These exhibitions are future-oriented and aspire to find new ways of advancing human development. One of the primary goals of such expositions is to educate. Held in the spirit of sharing and exchange, this event has lofty goals to encourage greater understanding and hence appreciation of different cultures and ways of life, fostering a greater degree of cooperation and rapport among nations. More than the Olympics or the United Nations, the World Expos expound the principle of universality because anyone, regardless of skill, abilities or profession, can participate.

World Expos seek also to entertain. Over the years, each event has found new ways to achieve this, inspiring a whole series of retail and entertainment concepts prevalent today, like department stores, theme parks and holiday villages.

Activities

A World Expo typically lasts six months. During that time, a host of activities will be run highlighting the theme of the Expo as well as the distinctive traits of each nation or organization. Exhibitions, shows, cultural activities and forums will be held throughout the site. To date, 24 cities in 13 countries have hosted the World Expo.

Theming

The concept of themed attractions so popular today originated from the world fairs. Theming was and continues to be one of the most important aspects of an event. A good theme has to be both a reflection of issues central to the development of the city at that point in time as well as of the loftier goals of a World Expo. Everything else, from the design of the site, to the exhibitions, to their marketing, stems from the theme.

Previous themes have centered around major issues, activities or events in a city. Shanghai Expo 2010 will focus on "Better City, Better Life", also the motto of the city, a poignant theme reflecting the yearning of Shanghainese, China and the developing countries at large for a better tomorrow. The central issue of urban life and its associated problems is also highly relevant to the developed world.

Bidding

World Expos are highly popular international events. Because of its extensive nature, the host nation stands to reap tremendous economic and social gains. Business opportunities abound and tourism is a prime motivator. Hence, many countries compete for the right to host the next World Expo.

The Application Process

An official notification of intent should be submitted to the BIE not earlier than nine years before the opening date of the next exhibit with an accompanying payment of 10% of the registration fee. The opening and closing dates, theme of the exhibit and legal status of the Organization Committee must also be included in the bid.

Six months following the initial submission, the BIE will conduct investigations to ascertain the feasibility of the proposals. Each inquiry will be conducted by several members of the BIE and all costs shall be borne by the organizers of the exhibit. The focus will be on the theme of the exhibit and its definition, the opening date, and duration; the logistical capabilities of the host nation in terms of location, area, and financial guarantees; the policies granted to exhibitors, attitude of the authorities and interested parties and the expected reach of the exhibit in terms of number of visitors.

When more than one country bids for the right to host a World Expo and all preparation works meet the requirements of the BIE, the selection will be subject to a secret ballot. A bidding country requires a 2/3 majority vote to win. Failing that, a second round of votes will be conducted after eliminating the country with the least number of votes in the first round. The same criteria apply and a 2/3 majority is needed. Successive rounds will be held until only two countries are left. In that final round, the country with the higher number of votes will win the bid.

Upon notification, the winning country must submit a formal application to register the exhibit at least five years before the opening date. This is also the time when the nation officially assumes the responsibility to meet BIE standards to ensure a smooth World Expo. Invitations will then be sent to other countries through diplomatic channels and the host country shall then pay the remaining 90% of the registration fee.

The Bureau of International Expositions (BIE) was formed in 1928 by thirty-one nations to regulate the fairs. Headquartered in Paris, France, it oversees the bidding process.

Economic Implications and Benefits

The success of Shanghai in its bid for World Expo 2010 will go a long way towards promoting Shanghai as an international metropolis, which fits in perfectly with the strategic goal of the city. The economic implications of this are also great. Hosting the event will provide a strong impetus for rapid growth. The pace of infrastructure development, especially of the transportation network will be sped up, and Shanghai's service industry (tourism in particular) will see tremendous expansion. With such attractive conditions, more foreign investments are expected for flow into the country.

Tourism industry

The World Expo will have a huge direct impact on tourism. In the case of Shanghai, the tourism sector is one of the fastest growing sectors of the economy. The number of tourists has been increasing, on average, at a rate of 8% every year since 1992 and this figure had risen sharply in 2001. Based on this, it has been postulated that Shanghai will be able to attract 130 to 150 million tourists in 2010, out of which 3.6 to 3.8 million will come from abroad. Come 2010, at least 70 million visitors are expected to attend the Expo, a further boost to the tourism industry.

According to the China Youth Daily, it is estimated that direct income from this sector will hit RMB 9.11 billion yuan (USD 110 million). Admission fees alone will rake in 7.3 billion while sale of food and beverages will contribute 1.3 million. The World Tourism Organisation predicts that each RMB spent on direct tourism income will further generate RMB 4.3 yuan in related industries such as transportation, electricity and telecommunications.

Showcasing superb architecture

There will be a continuous flow of domestic and international tourists throughout the six months of the exhibition. 70% of them will visit other places in China or other parts of Asia. The economic benefits of the World Expo hence trickle down to the rest of China and the region at large. It is an excellent opportunity for the tour operators of Shanghai and the neighbouring areas to cooperate and develop new tourism products and strengthen regional ties.

As seen from past experience, (the Flower Exhibition in Kunming 1999), tourism has generated income as much as RMB 16.9 billion yuan and the rate of growth for some of the economic indicators exceeded 30%. Shanghai's strategic location at the head of Yangtse will also encourage East China's participation in the event, fuelling the economic growth of the country as a whole.

Transport industry

The main concern of organising the World Expo lies in transportation. With a massive inflow of visitors expected in 2010, the current chaotic traffic system in Shanghai poses a big problem. It is important for Shanghai to ensure that there will not be any hiccups when ferrying the visitors from all over the city to the venue.

To overcome this problem, Shanghai has worked out a transport development plan for the international road-rail-air terminal based around Pudong International Airport with Hongqiao Airport playing a supporting role. A high-speed railway system which allows for 7 trunk lines running in 5 directions with yearly passenger capacity of 45 million trips will be constructed. This highway will eventually become the backbone of Shanghai's transport system. In line with this, Shanghai will also build an expressway network of approximately 650km, covering the city and neighbouring regions. This network will also link up cities in the Yangtse River Delta region. Besides revamping their public transport network, Tour-Guide Center will build 5 sub centers serving 98 road lines as well as set up the World Expo Special tour route to further enhance the visitor's experience.

Construction industry

The World Expo is a huge event requiring major construction works prior to the opening date. To host the World Expo, Shanghai will have to build an exhibition hall with a total area of 24 hectares between Lupu and Nanpu Bridge. This new exhibition hall will become the largest in China. The total exhibition area is approximately 10 hectares.

According to Professor Zhu Ronglin, each incremental 1000 square meters of exhibition space will generate an estimated 100 jobs. The World Expo in Hanover, for example, had created 100,000 jobs

More expressways needed

Social Implications for Shanghai & China

Five countries vied aggressively for the right to host World Expo 2010. The World Expos bring more than economic benefits; the social implications are tremendous. Great opportunities now lie for China to exhibit its achievements to the world.

Little is known in foreign lands of the Chinese culture. Because of the lack of outside contact throughout most of its long history, China has frequently been misunderstood. Winning the right to host the World Expo also gives Shanghai a valuable opportunity to present itself to the world. It is a chance for the city and its people to let others gain a deeper understanding of their rich culture.

The World Expos are held in the spirit of advancing human development, encouraging peace and prosperity. Hosting such an event will have a significant and positive impact on a country's image and international standing. It is also serves as a platform to enhance communications and hence, improve bilateral relationships.

Implications for Other Developing Countries

The door of opportunity has not only opened for China, it has in fact opened to the whole world including the developing countries. As the pioneer successful bidder amongst developing countries, China wishes to advance the interest of this group by bridging the gap between the developed and developing world through encouraging greater participation from the latter. A special unit has been set up for this purpose. China has set aside a fund of USD 100 million to promote the Expo amongst the developing countries. Part of the fund will be used to sponsor free exposition space, transportation, traveling and accommodation for the participants.

Non-Monetary Implications for Foreign Investors

In the case of the more developed countries, the Expo 2010 is a great occasion to showcase new innovations and technological breakthroughs. The exhibition provides huge exposure and serves as a 'test' market to gauge the reception of the new products.

Although trading inside the fair is not permitted, uncountable deals are always concluded outside the venue. The convergence of companies from all over the world will also generate many networking prospects that are previously unexplored.

The Long-Term Impact of World Expo 2010

Securing the right to host World Expo 2010 has opened up many doors for Shanghai. It is a big catalyst to growth and the development of the city dubbed 'the New York of the East' will see dramatic progress. The economic and social character of Shanghai will undergo tremendous change. Business opportunities abound. World Expo 2010, if successful, will be a critical turning point in the evolution of Shanghai into a bustling business capital.

BEIJING

The capital is also the site of Zhongguancun Hi-tech Zone (China's Silicon Valley) – the country's leading incubator of high-tech industries.

BEIJING Fact Sheet	2003
Area (km^2)	16,808
Population (mil)	14.6
GDP (RMB bn)	361.2
Gross capital formation (RMB bn)	201
Consumption expenditure (RMB bn)	170
~Household	105
~Government	65
No. of employed persons (mil)	7.98
Unemployment Rate	1.43%
Literacy Rate	97%
Government revenue (RMB bn)	59.3
Government expenditure (RMB bn)	73.7
Per capita annual	
~disposable income of urban residents (RMB '000)	13.9
~net income of rural households (RMB '000)	6.5
~living expenditure of urban residents (RMB '000)	11.1
~living expenditure of rural residents (RMB '000)	4.7
Actually Used Foreign Direct Investment (US$ mil)	2,150
Total assets (RMB bn)	298
Exports (USD mil)	16,850
~percentage of change from the same period of previous year	+33.6%
Imports (USD mil)	51,610
~percentage of change from the same period of previous year	+29.4%

Introduction

Beijing is the capital of the People's Republic of China, as well as the nation's political and cultural centre. Some 690,000 years ago, Peking Man lived at Zhoukoudian, 48 km southwest of Beijing. In 1045 B.C., a small town named Ji appeared on the present site of southwestern Beijing. At the beginning of the 10th century, it was the second capital of the Liao Dynasty. From then on, the city had been the capital of the Jin, Yuan, Ming and Qing dynasties until 1911. In the early 1920s, Beijing became the cradle of China's new democratic revolution. The May Fourth Movement against imperialism and feudalism began here in 1919.

Beijing was known as Peking by the Western world before 1949. Although it is an ancient city and was often used as the capital during various dynasties, Beijing's modern history as a capital began in the Yuan dynasty (1271-1368) with Kublai Khan, grandson of Ghengis Khan. Marco Polo made Beijing his base when he visited and travelled here with the Khan. He spent over 20 years as a guest of the Khan before returning to Europe with his vivid descriptions of the great civilisation in the east. Most of what we see today in Beijing was built during the Ming dynasty (1368-1644).

Situated in the north-eastern part of China at an elevation of 43.5m above sea level, Beijing City is an independently administered municipal district. The climate in Beijing is defined as "continental monsoon", with cold and dry winters. January is the coldest month (-4°C), and July is the warmest (26°C). Winter usually begins towards the end of October. The summer months, June to August, are wet and hot with about 40 percent of the annual precipitation.

Travel Information

Beijing Airport

Beijing Capital International Airport is one of China's major gateways. Electronic display boards are installed throughout the airport, providing arrival and departure information in both Chinese and English. The Unisys Airport Passenger Processing System (APPS) is used at the airport. APPS put intuitive Windows-type graphical screens at the fingertips of airport personnel, enabling them to check in passengers and baggage and complete reservations and departure control processes more quickly and efficiently.

Beijing is served by international carriers such as Northwest, United, Canadian Airlines, Japan Airlines, ANA, SAS, Dragon Air, Lufthansa, British Airways, Malaysian Air, Austrian Airlines, Air France, Alitalia, Korean Air, Pakistan Airlines, Singapore Airlines, Thai International, Air China, China Southern, and China Northern.

Travellers will be able to stay in touch with the world via multimedia payphones conveniently located throughout the terminal. A phone card, available at airport counters, is required to make calls. There are no English-language travel books or maps available at the airport, but tourist information and maps can be found at the front desks of most hotels.

Banks & ATMs

There are more than 12 ATMs (available 24 hours) and four auto cash exchange machines conveniently located throughout

Beijing offers tourists great convenience

the terminal and they accept: Cirrus, American Express, Visa, Visa Interlink, MasterCard.

Travel Tax

Travellers departing Beijing on an international flight must pay a RMB90 airport construction tax. Those flying to domestic destinations must pay RMB50. Payment must be made at counters in the departure area prior to checking in for your flight. Keep your receipt.

Airport Transportation

The airport is 26 km, or 40 minutes, from the centre of Beijing. Modes of transport (available during normal flight arrival and departure times) include bus and taxi. The airport bus is available on the lower level just outside the Arrivals area. There is just one government-run airport bus shuttle. Many hotels run their own airport shuttle bus services. Taxis are available on the lower level just outside the Arrivals area. There is no real difference between the various taxi companies in Beijing.

When arriving at the airport, avoid drivers who approach you in the terminal or outside the terminal. These drivers are almost always price gaugers and they will always quote a price that is triple or more than the actual price. There is a taxi line just outside the terminal. Remember to insist that the driver use their meter; and make sure that the driver puts down the flag. This is to avoid drivers who say they forgot to put down the flag and ask for a ridiculous amount of money. The cost to midtown Beijing is normally around RMB70 depending on the type of taxi, plus RMB15 for the highway toll. There is no need to tip taxi drivers in Beijing unless they render extra assistance such as carrying your bags.

Most of the better hotels provide a card with the taxi's licence plate when you get into a taxi at the front door. Retain this card should you have a problem with the driver, or should you leave something in the taxi. If you lose something and do not have the number of the taxi, you could try either your destination or departure point as it is not unusual for taxi drivers to turn lost goods in at these places. It is advisable to always carry the name of your hotel and any destination in Chinese because very few drivers in Beijing speak English. You can ask the staff at the front desk of your hotel to write your destination in Chinese.

Tourist attractions abound

Banking hours

Banking hours vary from bank to bank in Beijing. However, most Chinese banks are open from 9 a.m. to 4 p.m. or 5 p.m. and have branches that are open on Saturdays and Sundays. The services offered by the small number of branches set up by international banks in China are quite limited under current government regulations. Only two foreign banks in China have ATMs and there are no drive-in ATMs in Beijing.

Visas

L-visas for single or multiple entries for tourists are valid for 30 to 60 days. F-visas for business travel can be valid for up to six months but may require the visitor to leave every 30 days. They are good for single, double or multiple entries. Those seeking business visas must obtain official invitation from a government office or a company authorised by the Ministry of Foreign Affairs.

Credit Cards

In Beijing, most major credit cards including American Express, Diner's Club, Federal Card, JCB, MasterCard and Visa are accepted at major hotels, restaurants and shops.

Tipping

Tipping is generally not expected in mainland China.

Electricity

The voltage is 220 volts, 50 cycles. Most luxury hotels have built-in converters in bathrooms for shavers, hair dryers, etc. Otherwise, come equipped, because a wide variety of plug types are in use.

Health

Potable water is available only at top hotels, so visitors should always ask to make sure. Prior to your trip, consult your doctor on immunisations you might need (e.g. tetanus, typhoid, cholera and hepatitis A and B) and about malaria suppressants if you're planning to go to rural areas. Bring all prescription and over-the-counter medicines you might require.

Time Zone

GMT +8 hours. The whole of China is set to Beijing Time.

Business Hours

Offices in Beijing generally open from 8:30 a.m. to 6 p.m., with a lunch break of about an hour. Government-stipulated workdays are from Monday to Friday. Banking hours and days vary from bank to bank in Beijing. However, most Chinese banks are open from

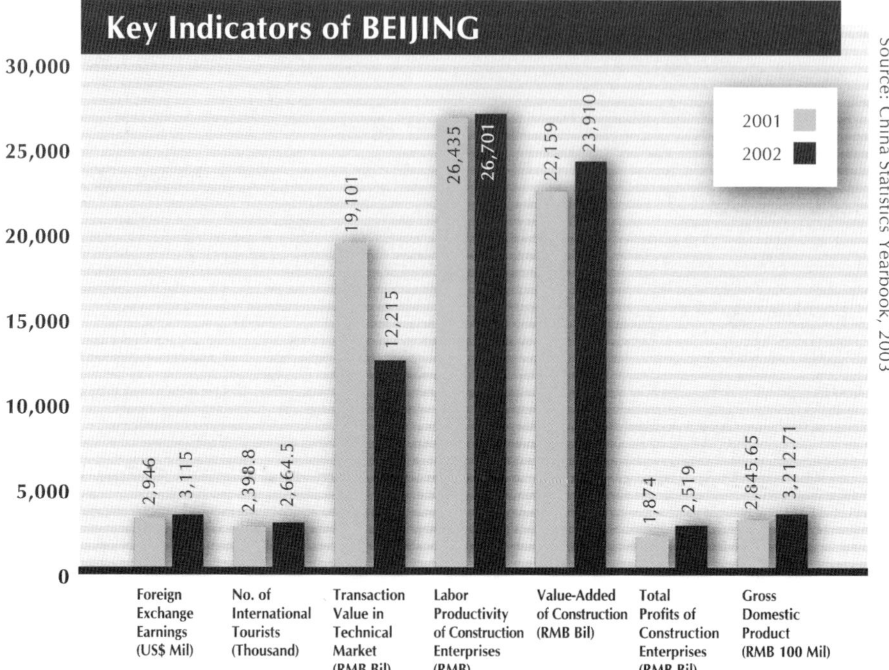

9 a.m. to 4 p.m. or 5 p.m. and have branches that are open on Saturdays and Sundays. Shops generally open at 9 a.m. and close at between 7 p.m. and 9 p.m. They are open on Sundays.

Business Attire

Normal Western business attire is considered appropriate for doing business in China.

Major Exports

Electrical machinery and equipment, machinery and mechanical appliances, textiles, garments, footwear, toys and sporting goods, household electrical appliances, telecommunication equipment, pharmaceuticals, steel products, general metalwares, coal and food stuffs.

Major Trading Partners

United States, Japan, Germany, South Korea, Netherlands, UK, Singapore, Taiwan, Russia.

Major Industries

Iron and steel production, machine-building, production of coal, armaments, textiles and apparel, petroleum, cement, chemical fertilisers, footwear, toys, cars, consumer electronics and telecommunication equipment, and food processing.

Ethnic Groups

The permanent residents of Beijing come from all of China's 56 ethnic groups. The Han nationality accounts for 96.5 percent of the total. The other 55 ethnic minorities claim a population of more than 300,000; most of them are from Hui, Manchu, and Mongolian nationalities.

Language

The official language is Mandarin (or Putonghua, based on the Beijing dialect). Local dialects include Yue (Cantonese), Hu (Shanghainese), Minbei (Fuzhou), Minnan (Hokkien-Taiwanese), Xiang, Gan, Hakka dialects, and other minority languages. Most tourist hotels have staff who are fluent in foreign languages.

Literacy Rate

97 percent of total population

Religion

China is officially atheist, but traditionally pragmatic and eclectic. Daoism (Taoism), Buddhism and Islam are practised by about two to three percent of the population and Christianity by one percent.

People

Beijing's people are quite friendly and outgoing in dealing with foreign guests, and most appear to enjoy interacting with foreigners. However, they are often quite reserved and cautious when dealing with foreigners in formal situations or in initial business relationships.

SHANGHAI

Its location has made it China's largest foreign trade port. In addition, it has diversified industries and a rapidly growing financial market.

SHANGHAI Fact Sheet	**2003**
Area (km^2)	6,340
Population (mil)	13.4
GDP (RMB bn)	625.0
Gross capital formation (RMB bn)	240.9
Consumption expenditure (RMB bn)	246
~Household	190
~Government	55
No. of employed persons (mil)	5.82
Unemployment Rate	4.9%
Literacy Rate	99.9%
Government revenue (RMB bn)	89.9
Government expenditure (RMB bn)	110.3
Per capita annual	
~disposable income of urban residents (RMB '000)	14.9
~net income of rural households (RMB '000)	6.7
~living expenditure of urban residents (RMB '000)	12.1
~living expenditure of rural residents (RMB '000)	5.8
Actually Used Foreign Direct Investment (US$ mil)	5.850
Total assets (RMB bn)	202.4
Exports (USD mil)	48.482
~percentage of change from the same period of previous year	+51.2%
Imports (USD mil)	63.915
~percentage of change from the same period of previous year	+57.4%

Introduction

Shanghai, also called "Hu" for short in Chinese, is situated at 31°41′ north latitude and 121°29′ east longitude. Bordering on Jiangsu and Zhejiang provinces in the west, Shanghai is flanked by the East China Sea on the east and Hangzhou Bay on the south. North of the city, the Yangtze River meets the East China Sea. It also occupies a central location along China's coastline. Thanks to its advantageous geographic location, Shanghai is an excellent sea and river port, boasting easy access to the vast hinterland.

Climate

With a pleasant northern subtropical maritime monsoon climate, Shanghai enjoys four distinct seasons, generous sunshine and abundant rainfall. Its spring and autumn are relatively short compared with summer and winter. The average annual temperature is 16°C. The city has

a frost-free period lasting up to 230 days a year, and receives an average annual rainfall of 1,200 mm. However, nearly 60 percent of the precipitation comes during the May-September flood season, which is divided into three rainy periods, namely, the Spring Rains, the Plum Rains and the Autumn Rains.

Area

The city covers an area of 6,340.5 km^2, 0.06 percent of China's total territory, which extends about 120 km from north to south and nearly 100 km from east to west. Shanghai has an urban area of 2,057 km^2, land area of 6,219 km^2 and water area of 122 km^2. The city's Chongming Island is the third largest island in China, covering an area of 1,041 km^2.

The City Emblem

The Standing Committee of the Shanghai Municipal People's Congress approved the design of the city emblem of Shanghai in 1990. The triangle emblem consists of a white magnolia flower, a large junk and a propeller. The propeller symbolises the continuous advancement of the city; the large junk, one of the oldest vessels plying Shanghai's harbour, represents the long history and bright future of the port, and the large junk is set against a white magnolia flower blossoming in the early spring.

The City Flower

In 1986, the Standing Committee of the Shanghai Municipal People's Congress passed a resolution adopting the white magnolia as the city flower. The white magnolia is among the few spring flowers in the Shanghai area. It is in full blossom in early spring and before the Qingming Festival, which usually falls on April 5. The flower has large, white petals and its eye always looks towards the sky. Therefore, the flower symbolises the pioneering and enterprising spirit of the city.

Water Resources

Dotted with many rivers and lakes, the Shanghai area is known for its rich water resources. Most of the rivers are tributaries of the Huangpu River. Originating from the Taihu Lake, the 113-km-long Huangpu River meanders through the downtown area of the city. The river is about 300 to 770m wide with an average width of 360m. The ice-free Huangpu River is the main waterway in the Shanghai area.

Administrative Divisions

Shanghai is divided into 19 districts. There are 205 towns, nine townships, 99 sub-district committees, 3,278 neighbourhood committees and 2,935 villagers' committees in the city.

Industry

Shanghai now has nearly 40,000 industrial enterprises, with about four million employees and over 400 industrial sectors. Shanghai's industry has many advantages such as comprehensive and diversified industrial sectors, ease of finding cooperative partners, supporting products and material, as well as easy access to domestic and overseas markets. Shanghai will expedite the development of three major high technology industries, i.e., integrated circuit and computer science, modern biology and new medicine, as well as new materials in the future.

Agriculture

Shanghai's rural economy has completed its transition from a small agriculture economy to a more diversified, integrated and industrialised suburban agricultural economy.

Foreign Trade and Finance

Shanghai has always been the nation's largest foreign trade port and its financial market is enjoying a rapid growth. A national financial market system is shaping up with the monetary, capital, and foreign exchange markets as its main components.

Infrastructure

There are two international airports; Shanghai Railway, one of the 10 railway hubs in China; Shanghai Port, the biggest port in the mainland, and water freight form the convenient transportation system. The inner city transportation is a three-dimensional system consisting of express main roads, elevated highway, tracks and cross-river roads. Shanghai Post and Telecommunications currently has formed a multidimensional communication network involving various means such as satellite, microwave and submarine cable.

Attractions

Longhua Temple

This is the biggest and oldest temple in Shanghai. Its main hall and all other halls are stately and splendidly structured. The chiming of "Longhua Bell" in the monastery is one of Shanghai's eight tourist attractions. The Longhua Pagoda, another imposing and splendid structure-with seven storeys, is octagonal in shape with upturned eaves and hanging bells on the eaves' corners.

Oriental Pearl TV Tower

One of the highest towers in the world, this stands erect on the other side of Huangpu River facing the Bund. Every visitor will invariably be overwhelmed by its serenity and grandeur. The glittering light on the top sparkles at night, radiating rays of hope to everyone who views it.

Oriental Pear Tower: Symbol of progress

People's Square

The centre of Shanghai is a square that every tourist visits. Dotted with a variety of flowers from various seasons, the plaza brims with vigour and vitality. Swift dancers follow the rhythmic beat of the music fountain in front of the City Hall; children express their love for animals by feeding hopping pigeons with corn; families of three stroll along the winding lanes; Shanghai Museum, surrounded by greenery, attracts thousands of museum-lovers daily.

Pudong New District

Situated in the east of the Huangpu River, the southwest of the mouth of the Yangtze River, and adjacent to the urban districts of Shanghai, Pudong New Area covers 520 km^2 with a population of more than 1.4 million. The area, which borders the East China Sea in the east and the Yangtze River in the north, occupies a position at the intersection of China's so-called golden coast and golden waterway. It is opposite to the famous "Bund" across the Huangpu River. With the advantages of favourable geographical position, firm economic foundation and rich resources, Pudong now has become a bustling land of attraction at home and abroad.

Pudong is along the estuary of the Yangtze River and opposite to the centre of Shanghai on the west side of the Huangpu River. It has sound natural geographical conditions and economic foundation, which is a treasure land with broad prospects remaining to be developed.

The Pudong New Area is a triangular area adjacent to the city proper, stretching to the east of the Huangpu River, to the southwest of the Yangtze estuary, including the former country of Chuansha and former Sanlin village of Minhang district. The north of this area is within 15 km of the city's downtown area. It covers 522 km^2 and has a population of 1,400,000. At present it is home to the four national development zones in Shanghai. They are Lujiazui Finance & Trade Zone, Zhangjiang High-Tech Park, Waigaoqiao Free Trade Zone, and Jinqiao Export Processing Zone.

Pudong borders on the sea in the east and on the Huangpu River in the west. It has fine deep-water ports with super conditions. The transportation facilities are as follows: along the east bank of the Huangpu River, there are now 157 berths, of which 33 can take 10,000-ton-class ships and 160 berths with a cargo handling capacity of 4.6million tons. The total length of existing roads is 437 km, of which urban roads make up 80 km and rural roads make up 357 km. For cross-river transportation, there are now two bridges, two river tunnels, 16 ferry lines for passengers and two ferry lines for motor vehicles.

Elementary public facilities in the Pudong New Area have been taking shape. The current capacity of daily tap water supply is 430,000 tons. The supply of electricity, with a maximum load of 410,000 kW, is mainly dependent on the electricity network of the city proper. The Pudong Gasworks with a daily capacity of producing two million cubic metres has been put into operation. A total length of 239 kilometres of gas pipes has been laid, with 35 percent of the households now using gas. The capacity of the telephone exchange system is 100,000 lines.

There already exists a sizable industrial and agricultural foundation in Pudong New Area. There are now 3,000 industrial enterprises, employing 460,000 people. The major industries include petrochemicals, ship building, iron and steel and building materials. The machine-building, light and textile industries in the area have also reached a moderate scale.

Social undertakings have been developed moderately in the area.

Over the past decade, apartment buildings with a total floor space of five million square metres have been bought and the residential areas are provided with commercial, educational, cultural and recreational facilities.

The Pudong New Area is an organic part of the economic and social development of Shanghai. Integrated with the overall urban planning of Shanghai, the development of Pudong will gradually proceed in a planned and phased way according to priority.

Impressive modern infrastructure

Infrastructure Construction

To attract investment from both home and abroad, a good investment environment is needed in Pudong. In the past five years, Shanghai made an investment of RMB25 billion in the 10 infrastructure projects, involving the first-phase project of a power plant, the Pudong section of inner-ring road connecting the two bridges, the Waigaoqiao harbour area, two flyovers, sewage project, the first phase of the Lingqiao Water Plant and modern telecommunications project.

Construction of other infrastructure projects has started, involving Lujiazui-Huamu Avenue, sewage discharge project in southern Pudong, modern telecommunications centre, new container harbour, and the Pudong section of outer-ring road. Besides, the preparation of the international airport and the No. 2 subway has also started. Thus, infrastructure facilities, centeringg on roads and transportation, are shaping a new modern city.

Social service

With the development of the economy, social progress has been made in the Pudong New Area as well. A great number of projects involving hospitals, schools, cultural and entertainment facilities have been completed. Besides, afforestation has been placed at the top of the government's agenda which improved the living quality of the residents.

Regulations of Shanghai Municipality for Encouragement of Foreign Investment

In order to encourage foreign investment in Shanghai, and especially in the Pudong New Area, Shanghai has formulated 74 local economic measures and adopted a series of preferential policies for foreign investment.

Projects which are encouraged include many types:

1. Projects dealing with transportation, energy, the processing of important raw materials and agricultural technology development, which are urgently needed by the state.

2. The projects which suit the needs of world markets, open new markets at home and abroad, as well as reconstruct existing Shanghai enterprises and increase the quality of products, in addition to exporting products to earn foreign revenue.

3. Projects provided with new equipment and new materials using imported advanced technology, which can improve the products, save energy and raw materials as well as increase the technological and economic benefits of the enterprises, and fill the gaps of production at home to meet the needs of the market.

4. Projects with new technology and new design that can make reasonable and compre

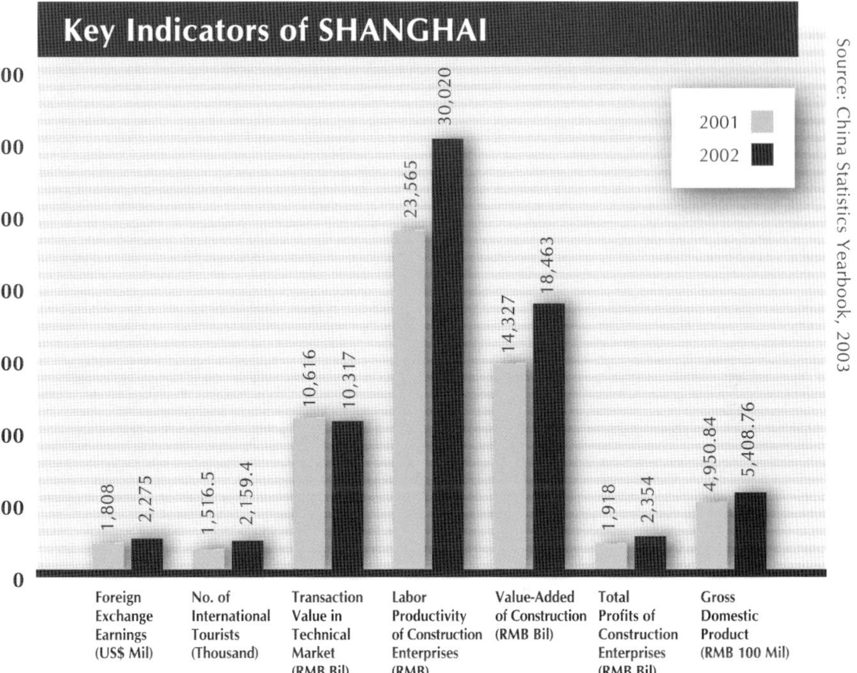

hensive use of resources and recycled resources.

5. Projects of new and high technology industry which suit the needs of international and domestic markets.

6. Projects which encourage foreign businessmen to invest and set up enterprises in Waigaoqiao Free Trade Zone dealing with import and export trade, international entrepot and the services for international trade such as processing, packaging, storage and transportation.

7. Projects which encourage foreign businessmen to invest and develop tract of land with the projects according to the unified plan of Shanghai and Pudong New Area; especially welcome foreign investors who reconstruct the old, simple houses in the original

urban districts, and projects which draw other investors.

Preferential Policies for Taxation

Income Tax

The income tax of Sino-foreign equity ventures, Sino-foreign cooperative joint ventures and wholly foreign-owned enterprises is 30 percent, plus 3 percent local income tax; the income tax of productive enterprises invested in by foreign businessmen in urban areas is 24 percent, and only 15 percent for productive enterprises invested in by foreign traders in economic development zones and in the Pudong New Area.

Booming economy attracts investors from all over the world

Enterprises scheduled to operate for periods of 10 years or more shall be exempted from income tax in the first two profit-making years and allowed a 50 percent reduction in the following three years. When the exemption period expires, export enterprises with foreign investment shall pay a rate reduced by 10 percent when their annual value of export good amounts to more then 70 percent of the total annual value of production. Foreign-invested, technologically advanced enterprises may pay the enterprise income rate reduced by 10 percent for another three years after the exemption period of enterprise income tax expires.

Foreign investors who reinvest their share of profits in their enterprises, or other foreign-invested enterprises, or in new foreign-invested enterprises, shall get a full refund of enterprises income tax paid on the reinvested amount.

Income tax for foreign invested enterprises engaged in energy, transportation and construction projects is 15 percent. Enterprises with operation period of over 15 years may be exempt from enterprises income tax for first five years and another 50 percent tax reduction from sixth to tenth year.

City Real Estate Tax

The tax is levied at an annual rate of 1.2 percent on the net original value of the real estate after 29 percent has been deducted. The tax rate is levied on the rental income. Newly-constructed buildings in the economic development areas, either self-built or purchased for private use by foreign-invested enterprises, shall be exempted from house property tax for five years when the construction is completed or the purchase is made.

Individual Income Tax

Wages and salaries earned by foreigners working in China shall be taxed according to progressive rates. Income of RMB 4,000 or less shall be exempted from tax. Over RMB 4,000, the individual income tax rate runs from 5 percent to 45 percent. With effective from August 1, 1987, wages and salaries received by foreigners have been taxed at 50 percent the original assessed amount.

Vehicle License Fees and Taxes

All vehicles owned and used by foreign-funded enterprises are subject to this tax according to "The Interim Regulations of the Vehicles and Vessels Operation License Tax".

TIANJIN

With excellent communication and transport facilities, this gateway to Beijing has rich natural resources, prospering industry and commerce.

TIANJIN Fact Sheet	2003
Area (km2)	11,305
Population (mil)	10.1
GDP (RMB bn)	205.1
Gross capital formation (RMB bn)	238.7
Consumption expenditure (RMB bn)	99
~Household	66
~Government	33
No. of employed persons (mil)	5.1
Unemployment Rate	3.8%
Literacy Rate	93.6%
Government revenue (RMB bn)	45.2
Government expenditure (RMB bn)	35.0
Per capita annual	
~disposable income of urban residents (RMB '000)	10.3
~net income of rural households (RMB '000)	5.9
~living expenditure of urban residents (RMB '000)	7.9
~living expenditure of rural residents (RMB '000)	3.0
Actually Used Foreign Direct Investment (US$ mil)	1,633
Total assets (RMB bn)	60.8
Exports (USD mil)	14,374
~percentage of change from the same period of previous year	+24%
Imports (USD mil)	14,997
~percentage of change from the same period of previous year	+33.5%

Introduction

As the gateway to China's capital, Beijing, Tianjin is an economic centre, hub of communications network and international seaport in North China, and one of the four municipalities directly under the central government. Located on the banks of the Haihe River and Yunhe (Grand Canal), Tianjin is also a major transportation hub in northern-central China. It is populated by almost 10 million people. Tianjin is well known for its 19th-century European-style buildings of the former concessions.

Although the harbour is poor, Tianjin is a leading international port of China and the collection and distribution centre for the North China plain. Tianjin is an important manufacturing centre with iron and steelworks, textile mills (cotton, woollen, and hemp), machine shops, a chemical industry based on salt, flour mills and other food-processing establishments, paper mills, plants making heavy machinery, cars, precision instruments, cement, fertiliser, rubber products, carpets, lubricants, computers and computer components. The city has been designated a special economic zone in order to increase foreign trade and investment. The banking and trade industries are vital to the economy. Strategically located on the overland route to Manchuria, Tianjin has been a frequent military objective since its rise to importance in the late 18th century. Tianjin was made a treaty port and a part of it was conceded for foreign settlements and garrisons, under an Agreement between China and British and French in 1860.

Tianjin is noted for its transport facilities - on land, by sea and by air. The New Harbour at Tanggu District is the largest seaport for foreign trade in North China. Two main railway lines intersect at Tianjin. One of them, the Tianjin-Pukou line, extends down south of the Yangzi River and the other, the Beijing-Shengyang line, reaches far beyond the Great Wall. The new Tianjin Railway Station is the largest in Asia. The Tianjin International Airport in the eastern suburbs provides facilities and service for giant cargo and passenger airplanes and is an alternative to Beijing International Airport.

Its richly endowed natural resources, solid foundation of the industry and commerce, and its excellent location as the hub of communication, provide excellent infrastructure for its development and construction.

Richly endowed natural resources, solid foundation of Tianjin's industry and commerce, and its excellent location as the hub of communications, provide excellent infrastructure for its development.

Five main tributaries in the North China, the South Canal, the North Canal, the Ziya, the Daqing and the Yongding, converge at Tianjin to form the Hai River, which, after meandering its way through the city, meets the sea. Several

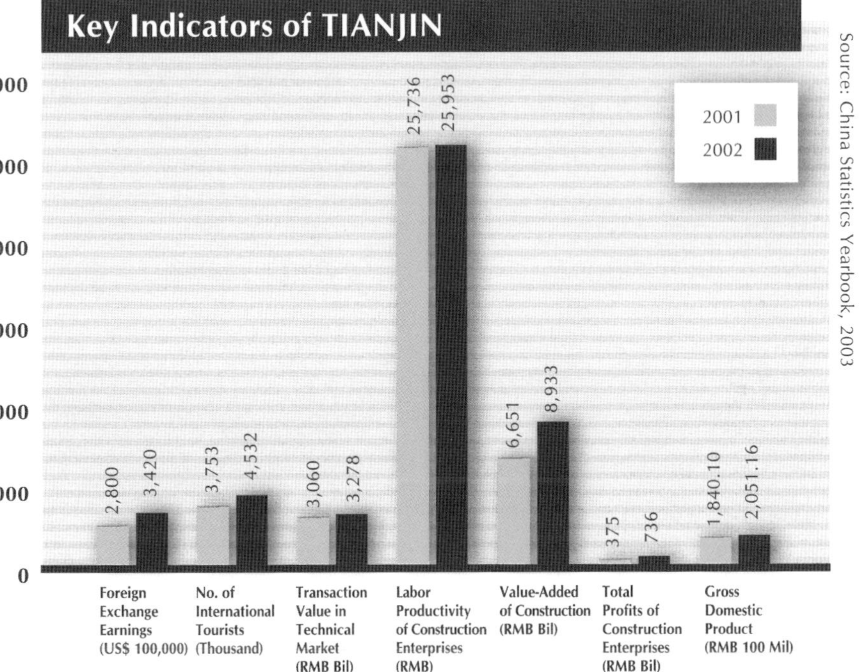

bridges over the Hai River, which are built in different styles, enhance the landscape of Tianjin. Tianjin is also known as a cultural city. The old town originally came from the people gathering along Shan-cha-kou, the port area on the convergence of three tributaries of Hai River.

CHONGQING

The cradle of Bayu culture and home to The Three Gorges is rich in natural resources.

CHONGQING Fact Sheet	2003
Area (km^2)	82,000
No. of Cities	4
Population (mil)	31.3
GDP (RMB bn)	225.0
Gross capital formation (RMB bn)	99
Consumption expenditure (RMB bn)	123
~Household	88
~Government	35
No. of employed persons (mil)	17.3
Unemployment Rate	4.1%
Literacy Rate	90.7%
Government revenue (RMB bn)	20.7
Government expenditure (RMB bn)	39.2
Per capita annual	
~disposable income of urban residents (RMB '000)	8.1
~net income of rural households (RMB '000)	2.2
~living expenditure of urban residents (RMB '000)	7.1
~living expenditure of rural residents (RMB '000)	1.6
Actually Used Foreign Direct Investment (USD mil)	310
Total assets (RMB bn)	29.2
Exports (USD mil)	1,585
~percentage of change from the same period of previous year	+45.3%
Imports (USD mil)	1,010
~percentage of change from the same period of previous year	+43.7%

Introduction

Bazhou and Yuzhou etc., got its present name 800 years ago, in 1189. One of the cradles of Changjiang Civilization, it is also called the cradle of Basu Culture.

Lying in hilly country, at the Jaling River and upper Yangtze River confluence, Chongqing is one of China's biggest municipalities as well as one of the largest cities in the world. As an economic centre, Chongqing is the hub of water, land, and air transportation in Southwest China with busy rivers and highways heading in all directions. Chongqing is also an inland river port with foreign trade in the west of China. It is an integrated industrial city with a balanced and developed agriculture industry.

Downtown Chongqing is magnificent, cut through by rivers and sprawling over hills. Chongqing is also great for Sichuan cuisine, like Zhang tea cooked duck, steamed carp, marinated beef, and bean curd. Silk, citrus fruit, tea, and grain are its main exports. Abundant mineral resources in the region facilitate local production of trucks, motorcycles, and metals. Chongqing's wider metro area is home to 10.2 million people, 40 percent of whom are industrial workers.

History

Chongqing is a famous cultural city with a history of 3,000 years and a glorious revolutionary tradition. It is the birthplace of Bayu culture. Towards the end of the Old Stone Age, approximately 20,000 to 30,000 years ago, mankind began to live in Chongqing. In Shang and Zhou Dynasties (c.11th century B.C.) Ba people founded Kingdom Ba and made Chongqing their capital. The domain of Ba in its most flourishing period was "to Yufu (present Fengjie) in the east, to Dao in the west, to Hanzhong in the north and to Qianfu in the south". Original Chongqing was the jurisdictional centre of East Sichuan, South Shanxi, West Hubei, Northwest of Hunan and North Guizhou. In all dynasties since Qing and Han, this region was for most of the time a unified administrative region with Chongqing as the centre. In olden times, Chongqing was called Jiangzhou. Then it was called Bajun, Chuzhou, Yuzhou and Gongzhou. In 581, Emperor Wendi of Sui Dynasty changed Chuzhou to Yuzhou, thus creating the short form Yu for Chongqing. In 1189, Emperor Guang Zhong of Song Dynasty was first conferred the title of prince and then ascended the throne. He called it double happiness, which is how Chongqing (double happiness) gained its name. It is almost 800 years old now. In 1891, Chongqing became an open port. In 1929, Chong-qing was formally designated as a city.

The establishment of Chongqing municipality marks a major breakthrough in China's initiatives to speed up economic development of the central and western regions.

In 1937, soon after Nanjing was invaded and occupied by the Japanese, the Kuomintang government moved from Nanjing to Chongqing and designated the latter as its wartime capital. Due to its important contribution during the Second World War,

Chongqing became one of the only four cities highlighted in the China map displayed in the great auditorium of the United Nations.

Chongqing has since gone through four phases of development. As the wartime capital of China, it began to develop into a modern industrial city at the end of the 1940s. In the 1950s, Chongqing's location at the Southwest Bureau and the Southwest Military and Political Committee under the Communist Party of China, as well as being the municipality directly under the People's Government, has strengthened its position as the political, economic and cultural centre of Southwest China. In the 1960s, the Third Front strategy brought a massive relocation of enterprises into Chongqing, particularly the military enterprises.

In the 1980s, Chongqing was earmarked in the First Five-Year Plan as one of the independent cities for economic reforms. Chongqing was upgraded to become the fourth municipality on March 14, 1997, together with Beijing, Shanghai and Tianjing.

The administrative jurisdiction of the Chongqing government was enlarged to include its neighbouring Fuling city, Wanxian city and the Qianjiang region.

The development of Chongqing municipality is expected to provide resettlement for more than one million people whose hometowns are swamped by the "Three Gorges Dam" project on the Yangtze River. About RMB70 billion will be needed to build towns, factories, irrigation facilities, roads and orchards for the relocation programme in both Chongqing and Hubei provinces. The establishment of Chongqing municipality marks a major breakthrough of China's initiatives to speed up economic develop-ment of the central and western regions.

Infrastructure

Water Transport

Chongqing is a major trading port on the upper Yangtze River. The Jialing River and Minjiang River are the two major rivers converging into the Yangtze River. Upon completion of the Three Gorges Dam project, vessels up to 10,000 tons can sail directly into Chaotianmen Port at high tide. Besides, the municipality is planning to develop its biggest deep-water berths at Changshou Port.

Railways

Chongqing is a major transportation hub in southwest China. Three major railways, Chengyu Lines: Chengdu-Chongqing, Chuanqian Lines: Chengdu-Guiyang and Xiangyu Lines: Xiangfan-Chongqing go through the city to connect with the national network, and to connect the municipality to China's major cities and ports.

Besides, the municipality plans to construct a railway running along the Yangtze River to Shanghai in the next five years. The new railway will cross various provinces and municipalities including Sichuan, Hubei, Jiangxi, Anhui, and Jiangsu, so as to bolster economic development along the Yangtze River.

Chongqing is also aiming to improve its city transport. One of the 10 key projects in the Great Western Development is the construction of Chongqing Metropolitan Transportation Railways.

Highways

One of the major highways include the Chengdu-Chongqing Expressway which connects Chongqing with the national highway network. Chongqing Lijiatuo Yangtze Bridge, Fengjiang Yangtze Bridge and a 10km ring road encircling Chongqing have eased traffic bottlenecks within the city. Other major highways include Yuchang Expressway, linking

Chongqing and Changshou, and an 53.5 km-long expressway from Chang-shou to Fuling, and the Yuqian Expressway from Chongqing to Guiyang.

Two key projects in the 10th Five-Year Plan are the Chongqing-Beihai Expressway and Chong-qing-Zhanjiang Expressway. These two highways are key components of the Southwest Sea Passage, which is expected to complete before 2005.

Air Transport

The Chongqing Jiangbei International Airport has been expanded in terms of capacity. The first direct air route between Chongqing and Seoul, capital of the Republic of Korea, was opened in June 2000. Currently, Chongqing has direct air routes to about 50 domestic cities and countries, including Hong Kong, Macao, Bangkok, Munich and Nagoya.

Telecommunications

Chongqing has direct-dial telephone and telegram links with most major overseas countries and regions. There were over 4.7 million installed telephone lines by end of 2003, linking the city with other domestic and overseas cities. The number of mobile telephones and Internet network subscribers reached 4,640,000 and 286,000 respectively at end of 2003.

Gas Supply

Construction of a new gas pipeline has begun. The gas pipeline will link the provinces of Sichuan and Hubei. The main part of the pipeline starts at Zhongxian County in Chongqing and ends in Wuhan. The whole project has been completed by now.

Oil Supply

Construction of Lanzhou-Chengdu-Chongqing oil pipeline has been completed. It passes through 30 counties and cities in Gansu, Shaanxi and Chongqing with an annual oil delivering capacity of more than five million tons. The long oil pipeline provides a major passage to deliver oil products from the northwest region to the southwest region.

Agriculture

Chongqing has a vast rural area. Chongqing is one of the country's major produces of grains and the producing base of commodity pork. Chongqing is also China's famous producing area of fine fruits, pickles, tung oil and tobacco. There are in Chongqing "Land of citrus" Jiangjin, "Land of pomelo" Liangping, "Land of yellow peach" Tongnan, "Land of pickles" Fuling, "Land of tung oil" Wanxian and "Tobacco base" Qianjiang. Chongqing's township enterprises are playing an important part in the city's economic development. Chongqing's hot summer is favourable for agriculture, including the production of jute. It is aiming to become the biggest spice producer in China by 2005.

Natural Resources

Chongqing is rich in natural resources. It has more than 40 kinds of minerals. Its coal reserve reaches 4.8 billion tons. The Chuandong Natural Gas Field in Chongqing is China's largest inland production base of natural gas, with deposits of 270 billion cubic metres, accounting for more than one-fifth of China's total. Chongqing also contains China's largest reserve of strontium, which is also the second largest in the world.

Industries

Chongqing has a strong industrial base. In 2002, the municipality's industrial output totalled RMB208.5 billion, an increase of 17.5 percent over 2001.

Chongqing is one of the four major car productions and one of the main military production bases of China. Car outputs grew strongly to 331,000 in 2002. Changan Automotive Corp and China Jialing Industrial

Corporation Group, a joint venture between Japan's Honda and Jialing Motorcycle, play important roles in the industry. Other major car producers include the Lifan Hongda Enterprise, Chongqing Longqin Industrial Group. In 2001, Chongqing became the "Motorcycle Capital" of China.

The municipality is also one of the nine biggest iron & steel production centres and one of the three major aluminium production bases of China. It produces more than 120 kinds of steel products and 13,000 kinds of specifications of aluminium goods. It is also one of the most important chemical and pharmaceutical production bases in China. Cars, metallurgical and chemicals will continue to be the pillar industries of the municipality. Other major industries include textiles, machinery, electronics, building materials and food processing.

Tourism

The Three Gorges on the Yangtze River in the most famous tourist attraction in Chongqing. Besides the Three Gorges, famous tourist attractions include: Jinyun Mountain, Fishing Fortress, Gold Buddha Mountain, Fengdu Ghost City, Dazu Rock Carving, Hongyan Revolution Memorial Museum, and five national forest parks. In 2002, Chongqing received 46.7 million tourists, including 461,500 foreigners and generated revenue of US$218 million.

Consumer Market

Retail sales of consumer goods rose by 8.7 percent to RMB75.9 billion in 2002.

Jiafangbei Commercial District, located in the Yu-zhong District, is Chongqing's traditional commercial centre. Most major state-owned and foreign-owned department stores are situated in this district. Major department stores and shopping centres include Chongqing Department

Store, Chongqing New Century Department Store, the Metropolis Plaza, Chongqing Qunying Shopping Centre, Chongqing Pacific Department Store, Chongqing Fu'an Department Store, Chongqing Wanyou Parkson Shopping Arcade, Chongqing Yangguang Department Store, Jiafangbei Central Shopping Centre and Carrefour Direct-sale Department Store.

Foreign Trade

Chongqing's exports reached US$1.6 billion in 2003, an increase of 45.3 percent compared to 2002. This increase is largely attributed to Chongqing's burgeoning motorcycle industry. The Lifan Hongda Enterprise had exported US$25.7 million in the first quarter of 2002, an increase of 101 percent compared to the same period in 2000. Other major export goods included textiles and garment, chemicals and pharmaceuticals, foodstuff, machinery and complete plant, hand tools and other light products.

Imports reached US$1.01 billion in 2003, an increase of 43.7 percent compared to last year. Imports of car and parts accounted for 34 percent of the total, while other major categories were electronic equipment, chemical materials, steel & iron, and light industrial products. Major import sources were Japan, Hong Kong, Germany, the US and Australia.

Foreign Investment

In 2003, Chongqing approved 210 foreign-invested projects with contracted foreign investment of US$557 million. The actually utilised foreign investment remained at about US$567 million that year. About 85 percent of the city's cumulative foreign-invested projects are involved in the manufacturing sector.

An increasing number of multinationals have set up operations in Chongqing. These include Nokia, ABB, Ericsson, American Standard, Rockwell,

Honda, Suzuki, Isuzu, and Yamaha from Japan; Mobil from the US; Hutchison Whampao and Watson's Group from Hong Kong; Gold Lion Group from Malaysia; and Samsung from South Korea.

Foreign investment in tertiary industries grew rapidly in the past two years. Major investment areas include tourism, commerce, finance, telecommunications, property, transportation and infrastructure development. Many Hong Kong firms have signed joint venture contracts to develop shopping centres, as well as commercial and residential complexes in Chongqing. The Cheung Kong Group invested about RMB1.2 billion to build the Metropolis Plaza and Yanghe Garden, and is interested in investing in other infrastructure projects. Other Hong Kong corporations, including Wharf Holdings, Henderson Land, New World, and Lai Sun Group have also increased their investment in the municipality to expand market shares. Other multinationals, including Sumitomo Bank, Mitsui Bussan, Sanwa Bank, Mitsubishi Shoji from Japan; Hyosung from South Korea; Standard Chartered Bank from the UK; and Mercedes & BMW from Germany.

Priority areas for foreign investment will be on the modernisation of old enterprises and hi-tech industries, as well as the development of the tertiary sector, including such areas as export promotion, infrastructure development, finance, tourism, education, and land development. However, projects involving high-energy consumption, heavy pollution, high transport cost, heavy industrial activities and hotel development are restricted.

To boost the development of the central and western regions in China, the State Council has granted further tax incentives to foreign-invested enterprises (FIEs) in China. Under the existing policy,

FIEs are entitled to a three-year tax reduction and exemption. The new policy allows foreign-invested enterprises in the central and western regions to enjoy another three years of preferential tax rate when the current preferential term expires. The tax rate can be further reduced to 10 percent if an enterprise is proved to export more than 70 percent of its annual output in terms of value.

Opportunities for Foreign Investment

Infrastructure construction projects

This includes highways, bridges, tunnels, medium-sized and small hydropower stations, renovation of water conservancy works, irrigation works, urban construction and sewage treatment, environmental protection, and real estate development.

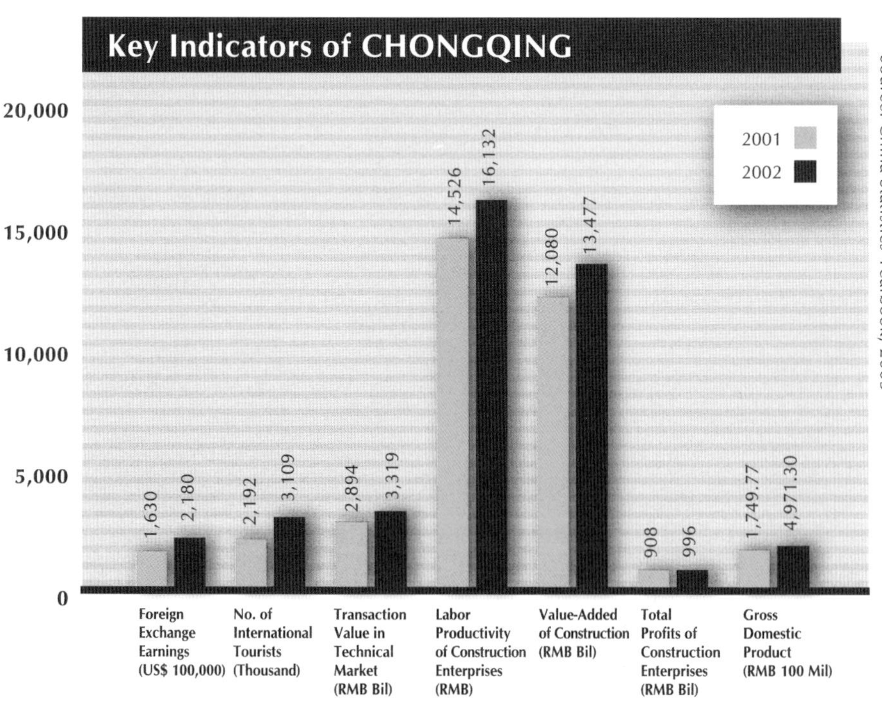

Resources development projects

Comprehensive development and in-depth processing of coal, natural resources and metal and non-metal minerals, production of raw materials.

Agricultural projects

Development of new breeds, preservation, processing, promotion and application of new technology in relation to quality grain, edible oil, vegetable and fruits; import, farming and processing of fine breeds of domestic animals, poultry and fish; development of export-oriented agricultural projects; harnessing and building of ecological environment.

Industrial projects

Readjustment and transformation of existing state-owned enterprises in industries of machinery, metallurgy, electronics, instruments, light industry, textile, chemical industry, food and building materials to improve their technological level and quality of products and enlarge their market shares; development of manufacturing industries related to electronic information facilities, environmental protection and biological medicine and of new industries with sound market prospects.

Development of tourism

Resources and construction of recreational facilities, including the development of scenic spots, improvement of travel transportation and tourist equipment, and development of tourist products.

Investment Information

Forms of Investment

Foreign investors may choose from the following alternatives:

- Enterprises solely owned by foreign investors.
- Equity joint venture.
- Contractual joint venture.
- BOT and BOO.

- Participations and domestic stock as well as the right of production.
- Leasing and contracting Chinese enterprises.
- Purchasing Chinese small and middle-sized enterprises.
- Running regional headquarters of holding companies, stock companies and multinational companies in Chongqing.
- Lending money to some Chinese enterprises.
- Other forms of investment allowed by Chinese laws.

Investment Modes

The investment of foreign funded enterprises may be paid in cash, in the form of factory buildings, equipment, other materials, land lease, industrial property rights of unique technology which are converted into money. The prices are determined by the principle of being fair and reasonable and with reference to the prices on the world market. They may also be assessed by some special institutions agreed on by both sides.

Investment Proportion

In general, the foreign funded enterprises should account for more than 25 percent of the total investment of the Joint Venture and Cooperation enterprises.

Registered Capital

The proportion of funds injected by the foreign JV partner vis-à-vis the local partner decreases with the amount of investment as follows:

Time Limit of investment

If the registered capital of foreign-funded enterprises is paid in instalments, both sides should pay 15 percent of the registered capital within three months after the business licence is issued. The rest of the investment capital shall be subscribed as follows:

- If the registered capital falls below US$500,000, the total investment should be paid up within one year after the licence is issued.

- If the registered capital is between US$500,000 and US$1 million, it should be paid up within 18 months after the licence is issued.

- If the registered capital is US$1-3 million, it should be paid up within two years after the licence is issued.

- If the registered capital is US$3-10 million, it should be paid up within three years after the licence is issued.

- If the registered capital exceeds US$10 million, the time limit is decided by the examination and approval authorities. If it is paid once, both sides should deliver the investment within six months after the licence is issued.

Duration of Contractual Joint Ventures

The duration of Contractual Joint Ventures depends on the trades and projects. It is to be negotiated by both sides. The duration of common projects is 10 to 30 years. Those projects with big investment, long-term construction and low returns could be extended to more than 30 years. The duration of the projects which acquire the right of land use through grant; transfer is decided by the duration of paid land transfer. If both sides intend to renew the limitation, applications should be submitted to the examination authorities six months before the limit is up.

Documents required in applying to establish a Foreign Invested Enterprise

Sino foreign joint venture and cooperative enterprises

Documents for establishing a project

- An application by the department in charge

- The project proposal

- An agreement signed by the partners. The legal person qualification credential and the business integrity credential of each party.

Documents for feasibility study

- An application from the department in charge for approving the feasibility report
- A project proposal and the approved document
- The feasibility report of the project signed by the partners
- The legal person qualification credential and the business integrity credential of each party.
- An asset-evaluation letter of the national asset administration on department for the Chinese state-owned enterprise if it invests through assets.

Documents for the approval of the contracts and provisions

- Reports from the departments concerned for the approval of the contracts and statutes
- A project proposal and approved documents
- A feasibility report of the project and approved document
- Contracts and statutes of the jointly-operated enterprise and relevant appendixes.
- The legal person qualification credential and the business integrity credential of each party.
- A list of imported equipment
- A name list of the board of directors of the jointly-operated enterprise, members of the board of directors, letters of appointment of the general manager and vice-general manager and their identity certificates.
- The approved notice of the name of the enterprise issued by the Administration department of Industry and Commerce for the Chinese state-owned enterprise if it invests through assets.
- An asset-evaluation letter of the national asset administration department

- Other relevant necessary documents

Wholly foreign-owned enterprise

Documents for establishing a project:

- A feasibility report of the project
- Legal certificate of foreign investor
- The capital credit certificate of a foreign businessman

Documents for the approval of statutes

- A feasibility report of the project and a written approval of relevant department
- An application form for establishing a foreign-invested enterprise
- Statutes of the foreign-invested enterprise
- The corporate organisation certificate and the capital credit certificate of the foreign business man
- The statement of income of foreign investors in the most recent three years.
- Plan for foreign exchange balance of the venture.
- A list of imported equipment
- A name list of the board of directors of the foreign-invested enterprise and the members of it, letters of appointment of the general manager and the assistant general manager and their identity certificates.
- The approved notice of the name of the foreign-invested enterprise issued by the Administrative Department of Industry and Commerce.
- Other relevant necessary documents.

Documents for Industrial and Commercial registration of foreign-invested enterprises

- an application form of the foreign invested enterprise

- an application letter of registration by the chairman of the board of directors of the foreign invested enterprise
- a feasibility report of the project and the approval
- an application form of establishing the foreign-invested enterprise
- Contracts, statutes, approvals and instruments of ratification
- The Corporate organisation certificate and the capital credit certificate of the investors
- A name list of the board of directors, members of the board of directors, letters of appointment of the general manager and the vice-general manager and their identity certificates
- Land-leasing documents
- Other necessary documents

Procedures for setting up offices of foreign enterprises

Preparing Documents

The following written documents should be provided if a foreign enterprise or economic organisation is to establish an office (or representative office) in Chongqing:

- Application signed by the chairman of the board of directors or the general manager.
- The legal certificate for registration is issued by its country (a duplicate).
- Capital credit certificate issued by the bank which has the business relation with the enterprise (an original).
- The letter of authority signed by the chairman of the board of directors or the general manager, the resume and ID card of the chief delegate (photocopy).
- Filling two forms "Application Form of setting up External Representative Offices of Foreign Enterprise" and the form "Declaration Form for the Personnel of the External

Representative Office of Foreign Enterprise"

- Other Materials required by the ratification authorities.

- The aforesaid documents and certificates should be five copies, either in Chinese or in English plus Chinese version. The letter of application should include: a brief introduction of the enterprise, the purpose of establishing the resident representative office, name, staff, range of business, time limits, the address and so on.

Application

With all the documents ready, the foreign enterprise shall entrust Chongqing Service Centre for Foreign Investors with the application procedures, or it can entrust the application procedures to a foreign trade business company economic organisation with the right of foreign trade. The entrusted units shall present the application documents, plus the official letter by the entrustee, to Chongqing Foreign Economic Relation and Trade Commission.

Ratification

Upon the receipt of the application documents for the establishment of representative office of foreign enterprises, Chongqing Foreign Economic Relation and Trade Commission shall, according to the regulations of the State, examine the application documents, ratify the application, and then issue the letter of ratification.

Registration

When the application for the establishment of external representative office of the foreign enterprise has been approved, one should within 30 days take the letter of ratification to the local administration office of Industry and Commerce for Registration, and obtain "Registration Certificate of External Representative Office of Foreign Enterprises" then go to public security bureau, taxes bureau, the customs office, exchange control administration and such govern-mental departments for the relevant formalities and procedures.

"One-Stop" Service Centre for Foreign Investment Service Range

- Receive and conduct the necessary procedures for the establishment of "Three Types of Enterprises with Foreign Investment", including the examination and ratification of project proposal and report on feasibility of project, the examination and ratification of company contract and company regulations, preliminary registration of company name and business registration, registrations with tax bureau, finance bureau and exchange control administration, registration for the customs for the record and so on.
- Provide consulting service and clarification of relevant policies.
- Accept pertinent complaints and coordinate in the solution of the problems concerned.
- Implement collectively the annual survey to the "Three Types of Enterprises with Foreign Investment".

Working Procedures

The Service Centre is located in the Foreign Trade Building, under the administration of Chongqing Foreign Economic Relation and Trade Commission. The range of services includes examination, ratification and administration of foreign investment enterprises in the Service Centre. The departments are Foreign Economic Relation and Trade Com-mission, Planning Commission, Economic Com-mission, Urban & Rural Construction Commission, Administration for Industry and Commerce, Finance Bureau, State Taxes Administration Bureau, Local Taxes Administration Bureau, Bureau of Labour, Exchange Control Administration, City Planning Bureau, Land Bureau, Administration of the Customs and Public Security Bureau.

Direct Service

All the procedures from the affirmation of project proposal to the receipt of licences and certificates of registration can be completed within the "One-Stop" Service Centre. The examination and ratification, the registrations of the foreign investment projects shall be completed within certain working days by the municipal governmental departments concerned. When the project proposed is in compliance with the regulations, the processing of the business permit will take up to nine working days to complete, while the processing of tax and custom registration will take up to five working days. If the project proposed need to be transferred to the departments of the Central Government to be examined and ratified, the transfer period may take up to nine working days.

Service through Agency

Foreign investors can engage the service of the accredited service agency on the implementation of related service work. Chongqing Service Centre for Foreign Investors and Chongqing Xingcheng Service Centre for Foreign Investors are the two accredited service agencies.

GUANGXI

This autonomous region's unique geographical advantages and sound foundation is the gateway for foreign investors and traders to southwest China.

GUANGXI Fact Sheet	2003
Area (km²)	236,660
No. of Cities	21
Population (mil)	48.6
GDP (RMB bn)	237.3
Gross capital formation (RMB bn)	87.7
Consumption expenditure (RMB bn)	170
~Household	116
~Government	54
No. of employed persons (mil)	26.01
Unemployment Rate	3.6%
Literacy Rate	91.4%
Government revenue (RMB bn)	20.4
Government expenditure (RMB bn)	43.9
Per capita annual	
~disposable income of urban residents (RMB '000)	7.8
~net income of rural households (RMB '000)	2.1
~living expenditure of urban residents (RMB '000)	5.8
~living expenditure of rural residents (RMB '000)	1.8
Actually Used Foreign Direct Investment (USD mil)	456
Total assets (RMB bn)	25.5
Exports (USD mil)	1,970
~percentage of change from the same period of previous year	+30.7%
Imports (USD mil)	1,222
~percentage of change from the same period of previous year	+32.2%

History

Towards the end of the Old Stone Age about 50,000 years ago, primitive men appeared in Guangxi. Today's Zhuang people are the descendents of the Xizhen and Luyue branches of the ancient Baiyue tribe, so they are Guangxi's oldest nationality. In 214 B.C., Qin Shi Huang set up three countries in Guangxi,namely, Guilin, Xiangjun and Nanhai. Guilin was the administrative centre of the region; hence the name of "Gui" for Guangxi. During the Song Dynasty, the whole country was divided into several regions, where the present Guangxi was the western part of the then Guangxi.

During the Song Dynasty, the whole country was divided into several regions. The present Guangxi was the western part of the then Guangnan region and was named the western Guangnan region, with its administrative centre in Guilin. "Guangxi" has since become an administrative region. After the founding of the People's Republic of China in 1949, the People's Government of Guangxi Province was established on 8th February, 1950. In 1958, with the approval of the State Council, Guangxi Zhuang Autonomous Region was set up.

Geography

Guangxi Autonomous Region is a provincial-level administrative region that lies on China's southwestern part. It is one of China's five provincial-level national autonomous regions. To its east is Guangdong province, and the Beibu Bay of the South China Sea lies along its southern coastal region with its southwest borders Vietnam. The Autonomous Region has an area of 236,700 km^2. Situated in the southeast ring of the Yunnan-Guizhou Plateau, the highest point of Guangxi stands at 2,141 metres above sea level. It shares a 1,020 kilometres border with Vietnam.

Guangxi also has a coastline, including many bays and estuaries, of 1,595 kilometres. Lying between Southwest Asia and the rest of southwest China, it is an increasingly important gateway connecting these regions. In May 1992, the Chinese government decided to "let Guangxi play its full role as a passage to the coast for the southwestern region". As a result, Guangxi has since reaffirmed its strategic position in boosting a coordinated development of the southwest China in the country's opening-up drive. Guangxi is also the only ethnic autonomous region that has access to both a sea and a land border.

Climate

Guangxi has a humid subtropical monsoon climate, which is characterised by plenty of sunshine, moderately high temperatures and abundant precipitation. The Tropic of Cancer runs across its central part. The average annual temperature ranges from 16°C to 22.7°C. Winter is mild and short. Spring usually comes early and the summer tends to be quite hot. Its warm climate is ideal for subtropical plants and crops. Even in winter, when much of the rest of the country is covered in snow, most places in Guangxi are still luxuriantly green.

Ethnic Groups

There are 12 nationalities in Guangxi, the Zhuang, Han, Yao, Miao, Dong, Mulao, Maonan, Jing, Hui, Shui, Yi and Gelao. There are also 25 smaller ethnic groups in the region. Guangxi has a population of 48.6 million, of whom 15.18 million are Zhuangs, the largest of China's 55 ethnic groups. Each ethnic group has its own language, and their customs, food, housing and clothing vary greatly. The colourful traditional customs and diverse cultures add much to Guangxi's attractiveness.

Natural Resources

Guangxi is rich in mineral resources, especially high quality metal ores, Guangxi, one of China's 10 major metal production bases, is known as the "Home of Metals". About 100 types of minerals have been found and amongst them, about 70 of the reserves proven. The reserves of 53 such minerals are among the 10 largest in the country. The reserves of 14 minerals are the largest in China. (The region's reserves of manganese and tin accounts respectively for one third of the country's total.)

Ranking among the second and sixth are 25 such minerals, of which the reserve of antimony constitutes one fourth of China's total. Famous big mines include the aluminium base in Pingguo, the tin mine in Danchang and the manganese mine in Laibin. These mines have big potential for further development.

Guangxi has many torrential rivers with an estimated 21.33 million kW of hydraulic power, which could theoretically support 856 power stations each with a minimum generating capacity of 500kW. This would amount to an annual generating capacity of 78.8 billion kWh for Guangxi. The Hongshui River which is known as the "rich ore" of water resources in China, has an average annual flow 2.8

times greater than that of the Yellow River; 10 step hydroelectric stations could be built along this river. So far, six stations are being built along this river, with an annual generating capacity of over 56.2 billion kWh.

Guangxi has 129,200 km^2 of sea, which is rich in marine resources. It has nearly 600 different fish species, 50 species more than the East China Sea. In its shallow seabeds live 149 types of marine mammals and plants. Guangxi is also known for its Southern Pearls, which are both roundly plump and valuable. The basin area in the Beibu Bay of the South China Sea is also rich in oil and natural gas.

Guangxi's mild climate is ideal for a great variety of animals and plants. The region has over 1,670 genera of plants in 280 different families, nearly 8,000 types of plants. 34.37 percent of Guangxi is covered by forests, including over 30 types of rare and precious trees. Guangxi also has 729 species of vertebrates, 40 of which are under state protection. With over 700 types of fruit, Guangxi is a fruit lover's paradise: pineapples, litchi, longan and mango are the most popular.

Regional Autonomy

Guangxi Zhuang Autonomous Region was set up in 1958. Since then, a number of autonomous countries and townships have been established in the region for ethnic groups. Today, Guangxi has 12 autonomous countries and 62 minority tonwships. Six of them are Yao nationality autonomous countries, the Miao, Dong, Mulao and Maonan each has one county, and two countries are for a variety of ethnic groups.

Guangxi's regional autonomy is ensured by the Constitution of the People Republic of China and the Law of National Regional Autonomy of the People's government. The region is governed by the People's Congress of Guangxi Zhuang Autonomous Region, its Standing Committee and the People's Republic of

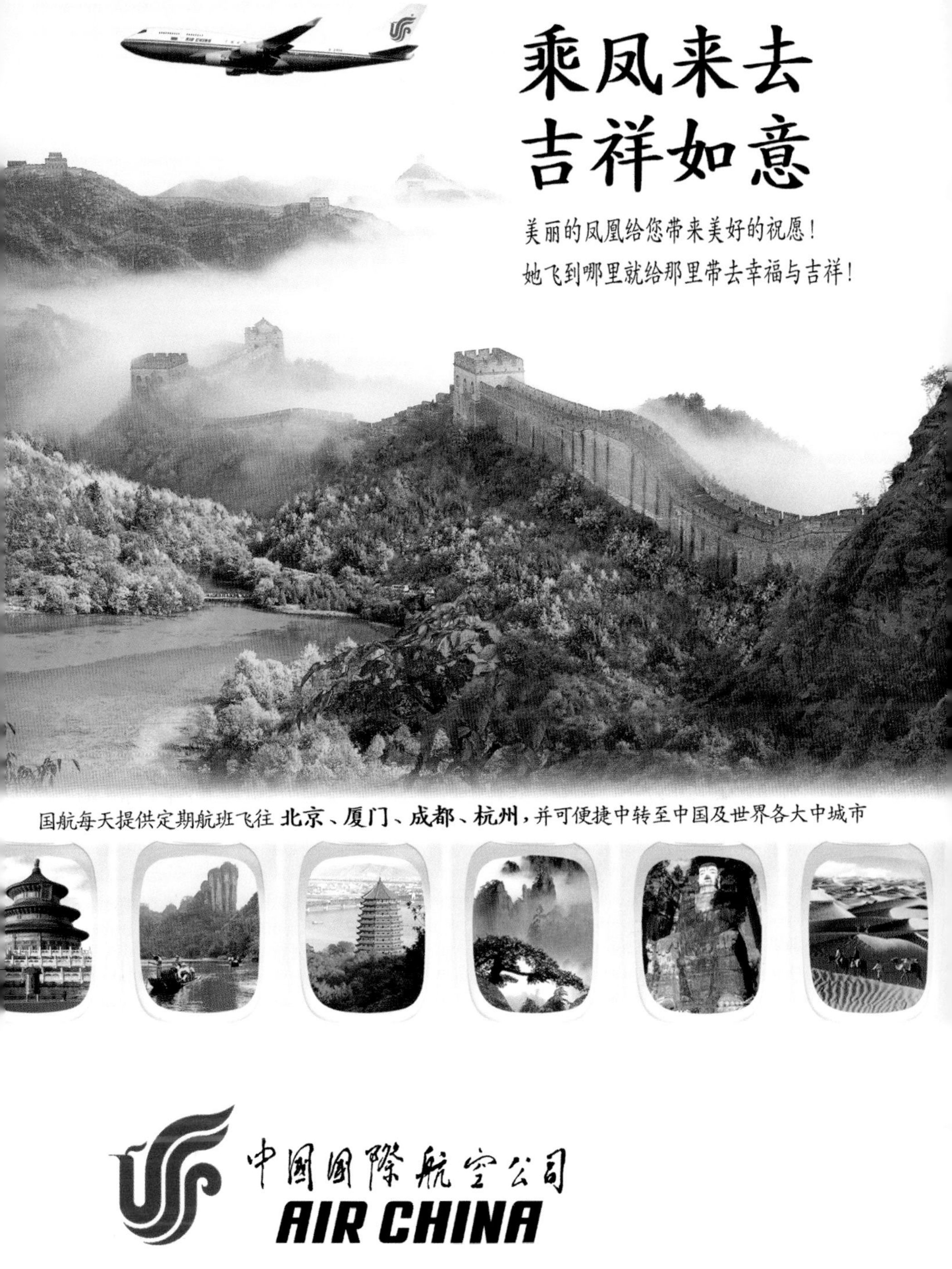

China. The right to autonomy is mainly embodied in the fields of politics, economics, finance, culture and education.

The election of delegates to the People's Congress of the Autonomous Region is arranged to ensure that the proportions of representatives from the Zhuang and other minorities are larger than their shares of the region's population. The region's government organs at various levels should have cadres from the Zhuang and other ethnic groups when there is a need or the possibility of doing so. As a result, ethnic groups account for 38 percent of the region's population, but delegates from ethnic groups constitute 46 percent of the delegates to the Autonomous Region's People's Congress, Cadres from ethnic groups amount to 39 percent of the region's total. The Guangxi government has paid great attention to the use and the development of the ethnic languages. In 1957, written Zhuang and Han became an official language used in communities, enterprises, institutions and schools.

Administrative Divisions

The Region has set up nine autonomous municipalities: Nanning, Liuzhou, Guilin, Wuzhou, Beihai, Qinzhou, Fangchenggang, Guigang and Yuling; six prefectures: Nanning, Liuzhou, Guilin, Hezhou, Baise and Hechi. There are 81 countries and cities, including 12 ethnic autonomous countries and 10 country-level cities. The region's capital is Nanning.

Science and Education

Forty years ago, Guangxi had only four research institutions and fewer than 100 professional technical workers. Now its science and technology work force is growing stronger every day. As many as 200 scientific research institutions are in operation, employing a total of 740,000 people. Guangxi set up more than 3,000 research associations at various levels that now boast a combined membership of over 400,000. The region has made remarkable achievements in natural science, technology, international cooperation, oceanic exploration, hydrology, meteorology, and social science. Some projects come up to advanced world standards.

These rapid advances in science and technology have been made possible by Guangxi's improvement in education. The nine years of compulsory education takes place in 16,077 primary schools and 3,055 high schools. The attendance rate of school-age children has reached 98.5 percent. Adults can pursue more advanced studies in 30 institutions of higher learning and 147 polytechnic schools. Adult residents of 96 percent of Guangxi's rural areas have access to the 1,272 village technical schools. In addition, a total of 533 schools throughout the region offer vocational training and 45 schools provide special education.

Of the 30 institutions of higher learning in Guangxi, nine offer post-graduate courses. They have advanced research facilities and serve to nurture the region's scientists and teachers. Guangxi has paid careful attention to education of its ethnic minority groups. In addition to the 11 preparatory schools, the region has established three universities, 31 junior colleges and 187 primary and high schools, all exclusively enrolling minority students. These students account for 39.8 percent of the student population in Guangxi, and minority teachers make up 36.7 percent of the whole faculty.

Opening Up to the Outside World

Since China adopted its policy of reform and opening, international trade in Guangxi has developed significantly, with 102.6 billion in 2002. Exports were expanded to include 17 product categories with more than 2,600 varieties of goods. Also in 2002, 1,363,400 overseas tourists visited the region, which accounts for a 7.6 percent increase over the previous year, bringing in foreign exchange income US$321 million, representing a decrease of 6.6 percent over 2001. The number of overseas investment contract signed as well as the number of active foreign investment projects in Guangxi both ranked among China's top in 2002. It has formed trade relations with over 5,000 companies from 130 countries and regions, and has established agencies with nearly 220 overseas trade organisations. Guangxi has also set up 62 trade units in a number of countries and regions, including the United States, Japan, France, Germany, Singapore, Panama, Gambia, as well as Hong Kong and Macau.

Liberalisation Policy

By the beginning of 1997, Guangxi had set up 14 open zones. These are the three coastal cities of Beihai, Fangchenggang and Nanning; the six coastal economic zones of Wuzhou, Yulin, Qinzhou, Cangwu, Dongxin and Hepu; a national tourism area known as Beihai; and two national high-tech development zones, i.e. Guilin and Nanning. There are also 34 development zones of various kinds, 16 first-grade open ports, 12 second-grade open ports, 12 border ports and 25 border trading sites.

Eight of Guangxi's counties, cities and districts share borders with Vietnam. Of the 12 border ports, Pingxiang, Youyiguan, Dongxing and Shuikou are classified as first-grade. In addition, there are 25 frontier trading sites. All border ports and trading sites are connected by highways,and the Hunan-Guangxi Railway links with Vietnam's railway so that trains can travel direct to Hanoi. The open border areas in Guangxi provide excellent opportunities for southwestern China to conduct bilateral or multilateral trade, and export processing with Vietnam and other South Asian countries.

Economic Development, Industries and Agriculture

With China's economic reform, Guangxi has been witnessing a rapid economic expansion. Its GDP grew at an average annual rate of 7.2 percent between 1980 and 2002. Since 1993, Guangxi has actively promoted an array of important reform measures, accelerating its market liberalisation and steadily raising people's living standards. From 1992 to 1997, the region's GDP increased at an average annual rate of 14.3 percent. In 2002, primary industry expanded 4.2 percent while secondary industry grew 8 percent. Tertiary industry, i.e., the service sector, increased 11.11 percent over the previous year.

Prior to 1949, there were only 706 workshops in Guangxi with very little mechanisation. Today, it

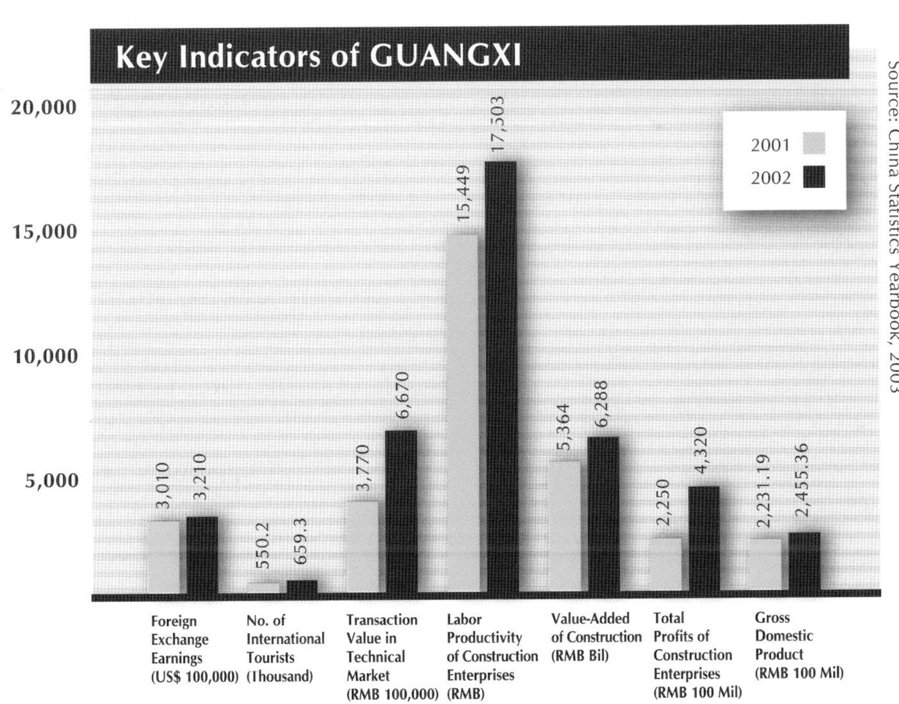

boasts a relatively complete industrial structure comprising coal, electricity, chemicals, medicines, light manufacturing, textiles, metallurgy, non-ferrous metals, machinery, cars, sugar refining, building materials, rubber, electronics and foodstuff. The region ranks first in China in terms of sugar refining with an annual production of over two million tons. Its production and sales of mini-cars and charging cranes also rank first in the country, with nationwide market shares of 25 percent and 20 percent respectively. Guangxi Yuchai Machinery Company Limited has developed into China's largest production base of diesel engines for mid-sized trucks. The region's production of non-ferrous metals and cement also leads the country. In 2002, Guangxi's industrial increment was RMB118 billion, up 44.6 percent over the previous year. "Heiwulei" foodstuff, "Sanjin" medicines and daily necessities from the "Liangmianzhen" company are famous throughout China.

Guangxi is a mountainous region. It has a pleasant, subtropical climate. With limited flat land, the potential for increasing grain yields is limited, so much of the agricultural effort goes into promoting industrial crops that suits the local conditions. It is one of China's top producers of sugar, meat, eggs, fruit, tea and aquatic products. In the meantime, Guangxi's township enterprises have quickened their structural reform; this has provided an important economic impetus for the whole region. It has also promoted the urbanisation of the rural areas. Farmers' incomes have increased greatly and their living standards have significantly improved. In 2002, the average net annual income of farmers was RMB1,944, up 4.3 percent over 1996.

Transportation and Telecommunication

Guangxi has very convenient telecommunication services. All post offices in the region offer efficient telegraph, fax, data exchange, domestic and international express mail srvice, domestic and international direct dial, money deposit and information services. Guangxi is connected with the country's main commercial, financial and academic data networks. The region is integrated into the national telecommunications systems through optic-fibre cable, satellites and microwave transmission.

The total installed telephone capacity in Guangxi is 4.2 million lines. Since 1993, program-controlled telephone systems were available in every county in Guangxi. The post office paging service now operates in almost all inhabited parts of the region. By the end of 1996, mobile phones could be used in every county, as every county was linked by fibre-optic cable. The telephone exchange network and digital network extend to all counties and cities in Guangxi. The total workload and the income of the telecommunications service are still above the national average. By 2002, the telephone network in the region was enlarged to a great extent, providing service to 4.1 million telephone customers, 4.3 million customers of mobile phone and 1,093,400 internet users. In 2002, telephone was available in 13,037 villages, accounting for 87.7 percent of the region's total.

With its vision to become "an important gateway to the sea in southwestern China", upgrading transportation infrastructure has therefore long been a priority for Guangxi. The region now has an integrated transportation system combining harbours, rivers, roads and air transport. The region has an excellent highway network, reaching out to almost every township. It also has expressways linking Guilin and Liuzhou, Qinzhou and Fangcheng. More first-class highways are being planned, some of which are already under construction.

Due to the mountainous terrain, transportation in Guangxi was very difficult in the past. Before the founding of the People's Republic, the region had only two railways with a total length of 573 kilometres. This has changed after 1949. The region now has three major railways linking with other parts of the country with numerous feeder lines reaching to almost every part of Guangxi. There are also six local railways and a group of specialised railways. This means the southwestern provinces and mountainous areas in the western part of Gaungxi can now transport their abundant raw materials and products to ports on the coast of Guangxi for shipment to other countries and parts of China.

Air transportation is convenient and fast. Guangxi now has airports at Guilin, Nanning, Beihai, Liuzhou and Wuzhou. All are equipped with advanced navigation and telecommunication systems. The region has opened 93 domestic and 3 international air routes. A network of routes is formed with Nanning and Guilin as the core airports linking with major cities of China. Guangxi has also opened up direct flights between Nanning and Hong Kong, Hanoi and Bangkok,; and from Guilin to Hong Kong, Macau, Fukuoka and Seoul.

Port Construction

The building of Guangxi's ports is a good example of the region's achievements in developing its economy and transportation. The region's opening up is greatly facilitated by its well-sheltered, deep water ports, 21 of which could be further developed. Beihai has already constructed four berths for 10,000-ton ships. Fangcheng, Qinzhou, Tieshan and Zhenzhu could also build berths for 10,000-ton vessels. Fangcheng Port has built 26 berths, of which nine can take at least ten 10,000-ton ships. In addition to its two berths for ships of 10,000-ton, Qinzhou Ports plans to build 18 berths, five of which will be for ships up to 10,000-ton ships. Guangxi's three major ports are among the best cargo trans-shipment centres in southwestern China, with regular routes to Hong Kong, Macau, Southeast Asia and Indo-Chinese Peninsula (it is about 500 nautical miles to Hong Kong, 150 nautical miles to northern Vietnam and 800 nautical miles to Ho Chi Minh City). There are also direct sailings to the Persian Gulf and Western Europe. The Nanning-Kunming Railway has gone into operation. Railways run to the three major ports of Beihai, Qinzhou and Fangcheng.

The region has also 106 inland river ports including Wuzhou, Guigang, Nanning, Liuzhou, Baise and Guiping. The Xinjiang River, running through Wuzhou, Guigang, Liuzhou, Nanning, Guilin and Baise, is regarded as a golden waterway linking the inland areas if southwest China with Guangdong, Hong Kong, Macau and Southeast Asia. After the realignment of the Xinjiang Waterway, 1,000-ton vessels can now sail directly from Nanning to Hong Kong and Macau. Wuzhou port is an inland river port of national standard. It is 436 kilometres by river from Wuzhou to Hong Kong and 384 kilometres to Macau. Giving full play to the Xinjiang Waterway will facilitate the opening-up drive in Guangxi and other parts of southwest China.

Development Plans

Southwestern China is a huge market with a population of 200 million people and abundant aboveground and underground resources. The Chinese government has adopted a strategy that gives priority to the economic development of central and western China, thus opening up a vast range of prospects for Guangxi's further advancement. The local government has established several goals striving to meet by the turn of the century. It seeks to boost total domestic output value to three times of the 1980 figure; per capita annual net income of 2,600 yuan for farmers; and per capita annual income of living expenses of 6,000 yuan for urban residents. Total domestic output value is projected to rise 10 percent annually from 1998 to 2010, while the region continues to bolster its comprehensive economic strength. To achieve these goals, Guangxi has examined local, regional, and global conditions and established its "Three Strategies, Six Breakthroughs" policy.

The Three Strategies

Regional Economy Strategy: set up five economic zones of various characteristics based upon local attributes and economic distribution.

They are:

1. Southern Guangxi Coastal Economic Zone, which focuses on port economy, marine industry and high-tech industry;
2. Central Guangxi Economic Zone, centering on industry;
3. Northern Guangxi Economic zone, which features tourism, farming and forestry;
4. Eastern Guangxi Economic Zone, which emphasizes modern agriculture, township enterprises and export industry;
5. Western Guangxi Economic Zone, targeting agriculture and mining industry.

Opening Promotion Strategy: Make full use of the geographical advantages of the coastal and border areas; open further to the outside world in both scope and level of contact; further develop the export-oriented economy; and absorb more foreign investment, technology, personnel and management techniques in order to speed the economic development of the autonomous region as a whole.

Major Breakthrough Strategy: Give priority to the key issues that are of vital importance to the region's overall reform and development. Work to modernize ideology, optimize the economic structure, transform the economic system, open further to the outside world, integrate science and technology with economic development, and train personnel.

The Six Breakthroughs

1. Emancipate the mind, be practical and realistic in work, and update ideology.

2. With agriculture as the base and rapid industrialisation as a focus, optimise the economic structure.

3. Step up reform and transform the economic system

4. With a strong base in the coastal areas, open further to international trade and investment.

5. Combine scientific and technological development with economic development.

6. Establish and perfect the employment mechanism by creating an ideal personnel training and employment environment.

Guangxi's designated coastal economic zones of Nanning, Beihai, Qinzhou and Fangchenggang will act as new industrial bases in southwestern China. They will also serve as important centers for China to open up Southeast Asian markets. The Guangxi regional government will adopt preferential policies for these areas and give priority to the development of the power industry, coastal industries and port trade. Now the region is working to establish the Beihai Bonded Area and the Nanning Economic and Technological Development Zone; improve the

Guangxi's designated coastal economic zones of Nanning, Beihai, Qinzhou and Fangchenggang will act as new industrial bases in southwestern China. They will also serve as important centers for China to open up to Southeast Asian markets.

traffic conditions from Beihai to Yulin and Wuzhou; and open expressways to Guangdong Province, Hong Kong and Macau.

In the next few years, by taking full advantage of its assets, Guangxi will conduct a number of major projects covering agriculture, forestry, water conservancy, power generation, telecommunications, tourism, trade, city construction, environmental protection and science and technology.

Key Industries

The dominant industries in Guangxi are:

- Power industry with hydropower as the mainstay;
- Non-ferrous metal industry (the output of 10 leading products came to 523,100 tons, worth 10.37 billion yuan);
- Building materials industry (cement, plate glass, ceramic, granite and marble); and
- Machinery industry (car, internal-combustion engine, engineering machines, agricultural machines, electric devices, petrochemical equipment, heavy-duty machines for mining, packaging equipment, equipment for sugar producing, power-generating equipment)

Opportunity for Foreign Investment

The sectors that local government encourages foreign investment include infrastructure, basic industries, high-tech industry, export-oriented production bases, comprehensive agriculture projects and technical innovation of old enterprises.

The local government encourages foreign investment in projects on the construction of Hongshui River hydropower station and other hydro and thermal power stations, river and sea ports, rail roads and high-grade highways. Those projects in which foreign investment has been permitted include real estates and the development of large pieces of land. Those belonging to the tertiary industry will be opened to foreign investment step by step, and include: finance, trade, transportation and tourism. Township and private enterprises are encouraged to make efforts to lure foreign investment or do manufacturing with imported materials and models.

The existing enterprises are encouraged to create technical innovation by using overseas funds. While establishing Sino-foreign joint ventures or corporations, the Chinese side is permitted to be a shareholding partner in terms of land, workshop, equipment and property. These enterprises may try a new system called one factory, two systems. Under this system, a state-owned enterprise may allow one or several of its subsidiaries to have joint venture with foreign partners. The foreign partner may contribute to the joint-venture via technology transfer. Foreign investors are encouraged to contractually run Chinese enterprises of state, collective and private ownership.

Foreign investors are encouraged to develop large stretches of land, where infrastructure has not been constructed yet. After acquiring land licenses, the foreign developers are permitted to do all the planning and designing, except post and tele-communication and port construction. Those construction projects in the foreign-developed zone, which do not fit in with the local government's general plan of civil engineering, should be submitted to the government departments concerned for examination and approval.

The land-use period for foreign developers may be as long as 70 years, during which time the land can be transferred, leased and mortgaged. The foreign developers are allowed to enjoy a 10-30 percent discount in paying the land-use fees.

INNER MONGOLIA

Its reserves of rare earth amount to 84 million tons, or 80 percent of the world's total.

INNER MONGOLIA Fact Sheet	2003
Area (km²)	1,180,000
No. of Cities	20
Population (mil)	23.8
GDP (RMB bn)	209.3
Gross capital formation (RMB bn)	84.7
Consumption expenditure (RMB bn)	109
~Household	83
~Government	27
No. of employed persons (mil)	10.1
Unemployment Rate	4.5%
Literacy Rate	88.1%
Government revenue (RMB bn)	13.8
Government expenditure (RMB bn)	46.9
Per capita annual	
~disposable income of urban residents (RMB '000)	7.0
~net income of rural households (RMB '000)	2.3
~living expenditure of urban residents (RMB '000)	4.9
~living expenditure of rural residents (RMB '000)	1.6
Actually Used Foreign Direct Investment (US$ mil)	368
Total assets (RMB bn)	14.5
Exports (USD mil)	1,160
~percentage of change from the same period of previous year	+43.3%
Imports (USD mil)	1,673
~percentage of change from the same period of previous year	+2.4%

Geography

It stretches 2,400 km (about 1,491 miles) from west to east and 1,700 km (1,056 miles) from north to south. Inner Mongolia traverses northeast, north and northwest China. The third largest among China's provinces, municipalities and autonomous regions, the region covers an area of 1.18 million km2 (about 455,598 square miles) or 12.3 percent of the country's territory. It is surrounded by eight provinces and regions in its south, east and west, and Mongolia and Russia in the north, with a borderline of 4,200 km (about 2,610 miles). Besides hills, plains, deserts, rivers and lakes, Inner Mongolia has plateau land forms. These land forms, includes the Inner Mongolia Plateau which is the second largest among the four major plateaus in the country, are mostly over 1,000 metres (about 13,780 feet) above sea level.

Climate

Inner Mongolia has a temperate

continental climate. The spring is warm and windy; summer short and hot with many rainy days; autumn usually sees early frost and plummeting temperature and the winter is long and bitter cold with frequent polar outbreaks. The region has an annual precipitation of 100-500 mm, 80-150 frost-free days and 2,700 hours of sunshine. The Greater Hinggan Mountains and the Yinshan Mountains divide the regions into areas with different climates. The area east of the Greater Hinggan Mountains and north of the Yinshan Mountains has lower temperature and less precipitation than the opposite area.

Natural Resources

Flora and Fauna

Inner Mongolia has 2,351 species of plants including vegetation of arbors, shrubs and herbs. It is home to over 117 species of wild animals and 362 species of birds. Among them, 49 species are under state and regional protection and 10 species are precious and rare.

Hydropower

Inner Mongolia has water resources of 90.3 billion cubic metres, of which 67.5 billion is surface water. Nearly 1,000 rivers run in the region with 107 of them averaging a valley area of more than 1,000 km^2 each. Inner Mongolia boasts of mineral water and springs with medical value. It has a total water area of 984,300 hectares, including 655,000 hectares of fresh water, which accounts for 10.68 percent of the country's total fresh water area.

Forests, Grasslands and Cultivated Land

The region has 7.22 million hectares (17,840,937 acres) of cultivated land which is equivalent to 6.11 percent of the country's total cultivated land; 86.66 million hectares of grasslands, equivalent to 73.3 percent of the country's total grasslands, and 18.66 million hectares of forests, which is 15.8 % of the country's total forests.

Minerals

More than 120 kinds of the world's total 140 minerals have been found in the region. Five of them have the largest deposits in China and 65 of which rank among the top 10 of their kinds in the country. The reserves of rare earth amount to 84.59 million tons, which is equivalent to 80 percent of the world's total and over 90 percent of the country's total. The proven deposits of coal hit 224.75 billion tons, the second largest in the country.

The region has large reserves of ferrous metals, non-ferrous metals, precious metals, industrial chemicals and non-mental minerals. It also has abundant oil and natural gas. 13 large oil and gas fields have been discovered with expected oil reserves of 2-3 billion tons and gas reserves of 1,000 billion m^3. The minerals (excluding oil and natural gas) in the region have a potential value of RMB13,000 billion, accounting for 10 percent of the country's total volume and the third largest in the country.

Tourism

Inner Mongolia is rich in tourist attractions. With its colourful ethnic culture, grassland scenery, virgins forests in the Greater Hinggan Mountains, grand views along the Yellow River, the majestic Xiangsha Gulf, rivers, lakes and springs, these factors make Inner Mongolia a wonderful and interesting place to visit. Inner Mongolia is the home to the Mausoleum of Genghis Khan, the Zhaojun Tomb, the ancient Great Wall, Wudang Monastery at the bottom of the Yinshan Mountains, Wuta Monastery, Bailing Temple, and tomb murals dating back to the Eastern Han Dynasty (25-220).

Ethnicity

49 ethnic groups live in Inner Mongolia, including the Mongolian, Han, Manchu, Hui, Daur, Ewenki, Oroqen and Korean. The region is inhabited by 3.97 million Mongolians, 18.75 million

Hans and 900,010 of other groups. The rural population reaches 13.78 million with 11.87 million in villages and 1.91 million in pastoral areas.

Education

Inner Mongolia has 500,000 technicians, 140,000 of whom has received senior and middle-level technical certificates. It has 324 scientific and technological research centres. In 2000, 71 counties in the region had implemented the nine-year compulsory educational campaign to eliminate illiteracy among young and middle-aged people.

As many as 99.44 percent of children of school age receive school education, 96.6 percent of children of secondary-school age enter junior middle school and 60 percent of them graduates. Inner Mongolia has 72,000 university

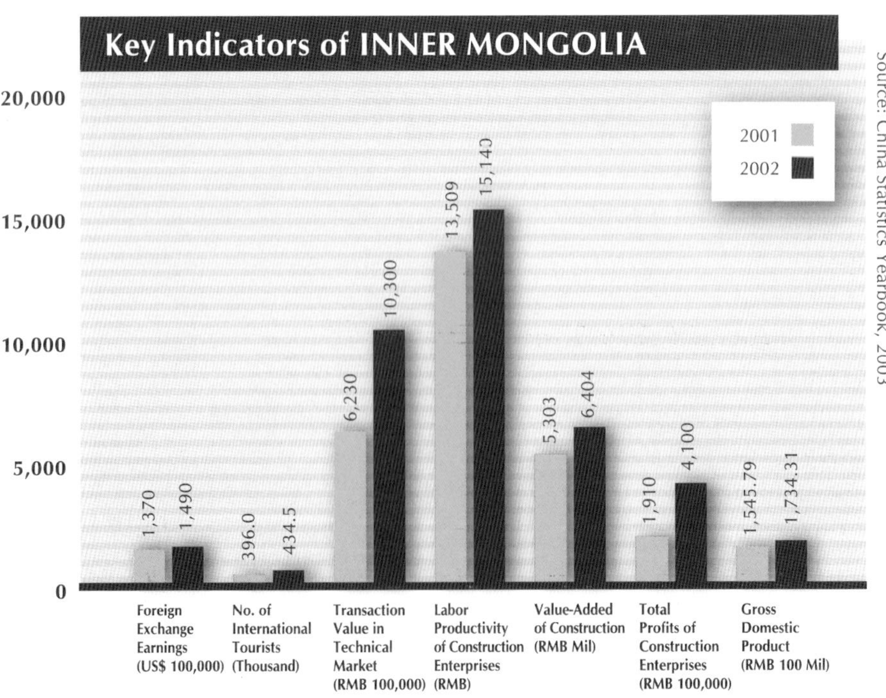

students. The percentage of literate middle-aged and young people has reached 96.8 percent.

In 2002, the region had 1,762 middle schools, including 1,381 junior secondary schools and 381 senior secondary schools; 425 polytechnic middle schools, including 269 junior polytechnic secondary schools and 156 senior polytechnic secondary schools; 21 universities and colleges, and 12 adult education schools.

Economy

Inner Mongolia has national iron and steel and coal production bases. In addition, it has industries of forest, farm produce processing, electricity, machinery, chemicals, electronics, textile, sugar, paper making and light industry. It has developed agriculture and animal husbandry. The region is a national production base of cash grain, oil and sugar. It is also an important animal husbandry base, ranking top among the five major pastoral areas in the country.

Key Industries

The key industries are farm production and processing as well as animal husbandry, energy, metallurgy and chemicals.

Urban and Rural Income

From 1989 to 1997, Inner Mongolia was the poorest in China in terms of the disposable per capita income of urbanites and rural residents. In 1999 it ranked 22nd in the country. In 2000 the disposable per capita income of rural residents hit RMB1950 (US$238), with an annual increasing rate of 5 percent.

Infrastructure

Railways

The region has 14 main national and 12 feeder railways as well as five local railways, with a total length of 7,083 km. The density is 59.9 km/10,000 km^2. The Beijing-Tonghua, Beijing-Baotou and Baotou-Lanzhou railways trasverse west to east through the province, which link the northeast, north and northwest of China.

Manzhouli and Erenhot, two large land ports in the region, connect the region with Russia and Mongolia, and European countries.

Inner Mongolia has conducted trade, economic and technological cooperation with nearly 100 countries and regions in the world. Trade with Russia and Mongolia thrives.

Highways

It has a total length of 63,000 km, with a density of 532.6 km/10,000 km^2. More than 95 percent of townships have access to highways.

Airports

It has seven civil airports, which are open to 20 domestic and two international air routes, with a total length of 67,000 km.

Post and Telecom

A modern post and telecom network has been set up which serves the whole region and links the region with the outside world. By the end of 1999, it had a fixed asset investment of RMB1.5 billion (US$181.2 million) in post and telecom and a postal length of 62,000 km. Towns and townships are accessible by postal communications and counties in the region offer computer-controlled postal service. Eight main express mail ways have been built to link the region with other cities such as Beijing. Its express mail can be delivered to the rest of the world.

Telecom and Telephones

So far, a digital telecom transmission network has been established in the region that features transmission via optical cable in addition to satellite and digital microwaves. The network has facilitated the construction of regional digital and information portals. The long-distance-call national A-grade cable includes the Beijing-Hohhot-Yinchuan-Lanzhou cable line and the regional Hohhot-Xi'an, Hohhut-Beihai, Zhalantun-Qiqihar, Ulanhot-Baicheng and Chifeng-Chaoyang lines. Its transmission facilities utilise updated SDH technology. The number of telephone users exceed 2.58 million and the mobile phone users are around 2.09 million.

Radio and TV Stations

The radio and television systems serves 81.3 percent of the total region.

Foreign Trade

Inner Mongolia has conducted trade, economic and technological cooperation with nearly 100 countries and regions in the world. Trade with Russia and Mongolia thrives. During the ninth Five-Year Plan, the region achieved US$7.58 billion in import and export, with an export of US$4.16 billion. In 2002 it obtained US$2.43 billion in foreign trade, the export being US$0.81 billion. The region has 18 opening ports (11 A-grade and 7 C-grade) as well as 16 development zones (4 state-level and 12 regional-level).

Foreign Investment

By the end of 2003, the region has 148 foreign invested enterprises and a contracted foreign investment of US$434 million in 2003. It received loans of US$1.72 billion for its 78 projects from international financial organisations and foreign countries, with a total of US$53 million from foreign governments for its 43 projects.

The projects cover over 70 counties in the region and involve agriculture, education, health, communications, energy and environmental protection. Foreign loans account for 5.1 percent of the total fund for fixed asset investment. It has actually utilised RMB177 million of foreign funds.

Opportunities for Foreign Investment

Foreign investments are invited in the following industries:

1. Deep produce processing of farming and animal husbandry and comprehensive development of agriculture and animal husbandry;

2. Infrastructure construction of water conservancy, electricity, communications, ports, urbanisation and public welfare undertakings;

3. Exploitation of rare earth products and development of bio-engineering projects, research and development of hi-tech industries planned by the regional scientific and technological department;

4. Development of tourism resources;

5. Environmental protection projects including improvement of barren mountains, barren slopes and other wasteland, and project of turning cultivated land into forests and grasslands;

6. Exploitation, extraction and processing of mineral resources;

7. Sophisticated chemical industry, petrochemical industry and processing of coal;

8. New building material development and recycling of waste and old resources;

9. Asset recombination of enterprises in Inner Mongolia in the forms of merger, purchase and shareholding.

The Advantages of Natural Resources of the Ulanqab League

Location

Situated in the north of China, the Ulanqab League, 458 km from east to west and 442 km from south to north, lies in the middle part of

Inner Mongolia Autonomous Region. It covers an area of 81,282 km2 and borders with Erenhot and Mongolia in the north, links up Zhangjiakou, Beijing and Tianjin in east, faces Dating in the south and neighbouring Huhhot and Baotou in the west. It is a communications hub connecting North China, Northeast and Northwest economic zones and an international channel to Mongolia, the Commonwealth of Independent States (CIS) and Eastern Europe. The Jinxing, where the government body of the Ulanqab League is located and 404 km to Beijing, 143 km to Datong, 195 km to Zhangjiakou, 155 km to Huhhot, 304 km to Baotou and 347 km to Erenhot, was granted the status of open city by the State Council.

Transportation and Telecommunication

There are four railway lines, namely: from Beijing to Bao, from Jınıng to Erehot, from Jo to Tong, and from Feng to Fun, running across the whole league. The station is divided into South Station and North Station. The Jining South Station, a cross point of Jing-Bao and Ji-Er railway, is a second grade station which conducts the transportation business of international and domestic passenger and goods. Everyday, 35 pairs of goods train and 12 pairs of coaches run past the station. Jining Railway Station, which undertakes the marshaling disintegration and transfer business, is an important communication hub of Ji-Er, Ji-Tong and Jing-Bao lines.

Since 1990, more than RMB100 million has been invested in the extension project and the transportation capacity has been increased rapidly. The road network has since taken shape. There are 128 different grade of road radiating from all directions, of which four national highways and 12 provincial ways are the main lines of communication. The well-developed railway and

road has facilitated much business activities. The Ulanqab League has advanced postal and telecommunication facilities. The automatic telephone and mobile telecommunication system are in full operation in 14 counties and cities. The international direct-dial telephone and fax have started their service in the Jining, Siziwang and Damao.

Energy Resources

The abundant energy resources provide the most favourable conditions for the economic development of the Ulanqab League. The generation of electricity is produced by a complete set of power network which also has the function of transmission. 110 kW and 220 kW of transmission lines which connect with the North China power network cross the whole League from east to west. There are eight substations of 110kW and two substations of 220kW in League. The Fengzhen power plant, with 0.8 million kW installed capacity, make an important contribution to the economic construction of Beijing, Tianjin and Tangshang.

The Dai lake and Qingshuihe power plant, with 2.4 million kW and 1.2 million kW installed capacities are placed on the construction agenda. Ulanqab League is rich in coastal resources. The discovered coal reserves are 91.54 hundred million tons and mainly in Damao, Jining, Qianqi, Wucuan, Xinghe, Zhongqi and Qingshuihe etc. The Ulanqab League also has abundant wind and sunlight energy resources. Due to the longer sunshine time and large day-night difference in temperature, it is very suitable for growing crops and grass.

Agriculture

The Ulanqab League has 17.41 million mu of cultivated land, of which 14 million mu are for growing grains and beans. The main produce are wheat, naked oats and potatoes. Each year the following approximate quantities are produced:

- 400 million kg of wheat;
- 100 million kg of naked oats;
- 3,000 million kg of potatoes;
- 80 million kg of oil materials;
- 20 million kg of buckwheat;
- eight million of barley; and
- 120 million kg of beans.

Of which coarse cereals are the main raw materials for producing health products. There are lots of health products with high quantity to be sold in domestic and foreign markets. The buckwheat fine dried noodles, bean flour noodle, cream millet stir-fried in butter, vermicelli, naked oats pieces and naked oats pastor, which are produced in Jining, Shangdu, Houqi and Liang county, are listed as major products. In addition, other green food health products awaiting development promise wide prospects.

Animal Husbandry and Products

There are 84.68 million mu of natural grassland in Ulanqab League. By the end of June 1993, the livestock on hand is eight million, of which cattle, horses and sheep are 6.53 million and pig is 1.47 million. About two million pieces of sheepskin, 11 million kg of sheep wool, 0.14 million kg of cashmere, 920 million kg of meat and 3,000 tons of bone have been produced every year. There are also two leading enterprises producing annually one million cattle, sheep and pigs in Ulanqab League. In addition to the milk powder, butter, milk-tea powder and other milk products have been produced in larger quantities, which has been exported to Western Europe, Eastern Europe, North America and South Asia regions. The production of bone glue, gelatin, capsule, woolen spinning, worsted spinning, carpet and biochemical pharmacy is taking shape.

Mineral

The Ulanqab has rich mineral resources. At present, 80 kinds of minerals have been discovered. Of which, 40 were in reserves and 85 in production places. About 30 kinds have been exploited and put into use. The geographical department estimates the potential economic value at RMB500 billion.

The graphite (49.25 tons in reserves), gold (yearly produce 937 kg), copper (133.3 million tons in reserves), zealot (30 million tons in reserves), iron (285.6 million tons in reserves), bentonite (150 million tons in reserves), kaolin (5.24 million tons in reserves) and diatomite (17 million tons in reserves) are listed as advantageous mineral products. Of these, the reserves of zealot is top in Asia, the grade of limestone holds highest position in South Asia, and the graphite is one of the largest production bases in China. In addition, the development of coal, silica, granite, marble, rare earth, phosphorus, magnesium, mirabilite and gypsum promise good prospects.

Building Material

Building materials is one of the pillar industries in Ulanqab League. The main products are cement, graphite products, granite and marble board, articles of everyday use, craft and construction ceramics. The quality of glazed tile, which is produced using high quality kaolin of Qingshuihe and a unique blend of materials, surpasses ministry standard. It is an appointed product in the construction of the Asian Games Gymnasium. The black ceramics are exposed to Paris and other foreign markets. The Xinghe county, also name "graphite city", produce 10,000 tons of scale graphite annually and the refined proceeding products are high carbon graphite, expansion graphite, flexible graphite, graphite electrode and graphite sealed piece etc. the Ulanqab League can produce 0.5 million tons of high quality cement. In brief, building materials occupy an important position in Ulanqab League. By the end of the "eight years plan", the production capacity of one million tons of cement, 0.7 million m^2 of granite board and 0.1 million tons of graphite will be reached.

Storage

The Ulanqab League has storage capability of grain, meat, petroleum, timber, fine hair and special railway lines. Storage capacity for grain and edible oil exceed 275 million kg and 5 million kg, and petroleum storage reached 0.21 million cubic metres. The storage capacity of meat also reaches 1,200 tons. There are 64,000m^2 of storehouses with special railway lines in the commercial department. In addition, the material department owned 0.5 million m^2 of storehouses for timber, light industry products and building materials.

Medicinal Material

With rich Chinese-Mongolia medicinal material resources, the Ulanqab League can produce 800 kinds of medical materials. Out of the 800, 653 are wild, 115 are cultivated, 60 are animals and nine are minerals. There are 50 kinds of medicinal material in Ulanqab League. The main varieties are 1.5 million kg of Chinese ephemera, 0.3 million kg of danelion, 60,000 kg of the root of large flowered skullcap, 50,000 kg of the root of the membranous mile vetch, 50,000 kg of licorice root, 40,000 kg of Chinese throwax, 30,000 kg of the root of common peony and 10,000 kg of large-leaved gentian. In addition, the biochemical pharmacy of livestock's viscera promises much development prospects.

Tourism

The Ulanqab League is a place with excellent landscape for tourism and vacation. Numerous scenic spots have been discovered and are awaiting future development. About 10 places are opening up for tourism, of which two places are scenic spots of state level and one is provincial. Situated in the north of Daging mountains, the Xilamuren which has lamasery built in Qing Dynasty 1796 lies in Damao. The Gegentala tour centre, located in the depths of Ulanqab League grassland and having a typical style and features of grassland, lies in soziwan banner. The Huitenxile tour centre and yellow flower gully, gathering the spirits of mountains and rivers, is located in Cayouzhougi. The "nine dragon bend" tour area, which covers an area of 100 km^2 and having 20 scenic spots, lies in Zuozi county. The Sumu Mountains forestry, which is 2,334.7 metres above sea level with a wide variety of plants, animals and birds, is located in Xinghe county. It is the biggest planted forestry in the middle and west part of Inner Mongolia. In Wuchua county is the Hada gate forest park, which covers 38 km^2 of primeval forest, where many kinds of wild plants, animals such as deer are found.

The Dai Lake and hot spring sanatorium is located in Liang county, which is blessed with pleasant weather and beautiful scenery. The spring can provide 2,732 tons of hot water at 38°C and is beneficial to human health. The "Quanyulin Reservoir" lies in Chayouqianqi and covers an area of 3000 mu with beautiful scenery. The Yellow River Bridge of Qingshuihe county, which is 580 metres long, is located in the cross point between Qingshuihe county and Zunger banner of Yi league.

NINGXIA

Land, water and sunshine have enabled Ningxia to develop its agriculture, animal husbandry and livestock breeding.

NINGXIA Fact Sheet	2003
Area (km^2)	66,400
No. of Cities	6
Population (mil)	5.8
GDP (RMB bn)	38.5
Gross capital formation (RMB bn)	24.5
Consumption expenditure (RMB bn)	25
~Household	15
~Government	10
No. of employed persons (mil)	2.91
Unemployment Rate (%)	4.4%
Literacy Rate (%)	85%
Government revenue (RMB bn)	3.0
Government expenditure (RMB bn)	10.6
Per capita annual	
~disposable income of urban residents (RMB '000)	6.5
~net income of rural households (RMB '000)	2.0
~living expenditure of urban residents (RMB '000)	5.3
~living expenditure of rural residents (RMB '000)	1.6
Actually Used Foreign Direct Investment (US$ mil)	71.9
Total assets (RMB bn)	4.5
Exports (USD mil)	510
~percentage of change from the same period of previous year	+56%
Imports (USD mil)	140
~percentage of change from the same period of previous year	+23.1%

Introduction

The Ningxia Hui Autonomous Region, which is called Ning for short, is located in northwest China on the upper reaches of the Yellow River. The Yellow River runs across the region from the west to the northeast for 397 km, and its basin covers nearly 75 percent of Ningxia's total land area. Ningxia borders the northern part of Shaanxi Province on the east, Inner Mongolia Autonomous Region in the north and Gansu Provinec in the south. With an area of 66,400 km^2, the region has four prefectures and prefecture level cities, and 18 counties and county-level cities, with Yinchuan as its regional capital.

Climate

The climate of this inland area is continental cold desert. Annual average temperature ranges from 5°C to 9°C.

Population

Of the 5.3 million strong population, 34.1 percent are people of the Hui ethnic group, accounting for one-fifth of China's total Hui population. The Han make up most of the rest of the population. Most of the Huis live in Tongxin, Guyuan, Xiji, Haiyuan and Jingyuan counties, as well as in Wuzhong City and Lingwu County.

Infrastucture

Railways

The Baolan Line (Baotou-Lanzhou Railway) and Baozhong Line (Baoji-Zhongwei Railway) run across the region's northwest area and have become an important part of the New Asia-Europe Land Bridge linking Asia and Europe. In northern Ningxia, the Pingluo-Rujigou feeder line of the Baolan Line plays an important role in transporting Ningxia's coal to other provinces. Construction of a new railway, the Zongtai line (Zongwei-Taiyuan Railway) linking eastern and western China is underway. The new railway will start from Zhongwei of Ningxia and cross Shaanxi and Shanxi.

Highways

Yinchuan is the centre of a network comprising 13 national and provincial highways, as well as more than 100 county and township highways. The network links all counties, cities, key mining and industrial production bases in the region. In 2001, the government invested RMB3 billion to improve the highways. A new expressway in the Xihaigu area will be built within five years, forming an integral part of the expressway between Yinchuan city and Wuhan of Hubei province. The Yinchuan-Wuhan Expressway will be one of the eight major highways in Northwestern China, planned as part of the Great Western Development Strategy. Another expressway, from Yinchuan to Qingdao, is also under construction. Upon completion, driving from Yinchuan to Qingdao, the nearest seaport, will take 14 hours.

Waterways

Six highway bridges have been built over the 397 km section of the Yellow River flowing through Ningxia, and construction of the 7th bridge is now underway. The Yellow River is the only inland river for water transportation in Ningxia, and is used mainly for the region's short distance cargo transportation. The central government is aiming to improve the water supply system, including Ningxia, by conducting water from the upper Yangtze River to the upper Yellow River. The first stage of this project is expected to be completed by 2010.

Airports

In September 1999, the Hedong Airport in Yinchuan went into operation, with regular scheduled flights to Beijing, Shanghai, Xi'an, Guangzhou, Foshan, Chengdu, Urumqi, Wuhan, Kunming, Shenyang, Lanzhou and Chongqing. A new civil airport in Guyuan is udner construction.

Telecommunications & Postal Services

Ningxia has invested substantially in upgrading its post and telecommunications network over the past few years. A major optic fibre cable connecting Beijing, Yinchuan, Huhehaote and Lanzhou has been completed recently. Another cable connecting Shizuishan and Taoyuan is under construction. At present, a digital mobile and wireless telephone network covers the whole autonomous region, and is connected with networks in other provinces and autonomous regions throughout China. There are telephone lines to all the villages, making Ningxia the first amongst the provinces and autonomous regions in the northwest to achieve this.

Electricity & Gas Supply

There are three thermal power plants and two hydroelectric power stations at Qingtong Gorge on the Yellow River. The Daba Power Plant, with a generation capacity of two million kWh, is under construction. More power plants will be built in Shapotou and Daliushu. The Shapotou power plant is one of the 10 key projects in the tenth Five-Year Plan. Another major project to improve electricity supply is the expansion of the Shizuishan power plant.

A major gas pipeline starting from the Tarim Basin in Xinjiang and ending at Shanghai is being constructed. It will run through the provinces of Gansu, Shaanxi, Shanxi, Henan, Anhui, Jiangsu and the Ningxia Hui Autonomous region. It aims to deliver gas from the country's western area, a major gas production base, to the central region as well as to the Yangtze River Delta areas and eastern regions.

Tourism

Ningxia has much to offer in terms of scenic beauty and history. Yinchuan and Qingtongxia are the major tourist sites. In 2002, about 2.8 million tourists visited the region and generated a foreign exchange revenue of US$2 billion. The Haibao Pagoda and Cheng Tian Temple Pagoda in Yinchuan are two ancient towers built in the fifth century AD and in 1050 during the Western Xia Regime respectively. The Western Xia Tombs, 7 emperor tombs and over 200 nobleman tombs are at the foot of Mount Helan, scattered over an area of about 40 km^2.

Shapotou , also known as the "Sand Capital", is at the southern tip of the Tengel Desert. The 80 m high sand dune overlooks the Yellow River flowing eastwards, while the Sand Lake is a natural formation of yellow sand and lake waters. Other sights not to be missed are the ancient carvings in Mount Helan, the Xumi Mountain Grottoes in Guyuan built during the Northern Sui and Tang Dynasties, the Lingwu Shui Dong Gou Stone Age relics, the Zhongwei High Temple, the Tong Xin Mosque, the ruins of the Great Wall of the Warring States and Ming Dynasty, and the Jing Yuan Dragon Pool.

There are plans to develop Shahu, Qingtongxia, Xuni Mountain, the Xixia Kings Mausoleum, Jinshui and Liupanshan into tourist zones in the coming years.

Agriculture

0.71 million hectares of uncultivated land in Ningxia is suitable for agriculture, while three million hectares may be used as pasture. The Weining

Plain, with an area of 0.37 million hectares, is irrigated with water diverted from the Yellow River. For years, the annual runoff of the Yellow River through Ningxia has remained at 32.5 billion cubic metres, and offers four billion cubic metres of usable irrigation water resources.

The land resources, gravity irrigation system and abundant sunshine have enabled Ningxia to develop its agriculture. Ningxia's main crops are wheat and rice, maize, beans, oil-bearing crops, sugar beet, Chinese wolfberry, melon and pumpkin seeds, melons, watermelons, apples, grapes, liquorice, hemp, flax and vegetables such as fa-cai (an edible black moss). Effort is also being put into developing the region as a major grain production base.

Animal husbandry and livestock breeding are well developed in Ningxia. Having substantial pasture, it is an important producer of sheepskin, lamb skin and wool in China.

Of the available water surface of 82,000 hectares, 10,000 hectares can be used for aquaculture, and there is great potential for further development. Currently, Ningxia produces various species of carp, river shrimp and river crabs.

Mineral Resources

Ningxia is rich in mineral resources with verified deposits of over 50 minerals, including coal, qypsum, oil, natural gas, pottery clay, quartz sandstone and barite. The verified deposit of gypsum exceeds 4.5 billion tons. In the Huojiakouzi deposit in Tongxin County, the 20 ton deposit has a total thickness of 100 meter.

There are abundant reserves of various kinds of coal and Ningxia is a sizeable coal producer. The quality of Ningxia coal is high and the nine varieties to be found include lignite, bituminous coal and cooking coal. The oil and natural gas reserve is ideal for the development of related chemical industries. Other minerals with industrial value are iron, copper, Helan stone (a special clay), pottery clay, firestone, limestone, silica, phosphorus, quartz sandstone, carbonate minerals and plaster.

Industry

The principal industries in the autonomous region are coal, pharmaceuticals, electricity, metallurgy, chemicals, textiles, papermaking, food processing, machinery and building materials. The gross value of industrial output in 2002 was RMB26.9 billion, an increase of 99.3 percent compared to the previous year. Industrial production bases in the region are located in the Yellow Rover basin along the Helan Mountain, mainly in Yinchuan, Qingtongxia, Shizuishan and Wuzhong cities. The northern part of the Helan Mountain Industrial Zone is the region's major coal production base.

The coal reserve in Ningxia is 31 billion metric tons. Its yearly output is about 16 million metric tons, which is distributed to other provinces and regions in addition to meeting local needs. The famous Taixi anthracite, with its specific properties, is a high quality coal and one of the main export commodities.

There are plans to further develop the core industries, urban infrastructure and communications facilities, as well as to explore the potential in the agricultural and energy resources. The five hydropower and thermal power stations have an installed capacity of 1,930,000 kW.

Foreign Trade

New effort is being put into expanding the export market and finding areas of growth. As a result, the annual import and export value in 2003 was US$650 million, an increase of 47.4 percent over 2002. In 2003, the volume of exports totaled US$510 million, an increase of 56 percent over the previous year.

A number of production bases for industrial and agricultural export products have been set up. Ningxia exports about 350 varieties of commodities to 70 countries and regions in the world. The main commodities include activated carbon, dicyandiamide, rubber tires, tantalum products, ferrosilicon, casting iron parts, iron alloys, magnesium ingot, electrolytic aluminium, alumna, abrasives, anthracite, Chinese wolfberry, licorice root, cashmere and wool.

In addition to the various import and export enterprises, there are also organisations such as the Ningxia Muslim International Economy and Technology Cooperative Company, the Ningxia Moslem International

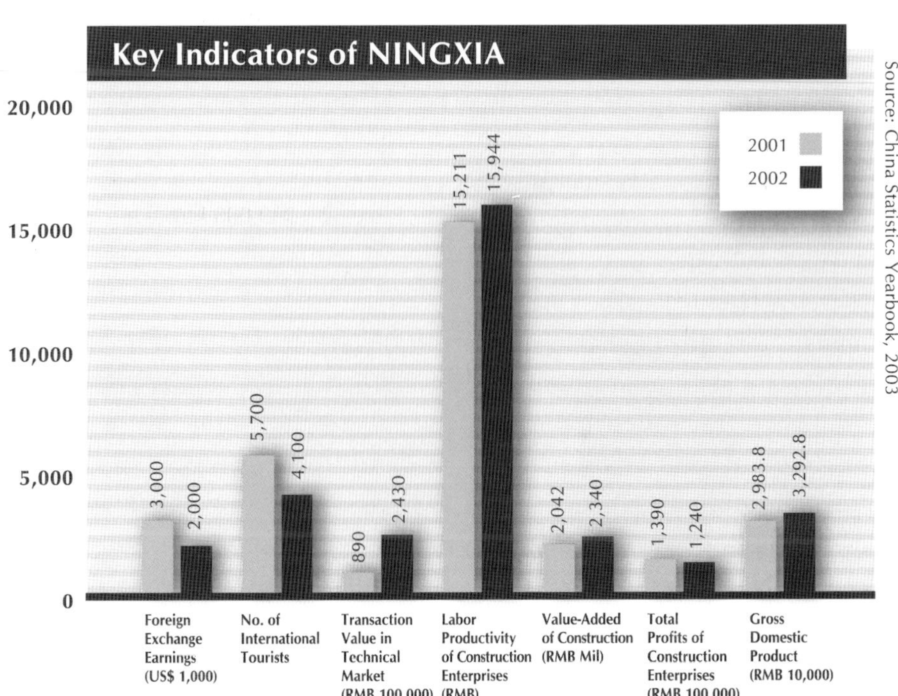

Source: China Statistics Yearbook, 2003

Trust Company, and service entities for commodity inspection, customs, insurance, finance, foreign exchange, taxation, international transport and advertising. Branches of these entities have been set up in some coastal cities and representative offices have been established in the United States, Singapore, Hong Kong and other regions. Hong Kong is Ningxia's largest trading partner, with other major trading partners being the USA, Japan, UK and Taiwan.

Foreign Investment

Foreign funds are raised from investment by foreign enterprises, loans from foreign governments and international financial organisations, as well as international commercial loans. Foreign investment is particularly encouraged in the fields of agricultural development, telecommunications, energy, transportation, machinery, metallurgy, pharmaceuticals, chemicals, textiles, construction materials and other light industries. As of the end of 2002, Yinchuan attracts the bulk of foreign investment as its contractual foreign capital and actual utilisation amounted to US$77 million and US$22 million respectively. In 1999, 20 new FIEs were approved in Yinchuan and the contractual value of US$44.3 million and actual utilisation value of US$10.21 million. Hong Kong is the largest investor in the province, followed by Taiwan, the USA and Japan. Mazak of Japan, a leading producer of high precision machine tools, has established a joint venture operation in Yinchuan.

To boost the development of the central and western regions in China, the State Council has granted further tax incentives to foreign-invested enterprises (FIEs). In 2000, the Ningxia government revised some of the policies to make the autonomous region more attractive to investors. Under the existing policy, FIEs are entitled to a five-year tax exemption and reduction.

In accordance with state policies on the economic development plan of the autonomous region, the government of the Ningxia Hui Autonomous Region encourages foreign businessmen to invest in the following fields:

1. Hi-tech industry and developing infrastructure such as energy, transportation and communications.

2. Advanced technology and equipment for the development of metallurgy, chemicals, machinery, building materials, agriculture and agricultural by-products processing and other pillar industries.

3. Technical transformations of the existing large and medium-sized industrial enterprises to upgrade product quality, reduce production cost and expand the range of export products.

4. Value-added export production, particularly in the Yinchuan Hi-Tech Development Zone.

5. The development of agricultural resources crop and plant cultivation, fish breeding, poultry raising and agriculture and agricultural by-products processing.

6. Energy-saving technology, technology for resource regeneration and comprehensive utilisation, environmental pollution control technology and projects, and construction of urban facilities.

7. The development of tourism, catering and information service industries.

TIBET

The mysterious land can become a major R&D centre for cosmic radiation, geothermal energy and traditional Tibetan medicine.

TIBET Fact Sheet	2003
Area (km^2)	1,200,000
No. of Cities	2
Population (mil)	2.7
GDP (RMB bn)	18.5
Gross capital formation (RMB bn)	7.2
Consumption expenditure (RMB bn)	10
~Household	6
~Government	4
No. of employed persons (mil)	1.32
Unemployment Rate	4.4%
Literacy Rate	62%
Government revenue (RMB bn)	0.8
Government expenditure (RMB bn)	13.8
Per capita annual	
~disposable income of urban residents (RMB '000)	8.1
~net income of rural households (RMB '000)	1.7
~living expenditure of urban residents (RMB '000)	7
~living expenditure of rural residents (RMB '000)	1
Total assets (RMB bn)	1.4
Exports (USD mil)	121.6
~percentage of change from the same period of previous year	+50%
Imports (USD mil)	39.49
~percentage of change from the same period of previous year	-19.8%

Introduction

Tibet is situated in the southwest of China, neighbouring Nepal and India. With an average elevation of 4,000 metres, Tibet is widely known as the "Roof of the World", an ancient but mysterious place in many people's minds. This 1.2 million km^2 land covers one-eighth of the country's total area and supports a population of 2.32 million. The regional capital is Lhasa. Tibet is the largest resident place in China for Tibetans who account for 96 percent of the region's population. Other places are Han, Hui, Mongolian, Monba, Lhoba etc.

Geography

The Himalayas, ranging from east to west on the southern edge of the Tibet Plateau, stretches along 2,400 kilometres with an elevation of more than 6,000 metres. Mount Qomolangma is the world's highest peak with an elevation of 8848.13 metres. The

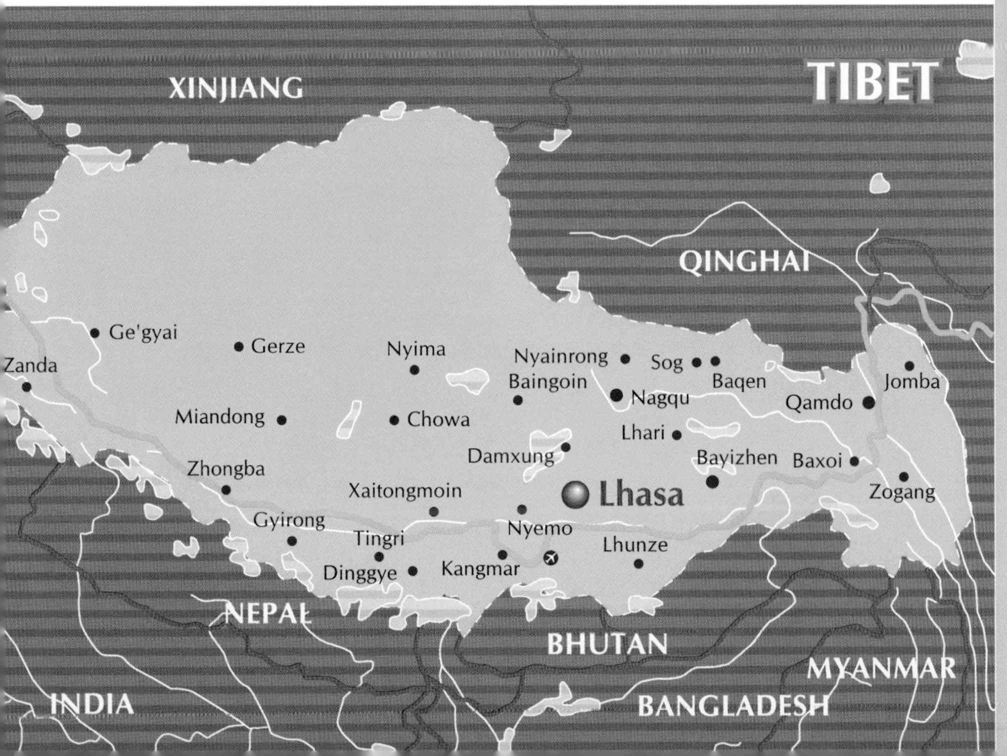

Yarlungzangbo Gorge is the world's deepest gorge with a depth of 5,382 metres.

Ethnicity

The Moinba people have lived on the Tibet Plateau since ancient times. Most of them are dsitributed in Moinyu in the south and some are scattered in Medog, Nyingchi and Cona counties.

The Lhoba people are mainly found in Lhoyu of southeastern Tibet, with some scattered in Mainling, Medog, Zayu, Lhunze and Nang counties. Most of the Hui people living in Tibet today are descendants of the Hui, who moved over from Gansu, Shaanxi, Qinghai, Sichuan and Yunnan provinces during the Qing Dynasty (1644-1911), with a minority coming from Central Asia. Most of them live in cities and towns of Lhasa, Xigaze and Qamdo. They work in commerce, handicrafts or animal slaughtering. Since the Qing Dynastry, many Han people have moved to Tibet. Some have been assimilated into Tibetan ethnicity. Today, most Han people living in Tibet are technicians, workers, teachers, medical workers and officials from other provinces, municipalities and autonomous regions.

Natural Resources

Minerals

There are more than 90 known mineral types in Tibet. Among them, 26 of the reserves have been proven and 11 of them rank among the top five in the quantity of reserves in China. The minerals include chromite, lithium, copper, gypsum, boron, magnesite, barite, arsenic, mica, peat, kaolin, salt, natural soda, mirabilite, sulphur, phosphorus, potassium, distomaceous earth, iceland spar, corundum, rock quartz and agate.

Energy

Tibet is rich in water, geothermal, solar and wind energy. It produces approximately 200 million kW of natural hydro-energy annually, which is equivalent to about 30 percent of the nation's total. It has 354.8 billion cubic metres of surface water resources which is equivalent to 13.5 percent of the nation's total and 330 billion cubic metres of glacial water resources. Tibet has about 56.6 million kW of exploitable hydro-energy resources, 15 percent of the nation's total. Tibet also leads China in geothermal energy. The Yangbajain geothermal field in Damxung County, Lhasa, is China's largest high temperature steam geothermal field and also one of the largest geothermal fields in the world.

Given Tibet's lack of coal and oil resources, plans are underway to build two major hydropower plants with a combined installed capacitiy of 160,000 kW by 2005 in eastern and central Tibet. The two hydropower plants to be located in Modrogongkar and Chamdu will absorb a total investment of up to 1.8 billion yuan (US$217 million). By 2005, the total installed capacity of power plants in the region is expected to reach over 500,000 kW from its current level of 360,000 kW. Most of the capacity comes from hydropower.

A number of production bases for industrial and agricultural export products have been set up. Ningxia exports about 350 varieties of commodities to 70 countries and regions in the world.

In addition, Tibet is actively lobbying the central government to build two more hydropower plants with a combined capacity of 46,000 kW in Nyingchi and Ari in the next five years. Investment in power plants is expected to reach RMB1.3 billion (US$157 million) in the coming years. The construction of dams and hydropower plants will help stop floods and improve local irrigation.

The region has decided to rely on its hydropower resources to help cope with power demand in its populous areas as Tibet's mountainous region is the least densely populated area in China and it is difficult to transmit power to the area. To solve the problem, the central government will invest RMB3 million (US$363,000) every year to fund household solar power generators for over 2,000 families in villages and meadows to meet their electricity needs.

Oil

Petroleum deposit spreading over 100 kilometres has been discovered in the north of Tibet by Chinese scientists. The Qiangtang Basin in Southwest China's Tibet Autonomous Region is expected to hold hundreds of millions of tons of oil. Laboratory research has confirmed the geologic age of the shale of the Qiangtang Basin to be around 180 million years, which has a bearing on the likelihood of oil deposits. The capacity of crude oil and gas in the Qiangtang basin is estimated to be somewhere between 4 to 5.4 billion tons.

Plants

Tibet is like a giant plant kingdom with more than 5,000 species of high-grade plants. It is also one of China's largest forest areas with intact primeval forests. Almost all the main plant species from the tropical to the frigid zones of the northern hemisphere are found here. Forestry reserves exceed 2.08 billion cubic metres and the forest coverage rate is 9.84 percent. Common species include Himalayan pine, alpine larch, Pinus yunnanensis, Pinus armandis, Himalayan spruce, Himalayan fir, hard-stemmed long bract fir, hemlock, Monterey Larix potaniniis, Tibetan larch, Tibetan cypress and Chinese juniper. There are about 926,000 hectares of pine forest in Tibet. Two species, Tibetan longleaf pine and Tibetan lacebark pine, are included in the listing of tree species under state protection. There are more than 1,000 wild plants used for medicine, 400 of which are commonly-used medicinal plants are Chinese caterpillar fungus, Fritillaria Thunbergii, Rhizoma Picrorhizae, rhubarb, Rhizoma Gastrodiae, Tian Qi (pseudo-ginseng), Codonopsis Pilosula, Radix Gentiane Macrophyllae, Radix Salviae Miltiorrhizae, glossy ganoderma and Caulis Spatholobi. In addition, there are over 200 known species of fungi, including famous edible fungi songrong, hedgehog hydnum, zhangzi fungus, mushrooms, black fungi, tremellas and yellow fungi. Fungi for medical use include teckahoes, songganlan, stone-like omphalias.

Animals

There are 142 species of mammals in Tibet, 473 species of birds, 49 species of reptiles, 44 species of amphibians, 64 species of fish and more than 2,300 species of insects. Wild animals include Ceropithecus, Assamese macaque, rhesus monkey, muntjak, head-haired deer, wild cattle, red-spotted antelopes, serows, leopards, clouded leopards, black bears, wild cats, weasels, little pandas, red deer, river deer, whitelipped deer, wild yaks, Tibetan antelopes, wild donkeys, argalis are all rare species particular to the Qinghai-Tibet Plateau and are under state protection. The white-lipped deer is a rare animal found only in China. The black-necked crane and the Tibetan pheasant are under the state's first-grade protection.

Tourism Resources

Tibet continually developed and exploited both its unique human and natural tourism resources. The region currently has four tourist areas of Lhasa, the west, southwest and south. The Lhasa tourist area includes Lhasa, Yangnajain, Damxung, Gyangze, Zetang, Xigaze and Yamzhoyum Co Lake. Lhasa itself is not only Tibet's political, economic, cultural and transportation centre, but also the centre of Tibetan Buddhism.

Major tourist sites include the Jokhang Temple, Ramoche Temple, Potala Palace, Barkhor Bazzar, Norbulingka Palace and three great monasteries of Ganden, Drepung and Sera. The Jokhang Temple, the Potala and Norbulingka palaces and Ganden, Drepung and Sera monasteries are key cultural relics under state-level protection.

Western Tibet is Nagari Prefecture, the so-called "rooftop atop the world's rooftop". The area draws visitors because of its great religious significance. Many tourists and pilgrims from Nepal and India come into Tibet through the Burang port of entry to visit the area's sacred mountains and lakes. The southwest Tibet tourist district is a place for mountaineers, many of whom are Nepalese who come to Tibet through Zhamu entry/exit port to enjoy the mountain scenery or do some climbing. In southern Tibet, at the area around Nyingchi, one can experience the four seasons of the year in a single day. There are snow-capped mountains, dense primeval forests, surging rivers and azalea-covered mountainsides. This beautiful scenery is made even more pleasant with the humid and mild climate.

New tourist routes and specialty tours have been added in recent years. New routes include Lhasa-Nyingschi-Shannan-Lhasa (eastern circle line) and Lhasa-Xigase-Ngari-Xigaze (western circle line). Specialty tours include exploration by car, trekking and scientific investigation tours. Other special events include the Shoton Theatrical Festival in Lhasa, the Qangtam Horseracing Festival in the North Tibet Plateau and the Yarlung Culture and Arts Festival in Shannan.

Infrastructure

China has approved some RMB31.2 billion (US$3.74 billion) for major construction projects in Tibet. One hundred seventeen projects have been ratified in areas important to Tibet. These include agriculture and animal husbandry, infrastructure (roads, bridges, rail lines and similar public works), science and technology education, ecological protection and construction of local government buildings.

The state also add new preferential policies for Tibet, while reviewing the current preferential policies which will be adjusted as needed. Tibet will also continue to be supported by its inland sister cities and provinces which are contributing an additional 70 construction programmes valued at RMB1.6 billion. Local governments in Tibet will give particular attention to developing the transportation, power supplies, telecommunication and irrigation facilities.

Railways

So far, this region is the only province that does not have a railway. The construction of the Qinghai-Tibet Railway, specifically the section from Golmud to Lhasa, is in progress. The Qinghai-Tibet Railway will stretch 1,118 km. It is the first key engineering project China has undertaken in the new century and one of the symbolic projects of the Great Western Development Strategy. The government is planning to invest RMB13.7 billion in this railway construction project, which is expected to boost the economic development of Tibet.

Highways

By the end of 2000, more than 1,000 permanent bridges with a total length of 30,000 metres had been built in Tibet and 22,500 km of roads put into operation. A highway network with Lhasa at its centre and supported by five national roads began to take shape. Except for Medog, all 72 counties in the region, 80 percent of towns and townships and 63 percent of administrative villages have access to roads. Tibet is now connected to other parts of the country via four roads:

- Sichuan-Tibet,
- Yunnan-Tibet,
- Qinghai-Tibet and
- Xinjiang-Tibet highways

The Sichuan-Tibet Highway is considered the most dangerous road in the world because it is subject to frequent landslides and mud-rock flows. The 2,122 km Qinghai-Tibet Highway stretches from Xining, capital of Qinghai Province, to Lhasa. Since it was built, it has undertaken the transportation of 85 percent of goods into and 90 percent of goods out of Tibet. To ensure smooth operation of this "lifeline", more than 1,500 road maintenance workers work along the section between Golmud and Lhasa all year round.

Between 2000 and 2005, Tibet will totally renovate the China-Nepal Highway, sealing the surface of the entire route with asphalt. Continuous construction will be done on two main roads leading to Tibet the South Sichuan Road and the No. 109 National Highway and asphalted roads will total 10,000 km.

The Xinjiang-Tibet Highway, the north section of the Sichuan-Tibet Highway and some sections of the Yunnan-Tibet Highway will also be reconstructed or renovated. By the end of 2005, highways in the region will total 27,000 km, of which roads at or above third class will account for 17 percent. The proportion of townships and administrative villages that have access to simply constructed roads will reach 90 percent and more than 70 percent respectively. A highway transportation network covering the whole region will be developed.

Air Transport

The Gonggar Airport and Bangda Airport provide more than 25 domestic and international air routes to Chengdu, Chongqing, Beijing, Xi'an, Xining, Kathmandu in Nepal etc. a new air route to Shanghai has been in operation since April 200 and it takes approximately four hours from Lhasa to Shanghai with a stopover in Xi'an.

Telecommunications

In 2002, there were 7.4 telephones per 100 persons. In May 2001, the Lhasa optic cable was constructed. Every region of Tibet is now reachable by telephone. Mobile telephone services are available in various Tibet cities such as Lhasa,Xigaza, Nyingchi, Qamdo, Naqu etc. In 2002, there were about 315,000 mobile telephone users in Tibet. The region has also started developing Internet service since March 1998 and Internet is making a big impact on the province as well. Lhasa now hs more than 100 internet cafes.

Electricity Supply

Yangbajing Station, the largest geothermal power plant in the country has an installed capapcity of 25,000 kWh. Because of its altitude, the region also has ample solar power resource. Currently, there are over 20 small and medium size solar power plants in a number of counties. At present, projects underway include the Yarnhog Yumco Lake Hydro-Electric Power Station and the Chaglung Power Station, which have a total installed capacity of 112,500 kWh and 10,800 kWh respectively. The expansion of the Yangbajing Geothermal Power Station provides an additional capacity of 50,000 kWh.

Water Projects

China will invest RMB4.8 billion to build water conservancy projects in southwest China's Tibet Autonomous region over the next five years from 2002 to 2006. Of the total sum, RMB4 billion will be provided by the central government and the rest will be raised by the local government. The funds will be used to build key water control projects, utilising water resources, upgrading irrigation systems and undertaking water conservation projects in Tibet.

The construction of Manlha Water Control Project, the largest water conservancy project in southwest China's Tibet Autonomous Region, has been completed at a cost of RMB1.45 billion (US$174 million). Manlha is located in Gyaze County in southwestern Xigaze Prefecture. The facility will contribute not only to irrigation and power generation, but also to flood control and the tourism industry in the region. The large project consists of a dam, flood water discharge tunnels and a power station, with the storage capacity of the reservoir hitting 155 million cubic metres and the power station's installed capacity reaching 20,000 kW. The project will provide irrigation for more than 43,000 hectares of farmland.

Weather Forecast

China will pour at least RMB60 million into the modernisation of meteorological research and weather forecast services in Tibet over the next five years from 2002 to 2006. The move is to ensure further economic growth and social progress.

The funds are double the amount that the central government invested in the area over the 1996-2000 period China's 9th Five-Year Plan. Instead of deploying many manual weather stations as China has done in inland areas, the funding boost will help Tibet introduce more advanced technologies into its weather services.

Covering more than 1.2 million km^2, which is equivalent to one-eighth of China's total territory, with an average elevation of over 4,000 metres, Tibet's meteorological research has far-reaching impacts. Tibet's atmospheric circulation not only affects China's affects China's climate changes but also has a strong impact on global weather changes. Experts say that at present there are major gaps in meteorological observation in Tibet, which currently has 39 conventional weather stations, about half of what is needed.

Industries

In 2002, Tibet's industrial output registered a 29.1 percent decrease from 2001, reaching RMB1.41 billion. The industries are mainly located at Lhasa, Nyingchi, Shannan and Xigaze. Tibet has more than 500 industrial enterprises which engage mainly in foodstuff, energy, timber processing, mineral, textiles and light industries. The region has established its own brand, including mineral water, Lhasa Beers, Chinese and Tibetan medicinal herbs, carpet etc.

Tourism

Tibet has abundant cultural and historical relics that can be explored to develop tourism. Some key cultural relics are under state-level protection, such as the Jokhang Temple, the Potala Palace, Norbulingka Palace, Ganden, Drepung and Sera monasteries, Octagons Streets, Guge Castle, the Tombs of the Ancient Kings and Samye Monastery. Potala Palace is listed in the World's Cultural Heritage by the UNESCO.

In 2002 over 142,300 foreign tourists (+11.9%) visited the region. It generated revenue of US$52 million which represented an increase of 13 percent from 2000.

Consumer Market

In 2002, retail sales totalled US$5.3 billion. As the largest consumer centre in Tibet, Lhasa accounts for 54 percent of the total retail sales. The second largest centre, Xigaze, accounts for about 15 percent of the total sales. At the end of 1999, Lhasa Department Store, the largest shopping centre in Tibet, was opened. The new shopping centre lies on a 12,000 m^2 area and carries about 20,000 kinds of commodities. Other major shopping centres include Lhasa Renyi Integrated Market, Saikang Business Centre.

Science and Technology

Tibet's high altitude makes it a research centre in certain areas. Recently, an international research laboratory on cosmic radiation opened at Yangbajing. Yangbajing is also China's research centre on geothermal energy. The rediscovery of Tibetan traditional medicines also led to several medical breakthroughs.

Foreign Trade

Tibet's exports increased by 50 percent to US$121.6 million in 2003. Major export products include agricultural and husbandry products, textiles, wool, Chinese medicinal herbs, carpet etc. Major export markets include Hong Kong, the US, South Africa and Brazil. Imports fell by 19.8 percent to US$39.49 million in 2003. Major import goods included building materials, mechanical and electronic products, chemical products etc. Major import sources were Russia, Republic of Korea, Japan, Australia and Nepal.

In 2003, Tibet's border trade was US$77.6 million, an annual increase of 26.3 percent. Major export goods were agricultural products, animal by-products, textiles, light industrial products, machinery and electrical products, building materials and medicine etc.

Foreign Investment

In 2002, the number of foreign-invested projects increased to 5 while accumulated contracted foreign investment reached US$183.8 million. Foreign investments mainly came from Hong Kong, Nepal, the UK, and the US. Major investments were engaged in the sectors of electrical & machinery, service industry, environmental protection, transportation and food processing.

In the coming years, the region plans to build 100 small towns along its major highways to accelerate the region's urbanisation

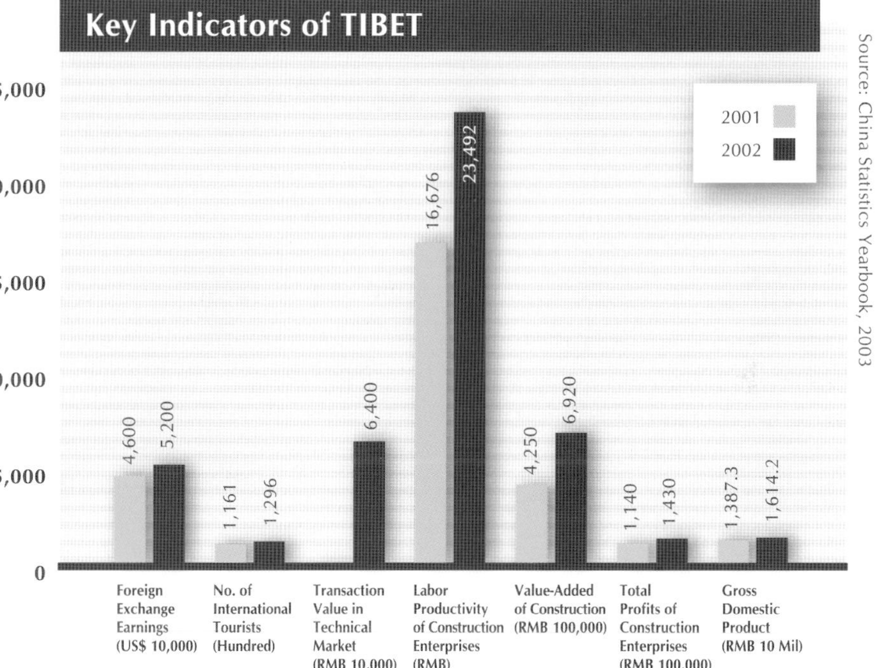

progress. Also, it will further develop industries in agriculture, tourism, Tibetan medicines, telecommunications, mineral products and infrastructure.

To boost the development of the central and western regions in China, the State Council has granted further tax incentives to foreign-invested enterprises (FIEs) in China. Under the existing policy, FIEs are entitled to a three-year tax reduction and exemption. The new policy allows foreign-invested enterprises in the central and western regions to enjoy another three years of preferential tax rate when the current preferential term expires. The tax rate can be further reduced to 10 percent if an enterprise exports more than 70 percent of its annual output in terms of value.

Science and Technology in Agriculture and Animal Husbandry

Agriculture has witnessed stable development, thanks to application of science and technology. Tibet now has 225,000 hectares of cultivated land. With the development of modern agroscience and technology, the traditional farming method has been replaced by modern techniques such as introducing improved strains, improving soil quality, building water conservancy projects, harnessing rivers, intensive cultivation, rational application of chemical fertilisers and agricultural chemicals. Gone are the days when Lamas were asked to pray for insects in the fields to be killed.

In 1990, the region carried out a project to establish four science and technology demonstration counties (cities) Gyangze, Xigaze, Lhunzhub and Gonggar. Their combined sown area of more than 30,000 hectares for grain crops accounted for 16.1 percent of the region's total. Grain yield totalled 152.7 million kg, amounting to 27.5 percent of the total, an increase of 24.6 percent or 30 million kg over the previous year. Moreover, grain output reached a record of 50 million kg in Gyangze and Xigaze. The 1995 total grain output in Tibet registered 700 million kg. All these were achieved without additional cultivated land and would have been impossible without science and technology.

While promoting agroscientific research, efforts have been made to breed improved seeds, transform the cultivation system, obtain a detailed survey of agricultural resources and soil, investigate the land use situation, develop a systematic cultivation, transform medium and low-yield farmland and popularise agrotechniques for dry-land farming. The popularisation of winter wheat planting, for example, is an important step forward. The efforts made in changing the old cultivation system, spreading improved strains and increasing grain productions have brought fundamental changes in agricultural production. Moreover, it laid a solid foundation for successive bumper grain harvests.

In 2001, the region's total gain output exceeded 0.98 million ton. At the same time, scientific workers also recorded tremendous progress in improving basic soil fertility through biotechnological means, the use of fertilisers and comprehensive prevention and control of plant weeds, diseases and insect pests. Research results such as the Survey of Agriculture-related Weeds, Diseases and Insect Pests and Their Natural Enemy Resources in Tibet and the Collections of Tibetan Crops Resources won awards for science and technology progress from the state and the autonomous region respectively. Studies on Comprehensive Survey and Use of Land Resources in the Tibet Autonomous Region filled vital gaps in knowledge of available land resources on the plateau, leading to the first establishment of the alpine soil order and classification of the soil system throughout the plateau. Research results, which attained advanced international level, won a special prize for science and technology progress from the autonomous region in 1993 and a second-class prize from the state in 1995. The Study on Systematic Cultivation Techniques for High-Yield Wheat Crops was demonstrated in areas in the Yarlung Zangbo, Lhasa, Nyang Qu and Nyang river valleys. Based on regional cultivation and systematic management, the experiments integrated study with demonstration and popularisation to create systematic scientific research materials.

Three years of research covered 77,200 hectares of systematic cultivated area which produced per-hectare grain yield of 5,500 kg per season. The result was a total increase of over 101.67 million kg of grain, produced more than 60.51 million Yuan of net income. In particular, the study of systematic cultivation of winter and spring qingke barley produced tangible economic, social and ecological returns.

In the final decade of the last century, Tibet undertook a significant Three-River Project, a comprehensive development of the middle reaches of the Yarlung Zangbo, Lhasa and Nyang rivers which cost RMB1 billion from the state. From 1991 to June 1995, the state had invested a total of RMB507.5 million and nearly 80 projects were completed, laying a solid foundation for further development. A decade of efforts will create four bases for commercial grain – (1) light industry; (2) textiles and handicrafts; (3) livestock products, vegetables and non-staple foods; and (4) scientific and technological demonstration. Ecological and economic returns in the area will reach a high level. This long-term programme, the largest ever in Tibet, will have far-reaching socio-economic significance.

Nowadays, the region's agricultural production has largely been mechanised with the aggregate power of farm machinery exceeding 500,000 kW. The per-capita power of farmers is nearly 0.6 kW, a rate close to the average for inland rural areas. The mechanised ploughed area accounts for 25 percent of the region's total and the sown area 65 percent, both equivalent to inland rural levels. Tibet today has abandoned backward and primitive agriculture to form an initial system based on modern science and technology.

One of the five large pastoral areas in the country, Tibet boasts 82.07 million hectares of grassland, 70.77 million hectares of which can be used to raise various kinds of domestic animals totalling 22.8 million. Animal husbandry is a basic and vital industry for the local economy and the growing prosperity of Tibetan people. Livestock products are key materials for both national handicraft and processing industries and an important source of export earnings. Over the past four decades, the government has paid great attention to livestock farming. Scientific research has achieved major results in selecting and breeding animal varieties, training veterinary surgeons and building up the grasslands.

Yaks, a symbol of highland animal husbandry, have long been trained on the Qinghai-Tibet Plateau and are deeply loved as a totem of Tibetan ethnic group. In return, yaks, as highland treasures, are raising the Tibetan people. In recent years, however, the variety of yaks has seriously deteriorated, directly influencing output and quality. Therefore, much effort has gone into seeking improvements. Linzhou County is in particular in the process of creating 614,000 Yuan of profits by playing a key role in the testing and manufacturing of frozen yak semen, as well as the study and practice of selective breeding. The economic returns are of great significance to Tibetan livestock farming.

The spread of the Lhasa white chicken has solved the reproductive problem of high-yield egg-laying chickens under highland conditions and formed an ideal egg-oriented breed. These efforts have solved the supply problem of egg and chicken meat, enriching the diet and improving people's lives. Science and technology in animal husbandry has made an important contribution to the region's poultry husbandry.

A breakthrough has been made in the study of the anal skin cancer in goats, opening a new way to cure skin cancer of domestic animals with medicinal herbs.

In the light of actual local conditions, scientific workers have given priority to the grass sector to introduce improved herbage and fodder, providing rich and reliable materials for artificial planting of forage grass. More than 1,000 hectares of land have been planted to help solve grass shortages in winter and spring.

In addition, cattle raising has a long history in Tibet. Cattle are used for milk, meat and work. Tangible results have been made in improving the variety and raising production properties since 1960. The creation of fine breeds has opened the way for the people to become prosperous. The breeding of half-fine-wool sheep has laid a solid foundation for creating a new variety. Production of formula feed has begun. Fish meal and additive production has bridged gaps in Tibetan fodder science and technology. The work of animal protection has basically reached the standard level.

Traditional Tibetan Medicine

Traditional Tibetan Medicine (TTM) has a history of over 2,000 years. TTM has been practised by Tibetan people for generations in their struggle against natural disasters and diseases. It is a resplendent jewel in the great treasure house of China's traditional medicine. With its unique theoretical system and rich clinical experience, TTM has made tremendous contributions to public health, especially to the reproduction of Tibetan ethnic groups. In addition, it has been developed into a science of its own, supported by years of research and empirical experiences. The classification and properties of medicinal herbs, as well as the prescription and preparation of herbal medicines, have been documented into a rich resource of Chinese medicinal practice.

The Central Government has always seen TTM as an important

part of its development plan. Famous ancient medical works such as Tibetan Medical Code and Four-Volume Medical Core have been collated, translated and published. A number of TTM monographs have also been published, including A New Compendium of Tibetan Medicinal Herbs and A New Compendium of Tibetan Medicine.

Rare traditional Tibetan medicine "Rannasangpei" has won gold medals twice at the International Conference on Traditional Medicine, while another medicine "Zuotai" has been honoured with a state patent. In 1993, the Ministry of Health held a symposium on Tibetan medicine standards in Lhasa. To date, 11 kinds of local medicinal herbs and 40 kinds of medicines have been endorsed with a quality standard, laying a key step for TTM to gradually enter into the domestic as well as the international markets.

Scientific Exchanges and Cooperation

Tibet has opened its doors to the outside world alongside the country's reform and liberalisation plan. In addition to extensive cooperation with domestic scientific and technological institutions, it has conducted exchanges and cooperation with more than 20 countries, including the United States, Japan, Germany, Austria and Nepal.

In 1987, the region's Bureau of Light Industry, Textile and Handicraft Industries imported dyeing techniques and formulae from Switzerland's Sandoz AG and invited Swiss experts to Tibet to hold a training course for carpet dying. The training course has helped solve a long-standing colour-fading problem and boosted the development of the local handicraft industry. The completed leather and shoe-making equipment and technology, imported from Germany in 1992 by the Lhasa

Tanyard, has laid a foundation for the best use of livestock resources.

The initial exploration of the local geothermal energy resources has attracted many domestic and overseas geologists and energy experts. United Nations and Italy invested US$9 million in the construction of geothermal fields of Yangbajain, Nyingzhong, Nagqu and Latogka, after affirming that there was huge potential for geothermal development in Tibet. A second-phase geothermal project, through grants from the UN Development Program and Italy, began construction in 1989. China, as well as various foreign parties, has conducted widespread exchanges on the exploration, development and use of geothermal resources. They have arranged many overseas investigation tours, training courses and participation in international geothermal conferences. In 1993, advanced technologies and equipment were imported for the construction of a dual-cycle geothermal demonstration power station at Nagqu. At the same time, advanced drilling machines and directional drilling tools were imported. Geothermal experts of Japan, the United States, Denmark, Iceland, Mexico, Australia, Canada and other countries have indicated interest to participate in the exploration of the Yangbajain Geothermal Field.

The Party Central Committee and the State Council have adopted a series of favourable policies to make Tibet a "special economic zone". In order to accelerate regional development, the Party Central Committee and the State Council held the Third Work Meeting on July 1994 in Tibet and approved 62 aid-Tibet construction projects. With a total investment of RMB2.38 billion, the projects covers trans-portation, energy resources, telecommunications, urban construction, agriculture, animal husbandry and medical and health services, as well as other sectors related to people's daily life.

With the implementation of the aid-Tibet policy, scientific and technological assistance was unveiled. The State Science and Technology Commission and provincial-level commissions respectively made plans to support Tibet. Besides providing human resource such as scientific workers and management personnel, assistance in capital and equipment were also provided. In the second half of 1996, the National Work Conference on Supporting Tibet with Science and Technology was held in Lhasa by the State Science and Technology Commission. This further confirmed the implementation of various projects to move Tibet onto a new phase of science and technology development.

Opportunities for Foreign Investment

Foreign investments are encouraged in energy, transportation, architecture, light industry, textiles, machinery and electronics, commerce, food, aquaculture, processing, tourism and in the development of agriculture, forestry and animal husbandry.

XINJIANG

The central government's preferential policies for this region make it economically more favorable than the coastal areas.

XINJIANG Fact Sheet	2003
Area (km²)	1,600,000
No. of Cities	22
Population (mil)	19.3
GDP (RMB bn)	187.5
Gross capital formation (RMB bn)	86.4
Consumption expenditure (RMB bn)	95
~Household	60
~Government	35
No. of employed persons (mil)	7.01
Unemployment Rate	3.8%
Literacy Rate	92.3%
Government revenue (RMB bn)	12.7
Government expenditure (RMB bn)	36.8
Per capita annual	
~disposable income of urban residents (RMB '000)	7.2
~net income of rural households (RMB '000)	2.1
~living expenditure of urban residents (RMB '000)	5.6
~living expenditure of rural residents (RMB '000)	1.4
Total assets (RMB bn)	49.3
Exports (USD mil)	2,542
~percentage of change from the same period of previous year	+94.3%
Imports (USD mil)	2,230
~percentage of change from the same period of previous year	+61.2%

Introduction

Xinjiang is officially known as Xinjiang Upper Autonomous Region. Separated by Tianshan Mountain, Xinjiang is divided into Nanjiang, Beijiang and Dongjiang. The world's largest inland basin, Tarim Basin and the second largest float desert, Takla Makan Desert are found in the region. The region's capital is Urumqi, which enjoys the same preferential policies as a coastal city.

Xinjiang is China's largest growing base of cotton and hops, with output that accounted for 33 percent and 80 percent of the country's total respectively in 2001. With the country's second largest pastureland, the region's capital is one of the major sheep farming areas and fine-wool producers in China. It provides more than 40 percent of the country's total fine-sheep wool output and its milk production in the region was ranked fourth in China in 1999. Besides, Xinjiang is a major agricultural base of gain, sugarbeet and fruits,, of which Yining apples,

Korla pears, seedless white grapes and honeydew are famous both at home and abroad.

Xinjiang is rich in energy resources. It has the largest reserves of oil, natural gas and coal in the country. Its coal reserves reach 27 million tons (40 percent of the country's total) and oil reserves amount to 30 billion tons. Crude oil output, which reached 19.5 million tons in 2001, was the third largest in the country. The oil and gas reserves found in tarim, Junggar and Turpan-Hami basins in the region account for one-fourth and one-third of the country's total respectively.

Like the energy resources, Xinjiang's mineral resources are equally huge. The region's natural reserves of beryllium and mica are the highest in China. The country's largest copper mine is also found in Xinjiang. There are 100 locations with a total of over one billion cubic metres of proven granite reserves.

History

Xinjiang's history is marked by a record of tumultuous events. It first came under Chinese rule in the first century B.C., when the Chinese army was sent by emperor Wu Di to defeat the Huns and occupy the region. In the second century A.D., China lost Xinjiang to the Uzbek Confederation, but reoccupied it in the mid-seventh century. It was conquered by Tibetans during the eighth century, overrun by the Uigurs, who established a kingdom there and subsequently invaded by Arabs during the 10th century. Xinjiang was passed to the Mongols in the 13th century. Subsequently, an anarchic period followed, until the Manchus established control.

The subsequent relations between China and Xinjiang were characterized by cultural and religious conflict, bloody rebellions and tribal dissensions. In the 19th century, this unrest was encouraged by Great Britain and czarist Russia to protect India and Siberia respectively. Xinjiang became a Chinese province in 1881, but somehow remained independent of the central government until the establishment of the Chinese republic in 1912. Chinese rule over Xinjiang was eased further after the rebellions in 1936, 1937 and 1944.

In 1949, Xinjiang came to terms with the Chinese Communists. In 1955, it was reconstituted an autonomous region, based on the fact that the Uigurs were the majority ethnic group comprising 74 percent of the population. Autotnomous districts were also created for the Kazakhs, Mongols, Hui and Kyrgyz. In the 1950s and 1960s, a large number of Chinese were sent by the central government to Xinjiang to help develop water conservancy and mineral exploitation schemes. This led to drastic alteration in the population composition, balancing the number of Chinese with the Uigurs. National defence is another strategic and sensitive issue in Xinjiang. In 1969, the Soviets and Chinese waged war along the border due to some frontier incidents. In the 1990s, the Turkish people of Xinjiang became increasingly discontented under Chinese rule. In 1997, the Muslims rioted in an attempt to fight for independence and troops were subsequently sent by the Chinese government to the region.

Location

Located in the northwestern corner of China, Xinjiang is China's largest province. It covers about one-sixth of the total area of China. It has contrasting landscape, ranging from the scorching Taklamakan Desert and the deep basins of Turpan to the mammoth ranges of the Heavenly Mountains.

Xinjiang was part of the old Silk Road and Kashgar and Turpan were once major cities on the route. Although its importance as a center for trade and commerce has diminished, Xinjiang remains a region uniquely rich in culture and tradition.

People

The Uighurs are the largest minority population in the province. They are ethnically and culturally distinct from the Han Chinese – they have Turkish roots and speak a language derived from Turkish. For over 1,000 years, their main religious belief was Islam, which is evidenced by the grand mosques in the area such as the Id Kah Mosque in Turpan. Other than the Uighurs, there are about a dozen other ethnic groups from the Central Asia regions. This diverse range of ethnic groups is due to Xinjiang's shared borders with Tibet, India, Kashmir, Afghanistan and Russia.

Economy

In the most populated areas, cotton and silk (both locally spun and woven) are produced. Wheat, rice, millet, potatoes, sorghum, sugar beets and fruit are grown. Traditionally, the Uigurs are excellent builders of canals and wells for supplying water to the fields. The Manas irrigation project in S Dzungaria is one of the several modern government attempts to expand the area under cultivation. Although extensive areas of grazing land have been converted to wheat farm, large-scale animal husbandry remains important and the number of livestock (sheep, goats, cattle, horses and camels) continues to grow. Many of the Kazakh and Mongol stock herders are still leading a semi-nomadic life.

Although Xinjiang is predominantly agricultural and pastoral, it has rich mineral resources. The vast oilfields at Karamay (Served by both highways and an airline) are among the largest in China and there are extensive deposits of coal, silver, copper, lead, nitrates, gold and zinc. New mines as well as associated industry such as refineries, ironworks, steel works and chemical plants are well established. Other industries include textile (the region produces large quantities of cotton and wool), cement production and sugar refining.

The region is linked to the Chinese rail network by lines from Lanzhou, Gansu to Urumqi (completed in 1963). The mode of transportation in the west and south of Urumqi is mainly highways that are built along two ancient roads: the north road, which skirts the southern edge of the Dzungaria and connects Urumqi with the Turkistan-Siberia rail line, and the south road, which surrounds the Tarim basin. Camels remain an important means of transport, but the use of trucks is increasing by the day.

Infrastructure

Railways

The region is served mainly by the Lanxin line: Lanzhou-Xinjiang, which links up with the Longhai line: Lanzhou-Lianyungang, and Nanjiang line: Korla-Kashi. Construction of Qinxin line: Gulmod in Qinghai and Korla in Xinjiang is at the planning stage. By the end of 2000, the total length of roads and highways in the region reached 35,600 kiliometres, covering over 99 percent of the counties, townships and villages. Major highways include TurUDai: Turpan-Urumqi-Daihuangshan, U-Kui Expressway: Urumqi-Kuitun, LanXin line: Lanzhou-Xinjiang, QinXin line: Qinghai-Xinjiang and XinTibet line: Xinjiang-Tibet.

Air Transport

Program-controlled telephones are available in 98 percent of township and 52 percent of administrative villages in Xinjiang. At present, there are about 1.7 million telephone users in the region. Direct dial service to Hong Kong and other major cities in the world is available. Mobile phone service is increasingly popular. At the end of 2002, 296,800 mobile telephone users were recorded in Urumqi. Xinjiang has built a digital microwave telecommunications trunk which links cities on both sides of Tianshan Mountain, a fibreoptic cable system leading to neighbouring countries with a total length of 25,000 kilometres and 10 satellite ground stations. The region has also set up a digital data network, a conference TV system, a smart terminal and a multimedia network. The number of data transmission users has risen to 105,000.

Wind Power

More than 200 power-generating units are in operation at the wind power center in Dabancheng. The generating capacity of the centre accounts for one-third of the total installed wind power capacity in the country.

Gas Supply

Under China's energy development strategy, a major gas pipeline running from the Tarim Basin to Shanghai with a total length of 4,167 kilometres has started construction for two years. The pipeline, which runs through Gansu, Shaanxi, Shanxi, Henan, Anhui and Jiangsu and Ningxia Hui Autonomous Region, will be able to transmit 12 billion cubic metres of gas annually from the west to the east.

Natural Resources

Land

About 42 percent of Xinjiang's total land area, i.e., 68 million hectares can be used for the development of agriculture, forestry and animal husbandry. Xinjiang is one of the nation's five major grazing areas.

Minerals

A total of 122 minerals, including more than 70 non-metal minerals, have been discovered. Xinjiang tops China's provinces and autonomous regions in deposits of beryllium, muscovite, natron saltpeter, pottery clay and serpentine. The identified reserves of iron, salt, mirabilite and natron saltpeter are 730 million tons, 318 million tons, 170 million tons and

2,326,000 tons respectively. Xinjiang is known for its muscovite, gemstone, asbestos and Hetian jade.

Energy

Xinjiang has an annual runoff of 88.4 billon cubic metres of surface water and 25.2 billion cubic metres of exploitable underground water. Glaciers stretch for 24,000 km^2 and contain 2,580 billion cubic metres of water. Sunshine in Xinjiang occurs for about 2,600 to 3,400 hours per year. The coal reserve in Xinjiang is estimated to account for 3737 percent of the nation's total. The petroleum and natural gas are estimated at 30 billion tons, which account for more than 25 percent of the nation's total.

Animal and Plants

There are 699 species of wild animals, including 85 species of fish, seven species of amphibians, 45 species of reptiles and 137 species of mammals. More than 4,000 species of wild plants grow in Xinjiang, of which more than 1,000 varieties, including the bluish dogbane and kok-saghyz, are of special economic value.

Pillar Industries

These include oil exploitation, petrochemicals, textiles, grain production, chemicals, machinery, electricity and forest industry.

Industries

In 2002, total added value of industrial output of the region was RMB76.3 billion, an increase of 19.2 percent over the previous year. The major industrial production centers in the region include Urumqi, Karamai, Korla and Tulufan.

Heavy industries like oil, petrochemicals and coal production formed a fundamental part of Xinjiang's industrial development, accounting for 69 percent of the region's total industrial output in 1999. Besides, the region has developed light industries like textiles and garments (especially wool and cashmere), leather processing, papermaking, sugar refining and carpet weaving. The Xinjiang government targets to accelerate development of its information, biotech, energy and environmental protection industries in the 10th Five-Year Plan period.

Tourism

Situated in the middle of the Silk Road, Xinjiang has abundant cultural and historical relics at Kashi, gaocheng, Jaiohe and Loulan. Other famous touristic spots include Tianshan Mountain, Tianchi Lake, Bizaklik Thousand-Buddha Caves, Flaming Mountains, etc. In 2002, about 275,400 overseas tourists visited the region and generated a total revenue of US$99million.

Consumer Market

Retail sales of consumer goods in the whole region rose by 9.1 percent to RMB44.3 billion in 2002. Major department stores and shopping centers in Xinjiang include Urumqi Tianshan Department Store, Urumqi Youhao Department Store, Xinjiang Department Store, Hongshan Shopping Arcade, Urumqi Dashizi Commercial Building, Tulufan Department Store, Hami Department Store and Xinjian Shengchan Jianshe Bingtuan Department Store.

Foreign Trade

Xinjiang exports rose by 94.3 percent to US$2.54 billion in 2003. Major exports items included canned food, cotton, garment, silk products, woolen yarn, etc. In addition to the traditional export markets like Kirghizistan, Kazakhstan, Hong Kong, Japan and the US, the region has diversified into new export markets in Southeast Asia, Korea, Latin America and Africa.

Imports rose by 61.2 percent to US$2.23 billion in 2002. Major import goods include aluminium and steel product, chemical fertilizer, paper and paper products, medical equipment, etc. Major import sources were Kazakhstan, Hong Kong, the US, Russia and Uzbekistan.

Xinjiang is the second largest border trade zone in China, after Heilongjiang Province. Border trade reached US$1.3 billion in 2000, an increase of 29 percent from previous year, and accounts for 58.3 percent of the region's total trade. There are 16 ports open for border trade with neighbouring countries. Major export goods include foodstuff, textiles, chemical fibre cloth, garment etc. major imports include raw materials, chemical fertilizer etc.

Foreign Investment

In 2002, there were 61 newly foreign-funded projects being approved, a decrease of 22.6 percent from 2001.

The contractual and utilized foreign investments have increased to US$149.9 million and US$18.9 million respectively. By the end of 2001, a total investment of US$400 million has been made in the region by 36 countries, of which Hong Kong, Macau and Taiwan collectively accounted for 63 percent. The investments are mainly in oil and gas exploitation, as well as manufacturing industries like foodstuff, textiles and pharmaceuticals.

The Urumqi Foreign Economic Relations and Trade Fair is a major annual event in Xinjiang to promote foreign trade and inward investment. In the coming year, the region will focus on expanding its border trade and attract foreign funds to develop its petroleum and natural gas resources facilities in the Tarim, Turpan-Hami and Junggar basins and infrastructure facilities. Other encouraged industries for foreign investments include agricultural, food processing, textiles, petrochemicals, mining, building materials, environmental protection and other industries using advanced technology.

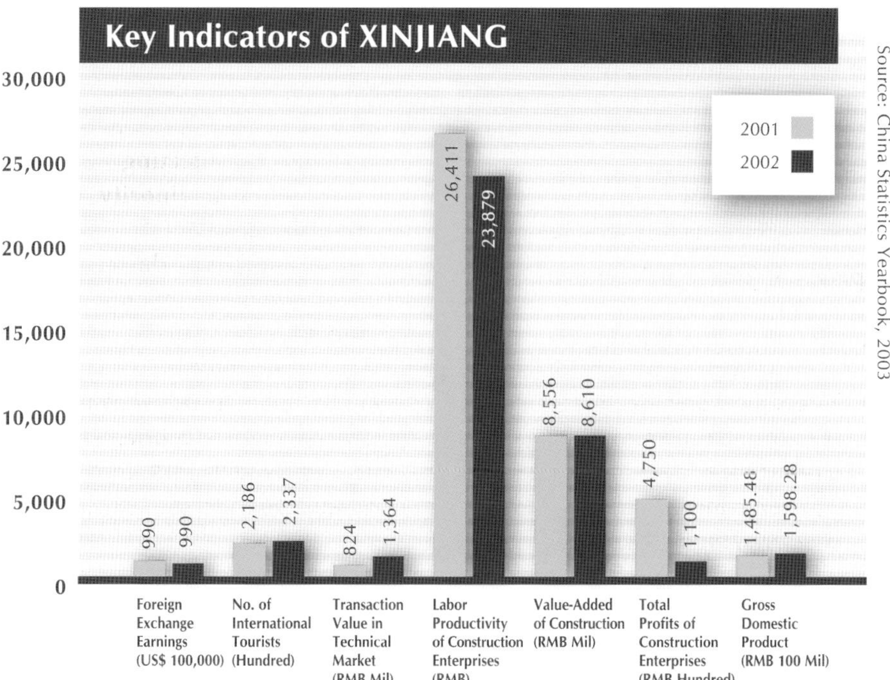

As part of the development plan for the central and western regions in China, the State Council has granted further tax incentives to foreign-invested enterprises (FIEs) in China. From January 2001, foreign-invested enterprises in the central and western regions enjoyed another three years of preferential tax rate at 15 percent on top of the existing preferential treatment (exemption of profit tax for the first two years and 50 percent reduction for three years thereafter). The tax rate can be further reduced to 10 percent when an enterprise exports more than 70 percent of its annual output in terms of its value. Besides, the region's government also exempts foreign investors from paying the three percent profit tax to the local government if the business has an operating period exceeding 10 years.

Opportunities for Foreign Investment

The following industries are opened to foreign investments:

- Infrastructure facilities
- Mechanical and electronics industry: electronic equipment, electronic meters, electronic instruments and products, high and middle grade household appliances production, computers, children's computer assembly and lines of products, integrated circuit, multi-functional electrical meters, information communication technology, genetic engineering technology, mechanical and electrical equipment production, assembly medium and small-sized power-operated instruments, new-type textile equipment, farming and stockbreeding mechanical products, petrochemical mechanical equipment and building machinery.
- Light and textile industry: paper and paper products, leather products, fur wear, synthetic detergent and raw materials, skin-protecting series of products, minority nationality special necessities, new-type daily ceramics and enamel ware, arts and crafts and small-sized universal machinery, cotton, yarn, linen and woolen silk processing production, new-type special chemical fibre and deep process.
- Building and chemical industry: new-type building materials, non-metal mineral products, new-type solid materials and roofing materials, new-type materials, building hygiene ceramics, petrochemical fine products.
- Pharmaceutical, agricultural chemicals, food process and medical care goods.
- Scientific research, business, trade, tourism and other tertiary industries.
- Projects initiated by investors should conform to the industrial policies of the zone.

ANHUI

The long-term industrial plans emphasise the development of its rich mineral resources.

ANHUI Fact Sheet	2003
Area (km^2)	140,000
No. of Cities	22
Population (mil)	64.1
GDP (RMB bn)	397.3
Gross capital formation (RMB bn)	131
Consumption expenditure (RMB bn)	226
~Household	183
~Government	43
No. of employed persons (mil)	35.45
Unemployment Rate	4.1%
Literacy Rate	85.3%
Government revenue (RMB bn)	41.2
Government expenditure (RMB bn)	50.6
Per capita annual	
~disposable income of urban residents (RMB '000)	6.8
~net income of rural households (RMB '000)	2.1
~living expenditure of urban residents (RMB '000)	5.0
~living expenditure of rural residents (RMB '000)	1.6
Actually Used Foreign Direct Investment (USD mil)	391
Total assets (RMB bn)	38.2
Exports (USD mil)	3,060
~percentage of change from the same period of previous year	+24.9%
Imports (USD mil)	2,880
~percentage of change from the same period of previous year	+66.6%

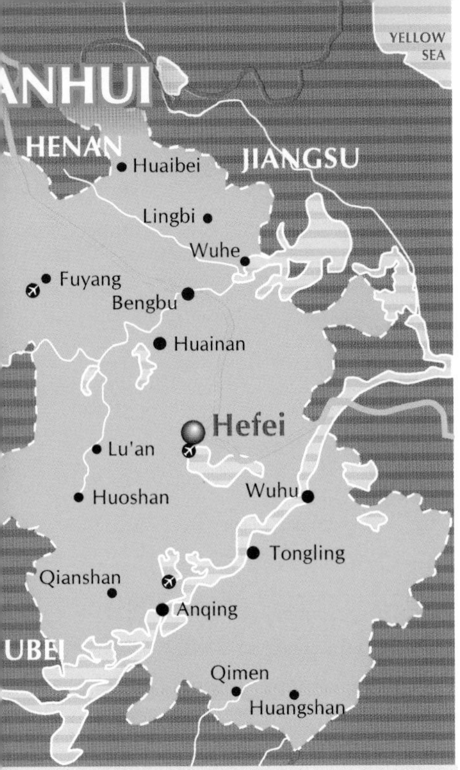

Introduction

Anhui has a complex physical topography. It is crossed in the north by Huaihe River and in the south by the Chang Jiang (Yangtze River) with alternating areas of plains, hills, mountains, and lakes and low-lying areas. Most of the inhabitants live on the plains near the Huai River in northern Anhui, and behind dykes on the right bank of the Chang Jiang. The Huang Mountains (Huang Shan) in southeast Anhui are favoured by poets and artists for its great beauty.

Anhui has abundant resources of aquatic products and forests, which are known for having many kinds of traditional Chinese herbs. Among the protected wild animals in Anhui are the Chinese (or Yangtze) alligator, Baiji (Yangtze River dolphin), South China tiger, and rhesus monkey.

History

Anhui was the first region of southern China settled by Han Chinese, who moved south in the 3rd century B.C. Although rich in agricultural potential, Anhui was economically backward in the past because of frequent floods and droughts. History records 8,614 natural disasters from 960 to 1949, including flood, drought, insects, wind, frost, and hail.

Today, Anhui is one of the most important agricultural provinces in China. The major staple crops are rice, wheat, beans, maize, sorghum and sweet potatoes. Cash crops include cotton, tobacco, peanuts, sesame, rapeseed, tea, hemp, silk, fruits, tung oil, and raw lacquer.

Anhui's industries have been built almost from scratch since the Communist revolution. From 1949 to 1980, the government reported an annual average growth in industrial output of 12.2 percent per year. Despite this growth, the industrial base is considered weak because of the dominance of small-scale enterprises. The long-term plans for Anhui's industries emphasise development based on its mineral resources, along the lines of the Ruhr Valley in Germany.

Language

Most natives of Anhui Province speak one of the Mandarin Chinese dialects. Inhabitants of extreme southeast Anhui and northwest Zhejiang Province speak Huizhou. It is previously considered to be part of the Lower Yangtze family of Mandarin dialects but now it is considered to be a separate major variety of Chinese. The dialects of Huizhou are said to differ greatly from each other.

Culture

The cultural traits of Anhui date back to the time of the Southern Song Dynasty (1127-1279), and are said to be marked by conservatism of language and art forms.

The Huizhou people of the mountains of southern Anhui are known for their commercial and clan traditions, and some linguists consider the Huizhou dialect to be a separate Chinese language, distinct from the Mandarin and Wu language spoken in the north and south.

Local specialties and handicrafts of the province include Gujinggong, Mingguang, and Suixi liquors, Xiaoxian wine, the "four treasures" of scholars (Anhui ink sticks, Shexian ink slabs, Xuan paper and Xuan brushes), as well as the wrought-iron pictures of Wuhu.

Two popular performing arts in Anhui are Huangmei Opera and Fengyang Flower Drum Opera, which originated in the folk traditions of the towns of Huangmei, Hubei Province, and Fengyang, Anhui Province, respectively.

Location Advantage

Anhui adjoins the Yangtze Delta Economic Development Region centred by Shanghai. Although it is an inland province, Anhui is near the coastal areas and lies along the Yangtze River. A readily accessible network of land, water and air transportation systems allows business firms to transport their products and technologies efficiently to markets at home and abroad. The Lianyungang Yili (Longhai) railway, also known as Eurasian transcontinental expressway, and the Yangtze River runs across north and south of the province respectively, making it possible for people to open up markets deep in the heart of China's mid-west.

Anhui's major ports, including Wuhu, Tongling, Maanshan and Anqing, also permit convenient access to the overseas market through Shanghai. China's major rail lines, including the Beijing, Shanghai railway, the Beijing Kowloon railway, all pass through Anhui in a north-south direction. The destinations of these two important arteries are Beijing, the nation's capital, Shanghai and Hong Kong, all cities of international reputation. Travel by coach from Hefei to Shanghai port via the Hefei Shanghai Expressway requires only five hours. Hefei has regular flights to more than 30 cities in China, including Beijing, Shanghai, Guangzhou , Shenzhen, Hong Kong and Xi'an.

Industry

Due to its advantage in energy, building materials, mineral and agricultural raw materials, Anhui has developed such industrial sectors as coal exploration, thermal power, cement, chemical raw materials, machinery manufacturing, household appliances, cement, textile, wine and etc. There are 370,000 industrial enterprises, of which

Anhui has established a relatively complete transportation system that includes railway, highway, water transportation and aviation. These accelerated developments in transportation were driven by the reform policy.

649 are large-scale enterprises. In 2002, the industrial enterprise value-added of RMB 194 billion was reported.

In the future, the province will enhance the overall quality of the industrial enterprises through technical innovation and transformation of management systems and at the same time strive to develop the electronics and information industries.

Agriculture

The north of Anhui, which is mostly plains, enjoys much sunshine throughout the year and an annual rainfall of 700mm, making it a favourable place for growing wheat, sweet potato, corn, sesame, ginger, garlic, apple, pear and grape. Cattle and goats produced here are a good source of raw materials for leather and food manufacturing, given their excellent quality of skin and meat. The highland areas of central Anhui, with an annual rainfall of 1,000mm, is suitable for growing rice, cotton, rapeseed, and hemp. The mountainous southern and western Anhui is abundant in timber, bamboo, tea and silk.

The area along the Yangtze River is of typical plain topology with an annual rainfall of 1,200mm. The fertile land, sufficient rainfall and criss-crossing rivers make the area a major producer of agricultural products. The plums produced here are of superior quality and are exported to the world.

Foreign Trade

Anhui has established broad trade relations with many countries in the world. Its major trading partners include North America, EU, Southeast Asia, Hongkong and Taiwan. Its trade value with Africa and South American countries is increasing annually. In 2003, total import and export value of Anhui reached US$5.94 billion, with exports US$3.06 billion and imports of US$2.88 billion. It is expected that after China's entry into WTO, Anhui's foreign trade will greatly increase.

Tourism Industry

Anhui boasts abundant tourism resources. Violent geological activities brought up the peculiar physiognomy in the mountainous area of southern Anhui. The world-renowned Huangshan scenic spots are just located in the mountainous area of southern Anhui. In western Anhui, where there are high mountains, thick forest and beautiful environment, due to the restrictions of transportation, there are relatively fewer travellers there and the tourism resources there are yet to be developed. Historically, Anhui was developed at a very early time with historical relics found everywhere in the province. In the mountainous area of southern Anhui, there is the well-preserved ancient residents village. In 2002, there were 238,800 foreign travellers coming to Anhui with a tourism income of US$124 million in foreign exchange. In China the tourism industry is still a new industry. With its abundance of tourism resources, Anhui's tourism industry has relatively greater potential for further development.

Open Ports

Anhui has nine open ports in terms of air, water and railway transportation. Exit and entry procedures can be directly transacted in Anhui for personnel and import & export goods. The

Chinese government has established customs offices in Level 1 open ports, dealing with exit & entry inspection procedures.

Transportation

Anhui has established a relatively complete transportation system that includes railway, highway, water transportation and aviation. These accelerated developments in the transportation system would not have been possible without the driving force of the reform policy. Currently, Anhui has four civil airports, namely Hefei, Huangshan, Fuyang and Anqin airports. Foreign travellers coming in and out of Anhui can also take advantage of neighbouring Nanjing, Xuzhou, Jiujiang airports.

As a province that boasts the highest railway density in China, Anhui has a railway length of 2,725 km. The railway intensity is 1.95 km per hundred km^2, ranking top in east China. The main railway lines that go through Anhui are Beijing-Shanghai line, Beijing-Kowloon line, Anhui-Jiangxi line, etc.

Anhui has set up a multi-level highway network, where nine national highways go through the province. There are also two expressways: Hefei Nanjing Expressway and Hefei Wuhu Expressway. The Tongling Yangtze River Highway Bridge is already in operation and permission has also been granted by the State Council for the construction of the Wuhu Changjiang Railway/Highway Bridge. The highway length of Anhui is 35,000 km, of which there are 211 km of expressway, 109 km of first class motor highway and 139 km of second class motor highway, 4,025 km of second class highway and 14,398 km of superior road. The highway intensity is 25.2 km per hundred km^2.

In Anhui there are three big rivers: Changjiang river, Huai river and Xinanjiang river; and more than 300 smaller rivers. The total length of the rivers is 15,000 km, of which 6,013 km is navigable, ranking seventh in China. The Zhujiaqiao Foreign Trade Harbour of Wuhu city is now open to foreign ships, where two 10,000 ton ships can anchor and 5,000 ton ships can navigate all the year round. Up to now, shipping lines have been made to Hong Kong, Japan, South Korea, Southeast Asia and Russia as well as to the coastal region of China.

Energy Resources

Coal

North of Huai River is abundant in coal reserves with an annual production of 45 million tons, which can meet the need of power plants and other sectors for coal.

Electricity

Mainly distributed in North Anhui and the areas along the Yangtze

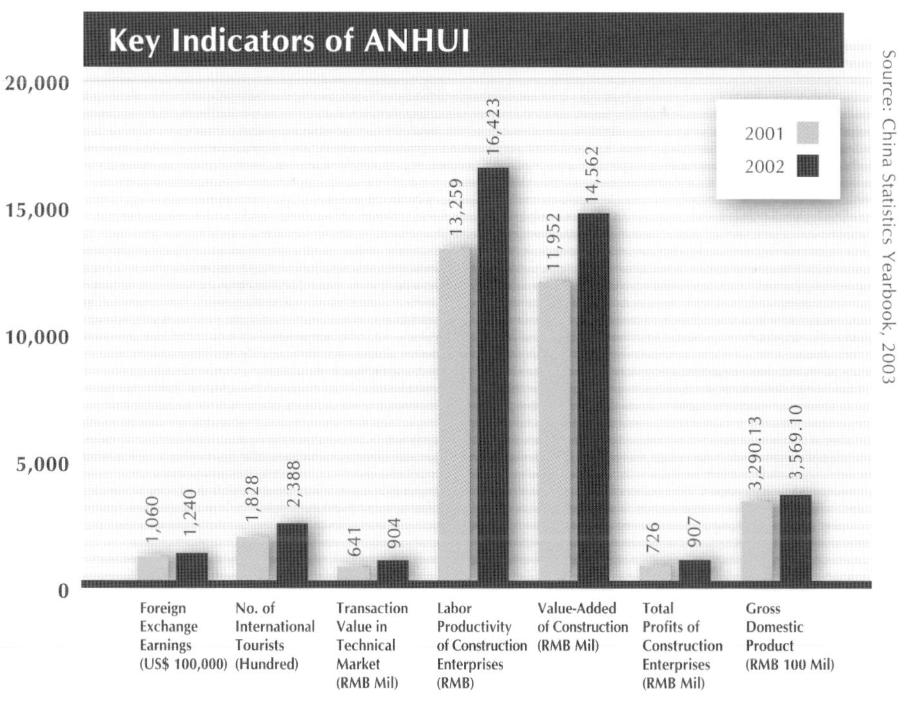

River, the province currently has a fire power plant capacity of 8.7 million kW, which can fully satisfy the need of industrial and agricultural production and people's daily life.

Geology

Anhui has undergone numerous earth sinkings and upheavals, resulting in various landforms and abundant mineral recourses. There are 75 kinds of mineral resources that have been proven. Coal, steel, copper, calcareousness lime and sulphur steel mines are the most abundant resources found in Anhui. This facilitates large-scale exploitation.

Telecommunications

After years of modification, Anhui has set up a modern telecommunication network of program controlled telephone and portable telephone, long distance transmission digital, radio location, group switching, digital data and teleconference. The population of local telephone users reach 3.21 million and mobile phone users 4.19 million. Now program controlled telephones have been installed in all the cities above county level and the 989 towns in Anhui. Direct call can be made to 1,600 cities in China and to 180 foreign countries and regions. The 900mhz mobile telecommunication system covers the whole province and automatic location within the country has been realised. Now there is a public radio location system with a total capacity of 1,319,000 units and a public network of group switching, automatic reversing direction which has covered all the cities above county level. Another network of digital data and teleconference has covered 16 cities at prefecture level, 108 service, sound message service and 200 service are provided in all the cities above county level.

Investment Guide

Types of Investment

- The foreign-funded enterprise
- Sino-foreign joint equity ventures

- Sino-foreign cooperative
- Contractual ventures
- Foreign-funded shareholding limited companies
- Equity investment in existing enterprises
- Contracted or leasing enterprises
- Develop single real estate projects
- Acquire the land use rights and develop the tracts of land
- Product processing with supplied materials and samples, assembling with supplied parts.

Approval Authorities

- The Planning Commission
- The Economic and Trade Commission
- The Foreign Economic Relations and Trade Commission of Anhui Province
- All their subordinate correspondents and the Administrative Commission of Hefei High-tech Development Zone and Wuhu Economic Development Zone are authorised to approve setting up Enterprises in Anhui Province with foreign investment within the total investment limit set up by the State.
- Those with total investment over US$30 million and those which require the approval from the responsible departments of the State Council are required to present their project proposals to the State Planning Committee for project approval by the provincial planning council after their preliminary examination, with contracts and articles of association subject to examination and approval by the Ministry of Foreign Trade & Economic cooperation (MOFTEC) after their preliminary Examination with the related departments in Anhui province.
- Those with total investment under US$30 million which are classified as a restrictive item by the State are required to present their project proposals to the Provincial Planning Committee or the Provincial

Economic and Trade Committee for their project approval, which the provincial Foreign Economic Relations and Trade Commission is authorised by the Government to give the approval for setting up enterprises.

- Any non-restrictive and promotional item with total investment under US$30 million will be examined and approved by the Prefectural and the Municipal Planning Commission or Economic and Trade Commission for the establishment of item and the establishment of the enterprises are to be approved by the local authority.
- The above two development zones are entitled to examine and approve the non-restrictive and promotional item with total investment underUS$30 million.
- The establishment of sole foreign invested enterprises will be examined and approved by the Foreign Trade and Economic Commission of different levels according to the above limits.

Documents Required

- Application for the establishment of a joint venture (investment application form for sole foreign funded enterprise) submitted by its Chinese partner;
- The feasibility study made and signed by all the investors and its official written reply;
- Enterprise name notice;
- Contract, agreements and articles of association signed and sealed by the legal representatives of all the investors or their authorised representatives (for sole foreign funded enterprise, only articles of associations);
- State owned Property Evaluation Report for Sino parties;
- Contract of leasing or purchasing of the premise for production and operation of the enterprises or contract of land use, signed with the municipal land administration or relevant district land administrative departments;

- The list signed by all investors of the imported machinery and equipment, office utilities and means of transport to be used exclusively by the enterprise (including description, model quantities, unit prices and gross value);
- The name list signed by all the investors of the Board of Directors (including name, sex, age, original position and the position in the ventures);
- Copies of valid business licence or other certificate of business operation issued by the government of the county or the region where investors reside; Credit Status Certificate issued by the bank with which the investors open the account (including company's name, A/C No, set up date, name of the legal person, formation of the organisation, deposit digits, and reputation). If the name of the legal person is not shown in the bank notice, a certificate of the name of the legal person issued by a lawyer is required; anyone who invests in his own name must provide copies of identification card and certificate of bank deposit.
- Technology transfer contract is requested if the relevant contract involves the transfer of technology.
- Written opinion of the department in charge of the Chinese partner with regard to their participation of the joint venture (not for wholly foreign owned ventures)
- Other supplementary documents deemed necessary by the approval authority.

Industry and Commerce Registration

- The foreign funded enterprise should go to the Municipal Industry and Commerce Bureau for registration one month after the ratification and provide the following documents:
- Ratifying documents and certificate for the setup of the enterprise
- Contract (Agreement)
- Enterprise's Regulations
- Project Proposal and written instructions

- Enterprise Feasibility Report and written instructions
- Name List of two chairmen of the board (a certificate should be presented from the Personnel Department of the high class for the Chinese parties which declares their positions in land)
- Legal Registration Certificate for the investors
- Capital Credit Certificate for the investors
- Enterprise's name examination and approval registration
- Housing Lease Agreement
- Relevant documents
- The registration department should decide whether or not to grant registration to the applicant within 20 days of the date receiving the application documents.

Registration Fee

- 5 percent for registered capital of RMB 10 million or more.
- Registration fee waived for registered capital of over RMB100 million.

The Administration of Foreign Exchange

Enterprises with foreign investment are required to register with duplicate copies of all related documents required at the local branch of the State's Administrative Bureau of foreign exchange (hereafter known as the local branch) to get the Exchange Registration Card for Enterprises with Foreign Investment within 30 days after their business licence is issued.

Enterprises with foreign investment are required to present their application to the local branch for their approval to open a foreign exchange account.

Enterprises with foreign investment should abide by Regulations on Exchange Control of the People's Republic of China and Regulations on the sale and purchase of and payment in Foreign Exchange in dealing with their receipts and payments.

FUJIAN

Electronics and food processing are the largest sectors. High-tech industries are becoming the new engine of economic growth.

FUJIAN Fact Sheet	2003
Area (km²)	121,700
No. of Cities	23
Population (mil)	34.9
GDP (RMB bn)	524.1
Gross capital formation (RMB bn)	211.9
Consumption expenditure (RMB bn)	243
~Household	170
~Government	73
No. of employed persons (mil)	17.46
Unemployment Rate	4.1%
Literacy Rate	88.1%
Government revenue (RMB bn)	30.5
Government expenditure (RMB bn)	45.2
Per capita annual	
~disposable income of urban residents (RMB '000)	10.0
~net income of rural households (RMB '000)	3.7
~living expenditure of urban residents (RMB '000)	7.4
~living expenditure of rural residents (RMB '000)	2.7
Actually Used Foreign Direct Investment (USD mil)	4,075
Total assets (RMB bn)	71.6
Exports (USD mil)	21,140
~percentage of change from the same period of previous year	+21.7%
Imports (USD mil)	14,195
~percentage of change from the same period of previous year	+28.7%

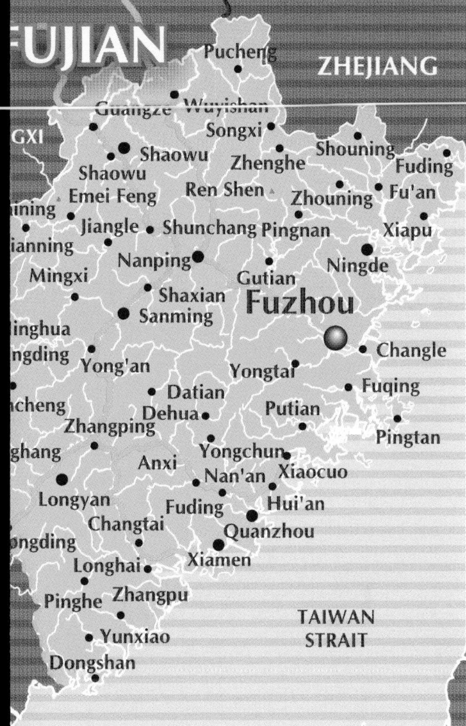

Introduction

Fujian Province, known as "Min", is situated along China's southeastern coast. It is separated from Taiwan only by the narrow Taiwan Straits. The province occupies an area of 121,700 km^2, with a population of 34.9 million. The provincial government has an immediate jurisdiction over nine administrative prefectures and municipalities, which are subdivided into 64 counties and cities.

Fujian is one of China's early experimental zones targeted for economic reforms. The province is opening to the outside world in various aspects, including economic special zones, economic and technological development zones, and coastal economic opening zones. Fujian is also a major hometown of overseas Chinese. Over the world, there are about eight million overseas Chinese of Fujian origin and 80 percent of Taiwan's population is of Fujian origin.

Fujian is known for its "eight mountains, one river and one tenth of Chinese Mu of rice field".

History

Fujian Province in southeast China has a long and rich history, dating back to the Warring States Period (475-221 B.C.). During that time, the State of Yue, located approximately in present-day Jiangsu and Zhejiang provinces, was defeated by the State of Chu, which ruled the areas of today's Hubei and Hunan provinces. After their defeat, the Yue people were forced to move southward and settled in the areas now known as Fujian, Guangdong, Guangxi and Vietnam. Those that went to Fujian were called Min Yue, and the province itself Dong Yue.

Fujian is also known as Min. People in the south of the province speak a dialect called the Minnan (southern Fujian) dialect. The natives of Fujian are therefore called the ancient Min people. No written records about them have ever been found, but the boat-shaped coffins at the Wuyi Mountains probably belonged to Xia Dynasty (c. 21st-16th century B.C.) Min people. A pictographic written language was discovered in a rock in the town of Hua'an, and is believed to be another relic of the ancient Min people from the Shang Dynasty (c.16th-11th century B.C.).

To reform the existing processing trade system and to go in line with international practice, the Chinese government has decided to set up export processing zones in 15 pilot cities.

Infrastructure

Water Transport

The coastal ports in Fujian have a combined annual throughput of over 69 million tons. Fuzhou's Mawei, Xiamen's Dongdu and Meizhou Bay are the most important harbours, with berths that can accommodate 10,000 to 50,000-ton-class vessels. Since January 1, 2001, direct shipping routes from Fuzhou and Xiamen to Quemoy and vice versa are available. Besides Taiwan, Xiamen has also opened other overseas routes linked to Europe, America, Japan, Singapore, Hong Kong and the Republic of Korea as well.

Railways

Fujian is well connected to northern and central China by railways. The province is connected to the Beijing-Kowloon railway via the 500-km Yingtan-Xiamen railway. The Wenfu

Railway has been completed and Ganglong Railway connecting Zhejiang and Jiangxi is expected to be completed by 2004.

Highways

Major highways include those linking Fuzhou-Kunming, Beijing-Fuzhou, Xiamen-Chengdu, and Fuzhou-Lanzhou. The existing class I highway within the province is Fuzhou-Quangzhou-Xiamen-Zhangzhou. Three new highways are under construction, they are the Wenzhou-Fuzhou highway, Zhangzhou-Longyan highway as well as the state-highway which links Beijing and Fuzhou.

Air Transport

The Changle International Airport in Fuzhou, the Xiamen International Airport and the airport in Wuyishan operate more than 90 domestic and international routes, linking the province with more than 40 domestic cities, as well as Hong Kong, Japan and the Philippines.

Telecommunications

Telecommunications sector is among the most developed in China. By 2002, there were 7.92 million and 2.50 million subscribers for mobile phone and Internet service in the province respectively.

Electricity

Fujian has abundant hydroelectric resources, with total electricity capacity estimated at over 4.04 million kWh a year. The major power stations are located at Shuikou, Shaxikou, Fuzhou, Zhangping and Yong'an. In Xiamen, a power plant is being built at Songyu.

Industries

In 2001, Fujian's total industrial output was RMB190.4 billion. Electronics and food processing are the largest sectors, and the province's output in canned food tops the country. Other major industries include footwear, garments, construction materials and aquatic products. Fujian is one of the largest electronics-manufacturing centres in China, and hi-tech industries have become the province's new economic growth engine.

Tourism

Fujian has two state tourist resorts, Wuyi Mountains and Meizhou Island, which are potential tourism development sites. Other major scenic spots include Gulangyu, Gu Mountains, Nanshan Temple, etc. Over 1.63 million foreign tourists visited the region in 2001, with generated revenue of US$942 million.

Consumer Market

The province's retail sales of consumer goods recorded RMB166 billion in 2002, which is an increase of 1.1 percent over the previous year. Among the cities in Fujian, Fuzhou was the largest consumer centre with retail sales of RMB35.2 billion, an increase of 11.6 % over 2001. Other major consumer centres are Quanzhou, Xiamen and Zhangzhou.

Xiamen is one of the 11 pilot cities in China for setting up sino-foreign joint venture department stores with import/export rights. Also, the first state-level market for trading with Taiwan was established in Xiamen in May 1999.

There are three commercial zones in Fuzhou: Dongjjekou, Wuyi Square, and Taijiang Pier. Major department stores in Fujian province include Xiamen Commercial Group, Fujian General Merchandise Department Store, Fuzhou Huadu General Merchandise Co., Fuzhou Xin Huadu Department Store Co., Ltd., Xindeco Dutyfree Market, Xiamen China, Xiamen Friendship Store Co., Ltd., Fuzhou Dongjiekou Department Store, Xiamen No. 1 Department Store, Zhangzhou Department Store, and Quanzhou Department Store.

Science and Technology

Xiamen Torch Hi-tech Development Zone was jointly set up by the State Science and

Technology Commission and Xiamen Municipal Government. It implemented a R&D programme which aims to facilitate commercialisation of new technological innovations. In addition, the zone focuses on the development of electronics, information industry and mechatronics industry. Multinational corporations which have set up their factories in the zone include Fuji Electric and Toshiba from Japan, ABB from Sweden and Bourns from the US.

Foreign Trade

In 2002, Fujian's total value of imports and exports was US$35.3 billion and exports value was US$21.1 billion. Major export goods included canned products, textiles and garments, footwear, handicrafts, electronics, chemicals and mineral products. US, Japan, Hong Kong, Germany

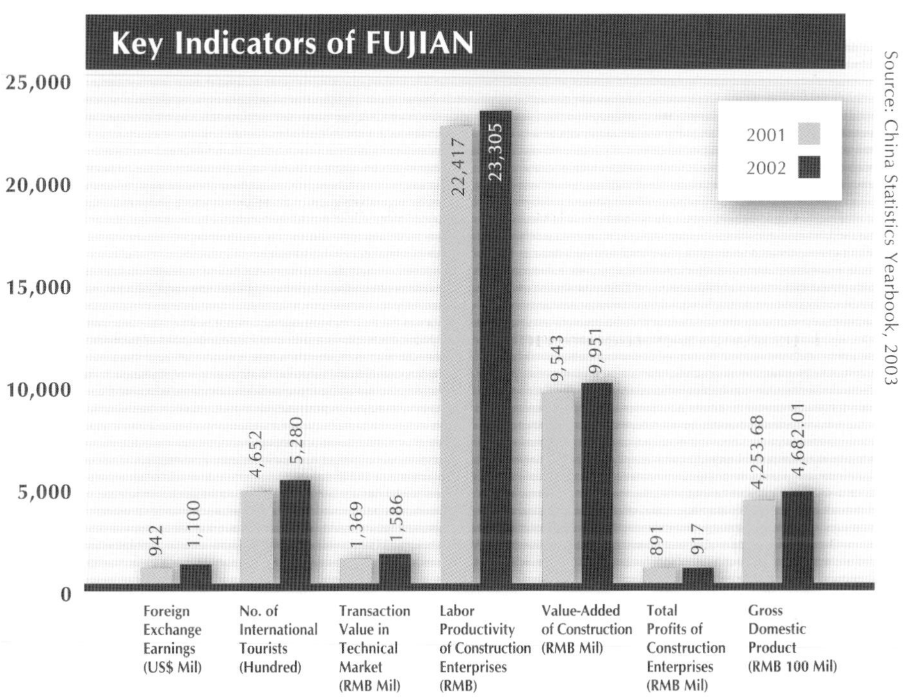

and the Netherlands are the major export markets.

Imports increased 28.7 percent to US$14 billion in 2003. Major import commodities included electronic raw materials, leather products, synthetic rubber, chemical raw materials, etc. Major imports come from Taiwan, Japan, Republic of Korea, the US and Germany.

Foreign Investment

By the end of 2003, Fujian approved 2274 foreign-invested projects. The corresponding contracted foreign capital was US$7.25 billion. Foreign investments are mainly from Hong Kong, Taiwan, the US, Japan and the UK. The investment projects are mainly in the fields of machinery, equipment, electronics, petrochemical, textiles, food processing, communications and telecommunications.

Taiwan is the largest foreign investor in Fujian. In 2000, the province approved 557 Hong Kong-invested projects with contractual and actual utilised foreign capital of US$1.8 billion and US$1.2 billion respectively. By end-2000, Fujian approved 16,414 HK-invested projects with contractual and actual utilised foreign capital of US$36.5 billion and US$17.6 billion respectively.

To reform the existing processing trade system and to go in line with international practice, the Chinese government has decided to set up export processing zones in 15 pilot cities. Xiamen is selected as one of the cities in this trial programme. Export processing zones are special restricted areas administered by Customs. Goods moving in and out of the zones are regarded as imports and exports. Enterprises involving in export processing, storage and transportation are allowed to be set up in the zones.

GANSU

Gansu is situated in the hinterland of northwestern China and at the upper reaches of the Yellow River.

GANSU Fact Sheet	2003
Area (km²)	390,000
No. of Cities	14
Population (mil)	26.0
GDP (RMB bn)	130.1
Gross capital formation (RMB bn)	53.8
Consumption expenditure (RMB bn)	68
~Household	51
~Government	17
No. of employed persons (mil)	15.11
Unemployment Rate	3.4%
Literacy Rate	81.9%
Government revenue (RMB bn)	8.6
Government expenditure (RMB bn)	30.0
Per capita annual	
~disposable income of urban residents (RMB '000)	6.7
~net income of rural households (RMB '000)	1.7
~living expenditure of urban residents (RMB '000)	5.1
~living expenditure of rural residents (RMB '000)	1.2
Actually Used Foreign Direct Investment (US$ mil)	39.0
Total assets (RMB bn)	17.8
Exports (USD mil)	878
~percentage of change from the same period of previous year	+59.9%
Imports (USD mil)	450
~percentage of change from the same period of previous year	+37%

Introduction

Gansu is situated in the hinterland of north-western China at the upper reaches of the Yellow River. It has a total area of 390,000 km2 and a population of 26 million.

With its long history and unique location, Gansu is known for various cultural relics and scenic spots, such as the world-known ancient "Silk Road" and Mogao Grottoes in Dunhuang, which is named by UNESCO as one of the world's cultural relics. In addition, the other grottoes, temples, scenic spots and historical sites, scattered across the province, sparkle like resplendent gems along the colorful ribbon of the "Silk Road" and attract great tourist interest both at home and abroad.

Lanzhou, the provincial capital with a population of 2.7 million, is a hub of transportation and communications as well as a centre of commerce and trade in north-

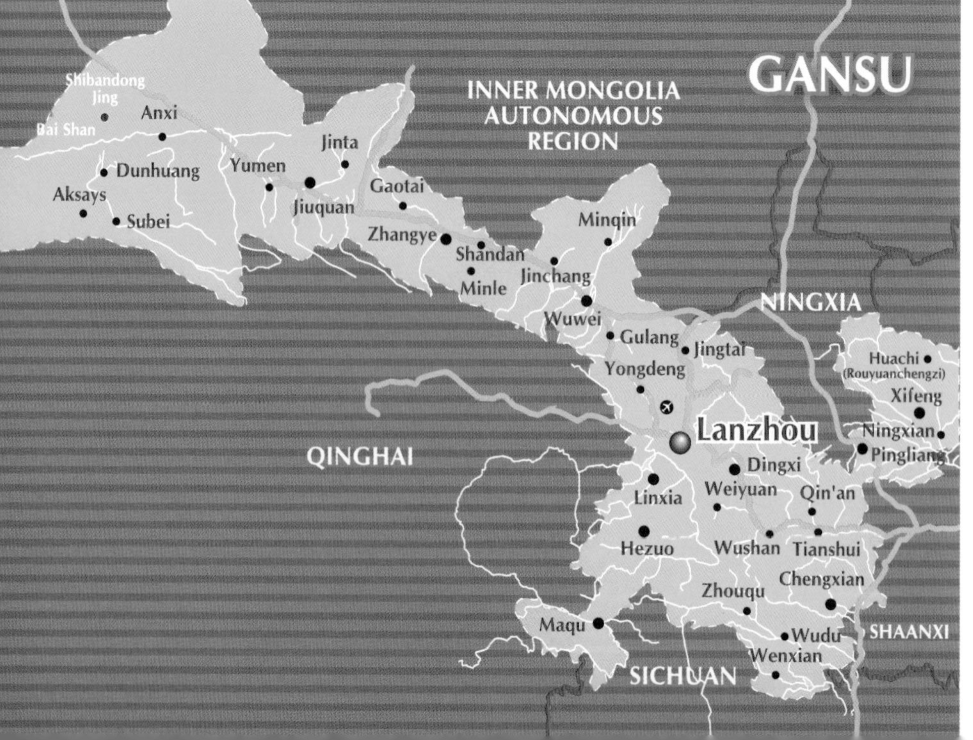

western China. The State Council approved Lanzhou as an inland open city in 1992, entitling it to the same preferential policies as the coastal open cities and the provincial-level administrative authority in economic management.

Gansu is abundant in resources, particularly its reserves of coal and oil. It is one of China's most important production bases of nonferrous metal such as copper, aluminium, nickel, lead and zinc. Eleven minerals resources have reserves ranking top in China. The exploitation scale of Jinchang copper and nickel mines ranks second in the world. Apart from supplying the domestic market, the province also supplies foreign markets such as the US, the UK, Japan and France. Gansu has natural advantages in developing agriculture. Apart from the famous watermelon, the province is a major agriculture base of Chinese medical herbs. Its output of flax is also high in the country.

The province also has favourable conditions for developing animal husbandry. Its pastoral area is one of the biggest in China and is good for grazing sheep and cattle. Its by-product of camel wool is famous.

Ethnicity

Gansu is inhabited by 20,515,000 Han people and 2,275,900 people of ethnic minority groups. They make up 91.7 percent and 8.3 percent of the province's population respectively. Other minority groups with a population of more than 1,000 each are the Hui, Tibetan, Dongxiang, Tu, Manchu, Yugur, Bonan, Mongolian, Salar, and Kazak.

Natural resources

Land

Gansu features a land area of 390,000 km2, including 3.53 million hectares of cultivated land or 0.14 hectare per capita, 16.64 million hectares of grassland, and 4.26 million hectares of forests with a standing timber reserve of 200 million cubic metres. In addition, there are one million hectares of wasteland suitable for agriculture, 6.66 million hectares of wasteland suitable for forestation, and 4.76 million hectares of mountain slopes suitable for livestock breeding.

Minerals

Nearly 3,000 deposits of 145 kinds of minerals have been found and the reserves of 94 kinds of minerals have been ascertained, including nickel, cobalt, platinum family elements, selenium, casting clay, finishing serpentine, and five other minerals whose reserves are the largest in the country. Gansu has unique advantages in accessing to 15 kinds of minerals such as nickel, zinc, cobalt, platinum, iridium, copper, stibium, barite, and baudisserite.

Energy

The water resources in Gansu are mainly distributed in nine river systems in the Yellow, Yangtze, and inland river drainage basins with an annual discharge of 61.4 billion cubic metres and a combined hydropower potential of 17.24 million kW. Gansu places ninth among China's provinces and autonomous regions in terms of hydropower potential. To date, 29 hydropower stations have been constructed in the province with an installed generating capacity of 30 million kW and an annual output of 23.565 billion kWh. The Liujiaxia, Yanguoxia, and Bapanxia hydropower stations on the upper reaches of the Yellow River and the Bikou Hydropower Station on the Bailong River have a total installed capacity of 212.5 kW. The proved reserves of coal are 8.92 billion tons, and those of petroleum, between 600 and 700 million tons. There is also considerable potential for the development of wind and solar energies.

Animals and plants

There are 659 species of wild animals, including the giant panda, snub-nosed monkey, antelope, snow leopard, deer, fawn, musk deer, bactrian (two-humped) camel, and 24 other first-class rare animals under state protection. There are 441 species of birds in Gansu Province. There are over 4,000 species of wild plants including 951 species of medical value. Of which 450 species, such as angelica root, rhubarb, hairy asiabell root, licorice root, fritillary bulb, marijuana, the bark of eucommia, glossy ganoderma, and Chinese caterpillar fungus, have been developed. Gansu holds second place among China's provinces and autonomous regions in the variety of medicinal herbs.

Environment

Gansu faces an adverse ecological environment an- acute shortage of water resources, sparse vegetation, and a serious water and soil loss. Every year, the section of the Yellow River in Gansu washes away more than 500 million tons of silt containing about 50 kilograms of organic matter. These include 3.5 kilograms of pure nitrogen and two kilograms of pure phosphorus. The silt washed away accounts for one-third of the annual silt that the Yellow River carries to the lower reaches.

In recent years, Gansu has spared no effort in using biological methods, construction projects, and technology measures to bring its soil erosion under control. The ecological environment on the Loess Plateau has been markedly improved. Cultivated land was restored into forest and grassland, so as to strengthen the protection and maintenance of the ecological environment. The readjustment of the agricultural structure will be stepped up. Emphasis will be placed on readjusting the variety of agricultural products, the ratio between the development of grain and cash crops, and the locations of the various economic sectors.

Infrastructure

Overall

To improve investment conditions, the Gansu government has invested huge amounts of fund to improve the province's infrastructure. In 2001, the government proposed 75 new infrastructure building projects, ranging from water supply, natural gas to electricity.

Railways

Lanzhou is a major transportation hub in China. It is the intersection point of four trunk railway lines (Lanzhou-Lianyungang/Longhai, Lanzhou-Xinjiang, Lanzhou-Baotao and Lanzhou-Qinghai). The international railway between Asia and Europe (the New Asia-Europe Continental Bridge which starts from Lianyungang and joins with the Siberia Railway) also runs across the province. The Lanzhou Western Goods Station (the largest station for freight transport in northwest China) is serving as the main transit and consolidation hub of containers on the New Asia-Europe Continental Bridge.

Besides, the government proposes to build a new double-track railway between Baoji of Shaanxi and Lanzhou. Travel time between the two cities is expected to shorten from the existing nine hours to 5.5 hours upon completion.

Highways

Lanzhou is also the hub of highways in the province. Five state-grade highways leading to other provinces including Xinjiang and Sichuan are being planned.

Air Transport

The Lanzhou international airport has services to 37 domestic and overseas destinations. Chartered flights from Lanzhou to Hong Kong are also available.

Telecommunications

Direct telephone services to over 100 overseas countries and regions are available. Currently, telephone subscribers reach 2.4 million. In 2002, total revenue from telecommunication reached RMB4.6 billion. More than 2.1 million people own cell phones and approximately 520000 users have access to the Internet. The government also starts to build an information highway connecting Taiyuan, Yinchuan and Lanzhou.

Water

By 2003, the Gansu government has exerted its plan to invest more than RMB 610 million for two years to improve the water supply system of the province. The central government is aiming to improve the water supply system of the north-western provinces, including Ningxia, by bringing water from the upper Yangtze River to upper Yellow River. The first stage of this project is expected to be completed by 2010.

Electricity

The Liujiaxia hydropower station is one of the largest in China, with a capacity of one million kWh. With the abundant hydropower resources of the Yellow river, Gansu is able to provide electricity for the neighbouring provinces, including Qinghai, Shaanxi, Sichuan and Ningxia.

Oil Supply

The Lanzhou-Chengdu-Chongqing oil pipeline will pass through 30 counties and cities in Gansu, Shaanxi and Chongqing with an annual oil delivering capacity of more than five million tons. Also, one of the key projects in the Tenth five-year plan includes the construction of an oil pipeline network connecting Xinjiang, Gansu, Henan, Hubei, Jiangsu, Jiangxi and Shanghai that has already been completed. The network extends as far as Turkmenistan and East Siberia and it provides a major passage for delivering oil products from the northwest region to the southwest region.

Gansu is an important base of oil refining and petrochemical industries. The roles of the Lanzhou Oil Refinery and the Lanzhou Company of Chemical Industry are significant in developing China's petrochemical industry.

Gas Supply

The new natural gas pipeline, Sebei-Xining-Lanzhou, linking Qinghai and Gansu provinces, runs 953 kilometres from Sebei Natural Gas Field in the Qaidam Basin, through Xining of Qinghai to Lanzhou. It will deliver two billion cubic metres of natural gas from northwest to the eastern parts of China.

Industries

In 2002, the added value of industrial output of the province totalled RMB68.8 billion and industries are mainly located at Lanzhou, Jinchang, Baiyin, Tianshui and Yumen.

Gansu is an important base of oil refining and petrochemical industry. The roles of the Lanzhou Oil Refinery and the Lanzhou Company of Chemical Industry are significant in developing China's petrochemical industry.

In order to accelerate development of its resource-based industries, the province has introduced incentives to encourage foreign investment in the mining, refining and processing of minerals.

Lanzhou and Tianshui are two major centres producing machinery. At present, the province supplies over half of the oil-drilling equipment in the country. Gansu is also the major industrial base of high-speed camera and imitated tape-making equipment. In recent years, the textile industry, including wool and cotton spinning, knitting and chemical fibres have also developed quickly.

Pillar industries

Pillar industries of Gansu include non-ferrous metals, electricity, petrochemicals, oil exploration machinery, and building materials.

Tourism

Gansu has good assets in developing tourism. Lanzhou is an important stop on the Silk Road, which connects the famous historic sites such as Dunhuang Grottoes, Bingling Temple Grottoes, Labuleng lamasery and Maiji Mountain Grottoes. Other tourist sites include Jiayuguan Pass at the westernmost end of the Great Wall and Tulu Gully.

In 2002, about 236,800 foreign tourists visited Gansu. This generated a revenue of US$54 million, which is an decrease of 20 percent over the previous year. The country has planned to build a new tourism economic zone in Dunhuang. The new zone will be located at the Yitang Lake and cover an area of five km2. The city has stipulated preferential policies to attract domestic and overseas investment for the zone.

Besides, Gansu will collaborate with nine other provinces and autonomous regions, namely Qinghai, Sichuan, Shaanxi, Shanxi, Henan, Shandong, Inner Mongolia and Ningxia, to establish a tourist information network. Under the collaboration project, a tourism fair will be organised every two years.

Consumer Market

Retail sales of consumer goods in Gansu rose by 9.8 percent to RMB43.4 billion in 2002. Lanzhou is the largest consumer centre that accounts for nearly half of the total sales. The second largest centre is Tianshui and Baiyin, each accounting for about 8 percent of the total sales.

Lanzhou has been developed into a major distribution centre of goods in northwestern China. The Lanzhou Commercial and Trade Center is the largest commercial building in Gansu. Besides, Lanzhou has over 300 commodities distribution markets including markets of non-ferrous metals, petrochemicals, machinery and electronics, building materials, fur and wool, grain, medicinal herbs, vegetables and fruits.

Major department stores and shopping centres in Gansu include Lanzhou Mingzhu Department

Store, Lanzhou Industrial and Commercial Shopping Centre, Lanzhou Hua Lian Supermarket. Baiyin Tongcheng Shopping Arcade and Jinda Daxia Co. Ltd.

Science and Technology

Although Gansu may not be as well developed as the eastern provinces, it is a leader in certain research areas in the world, including China. Jiuquan is one of the satellite launching centres in China. The particle accelerator RIBLL, built in 1997, is among the most advanced accelerators in the world.

Foreign Trade

Gansu's major export items include machinery, petrochemicals and garments. Major export markets were Japan, Hong Kong, the US, Republic of Korea and Germany. Total trade in 2002 reached US$621 million. To stimulate trade, the Gansu

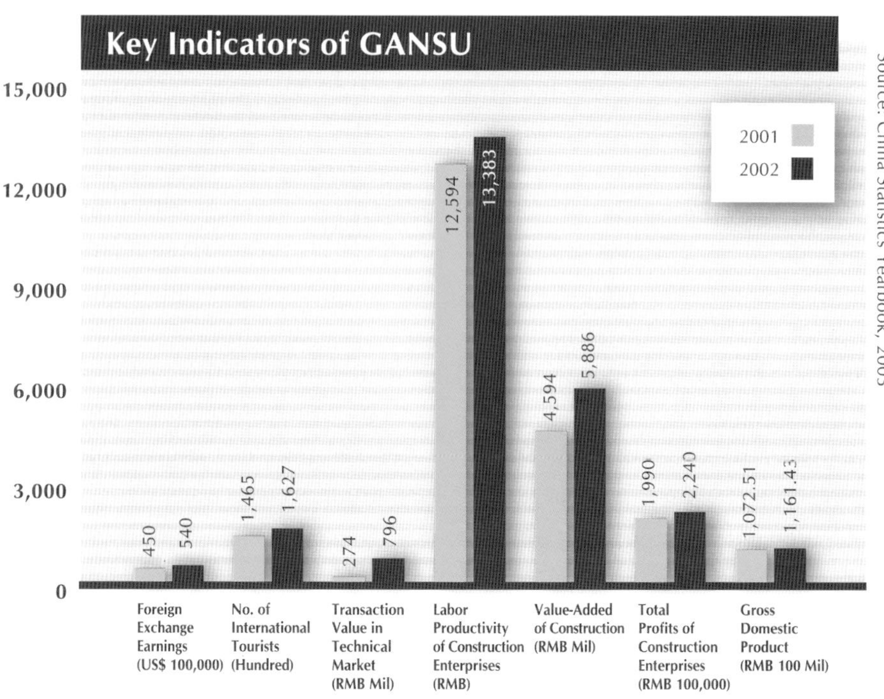

government has established 10 export industrial bases, ranging from IT industry to agriculture.

Export recorded US$326 million and import was US$295 million. Hong Kong was the largest import sources of Gansu, accounting for 31 percent of the total. Other import sources included Australia, the US, Germany and Japan.

The nearest seaport of Gansu is Tianjin, which is 2,000 km away. As an incentive for exports, the government decided to provide transportation subsidies to all exporting enterprises, including FIEs, in the province.

Foreign Investment

In 2003, the contracted amount was US$245 million. The actual utilised amount of foreign investment is US$39 million. Major sources of investment came from the US, Hong Kong, the UK, Philippines and Taiwan. Major foreign investments were mainly engaged in construction, property development, food and beverages, machinery, electronics, petrochemical, pharmaceutical, textile and other light manufacturing industries.

To boost the development of the central and western regions in China, the State Council has issued new investment regulation policies in early 2001. It gives FIEs national treatments and encourages FIEs to reform, merge, buy and join the state owned enterprises. Under the existing policy, FIEs are entitled to a three-year tax reduction and exemption. The new policy stated that foreign-in-vested enterprises in the central and western regions would enjoy another three years of preferential tax rate when the term expires. The tax rate can be further reduced to 10 percent if an enterprise is proven to export more than 70 percent of its annual output in terms of value.

GUANGDONG

This is the top province in attracting foreign direct investment. Many world-leading MNCs have established a presence there.

GUANGDONG Fact Sheet	2003
Area (km²)	178,000
No. of Cities	52
Population (mil)	79.5
GDP (RMB bn)	1,344.9
Gross capital formation (RMB bn)	415.6
Consumption expenditure (RMB bn)	670
~Household	445
~Government	225
No. of employed persons (mil)	42.10
Unemployment Rate	2.9%
Literacy Rate	93.6%
Government revenue (RMB bn)	120.2
Government expenditure (RMB bn)	152.1
Per capita annual	
~disposable income of urban residents (RMB '000)	12.3
~net income of rural households (RMB '000)	4.1
~living expenditure of urban residents (RMB '000)	10.3
~living expenditure of rural residents (RMB '000)	3.1
Actually Used Foreign Direct Investment (USD mil)	15,578
Total assets (RMB bn)	232.9
Exports (USD mil)	152.944
~percentage of change from the same period of previous year	+29.1%
Imports (USD mil)	130.702
~percentage of change from the same period of previous year	+27.3%

PROVINCES

Introduction

Guangdong is located in southern China adjacent to Hong Kong. It is a well-known hometown of overseas Chinese. More than 20 million overseas Chinese, scattered over more than 100 countries, were originally from Guangdong. This is particularly true for Hong Kong and Macao, where a majority of the citizens have their origins in Guangdong.

The province's capital city is Guangzhou. The major dialects in the province are Guangzhou, Hakka, and Chaozhou. More than half of Guangdong's people speak the Guangzhou dialects.

Guangdong was one of the two provinces in China that were first opened to foreign direct investment by means of special economic zones.

In 1980, three special economic zones (SEZs), i.e., Shenzhen SEZ, Zhuhai SEZ and Shantou SEZ, were established to attract technology transfers. To attract foreign investments, these SEZs were granted a high degree of autonomy by the State Council to manage their economic affairs and tax incentive schemes.

In 1985, the state designated the whole Pearl River Delta as an open economic zone. Most counties and towns of Guangdong are now open to foreign investors and enjoy favourable economic policies. The open zone includes Guangzhou, Shenzhen, Zhuhai, Shantou, Shaoguan, Heyuan, Meizhou, Huizhou, Shanwei, Dongguan, Zhong-shan, Jiangmen, Foshan, Yangjiang, Zhanjiang, Maoming, Zhaoqing, Qingyuan, Chaozhou, Jieyang.

Natural Resources

The province's abundant supply of sunshine and rainfall give the land enormous fertility and vitality all year round. The famous fruits found in the province include lychee, bananas, oranges, and pineapples, which are reputed to be the four finest fruits in South China.

Three-fifths of the province is covered by mountains and hills. There are 2.51 million hectares of cultivated land and 10.8 million hectares of mountainous areas.

The province is characterised by a great number of rivers, among these, the Pearl, Han-

jiang, and Jianjiang Rivers are prominent. The Pearl River comprises the Xijiang River, the Beijiang River, and the Dongjiang River at 2,129 kilometres. It is the third longest river in China.

The province boasts over 8,000 varieties of plants, and over 700 species of animals. Ten nature preserves for rare animals and plants have been set up, among which Ding Hushan Natural conservatory is regarded as a world-class reserve. The province also abounds in hydropower, with a potential capacity of 6.65 million kW.

The province's unique geological structure bestowed it with rich mineral resources. To date, 116 kinds of minerals have been discovered, most of which are nonferrous metals. Many of the minerals are among the largest in the country, such as charcoal, sulphur, iron, lead, bismuth, silver, thallium, oil shale, niobium molybdenum, and selenium. The oilfield in the South China Sea, which covers a huge area over the offshore basins at the Pearl River estuary and Beibu Bay, has an abundant reserve in both crude oil and gas, and promises to be an excellent site for future exploitation.

The vast sea territory of the province, combined with numerous natural bays and harbours, provides an ideal site for the fishing industry. There are 150 natural seawater fisheries, covering an area of 440,000 km2. There are 120,000 hectares of seawater and over 300,000 hectares of fresh water being deemed suitable for fisheries. The province is home to more than 800 fish varieties.

Infrastructure

Water Transport

Guangdong has more than 51 state-approved ports, which have seen rapid development in recent years. About 54 percent of Shenzhen's total container throughput was handled in Yantian, while 27 percent was handled in Shekou and 16 percent in Chiwan. Yantian International Container Terminals (YICT) has the capacity to handle the fourth generation container vessels. Yantian, which is now the second largest in China in terms of container handling capacity, is able to handle more than two million TEUs a year. When the planned Phase 3 expansion project is completed, Yantian will be able to play a more active role in promoting Shenzhen's overall port transportation service.

At present, there are regular direct calls at Shenzhen's ports by major shipping operators such as the Global Alliance, Hapag-Lloyd, P&O Containers, Maersk Line, Sea-Land Service, Hanjin Shipping, Hyundai, Merchant Marine,

Mediterranean Shipping Company, Norasia Lines and Madrigal Wan Hai Lines. Improvements in port services including computerisation of the inspecting network, which will help simplify the inspecting procedures and align the port's customs procedures with international practices.

Railways

The province is a major railway hub in southern China, providing easy transportation to most parts of the country. Major railways running through the province include the Beijing-Guangzhou Lines and the Beijing-Kowloon Railway. The opening of the Beijing-Kowloon Railway has reduced the travel time between Guangzhou and Beijing to only 27 hours.

Travel time from Guangzhou to Shantou was also shortened to about 10 hours with the Guangzhou-Meizhou-Shantou Line. A new railway, the Guangdong-Hainan railway connecting Zhanjiang in Guangdong with Sanya in the Hainan Island, is under construction. This is the first crossed-seas railway in China.

Highways

Road links have been greatly improved with the completion of Guangzhou-Shenzhen Expressway and numerous locally funded highways such as the Shenzhen-Shantou Expressway. The Humen Bridge which connects the Guangzhou-Shenzhen Expressway with the Guangzhou-Zhuhai Highway, has been completed and in operation. The Guangdong authorities also plan to build a network of 25 major roads linking major cities of the province with Hong Kong and Macau.

Air Transport

The province has seven civil airports (including Guangzhou Baiyun, Guangzhou Huadu, Zhuhai, Shenzhen, Shantou, Zhanjiang). Direct flight services are available to most major domestic cities. There are also international flight services to Manila, Bangkok, Singapore, Brisbane, Jakarta, Kuala Lumpur, Los Angeles, Melbourne, Sydney, Seoul, and Hong Kong at the Guangzhou Baiyun International Airport. A new Baiyun International Airport was approved by the State Council in July 1997 and is currently under construction. The expected completion date is in 2010 and it will handle 80 million travellers and one million tons of cargo annually.

Telecommunications

Guangdong has one of the most advanced telecommunication networks in the country. At the end of 2002, the number of mobile telephone subscribers in Guangdong exceeded 32.1 million, which is about 12 percent of the country's total. By the end of 2002, the number of subscribers of Internet services reached 57 million.

With a sophisticated telecommunications network, ATM systems are now adopted by the banks in Guangdong. Electronic data interchange (EDI) systems are also introduced in Guangdong to enhance communication between banks, manufacturing enterprises and the customs offices.

Electricity

There is ample electricity supply in the province. The total installed electric power generating capacity in the province was over 30 million kWh by end-1999. Besides the existing Daya Bay Nuclear Power Station, which has a capacity of 1.8 million kWh, the provincial government plans to build a second nuclear power station near Daya Bay.

Industries

In 2002, the province's total industrial output increased strongly to RMB1753.1 billion, which puts it top among the provinces in China. Major industrial production bases included Guangzhou, Shenzhen, Foshan, Huizhou and Zhuhai.

Guangdong is the largest light industry production base in China. Output of light industries accounts for over half of the province's total industrial output. Guangdong-made consumer products, including electrical appliances such as television sets, electrical fans and refrigerators, garments, bicycles, toys, shoes and electronics items, are popular among Chinese consumers.

Besides, Guangdong has developed into a major export-processing base for investors from Hong Kong, Macau and other foreign investors. Foreign-invested enterprises (FIEs) now account for about 60 percent of Guangdong's industrial output. However, Guangdong's industries rely heavily on other provinces and overseas for raw material supplies, such as cotton, coal, plastic chips and paper pulps.

In the coming years, the province will invest heavily in infrastructure projects. It plans to develop a strong production base of car, electronics, iron and steel, building materials, and expand the tertiary sector.

Tourism

Guangdong attracts a large number of business visitors each year due to its role as a trade centre in southern China. In addition, a number of theme parks, including the "the Window of the World" in Shenzhen, and "the Grand View of the World" in Guangzhou, have been developed in recent years to attract tourists. The province received more than 2.98 million foreign tourists in 2002, up 39.9 percent over 2000 and generated a total revenue of US$5.09 billion, up 23.8 percent from 2000.

Consumer Market

Guangdong has the largest consumer market in China despite having the fourth largest population among the provinces. Retail sales of consumer goods increased by 11.1 percent to RMB501.4 billion in 2002, which is 12 percent of the country's total.

Guangdong's retail sector is one of the most developed in China with a broad range of retail outlets including department stores, shopping malls, supermarkets, specialty stores, chain stores and warehouse clubs. Guangzhou and Shenzhen were selected by the State Council in 1992 as two of the 11 designated pilot cities to establish pilot Sino-overseas joint venture retail enterprises with import and export rights.

The Guangzhou Hualian-Broadway Co. Ltd., Guangzhou Zhengjia Enterprise (Commercial) Co. Ltd. and the Shenzhen Wal-Mart were approved by the State Council as three of the 19 pilot retail JVs in China. Other major overseas-invested cooperative retail enterprises approved by the local government include Chia Tai Makro from Thailand, Wal-Mart from the US in Shenzhen, Carrefour from France, Jusco from Japan, and dozens of franchised chain stores (such as U2, G2000, Baleno, Bossini, Fortei, etc.) from Hong Kong.

Major department stores and shopping centres in Guangdong include Guangzhou Friendship Department Store, Guangzhou Department Store, Guangzhou Xindaxin Co., Nanfang Shopping Centre, Dongshan Department Store, Shenzhen Duty Free Shop Enterprises Group, Guangzhou Chia Tai Makro Co., Zhuhai Duty Free Shop Enterprise Group, Shenzhen Wanjia Department Store Co., Fushan Xinghua Shareholdings Co., Shenzhen Tianhong Department Store Co., Guangzhou Huaxia Department Store, Zhuhai Department Store Co., Guangzhou Wangfujing Department Store Co., etc.

Guangdong has developed into a major export-processing base for investors from Hong Kong, Macau and other foreign investors. Foreign-invested enterprises (FIEs) now contribute about 60 percent of Guangdong's industrial output.

Foreign Trade

Guangdong's external trade totalled US$284 billion in 2003, accounting for 35.6 percent of the country's total and ranked top among all provinces and municipalities.

Exports amounted to US$153 billion in 2003. Major export items included agricultural products, chemicals, electrical appliances, electronics, textiles, garments, toys and shoes. Hong Kong is Guangdong's largest export market, accounting for 34 percent of the province's total. Other major markets included the US, the EU, Japan and Taiwan.

Imports totalled US$131 billion in 2003. Major imports included raw material and other resource-based intermediate goods, electronics, machinery, and complete sets of equipment. Major import sources included Japan, Taiwan, Republic of Korea, the US and the EU.

Foreign Investment

Guangdong ranked top in attracting foreign investment among all provinces and municipalities. In 2003, the province approved 11,472 (-2.0%) foreign-invested projects with contracted capital of US$24 billion (29.4%). Actual utilised foreign investment in the year increased by 14.2 percent to US$18.9 billion.

Foreign investments in Guangdong are mainly engaged in manufacturing industries, including computer accessories, computer, biological products, mechanical and electrical products, refined chemicals, toys, garments and hardwares. Many leading multinationals such as P&G, Amway, ICI, Erisson, Nestle, Pepsi, Coca-Cola and Mitsubishi have established their production bases in Guangdong. Foreign investments have increasingly been channelled into infrastructure, agriculture, property and capital-and technological-intensive projects in recent years.

Hong Kong is the largest source of foreign direct investment in Guangdong. Up to 1999, there were 63,144 investment projects being funded by Hong Kong companies with a total contractual foreign capital of US$119.3 billion.

Hong Kong's investments are mainly involved in electronics, toys, garments, shoes, plastic, computer and accessories, commerce, food catering, materials warehousing, distribution, real estate, and other infrastructure development. In recent years, Hong Kong's investment in Guangdong province has diversified from manufacturing to the services sector.

Other major investors in Guangdong were from Virgin Island, Taiwan, Singapore, and the US. FIEs played an increasingly important role in Guangdong's

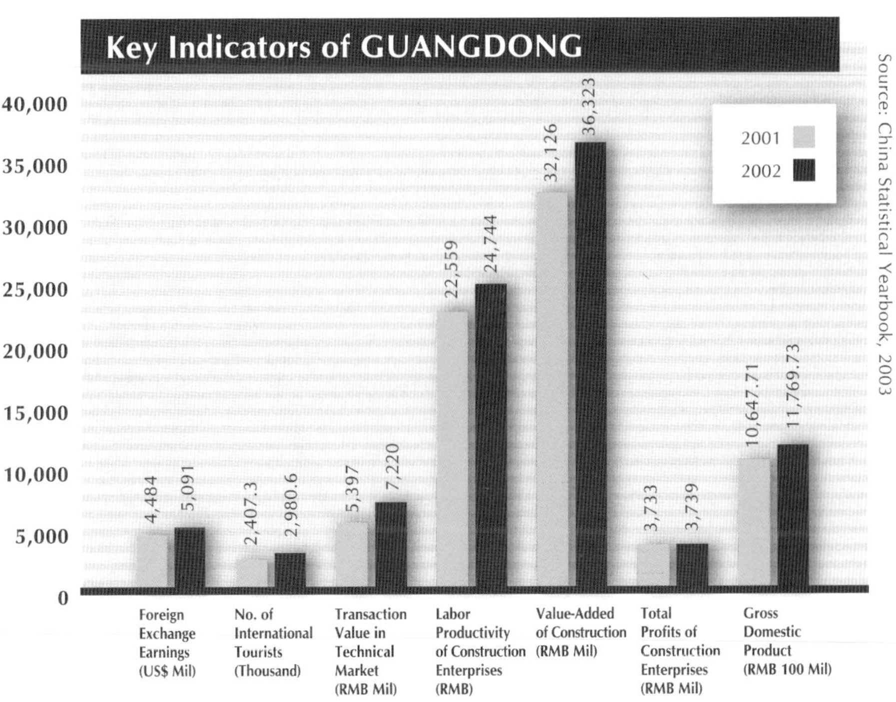

economy. Their exports in 2000 rose by 25.6 percent to US$49.5 billion, which accounted for 41 percent of all FIEs' exports in China and 53 percent of the province's total exports.

Foreign investments were mainly concentrated in Shenzhen, Guangzhou, Dongguan, Foshan, Zhuhai, Shantou and Huizhou. In 1999, Guangzhou's exports reached US$9.9 billion, accounting for12.7 percent of the province's total. Hong Kong was the major trading partner of Guangzhou, accounting for 33 percent of the city's exports in 1999. Hong Kong was also the largest foreign investors in the city, with contractual and actual FDI amounting to US$670 million and US$1.3 billion respectively in 1999.

According to Guangdong's strategies for the coming decade, Guangzhou, Shenzhen, Zhuhai, Foshan, Dongguan and Zhongshan (i.e., the centre of Pearl River Delta) will be developed into a commercial, trade, and hi-tech manufacturing centre; while Huizhou, Zhanjiang, and Shaoguan will become key production centres for cars, petrochemicals, iron and steel; and the relatively less developed mountainous regions of Heyuan, Shanwei, Meixian, etc., will strive to attract more overseas investments in order to exploit local natural resources and to take advantage of the region's low wages. Besides, Zhaoqing and Qingyuan will focus on the development of tourism, with participation by overseas investors.

To reform the existing processing trade system, the Chinese government has selected 15 pilot cities to establish export-processing zones. Guangdong is selected as one of the provinces in this trial programme. Export processing zones are special restricted areas administered by the Customs, which only engages in processing products for export. Enterprises concerned with export processing, storage and transportation are allowed to be set up in the zones.

GUIZHOU

The province will focus on using its abundant coal reserves and cheap electricity to become the power base of Southern China.

GUIZHOU Fact Sheet	2003
Area (km^2)	174,000
No. of Cities	13
Population (mil)	38.7
GDP (RMB bn)	134.4
Gross capital formation (RMB bn)	64.9
Consumption expenditure (RMB bn)	89
~Household	64
~Government	25
No. of employed persons (mil)	17.81
Unemployment Rate	4.1%
Literacy Rate	83.8%
Government revenue (RMB bn)	12.4
Government expenditure (RMB bn)	33.1
Per capita annual	
~disposable income of urban residents (RMB '000)	6.7
~net income of rural households (RMB '000)	1.6
~living expenditure of urban residents (RMB '000)	4.9
~living expenditure of rural residents (RMB '000)	1.2
Actually Used Foreign Direct Investment (US$ mil)	56.0
Total assets (RMB bn)	20.9
Exports (USD mil)	588
~percentage of change from the same period of previous year	+33.2%
Imports (USD mil)	396
~percentage of change from the same period of previous year	+58.8%

Introduction

Guizhou is situated in the mountainous part of the Yunnan-Guizhou Plateau in Southwest China. The province has an average altitude of 1,000 m above sea level. Mountaineous land constitutes 87 percent of the total area. The climate is subtropical with an average temperature of 25ºC in July and 5ºC in January. The province is very humid, with relative humidity above 70 percent throughout the year.

The population of ethnic minorities accounts for 40 percent of the total. Major groups include Miao, Buyi, Dong, Tujia and Yi.

The provincial capital is Guiyang, which has been approved by the State Council as an inland open city, giving it the privilege of the same preferential policies as in the coastal open cities and the provincial-level jurisdiction of economic management.

Guizhou has rich mineral resources. Out of its 120 kinds of minerals, 21 are ranked among the top three in the region. Its reserve of coal is the highest among southern Chinese provinces.

Guizhou has a strong agricultural sector, which has achieved significant improvement in the infrastructure of irrigation and terrace-farming. The province is a key producer of tobacco and its output ranks second in the country. Tea products and some exotic fruits such as star fruit are famous both at home and abroad. Guizhou also has large varieties of traditional Chinese medicinal herbs.

Natural Resources

Guizhou enjoys substantial rainfall. Rivers flow through steep terrain and generate huge hydropower of 18.74 million kW each year, putting the province sixth in the country. For each square kilometer, hydropower resources amount to 106,000 kW, which is the third largest in the nation. The province is also rich in gas stored in coal reserves. The abundant water and coal reserves make developing water and coal energy an important strategy for the province.

As one of the great reserves of minerals, Guizhou boasts more than 110 kinds of minerals, of which the size of reserves of 76 kinds have been ascertained. Guizhou has 42 kinds of minerals that ranked among the top 10 in the nation and 22 kinds that ranked among the top three. The province is particularly strong in reserves of coal, phosphorus, mercury, aluminium, manganese, antimony, gold , barite, raw materials for cement and bricks, as well as dolomite, sandstone and limestone.

With a reserve of 241.9 billion tons of coal, Guizhou has been known as the home of coal in south China. Its phosphorus reserve accounts for 44 percent of the national total, while the mercury reserve, after many years of extraction, still accounts for 38 percent of the country's total. The newly discovered gold reserve of 150 tons offers the country another gold production base.

Over 3,800 species of wild animals can be found in Guizhou. Over 1,000 of them are listed as rare species under state protection. More than 3,700 kinds of medicinal herbs, or 80 percent of the total number of medicinal herbs, are found in Guizhou.

Environment

In 1998, 75 incidents of environmental pollution costing RMB754,000 were documented. In the same year, total discharge of industrial wastewater was 311.13 million tons. Some 373 million tons of industrial wastewater was treated, with 41.49 million tons of treated industrial wastewater reaching the treatment standard. Also in 1998, total industrial waste air discharge was 33.47 million tons. In that year, waste air treatment capacity in the province was 23.3 million tons. Under construction in 1998 were 151 projects for dealing with industrial wastes, including 62 projects for treating wastewater and 29 natural reserves that protect a total area of 287,139 hectares.

Infrastructure

Railways

With the main capital Guiyang as the transportation hub, four main railways link Guizhou with Guangxi, Sichuan, Yunnan and Hunan. The Nankun railway, i.e., Nanning-Kunming railway, started operation in 1997 whilst the provincial railway, Shuibo railway (Shuicheng-Boguo), is under construction.

The construction of the Yuhuai railway, which is one of the landmark projects in the Great Western Development Strategy, has begun. It is targeted for completion in 2006. This railway and the Neikun line, Zhuliu line and Shuiguo line are key components of the Southwest Sea Passage. Guizhou has the densest network of railways in the western region, making it the de facto transportation centre in Southwestern China.

Highways

There are five state highways which form the highway network within the province. Externally, under the National Trunk Highway System (NTHS), the section of Shanghai-Kunming-Wanding and the section of Chognqing-Nanning will connect Guizhou with the seaports in Shanghai and Beihai. Guixin highway, which is a key section of the Southwest Sea Passage, has been built. Other major highways under construction, which are also key components of the Southwest Sea Passage, include: Guizhou-Bijie Expressway, Majiang-Kaili Expressway, Zunyi-Songxihe Expressway, Zhenning-Shuicheng Expressway, Yuping-Tongren Expressway, Guanling-Xingren Expressway.

Air Transport

Longdongbao Airport at Guiyang has more than 30 domestic air routes linking Guizhou to major cities in China. Direct flights to Hong Kong are also available. A new airport, Daxing Airport at Tongren, is under construction. Two new airports at Liping and at Xingyi are in the study stage.

Telecommunications

Telecommunication services have made remarkable progress. As at end 2002, subscribers for mobile telephone and Internet services reached 2.5 million and 4.3 million respectively.

Hydropower

Guizhou has a number of thermal and hydropower plants. Together with Sichuan and Yunnan, Guizhou has helped to establish the Southwest China power network. The completion of the Longtan Hydroplant will provide adequate electricity for Guizhou's industries.

Industries

Most of the industries are located at Guiyang and Zunji. In 2000, Guizhou's industrial ouput exceeded RMB68.7 billion, of which manufacturing industries such as tobacco-processing, pharmaceutical, metallurgy, chemical industry, etc., accounted for 83 percent. Guizhou is strong in tobacco and brewing industry. Maotai wine and Yantai beer are famous at home and abroad. Besides, Guizhou is also an important base of building material and chemical industries. In coming years, the province will focus on utilising its abundant coal and inexpensive electricity to become the power base of South China. Also, the province will further develop its building material industry like cement, glass and its finish working, sanitary ceramic wares etc.

Tourism

Guizhou is a popular tourist destination. Unique naturals scenery, rich ethnic traditions, colourful culture and history, as well as pleasant climate draw tourists to the province. It has eight state-level scenic spots and four state natural reserves such as Huangguoshu Waterfall, which is a world famous waterfall, Dragon's Palace, Zhijin Cave, Hongfeng Lake etc. Other provincial-level scenic spots include Wuyanghe River Scenic Spot and Zhangjiang River Scenic Spot in Libo County. The latter is one of the few remains of subtropical harst virgin forest in the world. In 2002, about 228,100 foreign tourists visited the province and generated a total revenue of US$80 million. These represent an increase of 23.9 percent and 31.1 percent respectively over the previous year.

Consumer Market

Retail sales of consumer goods of the whole province totalled RMB41.6 billion in 2002, an increase of 21.3 percent over 2000. Guiyang is the largest consumer centre, accounting for 31 percent of the total sales. The second largest centre is Zunyi, accounting for 15 percent of the total sales. Other department stores and shopping centres in Guizhou include Guizhou Department Store and Guiyang Department Store.

Through education and human resource development, Guizhou has over the years been adopting strategies in science and technology to vitalise its economic development.

Science and Technology

Through education and human resource development, Guizhou has over the years been adopting the strategies using science and technology to vitalise its economic development. To date, more than 474 scientific and technological projects at provincial level have been implemented. The number of non-governmental scientific and technological enterprises has exceeded 997.

Foreign Trade

Guizhou exported US$588 million worth of commodities in 2003, increasing by 33.2 percent over 2002. Major export products were non-ferrous metals, chemicals, tobacco and raw lacquer. Major export markets were Hong Kong, Japan, Republic of Korea, US and Taiwan.

In 2003 , the province's imports totalled US$396 million, up 58.8% from last year. Major import items included raw materials, machinery and plant equipment. Major import sources were the US, Hong Kong, Germany and India.

Foreign Investment

In 2003, the province aapproved 69 foreign-invested projects with contracted foreign investment of US$10.9 Billion. The province's actual utilisation of foreign capital for the year is US$56 million. Major sources of investment came from Hong Kong, Canada, the US, Myanmar and Malaysia. Foreign investments were mainly channelled into sectors such as the construction, mechanical and electronic industries etc.

In coming years, foreign investors are encouraged to invest in car parks, tourism and light industries, particularly in textiles, food-processing, medicines and health products. Guizhou is also eager to cooperate with foreign investors in upgrading its major industrial enterprises, developing hi-tech industries, transforming its old urban districts and improving its infrastructure.

To boost the development of the central and western regions in China, the State Council has granted further tax incentives to foreign-invested enterprises (FIEs) in China. Under the existing policy, FIEs are entitled to a three-year tax reduction and exemption. The new policy allows foreign-invested enterprises in the central and

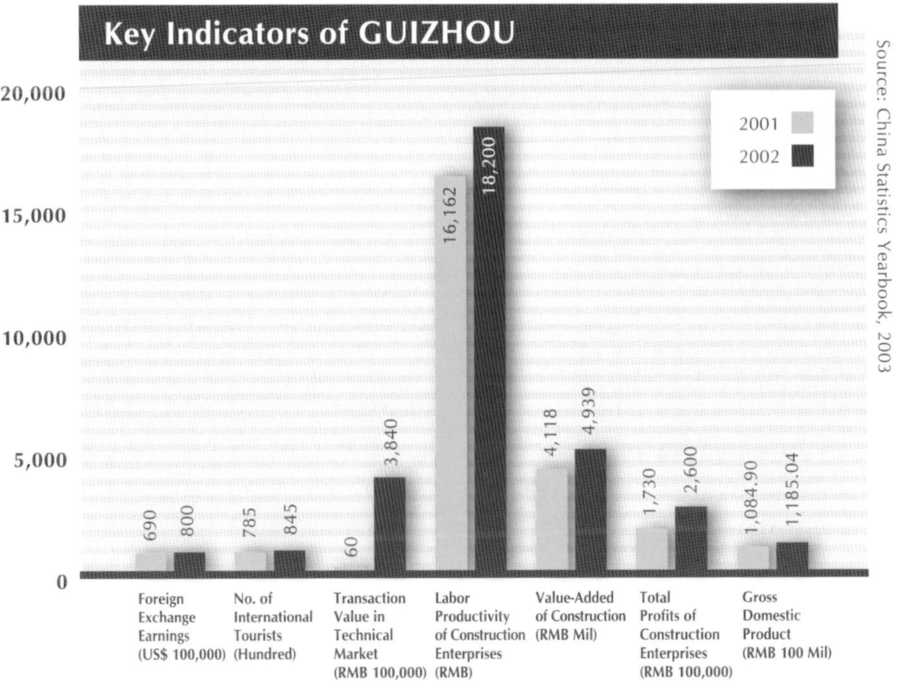

western regions to enjoy another three years of preferential tax rate when the current preferential term expires. The tax rate can be further reduced to 10 percent when an enterprise exports more than 70 percent of its annual output in terms of value.

Pillar Industries

Raw Material Industries

Total assets in this sector were worth RMB36 billion in 1998, including RMB8.2 billion for metallurgy, RMB7 billion for non-ferrous metals, RMB600 million for gold industry and RMB16 billion for chemical industry.

Machinery and Electronics

These include three military industrial bases of space, aeronautics and electronics. In addition, there are a number of large enterprise groups and backbone enterprises in the fields of car-making, grinding materials and tools, engineering machinery, internal combustion, industrial bearings, low pressure electric equipment, precision optical instrument, industrial meter and instrument, and precision machine tools for special use. Many products in these fields lead their counterparts in the nation in terms of technological level and quality. Guiyang is one of China's largest aluminium industrial bases, one of the five largest metre and instrument production bases, a major production base for grinding materials, grinding tools and cigarettes, and one of the top 10 electronic industrial cities in the western part of China.

Light and Textile Industries

These include name-brand liquors, cigarettes and mineral waters, cotton, woollen, linen, silk, synthetic fibre, leather processing and papermaking. The province holds an important position in the country in cigarette and liquor production. Its rich resources of mineral waters give the province a broad prospect for further development in the industry. Guizhou batik is gaining increasing favour of consumers both at home and abroad and they enjoy a brisk market in Japan, Africa, Europe and America.

Opportunities for Foreign Investment

The province invites foreign investment in the following areas:

- Processing and storage of grain, vegetable, fruit, poultry, meat and aquatic produce
- Cultivation of forest and introduction of fine breeds of trees
- Comprehensive utilisation of bamboo resources
- Rational tapping, utilisation and preservation projects for water resources
- Building and operation of highways, bridges and tunnels
- Development of applied technology for coal processing and production
- Technological transformation of enterprises of titanium smelting and processing
- Development of hard-to-open mines
- Technological transformation of enterprises of barium salt
- Mining and product processing of phosphorus
- Development and manufacture of new electronic parts
- Processing and production of traditional Chinese medicinal materials
- Development, construction and operation of tourist and scenic zones

HAINAN

The provincial capital, Haikou, is set to be a national base for pharmacy, tourism and tropical research.

HAINAN Fact Sheet	2003
Area (km^2)	33,940
No. of Cities	8
Population (mil)	8
GDP (RMB bn)	69.8
Gross capital formation (RMB bn)	27.5
Consumption expenditure (RMB bn)	33
~Household	25
~Government	8
No. of employed persons (mil)	3.54
Unemployment Rate	3.1%
Literacy Rate	92.1%
Government revenue (RMB bn)	4.6
Government expenditure (RMB bn)	9.2
Per capita annual	
~disposable income of urban residents (RMB '000)	7.3
~net income of rural households (RMB '000)	2.6
~living expenditure of urban residents (RMB '000)	5.9
~living expenditure of rural residents (RMB '000)	1.8
Actually Used Foreign Direct Investment (USD mil)	581
Total assets (RMB bn)	7.7
Exports (USD mil)	869
~percentage of change from the same period of previous year	+6.1%
Imports (USD mil)	1,410
~percentage of change from the same period of previous year	+34.6%

History

Hainan is one of the well-known sources of many overseas Chinese. Nearly two million overseas Chinese, including Chinese in Hongkong, Macao and Taiwan, came from the province. They are scattered all over in 53 countries and regions in the world, particularly in Thailand, Indonesia and Vietnam. There are one million overseas Chinese, and their relatives live in this province. The hometowns of overseas Chinese are mainly in Wenchang, Qionghai, Qiongshan and Wanning counties.

Hainan was established in September 1987, and was designated as the Hainan Special Economic Zone on April 13, 1988. This decision has profound impact in hastening the development of the province.

Located in the tropical region, Hainan Island is endowed with a vast land area and an abundant supply of sunshine, rainfall, as well as excellent weather. In terms of maritime space, Hainan province plays an important role in the national defence and economy given its strategic location. Standing at the key junction between Guangdong Province and Guangxi Province, it is a strategic passage for the entire south and hence controls coastal transportation and communications in South China.

Geography

Hainan Island is the second largest island of China, almost as large as Taiwan Island. The west of the island borders the Beibu Bay, with Vietnam visible in the distance. The east of the island is near to Hong Kong, Taiwan, and the Philippines in the southeast. The south of the island adjoins to Malaysia, Brunei, Singapore. Hainan City, the capital of Hainan, is 50 minutes by air from Hong Kong and 2-3 hours from the above foreign countries and regions.

It is situated in tropical and subtropical zones. The administrative areas of Hainan include Hainandao Island, Nansha, Xisha, Zhongsha Archipelagos and their sea area. It faces Leizhou Peninsula across Qiongzhou Channel to the north, Vietnam across the North Bay to the west, and Malaysia and Indonesia across the South China Sea to the south, and is closely joined by the South China Sea and islands. Hainan is China's second largest island, but its smallest province.

Ecological Environment

Hainan Island develops lately with well-protected natural environment. The forest covers 51.5 percent of Hainan Island. At present, there are five tropical primeval forest areas in Hainan Island: Wuzhishan Forest Area, Bawangling Forest Area, Jiangfengling Forest Area, Diaoluoshan Forest Area and Limushan Forest Area.

Transport

Hainan has two airports. Hainan Meilan Airport has opened the airlines to Macao, Hong Kong, Taiwan, Thailand, Singapore, Malaysia, and Burma as well as to the capitals of the important provinces and cities of China, and has been listed as one of the eight large airports of China. Meanwhile, Sanya Phoenix Airport has opened the airlines to Singapore, Malaysia, Thailand, Seoul, Osaka, Tokyo, Siberia, Macao, Hong Kong, Taiwan; a total of 10 international airlines providing air routes to 23 cities of China. In total, the two airports have opened more than 70 domestic and international air routes.

Hainan Island has formed a crisscrossing road network and built island-round expressway. Additionally, Hainan Island also expanded land and water transportation with many provinces and cities of China.

Agriculture

A new kind of tropical high yielding agriculture has seen spectacular growth in recent years, spurring tropical tourist agriculture, ecological agriculture and hi-tech agriculture. A significant base of China has taken root or is taking shape in Hainan. Cultivation will be centralised for natural rubber, seed breeding, vegetables, winter melons, tropical fruits, tropical flowers and plants, and marine aquaculture. The base has brought about a great deal of famous farm produce of high quality, and begun its transformation from superior farm produce to that of farm cash crops and to their processing industries. As a result, Hainan's status as China's agricultural base has been reinforced.

Industry

By focussing on market demand, increased application of new technology, and exploitation of rich resources, Hainan's new and traditional industries have seen significant innovation and growth. The province is building an industrial complex which caters to the following industries:

Hainan has a flourishing commercial sector with over 23,242 trading establishments and service centres, 92 markets and 2,140 wholesaling institutions. The local markets have ample supply of various commodities with a distinct local flavour.

natural gas, chemicals, building materials, beverage, foodstuff, medicine, chemical fibres, textiles, machinery, electronics, metallurgy, information, etc.

Natural Resources

Hainan is a tropical island and has a vast stretch of tropical primeval forests, mountain ranges, rivers and beaches. There are over 560 species of animals and 4,200 types of plants on the island. It has great mineral reserves and is rich in oil and natural gas. Among the proven deposits of minerals, iron ore and erinaceous quartz deposits are the most important resources to China; followed by natural gas, zirconium, nitrogenous fertiliser rock, gems, titanium and oil shale. Tourism has also become a leading industry in Hainan.

Investment Environment in Hainan

Established in the tide of economic reform and liberalisation, Hainan, the capital of the youngest province in China, is riding the tide well into a new phase of development. Strengthened economic cooperative ties with foreign countries have brought new technologies and foreign investments to Hainan, making remarkable economic and social achievements and improved investment environment. The GDP of the city in 2003 amounted to RMB69.8 billion, which is more than twenty-fold increase over the past 10 years since Hainan province was established. Through tenacity and vision, the provincial government has uphold the policy of opening-up the market since the founding of the province and SEZ, and enabled Hainan to make great progress in economic development.

Industry

In the past 10 years, Hainan has developed a comprehensive industrial system covering 32 different fields (if categorised by the State industry category), and the following five pillar industries: machinery and electronics, beverage and foodstuff, rubber and chemical industry, textile and chemical fibre, and pharmaceutical industry. Presently there are 176 industrial enterprises, including state-owned enterprises and other enterprises with independent accountability and a sales revenue exceeding RMB5 million. The total industrial output of the city in 2002 was RMB22.9 billion.

Agriculture

With favourable natural conditions and the policy of opening-up and reform, Hainan has maintained a continuous, stable and balanced growth in the agricultural sector in the past 10 years. As the cultivable land in Hainan is limited, the city mainly develops "suburb agriculture". Fruit and vegetables production weighs heavy in the city's agricultural development; other productions such as meat, milk, poultry, eggs and fish are also becoming large scale.

Domestic Trade

Hainan has a flourishing commercial sector with over 23,242 trading establishments and service centres, 92 markets and 2,140 wholesaling institutions. The local markets have ample supply of various commodities with a distinct local flavour. The total volume of retail in 2002 was RMB20.4 billion, an increase of 9.0 percent over the year 2001.

International Trade

In 2003, Hainan exported more than 208 kinds of commodities to 50 countries and regions, with an annual export volume of US$869million.

Tourism

Being a tourist resort with spring all year round, Hainan is rich in natural and man-made scenery. Major scenic spots are: the Memorial Temple to the Five Officials, The Mausoleum of Hairui, The Ancient Battery at Xiuying, The West Heaven Temple, The People's Park, The Golden Ox Park, the Zoo, the Wanlu Park, The Holiday Beach, The Baishamen Beach, etc. In 2002, 389,300 foreign tourists visited Hainan. That is a decrease of 14.8 percent over that in 2001. The whole tourism industry made US$93.2 million from foreign tourists in 2002, with a total tourism income of RMB9.54 billion.

International Communications

Hainan is enjoying a growing reputation at home and abroad. So far it has five sisterly cities in five different countries: Perth of England, Saint Nazaire of France, Oklahoma City of the USA, Darwin City of Australia, Zanzibar of Tanzania. There have been extensive communication and cooperation in various fields like economy, trade, science, technology and culture between Hainan and these cities.

Power Supply

Hainan has sufficient power supply. The present installation capacity in Hainan is 400,000 kW. The main transformer capacity, power supply and power consumption in 1998 were 593,500 kVA, 1.29 billion kWh, 1.20 billion kWh, increased by 8.9, 6, 6.1 times respectively from 60,000 kVA, 183 million kWh, 169 million kWh in 1988.

Telecommunications

Direct telephone calls can be made from Hainan to 947 foreign cities and 1,527 domestic cities and counties. The program controlled telephone switchboard in the city has a capacity of 313,000, 71.6 percent of all families in the city have installed telephones, which ranks No.1 among provincial capitals in China. There are more than 122,000 mobile telephone users in Hainan.

Harbour

At present, Hainan Harbour has 15 berths in use, including two berths of 10,000 tonnage and two berths of 5,000 tonnage, two berths of 3,000 tonnage, and seven berths below 3,000 tonnages. There are 23 international freight lines, 47 domestic lines linking all domestic seaports and more than 30 countries and regions, such as Korea, Japan, Australia, Singapore and Hong Kong, etc.

Railway

Approved by the State Council, Yuehai Railway, the first railway running across the

strait in China, started construction in August 30, 1998. The Railway starts from Zhanjiang City of Guangdong Province, runs across Qiongzhou Strait to Hainan, and then passes through Chengmai County and Danzhou City, finally arrives at Chahe town in Changjiang County. The proposed handling capacity of the Yuehai Railway is 11 million tons per year.

Highway

National and provincial routes in Hainan forms a highway web spreading in all directions, connecting every other city and county in the province. The expressways from Hainan to other cities or counties are now under construction. The eastern expressway from Hainan to Sanya was completed in 1995, and its expansion project has finished the part from Hainan to Qionghai in March 1998. The expressway from Hainan to Yangpu has been put into operation in 1996, and the Hainan to Wenchang section is under construction. There are 73 passengers transport routes everyday, covering 18 cities and counties and 37 major towns in Hainan.

Water Supply

The water supply capacity in Hainan has reached 725,000 tons. Hainan is rich in water resource.

Honorary National Titles

Since 1992, Hainan has been given the following honorary titles: one of the 50 cities strongest in comprehensive economic strength in China, one of the 40 cities with best investment hardware in China, City Advanced in Comprehensive Environmental Renovation in China, among the top ten cities in comprehensive environmental renovation, Sanitary City of China, excellent tour cities in China, the only city in China appointed by WHO and the Ministry of Health as A WHO Pilot Healthy City, etc.

Future Investment Outlook

In coming years, Hainan will focus on the following industries in her use of capital from home and abroad.

Hi-Tech Industry

Aiming to turn herself into a centre for high-tech enterprises and a base for high-tech research and development, Hainan has been focussing on high-tech development and industrialisation, accelerating the processes of commercialisation, industrialisation and internationalisation of high technology. Hainan possess the following advantages for the development of high-tech industry: comprehensive information networking facilities, rich talent resource brought by the high-tech enterprises running in Hainan, abundant tropical and marine resources providing Hainan with significant natural resources for the development of a high-tech industry with local flavour. Electronic information, biology, medical, marine development and ecological environment protection are key developing sectors in Hainan.

Pharmaceutical Industry

This is a pillar industry encouraged by Hainan City. The favourable natural resource of Hainan offers an excellent environment for developing the pharmaceutical industry. To date, more than 37 renowned medicine enterprises, such as Hainan Yangsheng-tang Co., Ltd, Hainan Qingqi Haiyao

Holdings Co., Ltd, Huakang Pharmaceuticals Co., Ltd. Hainan Sunbow Bio-product Co., Ltd etc., have been set up in Hainan. Their total annual production value exceeds RMB1.2 billion. Hainan is determined to turn herself into a national base for the pharmaceutical industry, trade, science and research. Enterprises producing pharmaceutical materials, new and special pharmaceuticals, bio-pharmaceuticals, and marine pharmaceuticals are greatly encouraged, as well as the development of products using local pharmaceutical resources.

Foodstuff Industry

Foodstuff of tropical crops, beverage of fruit juice, fruit processing and condensed fruit juice.

Chemical Fibre and Textile

High-tech, special or new fibre types, and the design and production of garments of famous brands.

Car Industry

Auxiliaries and spare parts for cars.

Rubber Industry

Tyres, rubber parts.

Electronics Industry

Electronic components, video & audio products, computer software and hardware.

Miscellaneous

High-class decorations, printing.

Agriculture, Husbandry, and Fishery

Water-economic agriculture and ecological agriculture; Bio-agricuture, Ocean fishing, aquaculture base and fishing boat technology upgrade.

Tourism

Tourism industry is set as the second pillar industry of Hainan. At present, a number of large-scale tourism projects are under construction or starting construction soon. Large-or-medium-sized projects making full use of Hainan's tropical resources or featuring tropical seaside scenic spots, tourism projects for business and vacationing, together with projects developing scenic spots with distinct features are greatly encouraged. Hainan is quickening its pace in tourism development and construction, with the following focuses: the development of Qiongzhou Strait Vacationing Resort, River & Sea Sport and Leisure Resort, and the development of bases for the production of tourism handicrafts, tropical flowers and plants.

Commerce

Wholesale markets, shopping streets, chain stores, delivery centres and warehouse stores.

Information Service Business

Hainan is speeding up the construction of the information resource networks, the development and improvement of information service system.

Urban Infrastructure

Projects involved in the development of transportation, telecom & postal services, water supply & drainage facilities and renovation of power supply network, afforestation and environment protection are all encouraged.

Social Welfare Utilities

The development of education, culture, health care, physical culture, etc. Restricted and forbidden industrial fields for foreign investment are specified in The Directive Category of Industries for Foreign Investment. (Excluding those specially stipulated by the government of Hainan Province or Haikou City.)

Protection for Foreign Investors

A foreign investor's investment, assets purchased, industrial property, investment profits and other legal rights in Hainan are protected by State laws and can be lawfully transferred or inherited. Investments and other assets belonging to the foreign investors should not be nationalised or requisitioned. Under special circumstances, for the sake of social public benefits, foreign-invested enterprises may be requisitioned with compensation through legal procedures. Should there be an investment protection agreement signed between PRC and the foreign government, the agreement should be carried out. No department or organisation has the right to overcharge the foreign-invested enter-prises, or collect fees that have not been approved by the State, the Provincial or the municipal government. Foreign-invested enterprises have the right to reject any unreasonable fees or charges. The foreign-invested enterprises take legal procedures in the Chinese courts when their investment or other legal rights are infringed.

HAINAN COMMERCE & ECONOMIC COOPERATION BUREAU

As an administrative body under the municipal government, Hainan Commerce and Economic Cooperation Bureau oversees commerce and foreign economic cooperation, with the following responsibilities: overall planning, introducing investment and project promotion, administration of international and domestic trade, administration of export quotas, approval and administration of foreign-invested enterprises, inspecting and guiding the use of foreign funds, ratification and management of representative offices of domestic provinces and cities, information provision and coordination. It was the first unit in China that has adopted an immediate service system and the promise system for social service. It has changed the approval procedures into registration procedures, provides follow-up service for big foreign-invested projects in Hainan, coordinates between different departments, resolves some existing problems and facilitated the development of some of the projects.

Address: 1/F, City Hall, No. 19 North Longkun Road, Haikou City, Hainan Province, P.R.China

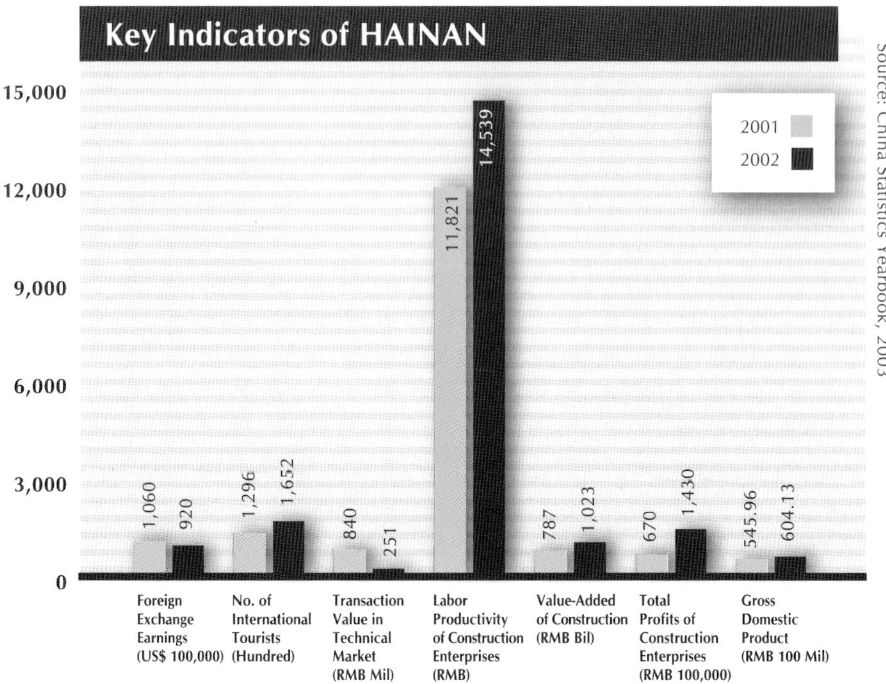

Postal Code: 570145
Tel: (86)(898) 6797781
Fax: (86)(898) 6798693
Information: (86)(898) 6797804, or 6709850

HAINAN INVESTMENT SERVICE CENTRE

Hainan Investment Service Centre is a professional organisation under the administration of Hainan Commerce and Economic Cooperation Bureau, provides a full array of investment services, aiming at improving Hainan's investment environment for foreign and domestic investors.

The centre offers the following services for investors at home and abroad:

1. Provides information on investment environment, law and regulations, policies, and relevant materials.

2. Introduces cooperative partners, offering help in project negotiation and directing investment.

3. Prepares feasibility reports, articles of incorporation, agreements, etc.

4. Provides services for the registration at administration of industry and commerce, tax bureau and customs, and annual assessment.

5. Handle the application for approval certificate and required permits for the customers.

6. Handle issues of taxation, export, passport and visa application, and providing translation and interpretation services.

7. Business consultation and conference receptions.

PROJECTS COOPERATION AND AGENCY

The centre provides services in the forms of contracts and takes pains to maintain a good reputation and high level of service quality. It had won enterprise awards given by Hainan Administration of Industry and Commerce for four years since 1993.

Address: B08 No. 19 North Longkun Road, Haikou, Hainan, China

Postal Code: 570145
Tel: (86)(898) 6794393/6705020/ 6716394

Investment Services

In order to offer the best service to develop the market economy, the Hainan municipal government has carried out special measures to wipe out the bureaucratic working style, improve work efficiency, and enhance service quality. Piloted by immediate service system, service-at-counters system and promise system for social services (known as three systems), great efforts have been made to establish a law abiding, efficient and honest governmental system with high transparency and standard management. The government interprets its administrative power as responsibilities and duties to serve. Under the above-mentioned system, even the most complicated matters will go through no more than three steps, all redundant procedures have been ended, and there's no need for investors to struggle through numerous formalities thanks to the good coordination between different government departments.

Forms of Investment

Investors can invest in factory buildings, equipment, other materials, land use right, industrial property rights and patented technology, as well as bank currency.

Investment Proportion

In general, the foreign partner should contribute no less than 25 percent of the total registered capital of the joint venture or cooperative enterprise.

Time Limit of Approval Process

The examination and approval process of each of the following issues: the project proposal, the contract, the articles of incorporation, business scope expansion, registration at the Administration of Industry and Commerce, should be concluded within seven working days after all required materials have been submitted.

Application Procedures for Utility Services for Foreign-Invested Enterprises

Electricity

The foreign-invested enterprise should prepare all required materials and fill in an application form at the application office of the Electricity Company. For low voltage power supply applications, the Electricity Company will work out the supply plan in seven days, and after relevant fees are paid, install an electricity meter and start power supply in four days for one-phase power consumers and 15 days for three-phase power consumers. For high voltage electricity applications, the Electricity Company will carry out field investigation in 10 days, work out the supply plan in 20 days, install electricity meter and start power supply in 10 days after the project is complete, checked and accepted, and all relevant formalities has been gone through.

Water

The foreign-invested enterprise should fill in an application form at the water consumption section of the Water Supply Company. If the application meets all relevant requirements, the office should issue an approval in five days and turn the application to the designing institute for reconnaissance and design work. After relevant fees have been paid and all formalities gone through, water consumption section should pass on the blueprint and relevant materials to the Labour Service Company for construction.

Drainage

The foreign-invested enterprise should first fill in an application form for drainage permit at the Waste Water Treatment Company, then go through relevant formalities at the drainage permit issuing office with the following materials besides the application form: documents on the drainage capacity (i.e. the receipt of the payment of tap-water rates in the last month or the month with biggest water consumption, or a copy of the document predicting the largest volume of waste water per day), document on the quality of waste water and the planar graph of the drainage pipe network.

Telecommunications

The foreign-invested enterprise should get the application form for the installation of telephone and fax machine at any business office of the Telecom Bureau. Once having received the application form with the seal of the enterprise, the Telecom Bureau will start the installation.

HEBEI

With its Jing-Jin-Ji Economic Zone, Hebei serves as a hub with a large interflow of population, commodities and information.

HEBEI Fact Sheet	**2003**
Area (km^2)	190,000
No. of Cities	33
Population (mil)	67.7
GDP (RMB bn)	709.5
Gross capital formation (RMB bn)	266
Consumption expenditure (RMB bn)	282
~Household	205
~Government	77
No. of employed persons (mil)	33.85
Unemployment Rate	3.9%
Literacy Rate	93.2%
Government revenue (RMB bn)	33.5
Government expenditure (RMB bn)	63.4
Per capita annual	
~disposable income of urban residents (RMB '000)	7.2
~net income of rural households (RMB '000)	2.9
~living expenditure of urban residents (RMB '000)	5.4
~living expenditure of rural residents (RMB '000)	1.6
Actually Used Foreign Direct Investment (US$ mil)	1,560
Total assets (RMB bn)	52.6
Exports (USD mil)	5,930
~percentage of change from the same period of previous year	+29.1%
Imports (USD mil)	3,050
~percentage of change from the same period of previous year	+47.2%

Introduction

Hebei Province derives its name from its geographical location, north of the lower reaches of the Yellow River. It covers an area of 190,000 km2 and has a population of 67.7 million. The province boasts not only a favourable location and many natural resources, but also a long history and rich culture.

Hebei Province is located between 36°3′ to 42°40′ N and 113°27′ to 119°50′ E. Lying in the North China Plain, it stretches to the south Inner Mongolian plateau and faces the Bohai Sea to the east. The topography of the province slopes down from northwest to southeast. While the northwest is a mountainous terrain with scattered basins and valleys, vast plains stretch over the central and southeastern regions. The coastline of the province is 487 kilometres long.

The area has been designated by the Chinese government as one of the major zones for liberalisation, in no small part due to its geographically advantageous location. As the only province surrounding Beijing and Tianjin, Hebei has long-standing ties with the two metropolises, a relationship all hope to plumb with the formation of the "Jing-Jin-Ji" (Beijing-Tianjin-Hebei) Economic Zone. Funds, trained personnel, technology and information in the two big cities are available to Hebei, while Hebei is an important source of commodities, raw materials and energy resources.

Climate

The province has a temperate continental monsoon climate which varies greatly due to its vastness, and most of the territory has distinct seasons. Its annual sunshine time is 2,400-3,100 hours, annual frost-free period is 120-200 days, annual precipitation is 300-800 mm, and annual average temperature is 0°C-13°C.

Population

By the end of 2003, the population of the province had reached 67.7 million, with a natural growth rate 5.16percent. The rural and urban labour resources added up to 43.5465 million, 77 percent of whom were employed. Hebei is a multinational province. Those of Han descent account for 96 percent of the total; the rest comprises peoples from the 53 ethnic minorities, including Manchu, Hui, Mongolian, Zhuang, Korean, Miao, and Tujia.

Administrative Districts

With Shijiazhuang City as the provincial capital, Hebei province consists of 11 municipalities directly under the jurisdiction of the provincial government. They are Shijiazhuang, Tangshan, Handan, Qinhuangdao, Xingtai, Baoding, Zhangjiakou, Chengde, Langfang, Cangzhou and Hengshui. Under the jurisdiction of these municipalities, there are 23 county-level cities, 115 counties and 34 urban districts in

As the only province between Beijing and Tianjin, Hebei has long-standing ties with the two metropolises, a relationship all hope to plumb with the formation of the "Jing-Jin-Ji" (Beijing-Tianjin-Hebei) Economic Zone. Funds, trained personnel, technology and information in the two big cities are available to Hebei.

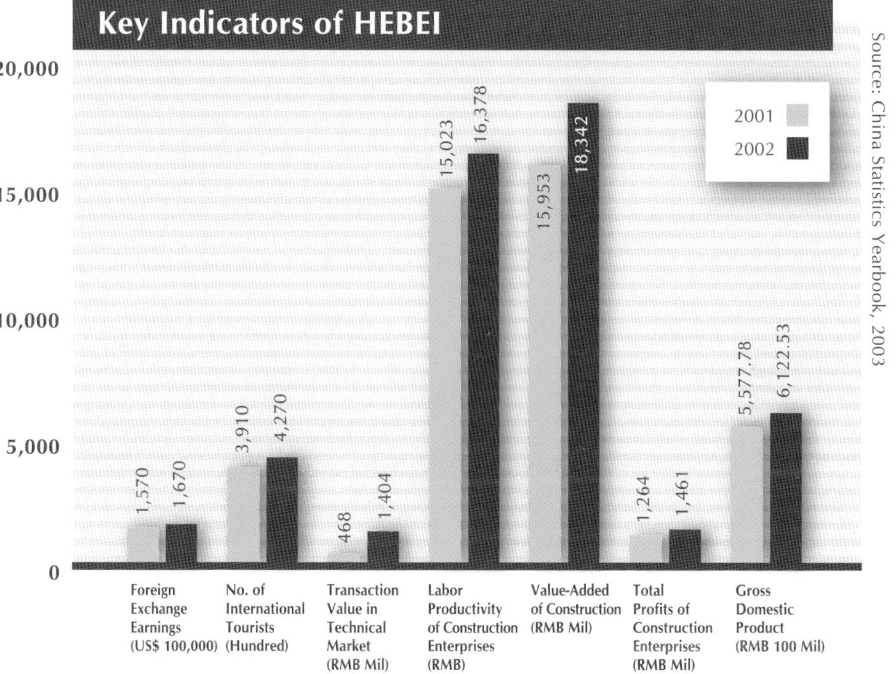

all. The province has 1970 townships and 50,201 village committees, which are its lowest-rung administrative units.

Guidelines on foreign investment

Projects are classified under encouraging, restricting and prohibiting foreign investment, in accordance with the Industrial Catalogue Guiding Foreign Investment approved by the State Council.

Projects encouraging foreign investment

This category includes projects concerning new farming techniques, the utilisation of agricultural resources, and important industrial raw materials; projects concerning new equipment and materials which require advanced technologies and are able to improve product performance, are energy-saving and efficient, increase economic returns, and meet the demands of the market where domestic production capacity is deficient; projects that meet the demands of the international market and improve product quality and export sales; projects based on new technology and equipment for the comprehensive utilisation of resources and renewable resources, and for the prevention and control of environmental pollution.

Projects restricting foreign investment

This category includes projects in which existing production capacity already satisfies domestic market demand; pilot projects launched by the state to attract foreign investments; projects in particular industries under monopolised sales of the state; projects concerning the prospecting and exploitation of rare or precious mineral resources.

Projects prohibiting foreign investment

This category includes projects that endanger the safety of the nation or damage social and public interests; projects that pollute the environment, destroy natural resources or impair the health of the human body; projects that occupy large tracts of cultivated land and are unfavourable towards future development of land resources; projects that endanger the safety and performance of military facilities.

Forms of investment and cooperation in Hebei Province

These include Sino-Foreign Equity Joint Ventures, Sino-Foreign Contractual Joint Ventures, Wholly Foreign-owned Enterprises, Foreign-funded Financial Institutions, BOTs (build-operate-transfer), compensation trade, processing and assembly, international leasing, mergers and acquisitions.

HEILONGJIANG

With its fertile black soil, good ecological health and low pollution, there is potential for green crop cultivation.

HEILONGJIANG Fact Sheet	**2003**
Area (km^2)	469,000
No. of Cities	31
Population (mil)	38.2
GDP (RMB bn)	443.3
Gross capital formation (RMB bn)	132.2
Consumption expenditure (RMB bn)	229
~Household	165
~Government	63
No. of employed persons (mil)	16.20
Unemployment Rate	4.2%
Literacy Rate	93.9%
Government revenue (RMB bn)	29.3
Government expenditure (RMB bn)	60.6
Per capita annual	
~disposable income of urban residents (RMB '000)	6.7
~net income of rural households (RMB '000)	2.5
~living expenditure of urban residents (RMB '000)	4.9
~living expenditure of rural residents (RMB '000)	1.8
Actually Used Foreign Direct Investment (USD mil)	1,050
Total assets (RMB bn)	34.5
Exports (USD mil)	2,870
~percentage of change from the same period of previous year	+44.6%
Imports (USD mil)	2,460
~percentage of change from the same period of previous year	+4.0%

Introduction

Heilongjiang Province is located in Northeast China, and is known for its sub-arctic climate, which can drop to -4°C in January. Covering 469,000 km^2 with a population of 38.2 million, the province lies next to the extreme eastern end of Russia, with whom it has had a turbulent history. About half of this area comprises mountainous terrain, including the heavily forested Da Xing-an and Xiao Xing-an Mountains. There are 19 cities and towns on both sides of the 3,000 km border. Harbin, the provincial capital, together with Heihe and Suifenhe, are the major economic centres of the province, followed by Qiqihar, Daqing and Mudanjiang.

Infrastructure

Water Transport

The port of Harbin is the province's largest inland transport centre on the Songhua River. There are 22 state-level ports in the province.

Railways

There are frequent train services to the ports of Dalian in Liaoning, and Vladivostok in Russia. Electrification of HaDa Railway: Harbin-Dalian was recently completed. A new railway network from Harbin to Changxing in Zhejiang is being built, which will link with the HaDa railway and a 170 km ferry passage from Dalian to Yantai in Shandong. From Shandong, the line extends to Zhejiang and runs through Shanghai and Jiangsu. Another major provincial railway, the Suidong, which links Dongning to major Russian ports in the east, is under construction.

Highways

The province has a well-developed transportation network radiating from Harbin. A major route is the Shenha Expressway, a four-lane highway, from Shenyang to Harbin. To expand border trade with Russia, the Heilongjiang government has embarked on construction of several highways

connecting Dongning to major Russian ports.

Air Transport

Harbin Airport has regular flights scheduled to Hong Kong and Russia. Other major airports in the province are located at Jiamusi, Mudanjiang, Heihe, and Qiqihar. Recent domestic air routes which have been opened go from Jiamusi City in Heilongjiang to Sanya City in Hainan, and from Jiamusi to Shenzhen in Guangdong.

Telecommunications

Communications are well-developed in Heilongjiang. By the end of 2002, there were 6.79 million mobile telephone users and 13 million internet users in Heilongjiang. Recently, Ericsson set up a new joint venture with the Heilongjiang Mobile Telecom Company. The new company, Heilongjiang Ericsson Technology Co. Ltd., engages mainly in R&D and technological services.

Electricity

There are 1,700 rivers in the province, providing ample resources for hydroelectric power generation. At present, the total capacity of hydroelectric power exceeds six million kWh, while the capacity of thermal power is about 3.6 million kWh.

Agriculture

Heilongjiang is one of the largest producers of beans, corn, fibre crops, beetroots and milk in China. The city's abundant pasture and large tracts of forested land provide good grazing conditions for livestock such as horses, cows, sheep, pigs and domestic fowl. The black soil of Heilongjiang is very fertile; some 18 billion kg of commodity grain is produced a year, one of the highest per capita outputs in China. Due to the low pollution levels and general ecological health, there is potential for green crop cultivation.

Natural Resources

One hundred and ten kinds of mineral and metal deposits have been identified in Heilongjiang, significant amongst which are deposits of gold, graphite, silver, copper, lead, aluminium, tungsten, zinc, molybdenum, crude oil, coal, soda, quartz, marble and mica. Petroleum is produced from Daqing Oilfield; in 2002, the output of crude oil had reached 69.4 million tons. The province is also endowed with a significant timber reserve.

Tourism

In 2002, the province received 669,500 foreign tourists and generated a revenue of US$297 million. Harbin's major tourist attractions include its picturesque Songhua River, the Confucius Temple, the Temple of Bliss, Huining, the ancient Capital of the Jin Dynasty, Yuquan Hunting Resort, Siberia Tiger Park, Mountain Songfeng, Zhalong Crane Natural Reserve and Jingbo Lake. Major festivities include the Harbin Summer Concert, Ice and Snow Festival, Ice Lantern Festival and winter swimming. Ecological tourism centred around the region's forests, lakes and rivers is being developed. Another tourism niche Heilongjiang hopes to cultivate is that of a ski resort destination.

Consumer Market

In 2002, retail sales of consumer goods increased by 10 percent to RMB132 billion. Major consumer markets are Harbin and Qiqihar.

In the coming years, Heilongjiang intends to direct interest to infrastructure development, agricultural processing, state-owned enterprises, export-oriented industries which are technology-intensive, and tertiary industries.

Industry

In 2002, Heilongjiang's industrial output rose to RMB147 billion. Industries are mainly located in Daqing, Harbin and Qiqihar. Key industries include oil extraction, timber, petroleum, the manufacture of airplanes, power generating equip-ment, railway wagons, large mechanical equipment and machine tools, textiles and food processing. Research is focused in the fields of ship-building, welding, computers, robots, sensor devices, wireless communications and organ transplants.

The electronics, cars and animal feed industries, all of which depend on imported capital and advanced technology, have become the province's pillar industries, along with heavy industry like mining. Future development will be focused on petrochemicals, cars and spare parts, electronics, foodstuffs and pharmaceuticals.

Foreign Trade

In 2003, exports increased by 44.6 percent to US$2.87 billion. Major export goods included textiles, clothing, electronic parts, soybeans and footwear. Imports amounted to US$2.46 billion, an increase of 4.0 percent over 2002. Major import goods were machinery, petro-chemicals, light industrial and textile products. Heilongjiang's major trading partners are Russia, Japan, Hong Kong, South Korea and Taiwan.

The Russian border trade is Heilongjiang's precinct by virtue of its geography; preferential policies in border trade are enjoyed in all 19 cities and counties along the

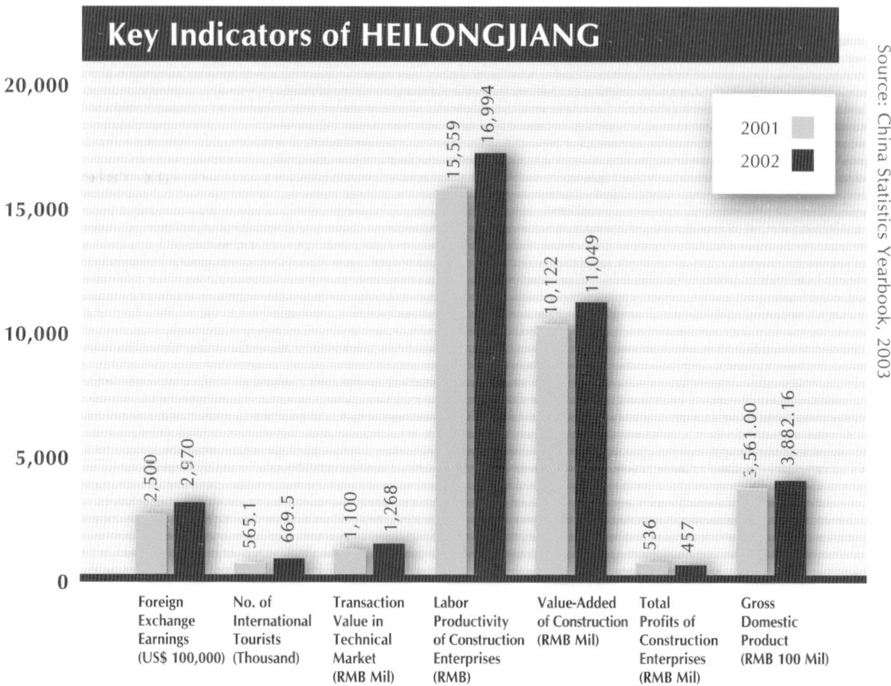

border. Mudanjiang is a major border trade centre, accounting for nearly 70 percent of the province's border trade. In 1999, Mudanjiang's border trade reached US$1 billion, the major export goods being light industrial products, textiles, electronic equipment, foodstuffs, vegetables, agricultural by-products and ornaments. Mudanjiang will be establishing an export processing zone to further boost exports to Russia by merging a smaller export processing zone, a hi-tech demonstration area and an economic development park. In light of Russia's demand for farm products, Mudanjiang may be developing export bases for fruits, vegetables, flowers, pork and processed pork.

Foreign Investment

In 2002, Heilongjiang approved 197 foreign investment projects, with contracted foreign capital of US$0.33 billion ; actual utilised foreign capital reached about US$355.1 billion in the same year. Investment came mainly from Hong Kong, Republic of Korea, USA, Taiwan and the UK. Harbin, Qiqihar and Mudanjiang attract the bulk of foreign investment.

To encourage foreign investment, Heilongjiang has been holding the annual Economic and Trade Fair of China in Harbin. In the coming years, Heilongjiang intends to direct interest to infrastructure development, agricultural processing, state-owned enterprises, export-oriented industries which are technology-intensive, and tertiary industries.

To accelerate the development of the central and western regions in China, the State Council has granted further tax incentives to foreign-invested enterprises (FIEs). The new policy allows FIEs in the central and western regions to enjoy another three years of preferential tax rates when the existing preferential tax period (three years) expires. The tax rate can be further reduced to 10 percent if an enterprise can prove that it exports more than 70 percent of its annual output in terms of value.

HENAN

It owns three famous ancient capital cities, Luoyang, Kaifeng and Anyang, which hold numerous relics of great historical value.

HENAN Fact Sheet	2003
Area (km^2)	167,000
No. of Cities	38
Population (mil)	96.1
GDP (RMB bn)	702.6
Gross capital formation (RMB bn)	254.6
Consumption expenditure (RMB bn)	344
~Household	247
~Government	97
No. of employed persons (mil)	56
Unemployment Rate	3.1%
Literacy Rate	92.2%
Government revenue (RMB bn)	29.7
Government expenditure (RMB bn)	62.9
Per capita annual	
~disposable income of urban residents (RMB '000)	6.9
~net income of rural households (RMB '000)	2.2
~living expenditure of urban residents (RMB '000)	4.9
~living expenditure of rural residents (RMB '000)	1.5
Actually Used Foreign Direct Investment (US$ mil)	561.0
Total assets (RMB bn)	60.1
Exports (USD mil)	2,980
~percentage of change from the same period of previous year	+40.6%
Imports (USD mil)	1,736
~percentage of change from the same period of previous year	+60.0%

Introduction

Henan lies in the central plains of China, between Yellow River and Yangtze River. Situated in the heart of the mainland, it is near Shanghai to the east, Wuhan to the south, Beijing and Tianjin to the north, and Shaanxi and Gansu to the west. Possessing a rich history, the remains of the Shang Dynasty, dated to 2000 B.C., have been found here. With a population of 92.6 million, Henan has an area of 167,000 km^2, and is divided into two prefectures and 15 cities under the jurisdiction of the provincial government. Most of the population is Han, with the other predominant ethnic groups being Hui, Mongolian and Manchu. Zhengzhou is the provincial capital, other major cities being Kaifeng, Luoyang, Xinxiang and Nanyang.

The landscape undulates with mountains and rivers. Henan is embraced by Funiu, Waifang, Xiong'er and Xiaoshan Mountains in the west, Taihang Range in the north, and Tongbai and Dabie Mountains in the south. Hilly terrain accounts for 44.3 percent of the total area of the province, and plains for 55.7 percent. Besides Yellow River, Huaihe, Haihe and Changjiang rivers also run through it. Vast alluvial plains formed by the flooding of Yellow River and Huaihe River make up the central and eastern parts of the province. There is hence a wealth of ground water resources; at the eastern foot of Tai-hang Mountain, there is an especially large underground reservoir.

Henan extends from the temperate zone to the subtropical zone. The climate is temperate with Henan extends from the temperate zone to the subtropical zone. The climate is temperate with heavy rainfall in summer. Average temperatures are: 30°C to 3°C in January, and 24°C to 29°C in July. The annual average rainfall is 500 to 900 mm.

Infrastructure

Water Transport

River transportation is available, with easy access to the Yellow River, Huaihe, Weihe and Hanshui rivers. To improve the system along the Huaihe, Henan has invested RMB50 million. Upon completion in 2004, the province's western region will become an important inland water transport hub.

Railways

The Beijing-Guangzhou line, the Jiaozuo-Zhicheng line and the Beijing-Kowloon line cross the province from north to south. Other railways include the Lanzhou-Lianyungang, the Jiaozuo-Xinxiang-Heze, and the Mengmiao-Baofeng-Luohe-Fuyang lines, which run through Henan from west to east. The

Euro-Asia Land Bridge also passes through from Lianyungang in Jiangsu to Rotterdam in Holland. The Zhengzhou North Railway Station is a significant marshalling yard in China, with a large freight handling capacity.

Highways

Major highways in Henan include the Luoyang-Zhengzhou-Kaifeng Expressway, the Zhengzhou-Luoyang Expressway, the Anyang-Xinxiang Expressway, the Zhengzhou-Xuchang expressway, the Xuchang-Luohe Expressway and the Luoyang-Sanmenxia Expressway. Construction of the Sanmenxia-Lingbao Expressway is underway, part of a project linking Lianyungang and Jiangsu in the east with Horgos and Xinjiang in the northwest. The expressway will link Henan with Shaanxi province to the northwest as well.

Air Transport

Henan has airports in Zhengzhou, Luoyang and Nanyang, with scheduled flights to Beijing, Shanghai, Guangzhou, Xi'an and other major cities in the mainland, as well as to Hong Kong, Macao and Taipei.

Telecommunications

Recently, Henan has set up a new broadband IP network. Program-controlled telephones have been installed in the entire province.

Electricity

With rich coal resources, Henan is a centre for thermal power generation. In 1999, the installed generating capacity was 14.8 million kWh. Power stations are located in the cities of Zhengzhou, Kaifeng, Luoyang, Pingdingshan, Anyang, Hebi, Xinxiang, Jiaozuo and Sanmenxia.

Tourism

There are three ancient capital cities in the province: Luoyang, Kaifeng and Anyang, all of which have numerous sites and relics of great historical value. Famous attractions include the ruins of the

Shang Dynasty in Zhengzhou, the Longmen Grottoes in Luoyang, the ruins of the Yin and Shang Dynasties in Anyang, the Shaolin Temple in Dengfeng and the White Horse Temple in Luoyang. In 2002, over 410,100 (+12.2%) foreign tourists visited the province, generating revenues of US$145 million (+9.0%). To further develop the tourism industry, the provincial government plans to invest RMB60-80 million annually, particularly in Zhengzhou, Luoyang and Kaifeng.

Consumer Market

In 2002, retail sales of consumer goods in Henan rose by 10.6 percent to RMB218.9 billion. Major consumer markets are Zhengzhou, Nanyang and Luoyang. Zhengzhou is a major distribution centre in central China. Recently, the Sino-US Henan McDonald's Food Co. Ltd. was set up jointly by the fast food giant and the local Zhengzhou Friendship Commercial Group Corp. There are plans to roll out up to 10 outlets in Henan in the coming years.

Agriculture

The arable land is 7.33 million hectares. There is great biological diversity in the province, with some 3,830 plant species and 418 animal varieties. With an arable land area of 7.33 million hectares, Henan is a big producer of farm products with the significant ones being wheat, corn, cotton, leaf tobacco and sesame seeds. Other products are millet, sorghum, rice, potatoes, sweet potatoes, peanuts, soybeans, sugar cane, rape, edible fungus, ambary hemp, tussah, flue-cured tobacco, oriental oak, apples, peaches, grapes, walnuts, gingko, and persimmons. Specialty produce include Lingbao Dates, Huaiyang Day Lily and Huanghe Common Carp.

Natural Resources

Of Henan's mineral resources, over 78 have been verified, of which 61 have been developed commercially. There are significant reserves of molybdenum, blue asbestos, natural alkali, refractory clay, aluminium, prearlite, cyanite, andalusite, bauxite, natural oilstone, cement limestone, tungsten, cesium, natural gas, nickel, graphite, gold, rubidium, quartzite, marble, petroleum, coal, chemical limestone, mica and zeolite.

In the coming years, Henan looks to improve its investment environment by improving infrastructure such as the transportation networks, telecommunications and energy supply, as well as by simplifying investment procedures.

In 1999, the province's coal output reached 80 million tons. The Zhongyuan oilfield is also one of the largest oilfields in the country.

Industry

In 2002, Henan's industrial output totalled RMB330 billion (+23.97%). The main industrial areas are Zhengzhou, Nanyang, Luoyang, Jiaozuo and Xinxiang. Henan has well-developed industries in coal, electricity, petroleum, metallurgy, chemicals, building materials, machinery, electronics, textiles, food processing and some other light industries. The bigger players are household brands in the mainland, such as "White Pigeon", "Peony", "Snowy Mountain", "Lotus", "Xinfei", "Dayang", "Shuanghui" and "Chundu". The province hopes to capitalise on its natural advantages and further develop the agricultural and food processing industries, as well as the production of raw materials and the energy sector.

Foreign Trade

In 2003, Henan's exports rose 40.6 percent to US$3.0billion. Major export goods included agricultural products and processed foodstuffs,

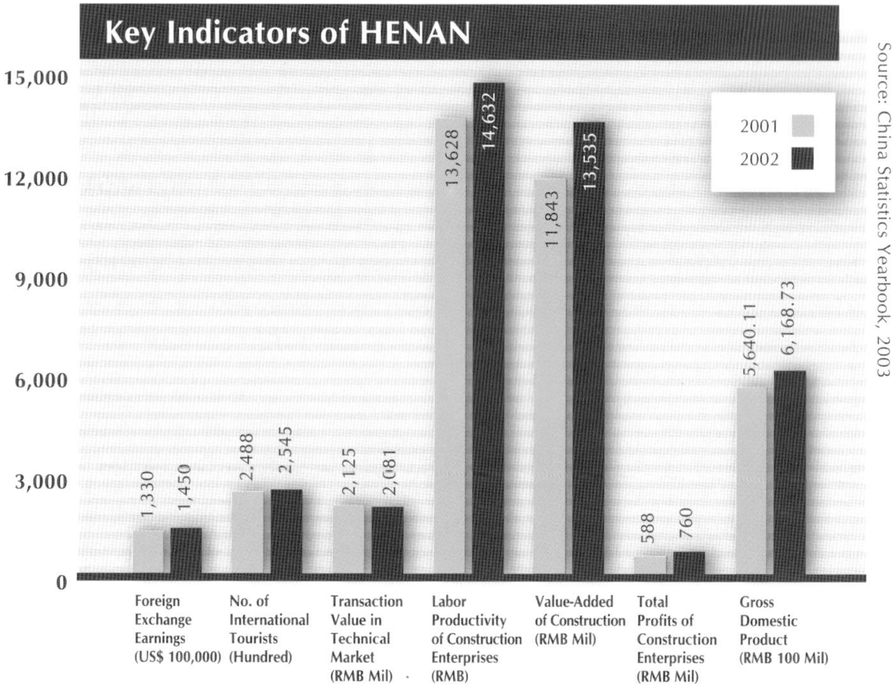

Key Indicators of HENAN

Indicator	2001	2002
Foreign Exchange Earnings (US$ 100,000)	1,330	1,450
No. of International Tourists (Hundred)	2,488	2,545
Transaction Value in Technical Market (RMB Mil)	2,125	2,081
Labor Productivity of Construction Enterprises (RMB)	13,628	14,632
Value-Added of Construction (RMB Mil)	11,843	13,535
Total Profits of Construction Enterprises (RMB Mil)	588	760
Gross Domestic Product (RMB 100 Mil)	5,640.11	6,168.73

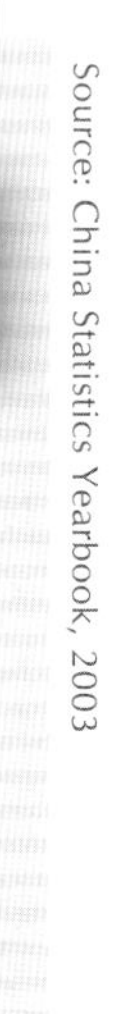

textiles, ceramics, machinery, metals and coal. Hong Kong was Henan's second largest export market; in 1999, Henan exports to Hong Kong amounted to US$178 million. Other major export markets were USA, Japan, EU, Russia and Republic of Korea. Imports rose by 60 percent to US$1.74 billion in 2003. Major import goods were electronic parts, chemicals, salt and copper, mainly from USA, Australia, Hong Kong, Japan and Holland.

Foreign Investment

In 2003, Henan approved 324 (11.7%) foreign-invested projects with contractual foreign capital of more than US$1,826 million (79%), of which more than US$561 million (24.3%) was actually utilised. Hong Kong is a major investor; in 1999, Hong

Kong investors signed 73 contracts with a contractual amount of US$258 million.

Other major investors are USA, Taiwan and Malaysia. Zhengzhou, Luoyang, Xinxiang, Nanyang, Xinyang and Shangqiu attract the bulk of foreign investment. High technology development zones have been set up in Zhengzhou and Luoyang, while economic development zones have been established in Xinxiang, Kaifeng, Luohe, Shangqiu, Hebi and other cities in the province. Foreign investment is concentrated in the sectors of agriculture, electronics, petrochemicals, energy, telecommunications, machinery, building materials, real estate and infrastructure.

A number of multinationals, such as Mitsui, Sumitomo and C Itoh and Co. Ltd. from Japan, General Electric and the International Telephone and Telegraph (ITT) from US, and Renault from France have invested in the province.

In the coming years, Henan looks to improve its investment environment by improving infrastructure such as the transportation networks, telecommunications and energy supply, as well as by simplifying investment procedures. Further, there are the preferential policies implemented by the State Council to boost development in the central and western regions.

Under existing policy, foreign-invested enterprises (FIEs) are entitled to a three-year tax reduction and exemption. The new policy allows FIEs in the central and western regions to enjoy another three years of preferential tax rate when the existing preferential term expires. The tax rate can be further reduced to 10 percent if an enterprise can prove that it exports over 70 percent of its annual output in terms of value.

HUBEI

The province has benefited greatly from the opening up of the Yangtze Economic Belt and the implementation of the Three Gorges Dam project.

HUBEI Fact Sheet	2003
Area (km^2)	187,700
No. of Cities	36
Population (mil)	60.0
GDP (RMB bn)	497.5
Gross capital formation (RMB bn)	199.4
Consumption expenditure (RMB bn)	267
~Household	211
~Government	56
No. of employed persons (mil)	34.76
Unemployment Rate	4.3%
Literacy Rate	87.6%
Government revenue (RMB bn)	26.0
Government expenditure (RMB bn)	53.8
Per capita annual	
~disposable income of urban residents (RMB '000)	7.3
~net income of rural households (RMB '000)	2.6
~living expenditure of urban residents (RMB '000)	5.6
~living expenditure of rural residents (RMB '000)	1.7
Actually Used Foreign Direct Investment (US$ mil)	2,529
Total assets (RMB bn)	68
Exports (USD mil)	2,656
~percentage of change from the same period of previous year	+26.5%
Imports (USD mil)	2,455
~percentage of change from the same period of previous year	+32.2%

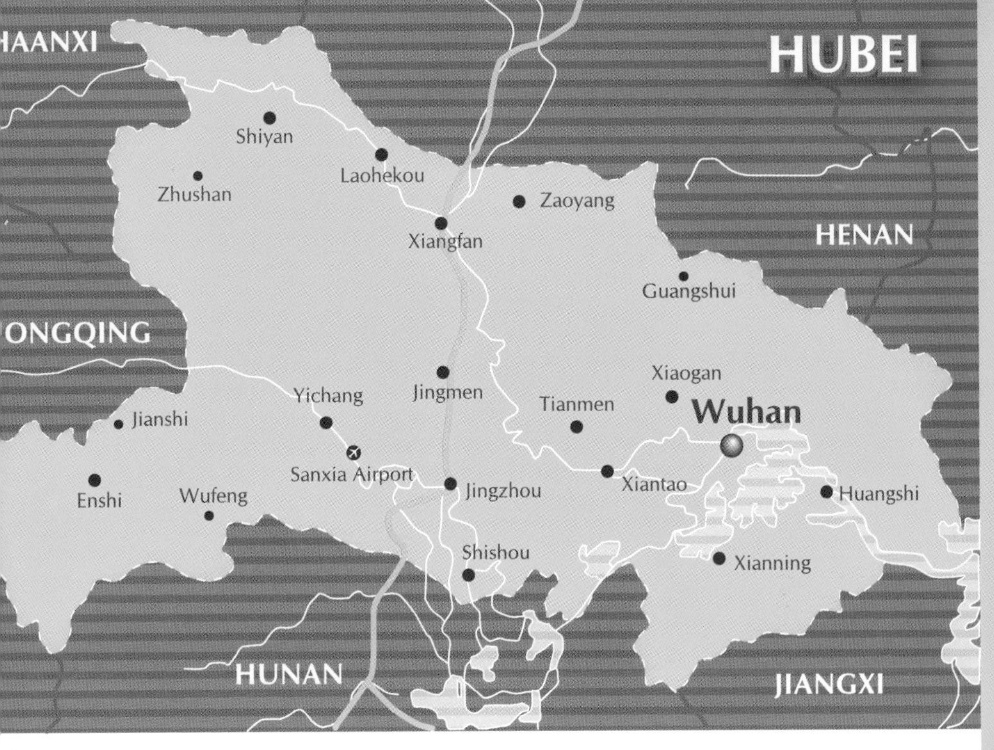

Introduction

Hubei province in central China has an area of 187,700 km^2, supporting a population of 60 million. There are 12 cities under the jurisdiction of the provincial government; Wuhan, Huangshi, Xiangfan, Jingzhou, Yichang, Shiyan, Xiaogan, Jing-men, Ezhou, Huanggang, Xianning and Suizhou. Wuhan, Huangshi and Yichang carry out economic policies that are equivalent to those practised by the coastal open cities.

Hubei was so named as it is situated to the north of Dongting Lake in the middle reaches of the Yangtze River; "hu" refers to lake and "bei" refers to the north. The Yangtze River Valley is the ancient cradle of the Chu Kingdom; the rich cultural legacy coupled with the scenic environs makes Hubei a popular visitor destination.

Hubei has benefited greatly from the opening up of the Yangtze Economic Belt, and the implementation of the Three Gorges Dam project, a cornerstone in the government's effort to direct economic growth from China's dynamic coastal open cities towards the less developed hinterland. Wuhan, the capital city of Hubei, is one of the most vibrant and cosmopolitan of China's interior cities.

Infrastructure

Highways

There are eight inter-province highways and 118 intra-province highways in total, covering all cities, counties and most villages and towns in the province. A new expressway in the Xihaigu area of the Ningxia Hui Autonomous Region is being constructed, forming an integral part of the expressway between Wuhan and the city of Yinchuan. Construction for the two major highways as approved by the central government's 10th Five-Year Plan is underway; the Beijing-Zhuhai and Shanghai-Nanning highways will both pass through Hubei.

Railways

Railways in Hubei include the Beijing-Guangzhou, Beijing-Kowloon, Shanghai-Wuhan, Wuhan-Chengdu and Jiaozuo-Zhicheng lines. The construction of the Shashi-Yueyang line and the Chongqing-Huaihua line are also underway. As part of the 10th Five-Year Plan, the central government plans to construct a railway running along the Yangtze River. The new railway will cross various provinces and municipalities including Sichuan, Hubei, Jiangxi, Anhui, Jiangsu, Chongqing and Shanghai so as to bolster the economic development along the Yangtze River belt.

Airports

There are seven airports in Hubei, including the Wuhan, Yichang, Sanxia, Xiangfan and Shashi airports. The largest one, Wuhan Tianhe Airport, operates an average of 230 flights (with daily flights to Hong Kong) each week with a total passenger handling capacity of 4.2 million.

Water Transport

Wuhan and Huangshi are the major ports on the Yangtze River, which are able to accommodate vessels of up to 3,000-5,000 tonnes in capacity. A frequent feeder service is also available between Wuhan and the ports along the Yangtze River to Shanghai and Chongqing.

Power and Gas Supply

Hubei has 33.1 million kW of installed capacity. Major sources include hydroelectric power plants such as the Gezhouba Power Plant and Danjiangkou Hydroelectric Power Station. The Three Gorges Power Plant, with a planned installed capacity of 18.20 million kW, is currently in construction and will boost the capacity significantly. Hubei is also developing a series of large and medium-sized thermal power plants, such as the Yangluo Power Plant, Xiangfan Power Plant, Erzhou Power Plant, Geheyan Power Station, Hanchuan Thermal Power plant and Yangluo Thermal Power Plant. Construction of a gas pipeline linking Wuhan to Zhongxian County in Chongqing is expected to be ready in 2003.

Tourism

Archeologists have discovered over 400 ruins and sites of historical value in the province, home of the ancient Chu culture. The remnants of the Dragon Tablet, excavated in Zhaoyang City, is dated to 6000 years ago. There are numerous visitor attractions, including the Wuhan East Lake, the Yellow Crane Tower in Wuhan, Yangtze River Three Gorges, the sacred Taoist Wudang Mountain, the Ancient City of Jingzhou from the Three Kingdoms Period, Dahong Mountain, Xiangfan Gulongzhong, Tongshan Dakou, Yuquan Temple in Dangyang City, Dalao Mountain in Yichang City, Longmen River in Singshan County, Lumen Temple, Xieshan in Gucheng County, Wuhan Jiufeng Mountain, and nature reserves such as Shennongjia and Sinluo. The magnificent Yangtze Three Gorges runs across two provinces, Hubei and Sichuan, for 201 km,

Wealth Centre – Beijing Finance Street (BFS)

As different international financial Centres, the Finance Street in London and the Wall Street in New York have written their own financial legends with different culture and economic background.

Inheriting the accumulated merits of the Chinese Tradition, the Beijing Finance Street has guided the Chinese financial powers into the international finance playground with RMB 13 Billion capital.

Financial Street Holding Co., Ltd.

Propellant of international Finance Commercial Zone

On December 14, 1992 established the finance Street Construction & Development Company. In May 2000, the company purchased Chongqing Huaya (0402), and the changed the name to Financial Street Holding Co., Ltd. (Stock Abbrev. 'Finance Street', code '000402'). As the sole development, the company has been committing itself to overall planning of the BFS area's land development, properly construction, and comprehensive management. Its business scope covers real estate development, commercial building sales, property management, investment and technological development of new technologies and projects, technical service, parking service, etc.

and is also known as the "Gallery of Landscape Paintings", while Shennongjia and Wudang Mountain are listed by UNESCO as world heritage sites. In 2002, over 755,700 (+39.2%) foreign tourists visited the province and generated a revenue of US$284 million (+53.5%).

Science and Technology

Hubei has a strong research community comprising 2,071 research institutions and laboratories. There is an emphasis on high technology fields such as lasers, optical fibre communications, bio-engineering, material sciences, computer software, electronic information, chemicals, medicine and environment protection.

Agriculture

The province has put much effort into industrialising the agricultural sector. There are 3.31 million hectares of arable land in the province, which produce an important share of the national outputs of grain, cotton and oil. The fertile Jianghan Plain is a major agriculture and aquaculture base. Produce for which Hubei is well-known for include rice, ramie, navel oranges, dried mushrooms, live pigs, Wuchang fish, tortoises, river crabs and shrimp. In 2002, the forest coverage rate of the province was 28 percent, half of which is timber forest.

Mineral Resources

Seventy-seven types of minerals have been found in Hubei. Amongst them, the reserves of both non-metallic and metallic minerals such as phosphorus, cement marl, silica, garnet, ratite, iron, copper, barite, gypsum, rock salt, gold, mercury, manganese, vanadium, cement limestone, dolomite, marble and refectory clay are sizeable.

Industry

In 2002, Hubei's industrial output totalled RMB328 billion. Along the Yangtze River, the eastern industrial base of Hubei is made up of Wuhan, Huangshi and Erzhou, while Yichang, Jingzhou, Jingmen are the key cities of the western industrial base. The former has a concentration of metallurgy, engineering, textile, chemical and building material industries, while the latter deals with electronics, oil, chemicals, textiles and light industry. In the north, the cities of Xiangfan, Shiyan focus on cars, electronics, textiles and light industry.

The iron and steel industries have been relatively well developed, covering most aspects including geological prospecting, designing, construction, mining, separation, smelting and rolling, over a 1,000 different iron and steel product specifications are produced. The Wuhan Iron and Steel (Group) Corp. is considered one of the local steel giants. Hubei is also one of the major car production bases in China; it produced over 132,400 vehicles in the first half of 2001, ranking third after Jilin and Shanghai. Big players include the Dongfeng Car Co. Ltd. and Citroen Automotive Co. By 2010, it is projected that Hubei would be producing over 900,000 vehicles a year.

Construction is another sector that has developed rapidly. In the wake of reform, major projects that have been approved include the Three Gorges Dam, the International Trade Center of Shenzhen, the Yellow Crane Tower of Wuhan, Yangtze River Bridge in Xiling and No.2 Yangtze River Bridge in Wuhan. Textiles have become a pillar industry. A comprehensive range of goods is produced, including cotton, wool, linen, silk, garments, knitwear and synthetic fibres. Other industries that have been established in Hubei include coal, oil, chemicals, building materials, electronics, food, leather, milling and ship building.

In the coming years, Hubei will give top priority to energy, telecommunications and raw materials production while further developing the car, machinery, and agricultural sectors along with tertiary industry.

Finance and Banking

The People's Bank of China Wuhan Branch, an agency of the central bank PBOC, supervises the financial system in Hubei, Hunan and Jiangxi provinces. National commercial banks in Hubei include Industrial and Commercial Bank of China, Agricultural Bank of China, Bank of China, China Construction Bank, Communications Bank, Merchants' Bank, Everbright Bank of China, Minsheng Bank, Huaxia Bank and CITIC Industrial Bank. Policy banks include the Agricultural Development Bank, Hubei branch, and the State Development Bank, Wuhan Office. In towns and rural areas, there are numerous credit cooperatives.

Foreign Trade

The total volume of exports and imports reached US$5.11billion in 2003, an increase of 29.2 percent over the previous year. Exports accounted for US$2.66billion, an increase of 26.5 percent, while imports accounted for US$2.46 billion. Major export commodities included agricultural products and sidelines, textiles and light industrial products, and chemical and heavy industrial products. Major export markets were Hong Kong, Japan, the USA, Germany and Taiwan. Major import goods included timber, textiles, machinery, chemicals and raw materials. Major import sources were Japan, Hong Kong, Australia, the US and the Republic of Korea. Hong Kong is Hubei's biggest trading partner.

The Chinese government has decided to set up export processing zones in 15 pilot cities; Wuhan has been selected as one of the cities in this trial programme. Export processing zones are special

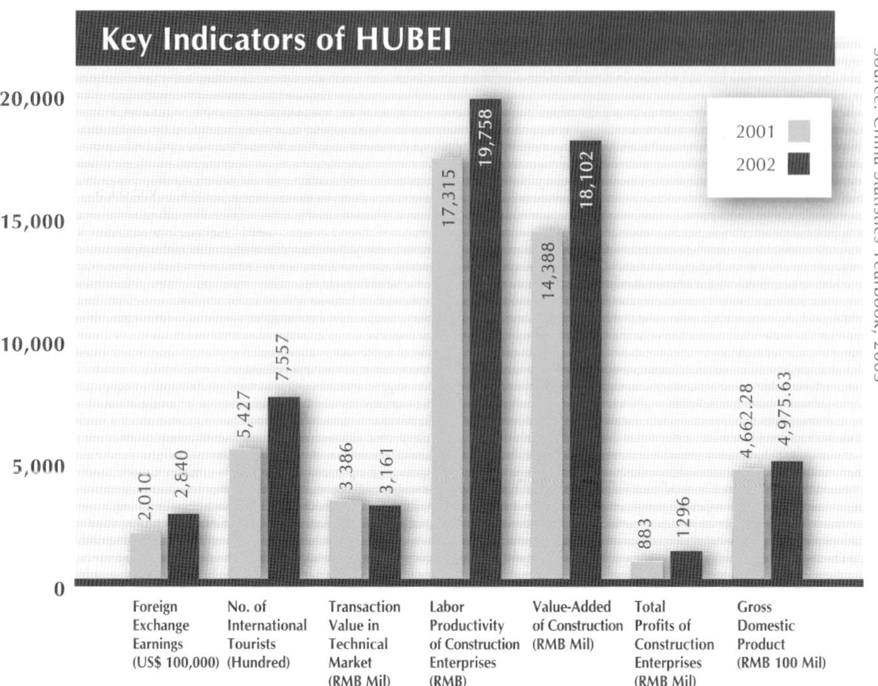

restricted areas administered by Customs, where all goods moving in and out of the zone are regarded as imports and exports respectively. Export processing, storage and transportation companies are allowed to be established within the zones.

Foreign Investment

In 2002, contracted foreign investment rose to US$9.79 billion. The number of newly established foreign-invested projects rose by 9.5 percent to 532, while actual utilised capital increased to US$2,529 million. Investments flowed in mainly from Hong Kong, the USA, Canada, Singapore and Taiwan, channelled into the sectors of medicine, telecommunications, chemicals, infrastructure and real estate.

MNCs which have invested in the province include Coca-Cola and McDonalds from the US, Siemens from Germany, Philips from the Netherlands, and Ericsson from Sweden. Wuhan attracts the most foreign investment; in the first half of 2001, actual utilised foreign capital came up to US$369 million in the city. Hong Kong and France are the two biggest investors in the city. French investment in Wuhan is mainly engaged in the car industry; the enterprises that have set up in Wuhan include PSA Peugeot-Citroen, Renault, Carrefour, Societe Generale and the Total-Elf Group. Yichang is another major city in Hubei to have attracted substantial foreign investment. In the first half of 2001, actual utilised foreign investment totalled US$64 million.

To boost the development of the central and western regions in China, the State Council has granted further tax incentives to foreign-invested enterprises (FIEs) in China. Under the existing policy, FIEs are entitled to a three-year tax reduction and exemption. The new policy allows FIEs in the central and western regions to enjoy another three years of preferential tax rate when the current preferential tax period expires. The tax rate can be further reduced to 10 percent if an enterprise can prove that it exports more than 70 percent of its annual output in terms of value.

In future, foreign investment will be encouraged in the following sectors: infrastructural facilities such as power plants in Jingman, Hanchuan, Huanggang, Erzhou, Yangtze bridge in Jingsha; modernisation of large and medium sized state-owned enterprises, especially those involved in textiles and car spare parts; agriculture; tertiary industry such as information, financial and insurance services.

HUNAN

Blessed with a subtropical climate and abundant rainfall and sunshine, large volumes of grain, tea, oranges and other agriculture products are produced each year.

HUNAN Fact Sheet	2003
Area (km^2)	212,000
No. of Cities	29
Population (mil)	66.6
GDP (RMB bn)	463.3
Gross capital formation (RMB bn)	157.2
Consumption expenditure (RMB bn)	276
~Household	199
~Government	77
No. of employed persons (mil)	35.2
Unemployment Rate	4.5%
Literacy Rate	92.8%
Government revenue (RMB bn)	23.1
Government expenditure (RMB bn)	53.3
Per capita annual	
~disposable income of urban residents (RMB '000)	7.7
~net income of rural households (RMB '000)	2.5
~living expenditure of urban residents (RMB '000)	6.1
~living expenditure of rural residents (RMB '000)	2.1
Actually Used Foreign Direct Investment (USD mil)	1,490
Total assets (RMB bn)	54
Exports (USD mil)	2,146
~percentage of change from the same period of previous year	+19.5%
Imports (USD mil)	1,590
~percentage of change from the same period of previous year	+47.1%

Introduction

Hunan is located to the south of the Yangtze River's middle reaches. Dotted with lakes and surrounded by mountains, the province lies on the Dongting Basin and is home to Dongting Lake, the second largest fresh water lake in China. Changsha is the capital city of Hunan. Along with Yueyang, the cities are the province's two inland open cities.

Infrastructure

Water Transport

The water transport network centres around Dongting Lake, with the Xiang, Yuan, and Li Zi rivers serving as major waterways. The annual handling capacity of the network exceeds one million tons. The Changlinji wharf on the bank of Dongting Lake in Yueyang city is the largest export shipping port in the province, and can berth a 5,000-tonne cargo ship.

Railways

The major railways include the Beijing-Guangzhou, Zhicheng-Liuzhou, Zhejiang-Jiangxi, Hunan-Guizhou and Hunan-Guangxi lines. Construction of the Shashi-Yueyang line, Chongqing-Huaihua line, and the Hunan section of the Datong-Zhanjiang line has begun.

Highways

Major highways include Changsha-Zhuzhou-Xiangtan,

Yueyang-Guangzhou, Changsha Zhangjiajie. The Xiang-Zi-Gui Highway, which links Hunan and Guangxi, was recently completed. Pipeline projects include the Xiang-Lai Line, Lai-Yi Line and Lin-Chang Line (the three are main sections of the Beijing-Zhuhai Expressway), the Tan-Shao Line, the Changsha Metro Superhighway, the Hengzao Line, and the Changde-Zhangjiajie Line.

In 2002, Hunan approved 413 foreign-invested projects with a contracted foreign capital investment of US$874.9 million. Actual utilised investment amounted to US$900 million in that year.

Air Transport

Hunan's international airport, Huanghua Airport in Changsha, operates regular domestic and international flights. There are domestic airports in Changde, Hengyang, Lingling and Zhangjiajie as well.

Agriculture

Blessed with a subtropical temperate climate and abundant rainfall and sunshine, Hunan produces large volumes of grain, tea and oranges. Well-known local products include day lily and lotus seeds, Niangxiang pork, West Hunan beef and lamb, Wugang goose, Lingwu duck and Liuyang's Sanhuang chicken. Hunan is also one of South China's important timber bases.

Mineral Resources

There are significant reserves of bismuth, rubidium, bone coal, fluorite, sepiolite, barite, monazite, manganese, vitriol, rhenium, mirabilite, arsenic, kaolin, zinc, aluminium, tin, tantalum, graphite and diamond in Hunan. Leading products include lead, zinc, hard alloys, salt fluorite, ramie textile products, tungsten, electric aluminium, electric zinc, mercury and pottery.

Industries

In 2002, Hunan's industrial output totalled RMB168 billion (+7%). The main industrial areas are in Changsha, Yueyang, Hengyang, Changde and Zhuzhou. Pillar industries in Hunan are metallurgy, machinery (including electric locomotives, tractors, heavy machine tools and high-precision electronic equipment) and electronics, foodstuffs, chemicals, textiles, energy and building materials. Major products are ferro alloys, household ceramics, machine tools, cars, motorcycles, electric motors, cement, chemical fertilisers, chemical fibres, pesticides and garments.

Tourism

Important historical sites in Hunan include Emperor Yan's Tomb in Yanling County, Emperor Shun's Tomb in Ningyuan County, the Memorial Temple of Qu Yuan in Miluo County, the Chuangwang Mausoleum, Yueyang Tower, Yuelu Academy from the Song Dynasty (960-1279A.D.), Aiwan Pavilion, and Mawangdui Tomb. Natural scenic spots include Mt. Hengshan, Dongting Lake, and the UNESCO-listed Wulingyuan in Zhangjiajie City. Shaoshan, Mao Zedong's birthplace, is a beautiful village to visit. In 2002, over 566,200 foreign tourists visited the province and generated a revenue of US$311 million.

Consumer Market

Retail sales of consumer goods in Hunan rose by 11.1 percent to RMB167.8 billion in 2002. Changsha and Yueyang are the largest consumer centres.

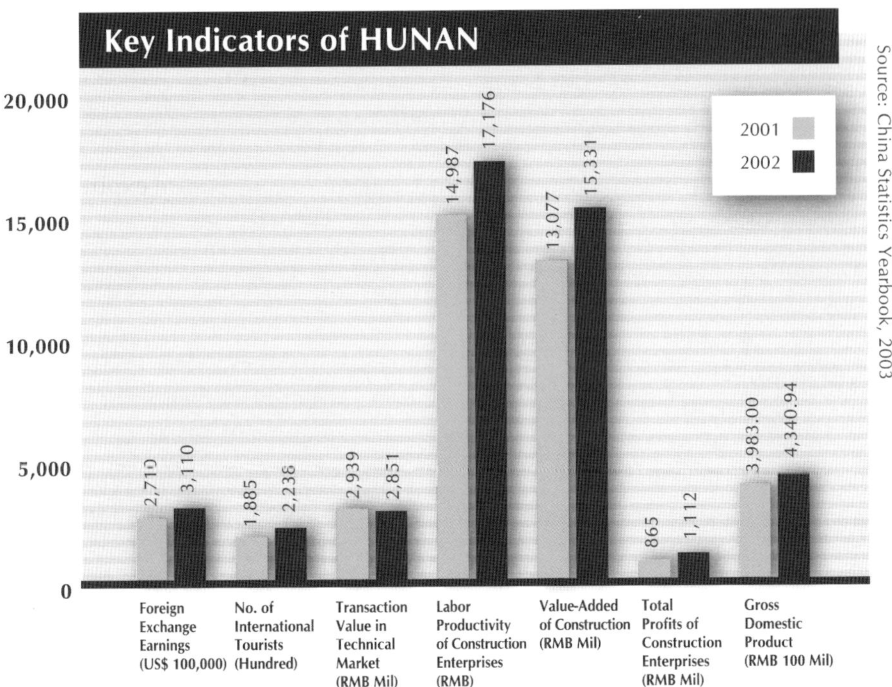

Foreign Trade

Exports from Hunan increased by 19.5 percent to US$2.15billion in 2003. Major export goods include garments, textiles, silk, rice, pottery, tea, live pigs, iron alloy and steel products. Manufactured goods accounted for some 85 percent of Hunan's total exports. Major export markets are Hong Kong, the USA, Japan, Germany and Republic of Korea.

Imports rose by 44.1 percent to US$1.59 billion in 2003. Major import goods include aquatic products, non-ferrous metals, steel, electronic equipment, chemical raw materials, tobacco, paper and chemical fertilisers. Major import sources are Hong Kong, the USA, Germany, Japan and Australia. Hong Kong is Hunan's largest trading partner; in 2001, exports to Hong Kong totalled US$264 million. In terms of imports, Hunan imported US$18.3 million worth of goods from Hong Kong.

Foreign Investment

In 2002, Hunan approved 413 foreign-invested projects with a contracted foreign capital investment of US$874.9 million. Actual utilised investment amounted to US$900 million in that year. Hong Kong is the biggest investor in Hunan; in 2001, contracted capital from Hong Kong was valued at US$329 million. Other major investors are the USA, Taiwan and the UK. Changsha, Hengyang and Zhuzhou attract the most foreign investment in the province.

To boost the development of the central and western regions in China, the State Council has granted further tax incentives to foreign-invested enterprises (FIEs) in China. Under the existing policy, FIEs are entitled to a three-year tax reduction and exemption. The new policy allows them to enjoy an additional three years of preferential tax rates when the current preferential term expires. The tax rate can be further reduced to 10 percent if an enterprise exports more than 70 percent of its annual output in terms of value.

JIANGSU

The China-Singapore Suzhou Industrial Park is the largest inter-governmental co-operation project between the two nations.

JIANGSU Fact Sheet	2003
Area (km^2)	102,600
No. of Cities	40
Population (mil)	74.1
GDP (RMB bn)	1,245.2
Gross capital formation (RMB bn)	480.8
Consumption expenditure (RMB bn)	480
~Household	348
~Government	133
No. of employed persons (mil)	44.69
Unemployment Rate	4.1%
Literacy Rate	87.6%
Government revenue (RMB bn)	79.8
Government expenditure (RMB bn)	103.0
Per capita annual	
~disposable income of urban residents (RMB '000)	9.3
~net income of rural households (RMB '000)	4.2
~living expenditure of urban residents (RMB '000)	6.7
~living expenditure of rural residents (RMB '000)	2.7
Actually Used Foreign Direct Investment (US$ mil)	15,800
Total assets (RMB bn)	138.9
Exports (USD mil)	59,140
~percentage of change from the same period of previous year	+53.7%
Imports (USD mil)	54,530
~percentage of change from the same period of previous year	+71.3%

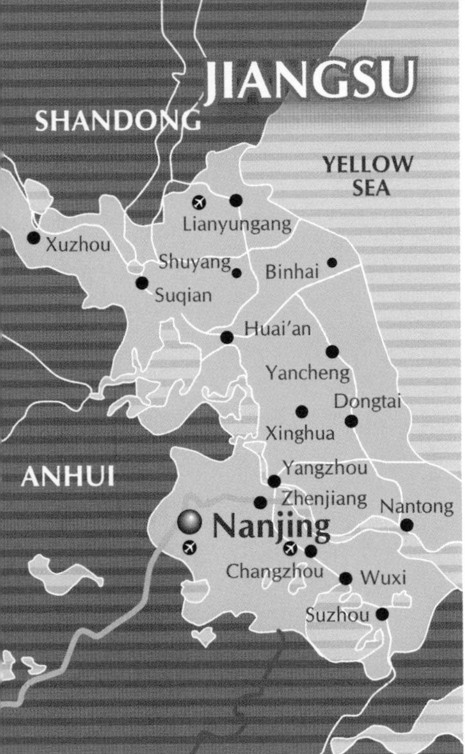

Introduction

Jiangsu is located at China's east coast at the lower reaches of the Yangtze River, adjoining Shanghai in the south. 17 percent of the province is covered with lakes and waterways. In terms of GDP, Jiangsu was second to Guangdong in China. 25 counties in the province were listed among the top 100 counties with the strongest economic strength in China, and seven of them among the top 10. The main economic centres are located in Nanjing (the capital city), Lianyungang, Nanton, Xuzhou (the coastal port cities), as well as the fast-growing industrial belt of Suzhou-Wuxi-Changzhou in the south.

The province is endowed with rich reserves of rare metal and resources for building materials like limestone and marble. Jiangsu also has the largest reserves of Kaoling in China. The 1,000 km-long coastline makes Jiangsu an ideal base for fishery activities, while the fertile soil gives it one of China's key agricultural production bases. The province's production of grain, cotton, silkworm cocoons, teas, and staples increased rapidly in recent years and gained important positions in the country.

Infrastructure

Water Transport

Jiangsu has the most advanced and convenient inland water transportation system in the country. While the Yangtze River flows through the province from the west to the east, the Grand Canal links Jiangsu with other provinces in the north and south. The ports of Lianyungang, Nantong, Zhangjiagang, Nanjing, Zhenjiang, Yangzhou and Jiangyin have formed a cluster of ports along the downstream of the Yangtze River and have been opened to foreign vessels as first-class ports of the state. Ocean freighters sail directly to ports in Hong Kong, Japan, Southeast Asia, Australia and Europe.

Railways

The province has a well-developed inter- and intra-provincial railway transportation network. Major railways running through the province include Jinghu Line: Beijing-Shanghai; Longhai Line: Lanzhou-Lianyungang; Ningtong Line: Nanjing-Tongling and Tianjin-Pukou. Of these, the Longhai Line is an important part of the New Asia-Europe Continent Bridge linking Lianyungang with the Siberia Railways to Europe. In the Tenth Five-Year Plan, the Jiangsu government plans to construct a railway linking Nanjing and Qidong. Also, several sections of the Chongqing-Shanghai Railway, which passes through Jiangsu, are under construction. The completion of the railway will greatly enhance economic development along the Yangtze River.

Highways

Jiangsu has invested substantially in upgrading its highway networks in recent years. The Nanjing-Lianyungang and Nanjing-Nantong Class-1 highways have started operation. Travel time between Nanjing and Shanghai is now shortened to about two and a half hours by the Shanghai-Nanjing Expressway. Several expressways and road bridges crossing the Yangtze River are under construction.

In the Tenth Five-Year Plan, Jiangsu focusses mainly on upgrading its existing highways into super-highways. There are also several new projects, including the Nanjing Yangtze River Underground Tunnel, the first Cross-River Tunnel under the Yangtze River and Nantong Yangtze River Bridge, which is going to be the longest bridge on the Yangtze river.

Air Transport

At present, there are eight airports (Nanjing, Suzhou, Changzhou, Xuzhou, Wuxi, Nantong, Lianyungang and Yancheng) in Jiangsu. The Nanjing Lukou International Airport serves Hong Kong, Japan, South Korea, the US and some European countries.

Telecommunications

Telecommunications have developed rapidly in recent years. Program-controlled telephones and cellular telephone networks have been incorporated into the provincial telecommunication system. The number of mobile telephone users in Jiangsu has exceeded 14.8 million, while there are 3.1 million registered internet users.

Education

Jiangsu enjoys educational and technological advantages. The number of high-learning institutions reaches 78 with total enrollment of 585,500. The number of research institutes is 2,821. In 2002, the number of projects honoured with great achievements for scientific and technological progress at the state and provincial levels were 16 and 322 respectively. The total number of technology contracts signed in 2001 was 31,000, with total value of RMB5.29 billion.

Industries

In 2002, Jiangsu's output rose to RMB1264 billion and ranked second in China after Guangdong province. The province is a major centre of light industries in China, particularly as its town and village enterprises grow rapidly in recent years.

Jiangsu's light industries are well developed, though the small and medium-sized enterprises dominate the industrial sector. Many cities in southern Jiangsu have become major production bases.

Jiangsu's light industries are well developed, though the small and medium-sized enterprises dominate the industrial sector. Many cities in southern Jiangsu have become major production bases of machinery, electronics, chemicals, car, and textile products. A number of national famous brands in electronics, machinery, food and textiles have been developed in Jiangsu.

Looking forward, the province aims to speed up the development of four pillar industries: machinery, electronics, petrochemical and car. In the medium-term, the areas along the Yangtze River and the Shanghai-Nanjing Railway will be developed into a new hi-tech industrial belt. In the long run, the province will see accelerated development and exploitation of coals, petroleum, iron ore, rock slat, and other mineral resources in northern Jiangsu, as well as the marine industries along its 1,000 km-long coastline.

Tourism

Jiangsu has abundant picturesque natural reserves, historical and cultural sites that make it an attractive tourism spot. Nanjing and Suzhou are the most important tourist sites in the province. In 2002, over 2.2 million foreign tourists visited the province and generated revenue of US$1050 million, representing an increase of 39 percent and 45 percent respectively from 2000.

The Suzhou Taihu Lake Tourist Resort and Wuxi Taihu Tourist Resort were approved by the State

Council to be developed into an international standard holiday and tourist resorts. The province continues to develop its tourism facilities (such as the "Ming Dynasty City" in Nanjing and a lake tourism zone in Xuzhou) in its bid to develop tourism into a pillar industry in Jiangsu in the coming years.

Consumer Market

One of the largest consumer markets in the China, Jiangsu recorded an 12 percent increase in its retail sales of consumer goods in 2002, amounting to RMB321.4 billion, and ranking it second after Guangdong. Major consumer markets are located in Nanjing, Suzhou, Wuxi, Changzhou and Xuzhou.

Overseas retailers, such as China Resources Co. Hong Kong Ltd, Pacific Concord, and Sincere have established department stores, chain stores or retail outlets in Nanjing and Suzhou to tap their rapidly growing consumer markets. Major department stores and shopping centres in Jiangsu province include the Nanjing Xinjiekou Department Store Shareholding Co., Nanjing Central Shopping Arcade Co., Nanjing Shopping Centre Co., Changzhou Department Store (Holdings), Xuzhou Department Store (Holdings), Yixing Sunan Shopping Centre, Suzhou Shopping Centre, Yixing Jiaoqiao Shopping Centre.

Foreign Trade

Jiangsu has established trade ties with more than 190 countries and regions. In 2003, its external trade grew 61.7 percent to US$113.7 billion. Exports soared by 53.7 percent to US$59.1 billion. Major export goods included food, textile, garment, silk, light products, petrochemical products, etc. Imports surged 71.3percent to US$54.5 billion. Major import commodities included chemicals, wool, synthetic fibres, steel, complete plant equipment and light industrial machinery.

Hong Kong is the fourth largest export market of Jiangsu. In 1999 Jiangsu exported US$1.4 billion worth of goods to Hong Kong. Other major export markets were Japan, the US, the Netherlands and Republic of Korea. Hong Kong is also the seventh largest source of import, and import from Hong Kong in 1999 was US$442 million. Other major sources of imports were from Japan, Taiwan, Republic of Korea, the US and Hong Kong.

Foreign Investment

Foreign direct investment (FDI) has been a major impetus for structural reform and economic growth in the province. In 2003, the number of new foreign-invested projects increased by 25.8 percent to 7.301. Both contractual and actual utilised foreign capital also increased by 56.6 percent and 52.4 percent to US$30.8 billion and US$15.8 billion respectively.

Foreign investments were mainly from Hong Kong, Taiwan, the US, Japan, etc. Those projects were mainly engaged in the sectors of textiles, electronics, telecommunications, engineering, banking, and tourism. Nanjing, Nantong, Suzhou are hot spots in attracting foreign funds.

In the coming years, overseas investments are encouraged in agricultural development, infrastructure, pillar manufacturing industries (textiles, chemical, petroleum-processing, pharmaceuticals, light industries, engineering, electronics, building materials, environmental protection, etc.), new and hi-tech sectors, as well as the tertiary sector.

To reform the existing processing trade system and to align it with international practice, the Chinese government has decided to set up export processing zones in 15 pilot cities. Kunshan and Suzhou are two of the selected cities in this trial programme. Export processing zones are special restricted areas administered by the Customs.

Goods moving in and out of the zones are regarded as imports and exports. Enterprises involved in export processing, storage and transportation are allowed to be set up in the zones.

Investment Environment

Located in the beautiful and fertile Yangtze delta in east China, Jiangsu province enjoys favourable natural and geographic conditions. It is one of the most developed coastal provinces in China in terms of economy, science, technology, culture and education. Its economy is among the most dynamic ones in China. With a population of 74.4 million, Jiangsu covers an area of 102,600 km^2. Its GDP reached RMB951 billion in 2001.

Under the national economic and social development plan, Jiangsu

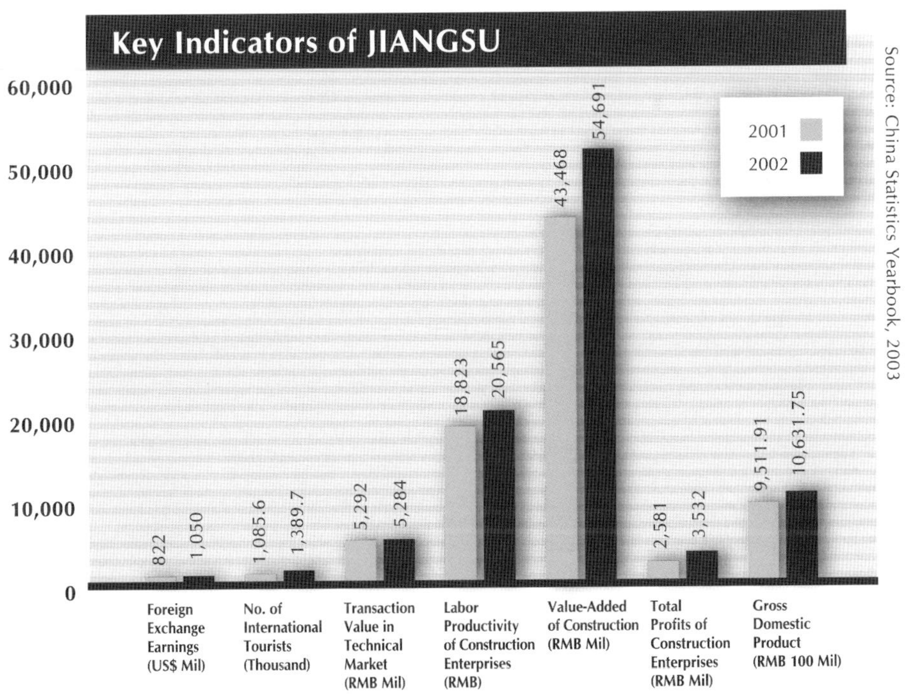

targets to complete its modernization plan by 2010. Four development strategies have been formulated, namely internationalization of economy, revitalize the economy through education, science and technology, common growth of different areas and sustainable development. The key way to internationalizing its economy lies in opening more economic zones to the outside world, thereby strengthening economic and technical cooperation and exchanges with the rest of the world. The five areas being earmarked for industrial development and foreign investment are as follows:

- Projects with new technology in agriculture, energy, communications, infrastructure, as well as having raw materials that are required by China.
- Projects which could improve product performance, save energy and cost of production, raise technology and economic efficiency.
- Projects that meet international standards in terms of product quality, open new markets, expand exports, increase foreign exchange earnings.
- Projects with new technology and equipment which could utilize resources, address environmental protection and pollution treatment.
- Projects covered by relevant state incentive policies.

JIANGXI

Pillar industries have been identified. Future development will be situated mainly in the areas along the Beijing-Kowloon Railway.

JIANGXI Fact Sheet	**2003**
Area (km^2)	166,600
No. of Cities	21
Population (mil)	42.2
GDP (RMB bn)	245
Gross capital formation (RMB bn)	99.9
Consumption expenditure (RMB bn)	146
~Household	111
~Government	35
No. of employed persons (mil)	21.31
Unemployment Rate	3.4%
Literacy Rate	90.9%
Government revenue (RMB bn)	14.1
Government expenditure (RMB bn)	34.1
Per capita annual	
~disposable income of urban residents (RMB '000)	6.3
~net income of rural households (RMB '000)	2.3
~living expenditure of urban residents (RMB '000)	4.5
~living expenditure of rural residents (RMB '000)	1.8
Actually Used Foreign Direct Investment (USD mil)	1,087
Total assets (RMB bn)	19.3
Exports (USD mil)	1052
~percentage of change from the same period of previous year	+1.3%
Imports (USD mil)	642.5
~percentage of change from the same period of previous year	+30.6%

Introduction

Jiangxi lies on the southern bank in the middle reaches of the Yangtze River bordering Fujian and Zhejiang. The provincial capital is Nanchang, while Jiujiang and Jingdezhen are inland open cities authorised by the State Council to enjoy preferential investment policies similar to coastal open cities.

The Boyang Lake is the largest freshwater lake in China, lying in the northern part of the province. It is known as the "Land of Fish and Rice" for its fertile land and rich aquaculture resources. Its products include rice, cotton, tea, sugarcane, oil-bearing seeds, beans, white lotus, melon seeds, ducks and chicken. Jiangxi is a major source of timber and bamboo products in China.

The province is also rich in metal deposits including copper, uranium, plutonium, tungsten, gold, silver, lead and zinc, all of which rank top in China. It has ample geothermal energy resources and mineral water.

Jiangxi has benefited greatly from the relocation of military industry from the coastal regions to inland provinces in the 1960s-70s. In 2002, Jiangxi's total industrial output was RMB1386 billion.

Infrastructure

Water Transport

Jiujiang is the only port city in the province. Situated at the superior location intersecting Yangtze River and the Beijing-Kowloon Railway, it is a major distribution centre for Jiangxi, Anhui, Hubei and Hunan provinces. Jiujiang is also a major inland water transportation centre at the middle reaches of the Yangtze River. The Jiujiang Port, now open to foreign trade, has an annual cargo handling capacity of more than three million

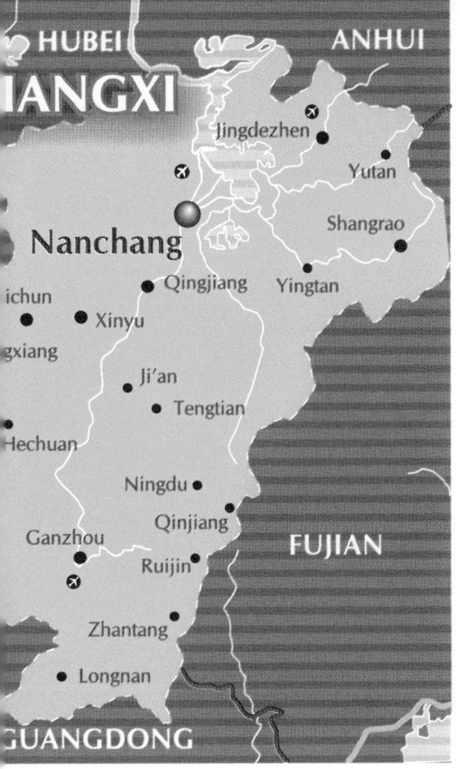

tons, and can accommodate 5,000-ton freighters sailing directly to Hong Kong, Japan and other Southeast Asian countries.

Railways

The province has a well-developed railway network. Major trunk railways include Jingjiu line: Beijing-Kowloon, Zhegan line: Hangzhou-Nanchang, Ying-xia line: Yingtan-Xiamen, Ninggan line: Nanjing-Nanchang, Xiangjiu line: Xiangtang-Jiujiang, Xiangji line: Xiangtang-Ji'an and Wujiu line: Wuhan-Jiujiang.

A new national trunk railway running along the Yangtze River is in the pipeline, which will cross various provinces and municipalities including Sichuan, Hubei, Jiangxi, Anhui, Jiangsu, Chongqing and Shanghai, and greatly enhance economic development of the Yangtze River Valley. Other railways under construction are: Gan-Long Line, Tong-Jiu Line.

Highways

Jiangxi's highway network including the Nanchang Bridge and the Nanchang-Jiaotan section of the Nanchang-Jinjiang motorway, Changzhang Expressway between Nanchang and Zhangzhou, the Jiujiang-Jingdezhen Expressway and the Ganyue Expressway linking Nanchang, Ji'an and Ganzhou with Guangdong province.

In the Tenth Five-Year Plan, Jiangxi will construct 1,000 km of new expressways and improve the conditions of over 10,000 existing expressways. The total amount of investment is expected to be over RMB50 billion.

Air Transport

There are five airports, located in Nanchang, Jiujiang, Jingdezhen, Ji'an and Ganzhou. Chartered flight from Nanchang to Hong Kong is available.

Telecommunications

All the places above the county level are equipped with program-controlled telephones. By end 2002, mobile telephone users in the province is expected to exceed 4.3 million, and internet users 1,193,100.

Electricity

Five large hydroelectric power stations and 10 thermal power plants make the province almost self-sufficient in electricity.

Industries

Jiangxi has benefited greatly from the relocation of military industry from the coastal regions to inland provinces in the 1960s-70s. In 2002, Jiangxi's total industrial output was RMB1386 billion.

Nanchang is a major heavy industry base of iron and steel, machinery, electronics, metallurgy, cars, textiles and petrochemicals. The Jiangling Car Co. Ltd., a joint venture between Isuzu and Nanchang Jiangling Car Factory, has become one of the largest light truck manufacturers in China.

Jingdezhen is a world famous city for chinaware and porcelain products. In recent years, the city has been developed into an important comprehensive industrial base. It covers many industries: car, household appliances, chemicals, coals, food processing, forestry, building materials and textiles.

The Dayu Uranium Mill is world famous, while the Dexing Copper Mill is one of the largest copper mines in Asia and nonferrous production bases in China. The coal industry in Pingxiang, Gaoan,

Fengcheng and Leping is also significant in China.

Future development focus will be on the areas along the Beijing-Kowloon Railway. Several industrial bases will be established in the "Golden Triangle Industrial Bases" of Nanchang, Jiujiang and Jingdezhen. Electronics, car, machinery, petrochemicals, pharmaceuticals, foodstuffs, textiles and building materials are the pillar industries targeted for the next 15 years.

Tourism

Jiangxi has a rich historical and cultural heritage, which has become a famous tourist attraction. Famous scenic spots include: Bailudong Academy, Mt. Dragon and Tiger in Jiangxi, Tengwang Pavilion, Capital of Porcelain-Jingdezhen Lushan, Jinggang Mountains and Poyang Lake. In 2002, 248,900 foreign tourists visited Jiangxi and revenue of US$72 million was generated.

Consumer Market

Retail sales of consumer goods in Jiangxi increased by 9.1 percent to RMB83.3 billion in 2002. Major consumer markets are located in Nanchang, Jiujiang, Pingxiang and Jingdezhen. Major department stores and shopping centres in Jiangxi include Nanchang Department Store Shareholdings Co, Nanchang Shopping Centre, Jiujiang Department Store and Jingdezhen Department Store, etc.

Foreign Trade

In 2002, Jiangxi's exports increased to US$10.5 billion. Major export goods included garment, porcelain, synthetic blended fabrics, tungsten ores, shoes, medicine, electrical appliances, rice, ammonium, fireworks and canned foods. Major export destinations are Hong Kong, the US, Japan, Germany and Republic of Korea. Imports jumped 30.6 percent to US$642 million. Major import commodities included chemicals,

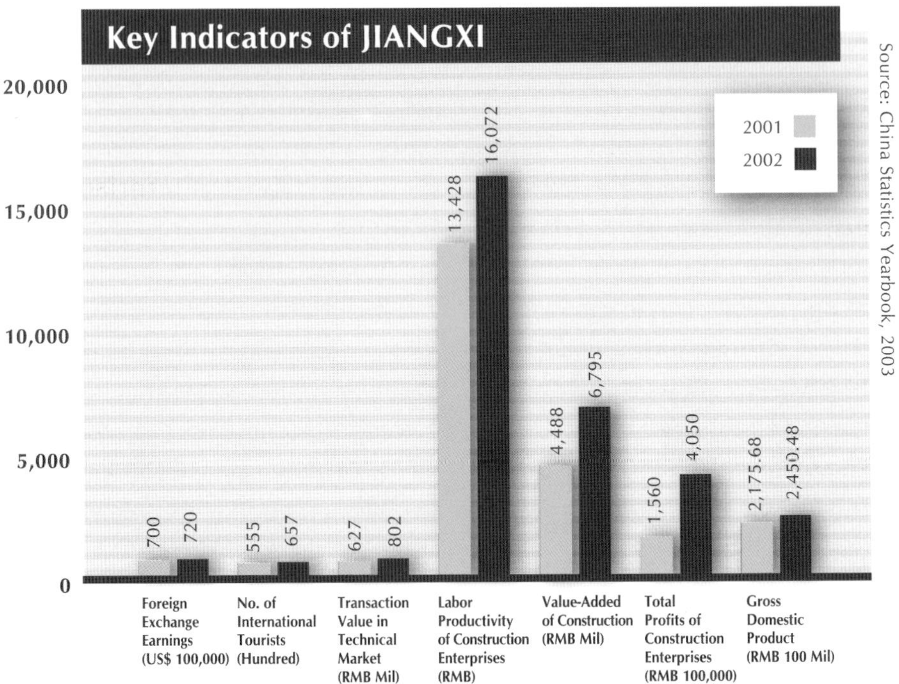

fertiliser, raw materials, synthetic fibre and machinery. Major import sources were Hong Kong, Japan, the UK and the US.

Foreign Investment

In 2002, Jiangxi approved 592 foreign-invested projects with contracted foreign capital of US$149 million. Actual utilised foreign fund decreased by 72.7 percent to US$108 million in the year.

By end-2001, the province had obtained a cumulative amount of foreign investment of more than US$5.3 billion from 58 countries and regions including the US, Japan, Singapore, Hong Kong and Taiwan. Some 5,000 foreign-funded enterprises were approved in transportation, energy, agriculture, electronics, cars, household appliances, food and pharmaceutical sectors.

Direct investment from Hong Kong has been diversified from hotels and processing and assembling industries in the early 1980s to infrastructure, manufacturing and tertiary industries in the 1990s. Hong Kong-invested projects such as the Qingshanhu Hotel, Jingdezhen Hotel, Lushan Hotel, Lushan Guest House, the No.105 State Highway in Ganzhou and the Longtan Hydropower Electricity Station.

In order to attract more Taiwanese investment, the government has established a Taiwanese investment zone in Gongqing City, aiming at developing electronics, machinery, garments, export-oriented agriculture, hi-tech and pollution-free industries. In addition, the Nanchang-Jiujiang Industrial Corridor, situated along the Nanchang-Jiujiang Expressway, is a popular spot for foreign investment.

To boost the development of the central and western regions in China, the State Council has granted further tax incentives to foreign-invested enterprises (FIEs) in China. Under the existing policy, FIEs are entitled to a three-year tax reduction and exemption. The new policy allows foreign-invested enterprises in the central and western regions to enjoy another three years of preferential tax rate when the current preferential tax period expires. The tax rate can be further reduced to 10 percent if an enterprise is proven to export more than 70 percent of its annual output in terms of value.

JILIN

The province is at the forefront in a series of research fields such as optics, applied chemistry, physics, biological engineering and automobile.

JILIN Fact Sheet	2003
Area (km²)	191,000
No. of Cities	28
Population (mil)	27
GDP (RMB bn)	252.2
Gross capital formation (RMB bn)	96.9
Consumption expenditure (RMB bn)	144
~Household	104
~Government	40
No. of employed persons (mil)	12.03
Unemployment Rate	4.3%
Literacy Rate	95.7%
Government revenue (RMB bn)	28.9
Government expenditure (RMB bn)	40.9
Per capita annual	
~disposable income of urban residents (RMB '000)	7.0
~net income of rural households (RMB '000)	2.5
~living expenditure of urban residents (RMB '000)	5.5
~living expenditure of rural residents (RMB '000)	1.8
Actually Used Foreign Direct Investment (US$ mil)	443.3
Total assets (RMB bn)	33.6
Exports (USD mil)	2,162
~percentage of change from the same period of previous year	+22.2%
Imports (USD mil)	4,010
~percentage of change from the same period of previous year	+107.3%

Introduction

Located in the centre of Northeast Asia, Jilin Province shares common borders with Russia and North Korea in the east and southeast, with Tumen River and Yalujiang River in the southeast. Songhua River is the longest waterway in Jilin, while the Songhua Lake, also known as Fengman Reservoir, is a renowned artificial lake. The border between the province and the two countries is over 1,4km long, and is dotted with counties and cities in which Sino-Russia and Sino-Korea border ports and official passageways have been established. Largely covered by grassland in the west and edged by the Changbai Mountains in the east, the central region is made up of hills, basins and valleys. The Western Plain and Liaohe Plain account for 30 percent of the province's total area. The Songliao Plain, a famed black soil area, is situated in the northwest of the province. With a total population of 26 million, there are 43 ethnic groups which inhabit

Jilin Province, the majority being made up of the Han, Hui, Korean, Manchu, Mongolian and Xibe.

The province has a territory of 187,400 km^2. There are eight cities (Changchun, Jilin, Siping, Tonghua, Liaoyuan, Baishan, Songyuan, Baicheng) directly under the jurisdiction of the provincial government, one autonomous prefecture (Yanbian Korean Minority Autonomous Prefecture), 41 counties and 19 districts under the jurisdiction of municipalities. Changchun is the capital of the province. With its verdant greenery, it is often called the "Spring City to the north of the Great Wall". Changchun and Hunchun, situated at the lower reaches of the Tumen River, are both open cities. The GDP of the province reached RMB203 billion in 2001, up 8.1 percent from the previous year.

With a continental monsoon climate, there are four distinct seasons in Jilin Province. Winters are cold and summers short and rainy, with average temperatures being -20°C to -14°C in January, and 16°C to 24°C in July. The annual average rainfall is 350-1,000 mm.

Administrative Divisions of Jilin Province

There are eight cities and one prefecture under the jurisdiction of Jilin Province:

Changchun City: Chaoyang District, Kuancheng District, Nanguan District, Erdao District, Luyuan District, Shuangyang District, Yushu City, Jiutai City, Dehui City, Nong'an County

Jilin City: Changyi District, Longtan District, Chuanying District, Fengman District, Huadian City, Jiaohe City, Shulan City, Panshi City, Yongji County

Siping City: Tiexi District, Tiedong District, Gong-zhuling, Lishu County, Yitong Manchurian Autonomous County, Shuangliao City

Liaoyuan City: Longshan District, Xi'an District, Dongfeng County, Dongliao County

Tonghua City: Dongchang District, Erdaojiang District, Meihekou City, Ji'an City, Tonghua County, Huinan County, Liuhe County

Baishan City: Badaojiang District, Linjiang City, Fusong County, Jingyu County, Changbai Korean Autonomous County, Jiangyuan County

Songyuan City: Ningjiang District, Changling County, Qianguo'erluosi Mongolian Autonomous County, Qian'an County, Fuyu County

Baicheng City: Taobei District, Taonan City, Da'an City, Zhenlai County, Tongyu County

Yanbian Korean Autonomous Prefecture: Yanji City, Tumen City, Dunhua City, Longjing City, Hunchun City, Helong City, Wangqing County, Antu County

Infrastructure

Water Transport

Inland water transport is available between April and November along the Songhuajiang River. Da'an Port, with an annual handling capacity of one million tons, is a first-class inland open port in China and has seven 1,000-ton berths. Direct sail to some ports in Russia is also available. A new land-water route, the Hunchun-Zarubino-Sogcho, linking China with Russia and the Republic of Korea (ROK), was opened in May 2000. The new route starts from Hunchun of Jilin and ends at Sogcho of ROK, passing through Zarubino of Russia. It takes approximately 17 hours for a one-way trip.

In addition to the usage of the harbours in Dalian and Yingkou, three new sea transportation routes have been opened starting from the border cities and going through the harbours in ROK and Russia to the Japanese Sea. The first one is from Hunchun to Poseit, Vladivostok and Pusan, the second goes from Tumen to Chong Jin and the harbours on the west coast of Japan, and the third from Hunchun to Lajin and Pusan. These sea routes cut short the distance from the northeast to the countries around the Japanese Sea and to ports around the Pacific Ocean. Some border cities in Jilin can directly enter the Japanese Sea through Korean and Russian ports.

There are 21 ports and passageways in the whole province. Sixteen are distributed along the border lines between China and ROK, while two are between China and Russia. Three of these are inland ports: Changchun Airport, Changchun Railway and Da'an Port. Classified by grade, there are 12 Grade A ports (national level), five Grade B ports (local level), and four for public service and goods transportation.

Classification of Ports and Passageways in Jilin Province

Grade A Ports: Changchun Airport; Da'an River Port; Hunchun Highway Port; Hunchun Railway Port; Quanhe River Port; Tumen Railway and Highway Port; Kaishantun Port; Sanhe Port; Nanping Port; Linjiang Port; Ji'an Port

Grade B Ports: Shatuozi Port; Guchengli Port; Changbai Port; Qingshi Port; Laohushao Port.

Public Service and Goods Transportation: Shuangmufeng Public Service Port; Badaogou Public Service Port; Sandaogou Goods Trans-portation Port (temporary and waterway); Ji'an Goods Transportation Port (temporary and waterway).

Railways

The Jingha Line is the most important trunk line in the province. Other major lines include Shenji Line, Simei line, Meiji Line, Changtu Line, Changbai Line and Pingqi Line, which link to major cities in northern China such as Shenyang, Tianjin, Dalian and Qinhuangdao. The railway networks handle more than two-thirds of the province's cargo transport. Access to Europe is also available by railways via Harbin and Manzhouli. A new railway line has been opened which links Hunchun in Jilin to Makhalino in Russia, thus speeding up cargo transport from China to Japan, Republic of Korea and North America.

Highways

Jilin's highway networks centre around Changchun, Jilin, Yanji and Tonghua. The construction of the YanBian-Tumen Expressway was

recently completed. The Shenha Expressway from Shenyang to Harbin that runs through Jilin is under construction.

To further develop foreign trade with Korea and Russia, the provincial government has invested in improving transportation in the Yanbian Korean Autonomous Area. As part of the project, the Chang-chun-Hunchun Expressway, the Yanji-Tumen Expressway, and Hunchun-Shucao Integrated Passage will be built. The expressway from Changchun to Siping, part of the expressway from Beijing to Harbin, the expressway from Changchun to Jilin City, that from Changchun to Yingchengzi, and the western section of the Changchun Round-City Expressway have already been put into use. Other projects underway include the expressways of Changchun to Lalinhe, Jilin to Jiangmifeng, Yanji to Tumen and the northern and southern sectors of the Changchun Round-City expressway.

Air Transport

Jilin has four airports in Changchun, Jilin, Yanji and Liuhe offering 47 domestic and international air routes. International flights to Hong Kong and Vladivostock, and chartered flights to Seoul, Sendai, Niigata, Irkutsk and Minsk, are available. A large international airport is in the pipeline.

Telecommunications and Postal Services

There are 1,400 post offices and postal agencies covering the whole province. Eighty-five percent of them are capable of handling international postal business. In 2002, population of telephone users reached 4.61 million, mobile phone users 4.61 million, and internet users are around 1,181,700.

Agriculture

Jilin is one of the main commodity grain bases in China, with an average output of 20 billion tons, the bulk of which is corn. There are about 2.96 million hectares of grassland in the northwestern part of the province, which makes it suitable for livestock breeding, animal husbandry and meat processing.

Jilin is rich in traditional medicinal resources, and is an important production base for herbal medicine. There are over 3,000 animal and plant species of commercial value in the eastern part of the province, of which ginseng, deer antler and sable fur are sought after. Jilin also produces soybeans, corn, sorghum, millet, rice, red beans, wheat, tubers, potatoes, sunflower seeds, sesame, mushrooms and edible fungus, mandarins, sugar beets, tobacco, flax, and silk cocoon. The provincial government aims to further industrialise the agricultural sector, and focus on intensified grain and livestock processing and by-product processing, as opposed to just churning out primary products.

The Changbai Mountain Forest Zone is one of the most important timber production bases in China. The 7.9 million hectares of forest produce an annual average output value that exceeds RMB1 million.

Natural Resources

Over 130 minerals have been discovered, with 83 kinds of mineral deposits verified. Significant ones include oil shale, silica, diatomite, bentonite, wollastonite, gas, coal, iron, nickel, molybdenum, cyanite, andalustie, talc, graphite, gypsum, cement rock, gold and silver.

Jilin has a fairly well developed energy industry. Apart from the output of coal, crude oil and gas, there are waterpower resources in the eastern mountains and wind power resources in the western plains.

Tourism

The foreign exchange earnings from overseas visitors amounted to

Jilin is rich in traditional medicinal resources, and is an important production base for herbal medicine. There are over 3,000 animal and plant species of commercial value in the eastern part of the province.

US$86 million, an increase of 13.54 percent over the last year. In 2002, over 294,000 foreign tourists visited the province and generated a revenue of US$86 million. Main visitor attractions include the Changbai Mountain Nature Reserve, the Xianghai Nature Reserve, Songhua Lake and Jingyue Pond.

Science and Technology

Jilin is at the forefront in the research fields of optics, applied chemistry, physics, biological engineering and cars. More than 11 key state-level laboratories are located in Changchun. The Changchun Institute of Applied Chemistry and Changchun Institute of Optics and Fine Mechanics are prestigious research institutes under the China Academy of Sciences.

A new optical electronics industrial park is being set up in the Changchun Economic Development Zone by the Institute of Optical Precision Machinery and Physics, the branch of the Chinese Academy of Sciences in Changchun. With a total investment budget of US$2.2 billion, it will focus on the optical electronics, instruments and information technology industries.

Industry

In 2002, Jilin's industrial output totalled RMB204 billion. Dominant industries are cars, petrochemicals, engineering, machinery, pharmaceuticals (including chemical drugs, TCM drugs, medical instruments and packaging), medicine, food, metallurgy, electronics, timber and wood processing. Leading products exported to other parts of China as well as overseas are cars, railway coaches (Changchun Railway Passenger Coach Plant), tractors, ferroalloy, carbon products, basic chemical raw materials, timber, sugar, machine-made paper, crude oil, vegetable oil, and medicine.

Light industry's added value amounted to RMB11.8 billion in 2001, an increase of 8.4 percent over the last year, while that for heavy industry was RMB43.9 billion, an increase of 17.6 percent. Cars and petrochemicals are the pillar industries in the province. The Changchun First Automobile Manufacturing Factory, in a joint venture with Volkswagen, manufactures Liberation trucks, Red Flag cars, as well as Audi and Jetta cars. The output of cars was up to 134,000 in 2001, an increase of 12 percent over the previous year. Jilin is also an important petrochemical production base, with the Jilin Oil Field and the Jilin Chemical Industry Corporation providing a variety of chemical materials for foodstuffs, medicine, textiles and other light industry.

Foreign Trade

According to Customs statistics, 2003's total volume of imports and exports amounted to US$6.2 billion, an increase of 66.7 percent compared to last year. Exports increased by 22.2 percent to US$2.16 billion. Major export goods included dried beans, vegetables, cars, garments, textiles, steel products, cement, frozen beef. Major export markets were Japan, Republic of Korea, the USA, Hong Kong, and North Korea. Imports increased by 107.3 percent to US$4.01 billion in 2003. Major import goods were car- parts, fertilisers, chrome ores and machinery, coming mostly from Germany, Japan, the USA, Italy and the Republic of Korea.

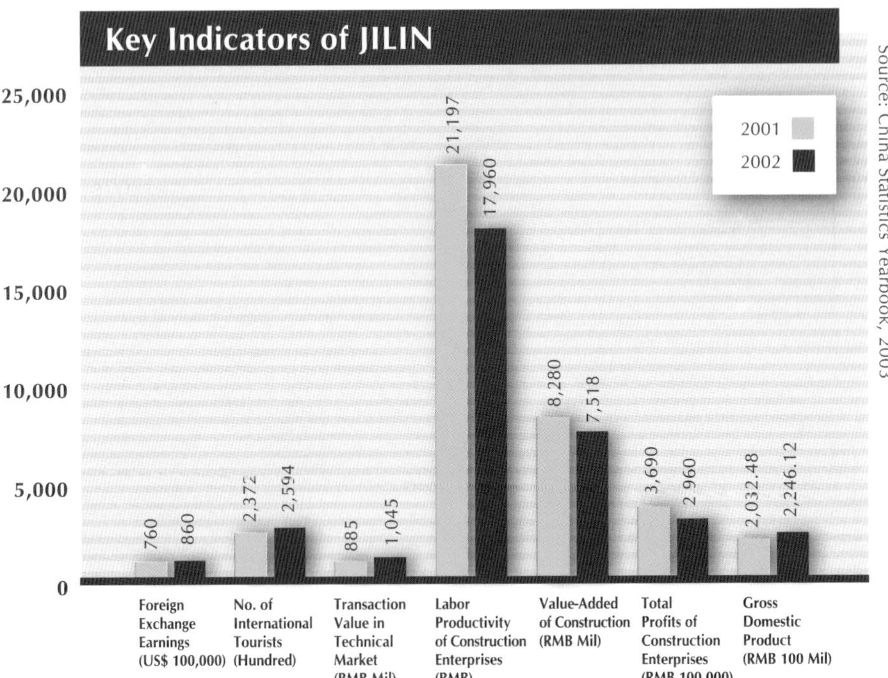

Foreign Investment

In 2002, the number of approved foreign-funded projects totalled 345 (-4.9%), with contracted foreign capital of US$493 million (-17.3%). Actual utilised amount came up to US$245 million (-53%) in that year. Procedures for foreign investment have been simplified, and a Service Centre for Foreign Investment has been set up. The Board of Foreign Investment of Jilin Province is responsible for all the foreign investment in the province, thus centralising the examination and approval system.

Foreign investments are mainly in manufacturing, agricultural processing and property development. Changchun, Jilin city and Siping attract the bulk of foreign investment. MNCs which have invested in Jilin include Pepsi-Cola, Ford and Chrysler from the US, Pilkington from the UK, and Siemens and Volkswagen AG from Germany. The Tumen River area is undergoing large scale development to turn it into a transportation hub in Northeast Asia, with a planned network of specialised ports. The Yanbian Chaoxian Autonomous Area and Hunchun are expected to benefit most from this project in terms of attracting overseas direct investment.

To reform the existing processing trade system, the Chinese government has decided to set up export processing zones in 15 pilot cities—Hunchun has been selected as one of them. Export processing zones are special restricted areas administered by Customs; goods moving in and out of the zones are regarded as imports and exports. Enterprises involved in export processing, storage and transportation are allowed to be set up in the zones.

To boost the development of the central and western regions in China, the State Council has granted further tax incentives to foreign-invested enterprises (FIEs) in China. Under the existing policy, FIEs are entitled to a three-year tax reduction and exemption. The new policy allows FIEs in the central and western regions to enjoy another three years of preferential tax rate when the current preferential term expires. The tax rate can be further reduced to 10 percent if an enterprise exports more than 70 percent of its annual output in terms of value. Foreign investment is encouraged in tertiary industry. The provincial government is taking action to create favourable conditions for foreign businessmen to set up in Jilin financial, insurance and commercial trade enterprises.

LIAONING

The province's long coastline possesses rich salt resources and offers a favourable condition for fishery activities. It is also rich in coal, oil and iron ore.

LIAONING Fact Sheet	
Area (km²)	146,000
No. of Cities	31
Population (mil)	42
GDP (RMB bn)	545.8
Gross capital formation (RMB bn)	183.5
Consumption expenditure (RMB bn)	303
~Household	214
~Government	89
No. of employed persons (mil)	18.42
Unemployment Rate	6.5%
Literacy Rate	95%
Government revenue (RMB bn)	40
Government expenditure (RMB bn)	69.1
Per capita annual	
~disposable income of urban residents (RMB '000)	6.5
~net income of rural households (RMB '000)	2.8
~living expenditure of urban residents (RMB '000)	5.3
~living expenditure of rural residents (RMB '000)	1.8
Actually Used Foreign Direct Investment (US$ mil)	3,411.7
Total assets (RMB bn)	107.9
Exports (USD mil)	12,366.6
~percentage of change from the same period of previous year	12.4%
Imports (USD mil)	9,373.1
~percentage of change from the same period of previous year	6.6%

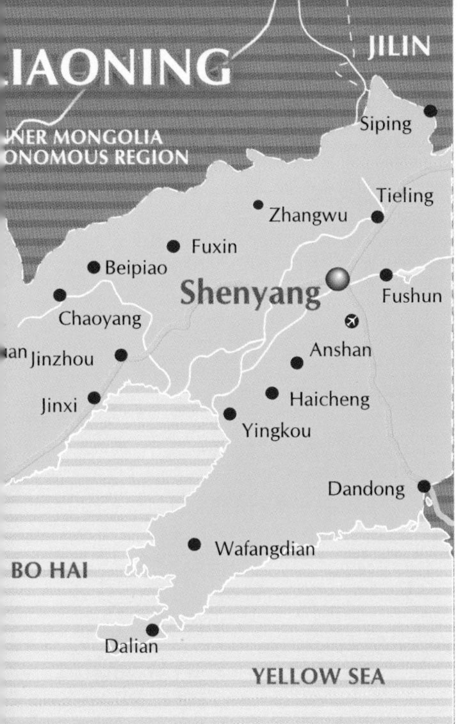

Introduction

Liaoning, abbreviated as Liao, is located in Northeast China bordering Democratic People's Republic of Korea (DPRK). Shenyang, the capital of the province, together with another major city, Dalian, are the two cities that enjoy preferential policies similar to the rest of the coastal cities in China.

Liaoning has rich mineral resources with huge deposits of coals and iron ores. The Liaohe Oilfield is one of the largest oilfields in China. Its output of crude oil ranked fourth in the country, reaching 14.3 million tons in 1999. Besides, Liaoning's output of steel and iron also ranked second and third in China in the year. Liaoning's reserve of boron, magnetite, diamonds and jade are also ranked top in China.

Liaoning possesses rich salt resources along its coastline. The province's long coastline offers a favourable condition for fishery activities. Luda is the famous fishery production base in China that supplies ocean fish and shellfish for the domestic markets as well as exports.

Infrastructure

Water Transport

The province has five foreign trade ports, namely Dalian, Yingkou, Huludao, Dandong and Jinzhou. Dalian is the fourth largest container port in terms of cargo handling tonnage in China and the port's throughput was 85.1 million tons in 1999. Inland water transport is seasonally available along the Liaohe and Yalujiang rivers. A new port in Panjin is located at the Bohai Rim with the primary function of handling commodities and oil products from the Liaohe Oilfield. In the Tenth Five Year Plan, the Lianning government plans to invest heavily to improve the facilities of its major ports. Two of the projects, the expansions of the Dalian port and Jinzhou port, are major items in the State Council's Five Year Plan and investors of these two projects will enjoy the same preferential policies granted to infrastructure building for the western provinces.

Railways

Liaoning has one of the densest railway networks in China. Major trunk railways include Jingha Line: Beijing-Harbin, Shenda Line: Shenyang-Dalian, Shenji Line: Shenyang-Jilin, Shendan Line: Shenyang-Dandong and Hada line: Harbin-Dalian. Construction of Qin-Shen line: Qinhuangdao-Shenyang, which links Hebei and Liaoning, is in progress. The electrification of the Harbin-Dalian line, making it the first electrified railway in Northeastern China, has been completed.

A new railway network, which covers 2,200 kilometres from Harbin to Changxing in Zhejiang, is under construction. The railway network will link the HaDa line and a 170-kilometre-long ferry passage from Dalian to Yantai in Shandong. It will further extend from Shandong to Zhejiang and running through Shanghai and Jiangsu. It will greatly improve China's existing railway network in the provinces of Heilongjiang, Jilin, Liaoning, Shandong, Jiangsu and Zhejiang upon completion.

Highways

Major highways in the province include Shenyang-Dalian Highway which links Shenyang, Fushun, Benxi, Tieling and Huancheng; Shen-Shan Express-way which links Shenyang with Shanhaiguan in Hebei. Besides, the Shenha Expressway from Shenyang to

Harbin has been completed. In the Tenth Five Year Plan, the Liaoning government plans to connect all 14 cities in the province with expressways. The last four major expressways of this project: Dandong-Benxi Expressway, Panjin-Haicheng Expressway, Jinzhou-Chaoyang, and Jinzhou-Fuxin have all been completed by 2002.

Air Transport

Liaoning has two international airports, the Shenyang Taoxian International Airport and the Dalian Zhoushuizi International Airport. There are also four provincial airports in Dandong, Jinzhou, Chaoyang and Changhai. Scheduled passenger services to Tokyo, Fukuoka, Seoul, Pyongyang, Moscow and Hong Kong, and chartered cargo flights to Japan, the US, Romania, Thailand, the Netherlands and Canada are available.

Telecommunications

Telephone penetration rate is high in Liaoning. At the end of 2002, the province had 9 million new mobile phone users. Internet users also reached more than 4.4 million.

Electricity

Liaoning has established one of the most developed electricity-supply networks within the country and it also takes the major part of the electricity-supply network in northeast China. A 500 kW electric cable from Suizhong in Liaoning to Qianxi in Tianjin has been constructed. This is the first cable that links the Northeastern China Electric Network with the Beijing-Tianjin-Tangshan Electric Network. It will provide relief to the future electricity supply shortage in the Beijing-Tianjin-Tangshan area.

Industries

Liaoning's industrial output was valued at RMB405 billion in 2002, a decrease of 8.2 percent over the previous year. Major industries included iron and steel, coals, petrochemicals, metallurgy, machinery, electronics, shipbuilding, building materials, paper making and textiles. Mechanical and electrical products are the province's main export products.

Liaoning is one of the most important heavy industry production bases in China. Shenyang and Dalian are the major industrial centres in the province. Some enterprises such as Shenyang FAW-Jinbei Co. Ltd., Dalian Iceberg Group, Dalian Shipbuilding Plant, Dalian Rolling Stock Plant, Anshan Steel Group, Fushun Petrochemicals Co. and Benxi Steel (Group) Co. Ltd. take significant roles in their own sectors, including electrical power, steel, cars, petrochemicals, aviation, shipbuilding and machinery.

Shenyang Aerospace Mitsubishi Motors Ltd is the largest car joint venture in recent years. The company, also the largest industrial joint venture in Liaoning, has a registered capital of US$88.92 million and total investment of US$263.8 million. Other well-known corporations such as General Motor, Ford, Mitsubishi also invested in the field.

The province's light industry mainly focuses on the development of textiles and clothing industries, which include cotton and wool spinning, chemical fibre, knitting, silk, garments and textile machinery. Dalian is a major fashion centre in China, and the China Dalian International Garment Fair has been an annual event in the industry.

In its future development plan, Liaoning will continue with the restructuring process in large and medium-sized state enterprises. The focus will be on its four pillar industries: petrochemicals, metallurgical, machinery and electronic sectors.

Bohai Bay Economic Belt, which is one of the strategic economic development areas in China, will be given much emphasis.

Tourism

As the historical site of the Qing Dynasty, Liaoning has rich cultural heritages. Famous tourist sites include: Shenyang Palace, the Mausoleums of the first three Qing emperors, Jiumenkou Great Wall and so forth. The annual China Dalian International Garment Fair is a well-known tourist attraction.

Shenyang Forest Wild Zoological Garden is one of the only two wild zoological gardens in China. With the approval of the State Council, the Dalian Jinshitan State Tourist Resort Development Zone was established in 1992 with the objective of boosting the province's tourism industry and to develop it into a world-class holiday and tourist resort. In 2002, the number of tourists and revenue generated increased by 28.3 percent and 19 percent respectively over the previous year.

Consumer Market

Liaoning's retail sales of consumer goods reached RMB226 billion in 2002, an increase of 7.2 percent from 2000, and ranking it the fifth largest among the provinces in China. Major consumer centres are located in Shenyang and Dalian.

In 1992, Dalian was selected by the State Council as one of the 11 designated pilot cities to establish one to two pilot Sino-overseas joint-venture (JV) retail enterprises with import-export rights. The Dalian International Commercial Trade Shopping Arcade Co., a JV retail store between the Dalian Shopping Centre and Japan's Nichii, was approved by the State Council as one of the 18 pilot JV retail enterprises. Dalian Friendship Group Corporation and Wal-Mart from US also formed a JV retail enterprise, Wal-Mart Dalian Supercentre. Covering 20,000 square metres, the Supercentre is the seventh store which Wal-Mart had invested in China.

Foreign Trade

In 2002, Liaoning recorded an external trade of US$21.7 billion. Its exports rose by 11.7 percent to US$12.4 billion in the year. Exports goods includes machinery, electronics, textiles, garments, silk, cement, soybeans, corn and seafood. Major export markets cover Japan, the USA, Republic of Korea, Hong Kong and Germany.

In the same year, imports increased by 7.7 percent to US$8.8 billion. Major import commodities include machinery, electronic equipment and components, fertilisers, raw materials and chemicals. Major imports are sourced from Japan, Republic of Korea, Hong Kong, Indonesia and the USA.

Foreign Investment

In 2002, the number of newly approved foreign invested projects increased by 2,147. Contracted foreign capital and actual utilised foreign investment also increased to US$1.24 billion and US$341 million respectively. Foreign investments are attracted mostly to Dalian and Shenyang, which are the major cities in Liaoning. Investments mainly came from Hong Kong, Japan, Republic of Korea, the US, Taiwan, etc. Well-known corporations such as General Electric from US, Siemens from Germany, Mitsubishi, Toshiba and Sanyo from Japan have invested in the province. The range of products include television, video recorder, air-conditioner, refrigeration equipment, cars, etc.

In the past two decades, more than 2,800 Taiwan-funded enterprises have been set up in Liaoning with total investment of more than US$2 billion. Accumulated to end-1998, there were 5,834 HK-funded investment projects with contracted foreign investment of US$10.2 billion, accounting for 32.4 percent and 33 percent of the province's total respectively. Apart from Dalian and Shenyang, HK investment started to expand in Anshan, Dandong and Yingkou. Famous Hong Kong enterprises such as Cheung Kong Group and New World Group also invested in the province. In the coming years, overseas investments are encouraged to invest in key industries such as machinery, metallurgy, electronics, chemical industry, textile, light industry, agriculture and infrastructure facilities, and the tertiary industry.

To reform the existing processing trade system and upgrade itself to international practice, the Chinese government has planned to set up export processing zones in 15 pilot cities. Dalian is selected as one of the cities in this trial programme. Export processing zones are special restricted areas administered by Customs. Goods moving in and out of the zones are regarded as imports and exports. Enterprises involving in export processing, storage and transportation are allowed to be set up in the zones.

Shenyang, Capital of Liaoning

Shenyang is the economic, cultural, financial and commercial centre of Northeast China. As an important industrial base and a famous historic and cultural city in China, it is a favourable choice for investments.

Shenyang is located in the southern part of Northeast China, in the centre of Liaoning Province, and in the inland area of Liaodong Peninsula. Located in the north of the Bohai Sea and southwest of the Changbai Mountains, it has a typical northern temperate continental climate with four distinct seasons.

Favourable Geographic Location

From a global point of view, Shenyang is situated in the central area of Northeast Asia, close to Japan, South Korea, North Korea, Mongolia and Russia.

Shenyang is located at the intersection of the Northeast China Economic Region and the Bohai Sea Rim Economic Region, which is surrounded by five provinces and two cities, namely, Liaoning, Hebei, Shanxi, Inner Mongolia, Shandong, Beijing and Tianjin. With regards to Liaoning province, Shenyang is surrounded by a number of cities, such as "Iron and Steel City" Anshan, 'Coal City" Fushun, "Chemical Fibre City" Liaoyang, "Coal and Iron City" Benxi and "Grain and Coal City" Tieling, which constitute an economic community in the middle part of Liaoning Province with Shenyang in the centre, where the economic exchanges are frequent enough with a big market and a promising future. The favourable geographic location makes Shenyang a key element in the opening and development of the Northeast Asia Economic Region and Bohai Sea Rim Economic Region.

Strong Industrial Foundation

Shenyang is an old industrial base funded by the central government for economic development during the first-five year plan period. Through years of development, Shenyang has over 5,800 industrial manufacturers with net fixed assets of RMB26.7 billion, covering over 140 industrial categories.

The types of industries include metallurgy, chemistry, pharmaceutical and textiles, electronics, cars, aviation, building materials and machine manufacturing. Among the industries, Shenyang's machine manufacturing industry is known worldwide. Its machine tools, power transforming and distributing equipment, universal equipment, large-sized mining machinery and car industries are key contributors to the nation's economy, and have the potential and capability to compete in the world markets.

Convenient Transportation and Communication

Shenyang is the transportation and communication hub which links the north-eastern part of China to the areas south of the Great Wall. Shenyang Taoxian International Airport is the largest airport in Northeast China, operating over 40 domestic and international lines with direct flights to major cities in China, and countries and regions 1ike Japan, Russia, Korea, and Hong Kong. Shenyang is also the largest railway hub In Northeast China with the highest railway network density in China. Apart from the six railway lines, including Shenyang-Shanhaiguan, Shenyang-Dandong, Shenyang-Jilin and Dalian-Harbin lines which all intersect here, there are also interconnecting lines with North Korea, Mongolia and Russia in Shenyang. The Shenyang-Dalian Expressway, which runs through and links seven cities along the Liaodong Peninsula, connects

Shenyang with port cities and other cities in the middle part of Liaoning province. Shenyong is also the largest information centre and communication hub in Northeast China, with easy-to-access advanced postal and telecommunication services.

Efficient Market System

Shenyang is the largest commodity distribution centre in Northeast China, possessing a complete set of efficient markets of three levels with the state-class markets in the leading position, the regional markets as supporters and local primary markets as supplementary.

The number of wholesale markets for consumer goods with an annual sales turnover of RMB100 million, has reached almost 185. There are 54 types of markets for productive materials trading, and a number of other attractive and specialised markets are being set up, such as steel, wood, coal and non-ferrous metal markets. Besides, 43 production related markets have been established, among which the markets for technology, human resources and labour have become state-categories.

In the meantime, Shenyang financial market is authorised by the People's Bank of China to be one of the largest financial centres in major Cities in China. Shenyang has become the largest exchange centre of capital, commodity, information and human resources in Northeast China.

Advance Science and Technology

With more than 550,000 engineers and technicians in all categories, and half of them in the fields of natural science, Shenyang tops the country in terms of human capital resource in science and technology. There are 578 college and/or university graduates for every 10,000 people in Shenyang, three times more than the national average. Among 30 colleges and/or universities and 400 scientific research institutes, Shenyang Metal Research Institute of Chinese Academy of Sciences, Forestry and Soil Research Institute, Shenyang

Chemical Research Institute of China Ministry of Chemical industry, and Shenyang Casting Research institute of are in leading positions in their areas of studies and research programmes, not only in China but in the world.

Rich Natural Resources

Rich natural resources such as energy resources, ferrous metals, and metallurgical materials can be found around Shenyang, with 25 million tons of iron ore reserves, two large coal mines of a verified reserve of 1.8 billion tons, and a proven crude oil deposit of 300 million tons, where three wells have been drilled with a daily output of about a thousand tons of oil. Besides, Shenyang also has natural resources of aluminium, granite and clay stone which would be used as building materials and processed for other industrial uses. Shenyang is also

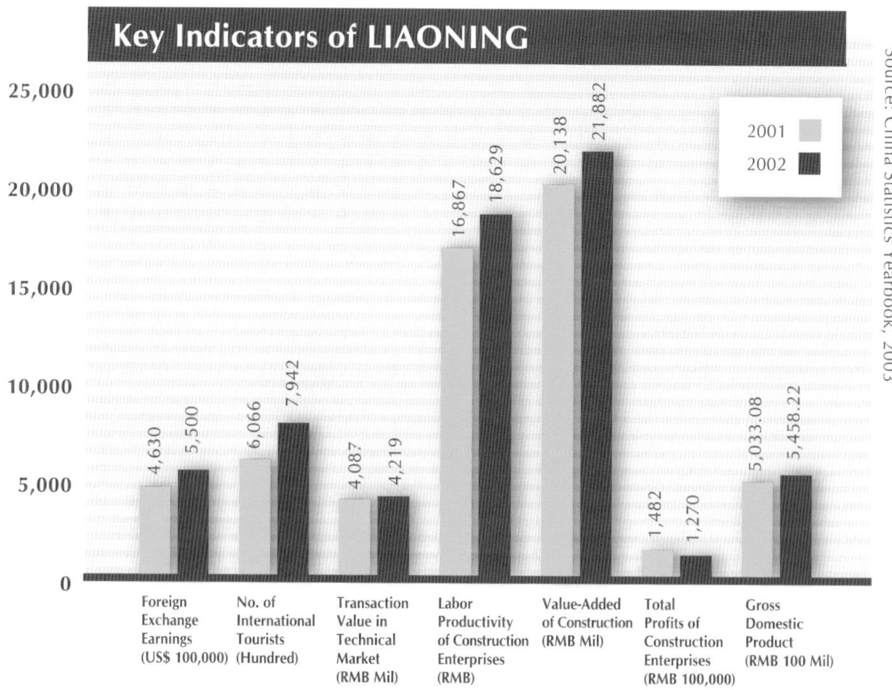

rich in agriculture, forestry, animal husbandry, by-products and fishery resources, which lay a solid foundation for Shenyang's economic development.

Investment Incentives

Since China's reform and opening to the outside world, Shenyang municipal government has spared no effort in implementing the country's preferential policies to encourage foreign investments.

The policies and measures expected to encourage foreign investment are:

- Three Openings
- Lowest Land-Use Fees
- Accrued Finance to Key Projects
- Rewards for Capital Raised
- Special Case with special Treatment
- Besides, flexible steps are taken to raise foreign capital. Apart from normal forms of investments such as joint ventures, co-management and sole proprietorship, the government also advocates and encourages the establishment of investment companies and "BOT" projects, issuing overseas bonds and stocks, and setting up stock companies, etc.

Infrastructure

Shenyang has a strong industrial base and the infra-structure to meet any requirement of new investments. The business conditions and facilities are improving day by day. The municipal government is spending huge budgets to make ready for future developments.

Labour Market

There are 2.4 million urban residents available for the labour market. Their wages are in the range of US$100 or less a month. There are 30,000 technical school graduates every year and they provide an ample source of excellent technical workers for businesses.

QINGHAI

Home to the famous ancient Silk Route, one of its major stops is Xining. The province is working with investors to develop tourism.

QINGHAI Fact Sheet	**2003**
Area (km^2)	720,000
No. of Cities	3
Population (mil)	5.3
GDP (RMB bn)	39.0
Gross capital formation (RMB bn)	24.5
Consumption expenditure (RMB bn)	22
~Household	14
~Government	8
No. of employed persons (mil)	2.95
Unemployment Rate	3.8%
Literacy Rate	77.8%
Government revenue (RMB bn)	4.4
Government expenditure (RMB bn)	12.3
Per capita annual	
~disposable income of urban residents (RMB '000)	6.7
~net income of rural households (RMB '000)	1.8
~living expenditure of urban residents (RMB '000)	5.0
~living expenditure of rural residents (RMB '000)	1.4
Actually Used Foreign Direct Investment (USD mil)	169
Total assets (RMB bn)	3.3
Exports (USD mil)	274
~percentage of change from the same period of previous year	+81.3%
Imports (USD mil)	65.0
~percentage of change from the same period of previous year	+43.1%

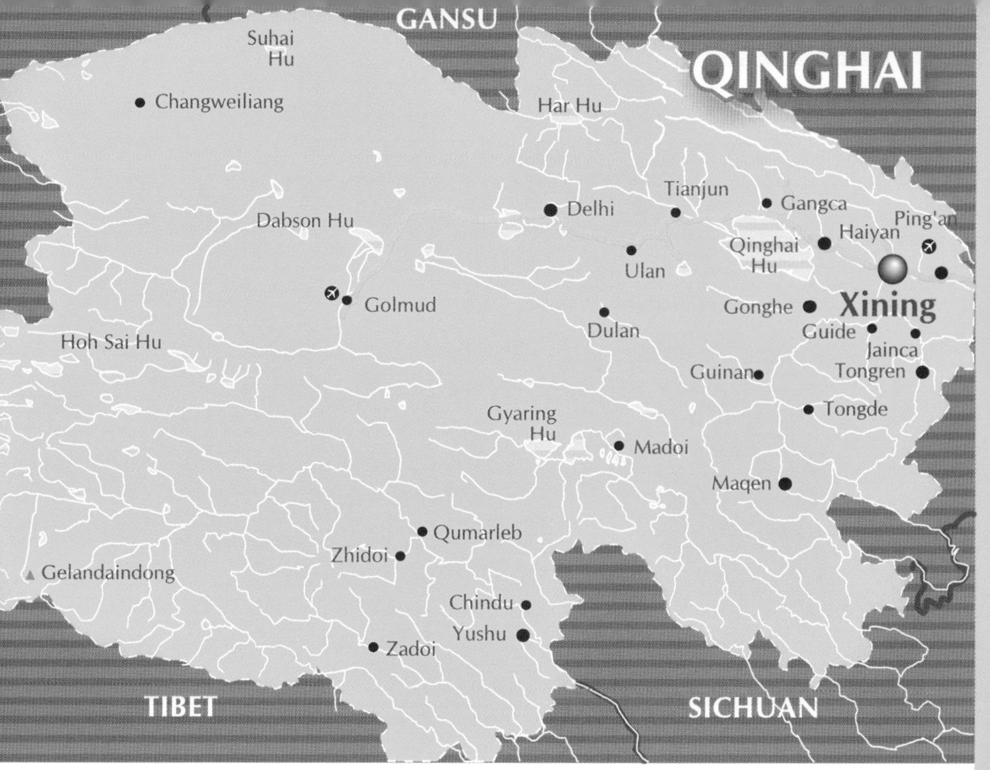

Introduction

Located on the north-eastern part of the Qinghai-Tibet plateau in western China, Qinghai province has a total area of 720,000 km^2. It is the source of the Yangtze River, the Yellow River and the Lancangjiang River. The province is named after Qinghai Lake, the biggest inland salt water lake in the country. The provincial capital is Xining, which was declared an inland open city by the State Council in 1992.

Population

Forty-four ethnic groups inhabit Qinghai province. Besides the Han, there are the Tibetan, Hui, Tu, Salar, Mongolian and Kazak ethnic groups. Ethnic minorities account for 43 percent of the total population.

Geography & Climate

The average elevation is more than 3,000 m above sea level, with 54 percent of the province being 4,000 to 5,000 m above sea level. The province is divided into the

Qilian Mountains, the Qaidam Basin, and the Qingnan Plateau. Qinghai has a continental climate with an average temperature of 10°C to 18°C.

Infrastructure

Railways

Qinghai's altitude and terrain limits the possibility of constructing a comprehensive railway network. Major railways include the Lanzhou-Qinghai railway, Qinghai-Tibet railway, QingXin railway, Qinghai-Xinjiang railway, YangXi railway, Yangpingguan-Xining railway, XiZhang railway and Xining-Zhangxe railway. The construction of the Qingzang Railway will greatly enhance accessibility in the region.

Highways

The three major highways are Qinghai-Xinjiang, Qinghai-Tibet and Gansu-Qinghai Highway. In line with the Great Western Development Strategy, Qinghai hopes to improve its highway network on a large scale. Twenty new projects were approved in 2001, eight of which were new highway constructions. Recently, the Pingxi Expressway, the first superhighway on the Qinghai-Tibet Plateau, was completed.

Airports

Golmud airport and Caojiabao airport at Xining offer flights to major cities in China, including Beijing, Xi'an, Shanghai, Guangzhou, Lanzhou, Chengdu, Urumqi and Lhasa.

Telecommunications & Postal Services

Computer-controlled telephone lines link Xining, and most prefectures and counties in the province to other parts of the country and to more than 160 foreign countries. Wireless services have also been developed. The transmission system utilises cables, microwave and satellite technology. The province is accessible via Internet.

Electricity & Gas Supply

The province has 178 hydropower stations with a total installed generation capacity of 21.66 million kWh and an annual generation capacity of 77 billion kWh. Major ones include the Longyiangxia and Lijiaxia hydropower stations. One of the key initiatives in the Great Western Development Strategy is the supply of natural gas from the four major gas reserve fields, including the Qaidam Basin Gas Reserve, to Eastern China. The first stage of the project, a natural gas pipeline linking Qinghai and Gansu provinces, was recently completed. The pipeline runs 953 km from Sebei Natural Gas Field in the Qaidam Basin, through Xining to Lanzhou of Gansu province.

Tourism

In 2002, over 39,700 foreign tourists visited the province and generated a total revenue of US$10 million, an increase of 42.9 percent over 2000. Xining is one of the main stops for travellers tracing the path of the ancient Silk Road trade route. Popular scenic attractions that are nearby include the Bird Island, the Mengda Nature Reserve, Ta'er Monastery, Dongguan Mosque, the snow-capped A-Nyemaqen Mountain, Sun-and-Moon Hill, and the Longyang Gorge Reservoir. To further develop its tourism resources, Qinghai is working closely with nine other provinces and autonomous regions, Sichuan, Gansu, Shaanxi, Shanxi, Henan and Shandong provinces as well as the Ningxia, Hui and Inner Mongolia autonomous regions.

Environmental Issues

Being the source of several rivers, Qinghai is pivotal to the ecological balance of the entire region. In the coming years, the province will focus on tackling soil erosion in the source area of the Yangtze and Yellow rivers, Qinghai Lake, the arid mountains in the east, the Longyang Gorge Reservoir, and the Qaidam Basin. Another critical issue is deforestation and the conservation of the native wildlife.

Measures are being taken to conserve the natural forests and grasslands, and shelter forests are being constructed.

Agriculture

Qinghai has 36.46 million hectares of pasture, ac-counting for 50.54 percent of the province's total area. It is a major husbandry base in China. Live-stock bred include cattle, donkeys, yaks, sheep, camels and horses. Xining wool is an important product.

Mineral Resources

Some 123 kinds of mineral deposits have been identified. these, there are large deposits of potassium chloride, nonferrous metals, rare metals, salt, magnesium chloride, lithium, boron and lead. The Qaidam Basin has abundant reserves of oil and natural gas. The Qinghai Oil Field is one of the largest in China. Qinghai has more than 30 salt lakes with a verified reserve of 70 billion tons.

Consumer Market

Retail sales of consumer goods totalled RMB10.3 billion in 2003, an increase of 11.5 percent over 2002. Xining is the largest consumer centre in Qinghai, accounting for 57 percent of total sales.

Industry

In 2002, Qinghai's industrial output was worth RMB12.3 billion. Industries are mainly located at Xining, Golmud and the Qaidam Basin. The large salt lake in the Qaidam basin, with its reserves of potassium, magnesium, lithium, natural gas and crude oil, provides the raw materials for the province's heavy industries. Major industries that have been developed in Qinghai are hydro-power, petroleum, natural gas, electricity, chemical salts, nonferrous metals, metallurgy, machinery, electronics, foodstuff, leather and textiles.

Foreign Trade

Qinghai's exports totalled US$274 million in 2003, an increase of 81.3

percent over the last year. Export products were mainly resource-based, with the share of non-ferrous metal and mineral products accounting for 55 percent of total export value. Other major export products were honey, textiles and metal silicone Qinghai's largest export market is Japan (US$23.1million), followed by Korea, the USA, Kazakhstan, Singapore and Hong Kong.

Imports totalled US$65.0million in the same year, a increase of 43.1 percent over the last year. Major import items included chemicals and telecommunications equipment.

Foreign Investment

In 2003, the province had approved the establishment of 44 foreign-invested enterprises with a contracted foreign investment capital of US$286 million. Actual utilised foreign investment also

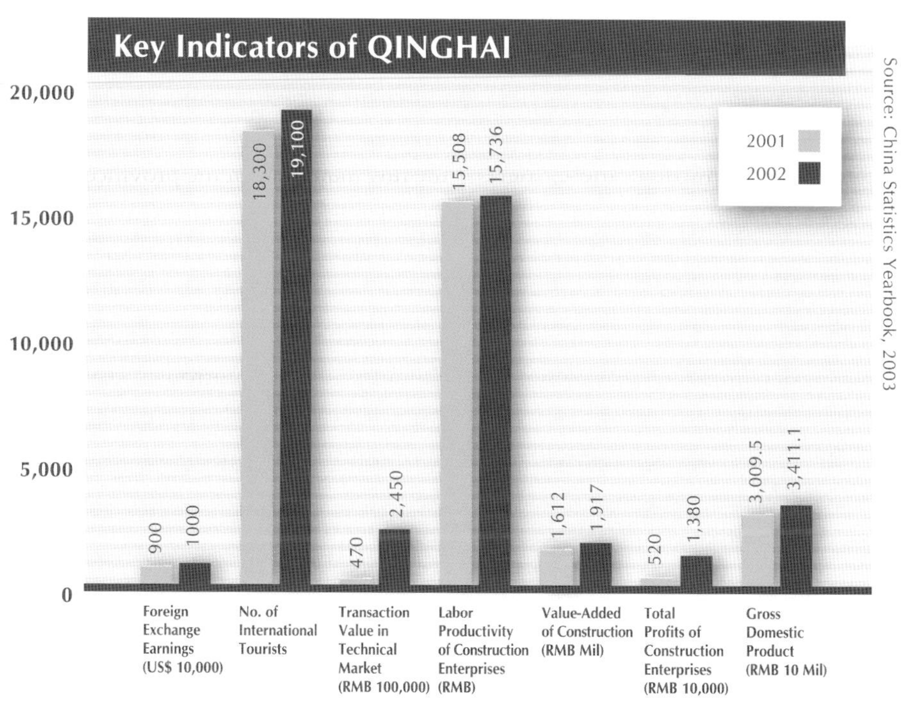

Source: China Statistics Yearbook, 2003

increased to US$169 million. The province had also received a total of US$63.26 million in international economic aid for 67 projects. These projects covered agriculture, livestock breeding, fishery, science, technology, education, culture, public health, and women's issues, and included the Haidong Agricultural Comprehensive Development Project, aided by the World Grain Program; the Qinghai Livestock Breeding and Potato Development Project, aided by the European Union; and the Qinghai Community Development Project, aided by Australia.

Xining attracts the bulk of foreign investment. In 1999, Xining's GDP reached RMB7.3 billion, an increase of 10.1 percent over 1998. The city drew US$11.8 million in foreign contracted investment, with an actual utilisation of US$5.6 million. Investment is particularly encouraged in the energy sector, chemical salt and raw material production, agriculture, livestock breeding and husbandry, machinery, electronics, communications, energy, textiles and food processing.

Foreign-invested enterprises (FIEs) are entitled to a three-year tax reduction and exemption. However, new policy allows for FIEs in the central and western regions to enjoy another three years of preferential tax rates when the current preferential term expires. The tax rate can be further reduced to 10 percent if an enterprise exports more than 70 percent of its annual output in terms of value.

Since the provincial government issued the Regulations of Qinghai Provincial People's Government on Encouragement of Foreign Investment in 2000, the Kunlun Economic Development zone in Golmud and the Qiaotou Economic & Technological Development Zone in Xining have been set up.

SHAANXI

The province is a natural base of energy resources and heavy chemical industries. It is blessed with rich reserves of coal, gas and petroleum.

SHAANXI Fact Sheet	2003
Area (km^2)	190,000
No. of Cities	13
Population (mil)	36.9
GDP (RMB bn)	239.9
Gross capital formation (RMB bn)	110.7
Consumption expenditure (RMB bn)	111
~Household	88
~Government	23
No. of employed persons (mil)	18.73
Unemployment Rate	3.5%
Literacy Rate	87%
Government revenue (RMB bn)	15
Government expenditure (RMB bn)	40.5
Per capita annual	
~disposable income of urban residents (RMB '000)	6.8
~net income of rural households (RMB '000)	1.7
~living expenditure of urban residents (RMB '000)	5.7
~living expenditure of rural residents (RMB '000)	1.5
Actually Used Foreign Direct Investment (US$ mil)	466
Total assets (RMB bn)	26.3
Exports (USD mil)	1,735
~percentage of change from the same period of previous year	+26.1%
Imports (USD mil)	1,049
~percentage of change from the same period of previous year	+23.6%

Introduction

Shaanxi is situated in the hinterland of the People's Republic of China adjacent to Shanxi and Henan. Provinces to the east, Gansu Province and Ningxia Autonomous Region to the west, Hubei and Sichuan provinces and Chongqing City to the South, and the Inner Mongolian Autonomous Region to the north. It is the gateway to the Northwest Region, as well as the hub of communications that links the east, the west, the northwest and the southwest.

There are seven cities, including Xi'an, Baoji, Xianyang, Tongchuan, Weinan, Hanzhong, and Yan'an, and three prefectures including Ankang, Shangluo and Yulin. There are 107 counties, cities and districts in the province, among which there are six county-level cities, 83 counties and 18 districts administered by the seven cities.

Among the 31 provinces, cities and regions in the People's Republic of China, Shaanxi is well known for its unique culture and long civilisation, its strong education and scientific capacity, its abundant natural resources and its strong industrial bases. All the above features provide a strong foundation for Shaanxi's future development.

Geography and Climate

With the completion of Xi'an-Baotou Railway, Xi'an-Ankang Railway and Xi'an-Nanjing Railway, Shaanxi Province will serve as an important economic and geographic link between the east and the west, and between the north and the south. It covers an area of 190,000 km^2, 2.1 percent of the total national area. It is 1,000 kilometres wide from the north to the west and 360 kilometres long from the north to the south. The land takes a strip-like form and the Guanzhong Plain is a low land and lies between the two highlands in the north and the south. The whole province can be divided into three natural regions from the north to

the south: the Northern Shaanxi Plateau, the Central Shaanxi Plain or the Guanzhong Plain, and the Qingling and Bashan Ranges. From the north to the south, it covers three different climate zones: the Temperate Zone, the warm Temperate Zone, and the Northern Sub-tropical Zone. Its average annual temperature ranges from 8°C to 16°C, its average annual precipitation is 300 to 700 mm and its annual frost-free period is between 150 to 270 days.

Rivers

The Qingling Ranges is a major water division line, passing through the province from the east to the west. The northern area to the Qingling Range belongs to the Yellow River system that comprises the Weihe River, the Jinghe River, the Luohe River and the Wuding River, while the southern area of the Yangtze River system comprises the Hanjiang River, the Danjiang River and the Jialingjiang River. The annual water flow in the whole province is 438 billion cubic metres and the total hydraulic power capacity in the province is more than 14 million kilowatts. The water conservancy resources in the province are distributed widely.

Xi'an, Capital of Shaanxi Province

Xi'an, the capital of Shaanxi Province, is the largest city in the northwest region of China and a regional centre of science, technology, finance, commerce, trade and tourism. It has a population of 6.7 million and an area of 9,983 km^2.

History and Culture

Shaanxi Province distinguishes itself as one of the cradles of Chinese civilisation. One million years ago, the Lantian Ape Man lived in this land. Six thousand years ago, the Banpo primitive man left an entire village in ruins. The tomb of the Xuan-yuan Huang Emperor, highly respected by all the Chinese, is located in Huangling County which is situated to the north of Xi'an. On tomb sweeping day, the Shaanxi Government commissioned by the State holds a public sacrifice ceremony here every year.

Before the tenth century, Shaanxi was the political, economic and cultural centre of China. Over a period of more than 1,100 years, Xi'an was the capital for 14 feudal dynasties, including the Zhou, the Qin, the Han, the Sui and the Tang. Shaanxi Province was also the cradle of the Chinese revolution in modern history. In the period of the Han and the Tang dynasties of the Middle Ages, the ancient capital city Chang'an was the starting point of the Silk Road, the international commercial and trade centre and the meeting place between the western and eastern cultures. From 1935 to 1948, Chairman Mao Zedong lived and worked in Yan'an and directed the Chinese revolution and founded the People's Republic of China.

Shaanxi Province has abundant cultural and historical relics. There are 35,750 identified historical sites across the region, with 55 at the state level and 372 at the provincial level. It houses 560,000 pieces of historical relics, with 3,526 at the first class level and 123 at the state level. The province ranks first in the national list of density, quantity and grade of cultural relics.

Shaanxi Province is reputed as a natural Chinese history museum, which houses a complete array of historical sites representative of different historical periods.

Among the famous historical relics are the site of the Lantian Ape Man over one million years of age; the site of a 6,000-year-old primitive village at Banpo; the Mausoleum of the Yellow Emperor (worshipped as the first ancestor by the Chinese people); the site of the capital city of the Zhou Dynasty: the first Qin Emperor's Mausoleum; Emperor Wudi's Mausoleum and its stone carvings; Sakyamuni's finger bones and the other treasures in the Underground Palace of the Famen Temple; Shaanxi History Museum with modern architectural features; Xi'an Forest Steles (known as "library of stone inscriptions" with high artistic value); Qianling Mausoleum for Empress Wu Zetian and Emperor Gao Zong (Li Zhi); Xi`an City Wall (the largest and most complete of its kind in China); the sacred revolutionary base, Yan'an and its relics. The world "Eighth Wonder", the Qin Warriors and Horses, has been included in the world cultural inheritance list by UNESCO.

Infrastructure

Transportation

To further improve the overall accessibility of the province, the provincial government will invest a total of RMB 52.3 billion in roads and highways in the 10th Five-Year Plan. Total road length of the province will increase by 4,000 kilometres to 48,000 kilometres by the end of 2005.

Railways

Shaanxi has 13 trunk and feeder railways across the province with a combined traffic length of 2,867 kilometres. Xi'an Railway Station and its 12 marshalling stations make up the largest hub of rail transport in the northwest region of China. The Xi'an Railway Station has 12 marshalling yards. It is a transportation hub in the northwestern region linking with the northwest, southwest, the east, and the north of China. Baocheng, Xiangyu and Longhai railway lines connect the northwest and southwest with East China. Xi'an-

Ankang and Yan'an-Shenmu railways are under construction. After their completion, a big passage, which traverses Shaanxi from the north to the south, will take shape. The state has planned to build 10 railway lines across the country over the years, four of which will cut through Shaanxi. They are Xi'an-Nanjing, Xi'an-Yangpiguan, Shenmu-Huanghua and Baoji-Chengdu railways.

The new Eurasian Continental Bridge from China's Lianyungang to the Netherlands' Rotterdam passes through the province. A new railway running north and south is under construction and will solve the transportation bottleneck in northern and southern Shaanxi.

Highways

With eight state-level highways and 56 provincial highways, its highway system extends from Xi'an in all directions. The province is constructing a highway transportation network comprising nine national highways with Xi'an at the core. The province has a total expressway length of 385 kilometres, and the highways now reach 95 percent of the villages.

Airports

The Xianyang Airport is the largest air hub in northwest China, and the expansion of the airport has started. The province has opened 119 domestic and international air routes and has flights to 51 cities in China. During the 10th Five-Year Plan, expansion and reconstruction works will be taken in a number of domestic airports at Hanzhong, An'kang, Yan'an and Yulin to improve air transportation in the province.

Civil aviation in Shaanxi has seen tremendous development in the past years. Xi'an-Xiangyang International Airport, a largest hub of air transport in the northwest of China, has opened more than 80 domestic and international airlines. The passenger and cargo dealing capacities rank eighth and sixth respectively in the country.

Energy Supply

At present, Shaanxi has 0.67 million kW installed capacity for power generation. In view of the abundant supply of coal, oil, natural gas and hydropower in Shaanxi, the government plans to construct a number of power plants to raise the electricity generation capacity to 1.0 million kW by 2005. A total of nine stations using coal, hydropower and natural gas will be built. Besides, a new oil pipeline (Lanzhou-Chengdu-Chongqing) will be constructed to transmit oil from the northwest region to the southeast region. The pipeline will pass through 30 counties and cities in Gansu, Shaanxi and Chongqing with an annual oil transmission capacity of more than five million tons and is expected to operate in June 2002.

Postal Services and Telecommunication

Shaanxi had invested billions of RMB in the fixed assets of the post and telecommunications system in 1990s. It had generated an income of RMB7.7 billion with an increase of 35.1 percent and income of RMB3 billion with an increase of 21.4 percent. To date, 10 local networks have been brought to completion. The total telephone capacity in the province increased from 1,700,000 lines in 1996 to 4.34 million lines in 2001 with a total number of 4.19 million users. There have been 2.91 million cellular phone users. There are five fabric cable trunks cutting through Shaanxi. Jinan-Taiyuan-Yulin-Yinchuan cable started opera-tion in 1997. The other four cables, Xi'an-Huhhote, Xi'an-Wuhan, Xi'an Hefei and Xi'an-Chengqing.

Natural Resources

Mineral Resources

Shaanxi Province is endowed with rich mineral resources. To date, 136 varieties of minerals have been discovered, and 91 out of them have had their reserves verified. In term of reserves, seven mineral varieties, including rhenium and alkali-contained limestone, rank first in China; nine varieties, including natural gas, molybdenum and mercury, rank second; 11 varieties including coal, magnesium, and asbestos, rank third; 58 varieties among the top 10 on the national list. The gold reserves rank fourth in China.

Animal Resources

Animal resources in the province are extremely abundant, with more than 700 species of wild animals. Seventy-nine of them are classified as rare animals under protection by the State and this number accounts for one third of that in the whole country. Twelve of them, including the giant panda, the golden-hair monkey, the antelope and the ibis, are listed as first-class animals under state protection. In recent years, milk goats have been raised in large numbers, ranking first on the national list. The Qinchuan cattle, the Guanzhong, Jiaxian and Mizhi donkeys are well bred.

Vegetation Resources

The 5,930,000 acres of forests in Shaanxi Province covers 28.8 percent of the province. There are many kinds of economic forests. The raw lacquer production ranks first in China. The Niuwang Lacquer is famous in both China and abroad. Jujube, walnuts and tung oil are the traditional provincial exports. There are more than 3,300 species of wild plants and herbs. Selenium-rich tea and shaji and jiaogulan plants are of great value.

Agriculture

Shaanxi Province, one of the major grain producers in China, has 3,360,000 hectares of arable land and 3,530,000 hectares of grassland. Over the past few years, the comprehensive agricultural production ability in Shaanxi has increased quickly and annual agriculture grows by 5.4 percent.

Its diversified economy has also developed in an all-round manner, with the completion of ten production bases for agricultural commodities, such as cereals, oils, cotton, tobacco, fruits, milk goats, Qinchuan cattle, silkworm cocoons, tea leaves, sheep and wool. Shaanxi Province is one of the important agriculture centres in China, producing high-grade apples and star fruit. There are 7,200,000 mu of apple land with a total production output of 2,840,000 tons, which ranks second in the country. The production value per capita ranked first in the country. Yantao covers an area of 230,000 mu with an annual total output of 20,000 tons, accounting for about 50 percent of the country's total. Egg and milk production in Shaanxi has been listed in the 10 largest egg and milk production provinces in China.

Industries

Since the founding of the People's Republic of China, Shaanxi has been an important industrial base in the country. During the 1950s, 25 of the 156 national key projects were built in Shaanxi. As a result of factories from the coastal areas moving to Shaanxi during the 1960s to 70s, coupled with the establishment of new enterprises during China's reform, the industrial system in Shaanxi has developed strongly.

The six key industries in Shaanxi are machinery, electronics, energy resources, chemical industry, medicine and food. These industries give rise to a series of pillar products, such as car, high-voltage transmission equipment, engineering machinery, new materials, household appliances, computers and telecommunication facilities. Industrial production has witnessed a two-digit growth rate in the past years. The industrial output value in 2002 is 125 billion Yuan, 54.3 percent more than that of the previous year. With 94.6 percent of all the products having been sold, there are a considerable number of products that have occupied a large proportion of the domestic market. There are 157 newly created brand products.

Machinery

Machinery industry is the largest industrial sector in terms of number of workers employed. Products in electrical engineering, electrical devices, meter, instruments, machine tools, heavy-duty trucks and engineering machinery are more competitive, and enjoy a larger domestic market share. Xi'an Electric Machinery Corporation is one of the two largest companies producing high and ultra-voltage transmission and transforming equipment. Xi'an Meter Factory ranks third in meter industry. Gears and spiral grinding machines produced by Qinchuan Machine Tool Factory and Hanjiang Tool Factory constitute more than 60 percent of total national production. Shaanxi Province's tremendous re-sources allows her to engage in the manufacturing of heavy-duty cars, high-powered bulldozers, precision digital machine tools, internal combustion fork trucks, large windmills, medium and small-sized rolling mills, se-wing machines of industry and petroleum machinery.

Electronics

Its electronic industry took shape in the 1970s, and has now become a pillar industry, with the ability to produce several hundred varieties of products within 11 categories including colour picture tubes, radio communication and navigation equipment, colour TV sets, refrigerators, air-conditioners, large integrated circuits, computers, electronic metres and devices. Rainbow Electronics Corp. Group ranks third nationwide in terms of its overall capacities and leads the country in colour picture tube production. Shaanxi Province leads the whole country in production and marketing of coloured deflecting coils, coloured deflecting cores, copper-clad plates and vacuum power switches. The 25-inch, 700-line colour picture tubes and the first improved digital sets with high fidelity developed by Xi'an Jiaotong University, Xi'an Electronics University, Huanghe Electronic Corp. and Rainbow Colour Tube Factory have been put into production and market. Xi'an Datang Telecommunication Corp. has developed and produced SP30 ultra-digital computerised-controlled telephone switches. The products have been sold in the province as well as the whole country. The instalment capacity in Shaanxi is more than 100,000 lines and 600,000 lines all over China, scattered in more than 20 provinces or cities. American Motorola Corp. has purchased the company's products of M30 mobile telecommunication exchange systems.

Medicine & Food

The medicine and food industry is a developing sector in the province. The most influential products in this sector are: medical products manufactured by Xi'an Janssen Pharmaceutical Company, Lijunsha antibiotic medicine produced by Xi'an Pharmaceutical Plant, healthcare products by 505 Group Corp. Ltd. and Sanbaoshuangxi Group Corp. Ltd, and medical products to cure brain and heart diseases. The famous beverages are: Xifeng Liquor, Taibai Liquor and Baoji Beer, Xi'an-Tsingtao Hans Beer and Rongshi drinks. Other famous products are finest cigarettes, Yanyousi foodstuff and milk products.

Energy Resources and Chemical Industry

Shaanxi Province is a national base of energy resources and heavy chemical industry, and is endowed with enormous amount of top-quality thermal coalmines, world-class self-contained natural gas fields, and abundant petroleum resources. The province focuses on the development and construction of its northern region as a national

Shaanxi Province is a national base of energy resources and heavy chemical industry, and is endowed with a large number of top-quality thermal coalmines, world-class self-contained natural gas fields, and abundant petroleum resources.

base of energy resources and heavy chemical industry.

Energy resources industry is the second largest industry in Shaanxi Province. Northern Shaanxi is the national heavy chemical industry base. In 2001 the province produced 45 million tons of raw coal, 14 million cubic metres of natural gas, 9.15 million tons of processed petroleum, and generated 25,12 billion kilowatt-hours.

Science, Technology & Education

Shaanxi Province is an important centre of science, technology and education in China, and also an important base of scientific research and production in the areas of aviation, aerospace, machinery, electronics, agriculture, metres and instruments. It ranks third in terms of overall R&D capability after Beijing and Shanghai. It has more than 2,000 science and technology research institutes, of which 50 are recognised as reaching the advanced level in the country. Besides, it has 10 key national labs and 50 specialised labs under government agencies. The province's research capabilities are particularly strong in military, space and agricultural technology. Output from hi-tech industry reached RMB 10.2 billion in 2000. As an important national centre of science, technology and education, Shaanxi ranks high among the provinces of China in terms of the number of colleges and universities, the ratio of technical personnel to workers, and in overall R&D capability.

Shaanxi is the country's first producer of civil aircraft, integrated circuit boards, carrier rockets, colour picture tubes, and 1,000,000-voltage air breakers. Great achievement has also been made in its agricultural sector, such as Xiaoyan No.6 well-bred wheat seed, Qingyou No.2 Cole seed and Qinbai series cabbage seeds. Shaanxi is leading the way in the development of new and high-tech products, such as the development of high-fidelity digital colour TV sets, visual CMOS core plates, light-fixed laser quick shapers, and ultra-fine vibration rubbing machines.

To accelerate development of hi-tech industries in the 10th Five-Year Plan period, five research and production bases will be established with focus on the following sectors: digital electrical appliances, computer and network products, mobile telecommunications, electronic accessories and parts, and electronic products. Through cooperation with research institutes like Xi'an Jiaotong University, Northwest Polytechnic University and Northwest University, the government will establish a software park in Xi'an Hi-tech Industrial Development Zone (XDZ) to enhance the development of the computer software industry.

Technology Development Plan

In order to rapid transform scientific achievements into productivity, Shaanxi Province has proposed the package of 1,851 scientific and technological economies. The package emphasised the development of high technology projects. It focuses on establishing Guanzhong high-tech economic zone with Xi'an City as its core and fostering eight back-bone industries. The industries include electronic information, electro-mechanical advanced technology, the development of new materials, energy resources and energy-saving technology, biological technology, new medical technology and environmental protection technology. The package is mandated to harness high technology to develop 50 key products to meet the challenges of the future. The package is envisaged to groom 10 large enterprise groups with annual output of more than a billion RMB.

National Defence

The defence industry is the strongest manufacturing sector in Shaanxi. Shaanxi Province ranks first in China in the scale of its national defence industry. In recent years, it has performed well in the development of civilian products and put large numbers of technology-intensive products into large-scale production. The Y-7 aircraft developed in Shaanxi dominates China's aviation industry. The Y-8 developed and produced by Shaanxi Aircraft Corp. is China's biggest medium-ranged and medium-sized cargo plane with a load of 20 tons and a maximum range of 6,515 kilometres. Shaanxi Province has secured an important position in the mass production of up-to-date textile machinery, refrigerators, air compressors, mini-buses, deluxe buses and tows.

Finance

All the state-run commercial banks and other financial institutions led by the People's Bank have formed a complete financial system in the province. There are 1,377 financial institutions, including 1,021 savings banks, 346 insurance companies, five trust companies, three security companies and three clearing firms. The remaining sum of the savings and loans was RMB320.5 billion and RMB253.8 billion with an increase of 20.4% -and 13.8% respectively. The sales of commodities were the main channel of withdrawal.

The capital markets have been linked with the national first class trading networks and the stock markets have made remarkable progress. The three major securities corporations have established 42 trading centres. There are 16 A-share companies whose stocks are being traded in Shanghai and Shenzheng stock markets. These companies raised 1.158-billion-yuan fund from the stock markets.

Commerce

There are 347,800 consumer goods wholesaling and retail centres employing 1,260,000 workers. The state, private and collective-owned centres take up 5.9 percent, 14.4 percent, and 79.7 percent respectively. The total retail volume of consumer goods in 2002 was RMB72.8 billion with an increase of 9.5 percent. There are 20 medium and large-sized retail trading corporations whose annual total trading volume exceeded RMB 100 million. The Minsheng Corporate Group Ltd. reached a total retail volume of more than RMB 104 million. The consumer market enjoyed rich varieties of goods with stable prices.

Consumer Market

In 2002, retail sales of consumer goods in Shaanxi increased by 9.5 percent to RMB72.8 billion. Major department stores and shopping centres in Shaanxi include Xi'an Minsheng Group and Xi'an Jiefang Department Store with total sales of RMB859 million and RMB725 million recorded in 1999 respectively, amongst the first 50th departments stores with the largest sales in the country.

Apart from department stores, chain stores and supermarkets have also expanded rapidly in the province. In 2000, Shaanxi Haixing Supermarket which operates 46 supermarket outlets recorded a sales revenue of RMB179 million and ranked 34th among all supermarket chains in China.

Travel Industry

Besides having long history, rich culture, picturesque landscapes, numerous historic relics, unique customs, Shaanxi has a rich cultural heritage of tourism. In recent years, the travel industry in Shaanxi has developed rapidly. The province boasts a complete range of tourist facilities, 120 tourist agencies in both domestic and international travel, more than 2,000 tour guides in the region, who can conduct guided tours in different languages, such as English, Japanese, French, German, Italian, Russian, Korean and Vietnamese. There are more than 90 hotels for overseas guests with 16,000 rooms, including four five-star hotels and five four-star hotels.

Travel industry in Shaanxi is characterised by its focus on culture appreciation and the combination of cultural and natural landscapes. The Xi'an Tourist Centre, the Four Travel Routes, the Ten Tourist Zones and the Ten Tourist Programme have been constructed and opened to tourists. The Four Routes are the Yellow River Tour, the Silk Road Tour, the Three Kingdoms Tour and the Loess Plateau Folklore Tour. The Ten Tourist Zones are: Xi'an Tourist Zone, Lintong Tourist & Economics Development Zone, Mount Hua Tourist Zone, Xianyang Imperial Mausoleum Tourist Zone, Famen Temple Buddhist Culture Tourist Zone, Mount Taibei Tourist Zone, Yan'an Tourist Zone. The Mausoleum of the Yellow Emperor, Hukou Falls, Folk Customs on the Loess Plateau, and the Sacred Revolutionary Base, Hanzhong "Han Dynasty & Three Kingdoms" Tourist Zone, Mount Zhongnan Tourist Zone and Yulin Desert Scenery Tourist Zone. The Ten Tourist Programme are the Religion & Culture Tour, the Root-hunting & Ancestral Worship Tour, the Folk Custom Tour, the Chinese Calligraphy Tour, the Health Care Tour, the Field Study Tour, the Business Tour and the Conference Tour.

In 1997, it generated an income of US$8.4 million from the travel industry, representing 6.3 percent of its gross national output value and 17.5 percent of the output value of the service industry. The travel industry has become one of the pillar industries in the province.

As a result of extensive marketing programmes, Shaanxi recorded significant growth in its tourism industry in recent years. In 2002, over 850,100 foreign tourists visited the region and generated revenue of US$351 million, an increase of 14 percent over 2001.

International Exchanges

So far, more than 120 heads of state have visited Xi'an. There are more than 2,818 foreign experts and 710 foreign students who are working and studying in Xi'an. To date, Xi'an has established sister relations with 30 cities in the world and set up good relations with more than 52 countries and regions.

Foreign Trade

In 2003, Shaanxi's exports increased by 26.1 percent to US$1.74 billion, of which exports of electrical products/machinery and garments soared by 49 percent and 69 percent respectively. The province's major exports included textiles, garments, machinery, electronic components and devices and medicinal raw materials, and its major export markets were Hong Kong, Japan, Malaysia, Singapore and Iran.

Imports increased slightly by 23.6 percent to US$1.05 billion in 2003. Major import items included synthetic fibre, machinery, chemicals and raw pharmaceutical material, electronic equipment and instruments, ferrous and non-ferrous metal. Major import sources were Japan, Hong Kong, the US, Germany and the UK.

Hong Kong was the major trading partner of Shaanxi. The total amount of goods exported to Hong Kong reached US$208 million in 1999 (+ 17.7%), the largest among all trading partners.

Foreign Investment

In 2003, the province approved 229 foreign-invested projects, an increase of 12.8 percent from previous year. The contracted foreign capital was US$834 million. The province's actual utilisation of foreign capital was US$466 million that year. By the end of 2003, many multinational corporations established joint ventures in Shaanxi, including Philips, Coca-Cola, Mitsubishi Electric Power Equipments Co. Ltd and Siemens.

In the coming years, foreign investors are encouraged to invest in infrastructure, chemicals and pharmaceuticals, metallurgy, machinery and electronics, food processing and building materials.

To boost the development of the central and western regions in China, the State Council has

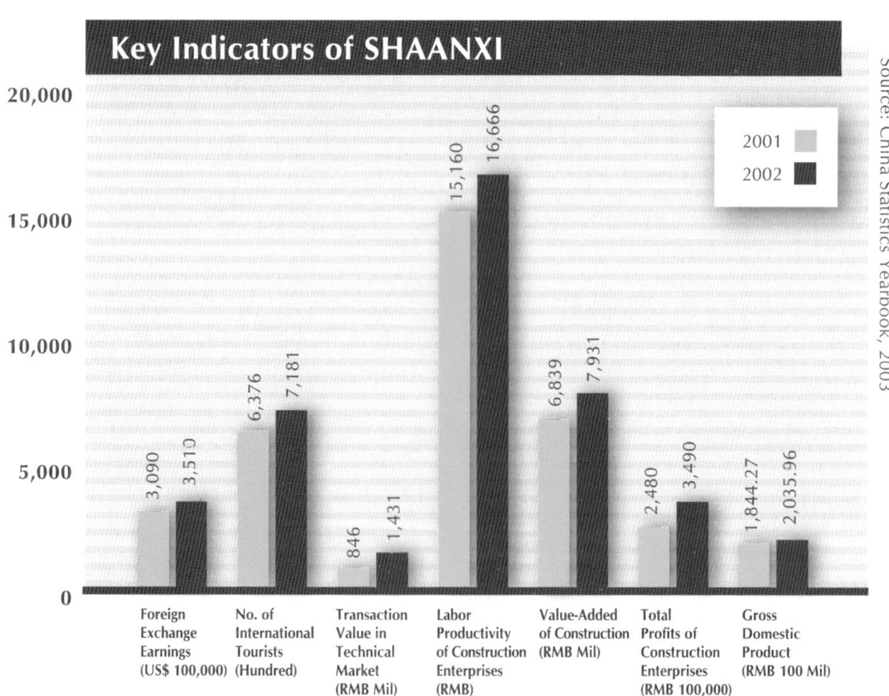

granted further tax incentives to foreign-invested enterprises (FIEs) in China. Beginning from January 2001, foreign-invested enterprises in the central and western regions would enjoy another three years of preferential tax rate at 15 percent on top of the existing preferential treatment (exemption of profit tax for the first two years and 50 percent reduction for three years thereafter). The tax rate can be further reduced to 10 percent when an enterprise is proven to export more than 70 percent of its annual output in terms of value.

Economic Development in the Middle and Western Parts of China

The state has proposed a series of policies and measures to foster economic development in the middle and western parts of the country. These include energy resource development, infrastructure projects, inter-provincial energy, and transportation and telecommunication projects. The major portion of the investment will come from the state. Other measures include the increase in state financial allocation and foreign funds. The state will strengthen its aid policies, such as extending approval rights for foreign investment, raising the proportion of products in the domestic market produced by foreign enterprises, remaking of foreign enterprises, no limitation to the projects once regulated in the national directory industry list. These enterprises will be supported by way of foreign loans, domestic funds, interest-free loans and tax return.

Economic Development Strategies

Shaanxi has the mandate to substantiate its overall economic developments strategies; that is, "giving priority to the development of education, and rejuvenating the local economy by harnessing science and technology", and "stimulating resource exploitation for an economic upsurge by adhering to the opening policies". By further opening to the outside world and making full use of its resources, technical and cultural advantages, Shaanxi will turn into "a highly-developed economy with technology-intensive industries and famous tourist attractions".

Shaanxi has been constantly struggling to conquer deserts and control soil erosion. Over the years, the ecological conditions have been markedly improved, together with economic development, and this has produced immense social and ecological benefits.

Plans have been laid to build a technology-intensive base of resources. Shaanxi will leverage on its advantages in energy, mineral, biological and cultural resources to increase its resources development by absorbing overseas investment and bringing in technological transfer.

There are also plans to enhance the industry standard of capital management and accelerate the re-capitalisation process. The property rights to the projects already completed or still under construction should be granted to the investors by means of transfer, transformation, lease and purchase, which will help liquidate the state-owned assets and convert them into cash to serve the needs of economic construction. In 1996, Shaanxi succeeded in selling to the investors part of operating rights of the Weihe Power Plant and those of Xi'an-Lintong Expressway for a period of 20 years. The proceeds from the sales were later invested in new power plants and highway construction projects.

With its market advantages, Shaanxi encourages overseas investors, especially multi-national corporations, to enter into joint ventures with its state enterprises to enhance the standard and skill level of the whole industry through technology transfer.

Five Big Events in the Development of Shaanxi

The five big events that are expected to boost the development of Shaanxi are: the construction of a beautiful Northern Shaanxi, Yangling Agriculture Town, Yulin Energy Base and the Guanzhong High-tech Development Belt. These events will give Shaanxi a promising future.

1. Construction of a Beautiful Northern Shaanxi

The region that covers 45 counties with an area of 108,000 km^2, situated in Northern Shaanxi and the Weibei Plateau, is an area hardest hit by soil erosion. For half a century, especially after the 1980's, the people of Northern Shaanxi have been constantly struggling to conquer deserts and control soil erosion. Over the years, the ecological conditions have been markedly improved, together with economic development, and this has produced immense social and ecological benefits. Altogether, there are 2.1 million hectares of forest, 250,000 hectares of grassland and 32,000 km^2 of controlled area hardest hit by severe soil erosion.

2. Construction of Yanliang Aircraft Town

Yanliang District, 45 kilometres from Xi'an, is China's most important aircraft research, production and testing base. It has processed and produced aircrafts and vertical tails for American, French, Italian and Canadian aircraft corporations. In 1997, the state invested $1.2 billion to build an aircraft assembly line in Yanliang to produce passenger planes with 100 seats developed by China, the Euro-bus Group, Italy, Singapore and other seven countries. This project will not only promote the development of Shaanxi's raw material industry, electronic instrument industry and machinery industry as well as improving modern management. Yanliang will be China's Seattle in the 21st century.

3. Construction of Yangliang Agricultural District

Yangliang District, 90 kilometres from Xi'an, is China's biggest agricultural base. Longhai Railway and Xi'an-Baoji Expressway transverse through the district. The Northwest Agricultural University of Science & Technology, and other 11 agricultural and forestry research institutes at the ministerial level and a group of modern national key laboratories are scattered here. There are more than 4,000 technicians and scientists in agriculture, forestry, irrigation and 70 other fields. More than 5,000 scientific achievements have brought a benefit of RMB200 billion.

The zone aims at developing improved varieties of crop, safe insecticides, biological medicines, chemical forestry products, and processed farm products. Efforts are made to strengthen international cooperation and introduction, utilisation and popularisation of new agricultural techniques.

4. Construction of Yulin Energy Base

Situated in the northern tip of Shaanxi Province, is a rich mineral area. Forty varieties of minerals of eight kinds have been discovered. The total amount of coal deposit is 142 billion tons. The coal is of high heat productivity but its contents of sulphur, phosphorus and ash are extremely low. In addition, abundant natural gas resources have been discovered in Northern Shaanxi, with 300 billion cubic metres of natural gas underground. It is a complete natural gas field. The total amount of discovered petroleum reserves is 600 million tons in 2002. The discovered rock salt, kaolin and bauxite reserves are more than 100 million tons, 680 million tons and 23 million tons respectively. The rich resources of coal, petroleum, salt and natural gas provide favourable conditions for the construction of an energy base.

Three larger enterprise groups have been set up to develop energy resources. Shenhua Group is responsible for the development of Shenfu Coal Field with an annual production capacity of more than 100 million tons. With an investment of RMB 90 billion, it is only second to the Three Gorges Project. China Natural Gas Corporation undertakes the development of natural gas. By 2,000, the total annual output capacity reached three billion cubic metres. China's Huaneng Group focuses its attention on the construction of large-scale thermal power plants. The planned electricity generating capacity is 4.5 millin kilowatts.

5. Construction of the Guanzhong High-Tech Development Belt

The Euro-Asian Continental Bridge traverses through the Guanzhong Plain. More than 40 universities and colleges, 340 scientific research institutes, 300 defence and civilian enterprises with 600,000 professionals are scattered in the Plain.

To take advantage of science and technology and speed up the conversion of scientific achievements, Shaanxi has decided to establish the Guanzhong High-tech Development Belt. Within the belt, there are Xi'an, Baoji and Yanliang high-tech zones at the state level, Weinan and Xianyang high-tech zones at the provincial level. The estimated completed floor space in the belt is 1.44 million square metres. There are 2,500 enterprises in the belt, of which 580 having been recognised as high-tech ones, 300 as foreign-funded, private-funded and joint ventured enterprises.

SHANDONG

The birthplace of Confucius is blessed with abundant agricultural and mineral resources, as well as a geographically strategic location.

SHANDONG Fact Sheet	2003
Area (km²)	156,700
No. of Cities	48
Population (mil)	91.3
GDP (RMB bn)	1,243.0
Gross capital formation (RMB bn)	494
Consumption expenditure (RMB bn)	502
~Household	358
~Government	144
No. of employed persons (mil)	47.51
Unemployment Rate	3.7%
Literacy Rate	89.9%
Government revenue (RMB bn)	210.9
Government expenditure (RMB bn)	100.9
Per capita annual	
~disposable income of urban residents (RMB '000)	7.4
~net income of rural households (RMB '000)	1.1
~living expenditure of urban residents (RMB '000)	6.1
~living expenditure of rural residents (RMB '000)	2.1
Actually Used Foreign Direct Investment (US$ mil)	7,090
Total assets (RMB bn)	130.6
Exports (USD mil)	26,570
~percentage of change from the same period of previous year	+25.8%
Imports (USD mil)	18,080
~percentage of change from the same period of previous year	+41.0%

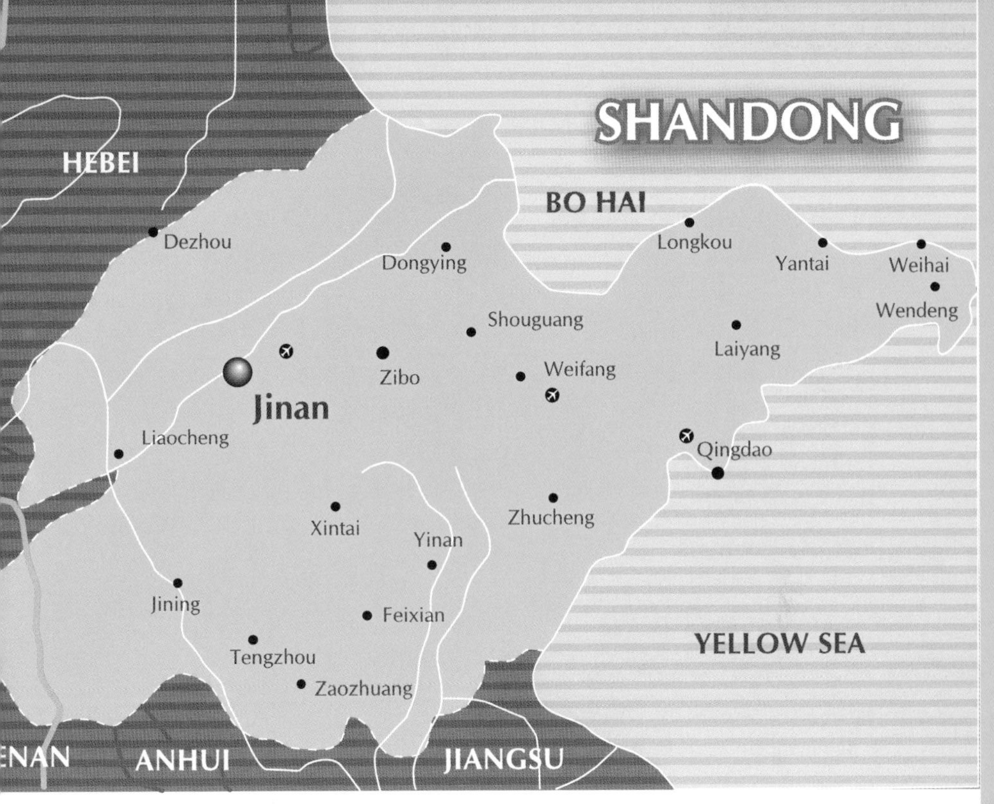

PROVINCES

Introduction

Shandong's history can be traced back to the genesis of the Chinese state. Confucius, the sage and philosopher, was born here and lived in Lu, one of the small states in the south of what is today known as Shandong. Mencius, his ideological successor, also hailed from the same region. The famous military strategist, Sun Wu, whose "Sun Zi: The Art of War" continues to be widely read today, was born in the region of the Yellow River Delta. An ancient city with a history dating back more than 2,600 years, the black pottery remains of the Longshan culture provide the earliest record of civilisation in the region.

Today, it is a significant coastal province in East China, blessed with an abundance of agricultural and mineral resources. Located in the lower reaches of the Yellow River, it is bordered by the Bohai and Yellow Seas. Shandong faces Japan and the Korean Peninsula to the east, and lies next to Hebei

Province in the northwest and Henan Province in the south. Lying between the Yellow River Economic Belt and the Bohai Ring Economic Area, its location is geographically strategic both within the mainland as well as in the East Asian and Asian-Pacific economic regions.

700 km wide from east to west and 420 km long from north to south, with a total land area of 156,700 km^2, it is the 19th largest province in the country. Central Shandong is mountainous, while hills undulate to the east and south. The alluvial plain of the Yellow River, part of the North China Plain, occupies the north and northwestern parts of Shandong. The whole province is criss-crossed by rivers and lakes. The Yellow River enters the province in the southwest, then flows into Bohai Sea in the northeast.

Administrative Divisions

Shandong Province was formally established in the Qing Dynasty (1644-1911), with its capital at Jinan. Today, the province has been administratively divided into 139 counties, cities and districts. More than 90.8 million people live in the province, which is the second most populous province in China after Henan.

Climate

Shandong is located in the warm temperate zone with a semi-tropical monsoon climate. The annual average temperature is 11 to 14°C. The annual average precipitation is 550-950mm. The frost-free period in the coastal area is more than 180 days, while in the inland it is more than 220 days.

Infrastructure

Highways

All the towns and 90.5% of the villages are accessible by road. Main arterial routes include the Jinan-Qingdao Expressway, Yimeng Highway, the Liuting Overpass in Qingdao, the Xiyuanzhuang-Liuting Bridge in

Qingdao, and the Nugushan Bridge in Qingdao.

Railways

Two major railways, the Beijing-Shanghai and Beijing-Kowloon railways, pass through from north to south of the province, while the Jiaozhou-Jinan and Yunzhou-Shijiazhuang railways go from east to west in the province. The newly-constructed Beijing-Kowloon line connects Shandong directly with the Hong Kong Special Administrative Region. Rizhao, a port city in the southeastern part of the province, has been approved by the state as one of the bridgeheads of the new Eurasia Continental Bridge.

Aviation

To date, nine airports including the international airports in Jinan and Qingdao, have been built, with more than 245 international and domestic routes. Yantai Airport is dedicated to international freight transport. Shandong Airline, which started operations in 1994, operates more than 100 flights every week.

Ports

Being a coastal province, port facilities are well developed in Shandong. The handling capacity has been improved with the construction of deep-water berths, specialised docks and land-island rotating transportation facilities. Currently, there are 26 ports in the province. The combined annual handling capacity of all the ports is 131 million tons. All the ports are open to foreign business. Qingdao Port ranks amongst the five biggest coastal ports in China. Yantai, Weihai and Rizhao are the other major harbours. Ambitious millennial projects include the development of the Yellow River Delta and the construction of "Shandong on the Sea".

Tourism

Tourism facilities such as tour agencies and hotels are readily found in Jinan, Tai-an, Qufu, Zoucheng and Weifang, as well as in the coastal cities of Qingdao, Yantai and Weihai. In 2002 alone, some 776,800 foreign tourists visited the province; revenue from international tourist is around US$472 million that year. There are many cultural relics and historical sites in Shandong Province. The Confucian Temple in Qufu and the sacred Taoist mountain Taishan have both been listed as UNESCO World Heritage Sites. Other famous attractions include Jinan, the ancient capital of the Qi State; Liangshan, home to the Liangshan Mountain heroes more than 1,000 years ago; and the Sulu King's Tomb in Dezhou.

The province enjoys a rich cultural life. Popular pastimes include the traditional local operas, ballad programmes such as Qinshu (storytelling through song with musical accompaniment) and Dagu (a versified story sung to the accompaniment of a small drum and other instruments), folk music and dance. The province is also known for folk art and handicrafts such as Weifang wood engraving and paper-cutting.

Economy

The economy in Shandong province has been developing healthily. In 2003, the GDP of the province reached RMB1,243 billion. The industrial sector, agriculture and the service industry contributed 53.5 percent, 12.1 percent and 34.4 percent respectively to the provincial GDP. By 2010, the provincial GDP is expected to be double that of 2000. To quicken the transformation into a socialist market economy, the province has implemented a strategy focusing on science and education, globalisation and sustainable development. It wants to revamp its traditional industries (chemicals, metallurgy, building materials, textiles, foodstuff processing, and papermaking), while continuing the development of the mainstay petrochemical, machinery, electronics, car and construction industries.

Agriculture

Agriculture has long been a key industry in Shandong's economic development. Recently, much effort has been put into improving the efficiency of agricultural production, including the forestry, animal husbandry and fishery industries.

Shandong is a leading supplier of grain, cotton, oil crops such as peanuts, soybeans, fruit, vegetables, meat and aquatic products. Famous produce from the region include Yantai apples, Laiyang pears, Yangxin pears, Feicheng peaches, Qingzhou peaches, Leling dates, Dazeshan grapes, Caozhou flowering quinces, Shandong peanuts, Longshan millet, Mingshui rice, Zhangqui green onions, Weixian turnips and Cangshan garlic.

The Shandong Peninsula has more than 3,000 km of golden sandy beaches. There are 299 islands in the offshore area, with a total area of more than 170,000 km^2. The waters teem with all manner of fish and crustaceans, with prawns, scallops, abalone, sea cucumber and sea urchins being amongst the top aquatic export products.

Mineral Resources

Over 140 kinds of minerals can be found in Shandong, among which 75 have large deposits. Reserves of gold, gypsum, natural sulphur, sand-stone, gabbros, granite and clay are the most significant. Shandong is one of China's major gold producers; reserves are found mainly in the eastern part of the province, particularly in the coastal city of Yantai. Weifang is rich in sapphires, while Linyi is well known for its large diamond deposit. Under the auspices of the Shandong Provincial Department of Geological Survey and Mineral Resources, a comprehensive group of enterprises look into geological survey, mineral prospecting, research, geological environment protection, management of mineral deposits, engineering, construction, contracting, international cooperation, high-tech development and other related services.

Shandong is an important energy base, with the Shengli Oil Field (which produces petroleum) in the Yellow River Delta, the Zhongyuan Oil Field and the Dongying Oil Field being located in the region. One third of the crude oil in China is produced here. Central Shandong is rich in iron ore and coal. The coal stratum exceeds 50,000 km2 in area, with the Yunteng Coal Mine, Tai'an, Jining and Zibo being important coal bases, while Laiwu is known for its iron ore.

Industry

The key industries are energy, chemicals, metallurgy, building materials, machinery, electronics, textiles and food. Major industrial products include coal, crude oil, concrete, and chemical fertilisers. Other main products are soda, caustic soda, salt, machine-made paper, wines and beer, cotton yarn and cloth.

Building and Construction

The added value of the building and construction industry exceeded RMB350 billion in which the impetus for infrastructural development is a key factor. Key projects from the last decade include the Qilu 300,000-ton ethylene project, Qianwan port, Xichi port in Yantai, Rizhao Port, Yunzhou-Shijiazhuang Railway, Jinan-Qingdao Expressway,

Progress is being made in the establishment of a long term capital market focusing on stocks and bonds. A stock exchange network, with the Shandong Stock Company at its heart, is beginning to take shape. A network for short term capital is also starting to be developed.

Dezhou Hualu Electric Power Plant, Jinan Huangtai Electric Power Plant, Feicheng Electric Power Plant, Huangdao Electric Power Plant and Zoucheng Electric Power Plant.

Real estate has also experienced healthy growth. Residential projects make up a significant proportion of new developments. Since the 1990s, more than 350 urban residential zones have been developed in the province, notable examples being the Foshan-yuan Residential Zone in Jinana, the Sifang Re-sidential Zone in Qingdao, and the Yanzishan Residential Zone in Jinan.

Banking & Finance

National banks in Shandong include the Industrial and Commercial Bank of China, the Agricultural Bank of China, Bank of China, the China Construction Bank, the Communication Bank, the CITIC Industrial Bank, and the Everbright Bank. These banks have more than 10,000 branches, and make up 60 percent of all the financial institutions in the province. In addition, there are over 6,000 rural credit cooperatives and 200 city credit cooperatives. Non-bank financial institutions such as trust and investment companies, stock companies, residential deposit banks and accountancy companies are beginning to make their presence felt. To meet the demands of liberalisation, many financial institutions, including the big banks, have begun providing foreign exchange services. So far, 11 foreign financial institutions have set up branches or representative offices in the province.

Progress is being made in the establishment of a long term capital market focusing on stocks and bonds. A stock exchange network, with the Shandong Stock Company at its heart, is beginning to take shape. A network for short term capital is also starting to be developed.

Foreign Trade

Shandong has seen a sustained increase in foreign trade volume. Since 1979, the export volume has been increasing at an annual average rate of 16.9 percent. The foreign trade volume in 2002 reached US$33.9 billion, making up 23 percent of the GDP of the whole province; US$12.8 billion came from imports, while US$21.1 billion came from exports. Important trade partners include Japan, Korea, the USA, Hong Kong, Germany, Singapore, the Netherlands, Britain, Russia and Italy. There has been a shift away from exporting crude products to manufactured goods. Major export commodities include grain, cooking oil, food, textiles, garments, medicine, light industrial products, machinery, electronic products, technology and handicrafts. Finished products made up 72.3 percent of total exports.

By 1993, eight cities at the prefecture level: Qingdao, Yantai, Weihai, Zibo, Weifang, Rizhao, Jinan and Dongying, have been listed as open coastal economic areas. At present, there are 31 open trade ports, including 25 seaports, three airports, highway stations and one railway station.

Grade A ports are: Qingdao Port, Yantai Port, Rizhao Port, Weihai port, Longkou Port, Lanshan Port, Shidao Port, Dongying Port, Penglai Port, Laizhou Port, Qingdao Airport, Jinan Airport and Yantai Airport.

Grade B ports are: Qingdao Qianwan Port, Yantai Local Port, Rongcheng Zhukou Port, Weihai New Port, Rongcheng Lijiang Port, Yantai Fishery Dock, Wendeng Zhangjiabu Port, Ru-shankou Port, Longkou Fishing Port, Weifang Yangkou Port, Rongcheng Longyan Port, Weifang Port, Nudao Port in Jimo City, Jimiya Port in Jinan City, Jinan Highway Trade Port, Jining Highway Trade Port and Heze Railway Trade Port.

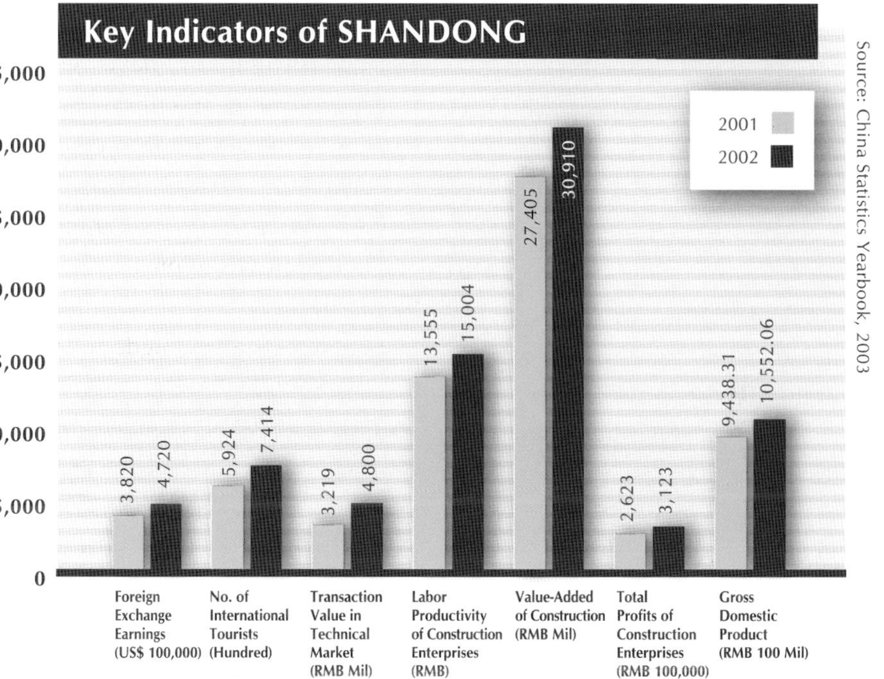

Qingdao plays a leading role, with Yantai, Weihai and Rizhao following closely behind. A number of other open areas are also emerging along the Huanhai High-way, the Jiaozhou-Jinan Railway, the Xinxiang-Shijiusuo Railway, the Jinan-Qingdao Highway, the Beijing-Shanghai Railway the Beijing-Kowloon Railway.

The Qingdao Customs Office is the department that supervises and administers entry and exit procedures from ports in Shandong. The Shandong Import and Export Commodities Inspection Bureau is responsible for inspecting commodities imported into, or exported from, the province. There is easy access to their services as both have branches spread across the province in a well-placed network centred on Qingdao and radiating to the inland and coastal areas.

Foreign Investment

The province has put considerable effort into improving its investment environment in order to develop the economy. In 2003, 5,305 new foreign-funded projects were approved, involving a contractual investment of US$13.4 billion. More than 10,000 foreign-invested enterprises have so far come into operation in Shandong. Korea, the USA, Japan, Singapore, Germany, France, Hong Kong and Taiwan are major investors. Multinational corporations such as Suzuki, Toyota Nissho lwai, Nestle, Siemens, Dae Woo, Sam Sung and Volvo have all invested in Shandong. Foreign-funded enterprises are playing a big role in the province's economic development; their export volume in 1998 came up to US$6.23 billion, making up 49.8 percent of the province's total export volume.

The utilisation of foreign capital has had a far-reaching impact upon economic and social development. It has enabled the agricultural sector to make increasing use of advanced technologies and superior strains, thus improving their export orientation and stepping up modernisation. The industrial sector has similarly benefited, particularly machine-building, textiles and building materials.

Last but not least, it has given birth to industries based on high technology, especially in the fields of machinery electronics, information processing and bio-engineering. In the foreseeable future, foreign investment will be encouraged in priority sectors such as infrastructure development, the ownership transfer of state-owned enterprises, tertiary industries, the industrialisation of agriculture, new and high-tech industries and urban public facilities.

SHANXI

Heavy industries, especially energy and chemicals, have an important place in the economy. Industrial areas are mainly in Taiyuan, Datong and Changzhi.

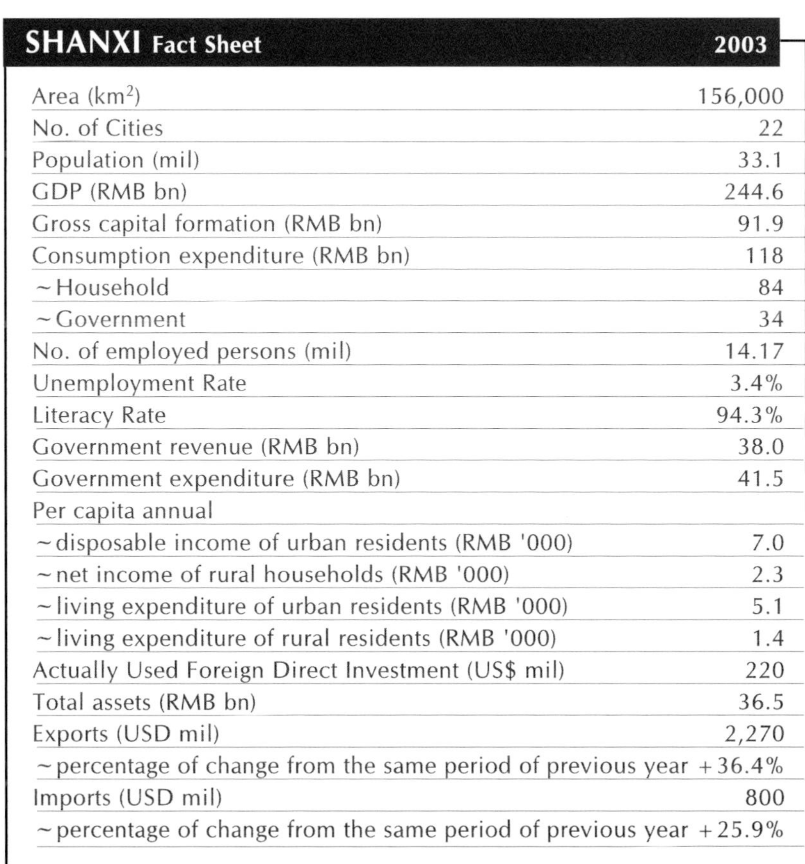

SHANXI Fact Sheet	**2003**
Area (km^2)	156,000
No. of Cities	22
Population (mil)	33.1
GDP (RMB bn)	244.6
Gross capital formation (RMB bn)	91.9
Consumption expenditure (RMB bn)	118
~Household	84
~Government	34
No. of employed persons (mil)	14.17
Unemployment Rate	3.4%
Literacy Rate	94.3%
Government revenue (RMB bn)	38.0
Government expenditure (RMB bn)	41.5
Per capita annual	
~disposable income of urban residents (RMB '000)	7.0
~net income of rural households (RMB '000)	2.3
~living expenditure of urban residents (RMB '000)	5.1
~living expenditure of rural residents (RMB '000)	1.4
Actually Used Foreign Direct Investment (US$ mil)	220
Total assets (RMB bn)	36.5
Exports (USD mil)	2,270
~percentage of change from the same period of previous year	+36.4%
Imports (USD mil)	800
~percentage of change from the same period of previous year	+25.9%

Introduction

Shanxi province is located in mid-west China, to the west of the Taihang Mountains and east of the Yellow River. It is called "San Jin" as well, meaning that the province comprises three parts. Located on the Huangtu plateau, four-fifths of the 156,300 km^2 province is hilly. It is landlocked, bordered by the provinces of Hebei, Henan, Inner Mongolia and Shaanxi. With a continental temperate climate, winters in Shanxi are cold and summers hot, with seasonal winds. The population of 31.7 million is mostly concentrated in the capital city Taiyuan and other major cities such as Datong, Yangquan, Changzhi, Jincheng and Shuozhou. Culturally and historically rich, Shanxi is also home to the ancient county seat of Pingyao, an ancient site listed by UNESCO.

Infrastructure

Railways

The railway network connects Taiyuan to Shijiazhuang, Beijing, Yuanping, Baotou, Datong, Menyuan and Jiaozuo. There are seven double-track electric railways extending to coastal ports such as Qinghuandao, Qingdao, Yantai and Lianyungang. The Shuozhou-Huanghua Railway links Shenchi county in Shanxi to Huanghua port in Hebei, and will be an important route for coal transportation from west to east in China.

province. The Taiyuan-Jiuguan Expressway joins the Beijing-Shijiazhuang expressway, Beijing-Tianjin-Tanggu expressway and Beijing-Shenzhen expressway, leading directly into Beijing and the Bohai Sea rim.

Heavy industry, especially energy and chemicals, has an important place in Shanxi's economy. In 2002, industrial output totalled RMB125.3 billion, with heavy industry accounting for over 80 percent of the figure.

Air Transport

Taiyuan Airport connects Shanxi to over 28 major domestic cities, including Beijing, Xian, Chengdu and Chongqing. International routes from Shanxi go to Hong Kong, Singapore, Russia and Japan. Construction on a new airport in Datong City has begun.

Gas Supply and Electricity

As part of the Great Western Development Strategy, a major gas pipeline starting from the Tarim Basin in Xinjiang and ending at Shanghai, is being built to run through the provinces of Gansu, Shaanxi, Shanxi, Henan, Anhui and Jiangsu and Ningxia Hui Autonomous Region. The purpose is to deliver gas from the country's major gas production bases in the western region to the central and eastern regions and the Yangtze River Delta area. Shanxi has an installed power capacity of 9.2 million kWh. A new thermal power plant is being built in Wangqu with an installed capacity of over 2.4 million kWh.

Natural Resources

Over 127 minerals have been discovered in Shanxi province, with 24 having significant deposits. Shanxi has an important coal reserve, estimates put it at 871 billion tons, and is also known as the "Coal Warehouse of China". Coalfields cover a total area of 64,800 km^2 in the province. Major coalfields are located near Taiyuan and Datong, which rank amongst the country's largest coal export bases.

Industry

Heavy industry, especially energy and chemicals, has an important place in Shanxi's economy. In 2002, industrial output totalled RMB125.3 billion, with heavy industry accounting for over 80 percent of the figure. Industrial areas are mainly located at Taiyuan, Datong and Changzhi. Taiyuan Iron and Steel Works is a big producer of special steel in the province, with an annual output exceeding 2.7 million tons. Aluminium is fast becoming an important industry as well. As for machinery and electronics, key enterprises include the Taiyuan Heavy Machinery Group Company, Taiyuan Mining Machinery Plant and Yuci Hydraulic Component Plant. Other industries that have been developed in the province include mining equipment, machinery, cars, metallurgy, chemical fertilisers, printing, paper-making, foods and textiles.

Tourism

Taiyuan, Datong, Wutai Mountain, Linfen, Yuncheng, Shangdang and Yangquan attract a fair number of visitors. There are many draws in Shanxi province, including Hu Kou Waterfall, Datong Yungang grottoes, Wutai Mountain, Guandi Temple, Xuankong Temple and the Yingxian Wooden Pagoda.. In 2002, the province attracted 248,000 foreign tourists and generated revenues of US$75 million. Shanxi will also be cooperating with several other provinces and autonomous regions namely Qinghai, Sichuan, Gansu, Shaanxi, Henan, Shandong, Inner Mongolia and Ningxia Hui autonomous regions in establishing a tourism information network. Tourists visit during certain times of the year to experience special festivals celebrated in Shanxi, such as the Guangong Cultural Festival held during 16-30 October in Haizhou Town, and the Yellow River International Drift Month held from 19 September to 18 October at Hukou Falls in Jixian County.

Banking

Banking institutions in Shanxi include the People's Bank of China, Taiyuan Branch; the Industrial and Commercial Bank of China, Shanxi Branch; the Agricultural Bank of China, Shanxi Branch; the Bank of China, Shanxi Branch; and China Construction Bank, Shanxi Branch.

Foreign Trade

Shanxi's exports increased by 36.4 percent to US$2.27billion in 2003. Major export categories were coke, coal, textiles, metals, minerals and chemicals. Major export markets were the USA, Japan, the Republic of Korea, and Germany. Imports rose by 25.9 percent to US$80.0 million in 2003. Major imported goods include iron grind, machinery, electronic equipment and chemicals from the USA, Hong Kong, Australia, Germany and Japan.

Foreign Investment

In 2003, Shanxi approved 89 foreign-invested projects with contracted foreign investment of US$480 million (50.8%). Foreign investments were channelled into infrastructure projects, light industry, and the food, metallurgy, textile, garment, machinery and electronic industries. Investment came mostly from Taiwan, the Virgin Islands, the USA and Hong Kong.

In the coming years, foreign investment will be encouraged in the fields of telecommunications, transportation, electricity, energy, raw material development, infrastructure construction (including two power plants Yangcheng and Yangquan, and the Wanjiazhai water control project), electronics and information technology, biological engineering,

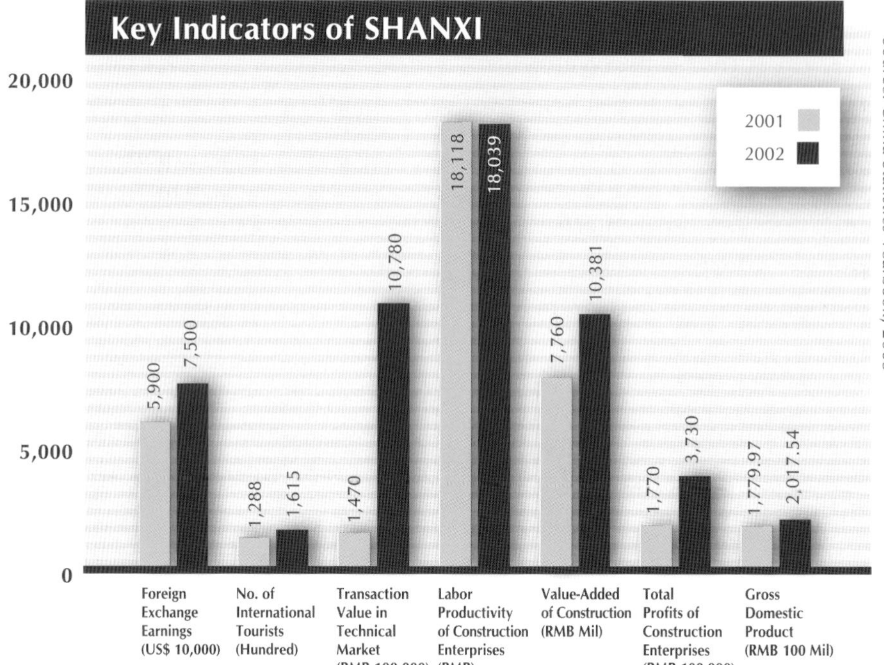

new material technology, radiation technology, new energy resources, energy efficiency, environmental protection, medicine, basic material science, and other new technologies. Incentives and preferential treatment will be given to enterprises investing in the processing and comprehensive utilisation of coal; smelting and processing of steel; textile industry; farming, forestry and animal husbandry by-product processing; and technological innovation.

To boost the development of the central and western regions in China, the State Council has granted further tax incentives to foreign-invested enterprises (FIEs) in China. Under the existing policy, FIEs are entitled to a three-year tax reduction and exemption. The new policy allows FIEs in the central and western regions to enjoy another three years of preferential tax rate when the current preferential term expires. The tax rate can be further reduced to 10 percent if an enterprise is proven to export more than 70 percent of its annual output in terms of value.

Foreign Investment Encouraged

1. Projects concerning infrastructural facilities: primary industry; energy; transportation; development of raw material industries; power industry; railway; highway; coal processing; metallurgy; aluminium; building materials; fine chemical products.

2. Projects utilising advanced technology: This refers to projects which introduce advanced technology and equipment to improve product properties, save energy and raw materials, enhance technological progress, reap economic benefits for enterprises, and manufacture new products to meet market demands.

3. Projects which are export-oriented: This refers to projects which expand the export market through product upgrading.

4. Projects which enhance the reform of large and medium sized state-owned enterprises in the five pillar industries in Shanxi (energy, machinery, metallurgy, chemicals and building materials).

5. Projects which develop agriculture, forestry and animal husbandry, as well as their by-products, and projects which concern new technologies in agricultural processing.

6. Projects which improve the comprehensive utilisation of resources and sustainable development, and projects concerning technology for environmental protection.

SICHUAN

The reserves of hydropower resources are second only to Tibet and the exploitable potential is greater than other places in China.

SICHUAN Fact Sheet	2003
Area (km^2)	488,000
No. of Cities	32
Population (mil)	87.0
GDP (RMB bn)	545.6
Gross capital formation (RMB bn)	197.6
Consumption expenditure (RMB bn)	289
~Household	222
~Government	68
No. of employed persons (mil)	46.8
Unemployment Rate	4.5%
Literacy Rate	95%
Government revenue (RMB bn)	29.2
Government expenditure (RMB bn)	70.2
Per capita annual	
~disposable income of urban residents (RMB '000)	7.0
~net income of rural households (RMB '000)	2.2
~living expenditure of urban residents (RMB '000)	5.8
~living expenditure of rural residents (RMB '000)	1.7
Actually Used Foreign Direct Investment (USD mil)	580
Total assets (RMB bn)	42.4
Exports (USD mil)	3,210
~percentage of change from the same period of previous year	+18.5%
Imports (USD mil)	2,430
~percentage of change from the same period of previous year	+38.1%

Introduction

Sichuan is located in the Southwest region and is known as the "Land of Abundance". The province's capital is Chengdu, which enjoys the same preferential policies as a coastal open city. Sichuan is one of the major agricultural production bases in China. Grain, including rice and wheat, is the major product, with output that ranked first in China in 2001. Commercial cash crops include rapeseeds, citrus fruits, peaches, sugar canes and sweet potatoes. Sichuan also had the largest output of pork among all provinces and the second largest output of silkworm cocoons in China in 2001.

Ethnicity

In addition to its majority, the Han people, Sichuan is also inhabited by many minority ethnic groups including the Yi, Tibetan, Qiang, Hui, Mongolian, Lisu, Manchu, Naxi, Bai, Buyi, Dai, Miao and Tujia. Each of the minority group

has at least 5,000 people. Sichuan is China's second-largest region inhabited by Tibetans as well as the largest region inhabited by the Yi ethnic group and the only region where the Qiang people live in homogeneous communities. The Yi ethnic group, which is the largest minority group in Sichuan, lives in the Greater and Little Liangshan mountains and the Anning River Valley. The Tibetans live in the Garze and Ngawa Tibetan Autonomous Prefectures and the Muli Tibetan Autonomous County in Liangshan Prefecture. The Qiang people, one of China's oldest ethnic groups, live mainly in Maoxian, Wenchuan, Heishui, Songpan and Beichuan on the upper reaches of the Minjiang River.

Natural Resources

The reserves of hydropower resources in Sichuan come to 150 million kW, second only to Tibet, and the exploitable potential is over 100 million kW, more than any other area in China.

Sichuan boasts 132 verified mineral resources and leads the country in the reserves of vanadium, titanium, calcium, mirabilite, fluorite, natural gas, and sulphur iron, and leads the world in reserves of titanium. Its reserves of vanadium ranks third in the world. The Panxi region alone possesses 13.3 percent of the reserves of iron, 93 percent of titanium, 69 percent of vanadium, 83 percent of cobalt of the whole country.

The pleasant climate provides a favourable environment for plants and animals. Forests cover a total area of 7.46 million hectares. Sichuan is home to one-fifth of the country's dawn redwoods and Cathaya argyrophylla, two species so old they are regarded as living fossils. It is also rich in animal resources. There are over 1,000 kinds of vertebrates, accounting for 40 percent of the country. Among them are 55 kinds of rare animals. The well-known giant pandas inhabit mainly in 36 counties and natural reserves of four mountain ranges within the territory of Sichuan.

Sichuan has three places on the World Cultural and Natural Heritage List: the Jiuzhaigou Scenic Area, the Huanglong Scenic Area, and Mount Ermei with the Leshan Giant Buddha; nine state-class scenic areas, including the Dujiang Dam Irrigation System, Qingcheng Mountain, the Sea of Bamboo in southern Sichuan; 11 national forest parks; 40 nature reserves, 44 provincial-class scenic areas. Almost every variety of tourist resources is available here: plateaus, mountains, ravines, basins, hills, plains, rivers, lakes, hot springs, waterfalls, limestone caves, and even danxia (red bed) formation.

Infrastructure

Railways

Chengdu is a major railway hub in China's central and western regions. Major railway lines such as the Baoji-Chengdu, Chengdu-Chongqing and Chengdu-Kunming link the city to different parts of the country. With two arterial railways, the Shanghai-Chongqing (via Sichuan) line and the Sichuan-Beihai line targeted to be completed in the 10th Five-Year plan period (2001-2005), railway transportation is expected to be improved significantly. Utilising domestic developed technology, the provincial government started the construction of the first magnetic levitation train rail at Chengdu-Qingcheng township in April 2000. The rail will be a 425-metre low-speed tourist trail line upon completion.

Highways

At the end of 2001, the total length of highways in Sichuan reached 92,000 kilometres, the longest among all the provinces in Western China. As an accelerated plan to develop the province's economy, the Sichuan provincial government has planned to invest RMB60 billion in highway development in the 10th Five-Year Plan, including the construction of the Chengdu Shanghai National Trunk, Chengdu Beihai National Trunk and highways linking Chongqing-

Sichuan is one of the major industrial bases in Western China. In 2002, added value of industrial output in Sichuan totalled RMB272.7 billion, an increase of 93.8 percent over 2001. In addition to heavy industries such as the coal, energy, iron and steel industries, the province has established a light manufacturing sector comprising building materials, wood processing, food and silk processing.

Changsha and Chengdu-Tibet. The total length of highways is expected to increase to 1,700 km by 2005 while the travel time between Chengdu and all other adjacent provinces (excluding Tibet) will be reduced to less than eight hours. With an extensive highway network linking major ports and provincial capitals, Sichuan is equipped with good facilities to position itself as the logistic centre for the western part of China.

Air Transport

Chengdu Shuangliu Airport is currently the largest international airport in Southwest China. International flights to Hong Kong, Bangkok, Singapore, Japan and the Republic of Korea are available. While the Shuangliu Airport is currently being modernised and expanded into a state-class hub airport, four new domestic airports are planned for in Guangyuan, Mianyang, Panzhihua and Jiuzhiguo.

Telecommunications

Sichuan has a fairly advanced telecommunications network comprising digital microwave, optic fibre, satellite, program-controlled telephones, pagers and mobile phones. At the end of 2002, the number of fixed line telephones in Sichuan reached 10.13 million. The number of mobile phones users has reached 86.2 million and internet users 1.26 million.

Hydropower

Sichuan tops the country in terms of hydropower resources with its estimated reserve of more than 110 million kWh. The Ertan Hydroelectric Project, with an installed capacity of 3.3 million kWh, had begun operation in 2000.

Industries

Sichuan is one of the major industrial bases in Western China. In 2002, added value of industrial output in Sichuan totalled RMB272.7 billion, an increase of 93.8 percent over 2001. In addition to heavy industries such as coal, energy, iron and steel industry, the province has established a light manufacturing sector comprising building materials, wood processing, food and silk processing. Chengdu and Mianyang are the production bases for textiles and electronics products. Deyang, Panzhihua and Yibin are the production bases for machinery, metallurgy industries and wine respectively. The wine production of Sichuan accounted for 21.9 percent of the country's total production in 2000.

To accelerate development of Sichuan into a high and new technology industrial base, investments are encouraged in electronics and information technology, machinery and metallurgy (including cars), hydropower, pharmaceutical, food and beverage industries.

Tourism

Sichuan's beautiful landscapes and rich historic relics have made the province a major centre for tourism. The Jiuzhaigou and Huanglong Temple are listed among the "World Legacies of Nature" by the United Nations. Other famous tourist spots included Leshan Buddha, Ermei Mountains, Dujiangyan, Qingcheng Mountain and Hailuogou.

In 2002, about 667,200 overseas tourists visited the region. Revenue of US$200 million was generated, which represent an increase of 17.6 percent over 2001. As tourism industry is one of the major focus areas in Sichuan's 10th Five-Year Plan, provincial government set up a Tourist Information and Advisory Services Centre in Chengdu in April 2001 to promote the industry. Besides, in order to attract new financial resources and management techniques to improve the industry performance, Sichuan government plans to transfer the operating rights of 10 selected scenic spots, including Jiuzhaigou and Huanglong Temple, to private operators.

Consumer Market

Sichuan's retail sales of consumer goods reached RMB185 billion in 2002, increasing by 10.1 percent over 2001. The largest consumer centre is located in Chengdu, which accounted for 36 percent of the province's total sales. There are about 60 shopping malls (over 5,000 sq.m.) in the province. In addition to local department stores and shopping centres like Chengdu Renmin Department Store, Chengdu Department Store and Chengdu Hualian Commercial Building, foreign investors have also entered the retail market to tap the vast markets of Sichuan and Chengdu in particular. Foreign retailers in Chengdu include Yokado Department Store, Lafayett Department Store and Carrefour.

Scientific Research Capacity

Sichuan is supported by 49 universities, 184 state-owned science and technology research institutes and more than 1.2 million scientists and engineers, giving it a leading edge in scientific research. The areas of scientific research include high-molecular chemistry, leather, nuclear technology, technology of aerospace and aviation, stomotological medicine, genetic engineering and optical fibre communication. Additionally, Xichang is the hi-tech research centre in rocket launches.

The West Software Park, approved by the Ministry of Science and Technology in 1997, is one of the four state-level computer software centres to develop domestic computer software industry. The park aims at developing applied software for state-designated key industries, providing specialised product training programmes for users and cultivating small and medium-sized software firms.

With a rich endowment in herbs (around 4,500 species), a large number of senior Chinese medicine doctors and research institutes like Chengdu University of Tradition Chinese Medicine (TCM), Sichuan is also strong in research and development of modern Chinese medicine. Sichuan's TCM output reached RMB4.6 billion in 1999, more than half of the province's medical and pharmaceutical industry of RMB8.7 billion, ranking it top in China.

More than 300 research projects are underway in Chengdu, many of which are close to success. These outstanding records have granted Chengdu the privilege to be selected by the Ministry of Science and technology to set up the first state-level Modernized Science and Technology Industry Base for TCM.

Given Sichuan's strength in science and technology development, and the preferential policies provided for hi-tech industrial investment by the provincial government, a number of internationally renowned IT companies such as Microsoft, Cisco, Intel, IBM and Motorola, have been attracted to

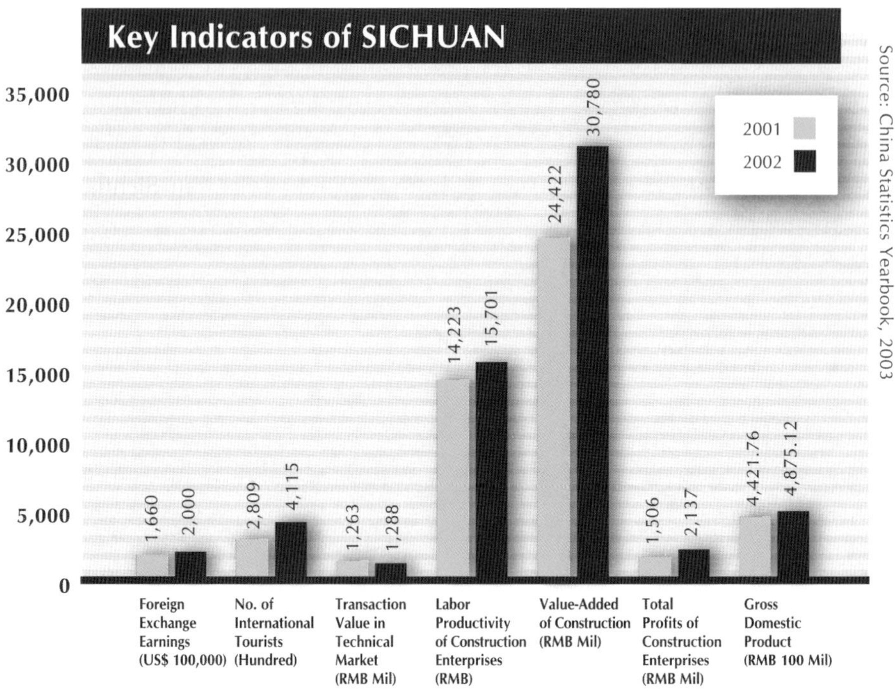

invest and set up their research and development centres.

Foreign Trade

Sichuan exports increased by 18.5 percent to US$3.21billion in 2003. Major exports included chemicals and industrial raw materials, steel products, garments and textiles, silk yarn and fabrics, electronics and power generation equipment. Major export markets were Hong Kong, Japan, the US, Iran and Russia.

Imports increased by 38.1 percent to US$2.43 billion in 2003. Major imports included aviation equipment, electronic components, electrical appliances, car spare parts, chemical raw materials, steel products, non-ferrous metals, electronics and machinery. Major import sources were Japan, Hong Kong, the US, France and Germany.

Hong Kong is one of the major trading partners of Sichuan. In 1999, the province's exports to Hong Kong totalled US$322.8 million, accounting for 18.6 percent of the total. As for imports, 17.2 percent of the province's imports was from Hong Kong, amounting to US$242.9 million.

Foreign Investment

By the end of 2003, 155 foreign investors invested in Sichuan, with the total accumulated contractual and utilised foreign investment reaching US$10.0 billion and US$0.93 billion respectively. Over 60 of the Fortune 500 companies like Siemens, Procter & Gamble, Shell, Nestle, Toyota and Motorola have established their presence in the province.

In 1999, there were 62 Hong Kong-invested projects with a total contracted investment amount of US$103.1 million in Sichuan. Actual utilised foreign investment was US$82.3 billion. Hong Kong's investments were mainly in manufacturing, real estate, transportation, telecommunications and construction industries.

In the 10th Five-Year Plan, Sichuan will concentrate on the improvement of product quality and competitiveness of its state-owned enterprises. The Sichuan government has decided to transform Chengdu into a hi-tech industrial centre, developing electronic information, bio-technology, new materials and integration of optics and machinery. Focus will be on five sectors; electronics and information technology, hydropower, machinery and metallurgy, chemical and pharmaceutical, food and beverage, with the aim to transform them into pillar industries. In addition, tourism industry is another key sector in Sichuan's future development plan.

YUNNAN

The province aims to develop itself into the largest flower production and export base in China and the whole of Asia.

YUNNAN Fact Sheet	2003
Area (km^2)	380,000
No. of Cities	16
Population (mil)	43.8
GDP (RMB bn)	245.9
Gross capital formation (RMB bn)	88.7
Consumption expenditure (RMB bn)	153
~Household	102
~Government	50
No. of employed persons (mil)	23.41
Unemployment Rate	4%
Literacy Rate	79.7%
Government revenue (RMB bn)	22.9
Government expenditure (RMB bn)	58.8
Per capita annual	
~disposable income of urban residents (RMB '000)	7.6
~net income of rural households (RMB '000)	1.7
~living expenditure of urban residents (RMB '000)	6.0
~living expenditure of rural residents (RMB '000)	1.4
Actually Used Foreign Direct Investment (US$ mil)	168
Total assets (RMB bn)	69.3
Exports (USD mil)	1,677
~percentage of change from the same period of previous year	+17.3%
Imports (USD mil)	991
~percentage of change from the same period of previous year	+24.3%

In the Tenth Five-Year Plan, Yunnan plans to promote trade with Southeast Asian countries. Hence, the construction work on the Southwest Cross Border Passage Railways to Vietnam and Myanmar is underway.

Introduction

Yunnan is situated at the southwestern part of China, lying at the threshold of Southeast Asia, bordering on Myanmar, Laos and Vietnam. Mountains and highlands constitute 94 percent of the province's total area. The ethnic minorities in Yunnan account for 34 percent of its total population, while the major ethnic groups include Yi, Bai, Hani, Zhuang, Dai and Miao.

The provincial capital is Kunming, which enjoys the same preferential policies as the coastal open cities. Other open cities include Ruili county, Wanding city and Hekou city.

Yunnan is one of the major production bases of copper, lead, zinc, tin and aluminium in China. Gejiu city is well known as "the Kingdom of Zinc", with reserves that ranked first in the country. The Yunxi brand of refined tin is one of the main products in Gejiu, and is registered on the London Nonferrous Metal Exchange. Besides, reserves of germanium, indium, zirconium, platinum, rock salt, sylvite, nickel, phosphate, mirabilite, arsenic and blue asbestos are also high.

The province is one of the major forest zones in China. Its forest area accounts for 24 percent of the country's total. Yunnan is also an important base of aromatic plants and flora in China, with more than 300 varieties of essential oil-bearing plants and 2,500 kinds of ornamental plants and flowers.

Yunnan aims to develop itself into the largest flower production and export base in China and Asia. Currently, Yunnan has three large flower production areas, including Kunming (a temperate fresh cut flower production area), Xishuangbanna and Yuanjiang (the tropical flower production area), and Diqing and Lijiang (a cold bulb flower production area). The annual flower output in the province reaches 1.1 billion bunches. Leveraging on its strength in floral resources, Kunming hosted the 14th International Horticulture Expo in 2000.

Yunnan's main agricultural crops are rice, corn, wheat, sugar cane and beans as well as rubber, tea, tobacco, walnut, cashew nuts and coffee. Some of the famous Chinese medicine herbs such as ginseng, danggui, fuling, tianma and sharen, are found in the province. It is the second largest sugarcane production base in China. Total output of sugar cane accounted for 18 percent of the country's total, reaching 15.3 million tons in 1999. The province has more than 40 fresh water lakes, including Dianchi, Erhai and Fuxian, which have the potential to be developed into aquaculture centres.

Minerals

More than 150 kinds of minerals have been discovered in the province. The potential value of the proven deposits in Yunnan is RMB three trillion, 40 percent of which comes from fuel minerals,

7.3 percent from metallic minerals, and 52.7 percent from nonmetallic minerals.

Yunnan has found deposits of 86 kinds of minerals in 2,700 places. About 13 percent of the mineral deposits are the largest of their kinds in China, and two-thirds of them are among the largest of their kinds in the Yangtze River valley and in south China. Yunnan ranks first in the country in the deposits of zinc, lead, tin, cadmium, indium, thallium, and crocidolite.

Hydro-energy

Yunnan is blessed with abundant rainfall. The annual water flow in the province is 200 billion cubic metres, three times the Yellow River. The rivers flowing from outside bring an additional 160 billion cubic metres into the province, which means more than 10,000 cubic metres of water for each person in the province. This is four times the average in the country. The rich water resources offer abundant hydro-energy.

Infrastructure

Water Transport

The Lancangjiang River, which connects the Mekong River, extends southward through Myanmar, Laos, Thailand, Cambodia and Vietnam to the South China Sea. Shipping services are also available from Zhaotong's Shuifu port to Shanghai. The landlocked province, however, relies very much on railways that lead to Guangxi's Beihai and other ports in Southern China. To foster the development of the economic development of the Mekong Valley, the first international commercial water transport route from Jinghong to destinations at Myanmar, Laos and Vietnam has been built.

Railways

Major railways in the province include Chengdu-Kunming, Guiyang-Kunming, Kunming-Hekou and Nanning-Kunming; other railways include Guangtong-Chuxiong, Guangtong-Dali and

Kunming-Yuxi. The new railway, Neijing-Kunming, which passes through several cities in Sichuan, Guizhou and Yunnan provinces, is an integral part of the Southwest Sea Passage.

In the Tenth Five-Year Plan, Yunnan plans to promote trade with Southeast Asian countries. Hence, the construction work on the Southwest Cross Border Passage Railways to Vietnam and Myanmar is underway.

Highways

Kunming and Dali are the major transportation hubs in Yunnan. Major highways include Yunnan-Guizhou, Yuannan-Guangxi, Yunnan-Sichuan and Yunnan-Tibet, which connect Yunnan with neigh-bouring provinces and autonomous regions. Three highways from Yunnan to Myanmar, Thailand and Vietnam will be upgraded. Yunnan plans to increase its investment in infrastructure projects in the Tenth Five-Year Plan. From January to May in 2001, Yunnan invested RMB3.7 billion on highway constructions, ranking it top among all western provinces and 5th overall in China.

Air Transport

The province has nine civil airports, including Kunming, Dali, Baoshan, Xishuangbana, Simao, Zhaotong, Lijiang, Diqing, etc. Besides, the Kunming Wujiaba International Airport offers direct flights to Hong Kong, Japan, Bangkok, Singapore, Yangoon, and Chiangmai.

Telecommunications

Telecommunication has developed rapidly over the past years. In 2002, the number of subscribers for mobile phone services exceeded 5.02 million.

Electricity

In addition to the existing thermal power plants, a number of staircase hydropower stations on the lower and middle-reaches of the Lancangjiang River are under construction. In 2000 the province generated 11.2 billion kW of electricity, ranking second in China.

Industries

In 2002, the province's industrial output amounted to RMB88 billion, which is an increase of eight percent from the previous year. The industries are located mainly in Kunming, Yuxi, Qujing and Honghe. Food processing is a key industry in the province. Yunnan Puer Tea is well-known at home and abroad. "Yunnan Cigarettes" are among the best brand names in the country. Other famous brands include "Hongtashan", "Ashima", "Yunyian" and "Hongmei". Yuxi is one of the most important tobacco production bases in China, and the nation's largest cigarette manufacturer, Hongta Group, is located in this city.

Yunnan is also one of the major coffee growing and processing bases in China. Famous coffee enterprises, Maxwell and Nestle companies, have both signed contracts with Yunnan to provide 10,000 tons of coffee beans annually. As of May 2001, Puer became the largest coffee plantation base in China.

Yunnan's textiles, clothing and leather industries are also thriving. Other major industries include tourism, rubber, forestry and papermaking, chemicals, building materials, machinery and other light industries.

In the Tenth Five-Year Plan from 2001 to 2005, the province has budgeted RMB 150 million or approximately US$18 million to develop the export of high-tech products in the fields of biological technology, medicine, new materials, electronic information, environmental protection and the optical-electromechanical field.

Tourism

Yunnan is one of the renowned tourist centres with more than 50 scenic spots in the province. Major tourist spots include the mysterious Xishuang-banna, the wonder of the world, Lunan Stone Forest, the Spring City, Kunming, the ancient kingdom capital, Dali, and the beautiful Lijiang under the snow-capped Jade Dragon Mountain. In 2002, over 1.3 million foreign tourists visited the region, generating revenue of US$419 million.

Consumer Market

Retail sales of consumer goods in Yunnan rose by 33.6 percent to RMB85.5 billion in 2002. A major consumer centre is located in Kunming, and its retail sales accounts for 37 percent of the province's total. The Kunming Department Store Co. Ltd is the largest retailer in Yunnan. Other major retailers include Kunming Wuhua Shopping Arcade, Kunming Cherry Shopping Centre, Kunming Yuandong Shopping Centre, (Wal-Mart of US is one of the major investors), Kunming Sakura Shopping Centre, Kunming Southwest Commercial Building, Kunming Panlong Building, Kunming Kundu Shopping Centre, Kunming Tianyuan Shopping Centre and Zhengyi Department Store, as well as the Xiaguan Department Store and Gucheng Shopping Centre in Dali. The Kunming International Flower Trade and Auction Center is the largest flower market in China.

Foreign Trade

Yunnan's exports rose by 17.3 percent to US$1,677 million in 2003. Major export goods were phosphates, jade ornaments, garments, kidney beans, tobacco, tea, tin and machine tools. Major export markets included Hong Kong, Myanmar, Japan, the US and Vietnam.

Imports grew by 24.3 percent to US$991 million in 2003. Major import goods were agricultural products, machinery for tobacco and raw materials.

Hong Kong was Yunnan's biggest trading partner, ranking second in Yunnan's exports and first in Yunnan's imports. In 2000, Yunnan's export and import to and from Hong Kong were US$210.9 million and US$130.9 million respectively. Other major trading partners of Yunnan include Myanmar, South Korea, US and Japan.

Yunnan has approved more than 28 counties located at Ruili, Wanding and Hekou, as border trade zones. In 2001, Yunnan's total border trade with Myanmar, Vietnam and Laos reached US$346 million, including exports of US$232 million. These represented a growth rate of 120 percent and 160 percent respectively over the previous year. Among these border counties, Ruili accounted for 70 percent of the province's border trade, which was also 34 percent of the total national border trade. Major export goods are sugar, beer, cigarette, garments, cement, oil products, paraffin wax, rubber, tropical fruits, etc. and major import goods included timber, Chinese medical herbs, etc.

Since 1979, the State Council

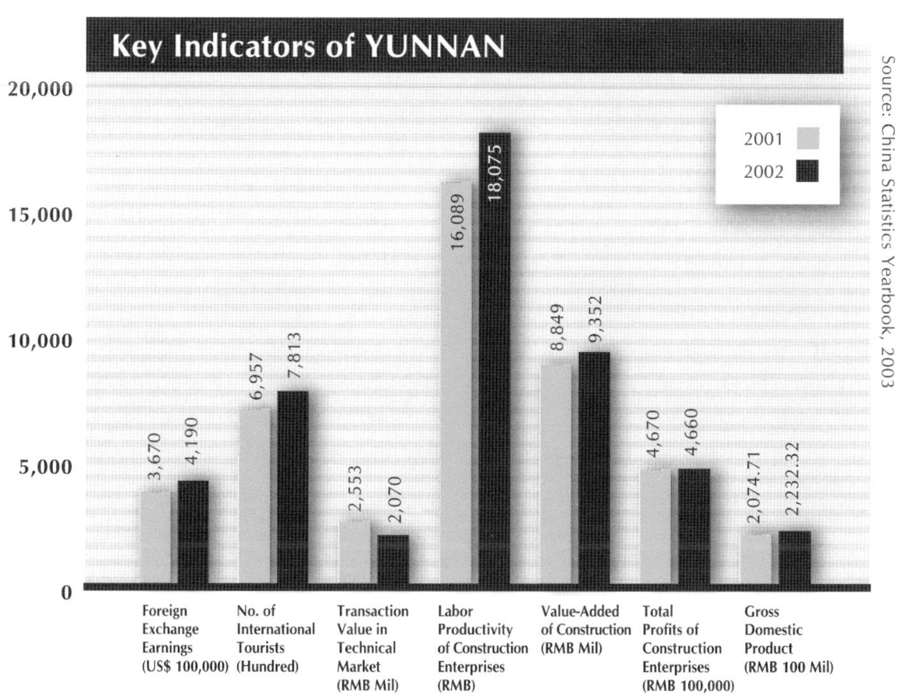

approved eight counties in Yunnan as state-level ports. The biggest of them, the Tengchong County, handled 126,000 tons of cargo amounted to RMB280 million in 1999.

Foreign Investment

In 2003, the number of approved foreign-funded projects totalled 167 with contracted foreign investment of US$544 million. US$168 million of the foreign capital was actually utilised in the year.

Hong Kong is the biggest investor in Yunnan. In 2000, the actual utilised investment from Hong Kong was US$75.3 million. Other major investors were from the Virgin Islands, US, Japan, Germany, Singapore and Taiwan.

Major invested sectors included metallurgy, machinery, electronics, textiles, light industry, printing, agriculture, animal husbandry and the tertiary sectors such as tourism, transport, post and telecommunications and real estates.

The Coca-Cola Company is one of the major investors in Yunnan. Recently, the company announced the opening of its 24th bottling plant in China. So far, Coca-Cola has invested more than US$1.1 billion in China since resuming its business in the country in 1979, when China started its opening policy.

To boost the development of the central and western regions in China, the State Council has granted further tax incentives to foreign-invested enterprises (FIEs) in China. Under the existing policy, FIEs are entitled to a three-year tax reduction and exemption. The new policy allows foreign-invested enterprises in the central and western regions to enjoy another three years of preferential tax rate when the current preferential term expires. The tax rate can be further reduced to 10 percent if the enterprise exports more than 70 percent of its annual output in terms of value.

ZHEJIANG

The area is noted for its high yield agriculture and aquatic products. It is also the fourth strongest industrial base in China.

ZHEJIANG Fact Sheet	**2003**
Area (km^2)	101,800
No. of Cities	33
Population (mil)	46.8
GDP (RMB bn)	920.0
Gross capital formation (RMB bn)	346.7
Consumption expenditure (RMB bn)	374
~Household	255
~Government	119
No. of employed persons (mil)	29.20
Unemployment Rate	4.2%
Literacy Rate	87.8%
Government revenue (RMB bn)	56.7
Government expenditure (RMB bn)	75
Per capita annual	
~disposable income of urban residents (RMB '000)	13.2
~net income of rural households (RMB '000)	5.4
~living expenditure of urban residents (RMB '000)	8.7
~living expenditure of rural residents (RMB '000)	3.7
Actually Used Foreign Direct Investment (USD mil)	5,450
Total assets (RMB bn)	147.6
Exports (USD mil)	41,600
~percentage of change from the same period of previous year	+41.5%
Imports (USD mil)	19,820
~percentage of change from the same period of previous year	+58.0%

Introduction

Archaeologists have excavated over 100 Neolithic sites in Zhejiang belonging to the Hemudu (c. 5,000 BC), Majiabang (c. 4,000 B.C.) and Liangzhu (c. 3,000 B.C.) cultures; there is a wealth of evidence showing that an ancient civilisation thrived here. In the 10th century, Zhejiang became one of the most prosperous and populous areas in China, thanks to rapid social and economic development. With its verdant landscapes and clear waters, this province steeped in history and culture is justly famed for its picturesque charm. Zhejiang has also long enjoyed the reputation of being a land of fish and rice, and the birthplace of silk and tea. A recent report by the United Nations on global city developments cited Hangzhou and Ningbo amongst China's most promising cities.

Located on the southeast coast of China, Zhejiang lies to the south of the Yangtze River Delta, with Shanghai bordering it on the north. The province contains a total land area of 1.018 million km^2, 23.2 percent is made up of plains and basins, 6.4 percent of rivers and lakes, and 70 percent of hills and mountains. There is 1,840.7 km of continental coastline. The 3,061 offshore islands each are over 500 m^2 in area. This brings the total coastline to 6,486 km, one of the longest in China; the Zhoushan fishing ground produces one of the biggest catches on the mainland's coastline.

Population

The province is administratively divided into the following areas: Hangzhou, Ningpo, Wenzhou, Jiaxing, Huzhou, Shaoxing, Jinhua, Quzhou, Zhoushan, Taizhou (the 10 administrative cities) and Lishui (an administrative area). The provincial capital is Hangzhou, one of the seven imperial capitals in ancient China. There are 41 counties, 23 cities and 23 towns, all administered at the county level. The province has a total population of 46.8 million; over 300,000 of them belong to 47 ethnic minorities. She and Hui are the two largest minority ethnic groups.

Natural Resources

The land is rich in mineral resources such as fluorite, alunite and lime. There are also considerable reserves of gold, silver, copper, aluminium, lead and zinc. In the continental shelf basin of the East China Sea, the petroleum and natural gas resources hold great promise. 393 km of the province's coastline is suitable for the construction of 10,000-tonnage deep-water berths, and 105 km is suitable for the construction of 100,000-tonnage berths.

Infrastructure

Water Transport

The inland water transport network along the rivers and canals is well developed. The Zhejiang government is investing RMB 2.3 billion to improve this network under the Tenth Five-Year Plan.

Ports

58 ports have been built along the coastline, of which the ports of Ningbo, Wenzhou, Shenjiamen and Haimen are open to foreign vessels. Ningbo was the second largest port in China in terms of cargo handling capacity, reaching 128 million tons in 2001. The port of Beilun in Ningbo is one of China's four major international transit ports in China, while the Aoshan Harbor in Zhoushan is able to accommodate oil transshipment from supertankers.

Railways

Zhejiang's railways are well developed. It is served by two national trunk lines, Hangzhou-Shanghai and Zhejiang-Jiangxi, as well as regional railways, including Hangzhou-Ningbo, Xiaoshan-Ningbo, Xuancheng-Hangzhou, and the Jinhua-Wenzhou. A new railway network will be built from Harbin in Heilongjiang to Changxing in Zhejiang.

Highways

The highway traffic network consists of six national and 69 provincial trunk highways. Major expressways include the Hang-Yong Expressway which links Hangzhou and Ningbo, and the Hu-Hang Expressway which links Shanghai and Hangzhou. The Yong-Tai-Wen Expressway (Ningbo-Taizhou-Wenzhou), which is an important section of the coastal expressway from Heilongjiang to Hainan, is under construction. The Wenzhou Shuangyu Highway Transport Station is also under construction; it will be the biggest highway transport station in the province. According to the Tenth Five Year Plan, Zhejiang will be investing a total of RMB13 billion to build new expressways and upgrade existing highways.

Air Transport

There are seven civil airports, Hangzhou, Ningbo, Wenzhou, Huangyan, Yiwu, Quzhou and Zhujiajian of Zhoushan, of which Hangzhou, Ningbo and Wenzhou are international airports. The construction of Hangzhou Xiaoshan International Airport has started.

Telecommunications

The province has built advanced public telecommunication networks for long distance program-controlled exchange, digital transmission, mobile communications, wireless paging, internet traffic, and video/telephone conferencing.

Electricity

Zhejiang utilises hydroelectric, thermal, wind, tidal and nuclear power resources. In addition to the thermal-power and hydroelectric power plants at Zhenhai and Taizhou, new nuclear power plants are also planned for Sanmen Bay, Xiangshan Port and Yueqing Bay.

Postal Services

International mail exchange bureaus have been set up in Hangzhou, Ningbo and Wenzhou, offering international air mail and parcel delivery.

Consumer Market

In 2002, Zhejiang's retail sales of consumer goods dropped by 20.8 percent to RMB202 billion and ranked fourth in the country. Major consumer markets are located in Hangzhou, Ningbo, Wenzhou, Shaoxing, Jinhua and Jiaxing. The average annual income of urban residents in Zhejiang reached RMB11,700 (US$1,261) in 2002, according to figures released by Zhejiang Provincial Statistical Bureau, ranking third after Shanghai and Beijing.

Tourism

Zhejiang is renowned for its beautiful scenery, West Lake, Fuchun River, Xin'an River, the Thousand-island Lake, Mount Yandang, Nanxijiang River, Mount Putuo, the Shengsi Islands, Mount Tiantai, Mount Mogan, Mount Xuedou, Shuanglong Cave and Mount Xiaodu count amongst China's most well known attractions. The province has devoted much effort to developing its tourism resources, particularly in Hangzhou. Trips to the breathtaking mountains, rivers and lakes in the west and the south, to the Buddhist precincts and water lands of the east coast, and to the historic culture sites of the north, have become part of the essential tourist itinerary. Visitors are also well serviced by the extensive network of hotels, tour agencies and guides. In 2002, Zhejiang received some 1,210,800 overseas tourists and 83 million domestic tourists.

Economy

Since the reform era, Zhejiang's economy has developed rapidly. In 2003, the provincial GDP reached RMB920 billion, an increase of 14 percent over 2002 and ranking it fourth amongst all the provinces in the mainland. medium and small-sized firms, urban collectives and township enterprises have undergone reform of their ownership and management structures, while the non-public sector of the economy has grown rapidly.

Zhejiang has worked out a comprehensive plan of economic targets for the future. Essentially, by 2005, it hopes to accomplish modernisation in nearly one-third of the municipalities and counties; by 2010, in nearly two-thirds; and by 2020, in the entire province.

Zhejiang has worked out a comprehensive plan of economic targets for the future. Essentially, by 2005, it hopes to accomplish modernisation in nearly one-third of the municipalities and counties; by 2010, in nearly two-thirds; and by 2020, in the entire province. Areas earmarked for improvement include the use of science and technology, education, infrastructure, tertiary industry, ownership and distribution structures, ecological and environmental sustain-ability, developing the agricultural base, urbanisation, and the continued reform of

Economic development is led by the coastal cities of Hangzhou, Inbo and Wenzhou, followed by the state and provincial level development zones. Public ownership is still the mainstay of the economy, developing alongside diversified ownership enterprises. The majority of state-owned investment, funds circulation, housing, endowment insurance and medical insurance systems.

Future economic development in Zhejiang will be concentrated in three economic belts: (1) from Beilun to Ningbo, and cities along the Shanghai-Hangzhou-Ningbo Expressway, including Shaoxing, Jiaxing and Huzhou (2) the coastal cities of Wenzhou (3) along the Zhejiang-Jiangxi, Wenzhou-Taizhou railways.

Agriculture

Zhejiang is an area noted for its high-yield agriculture. Grain and oil-bearing crops are the province's main agricultural products, but there are also other cash crops such as cotton, mulberry and silk cocoon, tea and fruits. The province also has one of the highest yields of fish and fresh water aquatic products in the country. In 2001 the output value of farming, forestry, animal husbandry and fishery altogether amounted to RMB69 billion. Recent years have seen an emphasis on the industrialised management of agriculture, with increased investment in agricultural machinery, and the mechanisation or semi-mechanisation of cultivation, irrigation and drainage, processing and transportation.

Industry

Zhejiang is the fourth strongest industrial production base in China after Guangdong, Jiangsu and Shandong. In 2002 the province's industrial output reached RMB1051 billion, an increase of 206 percent over the previous year. Industry is the predominant sector of Zhejiang's economy, its added value of RMB290 billion accounted for 48 percent of the province's GDP. The industrial growth rate stands amongst the highest in China. Industries in the northeast region of Zhejiang are more developed than those in the southwestern region. Major industrial production bases are located at Hangzhou, Ningbo, Wenzhou,

Jiaxing, Huzhou, Shaoxing, Jinhua, Quzhou, Zhoushan, Taizhou and Lishui region.

Machine building, electronics, chemicals and pharmaceuticals are the four pillar industries. The manufacture of textiles, silk, clothing, leather, food, drink, paper, common machines and non-metal mineral products are other key industries. Light industry dominates the sector, accounting for 62.8 percent of total industrial output value, some 15 percent higher than the national average. Light industry also accounts for two-thirds of the total output value of exports from Zhejiang.

Small-scale enterprises account for most of the industrial units in Zhejiang, employing 81 percent of the workers and producing 82 percent of the gross industrial output value. In the past two decades, township enterprises have been started all over the rural areas in the province, with the manufacture of textiles, clothing and leather accounting for 25 percent of the total output value of township industry. In recent years, due to the promotion and formation of large-scale enterprises, the proportion of the output value of large and medium-sized enterprises has increased.

Science and Technology

Zhejiang's research capability is amongst the most advanced in China. So far, it has 229 independent and 416 university sponsored research institutes. Key areas of research include silicon materials, nuclear science, computer science, fibre optics, electronics, recycling and industrial chemicals. The United Nations has also cooperated with Zhejiang to build the China Paddy Rice Research Institute, the International Center on Small Hydro Power, Hangzhou Bearing Laboratory, Hangzhou Light Building Materials Research and Development Center and the Pediatric Physical Growth and Mental Development Research

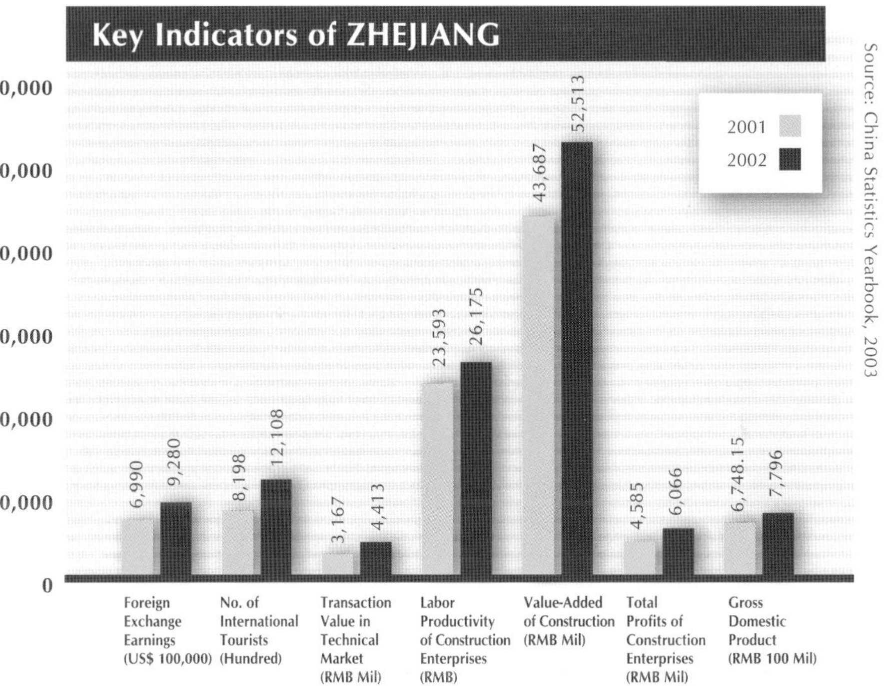

Center. Importance is placed on the application of scientific and technological advances to economic and social development.

Industry based upon new and advanced technologies is developing quickly. A high-tech industrial belt along the Shanghai-Hangzhou-Ninbo Expressway has been built. In 1998, 218 new and high-tech enterprises were set up in the Hangzhou High-Tech Industrial Development Zone, and another development zone was established on the south of Qiantang River in Hangzhou.

Foreign Trade

Zhejiang's exports rose by 41.5 percent to US$41.6 billion in 2003. Major export goods were foodstuffs, textiles, handicrafts, electronics, machinery, chemicals, pharmaceuticals, silk and mineral products. Imports amounted to US$19.8 billion in 2003. Major import commodities included fertilisers, petrochemicals, rubber, electronics, iron and steel, machinery and equipment. Major trading partners are the USA, Hong Kong, Japan, Taiwan, Germany and Italy.

Foreign Investment

In 1998, the provincial government established the Foreign Investment Administration of Zhejiang Province to take charge of foreign-related cooperation and investment. Every administration at the county level and above has an organisation in charge of foreign trade and investment, all of which are linked in a network. The provincial, municipality and prefecture authorities have delegated foreign-related examination and approval functions to the lower levels, thus simplifying the relevant proceedings.

A legal and regulatory framework safeguarding the autonomy of foreign investment has been established. This includes administrative rules and policy concerning the development of foreign trade, the establishment and management of economic development zones, favourable tax policies, loans, the right of use and transfer of state-owned land, real estate development, the management of foreign exchange, and simplification of entry and exit procedures.

In 2003, Zhejiang approved 4,442 foreign-invested projects with contracted foreign capital of US$12.05 billion, an increase of 77.5 percent over the last year. Actual utilised foreign investment increased by 72.4 percent to US$5.5 billion in the year. Ningbo was the main target for foreign investors, followed by Hangzhou, Jiaxing and Shaoxing. Over half of the FIEs in Ningbo came from Asian countries and those projects dealt with car parts, bio-engineering, infrastructure and education. Hong Kong was the biggest investor in Zhejiang. Other major investors were USA, EU, Taiwan and Japan.

In the coming years, foreign investors will be encouraged to look into the fields of chemicals, synthetic materials, new building materials, metal processing, textiles and light industry, machinery, electronics, communications, biological engineering, instruments, agricultural-processing, and new & advanced technologies. To transform the existing trade processing system, the Chinese government has decided to set up export processing zones in 15 pilot cities; Hangzhou has been selected as one of the cities in this trial programme.

HONG KONG

The HK SAR is ranked the freest economy in the world. It also has a huge stock exchange and one of the busiest international seaports.

Introduction

Hong Kong was once Britain's richest colony, and remained one at the start of the new century. Despite the economic downturn, it was admired and envied by many Chinese for being the richest and most stable part of China. With its unique position at the neutral point between East and West, being part of China yet not of it, Hong Kong was a key driving force for China's modernisation during most of its colony days.

History

For the Chinese residents in Hong Kong, the territory has for most of the past century been a home by necessity rather than choice. It was a place of temporary refuge for families in exodus from poverty or social and political instability in China. The political and economic upheaval has been the key engine driving Hong Kong's relentless quest for prosperity over its 150-year colonial interlude. Were it not for the Sino-Japanese wars, the Chinese civil war, the closing of China's economy for three decades from 1949, the Cold War, the disasters of the Great Leap Forward, and the excesses of the Cultural Revolution, all of which have severely impeded the social and economic progress of China, Hong Kong might still today be a second tier entrepot city on China's southern coast.

Hong Kong's economy has weathered dire challenges in the past century, but remained resilient and emerged even stronger after each event. During the Second World War in 1941, the Japanese Occupation reduced the territory's population by more than two-thirds. Hong Kong survived the trauma and re-emerged as an entrepot for trade between China and the world. In 1949, after the Communist's defeat of the Kuomintang, more than one million refugees from the Mainland poured into Hong Kong, causing severe strain to the land and resource scarce city. In 1950, the United Nations declared a blockade on China, which cut Hong Kong off from its natural hinterland in Southern China and shattered the entrepot trade that sustained its economy. Hong Kong's exports (90 percent were Chinese goods) fell by 34 percent

from 1951 to 1952. Many observers then doubted the territory's economic viability and survival.

The turning point for Hong Kong came when the barons of Shanghai's textile industries fled to Hong Kong, coupled with the support of British and other international bankers, which provided the foundation for Hong Kong to develop into a manufacturing powerhouse. Being close to the Mainland market, Hong Kong started building export-oriented and transnational production operations across Southeast Asia, laying the ground for a strong manufacturing sector which subsequently became the territory's economic engine.

The British and Mainland Chinese governments started negotiation on the future of Hong Kong in 1982, and resulted in an international treaty that called for the transfer of administration from the British to the Chinese on 1 July 1997. Under the Joint Declaration, Hong Kong would become a Special Administrative Region (SAR) of the People's Republic of China and its capitalist system and way of life would be preserved for 50 years. The "one country-two systems" framework under which Hong Kong is to be governed was further enshrined in the "Basic Law", the constitution for the Special Administrative Region after 1997.

The Return of Hong Kong

The return of Hong Kong to the motherland is both a great victory for the Chinese nation and a great event attracting global attention. It has wiped out the century-old humiliation of the Chinese nation and activated the proud national spirit. The smooth transition of power is a great tribute to the success of Deng's concept of "one country, two systems", which also facilitated the return of Macao to the motherland and the solution of the Taiwan issue, all with a view to achieving the complete reunification of the motherland.

Since Hong Kong's return, its previous socio-economic system and way of life have remained unchanged and its laws basically unchanged. The policies of "one country, two systems", "Hong Kong people administering Hong Kong" with a high degree of autonomy, and the Basic Law of the HKSAR have been implemented in an all-round way. Hong Kong now enjoys social stability, its residents have a sense of security and its economy is developing smoothly. The central government has given full support to the government of HKSAR in its work and in the measures it has taken for dealing with the impact of the Southeast Asian financial crisis.

Economic Developments

The Chief Executive announced in his Policy Speech 2001 a number of government initiatives to build up the territory for a prosperous future. Education is top on the agenda, plus other measures to improve the business environment of Hong Kong, and ways to relieve the economic hardship. The following key statistics give a snapshot of the territory's economic outlook:

- Real GDP rose to 1323.7 billion in 2002. The forecast of real GDP growth for 2002 is 2.3%.
- Foreign exchange reserves was US$112.3 billion at end of 2002.
- Retail sales fell by 0.8% in value despite a 1.7% in volume in the first 11 months of 2001.
- Unemployment climbed to 5.1% in 2002.
- Consumer prices dropped 3.1% at end of 2002.
- Inward direct investment reached US$404 billion at the end of 2002, up 80.6%.
- The number of tourists decreased 7.99% in the first eleven months of 2001.
- In 2002, total exports and imports fell by 7.4% and 11.5% respectively.

- The best lending rate was reduced to 5.125%following the US rate cut in December 2001.

Hong Kong is currently the world's freest economy, and the world's second highest per capita holding of foreign currency. It is the largest source of outward foreign direct investment in Asia, and also the top FDI recipient in Asia. It is the world's fourth largest foreign exchange reserves holding.

Real GDP has deteriorated steadily in 2001 from 2.2 percent in the first quarter to 0.8 percent in the second quarter and 0.3 percent in the third quarter. The slowdown of Hong Kong economy is largely due to the slower global demand, and has led to worsening employment conditions. The terrorist attacks in US led directly to weaker external demand, where merchandise exports declined by 4.0 percent. Exports of services were relatively better off, with a slower growth of 1.5 percent. While private consumption slowed to a 1.3 percent growth, investment spending increased 3.7 percent and government consumption spending maintained a 6.2 percent growth.

Consumer spending is much dampened by the lacklustre asset markets and the worsening labour market condition. The retail sales volume slowed to a 1.7 percent growth in the first 11 months of 2001, compared with the 8.1 percent upturn for the whole of 2000. Retail sales value fell by 0.8 percent in the 11-month period. Putting aside the factor of weak local demand, slowing retail sales were also due to the moderate inbound tourist spending. A high comparison base in early 2000, when the retail sales volume recorded double-digit growth, was another reason for the slowdown.

The Composite Consumer Price Index (CCPI) fell 3.8 percent in August 2002, less than the 0.2 percent in July 2002, despite the Housing Authority and Housing Society's waiver of public housing rentals for that month. For 2002, the CCPI was down 2.8 percent from the previous year. Due to the continued decline in import prices, overall consumer prices continued to slide.

The unemployment rate edged up to 8.7 percent in the three months ending July 2002. The government has planned training programmes for the next two years for both employed and unemployed workers, and is estimated to create 30,000 new jobs in the next few years.

Hong Kong's interest rates was pegged to the US's under the linked exchange rate system. On 3 July 2001, the interest rate was deregulated, all interest ceilings were lifted, and interest rates are subject to market forces.

The stock market has been sliding in tandem with the weak market performance in the US. At the end of 2002, the Hang Seng Index slid 24 percent from previous year to 11,397. The residential property market remained generally lacklustre, with deflated prices and rentals in the second quarter of 2001, down by 53 percent and 30 percent respectively from their peak in the third quarter of 1997. In a bid to revitalise the property market and stabilise market confidence, the amount of land supply has been restrained and certain anti-speculation measures relaxed.

The September 11 terrorist attack in US has also seriously affected tourism. The number of tourists increased by 5 percent in the first 11 months of 2002, significantly lower than the 20.7 percent increase for the whole of 2001. The average occupancy rate rose slightly to 84 percent in the first 11 months of 2002, from 79 percent a year ago. There are long term plans to develop new clusters and attractions, and upgrade of existing attractions to further enhance Hong Kong's position as a tourist destination. These initiatives will incur more than HK$18 billion in government investment in the coming five years, and include building the Hong Kong Disneyland and other tourist district enhancement schemes.

Future Directions

The Chief Executive of Hong Kong announced on 10 October 2001 a number of government initiatives to boost the territory's economy. To prepare Hong Kong for the knowledge-based economy, education is earmarked as the top priority in the economic development plan, with investment in the sector set to increase every year for the next five to 10 years. The education system will be undergoing significant reform, with emphasis on lifelong learning. Large-scale infrastructure projects, such as projects linking with the Pearl River Delta, will be developed. Other initiatives include increasing greening efforts to improve the living environment of Hong Kong.

The Policy Speech 2001 unveiled some government measures to improve the business environment of Hong Kong. Financial assistance worth $1.9 billion will be extended to small and medium enterprises through four new funds. These funds exceeded the budget by $600 million and are expected to benefit more than 100,000 enterprises. Other projects in the pipeline include:

- A new exhibition centre at Chek Lap Kok
- A Steering Committee on Logistics Development
- A Logistics Development Council

Following an agreement reached with the mainland authorities, the quota system will be abolished for the Hong Kong Group Tour Scheme from January 2002. The Policy Speech 2001 also targeted to create over 30,000 job opportunities in the short-term in areas including recreational and cultural facilities, housing estate management, education, environmental protection, public sanitation and greening.

The 2001/02 Budget delivered by the Financial Secretary on 7 March 2001 proposed no major change in Hong Kong's tax structure, with profit taxes and salary taxes remaining unchanged. Hong Kong will continue its policy direction to strengthen its status as an international financial and high-value-added services centre. The stamp duty on stock transactions has been reduced from 0.225 percent to 0.2 percent accordingly. The Budget also revealed the government's initiatives to strengthen economic partnership, such as infrastructural links with the mainland, especially the Pearl River Delta region. Investing for Hong Kong's long term growth, total expenditure on infrastructure and policy areas related to innovation and technology is set to increase much faster than other policy areas.

A deficit of HK$7.8 billion was recorded for the fiscal year 2000/01. The fiscal reserves were estimated at HK$430.3 billion at the end of March 2001. It is projected that the fiscal year 2001/02 will record a small deficit of HK$3 billion. Hong Kong has the world's fourth largest foreign currency reserves, after Japan, the Chinese mainland and Taiwan. At the end of November 2001, the amount of foreign exchange reserves held in the Exchange Fund was US$112.3 billion.

In an effort to foster technology development, the Chief Executive of Hong Kong appointed the Commission on Innovation and Technology in March 1998, which released its final report in July 1999. Recommendations were made on four major areas, namely institutional arrangements, human capital build-up, nurturing an innovation and technology culture, and creating an enabling business environment. To stimulate technology development and application in Hong Kong, the government's HK$5 billion Innovation and Technology Fund is open for applications from November 1999. A Cyberport housing technology-based enterprises including Motorola, Nortel, StarTV, Sybase, 3M and Vtech will be developed in partnership with the private sector at a cost of HK$13 billion.

Investment Flows

The total stock of direct investment in Hong Kong at end of 2002 was US$319 billion, 19.9 percent lower than end of 2001, equivalent to 256 percent of GDP in that year. One distinct feature of such direct investment was the flow of capital from non-operating companies in tax haven economies. British Virgin Island was the leading source of direct investment, accounting for 29 percent of the total. Excluding tax haven economies, the Chinese mainland was the most important source of direct investment in Hong Kong (26% of the total), followed by the Netherlands (6.6%), the UK (6.2%), USA (5.4%), Singapore (4.5%) and Japan (3.5%). The majority of investments was related to service industries such as real estate and business services, trading, banking, finance and communications.

On 2 November 1999, an agreement was reached with Walt Disney to build a theme park and a resort in Hong Kong. The Hong Kong Disneyland will be a key strategic infrastructure to strengthen Hong Kong's position as an international tourist destination. The Hong Kong government and Walt Disney will form a joint venture company and the government's total expenditure on this project will be HK$22.45 billion. The project will create around 6,000 jobs during the construction period and about 18,000 jobs at the opening of the park in 2005. It is projected that attendance during the first year of opening will be about five million, rising to a full capacity of about 10 million a year after 15 years.

Hong Kong ranked the largest source of outward foreign direct investment (FDI) and the top recipient of inward FDI in Asia in 2000, according to the United Nations' World Investment Report.

During the year, total investment outflows from Hong Kong climbed US$63.0 billion from US$19.3 billion, while total investment inflows to Hong Kong jumped US$64.4 billion from US$24.6 billion. The upsurge in investment flows was driven by a general improvement in the local business environment and transnational corporations' plan to invest on the mainland in anticipation of emerging business opportunities following China's accession to the WTO. It was also boosted by the cross-border M&A deal of China Mobile (Hong Kong) Ltd. to acquire seven mobile networks on the mainland. In terms of cumulative amount on approval basis, Hong Kong is the largest investor in the Chinese mainland, and is among the leading investors in Indonesia, Taiwan, Thailand, Vietnam and the Philippines.

Trading Industry

Hong Kong is the world's sixth largest (EU countries regarded as one entity) trading economy, and the world's ninth largest exporter of commercial services.

Exports rose 5.4 percent in 2002, after a 5.6 percent drop in the previous year. The rise was due to the global economic growth. Domestic exports fell by 14.7 percent and re-exports rose 7.7 percent.

The Chinese mainland, the US and the UK are Hong Kong's major export markets, which account for 31.6 percent, 32 percent and 5.8 percent of Hong Kong's total exports in 2002. Total exports to the Chinese mainland dropped by 16.5 percent in 2002 compared to 2001, while those to the US and the UK decreased by 11.9 percent and 11.5 percent respectively. The total exports to Japan in 2002 compared to 2001 decreased 26.9 percent, higher than exports to other countries, showing signs of worsening.

In 2002, imports to Hong Kong rose 5.4 percent after dropping 19 percent in 2001, leading to a trade deficit of US$59 billion, which is higher than the deficit of US$47.2 billion in the previous period. Hong Kong's sluggish macro-economic environment continued to affect retained imports, which account for around one-third of the imports. Import performance was affected by sluggish re-exports, which make up the remaining two-third of imports.

Guangdong's outward processing trade has fuelled Hong Kong's trade performance. In 2002, an estimated 70 percent of domestic exports and 50 percent of re-exports to the Chinese mainland were related to outward processing activities. As a whole, about 40 percent of Hong Kong's re-exports were destined for the Chinese mainland, and 60 percent of the re-exports were of Chinese origin. Nevertheless, the rise in direct shipments and transhipments has somewhat constrained the export performance of Hong Kong in recent years, although such cargo diversion effect has shown signs of easing.

Hong Kong is the world's leading exporter of toys, clocks, calculators, radios, hairdressing apparatus, telephone sets, travel goods and handbags, imitation jewellery and artificial flowers. It ranks second in the world as an exporter of clothing, fur clothing, textiles, watches, footwear and umbrellas.

Infrastructure Developments

The new airport at Chek Lap Kok was opened on 6 July 1998. The airport has a handling capacity of 35 million passengers and three million tonnes of air cargo a year, and is expandable in stages to 87 million passengers and nine million tonnes of cargo a year by 2040. With the second runway which started operation in 26 May 1999, the flight capacity has increased from 37 to 45 movements per hour.

Besides the new airport core projects, the government spent over HK$4.5 billion on other infrastructural improvements, including the construction of the Yuen Long Southern Bypass, the Ting Kau bridge, and the massive West Kowloon reclamation project. The government has also proceeded with the expansion of the rail network including the West Rail Phase 1 and the MTR Tseung Kwan O Extension Phase 1. Projects that will be launched at a later stage include the KCR East Rail extensions to Ma On Shan, Tsim Sha Tsui and Lok Ma Chau.

The first Kowloon-Canton Railway (KCR) inter-modal train started operation in 1994, and have trains that connect to Zhengzhou, Wuhan, Xian, Luoyang and Shijiazhuang every week, transporting freight from the Chinese mainland's inland provinces to Hong Kong's container ports.

The Lok Ma Chau border crossing started 24-hour operation in 1994. This arrangement provides an important link between just-in-time production in southern China and Hong Kong.

In September 1996, the Sino-British Joint Liaison Group planned the construction of container terminal number 9 (CT9). On completion, four berths for container vessels and two feeder berths for coastal vessels and barges will be added. The first berth is expected to be ready in May 2002. This project will increase the total capacity of Hong Kong's container terminals at Kwai Chung and Stonecutters Island from 11.5 million TEUs to 14.1 million TEUs per year.

The River Trade Terminal at Tuen Mun started operation in October 1998 to handle the rising volume of river boat transhipment from the Chinese mainland through Hong Kong. The terminal was designed to handle at least 2.1 million tonnes of cargo a year at the start of its operation, and to increase to 8.5 million tonnes within the next 18 months.

Connected to nine submarine cable systems, and with 36 satellite earth antennas that provide satellite-based telecommunications and television broadcasting services, Hong Kong is the largest teleport in Asia.

It also provides dedicated relay services for multinational companies, international press agencies and TV channels to download or upload their satellite signals over the Asia-Pacific region. Three overland systems have started operation to cater to the growing traffic between Hong Kong and the mainland. The Telecommunications Authority of Hong Kong has issued letters of intent to 13 companies in February 2000 for cable based External Fixed Telecommunications Network Services (EFTNS). An estimated investment of HK$9 billion is expected from these companies to set up seven new submarine cables and four new overland cables. These new cables will increase the band-width for external connections, which is an important part of Hong Kong's development as a regional telecommunications, internet and broadcasting hub.

Economic Relations with the Chinese Mainland

Hong Kong is the most important entrepot for the Chinese mainland, with 40 percent of the mainland's foreign trade going through Hong Kong. Out of Hong Kong's total re-exports of US$178.4 billion in 2000, 96 percent were either originated from or destined for the Chinese mainland. According to China's Customs statistics, Hong Kong ranked the third largest trading partner of the Chinese mainland, accounting for 11 percent of the country's total trade in 2000.

Of the 364,345 foreign-funded projects in the Chinese mainland as at end of 2000, more than half •

belong to Hong Kong investors. Contracted and utilised capital inflows from Hong Kong were US$328 billion and US$170.3 billion respectively, accounting for 48 percent and 49 percent of the national total.

Based on Hong Kong's official estimate, about 157,300 Hong Kong residents are working in the Chinese mainland, mostly in the manufacturing, commerce, restaurants and hotels and other business services.

On the other hand, the Chinese mainland is one of the leading investors in Hong Kong. According to official Chinese estimates, over 1,800 mainland-backed enterprises have registered in Hong Kong, with an estimated total asset value of US$205 billion at the end of 1998. The Bank of China and its 11 sister banks are now the second largest banking group in Hong Kong, after Hongkong Bank. The Bank of China also started to issue Hong Kong dollar banknotes in May 1994. In addition, China's other three specialised banks: the Industrial and Commercial Bank of China, the Agricultural Bank of China and the People's Bank of Construction of China have opened their first branch operations in Hong Kong. There are 19 Chinese banks in total operating in Hong Kong in terms of beneficiary ownership.

Hong Kong as a Regional Centre

Hong Kong's status as a regional centre is largely attributed to the following achievements:

- The world's busiest airport in terms of international cargo
- The world's busiest container port
- The best city for business in Asia
- Asia's largest gold bullion market, the fourth largest in the world

Asia's second largest stock market, the ninth largest in the world

- Asia's third largest foreign exchange market in terms of turnover, the seventh in the world

Following the Bank of China, the Industrial and Commercial Bank of China has moved its foreign exchange operations to Hong Kong. This further augmented Hong Kong's position as a foreign exchange centre. The banking sector plays a vital role in establishing Hong Kong as a major loan syndication centre in the region. Hong Kong is also a major source of venture capital in Asia.

Hong Kong is favoured by multinational companies as a regional business centre in the Asia Pacific, with 3,237 overseas companies having regional operations in Hong Kong, which is the highest number recorded in the past 11 years. Of these regional operations, 944 were regional headquarters, and 2,293 were regional offices. Japan has the largest total number of regional headquarters and offices in Hong Kong with 693 companies, followed by the US (641), the UK (253) and the Chinese mainland (242). In January 2001, the IMF established a sub-office in Hong Kong, underlining Hong Kong's position as a major international financial centre.

Hong Kong's trade with the Asia-Pacific region grew at an average annual rate of 16 percent since 1980 to reach US$233 billion in 1999. As a regional trading centre and entrepot, Hong Kong accounted for 20 percent of the intra-Asia

Pacific trade in 1999, despite its small population (about 0.2 percent of that of the Asia Pacific).

Hong Kong is an important banking and financial centre for the region. At the end of November 2001, there were 148 licensed banks, 48 restricted licensed banks and 55 deposit-taking companies operating in Hong Kong. At the end of October 2001, total loans to finance international trade amounted to US$12.1 billion, and other loans for use outside Hong Kong amounted to US$41.5 billion. According to a survey in 2001, Hong Kong's average net daily turnover of foreign exchange and derivatives transactions amounted to US$71 billion. Although this represents a 13.4 percent decline from 1998, Hong Kong remains a major centre for trading foreign exchange. Hong Kong was the seventh largest foreign exchange trading centre. Following the Bank of China, the Industrial and Commercial Bank of China has moved its foreign exchange operations to Hong Kong. This further augmented Hong Kong's position as a foreign exchange centre. The banking sector plays a vital role in establishing Hong Kong as a major loan syndication centre in the region. Hong Kong is also a major source of venture capital in Asia.

Hong Kong's stock market is highly internationalised, with a large number of international stock brokers. At the end of November 2001, there were 849 companies listed on the stock exchange, including 97 companies on the growth enterprise market (GEM), with a total market capitalisation of US$500 billion. Currently, 118 Chinese mainland enterprises are listed on the local stock market. At the end of April 2001, Hong Kong's stock market ranked the world's ninth largest in terms of market capitalisation.

With 0.17 million telephone lines (including 412,356 fax lines) as at end of 2002, Hong Kong is a leading telecommunications hub for the Asia-Pacific region IDD telephone services are available to over 230 overseas countries or regions and to over 2,200 Chinese mainland cities. From 1989 to 2000, the total international telephone traffic grew by an average of 15 percent per annum to 4.9 billion minutes in 2000. Seventy-three out of every 100 persons own a telephone set. Furthermore, the number of mobile telephone users grew rapidly to over 0.17 million at the end of August 2002 from about 0.067 million at the end of 1998.

With the increasing popularity of the internet, Hong Kong's dial-up internet traffic increased tremendously from 292 million-call minutes in January 1998 to peak at 1,441 million-call minutes in August 2000. However, due to the proliferation of broadband services, the number fell to 0.05 million in 2002. According to a government survey, 37.2 percent of business establishment had an Internet connection as of June 2001. The percentage was much higher for large establishments (86%) and medium establishments (64%).

Hong Kong's position as an international conferences and trade fairs centre contributes to the rising number of business visitors. More than 300 international conventions and exhibitions are held in Hong Kong each year.

MACAU

The service and tourism sectors are the main sources of revenue. Banking and insurance sectors are showing signs of rapid growth.

Introduction

As a colony of Portugal in the 16th century, Macau was the first European settlement in the Far East, and the oldest European colony in China. It became the Macau Special Administrative Region (SAR) of China on 20 December 1999, following an agreement signed by China and Portugal on 13 April 1987. China has promised Macau a high degree of autonomy in all matters except foreign and defence affairs, with its "one country, two systems" policy.

History

Macau was the name given by the Portuguese. In the first century of its existence, Macau became prosperous as a result of trading with China and Japan. After Japan terminated its contact with the rest of the world, Macau went into a steady decline.

No Chinese government had recognised the illegal occupation of Macau by Portugal until 1979, when China and Portugal established diplomatic relations and the Portuguese side affirmed that Macau was Chinese territory under Portuguese administration. On 20 December 1999, after 400 years of colonisation, China regained its sovereignty over Macau.

Macau has a long history with a rich and varied culture. The Macau Government and people attach and great importance to the preservation and development of Macau culture imbued with the feature of Sino-European cultures.

Location

Macau is situated at the sea coast of southeastern part of China to the west bank of the Pearl River Delta, surrounded by sea from three sides, linking the Zhuhai Economic Special Zone in the north of Guangdong Province, and facing Hong Kong which is an hour away to the east by hovercraft.

Macau comprises Macau Peninsula, Taipa and Coloane islands, with a total area of 23.5 km^2. More than 100 years ago, Macau was only the Macau Peninsula which occupied an area of only 2.78 km^2. After 100 years of land reclamation, the Macau Peninsula is now 9.1 km^2, and Taipa Island and Coloane Island are 6.33 km^2 and 8.07 km^2 respectively.

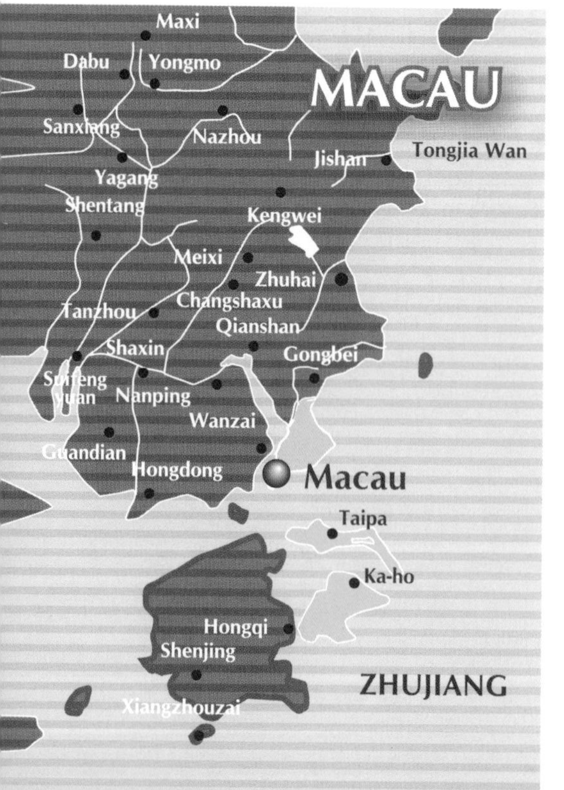

People

The Macau Peninsula is the political, economic, transportation and cultural centre of Macau, where 94 percent of the population and overwhelming majority of industrial and commercial industries are found.

Macau's total population is 0.4546 million, more than 96 percent of which are Chinese, and the rest mainly Portuguese. The locals, including the locally born Portuguese, speak Cantonese. The official languages are Portuguese

Chinese. English language is also commonly used.

Macau has seen significant demographic growth in the last two decades, with population increasing at an annual rate of around four percent. An average of 20,000 passengers enter Macau via the Outer Harbour ferry terminal each day, while around 50,000 people cross the Border Gates checkpoint at the border with mainland China.

Over 96 percent of Macau's population speaks Chinese, while Portuguese is spoken by around two percent. Cantonese is the most commonly used daily dialect but Mandarin is also widely spoken. Hokkien is another Chinese dialect commonly heard in Macau.

Over 80 percent of Macau's population has lived in the territory for over 10 years. 45 percent of the population was born in Macau, and another 45 percent was born in Mainland China, while less than 10 percent of the residents are from other places.

Climate

Macau has the monsoon climate of the East Asian Subtropical Zone. The average annual temperature is 22°C, the hottest month of the year falls in July, the average temperature is over 30°C; the coldest month falls in January, the average temperature of which is 14°C, the lowest, only a few degrees. The average annual relative humidity is 80 percent. Macau has typical foggy weather in Spring. Rainfall is frequent from July to September.

Political System

Macao People ruling Macao and A High Degree of Autonomy

The Government of the People's Republic of China resumed sovereignty over Macao on 20th December 1999, when the Special Administrative Region of Macao was established in accordance with

Article 31 of the Constitution of the People's Republic of China. In harmony with the principle of "one country, two systems", the previous capitalist system and way of life shall remain unchanged for 50 years.

The Government of the Macao Special Administrative Region ("MSAR") is the executive authority of the Macao Special Administrative Region. The Chief Executive is the head of the Government, and General Secretariats, Directorates of Services, Departments and Divisions are established in the Government of MSAR.

Economic Development

After the Asian financial crisis, Macau's economy began to show signs of recovery at the end of 1999, particularly in the tourism sector, which is a vital part of the local economy. In 2002, almost 115.3 million tourists visited Macau. Exports also recorded a total of over US$1 billion in 2002.

Macau's economy has been experiencing rapid growth since the 1980s. Gross Domestic Product (GDP) stood at US$1,287 million in 1998, growing to US$54 billion in 2002. Average per capita income stood at US$15,355 in 2002. Alongside economic development, the gambling, manufacture and export, finance and insurance, and real estate sectors have all carved significant roles in Macau's economy.

After the decline of the industrial sector due to competition from neighbouring regions, the service and tourism sectors have emerged as the main source of revenue for Macau. Since 1992, tourism revenue has surpassed income from exports. The tourism sector and related services employ 30 percent of the working population, generating 40 percent of the Territory's total revenue.

Casino gambling has a long history in Macau. Sociedade de Turismo e Diversoes de Macau (STDM) was granted the casino monopoly franchise in 1962 with a concession contract under which the concessionaire must pay an annual gambling tax which has been revised over the years and currently stands at 31.8 percent of gross gambling receipts. Revenue from Gambling accounts for 40 percent of government revenue. A series of regulations have been implemented to ensure a healthy development of the gaming industry after its liberalisation.

Macau's manufacturing industry has been much affected by the lower labour cost in regional countries. As such, the territory's manufacturing industry has been making the transition from traditional labour-intensive production to capital-intensive production. The increasingly competitive external conditions have threatened the continual growth of the territory's traditional industries, which will have to exploit new markets for top quality and upmarket products. In 2002, domestic exports decreased by 1.99 percent and re-exports increased by 27.3 percent respectively, and resulted in a trade deficit of US$140 million.

The United States of America and some countries in the European Union, France, Germany, the United Kingdom, the mainland China, Japan, Hong Kong and Australia are among Macau's biggest export markets (mostly for textiles and toys). On the other hand, Macau imports consumer essentials such as food, drink, tobacco, mostly from the mainland, countries in the European Union, the United States of America as well as from Japan. In addition to these goods, raw materials, semi-processed products, fuel and lubricants are also imported.

Macau has a stable finance system. Its quasi-central bank, the Macau Monetary Authority supervises the monetary, financial, banking and insurance markets. The currency pataca is pegged to the Hong Kong dollar at a fixed rate of 1.03MOP to one HK dollar, based on parity between the Hong Kong dollar and the US dollar.

As at end of 2002, the Exchange Reserves of SAR reached US$17.9 billion, together with the US$1.39 billion financial reserve that was transferred from the Land Fund to the SAR Government after its establishment, consolidating the stability of the SAR's currency and its public finance.

The banking and insurance sectors are showing signs of rapid growth. There are 22 licensed commercial banks and one offshore bank in Macau, using local capital, and capital from the mainland, Taiwan, and other countries and region. Total assets of the banking sector is US$1.84 billion. Total deposit had reached US$1.37 billion, while total credit equals US$6.4 billion. Bank of China and Banco Nacional Ultramarino are the two officially appointed banks sharing the function of note issuing.

Macau's manufacturing industry has been much affected by the lower labour cost in regional countries. As such, the territory's manufacturing industry has been making the transition from traditional labour-intensive production to capital-intensive production.

Currently, there are three financial companies, 26 insurance companies and nine companies providing exchange service in Macau. A series of international insurance groups, including one with capital equity of more than US$190 billion, have set up branches in the Territory. The insurance sector has recorded remarkable develop-ment over the last 10 years. At the end of 2001, net premium by insurance products reached a total of US$113 million. Growth in the insurance sector also leads to a constant increase in job vacancies. Besides, a Hong Kong based foreign exchange investment agent was also licensed to operate in Macau.

The real estate sector is experiencing stagnation after 10 years of rapid development, owing to changes in the region. As a means of stimulating the sector, the government of MSAR is planning measures to control land supply and offer incentives in investment immigration schemes. From 1990 to 2002, 40,529 units were built over an area of 472,200 m^2. Real estate transactions have risen to 4,209 units, and US$350 million.

Economic Integration in the Pearl River Delta Triangle

The Pearl River Delta economic triangle has resulted in intimate economic relations between the special economic zone of Guangdong Province and Hong Kong and Macau. In 2000, trade between Macau and Guangdong Province reached US$660 million. Investment in the Guangdong Province by companies in Macau increased 155 percent over the previous year, with over US$128 million in contracts, spreading

Macau is among Asia's advanced cities in terms of infrastructure facilities such as international airport, road network, new urban planning, the most advanced sewage treatment plants and solid waste incineration plants in Asia. Modern office tower and high class hotels, coupled with highly qualified workforce, make Macau an ideal place to work and live in.

over 6,366 projects from real estate road network, exhibition and consultative services.

Macau's investment environment is characterised by free competition and generous fiscal regime. Macau is an extremely desirable location for investments for the following reasons:

- The local system is free from foreign exchange restrictions
- Free circulation and exchange of currency
- Free repatriation of profits and assets
- Simple tax system
- Young work force
- Advanced telecommunications network
- Excellent transportation infrastructure for merchandise.

Macau's milestones for its domestic economic development are:

- Consolidate its role as a free port
- Ensure competitiveness and free competition for investments
- Speedy economic recovery
- Reduce the unemployment rate
- Maintain stability in the finance system
- Build up a modern, diversified, constantly developing economy
- Enhance Macau's image as a major international centre.

In terms of external economic policy, Macau is committed to the following:

- Foster economic cooperation with Hong Kong and Pearl River Delta regions
- Maximise each party's complementary advantages
- Introduce a system for economic coordination between governments, with focus on the opportunities arising from China's entry into WTO
- Continue to promote traditional trade relations

with the European Union and the Latin countries, while developing new international markets.

Macau is among Asia's advanced cities in terms of infrastructure facilities such as international airport, road network, new urban planning, the most advanced sewage treatment plants and solid waste incineration plants in Asia. Modern office tower and high class hotels, coupled with highly qualified workforce, make Macau an ideal place to work and live in.

Macau has committed itself to improving the physical investment environment, increasing international competitiveness and creating favourable conditions for regional cooperation. The major investment programmes are as follows:

- **Complementary infrastructures at TaipaColoane Land Reclamation Site**

Following the completion of Lotus Bridge and COTAI Border Checkpoint, subsequent projects will be on the main roads (to provide a basic link into the other urban roads) as well as the basic sewage and drainage systems, electricity supplies and telecommunications cables.

- **Olympic Swimming Pools**

An Olympic swimming pool estimated at US$15 million is being planned next to the Macau Stadium on Taipa Island in preparation for the 2005 East Asian Games. The swimming pool stadium will cover 7,200 m^2.

- **Renovation for the Border Gate Checkpoint**

Increasing contacts between Macau and Zhuhai has led to the Macau Government considering renovating the Border Gate Checkpoint. Construction of the new Border Gate Checkpoint started in 2001. The new Border Gate Checkpoint will cover 30,000 m^2. The number of counters for travellers and passages for vehicles will be increased. The Border Gate will be retained and a Border Gate Square will be built.

- **The Third Macau-Taipa Access**

With an increasing population, the traffic congestion of the two bridges, especially that of the Ponte Nobre de Carvalho, has worsened. Hence, another Macau-Taipa Access, a double deck bridge which will open in all weather conditions, is being planned.

- **Environmental Protection**

The Solid Waste Incineration Plant costing US$67 million started operation in 1992. Its technology for environmental protection is believed to be the currently most advanced in the Asia-Pacific region.

The Territory's third sewage treatment plant came into operation in April 1999. All the territory's waste water is given appropriate treatment (to avoid pollution) prior to being discharged into the sea. The first sewage treatment plant was built on the Macau peninsula and opened in 1996, while the second plant, on Taipa, was opened in 1996.

The Government of the MSAR is dedicated to continue environmental inspections, upgrade existing facilities for environmental protection such as the sound pollution network, provide forums to enhance public and corporate awareness on environmental protection, and comply with international conventions on environment protection to ensure sustained growth.

Infrastructure Upgrading

Macau International Airport

Costing US$1,200 million, the Macau International Airport was the largest and most important infrastructure project built in the territory in the 1990s. It is located on Taipa Island, where roads link it to Friendship Bridge and Lotus Bridge, providing access into the peninsula of Macau, the Chinese mainland, as well as the ferry terminal. The airport has the capacity for six million passengers a year, and air routes that cover the important cities in China and other countries.

Road networks and bridges

Two bridges and a six-lane highway link the peninsula of Macau to the islands of Taipa and Coloane, and have played an important role in the rapid development of the islands. Friendship Bridge is 4.5 km long and cost about US$75 million. It was built in 1994 and was the second bridge to link Macau to the islands. The isthmus that provides a road link between Taipa and Coloane was extended in 1998 and has three carriageways in each direction. Lotus Bridge, which cost about US$25 million, came into operation in March 2000. It connects Taipa and Montanha Island before linking to the highway between Guangzhou and Zhuhai. This new bridge established a new border between the MSAR and the Mainland and helps to ease the bad traffic conditions at Portas do Cerco Border Checkpoint.

Macau Ferry Terminal

The new ferry terminal started operation in 1993. With a capacity of 30 million passengers a year, it has significantly enhanced the Territory's capacity to handle tourists from Hong Kong and other regions in the Mainland. Jetfoils are the most commonly used form of transport by tourists visiting Macau.

Container and oil terminal

Operations at the new container began in December 1991, while that at the oil terminal started in June 1995. Both are at Ka Ho Port on Coloane Island. The new terminal bolstered Macau's role as a trading hub between the Chinese hinterland, neighbouring regions and the rest of the world. This project was crucial to keeping the Territory on the right track for development. The container terminal will be extended as required by Macau's economic development.

Nam Van Lakes Project

The largest private investment project since July 1991, this project costs US$1,875 million and covers 130 ha, which include two artificial lakes (with a total area of 80 ha) and five development sections. There are four zones covering 1,472,500 m2 being used for building construction. The Lake increase the land area of Macau peninsula by 20 percent.

The US$120 million Nam Van Tower, with a height of 338 metres, is an investment by Sociedade de Turismo e Diversoes de Macau (Macau Tourism and Amusement Company) in the Nam Van Lake area, and is due for completion soon.

Macau Cultural Centre

This project costs US$100 million. The Cultural Centre is located in the outer Harbour Land Reclamation zone near the Macau Ferry Terminal. In terms of size, it is one of the Territory's largest infrastructure projects and is visible from the ferry terminal. The superior facilities provide an excellent environment for cultural performances in the Territory.

FOREIGN AIRLINES IN CHINA

AIR CANADA	CONTACT NUMBER	
Beijing	86 10 6468 2001	
Hong Kong	852 2867 8111	
Shanghai Office	86 21 6279 2999	
AIR FRANCE		
Beijing	86 10 6588 1369	Customer Service
	86 10 6588 1388	Reservations
	86 10 6459 0129	Beijing Airport
Shanghai	86 21 6350 1496	Customer Service
	86 21 6360 6688	Reservations
	86 21 6835 5666	Shanghai Airport
AIR NEW ZEALAND		
Hong Kong	852 2524 9041	
ALITALIA		
Beijing	86 10 6567 2299	
ASIANA AIRWAYS		
Beijing	86 10 6468 4000	
Changchun	86 431 894 8948	
Chengdu	86 28 8676 7518	
Chongqing	86 23 6383 3908	
Hangzhou	86 571 8577 3699	
Harbin	86 451 234 4000	
Hong Kong	852 2523 8585	
Guangzhou	86 20 8760 9037	
Guilin	86 773 588 4000	
Nanjing	86 25 469 1595	
Shanghai	86 21 6219 4000	
Shenyang	86 10 6468 4000	
Tingji	86 431 894 8948	
Xi'an	86 29 870 3405	
Yantai	86 535 662 8000	
BRITISH AIRWAYS		
Beijing	86 10 8511 6699 / 5599	
FINNAIR		
Beijing	86 10 6512 7180 / 81	
Hong Kong	852 2117 1238	
Shanghai	86 21 5292 9400	
GARUDA AIRLINES		
Hong Kong	852 2840 0000	
Shanghai	86 21 5385 5398	
IRAN AIR		
Beijing	86 10 6512 0047	

JAPAN AIRLINES

Beijing	86 10 6513 0888
Guangzhou	86 20 8669 6688
Hong Kong	852 2523 0081
Kunming	86 871 315 8000
Qingdao	86 532 571 0088
Shanghai	86 21 6288 3000 / 4666
Tianjin	86 22 2313 9766
Xiamen	86 592 268 7777
Xi'an	86 29 870 8040

LUFTHANSA

Beijing	86 10 6465 4488
Shanghai	86 021 5830 4400

MALAYSIA AIRLINES

Beijing	86 10 6505 2681/ 2/ 3
Guangzhou	86 20 8335 8828/ 38
Hong Kong	852 2521 8181
Shanghai	86 21 6279 8607
Xiamen	86 592 210 8388/ 6088

PAKISTAN INTERNATIONAL

Beijing	86 10 6505 1681/ 82/ 83

PHILIPPINES AIRLINES

Hong Kong	852 2301 9300
Xiamen	86 592239 4729/ 30/ 65

QUANTAS

Beijing	86 10 6467 3337
Shanghai	86 21 6279 8660

ROYAL BRUNEI AIRLINES

Beijing	86 10 6465 1625 / 6
	86 10 6465 1576
Guangzhou	86 20 8612 3962
Shanghai	86 21 5298 6688 / 5240

SINGAPORE AIRLINES

Beijing	86 10 6505 2233
Guangzhou	86 20 8732 0600
Shanghai	86 21 6289 1000

THAI AIRLINES

Shanghai	86 21 5298 5555

VIRGIN ATLANTIC AIRWAYS

Shanghai	86 21 5353 4600

CHINESE AIRLINES OFFICES

AIR CHINA	CONTACT NUMBER	
Beihai	86 779 305 3468	
Beijing	86 10 6601 3336	Domestic Reservation
	86 10 6601 6667	International Reservation
	86 10 6605 0875	Night Reservation
Changchun	86 431 896 9746	Fax
Changsha	86 731 225 3354	
Chengdu	86 28 8665 6317 / 4321	
Dalian	86 411 480 1159	
Fuzhou	86 591 760 4867	
Guangzhou	86 20 8363 7523	
Guilin	86 773 281 2789	
Haikou	86 898 6672 5086 / 5186	
Harbin	86 451 233 4603	
Kunming	86 871 315 9165	
Lanzhou	86 931 887 7365	Fax
Nanjing	86 25 481 8747	
Qingdao	86 532 388 3650	
Shanghai	800 8201 999	Hotline
	86 21 5239 7227	
Shenyang	86 24 2318 0409	
Shenzhen	86 755 8377 9948	
Urumqi	86 991 588 1775	
Wuhan	86 27 8361 8666	
Xiamen	86 592 508 4377	
Xi'an	86 29 870 9689	
Yantai	860535 628 5744	
Zhengzhou	86 371 595 6285	Fax

AIR MACAU	
Beijing	86 10 6515 8988 / 9398
Guilin	86 773 286 5400 / 1
Haikou	86 898 6853 3269
Kunming	86 871 716 7378
Nanjing	86 25 679 9127 / 9
Shanghai	86 21 6248 1110
Xiamen	86 592 222 9260

CHINA NORTHERN AIRLINES		
Anshan	86 412 223 5817	
Changchun	86 431 272 5001	
Dalian	86 411 761 9290	86 411 281 8858
Harbin	86 451 362 5521	
Sanya	86 898 8827 7580	
Shenyang	86 24 2324 4137	86 24 2319 8713

CHINA SOUTHERN AIRLINES

Beijing	86 10 6459 0539 / 6490
Chengdu	86 28 671 2777
Guangzhou	86 20 8613 0870/ 3
Hainan	86 898 6671 9742
Hubei	86 27 8530 0477 / 1811
Hunan	86 731 455 7095
Shanghai	86 21 6211 3604
Shenzhen	86 755 605 6081 / 73

CHINA YUNNAN AIRLINES

Yunnan	86 871 711 2638

NORTHWEST CHINA AIRLINES

Shaanxi	86 29 8879 2299
	86 800 840 2 299 Toll Free

SHANGHAI AIRLINES

Beijing	86 10 6606 1260	86 800 820 1018
Chengdu	86 28 8612 7000	86 800 820 1018
Chongqing	86 23 6362 8000	86 800 8201018
Fuzhou	86 591 3300 721	86 800 820 1018
Guangzhou	86 20 8666 8800	86 800 820 1018
Guilin	86 773 282 7046	86 800 820 1018
Haikou	86 898 6679 1927	86 800 820 1018
Hangzhou	86 571 8511 9528	86 800 820 1018
Harbin	86 451 8263 7953	86 800 820 1018
Kunming	86 871 313 8502	86 800 820 1018
Nanjing	86 25 849 9757	86 800 820 1018
Qingdao	86 532 572 5519	86 800 820 1018
Sanya	86 898 8826 5322	86 800 820 1018
Shanghai	86 21 6255 0550	86 800 620 8888
Shenyang	86 24 2323 5858	86 800 820 1018
Shenzhen	86 755 8324 1431	86 800 820 1018
Taiyuan	86 351 413 9910	86 800 820 1018
Wuhan	86 27 8224 1008 ext 801	86 800 820 1018
Xiamen	86 592 221 0600	86 800 820 1018
Xi'an	86 29 8426 1630	86 800 820 1018
Macau	853 7878 77	

SHANDONG AIRLINES

Jinan	86 531 691 6737	86 531 852 9757 / 67
Shandong	86 531 873 0777	
	86 531 873 7888 Customer Service	
	86 531 96777 National Booking	
Qingdao	86 532 575 5658	

SOUTHWEST CHINA AIRLINE

Chengdu	86 28 8666 8080	86 28 8625 8800
	86 28 8625 9900	86 28 8522 6600

XIAMEN AIRLINES

Xiamen	86 592 573 9888

COURIER SERVICES

UPS

Beijing	86 10 6530 1234
Shanghai	86 21 6391 5555
Guangzhou	86 20 8348 6666

HOTELS

BEIJING	CONTACT NUMBER
Beijing Jinglun Hotel	86 10 6500 2266
Crowne Plaza Beijing	86 10 6513 3388
Grand Hyatt	86 10 8518 1234

Grand View Garden Hotel	86 10 6353 8899
Great Wall Sheraton Hotel	86 10 6590 5566
Holiday Inn Beijing - Lido	86 10 6437 6688
Prime Hotel	86 10 6513 6666
Scitech Hotel,Beijing	86 10 6512 3388
The St.Regis	86 10 6460 6688
Tianlun Dynasty Hotel	86 10 6513 8888

CHENGDU

Amara Hotel	86 28 8692 2233
Crowne Plaza Hotel	86 28 8678 6666
Huayang Garden City Hotel	86 28 8666 3388
Jinjiang Hotel	86 28 8550 6666
Minshan Hotel	86 28 8558 3333
Sheraton Lido Hotel	86 28 8676 8999
Tibet Hotel	86 28 8318 3388
Yinhe Dynasty Hotel	86 28 8661 8888

CHONGQING

Chongqing Guesthouse	86 23 6384 5888
Harbour Plaza	86 23 6370 0888
Hilton Chongqing	86 23 8903 9999
Holiday Inn Chongqing	86 23 6280 3380
Huang Jia Hotel	86 23 6352 8888
Marriott Hotel	86 23 6388 8888

DALIAN

Furama Hotel	86 411 263 0888
Hilton Dalian	86 411 252 9999
Ramada Dalian	86 411 280 8888
Shangri-La Hotel	86 411 252 5000
Swissotel Dalian	86 411 230 3388
Wanda International Hotel	86 411 362 8888

GUANGZHOU

Asia International Hotel	86 20 6128 8888
Baiyun Hotel	86 20 8333 3998
China Hotel	86 20 8666 6888
Garden Hotel	86 20 8333 8989
Holiday Inn City Centre	86 20 8776 6999
Ramada Pearl Hotel	86 20 8737 2988
Victory Hotel	86 20 8121 6688
White Swan Hotel	86 20 8188 6968

GUILIN

Guilin Bravo Hotel	86 773 282 3950
Guilin Plaza	86 773 588 2688
Guilin Ronghu Hotel	86 773 289 3811

Royal Garden Hotel	86 773 581 2411
Sheraton Guilin Hotel	86 773 282 5588

HAIKOU

Golden Coast Lawton Hotel	86 898 6625 9888
Golden Sea View Hotel	86 898 6853 7718
Huandao Tide Hotel	86 898 6626 8888

HANGZHOU

Hangzhou Tower	86 571 8515 3911
Holiday Inn Hangzhou	86 571 8527 1188
Ramada Plaza Haihua,Hangzhou	86 571 8721 5888
Shangri-La Hotel, Hangzhou	86 571 8797 7951
Wanghu Hotel, Hangzhou	86 571 8707 8888

JINAN

Crowne Plaza Hotel-Jinan	86 531 602 9999
Sofitel Silver Plaza Hotel	86 531 606 8888

KUNMING

Bank Hotel Kunming	86 871 315 8888
Harbour Plaza Kunming	86 871 538 6688
King World Hotel	86 871 313 8888
Kunming Hotel	86 871 316 2063
New Era Hotel	86 871 362 4999
Weilong Hotel	86 871 361 6688

NANJING

Central Hotel Nanjing	86 25 8473 3888
International Conference Hotel of Nanjing	86 25 8443 0888
Jinling Hotel	86 25 8471 1888
Nanjing Grand Hotel	86 25 8331 1999
Nanjing New Century Hotel	86 25 8540 8888
Nanjing Zhongshan Hotel	86 25 8336 1888
Ramada Yihua Nanjing	86 25 8330 8888
Shangri-La Dingshan, Nanjing	86 25 5880 2888
Sheraton Nanjing Kingsley Hotel & Towers	86 25 8666 8888
Xuanwu Hotel, Nanjing	86 25 8335 8888

NANNING

Mingyuan Xindu Hotel	86 771 211 8988
Yongjiang Hotel	86 771 218 0888

SANYA

Resort Horizon	86 898 8856 7888
Sanya Royal Garden Resort	86 898 8222 8888

SHANGHAI

Central Hotel	86 21 5396 5000
Cypress Hotel	86 21 6268 8868
Jing An Hotel	86 21 6248 1888
Jin Jiang Hotel	86 21 6258 2582
Oriental Riverside Hotel	86 21 5037 0000
Peace Hotel	86 21 6321 6888
Pudong Shangri-La	86 21 6882 8888
Radisson SAS Lansheng Hotel	86 21 5588 8000
Sofitel Jin Jiang Oriental Pudong Shanghai	86 21 5050 4888
St. Regis Hotel & Resorts	86 21 5050 4567

SHENZHEN

Crowne Plaza Shenzhen	86 755 2693 6888
Golden Lustre Hotel	86 755 8225 2888
LandMark Hotel	86 755 8217 2288
Nan Hai Hotel	86 755 2669 2888
Novotel Watergate Hotel	86 755 8213 7999
Panglin Hotel	86 755 2518 5888
Pavilion Hotel	86 755 8207 8888
Shangri-La Shenzhen Hotel	86 755 8233 0888
Sunshine Hotel	86 755 8223 3888

SUZHOU

Bamboo Grove Hotel	86 512 6520 5601
Gloria Plaza Hotel, Suzhou	86 512 6521 8855
Sheraton Suzhou Hotel & Tower	86 512 6510 3388

WUHAN

Holiday Inn Riverside Hotel	86 27 8471 6688
Shangri-La Wuhan Hotel	86 27 8580 6868
Wuhan Asia Hotel	86 27 8380 7777

XIAMEN

Hua Qiao Hotel	86 592 266 0888
Mandarin Hotel	86 592 602 3333
Marco Polo Xiamen Hotel	86 592 509 1888

XI'AN

Ana Grand Castle Hotel	86 29 8723 1800
Bell Tower Hotel	86 29 8760 0000
Dynasty Hotel	86 29 8862 6262
Grand New World Hotel	86 29 8721 6868
Hyatt Regency	86 29 8723 1234
Jianguo Hotel-Xian	86 29 8323 8888
Shangri-La Golden Flower Hotel, Xian	86 29 8323 2981
Sheraton Hotel, Xian	86 29 8426 1888

TRAVEL SERVICES

TRAVEL SERVICES	CONTACT NUMBER
China Air International Travel Service	86 10 6605 6434
China Business Travel	86 10 8152 8702
China Civil Int. Tourist Corporation	86 10 6447 6693
China International Travel	86 10 6601 2025
China National Tourism Administration	86 10 6520 1114
China Peace International Tourism Co.	86 10 6501 0234
CTS International Convention & Exhibition Co.Ltd.	86 10 6559 8489
Kingsway Incentives	86 10 6492 8745
BEIJING	
Beijing China International Travel Service	86 10 6515 0515
Beijing Overseas Tourism Co.	86 10 6515 8573
Beijing Travel Service	86 10 6512 2441
SHANGHAI	
Shanghai Dazhong International Travel Service	86 21 6353 2130
Shanghai Great World International Travel Service	86 21 6351 4293
Shanghai Qiangsheng International Travel Service	86 21 6258 2909
CHINA INTERNATIONAL TRAVEL SERVICE	
Anhui	86 551 281 2931
Chongqing	86 23 6582 4488
Fujian	86 591 337 0146
Gansu	86 931 886 1333
Guangdong	86 20 866 6889
Guangxi	86 771 280 2042
Guizhou	86 851 581 6348
Hainan	86 898 536 3161
Hebei	86 311 581 5102
Heilongjiang	86 451 366 1151
Henan	86 371 595 2072
Hubei	86 27 8783 2087
Hunan	86 731 228 0444
Inner Mongolia	86 471 692 4494
Jiangsu	86 25 342 8999
Jiangxi	86 791 628 8892
Jilin	86 431 565 6313
Kunming	86 871 313 2895
Liaoning	86 24 8680 6980
Nanjing	86 25 342 8999
Ningbo	86 574 731 2805
Ningxia	86 951 504 5555
Qinghai	86 971 613 3943
Shaanxi	86 29 526 2066
Shandong	86 531 296 5858

Shanxi	86 351 724 4312
Sichuan	86 28 667 3689
Suzhou	86 512 520 9362
Tianjin	86 22 2835 8349
Xinjiang	86 991 282 7467
Yunnan	86 871 351 4788
Zhejiang	86 571 515 2888

PROFESSIONAL SERVICES

ASCENDAS

Singapore	0065 6774 1033
Shanghai	8621 5878 2323
Beijing	8610 6787 8118
Suzhou	86512 6761 3388

INDUSTRIAL PARKS

MUNICIPALITIES

BEIJING

Beijing Economic-Technological Development Area

Situated in the southeast suburb of Beijing, the BDA is situated at the west of the entrance to the Beijing-Tianjin-Tanggu Expressway and south of the planned Fifth Ring Road. Four pillar industries: electronic & information industry, laser-machinery-electronic integrated industry, biotechnology and new pharmaceutical industry, new energy and material industry have taken shape in BDA.

Address: 4 Wanyuan Street, Beijing, China
Post Code: 100176
Tel: 86 10 6788 1105
Fax: 86 10 6788 1207
E-mail: webmaster@bda.gov.cn
Website: www.bda.gov.cn

Tianzhu Airport Industrial Zone

Tianzhu Airport Industrial Zone was founded in 1994, with a designated area of 6.6 km^2 and 1 km west to the Capital International Airport. After near ten years' of development and construction, a modern high-tech Zone has been formed with IT and modern logistics as the major industries, featured by foreign-oriented economy and based on high-tech enterprises.

Address: West of the Capital International Airport, Beijing, China
Post Code: 101312
Tel: 86 10 8048 9568/ 9922/ 9567
Fax: 86 10 8048 9568
E-mail: baizinfo@public.bta.net.cn
Website: www.chinabaiz.com

Zhongguancun Science Park

Zhongguancun Science Park is the first state-level high-tech development zone which was approved by the State Council in May 1988. It is China's biggest science park with a high concentration of scientific and technological institutions and intellectual resources. It is also the largest software development and production centre in China. Zhongguancun Science Park in fact is comprised of five science zones like Haidian Zone, Fengtai Zone, Changping Zone, the Electronic City Zone and Yizhuang Zone.

Address: 9 Daozhuomiao, Beijing, China
Post Code: 100080
Tel: 86 10 8269 0500
Fax: 86 10 8269 0506
E-mail: zgc@zgc.gov.cn
Website: www.zgc.gov.cn

SHANGHAI

Caohejing High Tech Park

Caohejing High Tech Park, established in 1991, is a state-level economic & technological development zone as well as a high-tech park. It is the only development zone in China to enjoy the preferential policy of being both an economic & technological zone, and a high-tech park. Currently, the main industries in the park are namely microelectronics, photoelectronics, computer software and new materials, forming the four centres: Research & Development, Network Operations, Financial Data and Technology & Innovation.

Address: 17F Technology Building, 900 Yishan Road, Shanghai,
China
Post Code: 200233
Tel: 86 21 485 0000
Fax: 86 21 485 0523
E-mail: webmaster@caohejing.com
Website: www.caohejing.com

Minhang Economic & Technological Development Zone

Established in 1983, Minhang Economic & Technological Development Zone was among the first 14 state-level development zones in China designated by the State Council in 1986. Topping the list among other development zones in six major economic indices, the Minhang Development Zone has set a successful example of mature development zones in China.

Address: 1251 Jiangchuan Road, Minhang Development Zone,
Shanghai, China
Post Code: 200245
Tel: 86 21 6430 0888
Fax: 86 21 6430 0789
E-mail: smudc@online.sh.cn
Website: www.smudc.com

Jinqiao Export Processing Zone

Jinqiao Export Processing Zone, located in the centre of Pudong New District, was approved in 1990 and enjoys the same preferential policies as those state-level economic and technological zones. The four pillar industries in the JEPZ include information electronics, automobile and its components, modern household electric appliances and biological medicines.

Address: 28 Jinqiao Road, Pudong New District, Shanghai, China
Post Code: 201206
Tel: 86 21 5899 1818/ 1951
Fax: 86 21 5899 1812
Website: www.pdjq.com/introduce/introg.htm

Waigaoqiao Free Trade Zone

Waigaoqiao Free Trade Zone is the country's biggest and oldest free trade zone approved by the State Council in June 1990. It incorporates various functions including free trade, export processing, and logistic warehousing and bonded commodities displaying.

Address: 2 Huajing Road, Waigaoqiao, Pudong New District, Shanghai, China
Post Code: 201204
Tel: 86 21 5046 1100
Fax: 86 21 5046 1441
Website: www.china-ftz.com

Zhangjiang High-Tech Park

The Zhangjiang High Tech Park was established in July of 1992 as a state-level park designated for the development of new and high technology. The Park's two leading industries are information technology and modern biotechnology and pharmaceuticals, and its principal focus is to develop innovation and entrepreneurship.

Address: 200 Longdong Avenue, Pudong New District, Shanghai, China
Post Code: 201204
Tel: 86 21 5080 1818
Fax: 86 21 5080 0686
E-mail: zjpark@zjpark.com
Website: www.zjpark.com

Songjiang State-Level Export Processing Zone

Songjiang State-level Export Processing Zone SJEPZ was approved on 27 April 2000 by the State Council for its establishment. It is the very first state-level export processing zones in China and presently is the only one in Shanghai area.

Address: 81 Rongle East Road, Songjiang, Shanghai, China
Post Code: 201613
Tel: 86 21 5774 1102
Fax: 86 21 5774 3188
E-mail: sjiz@public.sta.net.cn
Website: www.sjepz.com

TIANJIN

Tianjin Economic & Technological Development Area

Tianjin Economic & Technological Development Area TEDA, founded in Dec 1984, is located on the shore of the Bohai Sea in the east of Tianjin "golden belt". It is being built into the symbolic area of the Tianjin international port metropolis, together with the neighbouring Free Trade Zone of Tianjin Port. In addition, there are also three satellite development areas in the neighbourhood: the Yat-Sen Scientific Industrial Park, the Chemical Industrial Park and the Microelectronics Industrial Park.

Address: 19 Hongda Street, TEDA, Tianjin, China
Post Code: 300457
Tel: 86 22 2520 1111
Fax: 86 22 2532 8173
E-mail: teda@teda.gov.cn
Website: www.teda.gov.cn

Tianjin Export Processing Zone

Tianjin Export Processing Zone is located to the northeast of TEDA with a designated area of 2.54 km^2. It is a special enclosed zone where the Customs conduct 24-hour administration on commodities transported into and out of the zone and relevant places. This special economic zone is granted special preferential policies by the central government to attract enterprises in the business of processing and trade to invest in the zone.

Address: 3F, Zone A, 19 Hongda Street, TEDA, Tianjin, China
Post Code: 300457
Tel: 86 22 2520 1652
Fax: 86 22 2520 1021
E-mail: teda@teda.gov
Website: www.teda.gov.cn

Tianjin High-Tech Industrial Park

Tianjin High-Tech Industrial Park (THIP) was among the first State-approved state-level high-tech parks. It is made up of three different zones: Huayuan Industry Development Area (HIDA), Administrative Zone and Jingjintang Highway Region (inclusive of Wuqing Development Zone, Beichen Technological Industrial Park and Tanggu Ocean Technological Industrial Park).

Address: 8 Keyan West Road, Nankai District, Tianjin, China
Post Code: 300192
Tel: 86 22 2370 9365/ 9380
Fax: 86 22 2370 9365
E-mail: pangjh@eyou.com
Website: www.thip.gov.cn

Tianjin Port Free Trade Zone

Tianjin Port Free Trade Zone was established on the 12 May 1991 and is among the first specific economic open areas with a comprehensive nature and enjoys state preferential policies. It is the only free trade zone in China to have special railway lines connected to the Beijing-Shanhaiguan railway and is only 38 km from the Tianjin International Airport. It is a fast lane for international goods flow.

Address: Administrative Committee, Administration Building, 1
Tongda Square, Tianjin Port Free Trade Zone, Tianjin, China
Post Code: 300456
Tel: 86 22 2570 6932
Fax: 86 22 2570 6932
Website: www.tjftz.gov.cn

CHONGQING

Chongqing Economic & Technological Development Zone

Chongqing Economic &Technological Development Zone CETZ was approved by the State Council in 1993, and then becomes the first state-level economic & technological development zone in western China. The CETZ has attracted many domestic and foreign investors with its excellent investment environment and quality service.

Address: 76 Wanshou Road, Nanping, Chongqing, Sichuan,
China
Post Code: 400060
Tel: 86 23 6280 2780
Fax: 86 23 6280 2483
E-mail: kfgzsj@public.cta.cq.cn
Website: www.cetz.com

AUTONOMOUS REGIONS

GUANGXI

Dongxing Border Economic Cooperation Zone

Dongxing Border Economic Development Zone, covering an area of approximately 4 km^2, was approved by the State Council in September 1992 to develop border trade with Vietnam.

Address: Xinhua Road, Dongxing, Guangxi, China
Post Code: 538100
Tel: 86 770 768 3572
Fax: 86 770 768 6485

Nanning Economic & Technological Development Zone

Nanning Economic & Technological Development Zone was established in 1992, and was approved as a state-level economic & technological development zone in May 2001. It is a vibrant export-oriented development zone with major industries such as food processing, automotive parts, printing, fine chemicals etc.

Address: 76 Jiangnan Road, Nanning, Guangxi, China
Post Code: 530031
Tel: 86 771 451 7365/ 8883
Fax: 86 771 451 7365
E-mail: nndev.zo@163.net
Website: neda.gxi.gov.cn

Pingxiang Border Economic Cooperation Zone

It was approved as one of the national border zones by the State Council in Sept. 1992. The zone is located in the border between China and Vietnam, within the Asia-Pacific economic area, and is one of the main passages that connects Southwest China to Vietnam and countries in the Southeast Asia. International railway and No.322 National Road run through the area.

Address: 7 Nantian Street, Pingxiang, Guangxi, China
Post Code: 532600
Tel: 86 771 852 3099
Fax: 86 771 8523099

INNER MONGOLIA

Baotou National Rare Earth High Tech Industrial Development Zone

Baotou is situated in the central part of Inner Mongolia and has become a strategic area linking the Bohai Economic Zone to the northwest. Besides being the largest rare earth industrial base in China, it is also famous for its facilities for the production of iron and steel, machinery, non-ferrous metals, and textiles. Baotou National Rare Earth High Tech Industrial Development Zone is located in the southern part of Baotou, 6 km from the railway station and 16 km from the airport. Zonal roads are well-connected to the main roads of the city, providing convenient transportation for both passengers and goods.

Address: Administrative Committee, Qingnan Road, Baotou,
Inner Mongolia, China
Post Code: 014000
Tel: 86 472 515 6391/ 6779
Fax: 86 472 515 9784/ 6391
E-mail: xtgx@re-zone.gov.cn
Website: www.re-zone.gov.cn

Erlianhaote Border Economic Cooperation Zone

Erlianhaote Border Economic Cooperation Zone was approved as a national border zone among the open cities by the State Council in June, 1993. It is located in northern China, 1 km from the centre and 2.5 km from the nearest border. A conducive environment combined with accessible transportation, which will facilitate development and construction of the zone. It has participated in Erlianhaote Sino-Mongolia Free Trade Zone and hence was granted more privileges.

Address: Co-Inspection Building, Youyi Road, Erlianhaote, Inner Mongolia, China
Post Code: 011100
Tel: 86 479 752 3512
Fax: 86 479 752 1930

Huhhot Economic & Technological Development Zone

The Ruyi District of Huhhot Economic & Technological Development Zone, which was established in May 1992, is connected with the capital city — Huhhot of Inner Mongolia Autonomous Region in the west and lies in the economic circle around Bohai. It is a state-level economic & technological development area. The four existing important industries are bio-engineering, electronic information, fine textile and new materials.

Address: Administrative Committee, Sanwei Road, Ruyi District, Huhhot, Inner Mongolia, China
Post Code: 010010
Tel: 86 471 461 6551
Fax: 86 471 462 7630
E-mail: mcohetdz@hetdz.com.cn
Website: www.hetdz.com.cn

Manzhouli Border Economic Cooperation Zone

The biggest land trading port in China is located in Manzhouli and it was approved as a state-level border economic cooperation zone by the State Council in Sept 1992. Within the key economic zone in north-eastern Asia, it is the most important trading hub and distribution centre on the international main line of the Euro-Asia Bridge. Comprising of a high-tech park, industrial processing zone, warehousing bonded zone, commercial zone and others, it will gradually develop into a High Tech export processing base.

Address: Administrative Committee Building, 301 East Guodao, Border Economic Cooperation Zone, Inner Mongolia, China
Post Code: 021400
Tel: 86 470 622 5166
Fax: 86 470 622 0366
E-mail: WMTH99Q@public.hh.nm.cn
Website: www.manzhouli.net.cn

NINGXIA

Yinchuan Economic & Technological Development Zone

Yinchuan Economic & Technological Development Zone is the only state-level economic & technological development zone in Ningxia Autonomous Region. It is a new economic hotspot and western China's window to the outside world. Technology-based industries with research, development and testing, form the core of this comprehensive economic zone.

Address: 11 Xiqiao Alley, Yinchuan, Ningxia, China
Post Code: 750001
Tel: 86 951 503 3165/ 5058618
Fax: 86 951 505 8658
E-mail: postmaster@ycda.gov.cn
Website: www.ycda.gov.cn

TIBET

Lhasa Economic & Technology Development Zone

Lhasa Economic & Technological Development Zone LETDZ is approved by the State Council as a state-level ETDZ in September 2001. By making full use of the abundant resources of Tibet, LETDZ emphasizes on the development of its pillar enterprises such as farming and animal husbandry, and emerging industries like the new high-tech industry. At the same time, it also focuses on resource exploitation and material processing,

Address: Rm 502, Government Administrative Building, 22
Jiangsu Road, Lhasa, Tibet, China
Post Code: 850000
Tel: 86 891 634 3747
Fax: 86 891 632 4663

XINJIANG

Bole Border Economic Cooperation Zone

It was approved to be established as one of the national border economic cooperation zone by the State Council in Dec 1992. The zone is an important part of Bole city, the capital of Boertala Mongolia autonomous prefecture. Its industry section covers 4.85 km^2, which is 61.9% of the designated area. The zone is dependent on national first-level railway and highway port, the Ala mountain port, with good potential of development

Address: Chengdong Road, Bole, Xinjiang
Post Code: 833400
Tel: 86 909 222 3275

Shihezi Economic & Technological Development Zone

Shihezi Economic & Technological Development Zone was approved as a state-level development zone in April 2000. The zone has a developed area of 5.3 km^2. The SETDZ gives priorities to the development of new technologies, new processes, and new materials related to agricultural and husbandry production, and high-tech, high-value-added and high-return techniques and processes for processing agricultural products and by-products.

Address: 56 Beisi East Rd, Shihezi, Xinjiang, China
Post Code: 832014
Tel: 86 993 261 0868/ 1390
Fax: 86 993 261 1868/ 1370
E-mail: kfqgw-sh@xj.cninfo.net
Website: www.kfq.xjshz.com

Tacheng Border Economic Cooperation Zone

Tacheng city is located in northwestern Xinjiang and adjacent to Kazakhstan. The zone was approved to establish by the State Council in Dec. 1992. It adjoins the city in the east and near to the port in the west, covering 6.5 km^2 and is 12 km from the port of Baketu, the first-level national port. The zone is composed of commercial centre of border trading, import and export processing section, storing section and port service section.

Address: Guangming Road, Tacheng, Xinjiang, China
Post Code: 834700
Tel: 86 901 622 6163

Urumqi Economic & Technological Development Zone

Urumqi Economic & Technological Development Zone was approved to be one of the national development zones by the State Council in 25 Aug 1994. It is located in the capital city of Xinjiang. It enjoys easy accessibility and communications, rich resources, conducive investment environment, preferential policies, and comprehensive service providers.

Address: 68 Zhongya Boulevard, Urumqi, Xinjiang, China
Post Code: 830026
Tel: 86 991 371 6656/ 3238/ 3834
Fax: 86 991 3713116
Website: www.urumqi.gov.cn

Urumqi High-Tech Industrial Development Zone

Urumqi High-Tech Industrial Development Zone was set up in 1992. In the same year, it became a national one. Up to now, it is still the only national high-tech zone in Xinjiang. With good investment environment, superior geography location, flexible management mechanism and preferential policies, the zone has won great reputation from investors home and abroad.

Address: 5 Diamond City, Beijing South Road, Urumqi, Xinjiang, China
Post Code: 830011
Tel: 86 991 383 0834
Fax: 86 991 383 0834
E-mail: uctp@mail.xj.cninfo.net
Website: www.uctp.gov.cn

Yining Border Economic Cooperation Zone

It is a comprehensive economic zone with multiple levels, majoring in export-oriented and high technology business, industry and commerce. It was approved to be one of the national border economic cooperation zones by the State Council in June 1992.

Address: Business City, Beijing Road, Yining, Xinjiang, China
Post Code: 835000
Fax: 86 999 812 8184
E-mail: lfa-yn@mail.xj.cninfo.net
Website: www.ycatv.com.cn

PROVINCES

ANHUI

Hefei Economic & Technological Development Area

Hefei Economic & Technological Development Area (HETA) with a designated area of 39 km^2 and a population of 40,000, is located in the south of Hefei city, 9 km away from the downtown area. As a state-approved economic and technological area, as well as an experimental area for administrative and organization reform in China, HETA has been constantly attaching importance to the development of modern industry, foreign funded industry, export-oriented industry and high-tech industry since founding in April 1993.

Address: Pearl Square, South Suburbs, Hefei, Anhui, China
Post code: 230601
Tel: 86 551 381 1070/ 2989
Fax: 86 551 381 2940
E-mail: info@hetac.com
Website: www.hetac.com

Hefei High-Tech Industrial Development Zone

On 17 Oct 1997, Hefei High-Tech Industrial Development Zone witnessed its foundation stone laying ceremony. On March 1991, the State Council approved it as one of the state-level high-tech zones. On September 1997, the zone was ratified by the State Council as China APEC Science and Technology Industrial Park, which is specially open to all APEC members.

Address: 669 Jiangxi Road, Hefei, Anhui, China
Post Code: 230088
Tel: 86 551 531 2212/3264
Fax: 86 551 531 2961
E-mail: hfgxq@mail.hf.ah.cn
Website: www.hfnhz.com.cn

Wuhu Economic & Technological Development Zone

Wuhu Economic & Technological Development Zone was approved to set up by the State Council in Apr 1993. There are convenient communications and complete infrastructure facilities in this area. It lies in the adjoining part of East China and Middle-west China. It is the "golden start" for overseas investors promoting their business from East China to Middle-west China.

Address: 2F, Investment Promotion Bureau Building, Yinhu
North Road, Anhui, China
Post Code: 241001
Tel: 86 553 584 1555
Fax: 86 553 584 1876
E-mail: wuetdz@mail.ahwhptt.net.cn
Website:www.weda.gov.cn

FUJIAN

Dongshan Economic & Technological Development Zone

The DETDZ, established in January 1993, covers an area on 10 km^2. It is slated to be a comprehensive development zone, having several functional areas for industries, residential areas, commerce and green belt. Currently the first phase of the construction of industrial and trade start-up zone with the total area of 3.5 km^2 has been completed.

Address: Investment Promotion Bureau, Xipu Town, Dongshan,
Fujian, China
Post Code: 363400
Tel: 86 596 588 5867/ 5007
Fax: 86 596 588 5790
E-mail: jfj@detdz.com
Website: www.detdz.com

Fuqing Rongqiao Economic & Technological Development Zone

Fuqing Rongqiao Economic & Technological Development Zone, established in 1987 by the overseas Chinese from Fuqing, was the only zone to be established by overseas Chinese, and was approved to be a national Economic & Technological Development Zone by the State Council on 21 Oct 1992. FRETDZ engaged mainly in electronics, chemical fibre, plastics, car parts, garment and foodstuff. Major investment sources were Hong Kong, Singapore, Indonesia, Republic of Korea, Japan, Germany, USA, Taiwan and Macau.

Address: FRETDZ Administrative Committee, Fuqing, Fujian
Post Code: 350300
Tel: 86 591 537 7812/ 7819
Fax: 86 591 537 7820
Email: fredz@publ.fz.fj.cn

Fuzhou Economic & Technological Development Zone

Fuzhou Economic & Technical Development Zone FETDZ, with its 16 km^2 of area for industrial development. It was approved to be a national development zone by the State Council in Jan 1985. In this zone, there are several different sections: Fuzhou Bonded Zone, Fuzhou Taiwan Merchant Investment Zone, and Fuzhou Mawei High-Tech Industrial Park.

Address: 172 Junzhu Road, Mawei, Fuzhou, Fujian, China
Post Code: 350015
E-mail: mwwlzx@lublic.fz.fj.cn
Tel: 86 591 368 2135°°
Fax: 86 591 398 3505
Website: www.fdz.com.cn

Fuzhou Free Trade Zone

Fuzhou is engaged primarily in international trade, trade with Taiwan, bonded warehousing and export-processing. The zone has become an important goods distribution centre for foreign-invested enterprises in China's eastern coastal areas. Re-exports from the zone now extends to Japan, Republic of Korea, Southeast Asia and South America. Other major investment sources were USA, Italy and France.

Address: Luoxing Road, Mawei, Fuzhou, Fujian, China
Post code: 350015
Tel: 86 591 368 3954
Fax: 86 591 368 3954
E-mail: mwwlzx@public.fz.fj.cn
Website: www.fdz.com.cn

Fuzhou Mawei High-Tech Industrial Development Zone

Fuzhou Mawei High-Tech Industrial Development Zone was set up in 1988, and approved by the State Council in March 1991. In 1995 the government of Fuzhou decided to put aside 1.2 km^2 in the park so as to build a ten-billion electronic information city, which made it the leading business in electronic industry of Fuzhou. In 1999 the management committee was established and 5.6 km^2 was designated to be High-Tech Park.

Address: South Tower, Chuangye Building, 548 Gongye North Road, Fuzhou, Fujian, China
Post Code: 350002
Tel: 86 591 371 1234
Fax: 86 591 372 2394
E-mail: fzkjyfzb@pub5.fz.fj.cn
Website:www.fdz.com.cn

Xiamen Export Processing Zone

Xiamen Xinling Export Processing Zone was set up on April 2000 with the approval of the State Council and renamed as Xiamen Export Processing Zone on November 2001. It is situated in the Xiamen Haicang Taiwanese Investment Zone with a designated area of 2.24 km^2 and an area of 1.46 km^2 for the first phase. It started operations in January 2002.

Address: 2F, Jianxing, 170 Haicanghong Road, Xiamen, Fujian,
China
Post Code: 361021
Tel: 86 592 658 6665
Fax: 86 592 658 6664

Xiamen Torch High-Tech Industrial Development Zone

Xiamen Torch High-Tech is a high-tech product export base. The core estates in the zone are made up of Torch High-Tech Park Torch Software Park, Overseas Pioneering Park, Luqiao High-Tech Park, Beida Biology Park, Xiamen Software Park, Zhongzhai Science Park and Tongji Science Park.

Address: Administrative Committee, 2F Torch Plaza, Xiamen,
Fujian, China
Post Code: 361000
Tel: 86 592 603 5175
Fax: 86 592 603 5174
E-mail: hjgwh@xm.gov.cn
Website:www.xmtorch.gov.cn

Xiamen Xiangyu Free Trade Zone

Xiamen Xiangyu Free Trade Zone is located about 2 km^2 northwest of Xiamen, with Dongdu Harbour to the west, Harbour Railway to the east, Xiamen Bridge to the north and Xiangyu docks to the south. It is a test zone in accelerating the implementation of free port policies, The zone focuses on international trade, trade with Taiwan, transit trade, bonded storage and export processing, as well as other related businesses such as finance, insurance, commodity exhibitions, wharf management and transportation.

Address: Xiangyu Building, Xiangyu FTZ, Xiamen, Fujian, China
Post Code: 361006
Tel: 86 592 603 5822
Fax: 86 592 603 5831
Website: www.shinyco.com

GANSU

Lanzhou Economic & Technological Development Zone

Lanzhou Economic & Technological Development Zone LETDZ was established in 1993, and was approved as a state-level zone on 15 March 2002. The zone covers an area of

9.53 km^2. Lanzhou and its adjacent area hold abundant mineral resources. As one of China's key bases for scientific research, Lanzhou boasts of 700 various scientific research and development institutions

Address: 16 ETDZ, An'ning District, Lanzhou, Gansu, China
Post Code: 730070
Tel: 86 931 855 2462/ 2003/ 2507
Fax: 86 931 855 2003
Website: www.lzeda.com

Lanzhou High-Tech Industrial Development Zone

Lanzhou High-Tech Industrial Development Zone is one of the first 27 state-level high-tech industrial parks approved in 1991 by the state council. It has an area of 5.2 km^2, divided into the economic & trade section and industrial base. Science and technology, medical, electronics and chemical are some of the encouraged industries.

Address: 555 Zhangsu Bay, Chengguan District, Lanzhou, Gansu, China
Post code: 730020
Tel: 86 931 855 2003
Fax: 86 931 310 8830

GUANGDONG

Foshan High-Tech Industrial Development Zone

Foshan High-Tech Industrial Development Zone was one of the state-level industrial zones to be approved by the State Council in December 1992. The total area of the Zone is 10 km^2, consisting of Southern High-Tech District, Western High-Tech District and Shunde High-Tech District. The policy zone of Foshan High-Tech Development Zone was also set up.

Address: 3F, 10th Building, Municipal Government Square, Dafu Road, Foshan, Guangdong, China
Post Code: 528000
Tel: 86 757 338 6093
Fax: 86 757 335 5686
E-mail: hitech@fs-hitech.gov.cn
Website: www.fs-hitech.gov.cn

Guangzhou Economic & Technological Development Zone

Guangzhou Economic & Technological Development Zone is a state-level industrial zone approved by the State Council in 1984. At present, it has formed pillar industries such as plastics, chemistry, electronics, food processing and shipbuilding. The development of these industries will make it a base for industrial processing as well as a new economic growth point.

Address: Administrative Committee Building, Guangzhou,
Guangdong, China
Post Code: 510730
Tel: 86 20 8221 2242/ 0132
Fax: 86 20 8221 2242
Website:www.getdd.com.cn

Guangzhou Export Processing Zone

As planned, Guangzhou EPZ is situated in the east section of the Guangzhou Economic & Technological Development Zone. Taking up an area of 3.05 km^2, the EPZ enjoys a favourable location: the Guangzhou-Shenzhen Expressway is at its north; the Guangzhou- Shenzhen Highway is at its south.

Address: Rm 405, Central Tower, Administrative Committee
Building, Guangzhou EPZ, Guangzhou, Guangdong, China
Post Code: 510730
Tel: 86 20 8222 8063
Fax: 86 20 8222 8070
E-mail: web@getdd.com.cn
Website: www.getdd.com.cn

Guangzhou Free Trade Zone

Guangzhou Free Trade Zone was approved by the State Council in 1992. Guangzhou FTZ main development direction includes international trade, product processing, free trade & storage, bonded warehousing, transportation, financial services and telecommunications.

Address: International Building, Guangzhou FTZ, Huangpu,
Guangzhou, Guangdong, China
Post Code: 510730
Tel: 86 20 8221 7591
Fax: 86 20 8221 4382
E-mail: web@getdd.com.cn
Website: www.getdd.com.cn

Guangzhou High-Tech Industrial Development Zone

GHIDZ, with a total designated area of 28.14 km^2, lies in the east of Guangzhou. At present, it consists of Guangzhou Science Park, Tianhe Science & Technology Park, Huanghuagang Science & Technology Park, the Civilian Science & Technology Park and Nansha Information Technology Park. Higher education institutions, scientific research institutions and state-level laboratories are also located here.

Address: Administrative Committee Building, Guangzhou,
Guangdong
Post Code: 510730
Tel: 86 20 8221 2115
Fax: 86 20 8221 2115
E-mail: web@getdd.com.cn
Website: www.getdd.com.cn

Guangzhou Nansha Economic & Technological Development Zone

Guangzhou Nansha Economic & Technological Development Zone is at the heart of the Pearl River Delta region and a transportation hub. Deepwater seaports are its mainstay and a driving force for the growth of the tertiary industry. Protection of the bio-ecological environment is also highly emphasized, in an effort to achieve what would be "bright blue skies, clean unpolluted waters and luxuriant trees".

Address: Butterfly Park, Jingang Road, Nansha, Panyu,
Guangdong, China
Post Code: 511458
Tel: 86 20 8468 8220/ 8120
Fax: 86 20 8468 7763
E-mail: nansha@panyu.gd.cn
Website: www.nansha.gov.cn

Huizhou Daya Bay Economic & Technological Development Zone

Established in May 1993, Huizhou Daya Bay Economic & Technological Zone lies in the south of Huizhou city and faces the South Sea. The zone is situated in Pearl River Delta area with rapid economic development and adjacent to Shenzhen and Hong Kong. It is an ideal place to develop modern industries by the sea and tourist industry, because of its flat terrain, unique tourism resources and abundant fresh water resources.

Address: Daya Bay Development Zone, Huizhou, Guangdong,
China
Post Code: 516081
Tel: 86 752 557 7760/ 9462
Fax: 86 752 557 7620
E-mail: hzdywic@pub.huizhou.gd.cn
Website:www.dayawan.gov.cn

Huizhou Zhongkai High-Tech Industrial Development Zone

Huizhou Zhongkai High-Tech Industrial Development Zone is one of the 53 National High-Tech Industrial Development Zones approved by the State Council in November 1992.The High-Tech Zone is located in the southwest of Huizhou city, between Huishen Expressway and Beijing-Kowloon Railway Haizhou section, which enjoys geographical advantages and convenient transportation. The zone has a designated area of 8.8 km^2 of which 4.6 km^2 have been developed.

Address: Administrative Committee, Huizhou, Guangdong,
China
Post Code: 516000
Tel: 86 752 260 0059
Fax: 86 752 260 0059
E-mail: hzzk@pub.huizhou.gd.cn
Website: www.hzzk.org

Shantou Free Trade Zone

Shantou FTZ provides investors a comprehensive export processing, transit trade and bonded warehousing services, with basic infrastructure support. It is well connected to other parts of China, Hong Kong and Taiwan, by land, air and sea.

Address: Administrative Committee, Shantou, Guangdong,
China
Post Code: 515071
Tel: 86 754 759 0271
Fax: 86 754 759 0127
E-mail: ftzst@pub.shantou.gd.cn
Website: www.stftz.gov.cn

Shenzhen Futian Free Trade Zone

Futian Free Trade Zone, bridging Hong Kong to Shenzhen, was approved by the State Council in May 1991. Overseas investment projects in import and export trade, information, consultancy services, commodities exhibition, transaction and membership market, high-tech and export-oriented manufacturing, high value-added assembling and compensation trade, bonded warehousing, finance, telecommunications and other tertiary industries are especially encouraged.

Address: Administrative Building, 1 Guihua Road, Shenzhen,
Guangdong, China
Post Code: 518000
Tel: 86 755 8359 0915
Fax: 86 755 8359 0767
Website: www.szftz.gov.cn

Shenzhen High-Tech Industrial Development Zone

In September 1996, with the approval of the State Science and Technology Commission, Shenzhen Municipal People's Government decided to set up Shenzhen High-Tech Industrial Development Park SHIP, exercising the "management system of one-park for several estates".

Address: 4F, Comprehensive Services Building, Nanshan District,
Shenzhen, Guangdong, China
Post Code: 518057
Tel: 86 755 2655 1703
Fax: 86 755 2655 1526
E-mail: dcj@ship.szptt.net.cn
Website: www.shipgov.net

Shenzhen Shatoujiao Free Trade Zone

Shenzhen Shatoujiao Free Trade Zone was established in Dec 1987, and was approved by the State Council in May 1991. Export processing industry is mainly developed in the zone. Concurrently, industries of import & export, entrepot trade, warehousing &

transportation, real estate, and other related items are encouraged to develop. It was the earliest bonded zone with the best results in China.

Address: Yantian District, Shenzhen, Guangdong, China
Post Code: 518081
Tel: 86 755 2526 0223
Fax: 86 755 2526 0389
Website:www.szftz.gov.cn

Shenzhen Yantian Port Free Trade Zone

Shenzhen Yantian Port Free Trade Zone was approved by the State Council in Sept 1996. It sits on the shores of Dapeng Bay, eastern part of Shenzhen city. It faces the Kowloon Peninsula of Hong Kong to the south, and is located in the area of Yantian Port, one of the important deep-water container ports in South China.

Address: 16F Haigang Building, Yantian Port, Shenzhen,
Guangdong, China
Post Code: 518081
Tel: 86 755 2529 1941/ 2528 1203
Fax: 86 755 2529 1523
Website: www.ypf.com.cn

Zhanjiang Economic & Technological Development Zone

Zhanjiang Economic & Technological Development Zone (ZETDZ), established on 29 Nov 1984 with approval from the State Council, was ranked as the first batch of 14 economic & technological zones in coastal cities. It adopts preferential policies similar to that of Special Economic Zones but with a new administration system. An industrial system focused on biomedicine, chemical materials, mechanic and electronics, telecommunications, textiles and garments, office equipment and appliances, subsidiary agricultural products and food processing has been formed.

Address: No.2 Bridge, Renmin Boulevard, Zhanjiang,
Guangdong, China
Post Code: 524022
Tel: 86 759 338 1573
Fax: 86 759338 0349
E-mail: admin@zetdz.gov.cn

Zhongshan Torch High-Tech Industrial Development Zone

Zhongshan Torch High-Tech Industrial Development Zone lies at the heart of Pearl River Delta, with a clean and beautiful environment, convenient transportation networks and comprehensive infrastructure. "Guangdong Model Industrial Park with Excellent Practice" was awarded to Zhongshan Torch High-Tech Industrial Development Zone in 2002.

Address: Administrative Building, Kangle Boulevard, Zhongshan
Harbour, Zhongshan, Guangdong, China
Post Code: 528437

Tel: 86 760 559 7902
Fax: 86 760 559 7917
E-mail: info@zstorch.gov.cn
Website: www.zstorch.gov.cn

Zhuhai Free Trade Zone

Zhuhai Free Trade Zone was founded on 13 Nov 1996 with the approval of the State Council. It covers an area of 3 km^2. It is situated in southern Zhuhai, along Wanzai Port and faces Macau across the straits. It connects Macau by land through Hengqing Bridge and the Lotus Bridge. Zhuhai FTZ is about 11 km away from the downtown, 44 km away from Zhuhai Port, 18 km away from Jiuzhou Port, 40 km away from Zhuhai Airport, 5 km away from the future Zhuhai Railway Station, and only 36 nautical miles from Hong Kong.

Address: Hongwan, Zhuhai, Guangdong, China
Post Code: 519030
Tel: 86 756 882 5123
Fax: 86 756 882 4166
E-mail: zhftz@pub.zhuhai.gd.cn
Website: www.zhfreetradezone.org

Zhuhai National High-Tech Industrial Development Zone

Zhuhai National High-Tech Industrial Development Zone, a state-level development zone, is made up of four technological & industrial parks: Nanping, Sanzao, Xinqing and Baijiao, as well as Zhuhai Demonstration Base for the Industrialization of Technological Achievements. The high-tech zone is bestowed with double preferential policies of both the special economic zone and state-level high-tech zone.

Address: 230 Hongshan Rd, Zhuhai, Guangdong, China
Post Code: 519001
Tel: 86 756 261 6299
Fax: 86 756 261 6099
E-mail: zhhitech@pub.zhuhai.gd.cn
Website: www.zhuhai-hitech.com

GUIZHOU

Guiyang Economic & Technological Development Zone

The zone was established in 1993 and regards, foreign funds as an important factor in the development of high technology. At present, Guiyang ETDZ has an industry system based on engineering & mechanics, electronics, auto-machines & machine fittings, automotive and aviation parts.

Address: 443 Huanghe Road, Xiaohe District, Guiyang, Guizhou,
China
Post Code: 610012

Tel: 86 28 485 3233/ 3592
Fax: 86 28 487 2887
E-mail: admin@geta.gov.cn
Website: www.geta.gov.cn

Guiyang High-Tech Industrial Development Zone

Guiyang High-Tech Industrial Development Zone was approved to be a national development zone by the State Council in October 1992 with a designated area of 11.32 km^2. In 2000, the government made certain planning adjustments. Now it is a "one zone, two parks and a street", namely, Jinyang Science and Technological Industrial Park, Xintian Industrial Park and Shenqi Road.

Address: Torch Administrative Building, Xintian Boulevard,
Guiyang, Guizhou, China
Post Code: 550018
Tel: 86 851 646 0673
Fax: 86 851 646 0673
Website: www.guz.cei.gov.cn/kfc/home.htm

HAINAN

Haikou Free Trade Zone

Haikou Free Trade Zone (HFTZ) was founded on 21 Oct 1992 with the approval of the State Council and began operations on 13 April 1993. It encourages the development of the export processing industry, free trade storage, international trade, finance & insurance, information & consulting etc. As a comprehensive opening-up oriented special economic area, the zone is under the supervision of Customs.

Address: 168 Industry Boulevard, Haikou, Hainan, China
Post Code: 570216
Tel: 86 898 681 7087
Fax: 86 898 681 4885
E-mail: invest@hkftz.gov.cn
Website:www.hkftz.gov.cn

Hainan High-Tech Industrial Development Zone

Hainan International Science Park was set up in 1991 with the approval of the State Council. It is situated in the Xiuying District of Haikou city, covering an area of 4.67 km^2. As a national High-Tech Industrial Zone, it offers investors not only the preferential policies for the Hainan Special Economic and High-Tech Industrial Zone, but also more favourable policies in export and import, financial support, land transfer etc.

Address: Yuke Building, Technology Boulevard, Haikou, Hainan
Post Code: 570314
Tel: 86 898 686 64518
Fax: 86 898 686 55212

Baoding High-Tech Development Zone

In November 1992, examined by the State Science and Technology Commission the Baoding High-Tech Industrial Zone was established with the approval of the State Council and it is the key investment and construction zone in China. Its total designated area is 10 km^2 and divided into three estates, which are Central Science Park, North China Industrial Park and Bada Industrial Park.

Address: 118 Huaxian Road, High-Tech Zone, Baoding, Hebei, China
Post Code: 071051
Tel: 86 312 310 8801/ 8800
Fax: 86 312 310 8830
E-mail: gxq@bd-ctp.net.cn
Website:www.bd-ctp.net.cn

Qinhuangdao Economic & Technogical Development Zone

Qinhuangdao Economic & Technological Development Zone QETDZ was firstly approved in 1984 as one of the devlopment zones of 14 coastal cities. It is the only state-level development zone of Hebei province. A high-tech industrial system, with electromechanical integration, biological engineering, new materials, new energy sources and information industry as major industries, has been basically formed.

Address: Investment Promotion Bureau, Qinhuangdao, Hebei, China
Post Code: 066004
Tel: 86 335 805 1739
Fax: 86 335 8051519
E-mail: info@mx.qetdz.com
Website: www.qetdz.com.cn

Shijiazhuang High-Tech Industrial Development Zone

Shijiazhuang was set up in March 1991 by the State Council, among the first batch of national high-tech industrial zone. Now many countries and regions in the world including America, Germany, Britain, Hong Kong have invested in the zone. In the established enterprises, the output value of electronic information, biology and medicine and new material accounts for over 70% of the total.

Address: 151 Huanghe Boulevard, High-Tech Zone, Shijiazhuang, Hebei, China
Post Code: 050035
Tel: 86 311 596 1924
Fax: 86 311 596 3266
E-mail: public@shidz.com
Website: www.shidz.com

HEILONGJIANG

Daqing High-Tech Industrial Development Zone

Daqing High-Tech Industrial Development Zone was broken ground formally on 10 Apr 1992, and was approved to be a state-level zone on 9 Nov in the same year. It is one of the 53 key national development zones. The designated area of the zone is 16 km^2. Petrochemical and electronics industry are the encouraged industries.

Address: Administrative Committee, High-Tech Zone,
Dongcheng District, Daqing, Heilongjiang, China
Post Code: 163316
Tel: 86 459 628 2929/ 1237
Fax: 86 459 628 2082
E-mail: BGS@dhp.gov.cn
Website: www.dhp.gov.cn

Harbin Economic and Technology Development Zone

Facing Russia in the north and connected to the Chinese coastal open cities, Harbin is an important domestic viaduct. There are rich natural resources of wood, petroleum, coal, corn etc. in this area. Foreign investment in the zone is particularly encouraged in infrastructure development, textiles, petrochemicals, machinery, electronics, medical equipment, automobiles, construction materials, and new and advanced tertiary industries such as finance, insurance, real estate and information services.

Address: Administrative Building, 368 Changjiang Road, Harbin,
Heilongjiang, China
Post Code: 150090
Tel: 86 451 228 1107
Fax: 86 451 231 0931

Harbin High-Tech Industrial Development Zone

Harbin High-Tech Industrial Development Zone consists of Nangang convergence quarter, Yingbin Road convergence quarter, bungalow convergence quarter and four university quarters. Except for Yingbin Road convergence quarter which is located near the airport, the other quarters are located in the centre of the city, which enjoys convenient transportation and abundant manpower resources.

Address: Building 26, High-Tech Zone, Songshan Road, Nangang
District, Harbin, Heilongjiang, China
Post Code: 150036
Tel: 86 451 231 2267
Fax: 86 451 231 7807

Heihe Border Economic Cooperation Zone

Heihe city is one of the first batch frontier opening cities of China, situated in the northeast border of China. Its direct neighbour is the Amure Prefecture of Russia by the Heilongjiang River. An export-processing district has been established to promote border trade. The zone focuses on the development of tourism, high-tech industries and tertiary industries. Major trading partners include Russia, Japan and Republic of Korea.

Address: 8 Tongjiang Road, Heihe, Heilongjiang, China
Post Code: 164300
Tel: 86 456 822 5705
Fax: 86 456 822 3391
E-mail: hhzfmqb@mail.hl.cn
Website: www.heihe.gov.cn

Suifenhe Border Economic Cooperation Zone

Approved by the State Council in 1992, it is connected to Russia by one railway and two highways. Its main activity is border trade with Russia, along with initiatives for economic and technological cooperation, export processing, warehousing, transportation, real estate and tourism.

Address: 2F Governmental Building, Suifenhe, Heilongjiang,
China
Post Code: 157300
Tel: 86 453 392 4494
Fax: 86 453 392 2560
E-mail: sfhzf@mail.hl.cn
Website: www.suifenhe.gov.cn

HENAN

Luoyang High-Tech Industrial Development Zone

Based on a good institutional research foundation, the zone is aimed at developing industries such as new materials, photo-electricity and electro-mechanics, electronic information and bio engineering.

Address: 2 Nanchang Road, Luoyang, Henan, China
Post Code: 471003
Tel: 86 379 490 2651
Fax: 86 379 490 2654
E-mail: bgs@lhdz.gov.cn
Website: www.lhdz.gov.cn

Zhengzhou Economic & Technological Development Area

Zhengzhou Economic & Technological Development Area (ZEDA) was set up in April 1993, and approved to be a state-level economic & technological area by the State Council on 13 February 2000. It is the only national economic and technological development area in Henan. The zone is 107 km from the No.107 National Highway. Longhai Railway also crosses the zone in the north. There are rich underground water resources in the area.

Address: East Hanghai Road, Zhengzhou, Henan, China
Tel: 86 371 678 1251/ 1252
Fax: 86 371 678 1248
E-mail: zzetda@public.zz.ha.cn
Website: www.zz-economy.gov.cn

Zhengzhou High-Tech Industrial Development Zone

The focus of the zone is on developing technology and production based on new materials, electronic information and biological engineering. Priority is given to high-tech industries such as electronics and electronic information, material science, medicine, biomedical engineering, computers and software and artificial diamond composites.

Address: 6 Guohuai Street, High-Tech Zone, Zhengzhou, Henan,
China
Post Code: 450001
Tel: 86 371 798 1354
Fax: 86 371 798 1424
E-mail: Zhx706@public.zz.ha.cn
Website:www.zzgx.gov.cn

HUBEI

Wuhan East Lake High-Tech Industrial Development Zone

This zone is also known as the "Silicon Valley of Central China". Home to some 23 universities and colleges, 56 research and design institutions, 10 key laboratories and four national technological centres, pillar industries in the zone include telecommunications, bioengineering, new materials, software and laser technology. The zone has become an important R&D hub in Wuhan.

Address: High-Tech Building, Donghu High-Tech Zone, Wuhan,
Hubei, China
Post Code: 430040
Tel: 86 27 8756 1810
Fax: 86 27 8756 1266
E-mail£ʃdhgx@public.wh.hb.cn
Website: www.elht.com

Wuhan Economic & Technological Development Zone

Wuhan, the capital of Hubei Province, is 15 km away from the downtown Wuhan city and the cultural and economic centre in Central China. The zone is located on the north bank of the Yangtze River and has advanced transportation facilities. It also consists of the Wuhan Export Processing Zone, which has a designated area of 2.7 km^2. Citroen, Motorola, Coca-Cola and Henkel represent the pillar industries of the zone, i.e. automobile, beverage and food processing, machinery and bio-pharmaceuticals.

Address: Tunyang Plaza, Wuhan, Hubei, China
Post Code: 430056
Tel: 86 27 8489 1006/ 2700
Fax: 86 27 8489 1934/ 9673
E-mail: wetdz@public.wh.hb.cn
Website: www.wedz.com.cn

Xiangfan High-Tech Industrial Development Zone

Asia's only passenger plane-seats manufacturing base, China's only research centre on aviation life-saving equipment and China's biggest special optical glass manufacturing base, are all located in Xiangfan High-Tech Industrial Development Zone. Investment is particularly encouraged in the automobile industry, as well as the industrialization of the agricultural sector.

Address: 5F Torch Plaza, 2 Chunyuan West Road, Xiangfan,
Hubei, China
Post Code: 441003
Tel: 86 710 322 0246
Fax: 86 710 324 1044
E-mail: xfhdz@263.net
Website: www.xfhdz.org.cn

HUNAN

Changsha Economic & Technological Development Zone

Changsha National Economic & Technical Development Zone was established in August 1992 and approved by the State Council in February 2000 as one of China's state-level economic development zones. The zone encourages investment in the development of industry, high technologies and the service trades. There is a particular emphasis on micro-electronics, new materials, bioengineering, information and communications, and new energy sources.

Address: Xingsha Town, East Suburbs, Changsha, Hunan, China
Post Code: 410001
Tel: 86 731 401 1101
Fax: 86 731 401 6143

Changsha High-Tech Industrial Development Zone

Changsha High-Tech Industrial Development Zone (CHIDZ) was founded in October 1988. It has a total designated area of 18.6 km^2. Changsha Development Zone consists of four parks: Yuelushan High-Tech Park, Xingsha High-Tech Industrial Park, Longping Agricultural High-Tech Park, Yuanda High-Tech Park. Yuelushan High-Tech Park is situated on the west bank of the Xiang River by the National Highway No. 319.

Address: Tongxinbo, Hexi, Changsha, Hunan, China
Post Code: 410005

Tel: 86 731 880 6521
Fax: 86 731 880 6540
E-mail: cshtz@cshtz.com
Website: www.cshtz.gov.cn

Zhuzhou High-Tech Industrial Development Zone

Zhuzhou High-Tech Industrial Development Zone was established in Feb 1992, and approved to be a state-level high-tech development zone by the State Council in Dec 1992. Its total designated area is 35 km^2, including a 1.78 km^2 Science Industrial Park complete with comprehensive infrastructural facilities. The development of aviation and space technologies, chemical industry and other high-tech industries are encouraged.

Address: Torch Plaza, Huanghe North Road, Hexi, Zhuzhou,
Hunan, China
Post Code: 412007
Tel: 86 733 881 8549
Fax: 86 733 881 8549
E-mail: zsj@zzhitech.com
Website: www.zzhitech.com

JIANGSU

Changzhou High-Tech Industrial Development Zone

Changzhou enjoys a solid industrial foundation and a complete industrial system. It is one of "China's Top 50 Cities" in comprehensive strength. Changzhou High-Tech Industrial Development Zone is in the north of Changzhou city and is the biggest high-tech radiation sources industrial base. Currently, there are about 300 foreign investment enterprises established by investors from USA, Germany, Switzerland, Italy, Japan, Hong Kong, Taiwan etc.

Address: 85 Hehai Middle Road, Changzhou, Jiangsu, China
Post Code: 213022
Tel: 86 519 510 0668/ 7992
Fax: 86 519 510 5661
E-mail: cndfi@public.cz.js.cn
Website: www.cznd.org.cn

Kunshan Economic & Technological Development Zone

Parks in the zone include Kunshan Export Processing Zone, China Kunshan Business Incubator for Overseas Chinese Scholars, Jiangsu International Business Centre, and Kunshan Industrial Park for Japanese Companies. More than 900 companies have been set up with investments from 38 countries and regions across the world, mainly in the IT business, and the production of precision machinery and daily necessities.

Address: Investment Promotion Bureau, 1F, International Building, 167 Qianjin Middle Road, Kunshan, Jiangsu, China
Post Code: 215300
Tel: 86 512 5730 3999 / 3777
Fax: 86 512 5732 9191
E-mail: ketd@ketd.gov.cn
Website: www.ketd.gov.cn

Kunshan Export Processing Zone

This is an ideal location for businesses requiring prompt and easy customs clearance procedures. This zone, one of the first 15 export processing zones approved by the State Council in April 2000, is a duty-free zone located in KETDZ. With around-the-clock service provided by the Customs, and the banking, transportation, warehousing and freight inspection and quarantine establishments stationed in the zone, enterprises in KEPZ can fully enjoy a one-stop shopping for services to handle the import and export procedures.

Address: KETDZ, Kunshan, Jiangsu, China
Post Code: 215300
Tel: 86 512 5732 9158
Fax: 86 512 5731 3888
E-mail: ketd@ketd.gov.cn
Website: www.ketd.gov.cn

Lianyungang Economic & Technological Development Zone

Lianyungang Economic & Technological Development Zone was approved to be a state level development zone by the State Council in December 1984. It is the east entrance of the Euro-Asian Continent Bridge and is located only 5 km away from Lianyungang Port, one of the eight biggest sea ports in China. Enterprises are involved in the medical, textiles, foodstuff, construction materials industries etc.

Address: Investment Promotion Bureau, Lianyungang, Jiangsu, China
Post Code: 222047
Tel: 86 518 234 1427
Fax: 86 518 2349001
E-mail: admin@lygetdz.gov.cn
Website:www.ldz.gov.cn

Nanjing Economic & Technological Development Zone

Nanjing Economic & Technological Development Zone is adjacent to the railway, port and the Second Nanjing Changjiang Grand Bridge. It has a set of integrated checkout institutions for the customs, frontier defence, commodities inspection, sanitary inspection etc. The development zone makes commercial transaction with about 160 ports of more than 70 countries worldwide via the Nanjing port. In July 1, 2003, the zone successfully obtained the ISO14001 certification.

Address: Xinshengyu, Foreign Trade Port, Nanjing, Jiangsu, China

Post Code: 210038
Tel: 86 25 580 0800
Fax: 86 25 580 0900
E-mail: zsc@xggk.com
Website: www.njxg.com

Nanjing High-Tech Industrial Development Zone

Nanjing High-Tech Industrial Development Zone was ratified as a national high-tech industrial development zone by the State Council on 6 March 1991. The zone is the concentrated area and the industrial base of the two large industries — electronics & information, and the bioengineering & pharmaceutical.

Address: Administrative Committee, Daqiao North Road, Pukou District, Nanjing, Jiangsu, China
Post Code: 210061
Tel: 86 25 884 3666
Fax: 86 25 884 3843
E-mail: njhnza@public1.ptt.js.cn
Website: www.njnhz.com.cn

Nantong Economic & Technological Development Zone

Nantong Economic & Technological Development Area NETDA is one of China's first 14 coastal development areas to be opened to the outside world. The state-level development area now serves as the important gateway of both the Yangtze Delta and the Yangtze River valley. Its superior geographical location, steadily improved investment environment, existing industrial foundation as well as advantages in ports, fresh water, policies and talents, etc. all help to made the development area an ideal land for investment.

Address: Administrative Committee, Fumen County, Nantong, Jiangsu, China
Post Code: 226009
Tel: 86 513 592 2110
Fax: 86 513 359 6003
Website: www.netda.com

Suzhou High-Tech Industrial Development Zone

Suzhou High-Tech Industrial Development Zone was approved as a state-level high-tech industrial development zone by the State Council in Nov 1992. It was appointed as one of the first APEC science parks in China in 1997 and designated by the State Environmental Protection Bureau.

Address: 8 Yunhe Road, Suzhou New District, Jiangsu, China
Post Code: 215011
Tel: 86 512 6825 1888/ 2677
Fax: 86 512 6825 1579
E-mail: webmaster@cs-snd.com.cn
Website: www.cs-snd.com.cn

Suzhou Industrial Park

Suzhou Industrial Park is a cooperative project between the Chinese and Singapore governments. It has created a new model for Sino-foreign economic and technological cooperation. Its Master Plan, under which the 70 km^2 China-Singapore Suzhou Industrial Park (CS-SIP) is being developed in three phases, has adopted the advanced urban construction experience of Singapore and other countries in the world. Suzhou Export Processing Zone was also set up inside here in April 2000.

Address: International Building, 2 Suhua Road, Suzhou Industrial
Park, Suzhou, Jiangsu, China
Post Code: 215021
Tel: 86 512 6288 1822
Fax: 86 512 6288 1899
E-mail: editor@sipac.gov.cn
Website: www.sipac.gov.cn

Wuxi High-Tech Industrial Development Zone

Approved by the State Council, Wuxi National High-Tech Industrial Development Zone was established in 1992. The zone enjoys all the preferential policies as stipulated by the local and the central authorities. After years of hard efforts, combined with the high speed and standards of internationalization process, the zone has been crowned as the most successful science industrial park by the British magazine "*Corporate Location*" for three consecutive years.

Address: 5 Tianshan Road, Wuxi, Jiangsu, China
Post Code: 214028
Tel: 86 510 521 3201/ 7777
Fax: 86 510 521 1327
E-mail: wnd@wnd.gov.cn
Website: www.wx-wnd.com.cn

Zhangjiagang Free Trade Zone

Zhangjiagang Free Trade Zone, approved by the State Council in Oct 1992, is the only free trade zone of a inland river port in China. The zone possesses unique geographical advantages of being connected both with the Yangtse River and the sea, excellent harbour conditions, developed transportation network, special functional superiority as well as a broad economic hinterland and flexible favoured policies

Address: Administrative Committee Building, Zhangjiagang,
Jiangsu, China
Post Code: 215634
Tel: 86 512 5832 0702
Fax: 86 512 5832 0295
E-mail: ftz@zjg.sti.js.cn
Website: www.zjgftz.gov.cn

JIANGXI

Nanchang Economic & Technological Development Zone

Nanchang Economic & Technological Development Zone is a state-level economic zone, covering 9.8 km^2 and has comprehensive infrastructure facilities. Some of the encouraged industries are textile and clothing, automotive components, electronics and appliances, medical supplies and equipment, foodstuff, bamboo and wood processing etc. Foreign investments mainly come from USA, Japan, France, UK and Germany.

Address: Fenglin Street, Changbei, Nanchang, Jiangxi, China
Post Code: 330013
Tel: 86 791 703 9808/ 9812
Fax: 86 791 703 9936
E-mail: contact@nc-tdz.com
Website: www.nc-tdz.com

Nanchang High-Tech Industrial Development Zone

Nanchang High-Tech Industrial Development Zone was founded in 1991, and approved by the State Council as a state-level industrial zone in Nov 1992. Backed by strong R&D support of Jiangxi's major scientific research institutes or universities, the zone has immense potential in developing high-tech projects. Information technology, bioengineering and fine chemistry form the pillar industries.

Address: Torch Plaza, Gaoxin Road, Nanchang, Jiangxi, China
Post Code: 330029
Tel: 86 791 810 3024/ 0284
Fax: 86 791 810 4528
E-mail: info@nchdz.com
Website: www.nchdz.net

JILIN

Changchun Economic & Technological Development Zone

Approved as a state-level economic and technological zone by the State Council on April 1993, the growing pillar industries of the zone are automotive components, corn processing, photoelectron and electronics, bio-pharmaceutical and new materials.

Address: Administrative Committee, 118 Ziyou Road,
Changchun, Jilin, China
Post Code: 130031
Tel: 86 431 464 4211
Fax: 86 431 464 4215
E-mail: cetdz@mail.cetdz.com.cn
Website: www.cetdz.com.cn

Changchun High-Tech Industrial Development Zone

Changchun High-Tech Industrial Development Zone was one of the first 27 national high-tech development areas that were approved by the State Council in March 1991.With more than ten years of development, the zone has made much progress. The five key industries include automotive, bio-pharmaceutical, photoelectron, new materials and electronic information.

Address: 95 Qianjin Street, Changchun, Jilin, China
Post Code: 130021
Tel: 86 431 517 1636/ 567 1352
Fax: 86 431 517 1636/ 567 1348
Website: www.chida.gov.cn

Huichun Export Processing Zone

Huichun Export Processing Zone is located in the 5 km^2 Border Economic Cooperation Zone approved by the State Council. Its industrial development direction is foodstuff, textile, medicine, construction materials etc. electronics and communication technology industries are also developing rapidly.

Address: Administrative Bureau, Huichun, Jilin, China
Post Code: 133300
Tel: 86 440 761 2219
Fax: 86 440 761 2218
E-mail: webmaster@hcexport.com
Website: www.hcexport.com

Jilin High-Tech Industrial Development Zone

Jilin High-Tech Industrial Development Zone is a national economic zone approved by the State Council in November 1992. The zone encourages the development of the following industries: machineries, electronics, bio-pharmaceutical, new materials etc. and takes the lead in implementing and improving the market economic structure.

Address: Torch Plaza, 6 Shenzhen Street, Jilin, China
Post Code: 132000
Tel: 86 432 479 8186/ 8019
Fax: 86 432 479 8000
E-mail: webmaster@jlhitech.com
Website: www.jlhitech.com

LIAONING

Anshan High-Tech Industrial Development Zone

Anshan High-Tech Industrial Development Zone was approved by the State Council in 1992. It is situated in the eastern part of Anshan city with a designated area of 7.9 km^2. The first development area is 3.4 km^2, comprising of four functional districts: science and development centre, high-tech industrial district, education district and service district.

Address: 288 Qianshan Road, Anshan, Liaoning, China
Post Code: 114044
Tel: 86 412 521 1018/ 1028
Fax: 86 0412 521 1056
Website: www.asht-zone.gov.cn

Dalian Economic & Technological Development Zone

Dalian Economic & Technological Development Zone is the first economic and technological development area in China approved by the State Council in September 1984. Being located in the central part of China's Bohai Sea Economic Rim, it has immense regional market potential, reaching out within the economic rim and to the vast hinterland of Northeast China.

Address: Administrative Committee, Jinma Road, Dalian,
Liaoning, China
Post Code: 116600
Tel: 86 411 762 2666
Fax: 86 411 761 1284
E-mail: info@mail.ddz.gov.cn
Website: www.ddz.gov.cn

Dalian Export Processing Zone

Dalian Export Processing Zone is one of the 15 Export Processing Zones approved by the State Council in April 2000. It is one of the three pilot zones among the 15 and it is the only one in the coastal open cities in Northeast China.

Address: Taihua Plaza, Dalian, Liaoning, China
Post Code: 116600
Tel: 86 411 731 0295
Fax: 86 411 731 6565
E-mail: huiminli@online.ln.cn
Website:www.dlftz.gov.cn

Dalian Free Trade Zone

Dalian Free Trade Zone, the only one of its type in Northeast China, offers easy access to the Chinese market and lowers the cost of investment in China. Main functions of the zone are: international trade, export processing, bonded warehousing, bonded exhibition, entrepot trade and processing of imported materials.

Address: Taihua Plaza, Dalian, Liaoning, China
Post Code: 116600
Tel: 86 411 730 2951
Fax: 86 411 730 2951
E-mail: huiminli@online.ln.cn
Website: www.dlftz.gov.cn

Dalian High-Tech Industrial Development Zone

Dalian High-Tech Industrial Development Zone is among the first batch of high-tech industrial zones approved by the State Council. The zone covers an area of 35.6 km^2, composed of Qixianling Industrial Base, Double D Port, Overseas Park, Software Park and Huanghelu Science Park.

Address: 1 Gaoxin Street, Qixianling Industrial Base, Dalian,
Liaoning, China
Post Code: 116025
Tel: 86 411 479 3602/ 2100
Fax: 86 411 479 3639
E-mail: dlhizic@dalian-gov.net
Website: www.ddport.com

Dandong Border Economic Cooperation Zone

Dandong Border Economic Cooperation Zone is a state-level economic zone approved by the State Council. It is located in Dandong city, the largest border city in China, and near the Yalu River and Yellow Sea, facing the city of Sinuiju of the Republic of Korea across the river, thus enjoying geographical advantages.

Address: 3F Fangbeihao, Dandong, Liaoning, China
Post Code: 118000
Tel: 86 415 312 7399
Fax: 86 415 312 3154
E-mail: dbecz@mail.ddptt.ln.cn
Website: www.dbecz.ddppt.ln.cn

Shenyang Economic & Technological Development Zone

Established in June 1988, the Shenyang Economic & Technological Development Zone (SETDZ) was designated as a state-level zone in April 1993 by the State Council. The zone has a designated area of 32 km^2 bounded by an expressway that encircles Shenyang city. The growing pillar industries of the zone are automotive, chemicals, foodstuff and medicine.

Address: Administrative Committee, Huahai Road, Yuhong
District, Shenyang, Liaoning, China
Post Code: 110141
Tel: 86 24 2581 0324
Fax: 86 24 2581 2748
E-mail: sydz@sydz.gov.cn
Website: www.sydz.gov.cn

Shenyang High-Tech Industrial Development Zone

Shenyang High-Tech Industrial Development Zone was set up in May 1988, and approved to be a national one in March 1991 by the State Council. It is situated in the southern part of Shenyang city with an area of 34.2 km^2. The zone houses Shenyang Cross-Straits Science Industrial Park, College Science Park, Overseas Pioneering Park and Environmental Protection Industrial Park.

Address: 1 Shiji Road, Hunnan Industrial Zone, Shenyang, Liaoning, China
Post Code: 110003
Tel: 86 24 2374 5010
Fax: 86 24 2389 2622
E-mail: sygx@sygx.gov.cn
Website: www.hunnan.gov.cn

Yingkou Economic & Technological Development Zone

Yingkou Economic & Technological Development Zone (YETDZ) is located in the middle of Liaodong Peninsula on the east bank of Bohai Bay, and in the south of Yingkou city. The zone is 210 km north of Shenyang and 180 km south of Dalian. There are rich deposits of oil and gas in the area. Located in the zone, the Yingkou Port is one of the top ten key ports of China.

Address: 8 Qiantangjiang Road, Yingkou, Liaoning, China
Post Code: 115007
Tel: 86 417 625 7957
Fax: 86 417 625 1028
E-mail: gov@ykdz.gov.cn
Website: www.ykdz.gov.cn

QINGHAI

Xining Economic & Technological Development Zone

Xining Economic & Technological Development Zone was approved as a state-level economic zone on 3 July 2000. It is focusing its efforts in developing high-tech processing industries such as salt-lake chemicals, nonferrous metals, petroleum natural gas etc and plans to develop niche industries such as Chinese-Tibetan medicine. Emerging industries involving ecological protection, new high technologies, new materials and information technology are established.

Address: 36, Bayi West Road, Xining, Qinghai, China
Post Code: 810000
Tel: 86 971 812 5306
Fax: 86 971 812 5196
E-mail: xnjfj@163.com
Website: www.xnkfq.com

SHAANXI

Baoji High-Tech Industrial Development Zone

Baoji High-Tech Industrial Development Zone, divided into East and West zone, is a state-level industrial zone approved by the State Council in November 1992. The developing key industries in the zone are electronic information, machinery and electronics, new materials etc. The zone has become the technology innovation centre of Baoji city.

Address: 19 Huoju Road, Baoji, Shaanxi, China
Post Code: 721006
Tel: 86 917 331 2952
Fax: 86 917 331 9818
Website: www.bj-hightech.com

Xi'an Economic & Technological Development Zone

Xi'an Economic & Technological Development Zone is situated at the north suburbs of Xi'an city. It lies on a flat terrain, enjoying distinct superiority of its location and convenient transportation. The zone is based on high-technology orientation and the pillar industries have basically been formed: mechanical electronics, foodstuff, biopharmaceutical and new materials.

Address: Gangjiazha, North Suburbs, Xi'an, Shaanxi, China
Post Code: 610012
Tel: 86 28 485 3233/ 3592
Fax: 86 28 487 2887
E-mail: cdetdz@mail.sc.cninfo.net
Website: www.xetdz.com.cn

Xi'an High-Tech Industrial Development Zone

Xi'an High-Tech Industrial Development Zone was founded in May 1988, and approved as a state-level industrial zone by the State Council in March 1991. It is one of the economic zones open to APEC members. Five pillar industries have emerged: electronic telecommunication, energy-saving refrigeration, IT and computer, machinery and electronics, and new materials.

Address: Torch Plaza, Gaoxin Road, Xi'an, Shaanxi, China
Post Code: 710075
Tel: 86 29 823 8431
Fax: 86 29 821 0481
E-mail: xdz@xdz.com.cn
Website: www.xdz.com.cn

Yangling Agriculture High-Tech Development Zone

Yangling Agricultural High-Tech Development Zone was set up on 13 July 1997 with the approval of the State Council and it is the only agricultural high-tech zone in China. It enjoys the preferential and supporting policies for the agricultural industry. Without industrial pollution, the zone boasts of a superior geography location, convenient transportation, rich water resources, fresh air, good environment and abundant tourist resource.

Address: International Exhibition Centre, 1 New Bridge North Road, Yangling, Shaanxi, China
Post Code: 712100
Tel: 86 29 703 6900
Fax: 86 29 703 6882

E-mail: ycheng@ylagri.gov.cn
Website:www.ylagri.gov.cn

SHANDONG

Jinan High-Tech Industrial Development Zone

Jinan High-Tech Industrial Development Zone, approved as a state-level industrial zone in March 1991 by the State Council, is situated in the eastern part of Jinan city. Currently, there are several parks in the zone: Overseas Entrepreneur Park, Qilu Software Park, University Technological Park, Qilu Software Academy, Environmental Technology Park, Export Processing Zone etc.

Address: Administrative Committee, 28 Gongye South Road,
Jinan, Shandong, China
Post Code: 250101
Tel: 86 531 887 1617
Fax: 86 531 887 1600
E-mail: wj@jctp.gov.cn
Website: www.jctp.gov.cn

Qingdao Economic & Technological Development Zone

Qingdao Economic & Technological Development Zone was approved by the State Council in October 1984. Qingdao Free Trade Zone, Qingdao Hi-tech Industrial Development Zone and Xuejiadao Holiday Resort have been established within the Area. The pillar industries such as electronic information and home appliance, chemical fibres, machinery, building materials have already been developed in the zone.

Address: Zeren Mansion, 369 Changjiang Middle Road, Qingdao,
Shandong, China
Post Code: 266000
Tel: 86 532 609 2801
Fax: 86 532 698 8629
E-mail: propro@bestinvest.org
Website:www.qdhtz.com

Qingdao Free Trade Zone

Qingdao Free Trade Zone, a unique free trade zone along the Yellow River, represents one of the 15 Free Trade Zones in China. The zone has easy access to Qianwan Port, Huangdao Oil Port, and Qingdao Port. Qianwan Port boasts a 22 million-ton wharf for coals, ores, and bulk cargoes, a 5.1 million-ton containers wharf, and a 200,000-ton wharf specialized for loading and unloading mineral ores — which is Asia's largest and world's second largest of its kind. Huangdao Oil Port has a 30 million-ton wharf for crude and refined oils.

Address: Xingshan Road, Qingdao, Shandong, China
Post Code: 266555
Tel: 86 532 689 4097

Fax: 86 532 689 4090
E-mail: qingbsq@public.qd.sd.cn
Website: www.qdftz.com

Qingdao High-Tech Industrial Development Zone

Qingdao High-Tech Industrial Development Zone is mainly composed of two sections: National High-Tech Development Zone and Shilaoren National Tourism Resort. Qingdao Hi-Tech Industrial Park provides convenient transportation and communication systems, a beautiful environment and all the necessary facilities for modern high-tech industries.

Address: Administrative Building, Laoshan District, Qingdao,
Shandong, China
Post Code: 266061
Tel: 86 532 899 6529
Fax: 86 532 899 6530
E-mail: propro@bestinvest.org
Website:www.qdhtz.com

Weifang High-Tech Industrial Development Zone

Weifang High-Tech Industrial Development Zone is situated in Weifang city, which is in the centre of Shandong Peninsula and lies on the vital communication line connecting Shandong Peninsula and the inland area. Established in 1993, the development area has a designated area of 18 km^2.

Address: Torch Plaza, Beigong East Street, Weifang, Shandong, China
Post Code: 255005
Tel: 86 536 878 6638
Fax: 86 536 888 2507
E-mail: tjxx@public.wfptt.sd.cn
Website: www.wfgx.gov.cn

Weihai Economic & Technological Development Zone

Weihai Economic & Technological Development Zone was established on 21 Oct 1992 with approval from the State Council. Some foreign-invested projects with high added value such as Daewoo Automobile Components, Daewoo Electronics, Weidongri Foodstuff, Howden fans, Wooseak Semiconductor and Taikang Digital Technology, have been put into operation successively, forming eight pillar industries including automobile, electronics, food, textiles, pharmaceutical, chemical, building materials and machinery industry.

Address: Jianshe Building, Huangshan Road, Weihai, Shandong,
China
Post Code: 264205
E-mail: webmaster@eweihai.net.cn
Tel: 86 631 598 0100
Fax: 86 631 598 2200
Website: www.eweihai.net.cn

Weihai Export Processing Zone

Weihai Export Processing Zone was set up with the approval of the State Council on 27 April 2000. It is located inside th Weihai Economic & Technological Development Zone with a designated area of 2.6 km^2. Weihai EPZ is a comprehensive export processing zone, enjoying complete infrastructure and superior geographical advantages.

Address: Administrative Bureau, Qilu Boulevard, Weihai,
Shandong, China
Post Code: 264205
Tel: 86 631 598 1673
Fax: 86 535 684 0880
E-mail: netwhepz@163.com
Website: whckjgq.51.net

Weihai Torch High-Tech Industrial Development Zone

Weihai Torch Hi-Tech Industrial Development Zone, one of the three torch high-tech industrial development zones in china, was established with the approval of the State Council in March 1991. It is also one of the first 16 export base for high-tech products authorized by the National Science & Technology Ministry and Foreign Economic & Trade Ministry.

Address: Torch Plaza, 198 Wenhua West Road, Weihai, Shandong,
China
Post Code: 264209
Tel: 86 631 568 0118
Fax: 86 631 568 0118
E-mail: webmaster@whtdz.com.cn
Website: www.whtdz.com.cn

Yantai Economic & Technological Development Zone

Yantai Economic & Technological Development Area is one of the first 14 state-level development zones approved by the State Council in 1984 and began its construction in March 1985. Pillar industries comprising of machinery, automobile and components, electronic information, chemicals, textile and biopharmaceutical have been formed in the zone.

Address: 1 Changjiang Road, Yantai, Shandong, China
Post Code: 264006
Tel: 86 535 637 7777/ 639 6111
Fax: 86 535 639 6999
E-mail: yeda@public.ytptt.sd.cn
Website: www.yeda.gov.cn

Yantai Export Processing Zone

Yantai Export Processing Zone is one of the first 15 export processing zones approved by the State Council. It lies in the northern part of Yantai city, and faces Japan and Korea across the sea. To its south, it is adjacent to Yantai Railaway Station; to its east is Yantai Harbour; and to its west is the urban residential area. The zone has attracted foreign investors from Japan, Korea, Singapore, Hongkong, Taiwan, Sweden, USA, Canada etc. and also domestic enterprises.

Address: Administrative Comprehensive Building, 88 Huanhai
Road, Yantai, Shandong, China
Post Code: 264000
Tel: 86 535 680 0049
Fax: 86 535 684 0880
E-mail: office@yantaiepz.gov.cn
Website:www.yantaiepz.gov.cn

Zibo High-Tech Industrial Development Zone

Zibo High-Tech Industrial Development Zone is one of the 53 state-level development zone approved by the State Council in November 1992. The zone has a total area of 115 km^2, in which 70 km^2 of area can be used for industrial development and construction.

Address: Torch Plaza, Northern End of Liuquan Road, Zhangdian
District, Zibo, Shandong, China
Post Code: 255086
Tel: 86 533 358 0205
Fax: 86 533 358 3091
E-mail: webmaster@china-zibo.com
Website: www.china-zibo.com

SHANXI

Taiyuan Economic & Technological Development Zone

Taiyuan Economic & Technological Development Zone has a developed area of 0.66 km^2. The following industries are encouraged: food processing, medicine and electronics, machinery, light industry and packaging, refined chemicals, agricultural produce processing, bonded zone, storage and warehousing, and the centre will be comprehensively developed in terms of trade, commerce, finance, services and recreational facilities.

Address: Administrative Committee, Chuangye Street, Sub-
District 128, Taiyuan, Shanxi, China
Post Code: 030000
Tel: 86 351 709 8055
Fax: 86 351 709 8043

Taiyuan High-Tech Industrial Development Zone

Taiyuan High-Tech Industrial Development Zone was set up in July 1991 and was approved as a national development zone by the State Council in November 1992. It is Shandong's only national high-tech zone, with a total designated area of 60.8km². The key five pillar industries in the zone are microelectronic information, photoelectronics, new materials, energy-and-environmental friendly, medical and bioengineering industries.

Address: Administrative Committee Building, Xuefu West Road,
Taiyuan, Shanxi, China
Post Code: 030006
Tel: 86 351 702 7087
Fax: 86 351 702 4897
E-mail: webmaster@tyctp.com.cn
Website:www.tyctp.com.cn

SICHUAN

Chengdu Economic & Technological Development Zone

Chengdu Economic & Technological Development Zone was founded in July 1990 and was approved to be a state-level one by the State Council in February 2000. The zone, which is nicknamed "Pudong of Chengdu", has a designated area of 9.94km². It enjoys a developed transportation infrastructure and is well-connected to Chongqing, Kunming and other parts of China.

Address: 3 Longdu South Road, Longquanyi, Chengdu, Sichuan,
China
Post Code: 610012
Tel: 86 28 485 3233/ 3592
Fax: 86 28 487 2887
E-mail: cdetdz@mail.sc.cninfo.net
Website:www.cdetdz.com

Chengdu Export Processing Zone

Chengdu Export Processing Zone was established on 27 April 2000. It was one of the first batches of export processing zones in the country and the only state-level EPZ in western China. The zone is located south of Chengdu city, with a designated area of 3km².

Address: 5 Chuangye Road, Gaoxin Boulevard, Chengdu,
Sichuan, China
Post Code: 610041
Tel: 86 28 518 0019
Fax: 86 28 532 1788
E-mail: info@scepz.gov.cn
Website: www.scepz.gov.cn

Mianyang High-Tech Industrial Development Zone

Mianyang High-Tech Industrial Development Zone, founded in 1992 with the approval of the State Council, has a designated area of 6.1 km². It is situated in the western part of Mianyang city. With electronic information, fine chemical, new materials and biopharmaceutical industries as its four key pillars, it is fast evolving into an important economic growth point.

Address: Torch Plaza, 40 Mianxing Road, West Section,
Mianyang, Sichuan, China
Post Code: 621000
Tel: 86 816 253 1536
Fax: 86 816 253 2610
Website: www.myship.gov.cn

YUNNAN

Hekou Border Economic Cooperation Zone

The zone is separated from the Laojie city of Vietnam only by a bridge, and is linked to Xigong and Henei by the Dianyue Railway, Kunhe Highway and Red River. With convenient land and sea transport, it is Southwest China's gateway to Vietnam and Southeast Asia.

Address: Beishan Road, Hekou County, Gejiu, Yunnan, China
Post Code: 661300
Tel: 86 873 342 1158
Fax: 86 873 342 1821

Kunming Economic & Technological Development Zone

Kunming Economic & Technological Development Zone was founded in 1992 and was approved as a state-level development zone by the State Council on 13 February 2000. It lies in the east suburbs of Kunming city, about 4 km away. After ten years of development, a complete industry structure has formed, including manufacturing, scientific and technological innovation, commerce, real estate and education.

Address: Changhong Road, Kunming, Yunnan, China
Post Code: 650021
Tel: 86 871 727 5011/ 5008
Fax: 86 871 727 5005
E-mail: ketdz@public.dm.yn.cn
Website: www.ketdz.gov.cn

Kunming High-Tech Industrial Development Zone

Approved by the State Council in 1992, Kunming High-Tech Industrial Development Zone occupies a total designated area of 11.5 km² and is made up of the New District, Jinding Science and Technology Park, Yunnan Non-State Science and Technology Garden and Technology Street. The pillar industries in the zone are bioengineering, electronic information technology, photoelectronics, and new materials industries.

Address: Administrative Committee, Kunming, Yunnan, China
Post Code: 650106
Tel: 86 871 831 1306
Fax: 86 871 832 0518
E-mail: kmgx@kmhnz.gov.cn
Website: www.kmhnz.gov.cn

Ruili Border Economic Cooperation Zone

Approved by the State Council in 1992, the zone adjoins to Ruili city in the north and Mojie city of Burma in the south. Today it is the national port of trade to Burma as well as enterprise trade from the Burmese. The import & export trading, processing industry, local agriculture and biological resources of subtropical and tropical zone within the area are very promising.

Address: Administrative Committee, South Suburbs, Ruili,
Yunnan, China
Post Code: 679600
Tel: 86 692 414 8655
Fax: 86 692 414 8059

Wanding Border Economic Cooperation Zone

Wanding city is one of the Chinese border cities, which is located in the Sino-Burma border area. It is the terminal of No. 320 National Highway. The zone was established with the approval of the State Council in 1992, covering 5 km^2. It focuses on the development of trade, processing, agriculture resources, international cooperation of labour and tourism, making full use of Chinese and Burmese raw material and markets.

Address: 118 Minzhu Street, Wanding, Yunnan, China
Post Code: 678500
Tel: 86 692 515 1404
Fax: 86 692 5151 394

ZHEJIANG

Hangzhou Economic & Technological Development Zone

Hangzhou Economic & Technological Development Zone, approved by the State Council as a state-level indsutrial zone, is located east of Hangzhou city. It has a total designated area of 104.7 km^2. To date, five pillar industries have been established in HETDZ, namely machinery & electronics, biopharmaceutical, textile & chemical fibres, light industrial foodstuff and high-tech chemicals. Hangzhou Export Processing Zone is also located inside here.

Address: Yindu Commercial Building, Hangzhou, Zhejiang,
China
Post Code: 310018
Tel: 86 571 8691 0312/ 0297

Fax: 86 571 8283 5866
E-mail: xetdza@xsptt.zjpta.net.cn
Website: www.xetdz.com

Hangzhou Export Processing Zone

Hangzhou Export Processing Zone, one of the first batches to be approved by the government, was established on 27 April 2000 with approval from the State Council. With a total designated area of 2.92 km^2, it is also the only EPZ in Zhejiang province.

Address: Yindu Commercial Building, Hangzhou, Zhejiang,
China
Post Code: 310018
Tel: 86 571 8691 0312
Fax: 86 571 8691 1467

Hangzhou High-Tech Industrial Development Zone

The founding of Hangzhou High-Tech Industrial Development Zone was established in March 1990, and approved as a state-level high-tech zone by the State Council in the next year. It is mainly engaged in electronic information, new materials, medicine and biological technology, new energy, energy-saving and environmental protection.

Address: 199 Wensan Road, Hangzhou, Zhejiang, China
Post Code: 310000
Tel: 86 571 8806 0686/ 1990
Fax: 86 571 8806 0687
E-mail: gwh@hhtz.com
Website: www.hhtz.gov.cn

Ningbo Economic & Technological Development Zone

Ningbo Economic & Technological Development Zone was founded with approval of the State Council in October 1984, covering 29.6 km^2. The zone is located alongside Beilun Port, one of China's top four natural deep-water ports. It mainly engages in petrochemicals, paper, textiles, oil, shipping, iron and steel industries.

Address: Chuangye Mansion, 477 Mingzhou Road, Beilun,
Ningbo, Zhejiang, China
Post Code: 315800
Tel: 86 574 8688 1172/ 8685 0225
Fax: 86 574 8688 1816
E-mail: webmaster@netd.com.cn
Website: www.netd.com.cn

Ningbo Free Trade Zone

Approved by the State Council, Ningbo Free Trade Zone was established on 19 Nov 1992. It mainly handles international trade, export-oriented processing and bonded storage services. A high-tech industrial park is taking shape within the zone, which will focus on information technology, machinery and bioengineering.

Address: Baoshui Building, Ningbo FTZ, Ningbo, Zhejiang, China
Post Code: 315800
Tel: 86 574 8688 4850
Fax: 86 574 8688 3518
E-mail: yaoli@nftz.gov.cn
Website: www.nftz.gov.cn

Wenzhou Economic & Technological Development Zone

Wenzhou Economic & Technological Development Zone, approved by the State Council on 16 March 1992, is the only state-level development zone in the south of Zhejiang. A planned area of 5.11 km^2 has been completely developed and it is fast becoming the modern industrial base and new economic growth point in Wenzhou city. It encourages the development of biological technology, genetic engineering, medicine, electronic information, new materials and new energy industries.

Address: Development Zone Building, Tangjia Qiaonan Road, Wenzhou, Zhejiang, China
Post Code: 325011
Tel: 86 577 8891 0701/ 0212
Fax: 86 577 8891 0803
E-mail: wetdz@wetdz.gov.cn
Website:www.wetdz.gov.cn

Xiaoshan Economic & Technological Development Zone

Xiaoshan Economic & Technological Development Zone is located at the southern flank of the Yangtze River Delta and within the boundaries of Xiaoshan District of Hangzhou. It is very near to the Shanghai-Hangzhou-Ningbo expressway and Hangzhou-Jinhua-Quzhou expressway. Capital or technology intensive industrial projects such as electronics, communications, electrical and mechanical, pharmaceutical, biotechnology, textile, fine chemistry, machinery etc. are encouraged to invest in the zone.

Address: 99 Shixin North Road, Xiaoshan District, Hangzhou, Zhejiang, China
Post Code: 311200
Tel: 86 571 8283 5906/ 5908
Fax: 86 571 8283 5866
E-mail: xetdza@xsptt.zjpta.net.cn
Website:www.xetdz.com

GOVERNMENT AGENCIES

MINISTRIES	CONTACT NUMBER
Ministry of Civil Affairs	86 10 6513 5333
Ministry of Commerce	86 10 6512 1919
Ministry of Communications	86 10 6529 2114
Ministry of Construction	86 10 6839 4114
Ministry of Culture	86 10 6555 1432
Ministry of Education	86 10 6609 6114
Ministry of Finance	86 10 6855 1624
Ministry of Foreign Affairs of the People's Republic of China	86 10 6596 1114
Ministry of Health	86 10 6879 2114
Ministry of Information Industry	86 10 6601 4249
Ministry of Labour Relations	86 10 6612 7001
Ministry of Land Resources	86 10 6612 7001
Ministry of Rail	86 10 6324 4150
Ministry of Science & Technology	86 10 6851 5500
Ministry of Water Resources	86 10 6320 3069
COMMISSIONS	
National Development and Reform Commission	86 10 6850 1111
National Population and Family Planning Commission of China	86 10 6204 6622
State Economic & State Commission	86 10 6319 2154
The People's Bank of China	86 10 6601 5378
STATE BUREAUS OF MINISTRIES & COMMISSIONS	
Chinese Cultural Heritage	86 10 6401 2636
China Post	86 10 6831 5859
China Tobacco	86 10 6360 5678
State Administration of Foreign Exchange	86 10 6840 2255
State Administration of Foreign Expats Affairs	86 10 6894 8899
INSTITUTIONS DIRECTLY UNDER THE STATE COUNCIL	
Chinese Academy of Sciences	86 10 6859 7114
Chinese Academy of Social Sciences	86 10 6513 7744
Chinese Academy of Engineering	86 10 6851 8822
China Internet Information Centre	86 10 6832 6688
China Meteorological Administration	86 10 6217 4239
China Securities Regulatory Commission	86 10 6621 1188
Development Research Centre of the State Council of PRC	86 10 6513 5566
Xinhua	86 10 6307 1114

FOREIGN-CHINA BUSINESS ASSOCIATIONS

ASSOCIATION	CONTACT NUMBER
American Chamber of Commerce	86 21 6279 7119
AustCham Shanghai	86 21 6248 8301
Belgian Business Association	86 21 5879 1599
Benelux Business Association	86 21 3423 0084
British Chamber of Commerce	86 21 6219 8185
Canada China Business Council	86 21 6390 6790
Canadian Business Forum	86 21 6279 8400 ext 5592
China Australia Chamber of Commerce	86 21 6248 8301
China Britain Business Council	86 21 6218 5183
China-Italy Chamber of Commerce, Shanghai	86 21 3222 0891
ChinaLink Liverpool Chamber of Commerce	86 21 6323 7703
Danish Business Association	86 21 6219 2711
Delegation of German Industry & Commerce	86 21 6330 9791
Dutch Business Association	86 21 6437 6598
Finland Trade Centre	86 21 6471 0388
Foreign Business Development Association for the DPRK	86 10 6599 5262/3
French Chamber of Commerce	86 21 62813618
French Trade Commission	86 21 5306 1100
German Centre of Industry & Trade	86 21 6501 5100
Hong Kong Chamber of Commerce	86 21 5306 9533
Hong Kong Trade Development Council	86 21 6352 3453
Italian Institute for Foreign Trade Shanghai	86 21 6248 8600
Japanese Chamber of Commerce	86 21 6275 2001
Russian Federation Chamber of Commerce	86 21 6228 1304
Shanghai-Japan Club for Commerce & Industry	86 21 6278 0416
Shanghai Singapore Business Association	86 21 6437 0511
Swedish Trade Council	86 21 6474 3533
United Kingdom	86 21 6279 7650
US-China Business Council	86 21 6415 2579

FOREIGN EMBASSIES & CONSULATES

BEIJING

EMBASSY / CONSULATE	CONTACT NUMBER
Afghanistan	86 10 6532 1582
Albania	86 10 6532 1116
Algeria	86 10 6532 1231/ 2
Angola	86 10 6532 6968
Argentina	86 10 6532 2090
Australia	86 10 6532 2331/ 7
Austria	86 10 6532 1777
Azerbaijan	86 10 6532 4614
Bahrain	86 10 6532 5025/ 8
Bangladesh	86 10 6532 2764

EMBASSY / CONSULATE	CONTACT NUMBER
Belarus	86 10 6532 6426
Belgium	86 10 6532 1736/ 8
Benin	86 10 6532 2741
Bolivia	86 10 6532 4370
Botswana	86 10 6532 5751/ 6
Brazil	86 10 6532 2881
Brunei Darussalam	86 10 6532 4094
Bulgaria	86 10 6532 1462
Burkina Faso	86 10 6532 2550
Burundi	86 10 6532 2328
Cambodia	86 10 6532 1889
Cameroon	86 10 6532 1828
Canada	86 10 6532 3536
Central African Republic	86 10 6532 1789
Chad	86 10 6532 1295/ 6
Chile	86 10 6532 1287
Columbia	86 10 6532 3377
Congo	86 10 6532 1658
Cote D'ivoire	86 10 6532 1223
Croatia	86 10 6532 6241
Cuba	86 10 6532 2129
Cyprus	86 10 6532 5057
Czech	86 10 6532 1531
Denmark Danish	86 10 6532 2431/ 2
Ecuador	86 10 6532 3158
Egypt	86 10 6532 1920
Equatorial Guinea	86 10 6532 3679
Eritrea	86 10 6532 6534
Ethiopia	86 10 6532 1782
Finland	86 10 8529 8626
France	86 10 6501 4868
Gabon	86 10 6532 2810
Germany Building 1	86 10 6532 2161/ 5
Germany Building 2	86 10 6532 5556/ 61
Ghana	86 10 6532 1319
Greece Hellenic	86 10 6532 1317
Guinea	86 10 6532 3649
Guyana	86 10 6532 1337™
Hungary	86 10 6532 3845
Iceland	86 10 6532 6881
India	86 10 6532 3127
Indonesia	86 10 6532 5489
Iran	86 10 6532 2149
Iraq	86 10 6532 3385
Ireland	86 10 6532 2888
Israel	86 10 6505 0328
Italy	86 10 6532 2131/ 5

EMBASSY / CONSULATE	CONTACT NUMBER
Japan	86 10 6532 2361
Jordan	86 10 6532 3906
Kazakhstan	86 10 6532 6536
Kenya	86 10 6532 3381
Korea People's Democratic	86 10 6532 1186
Korea	86 10 6505 2608/ 9
Kuwait	86 10 6532 2216
Kyrgyzstan	86 10 6532 6458/ 9
Laos	86 10 6532 1224
Lebanon	86 10 6532 2197
Lesotho	86 10 6532 6842
Libya	86 10 6532 3666
Lithuania	86 10 6532 4421
Luxembourg	86 10 6513 5937
Macedonia	86 10 6532 6282
Madagascar	86 10 6532 1353
Malaysia	86 10 6532 2531/ 3
Mali	86 10 6532 1704
Malta	86 10 6532 3114
Marshall Islands	86 10 6532 5819
Mauritania	86 10 6532 1346
Mexico	86 10 6532 2574
Mongolia	86 10 6532 1952
Morocco	86 10 6532 1796
Mozambique	86 10 6532 3664
Myanmar	86 10 6532 1584
Namibia	86 10 6532 4810
Nepal	86 10 6532 1795
Netherlands	86 10 6532 1131/ 4
New Zealand	86 10 6532 2731/ 3
Nicaragua	86 10 6532 3014
Niger	86 10 6532 2768
Nigeria	86 10 6532 3631/ 3
Norway	86 10 6532 2261/ 2
Oman	86 10 6532 3276
Pakistan	86 10 6532 2581
Palestine	86 10 6532 1361
Papua New Guinea	86 10 6532 4312
Peru	86 10 6532 2976
Philippines	86 10 6532 2794
Poland	86 10 6532 1235
Portugal	86 10 6532 3497
Qatar	86 10 6532 2231/ 5
Romania	86 10 6532 3442
Russia	86 10 6532 2181
Rwanda	86 10 6532 2193
Saudi Arabia	86 10 6532 4825

EMBASSY / CONSULATE	CONTACT NUMBER
Senegal	86 10 6532 2593
Sierra Leone	86 10 6532 1222
Singapore	86 10 6532 3926
Slovak	86 10 6532 1531
Slovenia	86 10 6532 6356
Somali	86 10 6532 1752
South Africa	86 10 6465 1941
Spain	86 10 6532 2072
Sri Lanka	86 10 6532 1861/ 2
Sudan	86 10 6532 3715
Sweden	86 10 6532 3331
Switzerland	86 10 6532 2736
Syria	86 10 6532 1372
Tanzania	86 10 6532 1491
Thailand	86 10 6532 5058
Togo	86 10 6532 2202
Tunisia	86 10 6532 2435/ 6
Turkey	86 10 6532 2347
Turkmenistan	86 10 6532 6975
Uganda	86 10 6532 1708
Ukraine	86 10 6532 6359
United Arab Emirates	86 10 6532 2112
United Kingdom and Northern Ireland	86 10 6532 1961/ 4
United States of America	86 10 6532 3831
Uruguay	86 10 6532 4445
Uzbekistan	86 10 6532 6854
Venezuela	86 10 6532 1295
Vietnam	86 10 6532 1155
Yemen	86 10 6532 1558
Yugoslavia	86 10 6532 3516
Zaire	86 10 6532 1995
Zambia	86 10 6532 1554
Zimbabwe	86 10 6532 3665

SHANGHAI

EMBASSY / CONSULATE	CONTACT NUMBER
Australia	86 21 6279 8098
Austria	86 21 6474 0268
Belgium	86 21 6437 6579
Brazil	86 21 6437 0110
Canada	86 21 6279 8400
Chile	86 21 6249 8000
Cuba	86 21 6275 3078
Czech Republic	86 21 6471 2410
Denmark	86 21 6209 0500
Finland	86 21 6474 0068
France	86 21 6437 7414

EMBASSY / CONSULATE	CONTACT NUMBER
Germany	86 21 6433 6951
India	86 21 6275 8885
Iran	86 21 6281 4666
Israel	86 21 6209 8008
Italy	86 21 6471 6980
Japan	86 21 6278 0788
Korea	86 21 6219 6420
Mexico	86 21 6437 9585
Netherlands	86 21 6209 9076
New Zealand	86 21 6471 1127
Norway	86 21 6323 9988
Poland	86 21 6433 9228
Russia[M]	86 21 6324 2682
Singapore	86 21 6437 0776
Sweden	86 21 6474 1311
Swiss	86 21 6270 0519
Thailand	86 21 6321 9371[M]
Turkey	86 21 6474 6838
United Kingdom and Northern Ireland	86 21 6279 7650
United States of America	86 21 6433 6880
Yugoslavia	86 21 208 1388

GUANGZHOU

EMBASSY / CONSULATE	CONTACT NUMBER
Australia[M]	86 20 8331 2738[M]
Cambodia	86 20 8333 8999
Canada[M]	86 20 8666 0569[M]
Denmark	86 20 8666 0353
France	86 20 8330 3405
Germany	86 20 8192 2566
Japan[M]	86 20 8334 3009[M]
Malaysia	86 20 8739 5660
Netherlands	86 20 8330 2067
Poland	86 20 8886 2872[M]
Thailand	86 20 8188 6968
United Kingdom and Northern Ireland	86 20 8333 6520
United States of America[M]	86 20 8667 7842[M]

AREA & ZIP CODES

Country Code: 86

MUNICIPALITIES	AREA	AREA CODE	ZIPCODE
Beijing	Beijing	10	100000
	Changping	10	102200
	Daxing	10	102600

MUNICIPALITIES	AREA	AREA CODE	ZIPCODE
	Fangshan	10	102400
	Huairou	10	101400
	Mentougou	10	102300
	Miyun	10	101500
	Pinggu	10	101200
	Shunyi	10	101300
	Tongzhou	10	101100
	Yanqing	10	102100
	Ba'nai	23	401320
	Beipei	23	400700
	Bishan	23	402760
	Changshou	23	401220
	Chengkou	23	405900
Chongqing	Chongqing	23	400000
	Dazhu	23	402360
	Dianjiang	23	408300
	Fengdu	23	408200
	Fengjie	23	404600
	Hechuan	23	401520
	Jiangjin	23	402260
	Kaixian	23	405400
	Leedu	23	408100
	Liangping	23	405200
	Nanchuan	23	408400
	Nantongkuang	23	400800
	Peiling	23	408000
	Pengshui Miaozu Tujiazu	23	409600
	Qianjiang Tujiazu Miaozu	23	409000
	Rongchang	23	402460
	Shizhu Tujiazu	23	409100
	Shuangqiao	23	400900
	Tongliang	23	402560
	Tongnan	23	402660
	Wangxian	23	404000
	Wangxian	23	404100
	Wulong	23	408500
	Wushan	23	404700
	Wuxi	23	405800
	Xijiang	23	401420
	Xiushan Tujiazu Miaozu	23	409900
	Yongchuan	23	402160
	Youyang Tujiazu Miaozu	23	409800
	Yubei	23	401120
	Yunyangxian	23	404500
	Zhongxian	23	404300
Shanghai	Baoshan	21	201900
	Chongming	21	202150

MUNICIPALITIES	AREA	AREA CODE	ZIPCODE
	Fengxian	21	201400
	Jiading	21	201800
	Jinshan	21	201500
	Minxing	21	201100
	Nanhui	21	201300
	Pudong New District	21	200120
	Qingpu	21	201700
	Shanghai	21	200000
	Shanghai Jinjiao	21	200100
	Songjiang	21	201600
	Wenxing	21	201100
Tianjin	Baodi	22	301800
	Hanggu	22	300480
	Jinghai	22	301600
	Ninghe	22	301500
	Tanggu	22	300450
	Tianjin	22	300000
	Wuqing	22	301700
	Yuxian	22	301900

AUTONOMOUS REGION	AREA	AREA CODE	ZIPCODE
Guangxi	Baise	776	533000
	Fangchenggang	770	538000
	Guilin	773	541000
	Hechi	778	547000
	Liuzhou	772	545000
	Nanning	771	530000
	Qinzhou	777	535000
	Wuzhou	774	543000
	Yulin	775	537000
Inner Mongolia	Baotou	472	014000
	Chifeng	476	024000
	Dongsheng	477	017000
	Hailaer	470	021000
	Huhhot	471	010000
	Jining	474	012000
	Linhe	478	015000
	Qiqihaer	470	162650
	Tongliao	475	028000
	Wuhai	473	016000
	Wulanhaote	482	137400
	Xilinhaote	479	026000
Ningxia	Guyuan	954	756000
	Shizuishan	952	753000
	Yinchuan	951	750000
Tibet	Arikaze	892	857000
	Changdu	895	854000

AUTONOMOUS REGION	AREA	AREA CODE	ZIPCODE
	Lhasa	891	850000
	Linzhi	894	860000
	Naqu	896	852000
	Shiquanhe	873	859000
	Zedang	893	856000
Xinjiang	Ahletai	906	836000
	Akesu	997	843000
	Hami	902	839000
	Hetian	903	848000
	Kashgar	998	844000
	Kelamayi	990	834000
	Kuerle	996	841000
	Shihezi	993	832000
	Tulufan	995	838000
	Urumqi	991	830000
	Wusu	992	833000
	Yining	999	835000

PROVINCE	AREA	AREA CODE	ZIPCODE
Anhui	Anqing	556	246000
	Bengbu	552	233000
	Chaohu	565	238000
	Chuzhou	550	239000
	Fuyang	558	236000
	Hefei	551	230000
	Huainan	554	232000
	Huangshan	559	245000
	Liu'an	564	237000
	Suzhou	557	234000
	Wuhu	553	241000
Fujian	Fu'an	593	355000
	Fuzhou	591	350000
	Longyan	597	364000
	Nanping	599	353000
	Quanzhou	595	362000
	Sanming	598	365000
	Shaowu	599	354000
	Xiamen	592	361000
	Zhangzhou	596	363000
Gansu	Dingxi	932	743000
	Gannan Zangzu	9412	747000
	Hexi Bao	935	737000
	Jiuquan	937	735000
	Lanzhou	931	730000
	Liaoyuan	913	736000
	Pingliang	933	744000
	Tianshui	938	741000

PROVINCE	AREA	AREA CODE	ZIPCODE
	Wudu	939	746000
	Wuwei	935	733000
	Xifeng	934	745000
	Zhangye	936	734000
Guangdong	Guangzhou	20	510000
	Huizhou	752	516000
	Meizhou	753	514000
	Shantou	754	515000
	Shaoguan	751	512000
	Shenzhen	755	518000
	Yingde	763	513000
	Zhanjiang	759	524000
	Zhuhai	756	519000
Guizhou	Anshun	853	561000
	Duyun	854	558000
	Guiyang	851	550000
	Kaili	855	556000
	Liupenshui	857	553500
	Yuping Tongzu	856	554000
	Zunyi	852	563000
Hainan	Haikou	898	570000
	Sanya	899	572000
	Yanpu	898	578000
Hebei	Baoding	312	071000
	Cangzhou	317	061000
	Chengde	314	067000
	Hengshui	318	053000
	Langfang	316	065000
	Qinhuangdao	335	066000
	Shijiazhuang	311	050000
	Tangshan	315	063000
	Xingtai	319	054000
	Zhangjiakou	313	075000
Heilongjiang	Daqing	459	163000
	Daxing Anling	457	165000
	Harbin	451	150000
	Jiamusi	454	154000
	Mudanjiang	453	157000
	Qiqihar	452	161000
	Suihua	458	152000
Henan	Anyang	372	455000
	Kaifeng	378	475000
	Luohe	395	462000
	Luoyang	379	471000
	Nanyang	377	473000
	Pingdingshan	375	467000
	Sanmenxia	398	472000

PROVINCE	AREA	AREA CODE	ZIPCODE
	Shangqiu	370	476000
	Xinxiang	373	453000
	Xinyang	376	464000
	Xuchang	374	461000
	Zhengzhou	371	450000
	Zhoukou	394	466000
	Zhumadian	396	463000
Hubei	Enshi	718	445000
	E'zhou	711	436000
	Huangshi	714	435000
	Puxi	715	441000
	Shashi	716	434000
	Shiyan	719	442000
	Wuhan	27	430000
	Xianning	715	437000
	Yichang	717	443000
Hunan	Binzhou	735	423000
	Changde	736	415000
	Changsha	731	410000
	Hengyang	734	421000
	Huaihua	745	418000
	Jishou	743	416000
	Loudi	738	417000
	Shaoyang	739	422000
	Yiyang	737	413000
	Yongzhou	746	425000
	Yueyang	730	414000
	Zhangjiajie	744	427000
	Zhuzhou	733	412000
Jiangsu	Changzhou	519	213000
	Huaiyang	517	223000
	Lianyungang	518	222000
	Nanjing	25	212000
	Nantong	513	226000
	Suzhou	512	215000
	Wuxi	510	214000
	Xuzhou	516	221000
	Yancheng	515	224000
	Yangzhou	514	225000
	Zhenjiang	571	212000
Jiangxi	Fuzhou	794	344000
	Ganzhou	797	341000
	Ji'an	796	343000
	Jingde	798	333000
	Jiujiang	792	332000
	Nanchang	791	330000
	Pingxiang	799	337000

PROVINCE	AREA	AREA CODE	ZIPCODE
	Shangrao	793	334000
	Yichun	795	336000
	Yingtan	701	335000
Jilin	Baicheng	436	137000
	Changchun	431	130000
	Jilin	432	132000
	Meihekou	448	135000
	Siping	434	136000
	Songyuan	438	138000
	Tonghua	435	134000
	Yanji	433	133000
Liaoning	Anshan	412	114000
	Benxi	414	117000
	Dalian	411	116000
	Dandong	415	118000
	Fushun	413	113000
	Fuxin	418	123000
	Jinzhou	416	121000
	Panshan	427	124100
	Shenyang	24	110000
	Tieling	410	112000
	Yingkou	417	115000
	Zhaoyang	421	122000
Qinghai	Delingha	979	817000
	Geermu	977	816000
	Jiuzhi	9855	624700
	Maqing	975	814000
	Xining	971	810000
	Yushu	976	815000
Shaanxi	Ankang	915	725000
	Baoji	917	721000
	Hanzhong	916	723000
	Shangzhou	914	726000
	Suide	912	718000
	Tongchuan	919	727000
	Weinan	913	714000
	Xi'an	29	710000
	Yan'an	911	716000
	Yulin	912	719000
Shandong	Dezhou	534	253000
	Dongying	546	257000
	Heze	530	274000
	Jinan	531	250000
	Liaocheng	635	252000
	Linqi	539	276000
	Qingdao	532	266000
	Tai'an	538	271000

PROVINCE	AREA	AREA CODE	ZIPCODE
	Weifang	536	261000
	Xuecheng	632	277000
	Yantai	535	264000
	Yanzhou	537	272000
	Zibo	533	255000
Shanxi	Changzhi	355	046000
	Datong	352	037000
	Houma	357	043000
	Linfen	357	041000
	Lishi	358	033000
	Ningwu	351	036000
	Pucheng	356	048000
	Taiyuan	351	030000
	Xizhou	350	034000
	Yangquan	353	045000
	Yuncheng	359	044000
Sichuan	Chengdu	28	610000
	Daxian	818	635000
	Deyang	838	618000
	Guangyuan	839	628000
	Kangding	836	626000
	Leshan	833	614000
	Luzhou	830	646000
	Maerkang	837	624000
	Mianyang	816	621000
	Nanchong	817	637000
	Neijiang	832	641000
	Panzhihua	812	617000
	Suining	825	629000
	Wenchuan	8489	623000
	Xichang	834	615000
	Ya'an	835	625000
	Yibin	831	644000
	Zigong	813	643000
Yunnan	Baoshan	875	678000
	Chuxiong	878	675000
	Dali	872	671000
	Huaping	888	617300
	Kaiyuan	873	661000
	Kunming	871	650000
	Lincang	883	677000
	Qujing	874	655000
	Simao	879	665000
	Wenshan	876	663000
	Zhaotong	870	657000
Zhejiang	Hangzhou	571	310000
	Huzhou	572	313000

PROVINCE	AREA	AREA CODE	ZIPCODE
	Jiaxing	573	314000
	Jinhua	579	321000
	Lihai	576	317000
	Lishui	578	323000
	Ningbo	574	315000
	Quzhou	570	325000
	Shaoxing	575	312000
	Zhoushan	580	316000

USEFUL HOTLINES

SERVICE	CONTACT NUMBER
Police	110
Local Telephone Number Inquiry	114
Domestic Long Distance Inquiry	116
Time Inquiry	117
Fire	119
Ambulance	120
Weather Forecast	121
Traffic Police	122
Post Code Inquiry	184
Emergency Mail	185

CREDIT CARD HOTLINES IN BEIJING

American Express International	86 10 6505 2888
Diner's Club	86 10 6510 1868
Mastercard International	86 10 6510 1090-95
Visa International	86 10 6506 4371

TRADE EVENTS

BEIJING

Date	Exhibition	
Feb 10 - 12	China International Fishing Tackle & Trade Exhibition	China World Trade Centre
Mar 02 - 05	International Exhibition on Furniture Manufacturing (FURNIWOOD CHINA)	China International Exhibition Centre (CIEC)
Mar 02 - 05	Exhibition for Woodworking, Furniture and Building Industries (W.M. FAIR CHINA)	China International Exhibition Centre (CIEC)
Mar 02 - 05	Wood Machinery Fair China & Furniwood China 2004	China International Exhibition Centre
Mar 03 - 06	The 11th China Automotive Maintenance & Test Technology, Tools and Equipment Exhibition	National Agricultural Exhibition Centre (NAEC)
Mar 7 - 10	Chinawood Beijing 2004	Beijing Exhibition Centre
Mar 15 - 17	International Exhibition for the Food, Drinks, Hospitality, Foodservice, Bakery and Retail Industries (FHC BEIJING)	China International Exhibition Centre (CIEC)
Mar 23 - 25	China Cable Broadcasting Network (CCBN)	China International Exhibition Centre
Mar 30 - Apr 01	China Int'l Clothing & Accessories Fair (session 1)	China Int'l Exhibition Centre
Mar 31 - Apr 02	Yarn Expo China International Trade Fair for Fibres and Yarn	National Agricultural Exhibition Centre
Mar 31 - Apr 02	Intertextile Beijing	Beijing Exhibition Centre
Apr 05 - 07	China Int'l Clothing & Accessories Fair (Session 2)	China Int'l Exhibition Centre, Beijing
Apr 10 - 13	Photograph & Electrical Imaging Machinery and Technology Fairs (IMAGING EXPO)	China International Exhibition Centre (CIEC)
Apl 11 - 14	China International Glass Industrial Technical Exhibition (CHINA GLASS)	China International Exhibition Centre (CIEC)
Apr 21 - 23	INTER AIRPORT ASIA	China International Exhibition Centre (CIEC)
Apr 21 - 23	International Trade Fair for Intensive Animal Production (VIV CHINA)	China International Exhibition Centre (CIEC)
Apr 26 - 29	Medical Instruments and Equipment Exhibition (CHINA MED)	China International Exhibition Centre (CIEC)
May 11 - 15	6th International Exhibition-Congress on Chemical Engineering and Biotechnology (ACHEMASIA)	China International Exhibition Centre (CIEC)
May 24	The 13th China International Exhibition of Pro Audio, Light Music & Technology	China International Exhibition Centre
Jun 09 - 16	AUTO CHINA	China International Exhibition Centre (CIEC)
Jun 23 - 26	CHINA POLICE - China International Exhibition on Police Technology & Equipment	Beijing Exhibition Centre

Jun 29 - Jul 02	International Plastic Industries Exhibition (CHINAPLAS)	China International Exhibition Centre (CIEC)
Jul 07 - 10	International Exhibition on Electrical Engineering, Electrical Equipment and Contractors' Supplies (ELECTRICAL CHINA)	China International Exhibition Centre (CIEC)
Jul 07 - 10	International Exhibition on Electric Power Equipment and Technology (EP CHINA)	China International Exhibition Centre (CIEC)
Aug 21 - 24	SEARCH & RESCUE CHINA	China International Exhibition Centre (CIEC)
Sep 01 - 04	China International Occupational Safety & Health Exhibition (COS+H)	China World Trade Centre
Sep 01 - 23	China International Nonwovens, Techtextiles and Machinery Exhibition and Conference (CINTE)	China International Exhibition Centre (CIEC)
Sep 06 - 10	CHINA BREW - CHINA BEVERAGE International Brew & Beverage Processing Technology and Equipment Exhibition for China	China International Exhibition Centre (CIEC)
Sep 14 - 17	China International Trade Fair for Sanitation, Heating, Air-Conditioning, Bath & Kitchen (ISH CHINA)	China International Exhibition Centre (CIEC)
Sep 21 - 24	AIRPORT & AIR TRAFFIC EXPO CHINA	China International Exhibition Centre (CIEC)
Sep 21 - 24	Aviation Expo China	China International Exhibition Centre (CIEC)
Oct 12 - 16	China International Textile Machinery Exhibition (CITME)	China International Exhibition Centre (CIEC)
Oct 13 - 15	International Trade Show for Machinery, Equipment, and R&D in Agriculture and Animal Husbandry (AGRO-NEWTECH CHINA)	China International Exhibition Centre (CIEC)
Oct 26 - 30	Telecommunications, IT, Internet and Wireless Technology Exhibition and Conference (PT/EXPO COMM CHINA)	China International Exhibition Centre (CIEC)
Nov 01 - 05	Commercial Exhibition on Optics, Lasers, Biomedical Optics, Opto-electronic Components, and Imaging Technologies (PHOTONICS ASIA)	China International Exhibition Centre (CIEC)

CHONGQING

Date	Exhibition	Location
Apr 07 - 10	The 3rd China International Motorcycle & Accessories Exhibition	Chongqing Exhibition Centre

DALIAN, LIAONING PROVINCE

Date	Exhibition	Location
Mar 25 - 28	DIECF	Dalian Xinghai Convention & Exhibition Centre
May - 04	China Dalian International Port & Shipping Machinery & Equipment Exhibition	Dalian Xinghai Convention & Exhibition Centre
May - 04	Dalian International Electronic Product Exhibition	Dalian Xinghai Convention & Exhibition Centre

May - 04	Dalian International Electronic Product Exhibition	Dalian Xinghai Convention & Exhibition Centre
May - 04	Dalian International Rubber & Plastic Industry	Dalian Xinghai Convention & Exhibition Centre
May - 04	Dalian International Special Steel Exhibition	Dalian Xinghai Convention & Exhibition Centre
Jun 25 - 28	SHIPORT CHINA	Dalian Xinghai Convention & Exhibition Centre

DONGGUAN, GUANGDONG PROVINCE

Date	Exhibition	
Mar 24 - 26	Matech China	Guangdong Modern International Exhibition Centre
Apr 06 - 09	China Shoes	Dongguan International Conference and Exhibition Centre
Apr 06 - 09	China Shoetec	Dongguan Conference and Exhibition Centre
Apr 23 - 26	Dongguan Fair	Dongguan International Conference and Exhibition Centre

GUANGZHOU, GUANGDONG PROVINCE

Date	Exhibition	
Feb 25 - 28	Dental South China	Chinese Export Commodities Fairground (CECF)
Mar 3 - 6	Automation International Guangzhou	Chinese Export Commodities Fairground (CECF)
Mar 3 - 6	CHIFA	Chinese Export Commodities Fairground (CECF)
Mar 3 - 6	PTG	Chinese Export Commodities Fairground (CECF)
Mar 9 - 11	Personal Care Ingredients Asia	Jinhan Exhibition Centre
Mar 10 - 13	AWC	Chinese Export Commodities Fairground (CECF)
Mar 10 - 13	PVP	Chinese Export Commodities Fairground (CECF)
Mar 10 - 13	Water China	Chinese Export Commodities Fairground (CECF)
Mar 30 - Apr 2	Digital Imaging South China	China Foreign Trade Centre

Mar 30 - Apr 02	Sino-Pack	Guangzhou Fair Exhibition Centre
Mar 30 - Apr 02	China Drinktec	Guangzhou Fair Exhibition Centre
May 4 - 6	Interbake China	Guangzhou Fair Exhibition Centre
May 26 - 28	China Optics	Guangzhou Fair Exhibition Centre
Jun 15 - 18	Ceramics China	Guangzhou Fair Exhibition Centre
Jun 23 - 25	Retail China	China Foreign Trade Centre
Jun 23 - 25	FHC South China	Jinhan Exhibition Centre
Jun 23 - 25	Food & Hotel South China	Jinhan Exhibition Centre
Jul 6-9	CBD	Chinese Export Commodities Fairground (CECF)
Jul 15 - 17	SLM Expo	Guangzhou Fair Exhibition Centre
Sep 3 - 5	Cycle International Guangzhou	Chinese Export Commodities Fairground (CECF)
Nov 5 - 7	GDBN	Jinhan Exhibition Centre
Nov 5 - 7	Expo Card	Jinhan Exhibition Centre
Nov 5 - 7	Scan Guangzhou	Guangzhou Jinhan Exhibition Centre
Nov 18 - 21	Expo Comm China South	Guangdong Foreign Exhibition Centre
Dec 10 - 13	IT Expo South China	Jinhan Exhibition Centre

HARBIN, HEILONGJIANG PROVINCE

Date	Exhibition	
Apr 11 - 14	3rd China Harbin Int'l Building Fair	Heilongjiang International Convention & Exhibition Centre
Jun 15 - 19	The 15th China Harbin Fair for Trade and Economic Cooperation (CHTF)	Heilongjiang International Convention & Exhibition Centre
Sep 23 - 26	China International Winter Sports Goods & Garments Exhibition	Harbin International Exhibition Centre

HONGKONG

Date	Exhibition	
Feb 2 - 4	International Housing Conference in Hong Kong 2004	Hong Kong Convention & Exhibition Centre
Feb 4 - 7	The 6th Biennial Meeting of the Asian-Pacific Society of Neurochemistry	Hong Kong Convention & Exhibition Centre

BUSINESS DIRECTORY

Feb 7 - 8	Education UK Festival	Hong Kong Convention & Exhibition Centre
Feb 7 - 9	MDRT Experience - Hong Kong	Hong Kong Convention & Exhibition Centre
Feb 10 - 13	HOFEX 2004	Hong Kong Convention & Exhibition Centre
Feb 13 - 15	Wellness Hong Kong	Hong Kong Convention & Exhibition Centre
Feb 14 - 17	Hong Kong - Shanghai International Liver Congress 2004	Hong Kong Convention & Exhibition Centre
Feb 17 - 18	Integrated Security Conference & Expo Hong Kong 2004	Hong Kong Convention & Exhibition Centre
Feb 18 - 20	Sign Asia: Latest Technologies for Asia's Sign and Graphic Imaging Industries	Hong Kong Convention & Exhibition Centre
Feb 18 - 21	21st ICDE World Conference on Open Learning & Distance Education	Hong Kong Convention & Exhibition Centre
Feb 19	Best Practices: Decision Making Under Fire	JW Marriott Hotel Hong Kong
Feb 19 - 22	Education & Careers Expo 2004	Hong Kong Convention & Exhibition Centre
Feb 23 - 24	The 17th Asian Trade Promotion Forum (ATPF) in Hong Kong	Hong Kong Convention & Exhibition Centre
Feb 28 - Mar 02	2004 Hong Kong International Fur and Fashion Fair	Hong Kong Convention & Exhibition Centre
Mar 2 - 5	Hong Kong International Jewellery Show 2004	Hong Kong Convention & Exhibition Centre
Mar 05 - 14	Hong Kong Flower Show 2004	Victoria Park
Mar 12 - 15	11th Hong Kong International Packaging Exhibition 2004	Hong Kong Convention & Exhibition Centre
Mar 12 - 15	16th Hong Kong Int'l Machine Tool	Hong Kong Convention & Exhibition Centre
Mar 12 - 15	12th Hong Kong International Plastics Exhibition 2004	Hong Kong Convention & Exhibition Centre
Mar 17 - 18	Carriers World Asia 2004	Conrad Hong Kong
Mar 19 - 21	Hong Kong Wedding, Banquet & Honeymoon Travel Expo 2004	Hong Kong Convention & Exhibition Centre
Mar 22 - 26	43rd IFATCA Conference	Hong Kong Convention & Exhibition Centre
Mar 29 - Apr 1	Materials, Manufacturing and Technology (an APLF fair)	Hong Kong Convention & Exhibition Centre
Mar 30	Storage Networking World 2004/ Hong Kong	Hong Kong Convention & Exhibition Centre
Mar 30 - 31	Business Travel Expo Hong Kong 2004	Hong Kong Convention & Exhibition Centre

Apr 13 - 16	InterSource Hardware Asia 2004	Hong Kong Convention & Exhibition Centre
Apr 14 - 17	Hong Kong Electronics Fair 2004 (Spring Edition)	Hong Kong Convention & Exhibition Centre
Apr 1 4- 17	International ICT Expo 2004	Hong Kong Convention & Exhibition Centre
Apr 21 - 24	Hong Kong Houseware Fair 2004	Hong Kong Convention & Exhibition Centre
Apr 23 - 27	Made in China Gifts, Toys, Premium & Household Fair	Hong Kong Convention & Exhibition Centre
May 5 - 7	The Asian Banker Summit 2004	Hong Kong Convention & Exhibition Centre
May 8 - 11	Hong Kong SARS Forum & Hospital Authority Convention 2004	Hong Kong Convention & Exhibition Centre
May 18 - 20	Logistics Hong Kong Exhibition & Conference	Hong Kong Convention & Exhibition Centre
May 20 - 23	CEhk	Hong Kong Convention & Exhibition Centre
May 28 - Jun 01	26th Asia Pacific Dental Congress	Hong Kong Convention & Exhibition Centre
Jun 9 - 11	SME Market Day 2004	Hong Kong Convention & Exhibition Centre
Jun 10 - 13	ITE Hong Kong 2004 - The 18th International Travel Expo Hong Kong	Hong Kong Convention & Exhibition Centre
Jun 15 - 18	Asian Building Technologies 2004	Hong Kong Convention & Exhibition Centre
Jun 15 - 18	Asian Elenex 2004 / Asian Securitex 2004 / Asian Building Technologies 2004	Hong Kong Convention & Exhibition Centre
Jun 24 - 27	Asia's Fashion Jewellery & Accessories Fair 2004	Hong Kong Convention & Exhibition Centre
Jul 6-8	Hong Kong Licensing Show & Conference 2004	Hong Kong Convention & Exhibition Centre
Jul 13 - 16	Hong Kong Fashion Week for Spring/Summer 2005	Hong Kong Convention & Exhibition Centre
Jul 21 - 26	Hong Kong Book Fair 2004	Hong Kong Convention & Exhibition Centre
Aug 12 - 16	International Conference & Exhibition of the Modernization of Chinese Medicine & Health Products	Hong Kong Convention & Exhibition Centre
Aug 12 - 16	Food Expo 2004	Hong Kong Convention & Exhibition Centre
Aug 21 - 23	2nd CitiHomex 2004	Hong Kong Convention & Exhibition Centre
Aug 26 - 28	Print + Pack Expo 2004/SignEx 2004/Imaging Convergence Expo 2004	Hong Kong Convention & Exhibition Centre
Aug 26 - 28	SIGNEX 2004	Hong Kong Convention & Exhibition Centre

Aug 26 - 28	IMAGING CONVERGENCE EXPO 2004	Hong Kong Convention & Exhibition Centre
Sep 1 - 5	Hong Kong Watch & Clock Fair 2004	Hong Kong Convention & Exhibition Centre
Sep 28 - Oct 03	74th ASTA World Travel Congress	Hong Kong Convention & Exhibition Centre
Oct 5 - 7	Restaurant & Bar Hong Kong 2004	Hong Kong Convention & Exhibition Centre
Oct 6 - 8	Fashion Access - Handbags, Travelware, Footwear, Leather Garments and Fashion Accessories (an APLF fair)	Hong Kong Convention & Exhibition Centre
Oct 13 - 16	electronicAsia 2004	Hong Kong Convention & Exhibition Centre
Nov 3 - 5	Hong Kong Optical Fair 2004	Hong Kong Convention & Exhibition Centre
Nov 25 - 28	The 12th Hong Kong International Jewelry Manufacturers' Exhibition	Hong Kong Convention & Exhibition Centre
Dec 8 - 11	SOLUTIONS EXPO 2004Hong Kong	Hong Kong Convention & Exhibition Centre
Dec 18 - 26	2nd Hong Kong Mega Showcase	Hong Kong Convention & Exhibition Centre
Dec 04	39th Hong Kong Products Expo	Hong Kong Convention & Exhibition Centre

HUNAN

Date	Exhibition	
May 30 - Jun 3	The 3rd Int´l Electron & Industry Instruments Exhibition	Hunan Fair Hall

JIANGSU

Date	Exhibition	
Mar 2 - 4	2004 East China Packaging & Printing Equipment and Screen Printing Equipment Exhibition	Wuxi Exhibition Centre
Mar 6 - 15	2004 Dalian Spring Fashion Clothing & Accessories Exhibition	Wuxi Exhibition Centre
Mar 17 - 22	2004 Wuxi Commercial Franchise Chains Exhibition	Wuxi Exhibition Centre
Mar 27 - 30	2004 Wuxi International Hair & Beauty, Cosmetics & Cleansers, Bridal Photography Exhibition	Wuxi Exhibition Centre
Apr 22 - 25	2004 Wuxi International Printing & Packaging Machinery Exhibition	Wuxi Exhibition Centre
Apr 22 - 25	2004 Taihu International Machine Tool & Mould and Plastics Industry Exhibition	Wuxi Exhibition Centre
May 1 - 9	2004 Labour Day Welcome Exhibition - Commercial Products	Wuxi Exhibition Centre
May 28 - Jun 6	2004 Children's Day Exhibition – Women's and Children's Commercial Products	Wuxi Exhibition Centre

Jun 15 - 18	2004 East China (Wuxi) Electrical Vehicles & Spare Parts Exhibition	Wuxi Exhibition Centre
Jun 25 - 28	2004 Wuxi Textile Machinery, Fabric and Accessories Exhibition	Wuxi Exhibition Centre

SHAANXI

Date	Exhibition	
Feb 18 - 27	The 5th Fashion Exhibition	Shaanxi International Exhibition Centre Machinery Hall
Feb 19 - 21	Talents Recruitment Drive	Shaanxi International Exhibition Centre
Feb 22 - 27	Medical Equipment Exhibition	Shaanxi International Exhibition Centre
Feb 29 - Mar 4	The 6th Industry, Manufacturing and Machine Tool Exhibition	Shaanxi International Exhibition Centre
Mar 5 - 11	Real Estate Exhibition	Shaanxi International Exhibition Centre
Mar 12 - 16	Sports Exposition	Shaanxi International Exhibition Centre Machinery Hall
Mar 12 - 16	Transport Logistics System Exposition Shaanxi	Shaanxi International Exhibition Centre
Mar 17 - 20	Talents Recruitment Drive	Shaanxi International Exhibition Centre Machinery Hall
Mar 17 - 23	The 4th Western Region Residential Area Technology Industry & Urban Construction Equipment Technology Exposition	Shaanxi International Exhibition Centre
Mar 21 - 25	Advertising Exhibition	Shaanxi International Exhibition Centre Machinery Hall
Mar 25 - 31	Power & Electrical Equipment Exposition	Shaanxi International Exhibition Centre
Apr 1 - 11	East-West Region Business Forum	Shaanxi International Exhibition Centre
Apr 12 - 21	Business Forum cum Surplus Products Exhibition	Shaanxi International Exhibition Centre Machinery Hall
Apr 18 - 22	Protection Safety & Fire Prevention Exhibition (PSFP)	Shaanxi International Exhibition Centre
Apr 23 - 29	The 6th Western China Communications Exhibition	Shaanxi International Exhibition Centre
May 4 - 8	Hair & Beauty Exhibition	Shaanxi International Exhibition Centre
May 10 - 15	The 6th Medical Equipment and Automobiles, Maintenance & Spare Parts Exhibition	Shaanxi International Exhibition Centre Machinery Hall

May 10 - 15	Furniture Fair	Shaanxi International Exhibition Centre
May 16 - 21	The 2nd Xi'an Textile Industry Exhibition	Shaanxi International Exhibition Centre Machinery Hall
May 16 - 21	The 5th Xi'an International Hotel Facilities & Products Exhibition cum The 5th Xi'an International Travel Products, Handicrafts & Gifts Fair	Shaanxi International Exhibition Centre
May 23 - 28	The 5th Petroleum, Petrochemical & Chemical Equipment Exhibition	Shaanxi International Exhibition Centre Machinery Hall
May 23 - 28	The 5th Heating & Warming Equipment, Pressure Vessels, Refrigeration & Air-conditioning, Natural Gas and Solar Power Exhibition	Shaanxi International Exhibition Centre
May 29 - Jun 3	Hair & Beauty Exhibition	Shaanxi International Exhibition Centre
May 31 - Jun 5	The 4th China (Xi'an) Petroleum, Natural gas, Petrochemical Industry, Mining Exploration Technology Exhibition	Shaanxi International Exhibition Centre Machinery Hall
Jun 8 - 11	College Consultation Fair	Shaanxi International Exhibition Centre
Jun 12 - 26	The 4th Hangzhou Silk Exhibition	Shaanxi International Exhibition Centre
Jun 28 - Jul 4	Education Fair, The 3rd Electrical Vehicles Exhibition	Shaanxi International Exhibition Centre

SHANXI

Date	Exhibition	Location
Jun 11 - 13	Int'l Exposition on Electronic Material, Components (MatCom)	Shanxi Int'l Exhibition Centre

SHANGHAI

Date	Exhibition	Location
Feb 11 - 12	7th Shanghai Int'l Spare Parts & Materials Purchase Fair	INTEX Shanghai
Feb 16 - 20	China Logistics 2004 Conference	Shangri-La Pudong Hotel
Feb 17 - 20	FurniTek China 2004	Shanghai Mart
Feb 17 - 21	WoodBuild China 2005	Shanghai Mart
Feb 18 - 20	ChemSpec China 2004	Shanghai Mart
Feb 19 - 22	World Travel Fair	Shanghai New International Expo Centre
Feb 25 - 28	The 5th China (Shanghai) International Wedding & Photographic Equipment Exhibition	Shanghai Everbright Convention & Exhibition Centre
Mar 1 - 2	Embedded System Conferences	Shanghai Mart
Mar 1 - 2	The 9th Annual International IC-China Conference & Exhibition	Shanghai Mart

Mar 1 - 2	Embedded System Conferences	Shanghai Mart
Mar 1 - 2	The 9th Annual International IC-China Conference & Exhibition	Shanghai Mart
Mar 1 - 7	East China Fair	Shanghai New International Expo Centre
Mar 9 - 12	Electronic China	Shanghai New International Expo Centre
Mar 10 - 12	CPCA 2004	INTEX Shanghai
Mar 11 - 13	China National Hardware Fair (Spring)2004	Shanghai New International Expo Centre
Mar 17 - 20	Garment Expo 2004	Shanghai New International Expo Centre
Mar 17 - 24	electronicChina	Shanghai New International Expo Centre
Mar 24 - 26	Biotech and Pharma	INTEX Shanghai
Mar 25 - 27	DESSOUS CHINA	Shanghai Mart
Mar 30 - Apr 2	HOTELEX SHANGHAI 2004	Shanghai New International Expo Centre
Mar 31 - Apr 2	GAS EXPO SHANGHAI 2004	INTEX Shanghai
Mar 31 - Apr 3	Expo Shanghai 2004	INTEX Shanghai
Apr 12 - Apr 16	CCMT 2004 (China CNC Machine Tool Fair)	Shanghai Everbright Convention & Exhibition Centre
Apr 13 - 15	China Sourcing Fair: Electronics & Components	Shanghai Mart
Apr 14 - 16	CHINA CYCLE 2004	Shanghai New International Expo Centre
Apr 15 - 17	China International Bicycle & Motor Cycle Fair	Shanghai New International Expo Centre
Apr 20 - 22	China Sourcing Fair: DIY & Home Improvement	Shanghai New International Expo Centre
Apr 20 - 24	National Electronic Fair	Shanghai Everbright Convention & Exhibition Centre
Apr 21 - 23	Expo Real China	Shanghai New International Expo Centre
Apr 26 - 29	CeBIT Asia 2004	Shanghai New International Expo Centre
Apr 26 - 29	NEPCON MICROELECTRONICS SHANGAI	Shanghai Everbright Convention & Exhibition Centre
Apr 27 - 29	Opto CHINA 2004	INTEX Shanghai
May 11 - 24	TRANSPORT LOGISTIC CHINA 2004	Shanghai New International Expo Centre

May 12 - 14	INFOCOMM CHINA	Shanghai Everbright Convention & Exhibition Centre
May 12 - 16	DIE & MOULD China 2004	Shanghai New International Expo Centre
May 21 - 24	International Building & Construction Trade Fair 2004	Shanghai New International Expo Centre
May 28 - 30	Bakery China	Shanghai Everbright Convention & Exhibition Centre
May 28 - 31	China International Sporting Goods Fair Exhibition	Shanghai New International Expo Centre
May 31- Jun 2	2004 Shanghai Int'l Water Supply, Drainage and Treatment Equipment Fair	Shanghai Everbright Convention & Exhibition Centre
Jun 5 - 9	The 10th Shanghai TV Festival	Shanghai New International Expo Centre
Jun 5 - 13	The 7th Shanghai International Film Festival-International Film and TV Market	Shanghai New International Expo Centre
Jun 5 - 7	China Int'l Exhibition on Cable & Wire Industry	Shanghai Everbright Convention & Exhibition Centre
Jun 8 - 10	CRC	Shanghai Exhibition Centre (SEC)
Jun 15 - 17	CPHI CHINA	Shanghai Everbright Convention & Exhibition Centre
Jun 16 - 18	METRO CHINA 2004	INTEX Shanghai
June 16 - 19	Advertise, Print, Pack & Paper Exhibition 2004	Shanghai New International Expo Centre
Jun 29 - Jul 2	International Trade Fair for Environmental Protection	Shanghai New International Expo Centre
Jul 9 - 11	CiEX: 2nd China Interactive Entertainment Expo	Shanghai Exhibition Centre
Jul 9 - 11	China Interactive Entertainment Expo (CIEX)	Shanghai Exhibition Centre
Jul 13 - 16	The 10th International Processing, Packaging and Printing Exhibition (PROPAK CHINA BEIJING)	SNIEC Shanghai Pudong
Jul 13 - 16	ProPak China	Shanghai New International Expo Centre
Jul 22 - 25	Shanghai Int'l Diamond Jewellery Fair '04	Shanghai International Convention Centre
Jun 23 - 26	CIT Shanghai 2004/ China ELECOMM 2004	INTEX Shanghai
Sep 1 - 3	Intertextile Shanghai Autumn (Home Textiles)	Shanghai New International Expo Centre
Sep 1 - 3	Cinte Techtextil China 2004	Shanghai Int'l Exhibition Centre

Sep 1 - 9	All China Leather Exhibition	Shanghai Everbright Convention & Exhibition Centre
Sep 7 - 9	China Paper-Shanghai	INTEX Shanghai
Sep 9 - 10	AnalyticaChina 2004	Shanghai New International Expo Centre
Sep 11 - 14	The 8th China International Furniture Expo	Shanghai New International Expo Centre & Shanghai Everbright Convention & Exhibition Centre
Sep 11 - 14	The 8th China International Furniture Manufacturing Expo	Shanghai New International Expo Centre & Shanghai Everbright Convention & Exhibition Centre
Sep 14 - 19	FHC - Food and Drink	INTEX Shanghai
Sep 15 - 18	Furniture China 2004	Shanghai New International Expo Centre
Sep 25 - 27	Fashion China	Shanghai New International Expo Centre
Oct 8 - 11	China International Building & Housing Expo 2004	Shanghai New International Expo Centre
Oct 11 - 13	China Sourcing Fair: Electronics & Components	Shanghai Mart
Oct 12 - 15	PTC (Power Transimission and Control)	Shanghai New International Expo Centre
Oct 12 - 15	INTERFOOD SHANGHAI 2004	INTEX Shanghai
Oct 12 - 15	Factory Automation	Shanghai New International Expo Centre
Oct 12 - 15	Metal Working China	Shanghai New International Expo Centre
Oct 19 - 22	Auto Parts & Equip Shanghai 2004	INTEX Shanghai
Oct 26 - 29	Shanghai International Plastics & Rubber Industry Exhibition	Shanghai New International Expo Centre
Nov 10 - 12	Tubetec China	INTEX Shanghai
Nov 10 - 12	Wire Asia	INTEX Shanghai
Nov 14 - 19	The 6th Int'l Welding & Cutting Fair (Beijing Essen Welding 2004)	Shanghai Everbright Convention & Exhibition Centre
Nov 15 - 18	The 64th National Electronic Fair	Shanghai New International Expo Centre
Nov 16 - 19	Bauma China	Shanghai New International Expo Centre
Nov 25 - 28	China tourism Fair	Shanghai New International Expo Centre
Nov 26 - 28	SuperStore China 2004	Shanghai Exhibition Centre (SEC)
Nov 29 - Dec 2	Shanghai Int'l Advertising Printing Industrial Exhibition (Autumn)	INTEX Shanghai

Dec 11 - 13	China National Medicine Trade Fair	Shanghai New International

SHENZHEN, GUANGDONG PROVINCE

Date	Exhibition	Location
Mar 1 - 4	Shenzhen Int'l Electronic Element Devices Exhibition & Orders Invitation Conference	China Hi-Tech Fair Exhibition Centre
Mar 8 - 9	Embedded System Conferences - Shenzhen	China Hi-Tech Fair Exhibition Centre
Mar 8 - 9	The 9th Annual International IC-China Conference & Exhibition	China Hi-Tech Fair Exhibition Centre
Mar 9 - 12	The 5th China International Exhibition on Plastic Industry	China Hi-Tech Fair Exhibition Centre
Mar 25 - 28	SIMM 2004: 5th China Shenzhen Int'l Machinery & Moulds Industry Exhibition	China Hi-Tech Fair Exhibition Centre
Apr 25 - 28	15th China Watch Jewellery & Gift Fair (CWJF)	China Hi-Tech Fair Exhibition Centre
Jun 10 - 14	Food & Agro Expo China 2004	Shenzhen Int'l Exhibition Centre
Jun 20 - 23	The 6th China International Building Decorating Exhibition	China Hi-Tech Fair Exhibition Centre
Aug 2 - 5	Shenzhen Int'l Electronic Element Devices Exhibition & Orders Invitation Conference	Shenzhen Int'l Exhibition Centre
Aug 26 - 29	NEPCON/ Microelectronics Shenzhen	China Hi-Tech Fair Exhibition Centre
Sep 6 - 9	China Int'l Photoelectronic Expo	China Hi-Tech Fair Exhibition Centre
Oct 12 - 17	The 6th China Hi-Tech Fair / Biotech 2004	China Hi-Tech Fair Exhibition Centre
Nov 6 - 9	The 5th China International Stone Fair	China Hi-Tech Fair Exhibition Centre

SUZHOU, JIANGSU PROVINCE

Date	Exhibition	Location
Sep 9 - 11	Int'l Exposition on New Components	Suzhou Int'l Convention & Exhibition Centre

TIANJIN

Date	Exhibition	Location
May 9 - 11	The 5th Tianjin Int'l Exhibition on District Heating & Ventilation and Refrigeration Technology and Equipment	Tianjin International Exhibition Centre
Mar 17 - 20	2004 Tianjin Printing & Packaging Equipment Exhibition	Tianjin International Exhibition Centre
Mar 18 - 20	2004 China Tianjin International Cities & Residential Areas Construction Exhibition	Tianjin International Exhibition Centre
Mar 26 - 28	Northern China International Bicycles Exhibition	Tianjin International Exhibition Centre

Apr 4 - 7	2004 Household Paper International Technology Exhibition cum Conference	Tianjin International Exhibition Centre
Apr 12 - 14	2004 Tianjin International Plastic Packaging Industry Exhibition	Tianjin International Exhibition Centre
Apr 18 - 22	China (Tianjin) Spring Exported Commercial Products Exchange Fair	Tianjin International Exhibition Centre
May 18 - 20	The 4th Large Urban Cities Heating, Gas, Water Supply & Rationing, Water Treatment and Air-conditioning Combined Exhibition	Tianjin International Exhibition Centre
May 19 - 22	International Instruments & Meters and International Electric Power Automation Exhibition	Tianjin International Exhibition Centre
May 19 - 22	International Computer Systems & Communication Devices Exhibition	Tianjin International Exhibition Centre
May 28 - 31	Tianjin International Petroleum, Petrochemical, Natural Gas & Chemical Technology Exhibition	Tianjin International Exhibition Centre
May 28 - 31	Tianjin International Paint & Coating and Surface Treatment Exhibition	Tianjin International Exhibition Centre
Jun 3 - 5	2004 Tianjin International Light Industry Machinery Exhibition	Tianjin International Exhibition Centre
Jun 8 - 10	Tianjin International Modern Logistics and Warehousing Port Facilities Exhibition	Tianjin International Exhibition Centre
Jul 15 - 17	2004 China Automobile Electronic Parts & Components Exhibition	Tianjin International Exhibition Centre
Aug 28 - 30	2004 National Textiles & Fashion Exposition	Tianjin International Exhibition Centre
Aug 30 - Sep 2	China-Japan-Korea International Parts & Components Purchasing Forum	Tianjin International Exhibition Centre
Sep 8 - 11	The 6th Northern China International Mould & Machine Tools Exhibition	Tianjin International Exhibition Centre
Sep 8 - 11	The 5th Northern China International Plastics Machinery & Materials Exhibition	Tianjin International Exhibition Centre
Sep 15 - 18	2004 Tianjin International Information Technology Exhibition	Tianjin International Exhibition Centre
Sep 15 - 18	2004 AsiaPac Screen Printing & Graphic Imaging Exhibition	Tianjin International Exhibition Centre
Sep 15 - 18	2004 Tianjin New Advertising Techniques, Materials, Equipments & Medium Exhibition	Tianjin International Exhibition Centre
Sep 15 - 18	2004 China Screen Printing & Billboards Exhibition	Tianjin International Exhibition Centre
Oct 10 - 13	2004 Tianjin New Textile Products Exhibition	Tianjin International Exhibition Centre
Oct 26 - 29	The 4th Tianjin International Hotel Facilities & Products Exhibition	Tianjin International Exhibition Centre
Oct 27 - 30	China Ice-cream Dairy Products Ingredients & Processing Techniques Exhibition	Tianjin International Exhibition Centre

Nov 10 - 13	2004 China Machine Tools & Automation Exhibition	Tianjin International Exhibition Centre

WUHAN, HUBEI PROVINCE

Date	Exhibition	Location
Feb 17 - 22	China Wuhan International Biopharmaceutical & Disease Prevention Techniques Exhibition	Wuhan International Convention and Exhibition Centre
Feb 20 - 21	Wuhan Talents Networking Session	Wuhan International Convention and Exhibition Centre
Feb 25 - 28	2004 Wuhan Real Estate Exposition cum the 1st Wuhan Housing Exhibition	Wuhan International Convention and Exhibition Centre
Mar 2 - 4	2004 Wuhan Urban City Construction Exposition	Wuhan International Convention and Exhibition Centre
Mar 8 - 10	2004 Wuhan Equipment Manufacturing Exposition	Wuhan International Convention and Exhibition Centre
Mar 8 - 10	The 7th Wuhan International Industrial Controls & Automation Exhibition	Wuhan International Convention and Exhibition Centre
Mar 12 - 15	2004 Hubei Wuhan Real Estate Exposition and China Wuhan International Interior Furnishings & New Materials, Drainage Systems, Environmental Protection and Energy-saving Technological Products Exposition	Wuhan International Convention and Exhibition Centre
Mar 18 - 20	The 7th Central China Advertising, Printing & Office Facilities Exhibition 2004	Wuhan International Convention and Exhibition Centre
Mar 18 - 20	The 7th Hubei Advertising/Printing cum Video Technology Exhibition 2004	Wuhan International Convention and Exhibition Centre
Mar 19 - 21	2004 China Wuhan International Plastics Industry and Moulding Techniques & Equipment Exhibition	Wuhan International Convention and Exhibition Centre
Mar 19 - 21	Central China Plastics & Moulding Exhibition	Wuhan International Convention and Exhibition Centre
Mar 19 - 22	2004 International Beauty Festival	Wuhan International Convention and Exhibition Centre
Mar 23 - 25	Hubei (Wuhan) International Pharmaceutical Machinery & Medicine Exhibition cum the 20th Hubei (Wuhan) International Advanced Medical Equipment Exhibition	Wuhan International Convention and Exhibition Centre
Mar 28 - 30	The 2th Commercial Retail Trade Exhibition cum Chain & Franchising Exhibition 2004	Wuhan International Convention and Exhibition Centre

Apr 2 - 4	Home Furnishings Exhibition	Wuhan International Convention and Exhibition Centre
Apr 2 - 4	National Travel Exchange 2004	Wuhan International Convention and Exhibition Centre
Apr 2 - 4	Guangdong Branded Quality Commercial Products Exposition	Wuhan International Convention and Exhibition Centre
Apr 12 - 17	National Medical Equipment Exhibition	Wuhan International Convention and Exhibition Centre
Apr 19 - 22	The 13th China (Wuhan) International Hair, Beauty & Body Works Spring Exposition cum China (Wuhan) International Fashionable Consumer Goods Spring Exchange	Wuhan International Convention and Exhibition Centre
Apr 20 - 22	China Wuhan International Tobacco Technology Exhibition cum Forum	Wuhan International Convention and Exhibition Centre
Apr 20 - 22	Books Exposition	Wuhan International Convention and Exhibition Centre
Apr 20 - 23	Central China Dairy Industry & Food Additives Inaugural Exposition 2004	Wuhan International Convention and Exhibition Centre
Apr 23 - 27	The 3rd China (Wuhan) International Automation Industry Exhibition 2004	Wuhan International Convention and Exhibition Centre
Apr 30 - May 3	China Wuhan Housing Exposition 2004	Wuhan International Convention and Exhibition Centre
May 9 - 11	Hubei International Agricultural Products & By-Products Processing Techniques Exposition	Wuhan International Convention and Exhibition Centre
May 15 - 17	China Wuhan International Information Industry Exposition 2004	Wuhan International Convention and Exhibition Centre
May 21 - 24	Liaoning Province Business Forum	Wuhan International Convention and Exhibition Centre
May 27 - 29	China Wuhan International Traffic Construction cum Automobile Maintenance & Testing Equipment and Automobile Parts Exhibition 2004	Wuhan International Convention and Exhibition Centre
May 27 - 29	Wuhan Intelligent Building, Community & Residential Protection Safety, Refrigeration Techniques & Equipment Exhibition 2004	Wuhan International Convention and Exhibition Centre
Jun 1 - 4	Wuhan International Toys & Gifts Exhibition	Wuhan International Convention and Exhibition Centre

Jun 8 - 11	Wuhan International Refrigeration & Air-Conditioning Equipment Exhibition	Wuhan International Convention and Exhibition Centre
Jun 15 - 18	Central China Paper & Paper Products and Printing Equipment Exhibition 2004	Wuhan International Convention and Exhibition Centre

XIAMEN, FUJIAN PROVINCE

Date	Exhibition	
Sep 2004	China International Fair for Investment & Trade	Xiamen International Conference & Exhibition Centre
Sept 18 - 21	7th Building Decoration Material & Hotel Equipment Exhibition (Taiwan & China)	Xiamen International Conference & Exhibition Centre

ZHEJIANG

Date	Exhibition	
May 26 - 28	IGATEX Zhejiang	Zhejiang World Trade Centre

CONVENTION & EXHIBITION VENUES IN CHINA

China World Trade Centre

China World Exhibition Hall provides business traders with the most sophisticated forum for the promotion of international commerce, trade and information exchanges. With 10,000m^2 of exhibition space, the China World Exhibition Hall consists of three halls, i.e. Hall One (2,000m^2), which is 14-19m high and column free, Hall Two (3,500m^2), Hall Three (2,100m^2) and the Lobby (2,400m^2) which can be used either for exhibitions or for opening ceremonies.

CONTACT INFORMATION
TEL: (86) (10) 6505 2288 FAX: (86) (10) 6505 3260
E-MAIL: exhibition@cwtc.com
WEBSITE: www.cwtc.com
ADDRESS: 1 JIANGUO MENWAI AVENUE, BEIJING, CHINA 100004

China International Exhibition Centre

China International Exhibition Centre owns a total indoor exhibiting space of 60,000m^2, an outdoor space of 7,000m^2, a parking lot of 10,000m^2, a container-ground of 10,000m^2 and a Customs-bonded storage of 3,000m^2. All the exhibition halls have ready access to electricity and power, water supply and drainage, telecommunications, heating and air-conditioning systems, which can fully meet the requirements of the exhibitions. A general service building offers Chinese and western restaurants, seminar and meeting rooms and lecture halls. The exhibition can easily get the services they need in this exhibition complex such as the Customs, transportation, booth construction, business tour, hotel accommodation and article renting.

CONTACT INFORMATION

TEL: (86) (10) 8460 0000
FAX: (86) (10) 8460 0996
EMAIL: ciec@ciec-expo.com
WEBSITE: www.ciec-expo.com.cn
ADDRESS: 6 EAST BEISANHUAN ROAD, CHAOYANG DISTRICT,
BEIJING, CHINA 100028

Hong Kong Convention and Exhibition Centre

The award-winning multi-purpose Hong Kong Convention and Exhibition Centre is larger than any in Asia outside Japan — five exhibition halls, two ballroom-style convention halls, two world-class theatres, 52 various-sized meeting rooms, two large foyers for pre-function gatherings plus supporting amenities.

CONTACT INFORMATION

VENUE BOOKING HOTLINE: (852) 2582 1111
TEL: (852) 2582 8888
FAX: (852) 2802 7284
E-MAIL: info@hkcec.com
WEBSITE: http://www.hkcec.com
ADDRESS: 1 EXPO DRIVE, WANCHAI, HONG KONG, CHINA

Beijing International Convention Centre

The BICC is located in 8 Beichendong Road Chaoyang District, within the magnificent Asian Games Village. The main building faces the Huibin House on the north, the opposite is The National Olympic Sports Center, the east is Dongpei House and Youlian House, the other side is close to the Beichendong Road. As one of the Chinese biggest facilities specifically designed for conferences and exhibitions, the BICC has an area of 68802.54m^2 . It's an eight-floor building with two underground floors,

comprising of 50 conference halls and meeting rooms equipped to serve a wide variety of purposes with the capacity from 10 up to 2500 people, as well as indoor exhibition halls can accomodate as many as 300 international standard exhibition booths and dozens of offices. The Conference Building also has a business centre, an audio-visual studio, a post office, an information counter, spacious registration hall, public and VIP lounges and bars located on each floor.

CONTACT INFORMATION

TEL: (86) (10) 8497 3060
E-MAIL: sales@bicc.com.cn
WEBSITE: www.bicc.com.cn
ADDRESS: 8 BEICHEN EAST ROAD, CHAOYANG DISTRICT, BEIJING, CHINA 100101

Shanghai New International Expo Centre

SNIEC currently has seven halls with one-storey and column-free exhibition space. Each hall is 11,500m^2 big, thus amounting to a total of 92,000m^2 exhibition space. Halls one to four, and six to seven, is 11-17m tall, whereas hall five is 17-23m tall. SNIEC is being expanded. Upon full completion, the centre will have 18 halls with an integrated hotel and conference centre complex. The total exhibition area is up to 250,000m^2 (200,000m^2 of indoor and 50,000m^2 of outdoor).

CONTACT INFORMATION

VENUE BOOKING HOTLINE:
(86) (21) 2890 6856 (for overseas organizers)
(86) (21) 2890 6854 (for domestic organizers)
TEL: (86) (21) 2890 6666
FAX: (86) (21) 2890 6777

EMAIL: info@sniec.net
marketing@sniec.net (Venue Booking)
WEBSITE: www.sniec.net
ADDRESS: 2345 LONGYANG ROAD, PUDONG NEW DISTRICT, SHANGHAI, CHINA 201204

Shanghai Mart

Shanghai Mart, located in the major financial trade centre in China, is one of the largest exhibition and trade centers in Asia. Comprising of an international Trade Mart with 200,000m^2, an office tower of 42,000m^2, exhibition halls of more than 37,000m^2, a Sky Lobby of 2,000m^2 and several conference rooms of various sizes, Shanghai Mart houses a trade information centre, business centre, post office, bank, customs office, courier and catering services all under one roof.

CONTACT INFORMATION

TEL: (86) (21) 6236 6888 EXT 6368
FAX: (86) (21) 6236 0181
EMAIL: sam.fang@shanghaimart.com.cn
WEBSITE: www.shangmart.com.cn
ADDRESS: 2299 WEST YAN'AN ROAD, SHANGHAI, CHINA 200336

INTEX Shanghai

Covering 12,000m^2, Intex Shanghai provides both domestic and foreign exhibitors a perfect exhibiting place with all kinds of well-equipped facilities. The ground floor of 8.1 metres in height, can accommodate all kinds of special designs. Since its establishment in 1992, Intex Shanghai has undertaken more than 180 large-scale exhibitions over 150 of which were international ones. Apart from that there have been more than 560 seminars held in Intex .The annual occupancy has reached 49.2%.It has received more than

132,000 exhibitors and over 6 million visitors. All this made Intex Shanghai an ideal exhibition venue.

CONTACT INFORMATION

TEL: (86) (21) 6275 5800
FAX: (86) (21) 6275 7210
EMAIL: intex@public.sta.net.cn
WEBSITE: www.intex-sh.com
ADDRESS: 88 LOUSHANGUAN RD, SHANGHAI, CHINA 200336

Xiamen Int'l Conference & Exhibition Centre

XICEC occupies an area of 470,000m^2 and a total construction area of 150,000m^2 , composed of the main and wing buildings. Being 432m in length and 42.6m in height, the main building contains 5 floors. The height of the exhibition hall varies from 7.6m to 10m and 15m. It has a total of 3,3000m^2 area available for 2000 standardized booths. At two sides of the exhibition hall, there are two pillar-free exhibition units with an area of 6,560m^2 , a height of 15m and a 81m by 81m span grid system. The crescent-shaped ballroom on top of the main building is the most creative feature of the whole building. The International Conference Hall is equipped with simultaneous interpreting system of 6 languages. The wing building is a star-class hotel boasting 250 guest rooms.

CONTACT INFORMATION

TEL: (86) (592) 595 9898
FAX: (86) (592) 595 9201
EMAIL: infocenter@xicec.com.cn
WEBSITE: www.xicec.com
ADDRESS: NEW DISTRICT, XIAMEN, FUJIAN, CHINA 361009

Guangzhou International Convention and Exhibition Centre

Guangzhou International Convention and Exhibition Centre, the largest exhibition centre of Asia and the 2nd largest of this kind in the world after the Hannover International Expo Centre, is located at Bazhou in southwest part of Guangzhou with a total construction area of 700,000m^2, including an exhibition hall, international convention hall and so on. Subordinate facilities cover an area of about 600,000m^2 , with a floor space of about 400,000m^2 . The first phase of the project was completed in Dec.2002, with 15 exhibition halls (construction area 394,938m^2), which can hold 10,200 standard booths. Guangzhou International Convention and Exhibition Centre, which is extraordinarily grand, modern and advanced, is a symbal of futuristic the symbolic architecture of Guangzhou city.

CONTACT INFORMATION
ADDRESS: XIN'GANG EAST ROAD, BAZHOU, GUANGZHOU, GUANGDONG, CHINA

Guangzhou Jinhan Exhibition Centre

With 25,000m^2 of construction space, Jinhan Exhibition Centre consists of two halls: Hall 1 with 17,600m^2 and Hall 2 with 18,000m^2. Hall 2 is a new building with two levels in light steel structure and a holding capacity of 900 standard booths. Hall 2 which has 8 metre high walls, there are eight entrances, two groups of automatic lifts, three groups of elevators for guest and goods, eight walking staircases, multi-

functional conference halls, business centre, coffee shop, catering service for Chinese and western food, and a resting place. In addition, it is equipped amply with superior indoor ventilation, electricity, water facilities and 200 parking lots outside the centre. The exhibition layout is extremely convenient with simple space and full facilities.

CONTACT INFORMATION

TEL: 020-36235009 86018882 °°
FAX: 020- 36235687 86018836
EMAIL: info@jh-gz.com
WEBSITE: www.jh-gz.com
ADDRESS: 119 LIUHUA ROAD, GUANGZHOU, GUANGDONG, CHINA 510010

*ALL PHOTOS COURTESY OF THE EXHIBITION CENTRES.